SPECIAL INTEREST

SPECIAL INTEREST

Teachers Unions and America's Public Schools

TERRY M. MOE

BROOKINGS INSTITUTION PRESS
Washington, D.C.

Copyright © 2011
THE BROOKINGS INSTITUTION
1775 Massachusetts Avenue, N.W., Washington, DC 20036
www.brookings.edu

Library of Congress Cataloging-in-Publication data

Moe, Terry M.
  Special interest : teachers unions and America's public schools / Terry Moe.
    p.   cm.
  Includes bibliographical references and index.
  Summary: "Examines America's teachers unions—their historical rise to power, the organizational foundations of that power, the ways they have exercised it in collective bargaining and politics, and the consequences for American education and its reform"— Provided by publisher.
  ISBN 978-0-8157-2129-1 (cloth : alk. paper)
  1. Teachers' unions—United States—History—20th century. 2. Teachers— Professional relationships—United States. I. Brookings Institution. II. Title.
  LB2844.53.U6M64 2011
  371.1'04—dc22
                                                                          2011001359

9 8 7 6 5 4 3 2 1

Printed on acid-free paper

Typeset in Adobe Garamond

Composition by Cynthia Stock
Silver Spring, Maryland

Printed by R. R. Donnelley
Harrisonburg, Virginia

To My Dad
WALTER MOE

Contents

Acknowledgments

The writing of this book was the easy part. The preparation was the hard part. I spent years thinking about the teachers unions, studying their roles in collective bargaining and politics, carrying out my own research projects, writing articles, amassing information, and developing ideas about how to pull it all together into a consistent, comprehensive analysis of how the unions shape America's public schools. Throughout that process, however, I had plenty of help. I was supported—and challenged and inspired—by more colleagues, research assistants, educators, policy makers, and reformers than I can possibly mention here. I want to single out a few people, however, who have been especially influential in making this book a reality.

John Raisian, director of the Hoover Institution, has nurtured an organizational environment in which scholarship on important national (and international) policy issues is strongly valued and encouraged, with genuine respect for academic freedom—and thus for my own freedom to do the kind of research I want and to arrive at whatever conclusions I think are warranted given the evidence. He has been unfailingly supportive of my work, and has made it possible for me to have the time, resources, and collegial interactions that are so essential for productive research. I want to thank him for all this—and for his remarkable leadership.

In 1999, with substantial support from the Koret Foundation, John Raisian created the Koret Task Force on K–12 Education, whose purpose was to bring together outside-the-box thinkers to discuss, conduct research, and write on

American education reform—and hopefully, to influence the national debate and the direction of public policy. I have been fortunate to be a member of the Koret Task Force since its creation, and the opportunity to know and exchange ideas with the other members—all of them esteemed and lively thinkers, completely uninhibited about expressing their ideas—has been one of the most enjoyable and enlightening experiences of my academic career. Until a few years ago, I was joined on the task force by John Chubb, Bill Evers, Checker Finn, Rick Hanushek, E. D. Hirsch, Caroline Hoxby, Paul Hill, Paul Peterson, Diane Ravitch, and Herb Walberg. Recently, E. D. Hirsch and Diane Ravitch left the group, and Tom Loveless and Russ Whitehurst joined us. I want to thank all of these people for their friendship, support, and inspiration over the years, and for contributing immensely to my efforts to understand American education.

Finally, I want to express my gratitude to the research assistants who worked with me on this project. Because so much time went by from beginning to end, a great many research assistants were involved in helping me tackle various sorts of challenges, and I am enormously thankful to them all. But I want to extend special thanks to several who played central roles in bringing this book to fruition. They are (in alphabetical order): Natalie Ahn, Sarah Anzia, Catherine Kim, Jennifer Lawless, Angela Loc, Brendan Marten, Brad Smith, and Carol St. Louis. For their hard work, their insights, and their dedication to excellence, I am very much in their debt.

SPECIAL
INTEREST

1

The Problem of Union Power

Janet Archer painted watercolors. Gordon Russell planned trips to Alaska and Cape Cod. Others did crossword puzzles, read books, played chess, practiced ballet moves, argued with one another, and otherwise tried to fill up the time. The place was New York City. The year was 2009. And these were public school teachers passing a typical day in one of the city's Rubber Rooms—Temporary Reassignment Centers—where teachers were housed when they were considered so unsuited to teaching that they needed to be kept out of the classroom, away from the city's children.[1]

There were more than 700 teachers in New York City's Rubber Rooms that year. Each school day they went to "work." They arrived in the morning at exactly the same hour as other city teachers, and they left at exactly the same hour in the afternoon. They got paid a full salary. They received full benefits, as well as all the usual vacation days, and they had their summers off. Just like real teachers. Except they didn't teach.

All of this cost the city between $35 million and $65 million a year for salary and benefits alone, depending on who was doing the estimating.[2] And the total costs were even greater, for the district hired substitutes to teach their classes, rented space for the Rubber Rooms, and forked out half a million dollars annually for security guards to keep the teachers safe (mainly from one another, as tensions ran high in these places). At a time when New York City was desperate for money to fund its schools, it was spending a fortune every year for 700-plus teachers to stare at the walls.

Mayor Michael Bloomberg and Chancellor Joel Klein wanted to move bad teachers out of the system and off the payroll. But they couldn't. While most of their teachers were doing a good job in the classroom, the problem was that all teachers—even the incompetent and the dangerous—were protected by state tenure laws, by restrictive collective bargaining contracts, and by the local teachers union, the United Federation of Teachers (UFT), which was the power behind the laws and the contracts and the legal defender of each and every teacher whose job was in trouble.

With such a big defensive line, teachers who were merely mediocre could not be touched. So Bloomberg and Klein chose to remove just the more egregious cases and send them to Rubber Rooms. But even these teachers stayed on the payroll—for a long time. They didn't leave; they didn't give up; and because the legal procedures were so thickly woven and offered union lawyers so much to work with, it took from two to five years just to resolve the typical case. To put this in perspective, these proceedings went on much longer than the O. J. Simpson trial—just to decide if a single teacher could be removed from the classroom.

Sometimes it seems that public education operates in a parallel universe, in which what is obviously perverse and debilitating for the organization of schools has become normal and expected. As Bloomberg and Klein struggled to improve the city's schools, Rubber Room teachers responded with outrage at being taken out of the classroom. Paula Hawkes, for instance, was undaunted by the "unsatisfactory" ratings she received while working. She continued to earn more than $100,000 a year for doing nothing and said she was "entitled to every penny of it." What's more, she complained, "Until Bloomberg and Klein took over, there was no such thing as incompetence. . . . We talk about human rights in China. What about human rights right here in the Rubber Room?" This, of course, was supposed to be an indictment of Bloomberg and Klein. They were the ones in the wrong.[3]

The UFT agreed. It strongly supported its members in the Rubber Rooms, comparing them to prisoners at Guantanamo. And it strongly defended all the protections that make it virtually impossible to fire bad teachers, including those that required keeping teachers on the payroll for years while they did nothing. As UFT president Randi Weingarten artfully explained, "All we're looking for is due process." A New York City principal, acutely aware of the bad teachers that "due process" so completely protects, saw the same situation differently. "Randi Weingarten," he said, "would protect a dead body in the classroom. That's her job." And she did it well. Every teacher in New York City had more due process than O. J. Simpson. Because of it—and because of the union power that lay behind it—the city's children were being denied tens of millions of dollars every year: money that should have been spent on them, but wasn't.[4]

In April of 2010, Michael Bloomberg reached an agreement with the UFT to close down the Rubber Rooms.[5] Teachers unsuited to teach would henceforth be assigned to administrative work or other nonclassroom duties while their cases were pending, more arbitrators would be hired, and decisions would be made more quickly (in theory). But the teachers would still be paid full salaries and benefits, and, as the *New York Times* noted, "The union did not appear to sacrifice much in the deal. While the agreement speeds hearings, it does little to change the arduous process of firing teachers, particularly ineffective ones. Administrators still must spend months or even years documenting poor performance before the department can begin hearings, which will still last up to two months."[6] Observed Dan Weisberg, former labor chief of the city schools and now with the New Teacher Project, "The problem we should be trying to solve is that there are huge barriers that still exist to terminate chronically ineffective teachers. This agreement doesn't appear to address that at all."[7]

Educating Children

The purpose of the American public school system is to educate children. And because this is so, everything about the public schools—how they are staffed, how they are funded, and more generally how they are organized to do their work—should be decided with the best interests of children in mind.

But this isn't what happens. Not even remotely. The New York City school district is not organized to provide the best possible education to its children. As things now stand, it can't be. Why? If we could view the district's entire organization, we would doubtless find many reasons. But when it comes to bad teachers alone, the district is wasting millions of dollars because the rules it is required to follow in operating the schools—rules that are embedded in the local collective bargaining contract and state law—prevent it from quickly, easily, and inexpensively removing these teachers from the classroom. Getting bad teachers out of the classroom is essential if kids are to be educated effectively. Yet the formal rules prevent it.

These formal rules are part of the *organization* of New York City's schools. In fact, they are central to it. The district is literally *organized* to protect bad teachers and to undermine the efforts of leaders to ensure teacher quality. It is also *organized* to require that huge amounts of money be wasted on endless, unnecessary procedures. These undesirable outcomes do not happen by accident. They are structured into the system. They happen by design.

New York City may seem unusual. After all, it enrolls more than a million students in some 1,600 public schools, and over the years it has erected a gigantic administrative apparatus to govern it all.[8] So its dimensions dwarf those of the typical American school district, and its organizational perversities may be extreme as well. Whether they are or not, however, the *kind* of problem I've been discussing here is quite common. Almost everywhere, in districts throughout the nation, America's public schools are typically not organized to provide the nation's children with the highest quality education. It is virtually impossible to get rid of bad teachers in New York City, but it's also virtually impossible in other districts too, regardless of where they are.[9]

The public schools are hobbled by many other aspects of their organization as well. One example: salary schedules that pay teachers based on their seniority and formal credits and that have nothing whatever to do with whether their students are learning anything. Another example: rules that give senior teachers their choice of jobs and make it impossible for districts to allocate teachers where they can do the greatest good for kids. Another example: rules that require districts to lay off teachers (in times of reduced revenues or enrollments, say) in reverse order of seniority, thus ensuring that excellent teachers will be automatically fired if they happen to have little seniority and that lousy teachers will be automatically retained if they happen to have lots of seniority.[10]

These sorts of rules are not unusual. They are common. But who in their right mind, if they were organizing the schools for the benefit of children, would organize them in this way? No one would. Yet the schools do get organized in this way. Indeed, the examples I've given are the tip of a very large and perverse iceberg.

As a result, even the most obvious steps toward better education are difficult, if not impossible, to take. Researchers have long known, for example, that when a student is fortunate enough to have a teacher near the high end of the quality distribution rather than a teacher near the low end, the impact amounts to an entire year's worth of additional learning. Teacher quality makes an enormous difference.[11] Indeed, even if the quality variation across teachers is less stark, the consequences for kids can still be profound. As researchers Eric Hanushek and Steven Rivkin report, if students had good teachers rather than merely average teachers for four or five years in a row, "the increased learning would be sufficient to close entirely the average gap between a typical low-income student receiving a free or reduced-price lunch and the average student who is not receiving free or reduced-price lunches."[12] In other words, it would eliminate the achievement gap that this nation has struggled to overcome for decades.

Boosting teacher quality would also have much broader effects on students generally, and on the whole of American society. As Hanushek notes, summarizing the research, "The typical teacher is both hard working and effective. But if we could replace the bottom 5–10 percent of teachers with an average teacher—not a superstar—we could dramatically improve student achievement. The U.S. could move from below average in international comparisons to near the top."[13] These educational effects, in turn, would generate "astounding improvements in the well being of U.S. citizens. The present value of future increments to GDP in the U.S. would amount to $102 trillion."[14]

These findings are not so surprising. Good teachers matter, and they matter a lot. Yet despite the enormous benefits associated with teacher quality, our school system is organized to make it virtually impossible to get bad teachers out of the classroom, bases key personnel decisions on seniority rather than expertise, and in countless other ways erects obstacles to providing children with the best possible teachers.

So why does it happen? Why are the public schools burdened by ineffective organization? This is a question of profound significance, and the nation desperately needs an answer. The broad consensus among our policymakers—Democrat and Republican, liberal and conservative, from all corners of the country—is that the public schools are not delivering the goods and that something should be done about it.[15] This consensus began to emerge in the wake of perhaps the most famous educational report ever issued, *A Nation at Risk,* which warned in 1983 of a "rising tide of mediocrity" in America's public schools and led to a frenzied period of nonstop reforms that, it was hoped, would bring dramatic improvement.[16] As I finish this book, however, the era of education reform continues unabated: the dramatic improvement hasn't happened, and bold reforms are *still* needed to turn the schools around. The most intensive period of school reform in the nation's history has largely been a failure.

We now have two questions to ponder. To the first, which asks why the public schools are burdened by ineffective organization, we can add a second: why has the reform movement, which for a quarter century has been dedicated to bringing effective organization to the nation's schools, failed to do that? The answer to both questions, I will argue, is much the same: these problems are largely due to the power of the teachers unions. That is what this book is about.

Before I fill in the blanks, a few observations are in order about what I'm trying to do here. And what I'm not trying to do. Countless forces somehow affect the way schools are organized, as well as the politics of their reform; and any attempt to provide a complete account of these forces—to identify all the myriad, interrelated factors that might possibly have some causal influence—would inevitably conclude with something like "it's complicated." But this isn't very enlightening, and it doesn't really help us understand what's happening. In my view, as a social scientist, the way to understand the organization and reform of schooling—and most aspects of the social and political world, for that matter—is to focus on those aspects of the situation that appear to be especially important. The task is not to capture everything of any relevance. It is to get to the heart of the matter.

That is my approach here. I'm writing this book because I think that, to understand why the schools are not organized effectively and why reformers have been unable to do much about it, we need to pay close attention to the teachers unions, whose profound effects on both the organization of schooling and the politics of reform have a lot to do with why the nation is having such a difficult time with its public schools. I am not saying—and do not think—that the teachers unions are solely responsible for the nation's education problems.

I *am* saying that the teachers unions are at the heart of these problems and, therefore, that the unions themselves and the various roles they play in collective bargaining and politics need to be much better studied and understood.

This book is an attempt to do that. It pulls together a great deal of information on the teachers unions—on their historical rise to power, the organizational foundations of that power, the ways they have exercised it in collective bargaining and politics, and what the consequences appear to be for American education. It also attempts to make sense of it all by offering a simple, coherent way of thinking about all this—an approach that, although as basic as they come, helps to explain *why* the organization and reform of schooling have both become such serious problems in this country, and what can (and cannot) be done to bring about real improvement.

Union Power and America's Schools

On the surface, it might seem that the teachers unions would play a limited role in public education: fighting for better pay and working conditions for their members, but otherwise having little impact on the structure and performance of the public schools more generally. Yet nothing could be further from the truth. The teachers unions have more influence on the public schools than any other group in American society.

Their influence takes two forms. They shape the schools from the bottom up, through collective bargaining activities so broad in scope that virtually every aspect of school organization bears the distinctive imprint of union design. They also shape the schools from the top down, through political activities that give them unrivaled influence over the laws and regulations imposed on public education by government, and that allow them to block or weaken governmental reforms they find threatening. In combining bottom-up and top-down influence, and in combining them as potently as they do, the teachers unions are unique among all actors in the educational arena. It is difficult to overstate how extensive a role they play in making America's schools what they are—and in preventing them from being something different.[17]

It was not always this way. The rise of the teachers unions is a rather recent development. Prior to the 1960s, the power holders in America's public school system were the administrative professionals charged with running it, as well as the local school boards who appointed them. Teachers had little power, and they were unorganized aside from their widespread membership in the National Education Association (NEA), which was a professional organization controlled by administrators. In the 1960s, however, states began to adopt laws that for the first time promoted collective bargaining for public employees. When the American Federation of Teachers (AFT) launched a campaign to organize the nation's teachers into unions, the NEA turned itself into a labor union (and eventually kicked out the administrators) to compete, and the battle was on in thousands of school districts. By the time the dust settled in the early 1980s, virtually all districts of any size (outside the South) were successfully organized, collective bargaining was the norm, and the teachers unions reigned supreme as the most powerful force in American education.[18]

What accounted for their power? At the local level, their power in collective bargaining grew out of their ability to organize teachers, and thus their capacity to disrupt the operation of schools and hold back the labor of teachers—via strikes (even if illegal), work-to-rule, and other means of coordinated action—if district negotiators did not meet their demands. But the very existence of local organization also provided a guaranteed foundation of members and money that the unions could count on year after year to fuel their quest for *political* power: a quest that was inevitable and entirely rational on their part because their members were government employees working for government agencies, and virtually everything of value to them was ultimately a matter of political decision by state and national officials. Local organization was the unions' power base, but for them to limit their power to collective bargaining would have been a big mistake. They also needed to be thoroughly political organizations and to develop and hone their capacity for wielding political power. Which is exactly what they did, assiduously and with great success.[19]

This transformation—the rise of union power—created what was essentially a new system of public education. This new system has been in equilibrium for roughly thirty years, and throughout this time it has been vigorously protected—and stabilized—by the very union power that created it. In many ways, it looks very much like the original system of school boards, superintendents, and local democracy bequeathed to us by Progressive reformers nearly a century ago.[20] But what the Progressives envisioned and put in place was a system run by professionals, not a system of union power. This is a modern development, one with profound consequences that make the modern system qualitatively different from the one it replaced.[21]

What makes this seismic shift so consequential for America's schools is not solely that the teachers unions are now preeminently powerful. It is also that they *use* their power to promote their own special interests—and to make the organization of schooling a reflection of those interests. Like all special interest groups, they try to put the best face on their activities. They say that what is good for teachers is good for kids. And as a matter of public relations, they need to say that. But the simple fact—and it is indeed just a straightforward fact—is that they are not in the business of representing the interests of children. They are unions. They represent the job-related interests of their *members,* and these interests are simply *not the same* as the interests of children.

Some things are obvious. It is not good for children that ineffective teachers cannot be removed from the classroom. It is not good for children that teachers cannot be assigned to the schools and classrooms where they are needed most. It is not good for children that excellent young teachers get laid off before mediocre colleagues with more seniority. Yet these are features of the organization of schooling that the unions fight for, in their own interests.

When the unions use their power in these ways at the local level, through collective bargaining, they ensure that the schools are literally not designed to best meet the needs of kids. This is a fundamental problem. But the problem of union power is actually much bigger than this. For the organization of schooling extends well beyond the personnel rules of collective bargaining contracts to include all the formal components of the entire school system, as well as all the policies and reforms that lend shape to them. The issues range from accountability and choice to funding, class size, special education, and virtually anything else that policymakers deem relevant. These aspects of school organization are almost entirely determined by state and national governments, where they are fought out in the political process and where (as in any area of public policy) decisions are heavily determined by political power.

This is where the unions' great strength as political organizations comes into play. By any reasonable accounting, the nation's two teachers unions, the NEA and the AFT, are by far the most powerful groups in the American politics of education. No other groups are even in the same ballpark. Consider what they've got going for them. They have well over 4 million members. They have astounding sums of money coming in regularly, every year, for campaign contributions and lobbying. They have armies of well-educated activists manning the trenches in every political district in the country. They can orchestrate well-financed public relations and media campaigns anytime they want, on any topic or candidate. And they have supremely well-developed organizational apparatuses that blanket the entire country, allowing them to coordinate all these resources toward their political ends.[22]

No other group in the politics of education—representing administrators, say, or school boards or disadvantaged kids or parents or taxpayers—even comes close to having such weaponry. For perspective, though, it is important to add that the teachers unions are among the most powerful interest groups of *any* type in *any* area of public policy. Yes, the bankers have lots of money. Yes, the trial lawyers do too. And so do the National Association of Realtors, the Chamber of Commerce, and lots of other groups. But which groups—of all special interest groups of all types—were the nation's top contributors to federal elections from 1989 through 2009? Answer: the teachers unions.[23]

Money figures alone say nothing about all the other political weapons the teachers unions can unleash that other top-spending groups can't match. The trial lawyers have money, but they don't have countless thousands of activists in the political trenches. It is the combination of weapons that makes the teachers unions so uniquely powerful. These other elite power groups, moreover, have their own special interests to pursue and rarely get involved in issues of public education, whereas this is the single unifying focus for the teachers unions and the one arena in which they invest their massive political resources. In the politics of American education, as a result, the NEA and the AFT are the 800-pound gorillas.[24]

Superior power doesn't mean that the teachers unions always get their way in state and national politics or that they can impose whatever features they want on the public schools. The American system of checks and balances makes that impossible, because its multiple veto points ensure that getting new laws through the political process is extremely difficult. The flip side, however, is that *blocking* new laws is much, much easier, and this is how the teachers unions have used their political power to great effect in shaping the nation's schools: not by imposing every policy they want, but by blocking or weakening those they don't want. And thus preventing true reform.[25]

This is an extraordinary power with far-reaching consequences. It is a fact of great irony that the most influential call to reform in the history of American education, *A Nation at Risk,* burst onto the scene precisely when the teachers unions were consolidating their hold over the system and its politics. For the past quarter century, our nation has been dedicated to improving the public schools and boosting student achievement. Yet the hopes and dreams of reformers have been dashed, almost at every turn. Serious efforts at fundamental change—real accountability, real choice, pay for performance—are seen as major threats by the teachers unions. And they have used their power to stifle progress.

At the same time, the teachers unions have thrown their support behind mainstream approaches that carry the label of reform—bigger budgets, across-the-board raises, stronger certification, smaller classes (which require hiring more teachers), and the like—but leave the existing system, its perversities, and all of its jobs entirely safe and intact. Needless to say, these inside-the-box "reforms" have not led to significant improvement. America's schools are still not organized in the best interests of children. The reform era, stunted by union opposition, has not changed that.[26]

Throughout, the teachers unions have relied upon their alliance with the Democratic Party to gum up the reform process. This alliance makes good political sense, because both sides have much to gain from it. Democratic candidates receive almost all of the unions' substantial political contributions, their in-the-trenches manpower, and their public relations machinery for conducting electoral campaigns—resources that are enormously valuable. In return, the unions can usually count on the Democrats to go to bat for them in the policy process:

by insisting on bigger budgets, higher salaries, job protections, and other union-favored objectives—and, most important, by standing in the way of major reform. The teachers unions are the raw power behind the politics of blocking. The Democrats do the blocking.

Some of my Democratic readers may not like to hear such a thing, and may suspect that I am a Republican with an ax to grind. But I am not a Republican, and I have no stake in trashing the Democrats. My aim here is to understand the role of the teachers unions in American education and simply to tell it like it is. I don't care which party looks good or which party looks bad. I do care about getting the story right and presenting an accurate, unvarnished account.

I single out the Democrats for two reasons. First, the long-standing alliance between the teachers unions and the Democrats is absolutely central to this nation's politics of education, and any effort to understand what happens in the political process and why the era of reform has proved such a deep disappointment needs to pay serious attention to it. The failure of reform can't be attributed to a "lack of political will" or the complexity of the school system or too little money. It is, at its heart, a problem of power and self-interest. Reform has failed mainly because powerful interests, the teachers unions, *want* it to fail—and those interests are faithfully represented by the Democrats, who cast the official votes.

The second reason for highlighting this alliance is that the Democrats ought to be the party of education reform. Their history and ideals are progressive: they are the party of the New Deal, of civil rights, of Medicare, of poverty programs, of universal health care. They have always prided themselves, quite rightly, on standing up for the working class and the disadvantaged, and these are their core constituencies. In education, moreover, it is precisely *their* constituents—disadvantaged kids and families—who are stuck in the nation's worst schools and desperate for reform. But while the Democrats have been champions of the disadvantaged in virtually every other area of public policy, education is a glaring exception. In education, and in education alone, the Democrats are the party of conservatism. Throughout the modern era they have been immobilized, unable to pursue major change. Their alliance with the teachers unions has taken true reform off the table.[27]

With the teachers unions so powerful and with many Democrats sandbagging change, the reformist era never had a chance. And so, after a quarter century of perpetual reformist activity and rhetoric, the basic structure of the American education system remains pretty much the same, and its performance remains troubling:

—Scores on the National Assessment of Educational Progress (NAEP) indicate that achievement growth over the last thirty-five years has been modest (indeed, virtually nil for seventeen year olds) and that most of our children simply do not know what they need to know.[28] This, despite the fact that the nation is spending more than *twice* as much on education—per student, adjusted for inflation—as it spent in 1970 (and more than three times as much as in 1960).[29] In the wake of all this money, the 2009 NAEP study of reading proficiency among eighth graders showed that just 16 percent were proficient in Chicago, 10 percent in Baltimore City, and 7 percent in Detroit. How can kids learn if they can't even read?[30]

—Many urban school districts are in crisis, often failing to graduate even half of their students. The most recent figures (which are for 2007) show that the graduation rate is just 41 percent in Los Angeles, 46 percent in Albuquerque, and 48 percent in Philadelphia and Milwaukee.[31]

—Minority children consistently score much lower on tests of student achievement than white children do, and the differences are huge. On the 2009 NAEP examination, for example, black seventeen year olds—those who were still in school, which doesn't even account for the many who had dropped out—scored at about the same level as white thirteen year olds in reading.[32]

—Compared to students in other developed countries (members of the Organization for Economic Cooperation and Development, OECD), American students score above average in the early grades, but they lose ground by the middle school years and are near the bottom of the rankings by high school. In the Program for International Student Assessment (PISA) international study of fifteen year olds for 2009, released in December of 2010, the United States ranked fourteenth in reading, twenty-sixth in math, and sixteenth in science when compared with other OECD countries—and it was vastly outscored on all three dimensions by Shanghai, Hong Kong, and Singapore, which are not members of the OECD.[33] There is, however, one area in which the United States stands out: it *spends* more per pupil than almost any other developed nation.[34]

—Surveys of U.S. employers reveal a widespread perception that workers are too poorly educated to handle the flexibility and autonomy of the modern workplace. A 2009 survey of human resources professionals found that 44 percent rated recent high school graduates as "deficiently" prepared for even entry-level jobs.[35]

We all know, and have known for decades, why reform is necessary. Without good schools, the nation's children are less able to lead productive lives, to participate as informed citizens, or to realize their potential as human beings. Without good schools, social inequity persists and festers, as children who are poor and minority are systematically denied the opportunities that only quality education can provide, and are at risk for being unemployed, getting involved in drugs and crime, going to prison, and even dying at an early age. Without good schools, the nation as a whole is denied the latent talents and contributions of its people and cannot flourish as it should—in its economy, its society, its democracy.

These problems are all the more serious in international context. We live in an unforgiving world of global competition, technological change, and the rise of new economic superpowers—China, India, Brazil, and perhaps others. If the United States wants to maintain its economic preeminence and its status as a world leader, its success will depend most critically on its own human resources, and on having the kind of trained, flexible, well-educated workforce that the public schools are failing to provide.[36]

Defenders of the public school system often argue that our nation's low student performance is rooted in social factors—poverty, broken families, lack of health care, and poor nutrition—and that academic failure is the fault of society and its inequities.[37] There is, of course, some truth to this argument. It is quite true that millions of America's children are burdened by serious social disadvantages and that these problems affect their achievement.[38] It is also true that educators and reformers—and the teachers unions—are not responsible for the dysfunctions of our larger society. They are not responsible for poverty. They are not responsible for broken families. They are not responsible for inadequate health care and poor nutrition.

But what is the solution, if we want to significantly boost the achievement of America's children? The solution, many defenders say, is to stop blaming the schools for poor performance and to make attacking these social ills the top priority of American education reform. The real challenge of education reform, by these lights, is not to restructure the school system, but rather to ameliorate poverty, educate parents, and make schools into community service centers that can meet an array of health, dental, nutritional, psychological, family, and other social needs.[39]

Acting against society's inequities is a noble enterprise and a necessary one. But it cannot be allowed to distract from the pursuit of effective schools. Realistically, the education reform movement cannot be expected to solve all of society's problems. If that were its mission, it would never get around to fixing the very things in its own backyard—namely, the public schools—that it *can* fix. Yes, social inequities create disadvantages for many students. This is unfortunate, and something should be done about it. But still, the fact is that schools do have a big impact—their own independent impact, over and above the effects of social factors—on how much students learn. And *all children can learn,* including children laboring under social disadvantages. The distinctive challenge of American education reform is to make the public schools as effective as they can possibly be, so that America's children—all of them—can achieve at the highest levels.

Consider the remarkable track record of KIPP schools. Pioneered by Teach for America grads Mike Feinberg and David Levin, KIPP began in 1995 with two small charter schools, one in Houston and one in the South Bronx, dedicated to providing disadvantaged kids with quality education. It is now a national network of ninety-nine charter schools operating in twenty states and the District of Columbia, enrolling more than 26,000 students. Of these, 90 percent are African American or Latino.[40] The KIPP organizational model—followed in all of its schools—looks nothing like what we normally see in the regular public schools. KIPP schools are not unionized, and they can organize as they see fit. More time is devoted to learning: a longer school day (nine hours), a longer school week (half days on Saturday), and three weeks of school in the summer. Principals have control over budgets and personnel and thus are free to allocate funds to their best uses, to hire the best teachers they can find, and to weed out those who don't prove to be effective. Teachers, like students, put in many more hours—including being available at night, via cell phone, to help students with their homework—but they are also paid more than their counterparts in the regular schools. Students are held to uniformly high academic expectations and a strict behavioral code.

The results? Although KIPP students tend to be well behind district averages in achievement when they enter, their schools empower them to make extraordinary gains—gains that, according to an independent evaluation by Mathematica, are so large that they virtually wipe out the usual achievement gap separating disadvantaged from more advantaged kids.[41] Among KIPP's eighth grade graduates, moreover, a stunning 88 percent eventually go on to college.[42] And KIPP is not unique. A similar story of spectacular success with disadvantaged kids could be told for Aspire Public Schools—the largest charter network in California—whose twenty-five schools boast some of the most impressive test scores in the state and collectively outperform *every* large California school district with majority high-poverty enrollments.[43]

Social inequities are serious and consequential in this country. But it is a mistake to think that, because this is so, the public schools can somehow be held blameless when they fail to perform. There is no excuse for ineffective schools. Schools *can* be effectively organized. Disadvantaged kids *can* achieve at levels comparable to those of kids who are not disadvantaged. The challenge of American education reform is to *avoid* putting the blame on poverty or broken homes and to insist upon—and create—genuinely effective schools for all children.[44] Secretary of Education Arne Duncan sums it up succinctly: "It's obvious the system's broken. Let's admit it's broken, let's admit it's dysfunctional, and let's do something dramatically different, and let's do it now. But don't just tinker about the edges. Don't just play with it. Let's fix the thing."[45]

For the last quarter century, the United States has struggled to meet this challenge. And it has failed. The teachers unions are not solely responsible for that failure. But as the single most powerful group in American education by many orders of magnitude, they have played an integral role in it. Through their bottom-up power in collective bargaining, they have burdened the schools with perverse organizations that are literally not designed for effective education. Through their top-down power in the political process, they have blocked or weakened sensible reforms that attempt to bring change and improvement. The combination is devastating, creating a vise-like grip in which the nation's schools are systematically squeezed—and shaped to their organizational core—by the special interests of the adults who work in them.

From the beginning of the reform era, reformers have focused on the problem of ineffective schools, and thus on fixing the schools themselves. Yet they have failed to resolve this problem because there is *another* problem—the problem of union power—that is more fundamental, and has *prevented* them from fixing the schools in ways that make sense and have real promise. If our nation ever hopes to transform the public schools, this problem of union power must be recognized for what it is. And it must be resolved.

This simple point has been something of a third rail in the education reform movement. Until the last few years, most reformers haven't dared to touch it. Conservatives have been the exception: they have never been ideologically or politically wedded to the unions, and so have been free to criticize them. But most Democrats, liberals, and moderates, including the leaders of civil rights groups, others representing the disadvantaged, and many key people in think tanks and foundations, have gone out of their way to avoid saying anything that might put the unions in a negative light. Even when the facts have been staring them in the face.

This reticence is changing, as I discuss, but it hasn't gone away. Not by a long shot. Many of these players are ideologically sympathetic to unions, believe in collective bargaining (for all workers, not just teachers), and can't imagine having an education system that isn't thoroughly unionized. Others, particularly Democratic office holders, are politically dependent on the teachers unions and have incentives to be supportive (and stifle criticism). Still others, especially those in think tanks and foundations, are desperate to appear objective and balanced in the eyes of all "stakeholders."

The result is that, for decades, most reformers have basically ignored the elephant in the room. The reform movement has not been about the unions, and has not tackled the problem of union power at all. So it is hardly surprising that, in trying to transform the schools, it has made very little progress.

Resolving the Problem

The pivotal question for the future of American education is, will the problem of union power ever get resolved so that the nation's schools can actually be organized in the best interests of children? The answer, I believe, is yes. I explain why in the final chapter and leave the details for then. Here, very briefly, is what they come down to.

In the near term, union power will remain the reality. When a group is truly powerful, as the teachers unions are, efforts to undermine their power—by prohibiting collective bargaining in the schools, say—face formidable obstacles in the political process. Precisely because the unions already *are* powerful, they can almost always *use* their power to block these sorts of attacks. This is the baseline that any forecast of the future needs to deal with. Power is its own protection. It perpetuates itself. And this is true in any area of public policy, not just in education. The status quo is not stable by accident. It is stable because it is protected—by power. And power is stable because it is protected—by itself.

In normal times, reformers who try to change the system or its underlying power structure will almost always lose. Yet fortunately for the nation, these are *not* normal times. American education stands at what political scientists would call a critical juncture. Due to a largely accidental and quite abnormal confluence of events, the stars are lining up in a unique configuration that makes major change possible, and in fact will drive it forward. Two separate dynamics are at work. Both are already under way, but in their early stages.[46]

The first is arising "endogenously"—that is, it is arising *within* the education system and its politics—and should be readily apparent to anyone who has been following public education in recent years. More than at any other time in modern history, the teachers unions are on the defensive: blamed for obstructing reform, defending bad teachers, imposing seniority rules, and in general, using their power to promote their own interests rather than the interests of kids and effective organization. The key change, though, is that open criticism is coming not simply from conservatives, but also from liberals, moderates, and Democrats.

A struggle is going on within the Democratic Party. Key constituencies—notably, groups that represent the disadvantaged, along with leading liberal and moderate opinion leaders, such as the *Washington Post, Newsweek, Time,* the *New Republic,* and well-known columnists and education observers—have become fed up. Fed up with perpetually abysmal schools for disadvantaged kids. Fed up with the party's perpetual impotence with regard to reform. Fed up with what Jonathan Alter (of *Newsweek*) has called the "stranglehold of the teachers unions on the Democratic Party."[47] The demand is palpable for the party to free itself to pursue serious education reform in the best interests of children, especially those who need it the most. As Newark Mayor Cory Booker explained to a huge crowd at the 2008 Democratic National Convention, "We have to understand that as Democrats we have been wrong on education, and it's time to get it right."[48]

When the Democrats captured the presidency in 2009, the reformers apparently did too. President Barack Obama has attempted to take the lead, together with his reform-minded secretary of education, Arne Duncan, in putting the party on a very different educational path, one that the teachers unions do not like and have resisted for decades. His education agenda and its most forceful vehicle, the Race to the Top (which I discuss at length), are striking reflections of this reformist surge that is reshaping the contours of the Democratic Party. And the frenzy of reformist activity that they produced across the states in 2009 and 2010 is a striking indication of what can happen when the Democrats stop blocking reform and start promoting it.[49]

If all this wasn't bad enough for the unions, they took another hit in late 2010 with the release of *Waiting for Superman*, a documentary by Davis Guggenheim, who had won an Academy Award in 2007 for *An Inconvenient Truth*, about the crisis of global warming, and had now turned his attention to public education. In *Superman*, Guggenheim tells a heart-wrenching story of struggle and hope— and ultimately of crushing disappointment and searing inequity—about poor, minority families trying desperately to save their children's lives by escaping from their abysmal local schools. Along the way, he provides an avalanche of facts and figures on the problems of American education. And the teachers unions are featured, often through graphic footage, as heavily responsible—through their protection of bad teachers, their seniority rules, their opposition to charters, and more—for the sorry state of the system and for making change so difficult. It is no doubt a sign of the times that this film appeared at all. And even more so that, when it did, it received sensational coverage in the media. People were clearly ready to hear its message and, rather than dismiss it as antiunion—Guggenheim himself is politically liberal and a union member—to see it as a serious-minded revelation that the teachers unions actually *are* creating problems for the public schools. And for disadvantaged children and their families.[50]

This shift in the political tides is historic, and it is likely to continue. Even so, it *will not be enough* in future years, on its own, to bring about major education reform. Modest reform, yes. A real transformation, no. The brute fact is that, while the shifting tides will help to isolate the unions and force them into compromises they'd rather not make—indeed, this is happening even now— there is nothing here to subvert the fundamentals of their power. Absent some *other* dynamic, they will remain very powerful, with over 4 million members, tons of money, countless activists, and all their other weapons still intact; and the Democrats will continue to court their support and worry about alienating them. They will resist efforts to take the unions' power away. And they will only push reform so far before pulling up short.

This built-in resistance is exacerbated by a set of beliefs, widespread among Democrats and many in the reform community, that I refer to by the short-hand of "reform unionism" (and devote an entire chapter to). The basic notion is that the *power* of the unions is not itself a problem because, with sufficient enlightenment and pressure, union leaders can eventually be convinced to forgo their self-interested ways and start *using* their power to do what's best for children. In the end, by these lights, the nation can have collective bargaining, powerful unions, *and* schools that are organized to be maximally effective. For reasons I explain later, this line of thinking is unfounded. It is a have-your-cake-and-eat-it-too vision of the future that flatly misunderstands the fundamentals of union behavior. Nonetheless, it is surprisingly influential, and it prompts Democrats to pursue "reforms" that are inherently limited and flawed.[51]

Luckily, the ferment within the Democratic Party is not the only dynamic at work here. Another, completely separate dynamic is occurring at the same time. This one is an "exogenous" force—arising entirely from *outside* the educational and political systems—that will ultimately dovetail nicely with the political trends I've just discussed and generate a total effect that is devastating and decisive.

What I'm talking about here is the revolution in information technology: one of the most profoundly influential forces ever to hit this planet. It is fast transforming the fundamentals of human society, from how people communicate and interact to how they collect information, gain knowledge, and transact business. There is no doubt that it has the capacity to transform the way children learn, and that it will ultimately revolutionize education systems all around the world, including our own. John Chubb and I have explored these matters in great detail in a recent book, *Liberating Learning: Technology, Politics, and the Future of American Education.*[52]

As we argue in *Liberating Learning*, education technology is not a reform. It is not a new law. Reforms and laws are small things by comparison, and they can be blocked. Education technology is a tsunami that is only now beginning to swell, and it will hit the educational world—and the American public school system—with full force over the next decade and those to follow. The teachers unions can't stop it, although they will try (and, in fact, are already doing their best to keep it at bay through the politics of blocking). It is much bigger and more powerful than they are.

I leave the details for later. The key point is that the specific kinds of changes wrought by technology—among them, the massive substitution of technology for labor, the growing irrelevance of geography for teaching (which means that teachers can be anywhere, and no longer need to be concentrated in districts), and the huge expansion in attractive alternatives to the regular (unionized) public schools—are going to undermine the very foundations of union power, and make it much more difficult for them to block reform and impose their special interests through politics. This will lay the groundwork, over a period of decades, for truly massive reforms—and for the rise of a new system of American education: one that is much more responsive to the needs of children and much better organized to provide them with the quality education they deserve.[53]

Long term, then, the problem of union power will be resolved, and reform will come to fruition. But it will only happen because of a historical accident, a force from the outside that will hit with explosive impact. Were the system's fate left up to the self-generated forces from within, the future would look very different indeed. And not nearly as bright.

Thinking about Unions and Public Education

Although the teachers unions have tremendous influence over the nation's schools, they have been very poorly studied. Indeed, during the entire reform era of the last quarter century, which saw literally hundreds of governmental and academic reports on how to improve the schools—many of which provided the basis for new reform legislation at both the state and national levels—the teachers unions have almost always been completely ignored as targets of reform, as though they are simply irrelevant to an assessment of problems and solutions.[54] This is a remarkable state of affairs, and a debilitating one for a nation desperate for effective schools.

The research situation has improved a bit in recent years, as more scholars and policy organizations—among them the New Teacher Project and the National Council on Teacher Quality—have begun to explore collective bargaining contracts and other aspects of union influence.[55] But all in all, the research literature is quite sparse indeed; and aside from rare studies, the teachers unions are mostly flying under the scholarly radar screen.

My purpose in this book is to bring the unions fully into view, and to shed light on the pivotal roles they play in public education generally. For the most part, I do this by providing pertinent information. But despite what people often think, the facts do not really speak to us. We need a way to make sense of them, a perspective for understanding what is going on. So I want to do more here than describe what is happening. I also want to explain *why* it is happening.

How to do that? I have been studying politics for a long time, and a good portion of my writing and research over the years has not been about public education, but rather about the presidency, the bureaucracy, Congress, interest groups, and political institutions more generally. All of this work, regardless of its specific subject matter, has the *same* analytic orientation—an orientation characteristic of what political scientists often refer to as "institutionalism." When I study education, then, I do not approach the subject in an idiosyncratic way that is somehow peculiar to education. I approach it in the same way I approach any institutional subject. And this is typical of what political scientists do throughout the discipline: institutionalism provides them with an analytic basis for approaching whatever institutions they happen to be studying—because it is designed to capture and explore the essence of what institutions in general are about.[56]

This book on the teachers unions is not intended to be theoretical, and it is not targeted at an audience of academics. So the institutional tools I employ here are quite basic. But they are also important for helping us think about the teachers unions—as well as their political and educational contexts—in a simple, clear, and focused way.

To see what this entails, let's begin by considering members of Congress. They are well known for engaging in pork barrel politics, and more generally for crafting legislation to advance the special interests of favored constituents and powerful groups and companies. Of the many ways they ply their trade, one is through the use of "earmarks" in appropriations bills. Perhaps the most infamous is the $225 million provision for the "Bridge to Nowhere"—linking an Alaska town of 14,000 to an island of just fifty people—inserted in an appropriations bill by Alaska Senator Ted Stevens.[57] But the "Bridge to Nowhere" is just an egregious example of a common practice. The $1.1 trillion omnibus appropriations bill passed by Congress in December of 2009 contained more than 5,000 earmarks. The 2009 economic stimulus bill, which was Congress's opportunity to craft a potent, finely tuned program to boost an economy out of near-depression, was larded up with some 9,000 special interest earmarks—making it a Christmas tree bill that didn't even come close to providing a coherent economic program.[58]

As I write this, congressional Republicans have chosen to make earmarks a symbol of fiscal irresponsibility and are pressing for a "moratorium" that would (temporarily) end the practice. Maybe they will succeed, maybe they won't. But it doesn't matter, because earmarks are small potatoes—just one half of 1 percent of the federal budget—and members of Congress have many other, much more potent means of pursuing special interests.[59] Consider the nation's tax law, for example. It is filled with hundreds of special interest deductions and credits—generating benefits for oil companies, timber growers, NASCAR racetracks, you name it—that add up to some $1.2 trillion a year, almost as much as the entire budget. The tax code is crucial to the nation's economic growth and well-being, and should be designed as one of the linchpins of national economic policy; but instead, Congress uses it as a political vehicle for targeting benefits to special interests.[60] Or consider agriculture. The nation clearly needs an efficient farming sector, but Congress has long supported an archaic, grossly inefficient system of farm subsidies that pumps billions of dollars per year into the coffers of large farms and agribusinesses (while most farmers receive nothing).[61] Or consider the defense arena, where the nation's security hangs in the balance and one might think common interests would prevail. They don't. Congressional decisions about airplanes, ships, and weapons systems are heavily influenced by parochial political concerns about local jobs and subcontractors, and even the most liberal members sometimes find themselves demanding the continuation of unbelievably expensive programs—most recently, for the F-22 Raptor fighter—that the Pentagon has explicitly said *it does not want*.[62]

Examples are pervasive and easy to come by, because they simply reflect business as usual in the halls of Congress. So here is the question. Why don't members of Congress *stop doing these things*? Why don't they forgo pork barrel politics, rise above the special interests, and do what's best for the nation? The answer is simply that they have strong *incentives* to do exactly what they are doing. These incentives, moreover, are not a matter of choice. They are endogenous to the political system: they arise from the electoral and legislative institutions that members of Congress are part of and that determine their careers, their professional lives, and their ultimate success in office. Above all else, if these members want to get reelected—and, of course, they do—then they need to bring home the bacon to their districts and states, and they need to attract support from powerful, well-heeled interest groups.[63]

None of this has much to do with who they are as human beings. *Any* human being who wants to be a member of Congress—and wants to stay there—needs to play the game. That is to say, they need to respond wisely and efficiently to the incentives of their institutions. If they don't, they won't succeed. Congress is made up of 535 very different human beings, each with his or her own personality, family, moral values, past experiences, and all sorts of other distinctive baggage that shape how they think and feel. But these human qualities are *not* the keys to understanding how they behave as members of Congress. In that *one* role—but not in the rest of their lives—their behavior is highly structured by their institutional incentives. And that is how we understand what they do. We focus on their incentives, and on the institutions that give rise to those incentives.

This way of thinking is characteristic of institutionalism, and it is fundamental to how political scientists approach Congress—and the bureaucracy, the presidency, and all other political institutions. They don't do it for ideological reasons. They don't do it because they have an ax to grind or a favorite conclusion to embrace. They do it because it allows them to avoid getting buried in needless distractions and to lay bare the essence of what they are trying to understand.

The teachers unions can usefully be approached in exactly the same way. Like members of Congress, union leaders are elected to their organizational roles, and in those roles—but not in the rest of their lives—they have strong incentives to behave in very distinctive ways. Above all else, they must be centrally concerned with pleasing their members—their constituents—who are employees of the public school system, and who fully expect their unions to protect their jobs, to get them higher wages and better benefits, to push for teacher-friendly work rules, to oppose threatening changes, and in general, to fight for their basic job-related interests. As is true for members of Congress, moreover, the incentives for union leaders are not matters of choice. They arise from the organizational foundations of the unions themselves—their basic need to survive, their reliance on member solidarity, the ability of members to toss out ineffective leaders—and ensure that all union leaders will tend to approach their jobs in the same basic way: they will be special interest advocates for their members.[64]

This is not to say that union leaders, as human beings, are "self-interested." Although their qualities surely vary, they may care very deeply about children and want the best for them. They may also be very concerned about the quality of education and be convinced that significant improvement in the public schools is called for. More generally, they may be very good, public-spirited people. But these qualities are not of the essence when it comes to what they *do* in their jobs. As leaders, for reasons that are intricately woven into the warp and woof of their organizations, they have compelling incentives to represent the occupational interests of their members—and these special interests may require that they sometimes do things that are *not* in the best interests of children, quality education, or effective schools.

Recall from our tour of the Rubber Rooms what the New York City principal had to say about the leader of the local teachers union: "Randi Weingarten would defend a dead body in the classroom. That's her job." What he's saying is that Weingarten uses the union's resources to protect the jobs of bad teachers and keep them in the classroom. But he is also saying *why* she does it: she does it because *it is her job*. This is precisely my point. The fact that Randi Weingarten fights to protect the jobs of bad teachers does *not* mean that, as a human being, she doesn't care about kids. Nor does it mean she doesn't care about quality education or effective schools. It means she is responding to the incentives of her job and doing what anyone in that role would do—by acting as a special interest advocate for her members.

In the grander scheme of things, it should hardly come as a surprise that union leaders are special interest advocates and that the teachers unions are special interest organizations. The same is true of all unions. And in the private sector, the unions themselves are quite transparent about it. What's to hide? The United Auto Workers pushes hard to secure good wages and benefits for employees on the auto assembly lines, and it doesn't pretend to be concerned, first and foremost, with the welfare of the millions of consumers who buy cars. The Retail Clerks Union is concerned about the wages, benefits, and job protections of supermarket cashiers, not about the welfare of the consumers who buy food.[65] Unions are special interest advocates. They know it, and everybody knows it.

The teachers unions, however, are in the public sector. And in the public sector the rules of the game are different than in the private sector. The unions still have incentives to be special interest advocates for their members. But as organizations of employees who work for government, they are heavily dependent on the political process and thus on gaining democratic support for what they do and want. So to behave wisely in this institutional setting, they have incentives to convince the voting public that they are *not* self-interested, but in fact are fundamentally concerned about children and quality education—and that whatever they do to promote their own interests is actually good for children and schools too.

In the realm of politics, this camouflaging of special interests is quite normal. The teachers unions have incentives to do it. But so do all political interest groups, whether their interests are in guns or pharmaceuticals or telecommunications or agriculture. The drill is a familiar one: they all claim that the policies they favor are in the public interest, and they all routinely provide arguments (backed by cherry-picked evidence) about how ordinary Americans will be better off as a result. This is simply how the game of politics is played. The reality is that these arguments often have little or no bearing on why they take the policy positions they do. They *know* where they stand from the outset, because their stands are dictated by their *interests*. The arguments they make are simply tools for achieving those interests, and are chosen to try to convince *other* people to take the same stands. By and large, they often say anything that works. So as any sophisticated observer knows, it is best not to take what interest group leaders say at face value. To understand politics, we need to focus on what these groups *do*. And the way to explain what they do is to pay close attention to their interests.[66]

All of this applies across the board to the teachers unions. When they argue, for example, that charter schools should be opposed because of their poor academic performance, they may or may not be saying something accurate about the actual performance of charter schools. The more important fact is that this is not why they oppose charter schools in the first place. They oppose them because charters give kids alternatives to the regular public schools—allowing them to leave and threatening the jobs of unionized teachers. In the democratic arena, it obviously wouldn't go over well for them to simply say that. So their challenge, for this educational issue and all others, is to look around for arguments—any arguments—that might convince voters and potential allies to support their predetermined position. The themes, accordingly, are all about what's good for children and schools. Their special interests are carefully hidden inside a public interest package. That's how the game is played.

Again, this is entirely normal. The teachers unions are just doing what all political interest groups do. In one important respect, however, they have a big advantage over most other interest groups in being able to hide their special interests. The advantage is that their members are teachers, and Americans *like* teachers. They admire them, they trust them, they often interact with them personally, and they see them as caring about children and quality education.[67] The unions are well aware of this, and their political strategy, packaged with the help of public relations experts, is designed to put a human face—a teacher's face—on union behavior. Their strategy is to *personalize* it. They spend millions of dollars on media ads for and against political candidates and specific education policies; to listen to these ads, you would never know that a union is involved. The ads are about the *teachers* that Americans so trust and about the candidates and issues these *teachers* support—for the good of children and the public schools.[68]

Politics can be confusing. In part, this is because it's complicated. But it's also because many of the key players actually have incentives to confuse us—to camouflage the driving role of their own special interests—and they're very good at what they do. It's their job. This is where institutionalism is especially valuable, as it helps us keep our eye on the ball: by homing in on their incentives, the sources of those incentives, and the consequences for behavior. When we do that, we can see that what these players *say* is often very different from what they *do*, that appearances aren't always what they seem—and we are much better able to understand what is actually happening.

So let's readdress the question at hand. What role should we expect the teachers unions to play within American education? We now have a foundation for thinking about this issue, and here is a simple summary of the basics.

—The teachers unions are special interest groups.

—As the most powerful groups in American education, they *use* their power to promote these special interests—in collective bargaining, in politics—and this often leads them to do things that are not good for children or for schools.

—None of this has anything to do with union leaders or teachers being self-interested as human beings. The unions can be—and are—special interest groups, even though leaders and teachers may well care very much about children, quality education, and effective schools.

The same institutional logic applies to legislators and other public officials at all levels of government. Whatever their human values and beliefs may be in the greater scope of their lives, they have strong incentives in their institutional roles—if they want to stay in office and succeed—to be receptive to powerful interest groups. In the realm of public education, this means that politicians—especially Democrats, given the nature of their alliances—have incentives to be responsive to the very real power of the teachers unions, and thus to their special interests. This is another way of saying that, even if the Democrats are genuinely concerned about helping disadvantaged kids and improving urban schools, their incentives may often lead them to take actions that are not in the best interests of these kids and are not well designed to improve their schools. The problem isn't that these politicians are somehow bad people or self-interested. It is that they cannot escape their institutional incentives, and need to cater to the unions (at least some of the time) if they are to survive and prosper in their jobs.

Taken together, these elements make it unavoidable that public education is an arena of special interest power. When public officials make their decisions about the public schools, whether those decisions have to do with funding or personnel rules or new programs or major reforms, we cannot blithely assume that they are doing what is best for children and seeking out the most effective possible solutions. In fact, they are often responding to special interest groups. And the most powerful of these groups, by far, are the teachers unions.

To recognize as much is not to single out the education system for special criticism. No one who is familiar with American politics outside of public education should be at all surprised at what is happening inside of it, because, in their essential features, they are basically the same. Throughout American politics, in virtually every area of public policy, the norm is that special interest groups are active and influential. Politicians of both parties, meanwhile, are often open and receptive to interest group influence, because they have a lot to gain from what these groups have to offer and strong incentives to attract their support. To say that education is an arena of special interest influence, then, is simply to say that it is normal. It is like every other policy arena.[69]

Look at the nation's experience with health care legislation in 2009–10. Here was another noble idea that, in the policy process, turned into a train wreck with countless special interest groups struggling to shape the outcome. Insurance companies, pharmaceutical companies, hospitals, doctors, labor unions, trial attorneys—the list of powerful groups goes on and on, each with its own special angle and real power to wield. And members of Congress? They were quite responsive. The insurance companies defeated the "public option," which would have allowed the government to offer competing insurance policies. The pharmaceutical companies prevented Americans from gaining the right to buy prescription drugs from Canada. The trial attorneys headed off tort reforms that would have limited the malpractice liabilities (and crushing insurance premiums) of doctors. One special interest victory after another. The result was a piece of legislation that no one could really be proud of, and that never seriously tackled the critical challenge of reducing health care costs.[70]

Welcome to American government. Clearly, it would be impossible to understand this nation's attempt at health care reform without recognizing the extensive involvement and influence of special interest groups. The same is true for the struggles and events in any other area of public policy, including education. If education is at all different, it is because, unlike most areas of policy, *one* special interest is far more powerful than any others. By focusing on that one special interest, then, and by learning about the various roles it plays in shaping the public schools and the policies that govern them, we should be able to learn a great deal about the American education system —and why its serious problems have yet to be overcome despite a quarter century of national effort.

So that's the plan. And from an objective standpoint, as someone who has been teaching about and researching American political institutions for longer than I care to admit, it is a plan that strikes me as so straightforward that it borders on the obvious. With the teachers unions so clearly powerful in public education, there is *no excuse* for not studying them. How can we expect to understand the public schools—and the nation's deeply rooted education problems—if the teachers unions are routinely ignored? Yet, for decades, that is essentially what has happened. Education researchers have done next to nothing to make them a focus of serious, sustained inquiry.

This book is an attempt to change that. I don't claim to be writing a definitive work on the subject. And I don't claim to be omniscient. But I do hope to shed some useful light on the teachers unions, and on the education system as a whole. And I hope that other researchers, whether they agree with the specifics of this book or not, will soon bring the unions to center stage as important subjects for study.

2

The Rise of the Teachers Unions

Teachers are powerful because they are organized. Through organization, they can bargain with local school districts for better wages and benefits, job protections, and favorable work rules. Through organization, they can also take action in the political process to get favored candidates elected to office, lobby for desirable public policies, and block unwanted reforms.

The advantages of organization are hardly a mystery. The interesting point is that teachers went for so long *without* getting organized. Yes, many belonged to the National Education Association (NEA) during the first half of the 1900s. But the NEA was controlled by administrators, and thus by their own bosses. What the teachers didn't have were organizations that represented *them* and spoke and acted on *their* behalf.

Major obstacles stood in their way. Some of these obstacles were political: until the middle decades of the 1900s, labor law and political power were simply stacked against them. But other obstacles were arguably even more fundamental, as they arose from within the ranks of teachers themselves, due to the well-known "collective action problem" that plagues virtually all large groups as they seek to promote their common interests.

Eventually, of course, teachers did surmount these obstacles and get organized. In this chapter, I provide some historical background on how this came about, discuss some of the key issues involved in understanding how it happened, and present some basic data on historical trends in membership and collective bargaining coverage.

Along the way, I pay special attention to the collective action problem. The nature of this problem, together with how the unions and their political allies have tried to deal with it, is essential for understanding how the unions are organized today. It is especially relevant, moreover, to a key issue that has long been a matter of ideological and partisan controversy: the question of whether many teachers are *forced* to join—and thus of whether the unions have gotten organized not because teachers want to belong, but because they have to.

The Incentive to Free Ride

Teachers have much to gain from organization, so it is natural to think that this must be why they join unions in the first place and why they stay unionized. Yet social scientists have long known that there is something wrong with this line of reasoning. And unions have known it too. Indeed, they have known it for much longer than social scientists have studied it.

What they have known is that people who stand to gain by cooperating with one another—in this case, by joining and paying dues to an organization that pursues their common interests—often have compelling incentives, as individuals, *not* to contribute to the group effort. How can this be? And what, if anything, can be done about it? So much has been written about the collective action problem over the years that it would be impossible to cover all its dimensions, subtleties, and possible solutions without an extensive (and extensively abstract and theoretical) treatment. I want to avoid that here, so I just dwell on a few basic themes and apply them to teachers and unions.

To see the core problem, consider a hypothetical constituency of teachers who have common interests in winning policy concessions from the government: across-the-board pay raises, say, or reductions in class size. These teachers would benefit if they could join together to form (and pay for) an interest group that would lobby successfully for these sorts of objectives. All teachers would want such an organization to be created, but their incentives to contribute are another matter. Each of them knows in advance that, if such a group were to form and be successful, the policy benefits (higher pay, smaller classes) would take the form of collective goods—meaning that all teachers would get them, including those who had chosen *not* to contribute to the group effort. In fact, the free riders would be the big winners, for they would get the benefits without paying any of the costs. The flip side is that, if the organization's lobbying efforts were not successful, the teachers who contributed to its efforts would be worse off—they would have paid dues, but received nothing in return—while the free riders would again be in the better position: they would have gained nothing, but they would also have spent nothing. In either case, as individual teachers consider whether to contribute to the group effort, there are strong incentives—if they behave as rational actors—for them to free ride. And because everyone has the same incentives, no organization is likely to emerge to represent them. So this is the dilemma: individuals with common interests may fervently *want* an organization to lobby on their behalf, but each has strong incentives *not* to contribute to the group effort. They have incentives not to join.[1]

To keep things simple, I state the collective action problem rather baldly here, paying no attention to its underlying assumptions and possible solutions. The situation is not quite as bleak as I make it out to be. Nonetheless, the problem itself is very real: free rider incentives *do* undermine the formation of interest groups, and indeed they weaken the emergence of cooperative effort of virtually all kinds. They are of profound relevance throughout human society and are fundamental to an understanding of its organizations and institutions.[2]

As for teachers and their unions, the example given above focuses only on one aspect of what unions might do to promote the common interests of their constituents. Namely, they might act as political interest groups to secure policy victories. Another aspect of unions—which distinguishes them from other interest groups—is that they engage in collective bargaining. Does the free rider incentive inhibit the efforts of teachers to form collective bargaining organizations?[3]

The answer is clearly yes if the benefits of collective bargaining—as provided in the contracts negotiated between a union and its school district—are equally available to all teachers in the district, members and nonmembers alike. Were this so, the free rider incentive would obviously come into play from the outset. The union would have difficulty attracting members and, in the absence of some solution, would probably fail to get traction.

What would occur, then, if the union contract applies only to its members, and nonmembers are not covered? Here, it would seem, the free rider incentive is eliminated, as teachers can reap rewards only by joining and paying dues. Yet there are other reasons why the free rider incentive doesn't go away. One is that the employer, realizing the gains to be had, can simply announce in advance that any benefits negotiated with an emerging union will be offered to all employees, not just to union members—thus reintroducing the free rider incentive from the outset and undermining the union. Another arises because there are often substantial costs and risks involved in being among the first to participate in early union-organizing activities; there is hard work to be done, and even public employers (especially when the union is young and powerless) may find ways to retaliate against the early activists. If the union does get established, on the other hand, the remaining teachers can join *later* with very little cost or risk; and in return they will get whatever benefits the union and its contract provide. The union, moreover, has incentives to welcome them at that point, because its power and resources will grow as its membership grows. In the beginning, then, the typical teacher will have incentives to free ride on the early activists, letting them do the hard, costly, risky work and then joining the group once it is safe and easy to do so. This being so, unions will still suffer from collective action problems early on and may not get organized at all.

The free rider incentive is ubiquitous, affecting all types of groups that try to organize a constituency for collective action: environmental groups, women's groups, business groups, taxpayer groups, parent groups, you name it. Anyone who has ever tried to get large numbers of people to contribute to a cooperative effort—indeed anyone who has ever been asked to contribute to one—has experienced it firsthand. There are, however, ways to lessen its severity.

One avenue is that groups can provide members with tangible benefits, such as various forms of insurance specialized to their profession or newsletters carrying specialized information—anything of value that can be *withheld* from those who refuse to join. By their nature, then, tangible benefits overcome the free rider incentive. And not surprisingly, they are extremely common among interest groups of all types, including the teachers unions. As we see later, many teachers—especially in states without collective bargaining—say that they joined their union mainly to get the insurance benefits.[4]

Another solution has to do with personal values. The free rider incentive is rooted in self-interest, but other values clearly come into play as well. Some people may be especially ideological, for instance, or committed to a particular social goal, such as fighting cancer, helping children, protecting the environment, or promoting workers' rights. When people have such strong values, they may feel that they *should* support a group dedicated to promoting them. They may also believe that, if they stand to benefit personally from an organization's efforts, it is only *fair* that they should contribute too—that they should do their "fair share." When people have these sorts of other-oriented values, their calculations of costs and benefits depart from pure self-interest, and they may well decide to contribute rather than free ride.

Some portion of the constituency may contribute, then, simply because they embrace what the group is doing and feel an obligation to do their share in helping out. Laboratory experiments on collective action have repeatedly shown that norms of fairness and reciprocity are exceedingly common and that they induce more cooperative behavior than self-interest alone would lead us to expect.[5] Evolutionary psychologists have even made a strong case that humans are genetically disposed to these norms—because, among our primitive forebears, those who cooperated were better able to survive and reproduce than those who didn't cooperate.[6] Yet the question is not whether these norms and values are prevalent, but whether they are compelling (relative to self-interest) when people are deciding to join real-world interest groups. The answer, for the world of American interest groups, is that they seem to be very strong among the minority who emerge as activists, but less so among the masses. Many millions of Americans endorse the goals of environmentalism, after all, but only a tiny percentage of them belong to environmental groups. The same story could be told for many other constituencies.

The prospects are more favorable, however, when the constituencies are relatively small. This is typically the case for American unions, because they are organized into locals (which is probably not a coincidence). Even when locals have thousands of members, these people work together and often know one another. In such contexts, people are more likely to feel an obligation to support an organization that fights for their common interests, and thus to pay their "fair share" and not to free ride—for they are personally acquainted with colleagues who would be burdened and disappointed if they chose not to participate. The small context also makes it easier for them to observe one another's behavior, to coordinate their actions ("I'll join, but only if you will"), and to use social pressure to get stragglers on board.

Despite all these possibilities, however, there is nothing spontaneous or natural about the formation of unions. Workers may well have common interests in job security, higher pay, and a full range of occupational benefits and protections, but each worker also has an incentive to free ride on the group effort. This is unavoidable, and if unions are to form, leaders must find effective ways of dealing with it. The mechanisms I have discussed—tangible selective incentives, a sense of fairness, social pressure, tacit coordination—are partial solutions. Organizers can try to attract members by using as many of these tools as possible and by recognizing that different workers may be attracted for different reasons. But these measures are likely to vary considerably in their efficacy from place to place and from constituency to constituency. They are nothing like a general solution to the problem. What the unions clearly need if they are to be most successful at collective bargaining—and politics, for that matter—is to speak for all constituents, present a united front, and mobilize the resources of the entire constituency. They can't do that if left to cobble together their membership with inducements that are uncertain and undependable.

Yet they have one more iron in the fire, an approach to the collective action problem that is much more dependable than any of the others: workers can be *forced* to contribute to the group effort. This can be accomplished by union activists themselves, through violence, intimidation, and other means of making recalcitrants pay dearly for refusing to contribute. A good number of unions throughout American history have done just that: the Teamsters and the longshoremen's unions are famous for it.[7] But there is a more genteel and effective way of accomplishing the same thing, if public officials can be persuaded to go along—namely, to pass laws that, in one way or another, require workers to support unions. *Free riding then becomes illegal.* All constituents are required to pay their "fair share" of the group effort.

This sounds like coercion. It is coercion. But it also has a positive side. The free rider incentive, after all, is not a good thing for the people affected by it, because it prevents them from taking joint actions that would make them better off. They would be wise to eliminate the free rider problem if they could, and one way to accomplish that would be to support a law requiring all of them to contribute to the group effort. In deciding whether to support such a law, each person (calculating as a rational actor) would essentially ask himself, "If we *all* contribute, will the impact of our total contributions be sufficient to make *me* better off?" If the answer to that question is yes, then it would be quite rational for individuals to support a "coercive" law that forces them all to contribute— and *they would support it voluntarily.*

The additional advantage, of course, and it is a huge one, is that such a law applies uniformly across jurisdictions. Union organizers can't count on social pressure, fairness, and other inducements to be effective in every (or any) bargaining unit they seek to organize. But the law is in a realm of its own. If designed to do so, it can automatically ensure that all workers in all bargaining units join unions. From the unions' standpoint, then, a legal requirement is obviously the simplest, cleanest, most effective way of solving the collective action problem. It beats the other "solutions" hands-down.

Before moving on, I need to add a qualification. This discussion has been based on simplifying assumptions—that members have common occupational interests, that the unions will represent those interests, and so on—and given these (and other) assumptions, it is true that workers can be made better off if they are legally forced to join unions. There may be a good deal of slippage, however, between these assumptions and the real world. We need to acknowledge that. What if union leaders use their power to take advantage of their captive clientele and to promote certain policies or political candidates or political parties that members don't support? What about workers who see their occupational interests very differently (because they are especially talented, say, and want that talent recognized in merit-based promotions and raises) or who object to their union's partisan alliances (because they are Republicans) or who just don't want to join a union? Clearly, it is one thing to argue in the abstract, based on simple assumptions, that forcing workers into unions is a good thing. But it is quite another to apply that conclusion to all people in a constituency, some of whom may disagree very strongly and see it as a flagrant violation of their freedom.[8]

I return to these issues later on. They are part of what makes "forced unionism" a lightning rod of controversy in American society. For now, my aim is simply to provide some perspective on the collective action problem and to suggest why legal coercion—from the standpoint of the unions as well as many (but not all) workers—emerges as a particularly attractive solution.

The Growth of Public Sector Unions: Early History

Today, the NEA and the American Federation of Teachers (AFT) have well over 4 million formal members between them, and collective bargaining is the norm throughout most of public education. How did this happen? A good place to start is by recognizing that their rise to success, which took many decades, was not an isolated development in the history of the American labor movement. It was bound up with a much more broadly based struggle: the movement to organize all public sector workers into unions.

During the late 1800s and into the first half of the twentieth century, government workers had the same basic concerns as workers in the private sector: they wanted secure jobs, they wanted better wages and benefits, they wanted good pensions, they wanted favorable working conditions. But even when their organizing efforts focused (as they usually did in the early decades) on well-defined trades—teaching, police, fire, and the like—and even though these trades were naturally broken down into small work units in the districts and cities where they were located, the collective action problems of getting workers organized were often insurmountable. Activists and agitation were common at all levels of government, but with few exceptions—notably, among U.S. postal workers—public sector unions had little success in organizing the masses of ordinary public employees. In many cities and states, the unions (and professional associations) were large enough to achieve a measure of power and prominence. But they represented just a small percentage of the public workforce, and even as late as 1960 they could claim no more than 10 percent as members.[9]

Collective action problems would be normal in any event. But during this formative era in American history they were made considerably more debilitating for public workers because the government itself was a particularly hostile setting for unions. The private sector was hostile too, of course, and the battle in that realm to organize workers and establish collective bargaining was fierce, often bloody, and slow-going. Yet, if anything, labor's plight was actually *worse* in the public sector, where the employers—governments—not only resisted unionization, but also had the authority to make law. And to make it anti-union. Ordinary citizens, meantime, tended to be more supportive of unions in private disputes than in public disputes, for a strike in the public sector meant that their local public services would be disrupted—or that much worse might happen, as highlighted by the 1919 Boston police strike, which led to a frightening breakdown of social order and a drastic drop in support for public sector unions generally.[10]

At all levels of government—federal, state, local—public officials argued that collective bargaining amounted to an improper delegation of the government's "sovereign authority." Their duty, they said, was to faithfully represent the people—the true sovereigns—and they couldn't do that if they were bound by collective bargaining agreements. Accordingly, they not only refused to authorize collective bargaining for government employees, but often passed laws explicitly prohibiting it, which the courts routinely upheld. Needless to say, employee strikes in the public sector were often made illegal as well, denying unions their main weapon in the struggle to get established and win contracts.[11]

Even President Franklin D. Roosevelt, an ardent supporter of collective bargaining in the private sector, was opposed to it in the public sector. In his words, "All government employees should realize that the process of collective bargaining, as usually understood, cannot be transplanted into the public service . . . The very nature and purposes of government make it impossible for administrative officials to represent fully or to bind the employer in mutual discussions with government employee organizations. The employer is the whole people."[12]

Although "sovereign authority" was the official rationale for treating public sector workers differently, it was a rationale that reflected the prevailing structure of political power, and it would change once this structure gave way to something else over the decades. As Martin West insightfully argues, two evolutionary developments in American politics were especially important to this change in the power structure, and both were critical to the eventual rise of the public sector unions, which would come later in the 1960s and 1970s. One had to do with the replacement of patronage with civil service throughout American government. The other had to do with the cementing of a political alliance between the nation's unions and the Democratic Party. It wasn't until both these building blocks were in place that public sector unions were able to overcome their collective action problems and achieve takeoff on a grand scale. Here, very briefly, is why.[13]

From the late 1800s through the first several decades of the twentieth century, party machines and patronage held sway throughout much of American government. Under patronage systems, government jobs were controlled by party bosses and public officials, who used them as political currency to maintain their political machines. This meant that jobs were inherently insecure for many public employees; it also meant that these employees were dependent on the party in power and expected to be party loyalists, funders, and campaign workers. The main goal of the early public sector unions (and professional associations) was to put an end to these practices: to make jobs secure for public workers, to promote their occupational interests, and to mobilize independent power on their behalf. By the very logic of their being, then, the early unions came into direct conflict with the established political powers—and met with the fierce opposition of government.

Yet the currents of history were running in their favor. Around the turn of the century, the most powerful reform movement the nation had ever seen—the antiparty, antipatronage Progressive movement, fueled by the "good government" demands of the middle class and business—was reaching full tilt. At the heart of its agenda was civil service reform, which sought to replace patronage with a "merit" system based on tenure, job classifications, pay schedules, and other bureaucratic means of job protection. The early organizations of public sector workers eagerly signed on to the cause and, in league with Progressive reformers, became relentless and influential promoters of civil service. In the private sector, workers and their union leaders sought collective bargaining. But in the public sector, they focused on civil service. This was their main path to job protection and material well being.[14]

Change didn't come easily, because the party machines were entrenched and fighting for their very survival. There were early reformist victories—the 1883 Pendleton Civil Service Reform Act at the federal level and a surge of state and city adoptions around the turn of the century—but as the force of Progressivism died down in the 1920s, the advance of civil service stalled. During the first half of the New Deal it stalled even further, with Roosevelt creating large numbers of new agencies, filling them with Democrats, and resisting (for a time) the constraints that civil service would have imposed. As we all know, civil service eventually triumphed at all levels of American government. But the triumph came about with agonizing slowness, in fits and starts. It wasn't until the 1950s or so that most vestiges of patronage and old-style party organization were cleared away.[15]

For much of this time, patronage kept the Democrats and the early public sector unions apart. In some sense, they were natural allies, as both represented the working man. But they couldn't come into alliance as long as the Democrats depended on a politicized government personnel system that conflicted with the most basic demands of the unions. Indeed, the gulf between the Democrats and the union movement was even bigger than this suggests because the private sector unions were disconnected from the Democrats as well. Led for many years by the American Federation of Labor and its longtime president, Samuel Gompers, they championed a brand of "pure and simple unionism" that emphasized bread-and-butter bargaining between business and labor, the reliance of workers on their unions—rather than government—for social services and support, and an unwillingness to forge alliances with political parties.[16]

These barriers eventually came down. With the Depression and the New Deal, Gompers and other union leaders began to look much more favorably on governmental action and a mutually beneficial alliance with the Democrats. And as patronage slowly declined, the Democrats needed to find other sources of votes, money, and campaign workers—and a growing union movement was the obvious place to look. The Democrats, moreover, were in a position to offer valuable policy benefits in return: collective bargaining rights (in the private sector), civil service reforms, and social services targeted at working-class constituencies. Indeed, the Democrats had incentives to do more than just cater to their union constituency. They also had incentives to use the power of government to make that constituency bigger and more powerful—and in the process to enhance their own electoral prospects.[17]

The most immediate result of this new alliance was the National Labor Relations Act (NLRA) of 1935, which was designed to overcome the collective action problems that had long hobbled the labor movement, and thereby to promote unionism, collective bargaining—and the Democratic Party. Its focus was purely on the private sector. The public sector was still off limits. And its solution was precisely the one highlighted in the previous section: it set up a legal framework that essentially allowed workers in any given bargaining unit to vote on whether they should *all* be represented by a common union—their "exclusive representative." If a majority voted yes, the employer was legally bound to bargain collectively with that union. And all employees could be legally required to join and pay dues, and thus their "fair share" of having their common interests forcefully represented.[18]

The strategy was ingenious and worked beautifully: union membership in the private sector surged, jumping from 14 percent in 1935 to 24 percent in 1940 and to 35 percent in 1949.[19] The NLRA was modified by the Republican-inspired Taft-Hartley Act of 1947, which allowed (but did not require) the states to pass "right-to-work" laws eliminating the forced membership and "fair share" requirements. Many southern and border states soon did just that. But the overall impact of the NLRA was hugely beneficial to the labor movement throughout the rest of the nation, and by the mid-1950s American unions were a well-established presence in private sector employment, especially in the larger firms and key industries—automobiles, steel, coal. With massive organization and numbers, moreover, came awesome political capabilities: for raising money, campaigning, mobilizing voters, advertising, lobbying, and more. In a matter of less than two decades, unions became a tremendous power in American politics and the main organizational bulwark of the modern Democratic Party.[20]

The Growth of Public Sector Unions: Takeoff

By the mid-1950s, the stars were coming into alignment for public sector unions. Civil service had triumphed. Governments and parties (with some exceptions) were no longer rooted in patronage, and Democratic politicians were eager to curry favor with the unions and promote their causes. Private sector unions, meantime, had grown huge, wealthy, and politically powerful. The union-Democratic coalition, cemented and regularized during the New Deal, was now an integral part of American politics and the key to success for both its partners. The unions would help the Democrats to win office. The Democrats would use their authority to get more workers into unions, promote collective bargaining, and build and strengthen their own base of support.[21]

It wasn't so obvious at the time, however, that unionism in the public sector was about to take off. The coalition's ideas about how to proceed were in a state of flux and even confusion. Many organizations of public employees—often professional associations, often with histories of focusing on civil service protections—did not even support collective bargaining or strikes, which many public workers regarded as unprofessional. Given the state of the law (which was stacked against them), the high percentages of professionals and white-collar employees (who were traditionally less open to unions than blue-collar workers), and the advances of civil service (which had already responded to many worker concerns), even hard-core union leaders in the private sector were not convinced that their movement could ever succeed in the public sector. In 1959 George Meany, president of the American Federation of Labor–Congress of Industrial Organizations (AFL-CIO) and an avowed pessimist on the subject, could still say, "It is impossible to bargain collectively with government."[22]

But the combination of union activism, raw political power, and Democratic office holders—in a federal system that opened up countless opportunities for change—generated too much force to be contained. And in the late 1950s the coalition began to make tangible progress in the public sector. In 1957 the Democratic mayor of Philadelphia, Richardson Dilworth, recognized the American Federation of State, County, and Municipal Employees (AFSCME)—the largest public sector union in the country, which then had almost 180,000 members—as the exclusive bargaining agent for all (nonuniformed) public employees in the city. In 1959 the Democratic mayor of New York City, Robert F. Wagner Jr.—whose father, Robert F. Wagner, had authored the NLRA—extended collective bargaining rights to public workers in his city. Also in 1959 the state of Wisconsin—where Democrats had just taken control of government and where AFSCME had long been powerful (having originated there)—adopted the nation's first state-level labor law to allow for unionism and collective bargaining among public workers.[23]

This was the beginning of the end of the ancien régime. But it is probably fair to say that two events, more than any others, opened the floodgates. The first was a highly publicized and tumultuous strike by New York City teachers in 1962, led by local union president Al Shanker, which demonstrated to public workers throughout the nation just how successful they could be when strongly organized and willing to take militant action.[24] The second was President John F. Kennedy's landmark Executive Order 10988—issued in 1962 as fulfillment of a promise made to unions during the 1960 electoral campaign—which extended collective bargaining rights to the federal government workforce. This order proved to be of huge symbolic significance, signaling to public officials, unions, and public employees at *all* levels of government that collective bargaining in the public sector was legitimate and obtainable. The notion that government was somehow different, that collective bargaining called for an impermissible delegation of authority, had long been on the ropes. Now it was effectively dead.[25]

What followed was a period of turmoil and transformation that lasted roughly two decades. Throughout the nation—excluding, for the most part, the right-to-work South—many state and local governments began to adopt new labor laws explicitly designed to encourage the organization of public sector workers and their right to meet and bargain with their public employers. Unions were frenetically on the move, mobilizing public employees of all types and often competing with one another for exclusive rights to representation. Strike activity among public workers, almost nonexistent prior to 1960, became commonplace and seriously troubling, making "labor peace" a major political concern for state and local governments and (sometimes) forcing even Republican public officials to look more favorably on bargaining or meet-and-confer laws as ways to put out the fires.[26]

By 1980 the upheaval was essentially over, and a new equilibrium prevailed—one that has been extraordinarily stable ever since. From trivial levels in the 1950s, union membership and collective bargaining in the public sector soared beyond anything George Meany had ever dreamed possible. By 1983 union membership had climbed to 42 percent for local government employees, 28 percent for state government employees, and 19 percent for federal workers (excluding those in the postal system, which is thoroughly unionized). These levels have been maintained ever since, standing in 2009 at 43 percent for local, 32 percent for state, and 18 percent for federal workers.[27]

State legislation often takes the NLRA as its model, especially in the more heavily populated industrial states, where most government workers are. But it also varies considerably from state to state with regard to the duty to bargain, the scope of bargaining, union security provisions (that is, whether they allow "agency fees" to be imposed on nonmembers if they refuse to join), and the specific types of public workers who are covered. When it comes to teachers, for instance, only one state had a labor law in 1955 authorizing collective bargaining, but by 1980 some forty-three states had adopted such laws. In 1955 no states had labor laws for teachers that imposed a duty to bargain on their (school district) employers, but by 1980 thirty states had such laws—and again, these include most all the highly populated, industrialized states. The figures on both counts are somewhat lower, nationwide, for other categories of public workers such as police officers and firefighters, but they are still comparable, and the relevant state laws have generally remained quite stable over the last quarter century, as have membership levels.[28]

This is the basic history. All in all, then, what seems to account for the rise of public sector unions? Surprising though it may seem, given the importance of these unions to American government and public policy, this question has not been well studied. Labor scholars have focused overwhelmingly on unions in the private sector, and much of the research on public sector unions—what there is of it—was carried out in the 1980s, when the phenomenon was new and politically salient and when sophisticated quantitative studies of cause and effect were less common (and less possible) than they are now.

Most of the studies, as a result, are historical or sociological in nature, and their emphasis is on the sorts of traditional explanations for unionism that these disciplines had long provided—highlighting the frustration of public workers with their pay, benefits, and (before civil service) low job security; their goal of gaining more autonomy (and avoiding mistreatment) in the workplace; their willingness to take militant action; the role of ideology in motivating activists to take risks; and so on.[29] There is no doubt a good deal of truth to all these explanations, but the brute fact is that these sorts of forces were at work throughout the twentieth century. Public workers had a great deal to be frustrated about, much to motivate militant action, and strong ideological currents to drive their activism during the early 1900s. The same was true during the Great Depression. Yet they did *not* overcome their collective action problems in large numbers to form unions. These sorts of motivations and conditions were doubtless conducive to union success, and perhaps even necessary for it—but they clearly did not generate a breakthrough in all the years prior to 1960.

All things considered, the most reasonable conclusion is that the breakthrough came about because, beginning around 1960 and continuing into the 1970s, governments began passing new labor laws. These laws were specifically *sought* by unions (and their allies) to overcome their collective action problems, they were specifically *designed* to promote unionism and collective bargaining—and in large measure, they were successful. This is Richard Freeman's assessment, in the most widely read analysis of public sector unions in the research literature: "What changes led to the sudden organization of traditionally nonunionizable public sector workers? First and foremost were changes in the laws regulating public sector unions."[30]

Because so many factors are involved, the historical period is so long, and the causal issues are so difficult to sort out, social science can't prove definitively that Freeman is right. But a number of quantitative empirical studies suggest that he is, showing that legal changes within the states did indeed have a significant positive impact on public sector unionism.[31] It would be surprising if the research had shown otherwise.

Public Sector versus Private Sector

At the very time that unions were succeeding so dramatically in the public sector, they were stumbling badly in the private sector, in what was nothing short of an organizational (and therefore political) catastrophe for the labor movement. In the mid-1950s union membership in the private, nonagricultural workforce stood at a lofty 35 percent, and many observers expected it to head ever-higher. In fact, it was headed off a cliff. By 1983 union density had been cut in half, plunging to 17 percent. After that, the downward spiral simply continued, year after excruciating year, until by 2009 union membership in the private sector had fallen below 8 percent of the workforce.

With union membership in the public sector holding rock steady—37 percent of the public workforce (combining all levels of government) in 1983, 37 percent in 2009—the balance of power had clearly shifted. The "new" public sector unions had become the stable core of the union movement, which was increasingly dependent on them for members, money, and political clout. In the old days, the union movement was a private affair, controlled by private sector unions and their leaders. The engines of power were the United Auto Workers, the United Steelworkers, the United Mine Workers of America, the Communication Workers of America, the Brotherhood of Teamsters, and other unions representing the mainline private industries. But no more. Today, although public employees make up just 17 percent of the total labor force (excluding the post office and the military), they constitute *half* of all union members, and the new powers of the union movement are the major public sector unions—the NEA, AFSCME, the AFT, and the Service Employees International Union (SEIU).[32]

Why have teachers unions and other public sector unions done so well in recent decades, while private sector unions have done so poorly? After all, they both benefit from the same sorts of union-promoting legal frameworks. Experts disagree on the precise causes and their relative importance, but one factor seems clear: even with common legal frameworks, the two sectors offer starkly different contexts for union activity.[33]

In the private sector, business firms are beset by competition, and the unions cannot avoid its consequences. When unions impose additional wage and benefit costs on their own firms and when they impose restrictive work rules that make production, governance, and adjustments more difficult, they face the prospect of losing business and employment to nonunion firms. They are putting their own firms, and thus themselves, at a competitive disadvantage. Employers know this, of course, and it prompts them to resist unionization. As a general matter, then, competition breeds trouble for unions and limits their ability to organize, bargain, and wield power.

Over the last few decades, due especially to the explosion of technology and the globalization of economic activity, the private sector has become much more competitive than in the past. The 1940s and 1950s (and even the 1960s) were a very different time: automobiles, steel, communications, and many other industries were largely sheltered from competitive pressure, and their unions flourished in those safe environments. Costs could be jacked up and organizational rigidities imposed on firms by their unions, but consumers had nowhere else to go. Now they do. Competition has boomed, directly undermining union membership and power. It has undermined them indirectly as well by shaping the deeper structure of the American economy: for largely in response to competitive pressures, business and employment have shifted over time from manufacturing (highly unionized) to services (weakly unionized) and from the Rust Belt states (highly unionized) to the Sun Belt states (poorly unionized). These structural shifts, too, have had the effect of draining members from private sector unions and making their organizational missions more difficult.[34]

To say the least, the public environment is very different. Governments and public agencies usually have no competition, and they are not threatened by loss of business if their costs go up or their organizations are hindered by restrictive work rules. In normal economic times, public sector unions know they are not putting their agencies or jobs at risk by pressuring for all they can get—however costly, however disabling to productivity. They need to scale back their demands, of course, when times are bad and governments have no money; and the economic downturn that began in 2008 has brought about just such a situation. But in general, and even in bad times, they are far less disciplined by considerations of cost, efficiency, and competition than unions in the private sector are.

This difference between public and private is hugely important. But there is another difference that, if anything, is even more profound: the "employers" in the public sector are *elected* officials. To the extent that public sector unions can wield power in elections, therefore, they can literally *select* the "employers" they will be bargaining with, and who will make all the authoritative decisions about governmental funding, programs, and policy. Unlike in the private sector, then, the "employers" in the public sector are politicians who are *not independent* of the unions. Quite the contrary. In jurisdictions where unions have achieved a measure of political power, many public officials—especially Democrats, given their longtime political alliances with the unions—clearly have incentives to promote collective bargaining, give in to union wage and benefit demands, go along with restrictive work rules, add to the employment rolls, and protect existing jobs. That is so even if they know full well that the result will be higher costs and inefficiencies and that the larger population of citizens will not be well served.

Government is not always a union-friendly environment, of course. Some public officials, especially Republicans and especially in culturally conservative areas of the country like the South, respond to antiunion constituencies. And in some governmental settings, officials of both parties are forced to deal with hard budget constraints that (particularly in bad economic times) heighten their concern for costs, make them more resistant to unionization, and prompt them to pursue strategies (like the contracting out of public services) that unions abhor.

Even in government, then, the unions have opponents and costs do matter. But the bottom line is that, given the lack of competition, the dominance of politics over efficiency, and—remarkably—the golden opportunity for unions to participate in selecting their own "employers," they simply find it much easier to organize and prosper in the modern public sector than in the competitive, efficiency-conscious world of the private sector. It is no accident that the modern American labor movement has increasingly been driven (and kept afloat) by the resources, numbers, and leadership of the public sector unions. They live in a protected environment filled with solicitous "employers," and that environment allows them to flourish.[35]

Forced Unionism, Agency Fees, and the Law

Public sector unions did not become a powerful force in American politics and government because public employees suddenly decided they wanted to join unions or because conditions became so bad that they somehow needed unions more than ever before. The key to the spectacular growth of public sector unions is that the laws changed. And what the laws did was to make union organizing and collective bargaining much easier, largely by setting up legal frameworks that allowed for elements of coercion. Through majority vote, employees can "force" one another to accept a given union as their "exclusive representative," and except in right-to-work states (remember: the highly populated, industrial states are *not* right-to-work states), employees who choose not to join that union can still be legally required to contribute money to it.[36]

The topic of forced unionism has been a hot-button issue in American politics for many decades, but it remains poorly understood. Labor unions have historically sought collective bargaining laws that *do* force employees to join unions and pay dues. Since long before scholars began studying the dilemma of social cooperation, unions were well acquainted with the problem and dedicated to overcoming it. If unions try to represent the shared occupational interests of employees in collective bargaining, labor leaders argued, their organizing efforts will unavoidably be hampered by the free rider problem. Their solution was (and still is) to require all employees to join and pay their "fair share" of the costs (member dues)—a requirement that is in the employees' best interests and can make them all better off.[37]

As I've explained, there is a good and rational basis for this argument, but there are also reasonable arguments on the other side. Some employees, after all, may not want to join a union. They may object to collective bargaining, for example, because they do not want to be involved in an adversarial relationship with management or because they regard it as unprofessional or—if they are especially talented or meritorious, say—because they think union rules will prevent them from being rewarded for their good work. They may also object to the union's political activities, which may involve a brand of partisanship that they do not support. Or they may believe that their union is undemocratic or corrupt and will not represent their interests faithfully or effectively. These are all legitimate grounds on which individuals may prefer not to join a union. It is easily argued, then, that they should not be forced to do so against their will.[38]

During the halcyon years of American unionism, which were roughly the years leading up to the Wagner Act until the 1960s, American unions were generally successful in making forced membership a standard element of the collective bargaining system. Labor contracts for private sector workers—the public sector was still not unionized—frequently contained union security clauses that called for a union shop, requiring all employees in the bargaining unit to join the union once hired. This victory for the unions did not last, however. The U.S. Supreme Court effectively ended the union shop in its 1963 General Motors decision, and since then the law of the land has essentially been (enforcement failures aside) that *American workers cannot be forced to join unions*. Recognizing that employees may have all sorts of legitimate reasons for not wanting to become members, the court reasoned that forcing them to join would violate their constitutional rights to freedom of expression and association.[39]

Yet the court did not go all the way and instead chose to engage in a balancing act. In the General Motors decision, as well as a number of other decisions in subsequent years, it has embraced essential aspects of the unions' argument about the free rider dilemma. The court has ruled that, given the unions' duty to bargain for all employees in the workplace—exclusive representation—those employees who choose not to join the union can nonetheless be required to pay "agency fees": assessments that are presumed to represent their "fair share" of the costs of collective bargaining. In effect, then, the court has rejected forced membership, but in its place has substituted forced contributions, which it finds entirely acceptable based on "fair share" reasoning.[40]

Such is the state of labor law today.[41] Under the right conditions, this arrangement of forced contributions—often called the agency shop—can be quite a good deal for the unions and can work almost as well as forced membership. Yes, some employees may refuse to join. That is their constitutional right. But the unions can claim (and regularly do) that these employees' "fair share" of the collective bargaining costs is actually equal to member dues (or just slightly less), they can charge them accordingly, and the employees are legally required to pay (if such provisions are contained in collective bargaining contracts or state law). So little is lost, and union finances are hardly affected. Moreover, if employees know they are going to be charged an amount comparable to dues if they refuse to join, *they have strong incentives to join*—for by paying just a small extra amount, or maybe even nothing extra, they qualify for all the other benefits the union provides its members: insurance, newsletters, legal protection, and the like. When agency provisions are in place, then, the overwhelming majority of employees typically decide to join the union, and only those who have serious objections—because they are ideologically offended by union political activities, for example, or are personally opposed to unions—decide to opt out and pay agency fees instead.[42]

But while agency fees can serve as a comparable substitute for forced membership, not all unions can take advantage of them. The reason is that the court's embrace of the agency shop is merely permissive. Private sector collective bargaining contracts, negotiated within the legal structure of the NLRA, are allowed to include provisions for agency fees if the unions are strong enough to win such provisions. But the court does not require them and neither does the NLRA. In the public sector, where labor-management relations are covered by state laws (or federal laws, in the case of federal workers) rather than the NLRA, the court allows each state to make its own decision on agency fees—but many states do not allow them. Indeed, for both public and private sector employment, this is the hallmark of the "right-to-work" states: they do not allow agency fees. (They may still have labor laws that impose all the usual electoral machinery, such as exclusive representation, a duty to bargain, and so on.)

In addition, even when unions are allowed to charge agency fees, the Supreme Court has complicated their lives by weighing in on the amount they can charge. In its 1977 Abood decision, which was actually about teachers and their unions, the court ruled that agency fees could only be assessed to cover the collective bargaining services provided by the union and that nonmembers could not be required to pay for the union's *political* activities. The court failed, however, to set up any clear procedures by which dissident members could object to union fees or get a portion of their money back; and the unions, predictably, made it onerous and difficult—and thus rare—for them to do so.[43]

An attempt was made to remedy the situation in the Supreme Court's 1988 Hudson decision, which was again based on a case involving teachers. Here it ruled that the union must provide an independently audited breakdown of exactly how much it spends on collective bargaining, politics, and other things; that this information must be provided to all agency fee payers in explaining why they are being charged as they are; that the fee (following Abood) must be based on the collective bargaining costs alone; and that objections by the fee payers must be adjudicated by an independent arbitrator and not be treated as an internal matter for the union itself to decide.[44]

In principle, then, agency fee payers in the public sector have "Hudson rights" that put definite limits on what the unions can charge them. In practice, these rights do not work very well. It is the rare worker who really knows his rights and is willing to get informed about union finances, challenge the union's calculations (which typically claim that the union spends very little on politics), demand a refund, and pursue his case through formal channels. The unions, therefore, are not seriously constrained. Agency fee payers are still charged amounts that approximate member dues, and legal stipulations for such contributions still work to the unions' great advantage in gaining both members and money.[45]

The Historical Rise of Teachers Unions

This background on America's public sector unions takes us a long way toward understanding why today's public school system is so heavily unionized and why its teachers unions are so large, well financed, and powerful. It wasn't always this way. But with the legal changes of the 1960s and 1970s and with the explosion of union organizing and collective bargaining that they authorized and encouraged, public education entered a new era. An era of union power.

If there is a special twist to the education story, it is that the largest of today's teachers unions, the National Education Association, was not initially controlled by the teachers it now so forcefully represents. Established in 1857 as a professional association of educators, it quickly came under the control of superintendents, principals, and other administrators; and even though most of its members were teachers, it was not in the business of representing their interests (as the teachers understood them) or righting their grievances. Rather, it was in the business of carrying out what, by the turn of the century, would be regarded as the Progressive transformation of the American school system: by removing schools from the clutches of party machines and patronage (and thus from existing forms of neighborhood and community control, which were highly politicized) and placing them under the control of professionals in more centralized, more rule-governed organizations run by "experts"—that is to say, by the administrators themselves.[46]

As NEA leaders saw it, teachers needed to be professionalized—to meet high standards, to be well trained, to be paid a professional salary, to be protected by tenure, and the like—but they were also subordinates in a centralized hierarchy, in which the administrators were responsible for making the key decisions, overseeing teachers, controlling hiring and firing, and controlling classroom behavior. As an administrator-run organization, then, the NEA found itself representing the interests of teachers on some dimensions—lobbying state governments for higher teacher pay and better pensions, for instance, and for laws giving them tenure rights. But on other dimensions—having to do with who ran the show, and thus with major restrictions on teacher autonomy in the workplace—the NEA clearly was not a teacher advocate. It advocated teacher interests when they were consistent with administrator interests. Otherwise not. Throughout, it was inevitably opposed to teacher unionization, which it blasted as unprofessional and as out of keeping with the requirements of effective administration.

All in all, this approach worked well for the NEA during the first 100 years of its existence. Like many other public employees, teachers saw themselves as professionals and took a much more positive view of professional associations than unions, which they associated with blue-collar workers. Local administrators, moreover, often encouraged (and sometimes effectively required) teachers to join as part of their jobs. Given the coast-to-coast reach of the NEA and the huge numbers of teachers employed by the public school system, membership in the organization soared: from roughly 2,000 in 1900 to 53,000 in 1920, 203,000 in 1940, and more than 700,000 in 1960.[47] Meantime, it was by far the preeminent voice of public education in the political process and an active lobbyist at the state and national levels. A symbol of that: it moved its headquarters to Washington, D.C., as early as the 1920s.

While the NEA was achieving dominance as the premier organization of the education establishment, the early AFT and its affiliates were *unions* dedicated to representing the special interests of teachers—and they were struggling. Around the turn of the century, activist teachers tried to work within the NEA to achieve their goals, which included not only better pay and pensions but also more autonomy and job control in the workplace. But they ran into a wall of administrator power and had to go it alone by building their own movement outside the NEA. The world outside the NEA was hardly welcoming. There were, of course, all the usual collective action problems that inhibit social organization in almost any environment. But in addition, business was fighting hard against unions in the private sphere; parties and public officials often fought hard against them in the public sphere; and with the rise of Progressivism, school boards (which often were controlled by business leaders and representatives of the middle class) sometimes simply fired teachers who became union activists—indeed, sometimes fired ordinary teachers who merely chose to join. Most teachers, moreover, were women: they were even less inclined to join unions than men, and they couldn't vote at the time, making them even less threatening to politicians who defied them. To make matters worse, conflicts of interest within the teaching profession undermined solidarity—conflicts of interest between men (who tended to get paid more) and women and also between secondary teachers (who tended to get paid more and were more likely to be men) and elementary teachers.[48]

Understandably, progress was slow. But the union movement among teachers did get off the ground. The hotbed of union organization and leadership was in Chicago, where the Chicago Federation of Teachers was formed in 1897, followed in 1916 by the American Federation of Teachers, a national union chartered by the American Federation of Labor that, in the early decades of the 1900s, brought together all the major locals from around the country: from Chicago, New York City, Atlanta, Baltimore, Washington, D.C., Philadelphia, San Francisco, Boston, St. Paul, and Toledo, among others. Their memberships were disproportionately made up of activists rather than rank-and-file teachers, and their aggregated numbers were not large: 10,000 in 1920, 30,000 in 1940, and 59,000 in 1960.[49] Miniscule compared to the NEA. Throughout the first half of the century, moreover, they didn't have collective bargaining rights and didn't have the right to strike; in fact, their official policy (consistent with the legal and political tenor of the times) was that strikes were unacceptable. But they succeeded quite well in constructing an organizational and political base that would allow them to take advantage of future opportunities for dramatic expansion. Those opportunities did come. And when they did, the AFT was ready.[50]

Ground zero was New York City. In 1960 Mayor Robert Wagner promised that he would authorize an official election in which teachers could decide whether they wanted to bargain collectively through a union representative, but he backed away from his promise. The United Federation of Teachers (UFT), the local affiliate of the AFT, then staged a one-day walkout in protest. Although only 5,000 of the city's 50,000 teachers participated in the walkout—a reflection of the low membership levels that prevailed in the years before labor laws were enacted—the union won a big victory. Wagner soon authorized an election, and in 1961 New York City teachers voted to embrace collective bargaining and to endorse the UFT as their exclusive representative. The union then went to work, pressuring the city for "a substantial pay raise, free lunch periods, check-off for union dues, and one hundred and forty seven other items dealing with workplace conditions."[51] When the concessions weren't forthcoming, UFT leader Al Shanker (and his colleague in arms, David Selden, who was president of the AFT) called a strike. The strike was illegal under New York state law, but Shanker called for it anyway—and out the teachers went.

The result was a watershed in American labor relations. Although less than half of the teachers—20,000 of them—walked off the job, they won a sweeping victory: the nation's first major collective bargaining contract in public education, a large pay increase, a duty-free lunch, and other workplace concessions. The state's tough no-strike law was essentially ignored, and teachers throughout the country were shown—through the vivid spectacle of successful militancy—that by getting organized into unions and taking forceful action on their own behalf they too could win great victories. They could win better salaries and benefits. They could win better working conditions. They could win greater control over their work lives and take control away from "management." No longer would the administrators run the show. The balance of power was about to undergo a radical shift. This was a revolution in the making.[52]

The UFT triumph in New York City set off an aggressive AFT campaign to organize teachers in other big cities around the country. It also came right at the time that state governments were beginning to adopt new labor laws promoting unions and bargaining rights for public sector employees. Teachers outnumbered all other types of public employees—police officers, firefighters, nurses, park rangers, sanitation workers, and more—by orders of magnitude. Should they get organized, they clearly had the potential to be extraordinarily powerful, a potential that was hardly lost on the union movement and its Democratic allies as they pushed for changes in the laws.

With teacher unionism forcefully on the move, the NEA was put on notice that, if it didn't convert itself into a union and compete for teachers, the AFT was going to win over the entire constituency. Such a conversion was not easy for the NEA. With administrators at the helm for its entire history, its interests were simply incompatible with unionism, and the organization was riven with conflict over the matter. Survival imperatives soon won out, however, and the NEA—whose massive membership, after all, was made up primarily of teachers—turned itself to the challenge of organizing the masses of American teachers *for collective bargaining*. Although it didn't formally declare itself as a union until 1969, it began *acting* as a union during the early 1960s as soon as it became clear that its survival was on the line.

Throughout the 1960s and into the 1970s, the NEA went head-to-head with the AFT in disputed urban districts, where the two often fought on relatively equal terms. In the meantime, the NEA used its nationwide presence in the full range of districts—a presence the AFT did not have—to give it a huge advantage in representing teachers outside of the major urban centers. Both organizations grew tremendously. But while the AFT won impressive victories in Detroit, Philadelphia, Washington, D.C., and a number of other big cities—areas in which it had previously been organized and strong—it was the NEA that emerged triumphant from the early competitive struggle, gaining control over the lion's share of teachers and school districts and maintaining its stature as the leading force in American public education. From this point on, however, its leadership would reflect the distinctive interests of a labor union, rather than those of a more eclectic professional association.[53]

During this twenty-year period, the American education system underwent a massive transition. Until the early 1960s, only a tiny percentage of teachers were unionized, and school boards and other democratic authorities made all the key decisions about schools. Aggressive organization by the NEA and the AFT, accompanied by waves of teacher strikes and labor unrest, brought thousands of school districts under union control. By the early 1980s, just twenty years or so after the AFT's initial victory in New York City, the transformation of the system was largely complete. The turbulence of institutional change had subsided, dramatic increases in union membership had started to level off, and a new equilibrium had taken hold in which (outside the South) unionization and collective bargaining had become the norm. Today, a quarter century later, this same equilibrium continues to prevail and is clearly quite stable.

The New Equilibrium: The NEA and the AFT

Figure 2-1 presents the best available evidence on the percentage of teachers covered by collective bargaining and how it has varied over the years. The data for 1960 through 1978 were collected by economist Gregory Saltzman for his pioneering study on collective bargaining laws and the growth of teachers unions.[54] The data for 1993 through 2008 are from the more recent Schools and Staffing Survey (SASS) carried out by the National Center for Education Statistics. Together they show that the percentage of American teachers covered by collective bargaining increased dramatically during the period when state bargaining laws were being adopted, soaring from zero in 1960 to 65 percent in 1978 and then leveling off. It has remained virtually unchanged during the thirty years since, with coverage estimated by SASS to be 65 percent in 1993, 64 percent in 2000, 65 percent in 2004, and 63 percent in 2008.[55] This is nice documentation for the story told throughout this chapter. After two frenzied decades of spectacular growth, union organization expanded as far as it was going to go—given the institutional, political, and social conditions of modern times—and hit a steady state: the hallmark of a system in equilibrium.

Comparable data are not available during the early period for the percentage of teachers who *belong* to unions. But SASS shows that the percentage unionized was 80 percent in 1993, 80 percent in 2000, 79 percent in 2004, and 78 percent in 2008.[56] Because we know that very few teachers belonged to unions prior to 1960 and that membership grew tremendously during the 1960s and 1970s, these figures from the later period are again indication that the system is in a steady state. Note that the percentage of teachers covered by collective bargaining is lower than the percentage of teachers belonging to unions. The reason is that, in certain southern and border states—such as Texas, Alabama, and Georgia—there is little or no collective bargaining, but many teachers belong to unions. More on this later.

Figure 2-1. *Percentage of Teachers Covered by Collective Bargaining, 1960–2008*

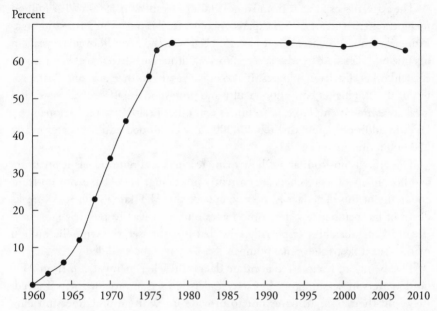

Sources: Data for 1960–77 are from Gregory M. Saltzman, "The Growth of Teacher Bargaining and the Enactment of Teacher Bargaining Laws," Ph.D. dissertation, University of Wisconsin, 1981. Data for later years are from the National Center for Education Statistics, Schools and Staffing Survey.

The situation today is that the vast majority of public school teachers are union members; and of these, all (essentially) belong to either the NEA or the AFT. In 1961, years before it became a union, the NEA claimed a total membership of 766,000 (not all of them active teachers, and including many administrators). It has more than quadrupled in size since then, expanding to 3.2 million members in 2009. The membership numbers have tended to grow over time because, even though the percentage of teachers unionized has stayed constant over the years, the size of the national teaching force has continued to increase: from 1.6 million in 1960 to about 3.3 million today, measured in full-time-equivalent positions. About 2.7 million of the NEA's members are "practicing" K–12 teachers—although some portion of these are substitutes or part-time teachers, not full-time classroom teachers (so the 2.7 million figure can't be compared to the 3.3 million figure for the nation as a whole, which refers to full-time equivalents).[57] Most of the rest of the NEA's members are retired teachers, instructional aides, and the like. There are no administrators. The NEA has affiliates in all fifty states, is politically active and powerful throughout the country, and is the largest union of *any* type in the United States.[58]

The AFT has expanded from some 59,000 members in 1960 to 1.4 million members in 2010. Part of this expansion, obviously, is due to its success in organizing classroom teachers. Yet it has also been actively involved over the years in organizing "classified" workers: secretaries, janitors, bus drivers, cafeteria workers, and other district employees. It also organizes, by its own account, "paraprofessionals . . . ; higher education faculty and professional staff; federal, state, and local government employees; . . . nurses and other health care professionals . . . [and, in addition] approximately 80,000 early childhood educators and nearly 250,000 retiree members."[59]

The NEA is up-front about how many teachers and nonteachers it organizes and how many of its teachers are currently practicing. The AFT is not up-front about any of this. The fact is, no one outside the AFT knows the exact breakdown of its membership. The union goes out of its way to publicize the *total size* of its membership—especially now that it has passed the symbolic million mark—but it keeps the actual number of *teacher* members hidden.

This being so, I requested accurate data on teacher membership from AFT headquarters in Washington, D.C. Its leaders refused to provide them. Indeed, they told their state affiliates not to provide me with any membership data either. The AFT is a teachers union that literally will not say how many teachers it represents.

The best any outsider can do, then, is to make reasonable estimates. Myron Lieberman, who is among the most knowledgeable observers of America's teachers unions, estimated in 1997 that practicing classroom teachers made up only about half of the AFT's total membership. He arrived at this estimate using unpublished membership information contained in AFT convention documents. I did my own estimate using a different method—which involves counting the number of teachers in AFT districts and merged AFT-NEA states—and came up with roughly the same answer.[60]

Double counting is a basic issue here. The NEA and AFT have merged their state affiliates in Florida, Minnesota, and Montana, as well as their local affiliates in Los Angeles, San Francisco, and a few other cities, and both national unions claim all these state and local union members as their own when tallying up their membership totals. Altogether, there are more than 250,000 teachers in these merged unions. One implication, of course, is that the grand total across the two unions is not just the sum of NEA and AFT membership totals; it must be adjusted downward to recognize the double counting. A second implication is that a little more than *a third* of the AFT's entire *teacher* membership—about 250,000 out of some 700,000—is shared with the NEA.

Thus, if we accept the AFT's own claims about its total membership numbers, assume that only half of its members are teachers, and adjust for double counting, we find that the AFT uniquely represents just 14 percent of organized teachers, that the NEA uniquely represents 78 percent, and that 8 percent are shared between the two of them.

There is also, it happens, a much more direct source of information about these matters: a nationally representative survey of more than 3,000 full-time public school teachers (which I discuss in the next chapter). When teachers are asked which union they belong to, the results are very much in line with the above calculations, with 17 percent of unionized teachers uniquely represented by the AFT, 74 percent by the NEA, and 9 percent shared. The survey also shows that fully 36 percent of the AFT's teacher members are shared with the NEA, which again is in line with the earlier conclusions.

These figures help to quantify the extent of NEA superiority. They suggest that, while the NEA is 2.3 times larger than the AFT in total membership, its dominance in the organization of practicing *teachers* is far greater than that. The AFT is only as big as it is because it organizes so many nonteachers and because it shares so many members with the NEA. The NEA's advantage, moreover, goes beyond sheer numbers. The NEA is truly a *national* organization, attracting teachers in all corners of the country and in districts of all shapes and sizes. The AFT is concentrated in big cities—places like New York, Chicago, Boston, Cleveland, Philadelphia—and roughly 30 percent of all its teacher members are located in the state of New York.[61] The NEA is representative of America's teachers in a way that the AFT clearly is not.

Such numbers are helpful in giving us a sense of how unionization and collective bargaining have taken hold in American education and how the two unions compare in size and coverage. It is worth emphasizing, however, that precise data on the levels of union membership and the prevalence of collective bargaining are surprisingly difficult to come by. Even the simplest questions must often be answered through sketchy information that is patched together from various data sources. The Department of Education, the Bureau of Labor Statistics, the Census Bureau, and other standard sources of information have done a poor job of collecting data on teachers unions and collective bargaining.

This is unfortunate. The teachers unions represent the government's own workers, they engage in collective bargaining with the government's own agencies, and they are integral components of the modern American public school system. Just as the government collects data on the public schools, so it should also collect basic, factual information about the teachers unions. For each school district, at a minimum, it should be a matter of public record which union (if any) has bargaining rights for teachers, what the collective bargaining contract contains, how many teachers belong to the union, and how many do not. This information should be gathered regularly, just as school data are, and kept in national databases that are readily available to researchers, public officials, parents, and other citizens.

A Closer Look: The Laws and Their Impact

Some of the best quantitative research on the rise of public sector unions was carried out in the 1980s by Gregory Saltzman, whose focus was specifically on teachers unions.[62] Using time-series data from 1960 through 1977 on the fifty American states, he showed that collective bargaining for teachers tended to be adopted earlier, and in stronger forms, in states that already had relatively well-organized labor movements and where Democrats had recently made political gains in control of the governorship and the legislature. He also showed that, once these laws were adopted, they did indeed serve to promote—as intended—the growth of teachers unions. Both findings make eminently good sense, and help to document the arguments developed here.

I won't recount Saltzman's statistical analysis. But it is enlightening to take a closer look at when these laws were adopted and how union membership was affected.[63] In table 2-1, using Saltzman's data, I single out those states in which there was a major legal shift from a very weak or nonexistent collective bargaining law to a full-blown collective bargaining law, one that included provision for an administrative agency to oversee elections and unfair labor practices. If laws really do have an impact on the rise of unions, these large, abrupt legal changes should give us a good opportunity to observe whether there was a corresponding rise in collective bargaining shortly thereafter.[64]

Because information on collective bargaining coverage is difficult to get, for exactly the reasons I have discussed, Saltzman only has biennial data for the 1960 to 1972 period and thereafter for 1975, 1976, and 1977. We do not, therefore, have the luxury of smooth yearly time series. Even so, the pattern shown in table 2-1 is quite striking. California, for example, adopted its collective bargaining law in 1975, and the portion of teachers covered by collective bargaining jumped from just 8 percent in 1975 to 51 percent in 1976 (and then 85 percent in 1977). In Michigan, the new law was adopted in 1965, and bargaining coverage soared from 18 percent in 1964 to 85 percent in 1966. Minnesota adopted its law in 1971, and coverage grew from 3 percent in 1970 to 47 percent in 1972 and 94 percent in 1975. In some of the states listed in the table, such as Oregon and Washington, there were nontrivial levels of coverage prior to the adoption of the full-blown collective bargaining law, indicating that other influences were at work as well.[65] The same is true for New York—but there, the pre-law numbers

Table 2-1. *Bargaining Laws and the Growth of Collective Bargaining, 1960–77*[a]

Percent of teachers covered by collective bargaining

State and date collective bargaining law was adopted	1960	1962	1964	1966	1968	1970	1972	1975	1976	1977
California (1975)	0	0	0	0	3	6	10	8	51	85
Florida (1974)	0	0	0	0	0	7	19	72	94	99
Hawaii (1970)	0	0	0	0	0	0	100	100	100	100
Indiana (1973)	0	0	0	0	12	33	33	89	91	93
Iowa (1974)	0	0	0	0	0	0	4	43	70	80
Maine (1969)	0	0	0	0	0	49	48	81	84	86
Massachusetts (1965)	0	0	0	35	78	88	92	98	99	99
Michigan (1965)	0	0	18	85	90	90	99	99	99	99
Minnesota (1971)	0	0	0	0	0	3	47	94	97	99
New Hampshire (1975)	0	0	0	0	0	20	40	51	66	78
New York (1967)	0	34	37	38	87	96	96	98	98	98
Oregon (1973)	0	0	0	0	0	22	46	95	96	96
Pennsylvania (1970)	0	0	13	12	14	21	68	91	94	95
Rhode Island (1966)	8	7	7	36	88	90	90	98	98	98
South Dakota (1973)	0	0	0	0	0	11	19	61	64	74
Washington (1975)	0	1	1	2	40	59	91	96	96	96

Source: Data from Saltzman, "The Growth of Teacher Bargaining and the Enactment of Teacher Bargaining Laws," PhD dissertation, University of Wisconsin, 1981.

a. Light gray denotes that the collective bargaining law was adopted during this year. Dark gray denotes that the collective bargaining law was in force throughout the year.

were specifically due to the AFT's early breakthrough in New York City, discussed earlier. Overall, though, the Saltzman data provide solid evidence that the laws themselves had a big impact on union success.

Modern Times: Union Strength across the States

Collective bargaining is now the norm in American education as a whole, but it is not established everywhere and its incidence varies sharply by region. The details, state by state, are set out in table 2-2. The data are from the Schools and Staffing Survey, and they represent average figures for unionization and bargaining coverage across 2004 and 2008. Averages are used because, for any given survey, the numbers of schools and districts may not be very large for some of

Table 2-2. *Unionization and Collective Bargaining among U.S. Teachers, 2004–08 Average*

State and stance toward collective bargaining and agency fees	Total number of teachers (thousands)	Percent unionized	Percent covered by collective bargaining	Percent covered by meet-and-confer arrangements
States that have collective bargaining laws and allow agency fees				
Alaska	8	90	99	1
California	305	96	98	1
Connecticut	41	100	95	0
Delaware	8	93	100	0
District of Columbia	6	93	100	0
Hawaii	11	98	100	0
Illinois	132	95	96	4
Maine	17	79	98	2
Maryland	57	86	100	0
Massachusetts	71	97	98	2
Michigan	97	99	94	3
Minnesota	52	99	93	6
Montana	10	85	90	4
New Hampshire	15	81	99	1
New Jersey	110	99	95	5
New Mexico	22	41	56	5
New York	214	99	95	4
Ohio	116	95	97	2
Oregon	28	97	99	1
Pennsylvania	128	96	98	2
Rhode Island	12	99	93	6
Vermont	9	84	98	2
Washington	53	98	97	1
Wisconsin	59	99	98	2
States that have collective bargaining laws but prohibit agency fees				
Florida	157	61	100	0
Idaho	15	66	95	3
Indiana	61	81	99	1
Iowa	35	75	98	2
Kansas	34	60	88	11

State and stance toward collective bargaining and agency fees	Total number of teachers (thousands)	Percent unionized	Percent covered by collective bargaining	Percent covered by meet-and-confer arrangements
Nebraska	21	85	93	3
Nevada	22	72	100	0
North Dakota	8	77	85	5
Oklahoma	43	59	63	7
South Dakota	9	56	88	7
Tennessee	62	65	84	5
States that do not have collective bargaining laws				
Alabama	54	84	2	37
Arkansas	32	36	17	8
Colorado	46	69	76	10
Kentucky	42	60	21	10
Louisiana	50	61	19	9
Missouri	67	76	8	45
Utah	23	70	84	7
West Virginia	20	75	0	11
Wyoming	7	56	40	34
States that prohibit collective bargaining				
Arizona	51	51	0	81
Georgia	107	55	0	9
Mississippi	33	35	0	2
North Carolina	98	49	0	13
South Carolina	47	28	0	6
Texas	306	65	0	14
Virginia	81	53	0	31
U.S. total	3,113	79	64	8

Sources: Data on collective bargaining laws are from the National Right to Work Foundation, "Teacher Monopoly, Bargaining, and Compulsory Unionism and Deduction Revocation Table" (National Right to Work Foundation, 2010). Data on teacher employment are full-time-equivalent measures and are from the National Center for Education Statistics, State Nonfiscal Survey of Public Elementary/Secondary Education, Common Core of Data, 2003–04 and 2007–08. Data on unionization and collective bargaining coverage are from the National Center for Education Statistics, Schools and Staffing Survey, 2003–04 and 2007–08.

the states, and by combining measures across years we get more reliable estimates (particularly because the true rates of unionization and coverage for each state are likely to be quite stable over this time period).

As the table shows, the vast majority of states—and all of the states in the Northeast, the upper Midwest, and the West Coast—have public sector bargaining laws for teachers. Within this large group, twenty-four states have laws that either require nonmembers to pay agency fees to unions (California, Hawaii, Minnesota, and New York) or, much more common, permit agency fees if they are imposed through local-level negotiations—which is often what happens, especially in the larger districts, because the unions push hard for them and make them a high priority. Another eleven states have collective bargaining laws but do *not* allow agency fees, even if school districts are willing to go along.[66]

The remaining sixteen states do not have collective bargaining laws. Of this group, nine *permit* collective bargaining to occur if local unions—unaided by the NLRA-like electoral and administrative machinery—can pressure local school boards into accepting it in their districts. They are Alabama, Arkansas, Colorado, Kentucky, Louisiana, Missouri, Utah, West Virginia, and Wyoming. The other seven not only have no public sector bargaining statute for teachers, but also *do not permit* collective bargaining by teachers: Arizona, Georgia, Mississippi, North Carolina, South Carolina, Texas, and Virginia.

In this last group of states that technically prohibit collective bargaining, something very much like it sometimes occurs, and this is quite often the case in the largest districts. In Texas, teachers in Houston, Dallas, San Antonio, and a number of other cities are heavily unionized and engage in something that resembles collective bargaining with their districts. But it isn't collective bargaining, legally speaking, and doesn't lead to legally binding contracts. Its results show up instead in district policies and regulations.

If any state stands out, however, it is Arizona, where most people in and around the education system, so far as I can tell, don't even know what the law is. No statute strictly prohibits collective bargaining. The prohibition derives from a key attorney general decision, which has been respected by the courts, and from a legal background (in statute as well as in court and attorney general decisions) that allows local governments to enter into "meet-and-confer" arrangements with employees. "Meet-and-confer" arrangements in Arizona are exceedingly common, far more so than in any other state (table 2-2). Some 81 percent of the state's teachers are covered by them, and they typically lead to "agreements" that look just like collective bargaining contracts and seem to be treated as such (although their legal status remains untested and unclear).[67]

Arizona, it seems, is neither fish nor fowl. In this chapter and the next, I classify it as a "prohibits collective bargaining" state for purposes of presenting the data, but I could have justified moving it into the "no law" category instead, based on the practicalities on the ground. Readers should keep this caveat in mind. This coding decision is a judgment call, but some decision had to be made one way or the other.

Figure 2-2 provides a map of the United States, showing more visually how these legal environments vary across the states. What can be observed, right away, is a familiar geographic pattern that looks a lot like the "red versus blue" map typically used to depict the nation's political division between Republicans and Democrats in recent presidential elections. Labor laws tend to be weaker in the more conservative, Republican areas of the country: the South, the Southwest, and the "heartland." They tend to be stronger in the more populous, more industrialized areas of the country that vote more liberal and Democratic: the Northeast, the upper Midwest, and the West Coast.

Let's go back now to the data presented in table 2-2 and discuss some of the details, starting with the percentage of teachers *covered* by collective bargaining (which, again, is different from the percentage of teachers joining unions). With the exception of New Mexico, such coverage is extremely high—between 90 and 100 percent—for all states that have collective bargaining laws *and* allow agency fees. New Mexico is an outlier, at just 59 percent, because it only recently joined this group, having adopted a new collective bargaining law with an agency fee provision in 2003 (thanks to the prolabor efforts of Democratic Governor Bill Richardson and his Democratic allies in the state legislature). Prior to 2003, it had no collective bargaining law, so its unions had a long way to go to catch up.[68]

In the next category of states—those that have collective bargaining laws but do *not* allow agency fees—the level of bargaining coverage is also extraordinarily high (although slightly lower, on average). The states in this group clearly have more conservative, more Republican cultures—plus they don't allow agency fees—yet collective bargaining in almost all these states is close to universal. It would appear, then, that the presence of agency fees has little impact on the percentage of teachers covered by collective bargaining. The key factor seems to be the presence of a collective bargaining law and the electoral and administrative machinery that goes along with one.

If we look at the nine states that allow collective bargaining but have no legal framework to promote and sustain it, this conclusion is reinforced: coverage is usually quite low. Colorado and Utah are outliers at 76 and 84 percent, respectively, but six of the remaining states range from 0 to just 21 percent, and the only other state, Wyoming, sports a measly 40 percent. When it comes to collective bargaining coverage, then, there is a giant gulf between the states that have labor laws and those that don't—an indication that these laws are critical to the ability of unions to win bargaining rights.

It is worth recognizing that, even in the *absence* of agency fee provisions, these labor laws have coercive elements that give unions—and coverage—a big

Figure 2-2. *Teacher Collective Bargaining Laws, by State, 2010*

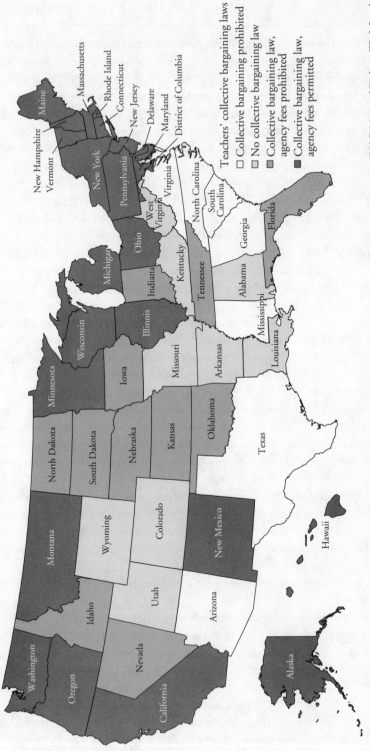

Teachers' collective bargaining laws

☐ Collective bargaining prohibited
☐ No collective bargaining law
▨ Collective bargaining law,
   agency fees prohibited
▨ Collective bargaining law,
   agency fees permitted

Sources: National Right to Work Legal Foundation, "Teacher Monopoly Bargaining, Compulsory Unionism, and Deduction Revocation Table" (National Right to Work Legal Foundation, 2010).

boost. On the teacher side, when a majority of teachers support a union in a legally sanctioned representation election, all teachers—including any who dissent—must accept that union as their exclusive representative, and all of them are covered by any collective bargaining agreement. The districts are coerced too: whether they want to or not, they are legally required to accept the union as the teachers' exclusive representative and to bargain with it. Assuming enough teachers are willing to vote yes, then, the administrative and electoral machinery of a collective bargaining law *makes coverage automatic* for all teachers in the district, and the district can't do anything to stop it.

In general, there is good reason to expect basic differences between coverage and *membership*. Different dynamics are involved. Once collective bargaining is adopted by a district, it tends to become institutionalized as the normal, routine way that districts and teachers do their business and conduct their lives. It is exceedingly rare for collective bargaining to be overthrown (by a teacher vote) years later. The districts that adopted collective bargaining thirty years ago still have collective bargaining. It is in institutional concrete. This sort of thing can't really happen in the same way, however, with teacher *membership* in unions. Each teacher makes his or her own decision about whether to join a union; and over the years there is a great deal of turnover in the teacher workforce, so new people are constantly coming in and making new membership decisions. The Supreme Court has ruled, moreover, that no one is required to join. So while a district may well have collective bargaining, there is no guarantee that the local union will have high levels of membership, or that those levels can be maintained over time. There is a lot less certainty about membership than about coverage.

Let's take a closer look, then, at the state-level data on membership. In the states with collective bargaining laws *and* agency fees, it is usually the case that more than 90 percent of teachers belong to a union. New Mexico is the major outlier, at just 41 percent, but that is because it had no labor law at all prior to 2003. It's a newcomer to this strong-law group of states. Maine, New Hampshire, and Vermont also have lower than average membership figures—79, 81, and 84 percent, respectively. But they are new to this group too: all three of them have become more politically liberal over the years, and all three have added agency fees to their collective bargaining laws since 2000.

Now check out the states with bargaining laws that do *not* allow agency fees. In these states, collective bargaining *coverage* is almost exactly the same as in the previous group, but union *membership* is quite a bit lower, often in the 60 to 70 percent range. It would appear, therefore, that while agency fees have little effect on the adoption of collective bargaining, they have a considerable impact on membership levels.

Another possibility is that these states have lower membership levels because they have more conservative cultures—which they clearly do—and thus more conservative teachers who are less likely to find unions attractive. It is quite clear that the legal imposition of agency fees gives *anyone*, conservative or liberal, a greater incentive to join; for nonmembers must pay an amount roughly equal to dues anyway, and by not joining they pass up all the other benefits (insurance, protection, and so forth) that unions have to offer. Yet when there are no agency fees and nonmembers pay nothing, this could free up conservative teachers to act on their ideology and refuse to join. So both factors may well be relevant. What we know for sure is that, in the more conservative states that have collective bargaining laws but no agency fees, the unionization rates are much lower on average. For the unions—and their funding and their power—this is a big deal.

An upside for the unions needs to be emphasized as well: although these are conservative states with no agency fees, 60 to 70 percent of teachers still choose to join unions. They don't have to. They aren't forced to. But they do. It is true that, with labor laws in place, the teachers in any district can vote to "force" themselves to accept collective bargaining (which applies to every teacher in the district) and to accept a specific union as their exclusive representative (which, again, applies to everyone). But each teacher is still free not to join that union, and is not induced by agency fees to do so—yet a big majority of them join anyway. This is an early indication that most teachers may well be involved in their unions for purely voluntary reasons.

We get another indication when we look at the remaining states, which not only don't have agency fees, but also are even more conservative and have weaker laws. Among the states that simply permit collective bargaining, but have no labor law to promote and encourage it, the levels of teacher unionization are somewhat lower than in the previous group, on average, but they are still typically in the 60 to 70 percent range—membership is a whopping 84 percent in Alabama. (Arkansas is the outlier on the low end, at 36 percent). The states in the bottom category—those that do not even permit collective bargaining—probably have the most conservative, antiunion political cultures in the country, and would seem to be the worst-case scenario for the teachers unions. Yet even in these contexts, surprisingly large percentages of teachers do belong to unions: 51 percent in Arizona, 55 percent in Georgia, 35 percent in Mississippi, 49 percent in North Carolina, 28 percent in South Carolina, 65 percent in Texas, and 53 percent in Virginia. These figures are much lower, on average, than those in the other states, and lower membership levels cannot help but have a major impact on the unions, affecting their money and power. Still, the differences with other states are not nearly what one might expect. Among ordinary teachers, there appears to be a lot of support for unions—support that is not legally "coerced" and appears to be voluntary—even in the nation's most antiunion settings.

Agency Fees and Union Membership

It seems to be a mistake, then, to think that somehow the great majority of teachers are forced to join unions because the laws push them into it. In the next chapter, I explore this issue in much more detail through a large national survey, and I show that voluntarism—while not totally universal—is almost surely the norm.

Nonetheless, as we've seen, there is good evidence that the laws have had a big impact on union success over the years. Teachers are much more likely to be *covered* by collective bargaining in states that have collective bargaining laws than in states that don't have such laws. And teachers are much more likely to *join* unions in states that legally allow for agency fees than in states that don't.

Yet as table 2-2 illustrates, and as our discussion inevitably reflects, it is not so easy to separate the effects of state laws from other possible influences on union success. States with prounion laws also tend to be more liberal, more union-friendly political environments in general, to have a more unionized private sector, and to be larger, more industrial, and wealthier. Differences in coverage and membership seem to be affected by state laws, but it would be helpful to be able to disentangle these influences and see if, once these other factors are controlled, the laws still appear to have important impacts.

Saltzman has already done as much for the percentage of teachers covered by collective bargaining, showing that the laws do have a big impact. But coverage is a very different animal from membership. For all intents and purposes, coverage became entrenched in districts of any size some thirty to forty years ago, and it has been institutionalized ever since. This is not true of membership: regardless of whether teachers are covered by collective bargaining, they are not required to join a union. Membership is uncertain. And in a sense, it is more interesting for precisely that reason.

Why is membership higher in some states than others? The underlying issues, as I've said, are very complicated, involving many factors and complex historical dynamics; and because this is so, definitive answers would require an extensive, in-depth study and some very sophisticated methods. I do not attempt that here, given all the other ground that needs to be covered. Instead, I carry out a simple analysis that helps to disentangle some of the basic factors I've been talking about, and thus to shed light on whether, once other influences are controlled, the laws seem to have their own impact on membership levels. Most readers, I suspect, are more interested in the bottom line than in the details, so the actual analysis is reported in appendix A. Here, I summarize its basic elements and findings.

The analysis is carried out separately on two entirely different data sets: one based on state-level aggregates (as in table 2-1), the other based on a national survey of more than 3,000 individual teachers. The latter is the better data source, as its information is more finely grained, and it allows us to look at the membership of individual teachers—and control for their personal characteristics—rather than dealing with state-level percentages. Nonetheless, having two data sources is a big plus, because if they point to common findings we can have greater confidence in what they show.

In both lines of analysis I control for an array of state-level factors, in addition to collective bargaining laws and agency fee provisions, that may have an influence on membership in teachers unions. These variables are: the state's vote for John Kerry in the 2004 presidential election (a proxy for liberal political culture), the log of the state's population, the log of the state's average household income, manufacturing as a percentage of gross state product (a proxy for industrialization), and the percentage of the state population living in urban areas. In the individual-level analysis I also control for each teacher's party identification, gender, ethnicity (nonwhite), age, location (urban, suburban, rural), and the size of his or her school district. Here is an overview of the basic findings:

—Both analyses show that labor laws have important impacts on membership in teachers unions. These impacts hold up when other state-level influences are controlled, and they have greater explanatory power than all these other influences combined.

—Agency fee provisions stand out as powerful determinants of union membership. The individual-level analysis shows, for example, that if we just look at teachers in districts that *do* have collective bargaining, the probability that a teacher will join a union is about 20 percent higher when agency fees are allowed than when they are not allowed.

—Collective bargaining laws, absent agency fees, also have an important role to play. They make it easier for unions to win collective bargaining rights, and teachers are more likely to join unions when their districts have collective bargaining.

—The personal characteristics of teachers make a difference for their membership decisions. Republicans, women, and younger teachers are less likely to join than their counterparts. Even so, these influences play a much smaller role in explaining membership decisions than state bargaining laws and agency fee provisions do.

There is, of course, more to the story. Political culture, industrialization, private sector unionism, and other state characteristics—the factors that take a back seat to state labor laws in explaining membership in the teachers unions—almost certainly played important roles, decades ago, in *giving rise* to those very labor laws. The point here is not that these other influences are somehow unimportant to an explanation of union membership, but rather that, once they succeeded in generating these labor laws (or not, depending on the state) years ago, the laws themselves have had *independent effects* on union membership—indeed they are the key prevailing influences.

More research is always needed. But these simple findings, and the logic behind them, make good sense. They also dovetail nicely with the larger body of evidence that suggests a strong connection between state laws and the rise and success of the teachers unions and other public sector unions.

Conclusion

As any close observer of American education is well aware, the nation's public schools are heavily unionized, and the unions are superbly organized and enormously powerful. This is the reality of our times—but it is also a reality that, in historical terms, is a rather recent development. The public school system began to emerge in roughly its present form a little over 100 years ago, and for most of its history it was a union-free zone: hardly any teachers belonged to unions, there was no collective bargaining, and neither teachers nor their unions had much political power. Large numbers of teachers across the country did belong to the NEA, and it was a powerful presence at all levels of government; indeed, it was widely recognized as the vanguard of the education establishment. But the NEA of that earlier time was a professional association run by administrators, and it was avowedly opposed to unions and collective bargaining.

Things are different now. Very different. In this chapter I offer some perspective on how the transition from this earlier era to the union era came about and what the lay of the land looks like in modern times. I won't summarize the details here, but a few basic points are worth underlining.

One is that the rise of the teachers unions was not simply due to conditions unique to the public education system—for example, that teachers were subject to arbitrary treatment, horrible working conditions, insecure jobs, and the like, and, as a result, became militant and sought out unions. Lots of workers across all industries, public and private, had similar complaints about their jobs, especially in the late nineteenth and early-to-middle twentieth centuries, and there is no reason to think that teachers were especially victimized. Nor is there any reason to think that these job-related dissatisfactions led to large-scale unionization, whether by teachers or most other workers. The key event that promoted unionization and collective bargaining is that the *laws changed*. They changed for private sector workers with the adoption of the NLRA in 1935. And they changed for public sector workers with the enactment of new labor statutes in most states during the 1960s and 1970s. Whatever the frustrations of teachers and other workers, they did not find expression in unions on a massive scale until the laws made such expression possible.

As a historical movement, then, the unionization of teachers was not some-how special, and it cannot be explained in a satisfactory way by focusing on edu-cation alone. Teachers unions arose when *other* public sector unions did: in the 1960s and 1970s. And they arose because they were empowered by new laws that, thanks to their Democratic allies and their union brethren in the private sec-tor, were purposely designed to promote unionization and collective bargaining.

Another key point is that the teachers unions, like other types of unions, were unavoidably faced with free rider problems that hindered their ability to get organized from the very beginning. These built-in problems ultimately shaped the kinds of solutions that were necessary if teachers were ever to become orga-nized and powerful on a national scale, and if collective bargaining was ever to become the norm. The solution that was best suited, by far, to overcoming the free rider problem was (and is) legal "coercion." That is the solution the early unions (and many professional associations) and their Democratic allies favored, fought for in the political process, and ultimately achieved. Were legal "coercion" not so effective a solution, we would not have laws calling for votes that bind all workers to collective bargaining, anoint one union as their exclusive representa-tive, and allow for agency fee provisions that require everyone to pay their "fair share." These "coercive" provisions are in the law because they work and because the unions and their allies know they work.

Coercion is clearly a two-edged sword. It is an infringement on the rights of teachers who don't want to support unions, and in that respect it is lamentable. Americans value freedom, needless to say, and individual freedoms are surely being restricted here. But coercion also has a positive side. The free rider prob-lem prevents people with common interests from freely joining together to make themselves better off, and the "coercive" aspects of these laws can be understood as simple mechanisms that allow individuals, through democratic votes, to bind themselves *voluntarily* to cooperative, mutually beneficial agreements.

An important question, then, concerns the balance that is struck: how many teachers see legal coercion as an unwanted infringement on their freedom, and how many see it as a mechanism they would voluntarily embrace in order to better pursue their common interests? So far, we don't have any hard-and-fast answers. But a look at the data on union membership across states and legal contexts suggests that most teachers are involved in their unions voluntarily. If some teachers are being forced into collective bargaining and supporting unions, they are probably a minority. To critics, this may be little consolation. It is never a good thing to deny someone freedom, and this is a nation whose Constitu-tion is dedicated to protecting minority rights. But the point is still an interest-ing and consequential one: legal coercion seems to have been crucial for the organizational success of unions, yet their success also seems to be rooted in the voluntary involvement of most teachers. For the majority, it appears, this is an instrumental form of coercion that works for them and that they support. (I have much more to say on this in the next chapter.)

One final point: although it is worthwhile to think about teachers, the nature of their membership, and whether legal "coercion" might be desirable and valuable to many of them, we have to remember that, at the end of the day, the rise of the teachers unions is a historic phenomenon whose impacts go way *beyond* whatever benefits they may hold for teachers. Children are also affected. So is the entire nation.

What the rise of the teachers unions has meant in the grander scheme of things, for all of us, is a radical shift in the structure of power in American education, and with it the emergence of what amounts to a new type of education system for the modern era: a system in which—as the rest of this book shows—the schools are heavily shaped by special interests, efforts to bring improvement are regularly blocked, and the new status quo is fiercely protected by entrenched power.

The rise of the teachers unions, then, is a story of triumph for employee interests and employee power. But it is not a story of triumph for American education.

3

Teachers and Their Unions

It might seem obvious that, if we want to understand the teachers unions—what they do, why they do it—we should focus on their leaders. After all, the leaders are in charge. They are the ones who make the official decisions in politics and collective bargaining, control all the money, and wield power. A focus on leaders also comes naturally. Most people tend to personify politics and organizations, and believe that leaders—whom we can see, watch, listen to, and psychoanalyze—are the keys to what is happening.

This fixation is only reinforced by common stereotypes. One, advanced mainly by conservative critics, is that the teachers unions are run by "bosses," who can do what they want and who use their power to trample the interests of ordinary members. A corollary notion—widely embraced and a favorite of public officials and education followers of all political stripes—is that we need to make a sharp distinction between union leaders and teachers: because union leaders often do things that are not in the public interest, but teachers are good and compassionate and public spirited. To the extent that unions cause problems for public education, then, the blame rests with union leaders. Not with teachers, who are essentially being taken for a ride and are not responsible.

These stereotypes don't come from nowhere. Union leaders do have a measure of autonomy, and sometimes they abuse it. The flamboyant Pat Tornillo, for instance, reigned over the Miami-Dade teachers union for some forty years until a Federal Bureau of Investigation raid revealed that between 1998 and 2001 he had systematically embezzled $650,000 of member dues money to pay for his own personal expenses, including lavish vacations that involved "first-class airfare, stays at luxury hotels, meals, gifts, and souvenirs in Australia, New Zealand,

New York City, the San Francisco area, and the Caribbean island of St. Barthélemy."[1] Meantime, his union was $2 million behind on its dues payments to the national AFT, as well as delinquent in repaying $2 million in loans to two banks that were demanding their money.

Tornillo was clearly a boss, and he clearly did bad things. But his malfeasance was dwarfed by the brazen thievery of Barbara Bullock, president of the Washington, D.C., teachers union. Between 1995 and 2002, she and a few cronies managed to siphon $5 million out of union coffers to support their lavish lifestyles, which included, for Bullock herself, $500,000 on custom clothing, $50,000 on fur coats, $100,000 on season tickets for professional football and basketball games, and various amounts on art, silver, jewelry, and other luxuries. As Bullock explained to a federal judge, "I love to shop."[2] Because she was shopping with member money, though, her union was behind in its dues to the national AFT and unable to pay its rent or phone bills.[3]

These are famous cases of union bossism and teachers being taken for a ride. There are less famous cases too. But they are not the norm, and to focus on them is to misunderstand the situation of the typical union. The point that needs appreciating is that—as is true for most organizations, especially member organizations—union leaders operate under *constraints* that heavily determine what they can and cannot do, and these constraints derive largely from their members.

In fundamental respects, leaders are extensions of their own organizations. The things that matter most to them—their positions of power, their reputations, the money they can wield, the staff they can hire, the perquisites and salaries that go along with the job—are all tied to their organizations' survival and prosperity and their members' satisfaction. When their organizations do well, they do well. To make themselves better off, therefore, they cannot simply do what they want, unless what they want is to reign over small, weaker, less powerful organizations or to be thrown out of office. They have compelling incentives to make the organizations' interests their own. As Miriam Golden notes, "Ordinary workers have only to pursue their individual interests, but union leaders have to pursue the interests of the organization itself; that is, they have to act as caretakers for the union or risk its demise."[4]

What this means, among other things, is that the power of leaders is rooted in the membership. Members are the source of most of the unions' money. They are the source of all their political activists. And if they are willing to cooperate, act with solidarity, and thus *follow* their elected leaders, they give leaders the leverage they need—via the threat of strikes, demonstrations, work disruptions, political contributions, and political activism—to be successful in collective bargaining and politics. Even if leaders could get members and money through coercive means, or something like it, they couldn't get activists that way, they couldn't get genuine followers that way, and their power in collective bargaining and politics would be inherently limited.[5]

To cultivate the full power of their own members, then, leaders have incentives to build support and thus to represent them by protecting and pursuing their interests. These incentives are only strengthened by the fact that union leaders are elected by these same members. Contested elections are common when leaders seem to be out of step with their members, and losses by incumbent leaders are not at all rare. In Cincinnati, for example, union president Rick Beck endorsed a (limited) pay-for-performance reform that his members disavowed, and he was soon tossed out of office. The same thing happened in Chicago when union president Deborah Lynch was faulted for being too "collaborative" and failing to fight hard enough for bread and butter issues.[6] Not all teachers unions are bastions of democracy. But even so, there are strong forces at work that forge a positive connection between what teachers want and what their leaders actually do.

If we aim to understand the teachers unions, then, we need to understand the nature of this connection. To help to do that, I commissioned a national survey of America's public school teachers, which was carried out by Harris Interactive in 2003. The sample consists of 3,328 teachers from all corners of the country. When properly weighted, it represents a national cross section of full-time, practicing public school teachers.[7] (For comparisons to the Schools and Staffing Survey data used in the previous chapter, see appendix B.)

Several surveys have been carried out on the attitudes and opinions of America's teachers over the years, but with few exceptions these studies do not explore the connection between teachers and their unions.[8] The exceptions—one by Public Agenda in 2003 and another by Education Sector in 2008—are helpful, and I cite them on occasion in the pages to follow.[9]

My own survey covers a lot of ground, and, although I have tried to keep the presentation simple and straightforward, it can be rather detailed at times. The details are important, however, and are not just separate findings that lead to some sort of encyclopedic listing of results. On the contrary, they fit together into a simple, coherent perspective on how members are connected to their unions, and they shed revealing light on the fundamentals of union organization. Here, as guideposts for what follows, are some of the basic themes.

The survey ultimately tells a story about teachers who, despite their personal differences in partisanship, ideology, and location, are bound together by *common occupational interests*. Whether Democrat or Republican, liberal or conservative, from the South or North or West, they join local unions because they *want* to, they are highly *satisfied* with what the locals (via leaders) do to promote their interests, and they are strongly focused on—and supportive of—local *collective bargaining*. They firmly believe, moreover, that collective bargaining has benign consequences for schools and children, and thus that the familiar union mantra—what's good for teachers is good for kids—is true.

These are the foundations of union strength. The NEA and the AFT are powerful organizations precisely because they are grounded in thousands of local unions that win the loyalty, attachment, and dues money of teachers by *representing their common interests*. Local leaders are not "bosses." They represent their members and, in so doing, are constrained by what their members want.

While collective bargaining is a bedrock of union strength and unity, politics is a source of internal problems. The teachers unions are (for good reason) closely aligned with the Democratic Party, and many Republican teachers aren't happy with this partisan tilt. Their alienation, however, is focused on the *state and national* organizations—whose activities are largely political—and has *nothing to do* with the local unions, which they *continue to support fully*. Moreover, their positions on educational policy issues that comprise the heart of union politics—regarding tenure, accountability, vouchers, charter schools, and the like—are in line with those of their Democratic colleagues, and with what the NEA and AFT actually do in the political process. Thus, while union politics is a source of dissatisfaction, it is ultimately (when focused on education) a reflection of the common occupational interests of members. Which means that in politics—as in collective bargaining—leaders are not "bosses" and are doing basically what their members want.

What the survey helps to show, then, is that the common stereotypes are very wide of the mark. To understand the teachers unions as organizations, we need to recognize that leaders are heavily constrained by their members. Whatever the unions may do in promoting their special interests—including things that are not good for schools or kids—these interests are the *teachers' own interests*, and the unions are generally doing things that *teachers want them to do*.

So this is where the discussion is going. Let's get to the survey and put the building blocks together.

Forced Membership

Historical evidence on the rise of the teachers unions seems to suggest that many and perhaps most teachers join unions voluntarily. But is this the case? By law, teachers cannot be forced to join. Yet if agency fees are required they may feel they have no rational alternative. After all, if they don't join, they lose the direct benefits of membership—liability insurance, for example, and legal protection (if threatened with dismissal or reprimand, say)—and are still required to pay fees comparable to dues. Under the circumstances, they may join but still feel forced. In addition, they may face social pressure from their colleagues at work, who may make them feel that, if they don't join, they will be shunned.

Table 3-1. *Voluntarism at Local, State, and National Levels, by Type of District and State*[a]

			State legal context				
	District type		CB law, AF allowed	CB law, no AF allowed	No CB law	CB prohib- ited	Total
Response	CB	No CB					
Reasons for joining union							
I belong because I really want to	77	80	76	79	78	83	78
I belong because I feel I have to or feel pressure to	23	20	24	21	22	17	22
N	2,097	351	1,662	335	181	270	2,448
If allowed, would member voluntarily join local union?							
Yes	94	92	94	93	93	93	94
No	6	8	6	7	7	7	6
N	1,985	329	1,568	320	174	252	2,314
If allowed, would member voluntarily join state union?							
Yes	80	88	80	82	81	90	81
No	20	12	20	18	19	10	19
N	1,784	320	1,410	286	163	244	2,104
If allowed, would member voluntarily join national union?							
Yes	67	75	67	60	72	76	68
No	33	26	33	40	28	24	32
N	1,584	292	1,233	270	154	220	1,876

Source: Harris Interactive survey conducted online between April 24 and May 20, 2003.

a. Figures in body of table are percentages, with the columns for each survey item adding to 100 percent within each type of district or state. *N* is the weighted number of observations. AF = agency fees. CB = collective bargaining.

The survey asked union members whether they belong because they "really want to" or because they "have to or feel pressure to."[10] Their responses, set out in table 3-1, show that the overwhelming majority of union members, more than three-quarters, said they join because they really want to. Importantly, even though we might expect a sense of forced membership to be much higher in states that allow agency fees (as compared to states that don't) and in districts that have collective bargaining (as compared to districts that don't), the evidence does not bear this out. Voluntary membership is the norm across all contexts, even when elements of legal coercion might appear to be present. This isn't to say that legal coercion doesn't increase membership, but rather that union members don't *see* themselves as being coerced.

One ambiguity here is that, when teachers join their local unions, they automatically join the relevant state and national unions at the same time, and the latter get a portion of their dues money. This "unitary" membership is *required* by both the NEA and the AFT: members have no choice. Obviously, teachers may feel rather differently about their local, state, and national unions, and it isn't clear which one(s) they are thinking about when they talk about their membership.

To pull these views apart, the survey first asked union members whether, if membership were purely voluntary, they would choose to join and pay dues to their local organization, and then asked the same question separately for the state and national organizations.[11] As the figures in table 3-1 vividly demonstrate, the voluntary involvement of members at the local level is truly stunning, with 94 percent of members saying that, given the opportunity to make a free choice, they would voluntarily join their local union. The figures are comparably high across all institutional settings, even where coercion might be a problem. This is not to say that all teachers want to belong to unions. They don't. Yet it is of great significance that, across all areas of the country, teachers who *do* choose to join unions are almost all doing it because they want to. This is even true in states that are quite conservative (although fewer teachers in those states choose to join).

Voluntarism falls off somewhat for the state unions, to 81 percent. And it falls off still more for the national unions, to 68 percent. An obvious reason—but not necessarily the most important one, as the evidence on politics will show—is that the locals are the source of most benefits, including collective bargaining. They are also located where teachers actually work and interact with others, and so are more relevant to teachers' everyday lives.

These numbers shed favorable light on the unions. At all three levels of organization, the great majority of union members are voluntarily involved. But there are also troubling implications. If one-third of the existing membership (which amounts to more than a million teachers) would voluntarily opt out of the national organizations given the opportunity, the NEA and the AFT would lose enormous amounts of money, and their operations would be heavily affected. This surely helps to explain why both unions have "unitary" dues structures that force members to join the national and state organizations when they join their locals. Most members don't need to be forced. But some do, and without them and their money the national unions would take a big hit.

Still, the basic story here is that coercion operates only at the margins. This being so, it would be interesting to know whether teachers support the concept of forced membership as a matter of public policy. Do they think it is right or desirable that all teachers be required to join a union, or at least pay fees to one?

As discussed in chapter 2, teachers have self-interested reasons to favor such a policy: they can overcome their collective action problem—and better pursue their common interests—by agreeing to a policy that forces all teachers to join or to pay their fair share. But maybe this rationale is too simplistic. Some teachers—those who are young, for example, or especially talented or ambitious—may not see their own interests as identical to those of their colleagues. Some may also have ideological, partisan, or professional objections to unions. And some may have moral qualms about forcing people to do things against their will. So it is surely legitimate to wonder, do most teachers see forced membership or fees as a good idea?

To see, the survey asked teachers which approach they would favor in districts with collective bargaining: "(1) All teachers in the district should have to belong and pay dues to the union, because the union represents them all. (2) Membership in the union should be voluntary, but teachers who don't want to join should still have to pay a fee to the union, because the union represents their interests too. (3) Membership in the union should be voluntary with no fees imposed on teachers who don't join, because they should not be required to support the union against their will."[12]

The responses are presented in table 3-2. Among teachers as a whole, a population that includes both members and nonmembers of unions, 54 percent favor some form of forced membership: with 16 percent favoring the union shop, which would literally force teachers to join (but has been declared illegal by the Supreme Court), and another 38 percent favoring the agency shop, which would require teachers to pay agency fees to the union.

There are, however, big differences across the states. Indeed, the states are essentially divided into two opposing camps. In states with strong collective bargaining laws—where the concept of forced payments to unions has become part of public policy—76 percent of teachers favor some form of coercion. In the remaining states, where the laws are weaker and agency fees are not allowed, more than 70 percent of teachers *oppose* any form of coercion—although many of these teachers, of course, are not union members.

It is reasonable to suspect that union members are much more sympathetic to coercion than nonmembers are, and thus that the pattern we've just seen is due in part to the fact that unionization is much more common in the first group of states. We can get a clearer picture by breaking the data down a bit further. Doing so, as the table shows, leads to three basic conclusions:

—Everywhere, union members are much more supportive of coercion than nonmembers are.

—In the states without strong laws, nonmembers (who are quite numerous) are massively opposed to coercion, at a rate of more than 90 percent. In the

Table-3-2. *Attitudes toward Voluntary Membership, by Type of State*[a]

Sample and attitude	CB law, AF allowed	CB law, no AF allowed	No CB law	CB prohibited	Total
All teachers					
All teachers must belong to union	23	4	10	7	16
All teachers must pay fees to union	53	28	20	14	38
Teachers should have free choice	23	68	70	79	46
N	1,787	501	347	693	3,328
Union members					
All teachers must belong to union	25	6	16	12	20
All teachers must pay fees to union	56	40	33	25	49
Teachers should have free choice	19	54	51	63	31
N	1,662	335	181	270	2,448
Nonmembers					
All teachers must belong to union	7	2	4	4	4
All teachers must pay fees to union	24	4	6	7	9
Teachers should have free choice	69	95	90	89	87
N	139	165	163	413	880

Source: Harris Interactive survey conducted online between April 24 and May 20, 2003.

a. Figures in body of table are percentages, with the columns for each survey item adding to 100 percent within each type of district or state. *N* is the weighted number of observations. AF = agency fees. CB = collective bargaining.

strong-law states, most nonmembers also take a dim view of coercion, but opposition is lower, at 69 percent.

—Support for coercion is confined largely to union members in the strong-law states, where 81 percent support it. (Union members in these states, however, constitute a majority of all unionized teachers nationwide.) An interesting finding is that 56 percent of union members in the remaining states actually *oppose* resorting to these elements of force.

The differences across states probably have something to do with political culture. The first group of states is more liberal and labor-friendly, the second is more conservative and antiunion, and these distinctive attitudes likely account (in part) for the different reactions to the concept of forced unionism. Indeed, these same attitudes probably also shape how citizens vote, so it is likely that the policies themselves—agency fees and strong laws in the first group, no agency fees and weak laws in the second—largely reflect the underlying political cultures from the get-go.[13]

The unions themselves are big proponents of coercion, and the cultural divide across states poses a big challenge for them. The areas of the country where they are weakest and most clearly need to attract members, mainly in the southern and border states, are precisely the areas where the cards are stacked against them. Not only are the laws weak, but teachers themselves—including those who belong to unions—do not support an approach to unionization that contains elements of coercion. This doesn't mean that they don't have interests in common with other teachers, and it doesn't mean that they don't want to act on them. It means that, for some teachers, *other values* come into play when coercion is being considered.

Just how important is coercion to union success? The survey cannot answer that question. We know that the vast majority of union members in all areas of the country see their own membership as voluntary. This is important for understanding the teachers unions as organizations and for debunking stereotypes about the tyranny of union bosses. Yet we also know that coercion is strategically used, and to good effect, to bolster the state and national organizations—which, it appears, would be seriously weakened if membership were made truly voluntary. And we also know that, in the more conservative states where voluntarism is enshrined in the law, most teachers exercise their freedom by choosing *not* to join, which is a huge problem for the unions. It may well be that, in those settings, coercive new laws—if they could get them—are actually necessary if the unions are to have any hope of ramping up their membership and power.

Why Do Teachers Join?

In the main, though, teachers join unions not because they are required to, but because of the positive things the unions can do for them. The recent survey by Education Sector highlights as much, showing that teachers see great advantages to getting unionized. A lofty 75 percent agree that "without collective bargaining, the working conditions and salaries of teachers would be much worse," a clear indication that they think unions are effective at promoting their occupational interests and making them better off. And 77 percent agree that "without a union, teachers would be vulnerable to school politics or administrators who abuse their power," a clear indication that they see themselves as needing the kind of protection a union can provide.[14]

Let's take a closer look, then, at the specifics of why teachers join their unions. My own survey asked union members about their main reason for joining and presented them with the following alternatives:[15]

Figure 3-1. *Reasons for Joining the Union, by Type of District*[a]

Percent

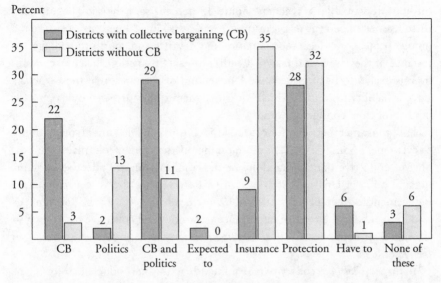

Source: Harris Interactive survey conducted online between April 24 and May 20, 2003.

a. Figures represent, for each type of district, the percentage of union members saying that this particular benefit or rationale is their main reason for joining the union.

—To support the organization's collective bargaining activities,

—To support the organization's political activities,

—To support both its collective bargaining and its political activities,

—Because other teachers expect me to,

—To get liability (and perhaps other) insurance,

—Because the union would protect me if I needed it,

—Because I have to,

—None of these.

Their responses are set out graphically in figure 3-1. The potential for coercion is greatest in districts that have collective bargaining, as most districts (of any size) do. In these districts, the evidence suggests once again that teachers do not regard their membership as forced. Very few said that they join mainly because they have to (6 percent) or are expected to (2 percent). Instead, almost all members pointed either to their support for collective bargaining and politics or to the direct benefits they receive, such as protection or insurance.

Direct benefits are quite effective as organization builders, because in giving members something tangible in return for their dues they help to bind teachers to their unions regardless of how successful their leaders are in collective bargaining or politics—activities that are fraught with uncertainty. Direct benefits are certain. They are elements of stability and attraction, and they are obviously quite valuable to teachers. Some 37 percent said they join mainly for these reasons: 9 percent to get insurance and a striking 28 percent to ensure the union's protection—legal representation in grievance and court proceedings, for instance, if they are ever threatened with dismissal or sanction. Insurance, moreover, is itself a form of protection. A basic kind of insurance that most teachers carry is liability insurance, which backstops them if they are sued by parents (or others) for their conduct at work.[16]

Still, most members join for collective goods: benefits that are supplied jointly to everyone.[17] Some 51 percent of union members said they join mainly in support of collective bargaining alone or the combination of collective bargaining and politics. Union political activities, however, are almost never the main inducement for membership, selected by just 2 percent, and this begins to tell us something about the relative importance of politics and collective bargaining in the minds of members. *Of all the motivations for joining, collective bargaining is the most salient.*

In districts *without* collective bargaining, then, this key inducement for membership is absent. Unions might try to convince teachers that, with a strong organization, they can win collective bargaining for themselves later on; but most districts are in a stable equilibrium, and those that don't have collective bargaining are almost surely not going to get it in the near future. Most teachers are surely aware of that fact and need to be attracted on some other basis. And indeed, this other basis is readily available: teachers who join unions in these districts do it primarily to get the direct benefits of insurance (35 percent) and protection (32 percent). Almost none join because they have to or are expected to. And tellingly, politics is relatively unimportant: these are unions that do not engage in collective bargaining at all, so politics is *the* major way that they are able to fight for the broader interests of teachers, yet it does little to attract members. Only 13 percent said they join mainly for politics, and another 11 percent said they join for the combination of politics and (presumably the hope of getting) collective bargaining.[18]

It is tempting to conclude that, in districts without collective bargaining, the unions are essentially just providing insurance and protection to members, and that collective bargaining just isn't important to them. But the data only tap the *main* reasons members join. The survey didn't ask whether other inducements might be relevant too. It did, however, ask the teachers in these nonbargaining settings, "Would you like to see collective bargaining adopted in your district?" A resounding 81 percent of union members said that they *would*. So although they obviously value the direct benefits their unions provide, they clearly want and value collective bargaining too.[19]

We can take this one step further. The survey results indicate that, of the teachers who have chosen *not* to join unions in these nonbargaining districts—and who are thus a rather extreme pool of teachers: nonmembers in what tend to be conservative, nonunion contexts—42 percent said that *they too* would like to see collective bargaining adopted. This means that, in the aggregate, collective bargaining actually has the support of 57 percent of all the teachers who work in nonbargaining districts, most of which are in southern and border states. The upshot is that *teachers everywhere are quite supportive of collective bargaining—even when they do not have it.*

Member Satisfaction with Their Unions

Because teachers join their unions voluntarily, it is reasonable to suspect that they are satisfied with what they are getting in return. The survey bears this out. When asked how satisfied they are with their union as a whole, an impressive 77 percent said they are either very or somewhat satisfied, and the percentages are virtually the same in districts that do and do not engage in collective bargaining.[20]

This reflects well on the unions, but it only scratches the surface. Because aside from the direct benefits they provide, the unions pursue member interests in two very different ways. They do it through collective bargaining, which is conducted locally. And they do it through politics, which is pursued mainly at the state and national levels through election campaigns and lobbying. These are the two key avenues by which the unions exercise power—and shape the public schools—so we need to learn more about their organizational foundations. The evidence thus far suggests that politics has less motivational value than collective bargaining in attracting members. The survey explored this further by asking members about their satisfaction with each realm.[21]

Responses show that members are quite satisfied on *both* dimensions, indicating that the unions are doing a good job of representing their constituents. Yet members are *more* satisfied with the unions' collective bargaining activities than with their political activities. Overall, 84 percent said they are satisfied with what their union is doing on collective bargaining; on politics 66 percent said they are satisfied. This figure for politics is surely respectable. But it is also considerably lower, and, indeed, looked at from another angle it is a sign of trouble—for the flip side is that, while just 16 percent of teachers are dissatisfied with union collective bargaining, more than twice as many, 34 percent, are dissatisfied with union politics. Thus, while the unions are satisfying most members politically, there is a fairly sizable alienated minority. The same is not true for collective bargaining, on which members are quite united.

We can also use these measures to get a sense of the *relative importance* that teachers attach to collective bargaining and politics when they evaluate their unions. When teachers are asked how satisfied they are with their unions overall, what aspects of their unions are they thinking about? Are they thinking mainly about collective bargaining, mainly about politics, or rather equally about both? One simple way to get at this is to use their satisfaction with collective bargaining and politics to try to predict their overall level of satisfaction. It stands to reason that, if collective bargaining is more salient to them, their satisfaction with collective bargaining will do a better job of predicting their overall level of satisfaction than their satisfaction with politics will. And vice versa.

When this is carried out through simple regression analysis—with controls for a host of other relevant variables (such as a teacher's age, gender, and ethnicity)—the findings show that collective bargaining is *far* more important than politics in predicting a teacher's overall satisfaction with the union.[22] Indeed, it has about three times the impact of politics in determining how members view their unions. For the most part, then, *members evaluate their unions as collective bargaining organizations*, and it is the performance of the unions on this score—not on politics—that mainly determines how satisfied they are with their membership overall.

Let's carry this analysis a bit further. The survey asked members to indicate how they feel about their local, state, and national unions by giving each a score from 0 to 100, with 0 being the most negative and 100 being the most positive. When their scores are aggregated, they yield a median score of 75 for local unions, a score of 60 for state unions, and a score of 55 for national unions. *Teachers like their local unions best.*

Why? What are they thinking about? An interesting way to get at this is to take the information we already have about member satisfaction with collective bargaining and politics and use it to predict how members feel about their local, state, and national organizations. The results are quite revealing. When the same form of regression analysis is carried out as before (with the same controls), we find that how members view their *local* union is much better predicted by collective bargaining than by politics—indeed, it has more than four times the impact. At the *state* level, in contrast, the predictive power of collective bargaining and politics is much more evenly balanced, with politics somewhat more important. And at the *national* level, members barely think of collective bargaining at all when they evaluate the union, and base their evaluations *almost entirely on politics.*[23]

Finally, let's carry out one more round of analysis, using member evaluations of their local, state, and national unions to predict their overall levels of satisfaction. Here the goal is to determine the relative salience that teachers attach to these parts of the organization as they arrive at summary evaluations of their union membership as a whole. All three levels are "performing," but how does each contribute to a member's overall satisfaction with the union? If we carry out the same sort of regression analysis as above, we find that *teachers are heavily focused on their local unions.* This is by far the main determinant of their satisfaction (or dissatisfaction) with the union as a whole. Specifically, the estimation indicates that what happens at the local level carries roughly five times more weight than what happens at either the state or national levels (with the latter two roughly equal to one another in impact).[24]

The picture that emerges from the data, then, is clear and consistent. Above all else, it highlights the key importance of *union locals* and *collective bargaining* in attracting teachers to their organizations and keeping them satisfied and attached. *These are the foundations of the unions' organizational success.* Although the unions are thoroughly political organizations—continuously active, armed with a vast array of weaponry, and quite powerful in elections and the policy process—politics is a secondary concern for most members. They are far less motivated by it. And they associate it, as they should, with the state and (especially) the national organizations, whose performance they see as much less relevant to their satisfaction.

In some sense, this asymmetry is good for the unions—because members are also *less satisfied* with politics than they are with collective bargaining. Collective bargaining is something they all tend to agree upon and that they weight heavily when assessing the value of their membership. They are less likely to agree on politics—but they also don't care about it as much, and this reduces the internal problems that any disagreements might cause.

Attitudes toward Collective Bargaining

When teachers contemplate unions and collective bargaining, they face an interesting moral dilemma. Collective bargaining is in their self-interest. But by pursuing their self-interest, they may be taking actions that—in some part, and perhaps in large part—work to the disadvantage of children, and saddle schools with costs and organizational perversities that undermine effective education.

The question is, what do teachers think about all this? Do they recognize that collective bargaining and the pursuit of their own interests may well come at the expense of the very children they are supposed to be serving? Or do they resolve the moral dilemma—the cognitive dissonance, as psychologists would put it—by believing that collective bargaining has no real downside and that there is a happy compatibility between their own interests and what is best for kids and schools?

Union leaders are vocal purveyors of the happy-compatibility theme. Their mantra is that what is good for teachers is good for kids—and thus that teacher benefits and restrictive work rules are justified on educational grounds, and are not simply means of advancing the self-interest of teachers (and unions). As leaders of public sector unions, dependent as they are on voter support and dollars, they need to say these things as a matter of simple strategy. That's how the game is played. They may believe it. They may not. It really doesn't matter much.

But what about ordinary teachers? The survey asked them two sets of questions about collective bargaining. The first singles out six basic dimensions of schooling—costs, academic performance, organizational flexibility (or rigidity), conflict (or cooperation), professionalism, and teaching—and asks whether they think the effects of collective bargaining in each case are positive, neutral, or negative.[25]

As table 3-3 reveals, union members overwhelmingly believe that collective bargaining is either positive or neutral in its consequences for public education and that it has no real downside. In their minds, there is indeed a happy compatibility of interests here: what is good for teachers is good for kids and schools, or at least is not harmful to them. Teachers therefore have nothing to feel guilty about in aggressively pursuing their own interests. The moral dilemma is resolved.

The teachers most directly involved, of course, are the union members in districts with collective bargaining. In this group, teachers are virtually unanimous in claiming that collective bargaining has no negative consequences for academic performance, teaching, or professionalism—arguably the three dimensions closest to the educational process. A mere 3 percent associate collective bargaining with lower academic performance, 5 percent associate it with worse teaching, and 9 percent associate it with less professionalism. These negatives are barely on the radar screen. The figures are a bit higher on dimensions teachers are likely to see as more distantly connected to education itself—cost, organization, and conflict—but these numbers too are quite low in any absolute sense. On all six dimensions, the vast majority of teachers see no real downside. When they engage in collective bargaining, they believe they are helping themselves without hurting anyone else.

As for whether collective bargaining actually has *positive* consequences for the larger system, rather than just being neutral, union members are rather split. They are most likely to see positive consequences for the dimensions that are most fundamental—academic performance (50 percent), teaching (48 percent), and professionalism (57 percent)—and are less likely to think it leads to more flexible organizations (26 percent), more cooperation (36 percent), or lower costs (6 percent). So union members are not uniformly convinced that collective bargaining is *good* for public education—although many do feel that way—but they *are* uniformly convinced that it is *not bad* and thus that their pursuit of self-interest does no harm.

Union members in districts *without* collective bargaining also have a benign view of collective bargaining. While they are less likely to see overtly positive consequences—they are, after all, from more conservative areas of the country—they almost always believe that collective bargaining has no negative consequences and thus can be pursued without undermining the quality of education.

Table 3-3. *Teacher Attitudes toward Collective Bargaining,
by Union Membership and Type of District*[a]

Attitude	Union member		Nonmember		*All teachers*
	CB	*No CB*	*CB*	*No CB*	
Perceived impact of CB on					
Costs					
Higher costs	22	25	31	42	26
No difference	72	68	64	53	68
Lower costs	6	8	6	6	6
Academic performance					
Lower academic performance	3	3	7	11	5
No difference	47	52	69	68	53
Better academic performance	50	45	24	21	42
Organization					
More rigid	23	29	37	39	28
No difference	52	46	46	48	50
More flexible	26	25	16	13	23
Conflict					
More conflict	29	35	48	56	36
No difference	35	31	34	27	33
More cooperation	36	34	18	17	31
Professionalism					
Less professionalism	9	11	23	24	13
No difference	34	33	44	50	38
More professionalism	57	56	33	26	49
Teaching					
Worse teaching	5	5	16	16	8
No difference	47	45	63	63	51
Better teaching	48	50	21	21	41
Contending arguments					
CB contracts					
Produce so many rules and restrictions that they make schools difficult to manage and lead	17	28	43	60	28
Produce reasonable rules and regulations that help schools promote learning	83	72	57	40	72
Transfer rights and seniority preferences					
Make schools less effective because they make it difficult to put the right person in the right job	30	33	65	47	37
Make schools more effective because they give teachers more options and prevent favoritism	70	67	35	53	63
Principals					
Need lots of discretion in order to manage their schools and promote learning most effectively	38	41	61	54	43
Can abuse their discretion, and it needs to be restricted in order to protect teacher rights	62	59	39	46	57
N	2,070	346	348	533	3,297

Source: Harris Interactive survey conducted online between April 24 and May 20, 2003.

a. Figures in body of table are percentages, with columns adding to 100 percent for each item. *N* is the weighted number of observations. CB = collective bargaining.

In general, then, *union members everywhere, regardless of where they live and work, tend to believe that collective bargaining has no downside for schools or kids.*

Now let's look at teachers who have chosen *not* to join unions. It is no surprise that their views are more negative than those of union members. But not by much. Except when it comes to organizational conflict, they believe that collective bargaining has effects that are either positive or neutral, and the majorities are quite lopsided. Thus, on these general measures, *even teachers who do not belong to unions are inclined to see the pursuit of teacher self-interest as having little downside for schools and children.* This is the case even though most of these teachers come from the more conservative states.

The survey also tapped teacher attitudes through a second set of measures. These items highlight three pairs of contending arguments, and for each pair teachers were asked to pick the position they agree with more. The three sets of arguments are as follows:

—Pair 1: Collective bargaining contracts produce so many rules and restrictions that they make schools difficult to manage and lead . . . (or) . . . Collective bargaining contracts produce reasonable rules and regulations that help schools promote learning.

—Pair 2: Transfer rights and seniority preferences make schools more effective, because they give teachers more options and prevent favoritism . . . (or) . . . Transfer rights and seniority preferences make schools less effective, because they make it difficult to put the right person in the right job.

—Pair 3: Principals need lots of discretion in order to manage their schools and promote learning most effectively . . . (or) . . . Principals can abuse their discretion, and it needs to be restricted in order to protect teacher rights.

These items do not allow teachers to take neutral positions. The issues are also much more specific than the earlier items, and teachers are presented with plausible arguments pro and con. Given the either-or framing, it is predictable that these measures will yield a larger portion of members who associate negative consequences with collective bargaining. But the real question here is, if they are forced to say that collective bargaining has either positive or negative effects, which will they choose?

Under this framing, as table 3-3 (bottom portion) shows, union members in districts with collective bargaining said overwhelmingly that collective bargaining has positive effects: 83 percent think that contract rules promote student learning, 70 percent think that seniority-based transfer rights make schools more effective, and 62 percent think that principals can abuse their discretion and need to be restricted by contract rules. Similar responses were given by union members in districts without collective bargaining. The theme of the story remains the same: the vast majority of union members, wherever they are located, see their pursuit of self-interest as consistent with what is good for kids and schools.

By these measures, however, there is a bigger gap between members and non-members, with the latter much more likely to see the downside of collective bargaining. If we put this rather jaundiced view of collective bargaining together with the earlier evidence, then, it is fair to say that nonmembers are conflicted. The vast majority of them do not think that collective bargaining has bad outcomes for academic performance, the quality of teaching, and other basics of public education. But they do think that, in specific ways, it can cause problems.

Politics

Collective bargaining is an organizational winner for the teachers unions. In districts that have it, members are overwhelmingly satisfied with what they are getting, are bonded to their local unions, and are convinced that the consequences for schools and students are benign. In districts without collective bargaining, union members overwhelmingly want it and are just as positive in their assessments. For teachers unions throughout the country, collective bargaining is a source of unity and organizational success. The key to all this is that collective bargaining is narrowly focused on the occupational interests of teachers, and these are interests that, at least in large measure, all teachers share.

The teachers unions also engage in politics. As we have seen, most union members are satisfied with what their organizations are doing politically, but they are distinctly *less* satisfied than they are with collective bargaining, and a sizable minority are dissatisfied. This is not an accident. Politics is problematic in ways that collective bargaining is not.

If the teachers unions want to maximize their power in politics, especially in elections and legislatures, they cannot act alone. They need allies. To get them, they have followed a strategy that the AFL-CIO and almost all politically active unions have followed for many decades: they have planted themselves at the heart of the Democratic Party and made themselves indispensable supporters. In elections, they endorse, finance, and actively campaign for Democratic candidates. These candidates tend to support unionization, collective bargaining, higher spending on education, and other teacher interests, and so are enormously helpful once in office. But they also have much broader agendas—on abortion, gun control, gay marriage, and other important issues of the day—that go well beyond educational issues. When the teachers unions support Democratic candidates, then, they are putting their weight behind the whole package—a liberal package that doesn't deal solely with education.

The same thing happens in their coalitional relations with other interest groups. In the legislative policy process, for instance, they enhance their own power—and attract support for their own educational objectives—by broadening their network of interest group allies and taking a lead role in the liberal policy coalition. This gets them actively involved—alongside such groups as the National Association for the Advancement of Colored People, the American Civil Liberties Union, the trial lawyers, People for the American Way, and many labor unions—in supporting the liberal policy agenda more generally. In return, the teachers unions can expect liberal allies to come to their aid in education and help them win. But notice how the formula works: to be winners in education, the unions can't focus just on education. They need to be part of larger coalitions and involved in a broader range of issues.

Internally, this is a source of problems. Republican and conservative teachers surely want their unions to be politically successful in advancing their occupational interests. But it is inevitable that, at least for some, the unions' close association with liberal policies and the Democratic Party will be a source of dissatisfaction and even alienation and antagonism. In an important sense, there is nothing the teachers unions can do about this. It is a built-in tension. As human beings, Republican and conservative teachers have values and concerns that go well beyond their narrow occupational interests; and in the grander scheme of life, they may want Republican candidates elected and liberal policies defeated. But the union is not, and cannot be, in the business of representing its members as full-blown human beings. It is in the business of representing their much more narrow interests as employees. And when it does so, some of these human beings are going to feel that their *other* values and concerns are not being met.

Partisanship and Ideology

To explore the political side of union organization, I begin by putting together some basic evidence on where teachers stand politically. What is the political profile of America's public school teachers, and how do they compare on political grounds to ordinary American citizens? Are teachers more liberal and Democratic than other citizens are, on average, or is it possible that teachers are actually quite mainstream in their political leanings, and that the teachers unions are much more liberal than their members?

The survey contains information on the partisanship, ideology, and voting behavior of teachers. To get data on citizens generally, I turn to the National Election Study (NES), which has been carried out regularly for more than half a century and is the best single source of information on American political attitudes and voting behavior.[26] In comparing teachers to ordinary citizens, it is important to remember that teachers are unusually well educated—all have college degrees, roughly half have master's degrees—and education is an important determinant of political attitudes. Also, the teaching force is disproportionately female, and American women tend to be more liberal and Democratic than American men.[27] In judging whether teachers are politically different (or not)

Table 3-4. *Party Identification, Ideology, and Voting among Teachers and the General Public*

Percent unless otherwise noted

Variable	Educated voters (NES, 2000–04)			Teachers (2003)								
				Union Members			Nonmembers			All teachers		
	All	Women	Men	All	Women	Men	All	Women	Men	All	Women	Men
Party identification												
Democrat	31	36	27	51	54	43	30	31	28	45	47	40
Independent	32	29	35	24	21	32	24	23	26	24	21	31
Republican	37	36	39	25	25	25	46	46	46	31	32	29
N	1,225	608	617	2,419	1,720	699	840	647	193	3,290	2,391	899
Ideology												
Liberal	31	37	25	48	48	48	30	30	32	43	42	45
Moderate	24	24	23	22	23	18	24	27	12	22	24	17
Conservative	46	39	52	31	29	34	46	44	56	35	34	38
N	943	461	482	2,448	1,740	708	849	651	198	3,328	2,415	913
2000 vote												
Bush	48	43	52	34	34	35	60	60	61	41	42	40
Gore	48	53	42	61	63	58	36	37	33	55	55	54
Nader	4	3	5	3	2	5	2	2	3	3	2	5
Other	1	1	1	2	2	2	1	1	2	2	2	2
N	387	191	196	2,376	1,682	694	817	627	190	3,222	2,331	891

Source: Data for the American public are from the National Election Study (NES). Data for teachers are from Harris Interactive survey conducted online between April 24 and May 20, 2003.

a. Data for the American public are based on a weighted average of respondents from 2000, 2002, and 2004 and include only those who have a college degree or beyond and who are between the ages of twenty-six and sixty-nine. *N* is the weighted number of observations.

from the rest of the population, then, it is best to compare them to the subset of the American adult population that is well educated, and to break the data down by men and women.[28]

Using a subset of the data greatly reduces the number of observations in the NES data set—there are typically about 300 well-educated respondents a year—so I have combined the NES surveys for 2000, 2002, and 2004 to arrive at the relevant figures for educated American adults. These years were selected because my own survey was carried out in 2003, and we need to compare teachers with their contemporaries.

The political profiles are set out in table 3-4. Consider the findings on party identification. Among Americans with college degrees, the 2003 partisan balance favors Republicans over Democrats by a margin of 37 to 31 percent, with another 32 percent calling themselves Independents. This Republican advantage, it turns out, is entirely due to the differing partisan orientations of women and men: educated women are evenly split between the two parties, but educated men are heavily Republican. *The pattern for teachers is very different.* For the population of public school teachers as a whole, Democrats far outweigh Republicans, by 45 to 31 percent. The differences across women and men, moreover, are slight. Even the *men* are much more likely to be Democrats than Republicans.

If we look just at teachers who are union members, the partisan advantage for Democrats is greatly magnified: Democrats outnumber Republicans by two to one, 51 to 25 percent. The disproportion is greater among women than men, but the men are still overwhelmingly Democrats and just as unlikely to be Republicans as the women are. These union members are entirely responsible for the Democratic tilt within the larger population of teachers. In fact, teachers who do *not* belong to unions are markedly skewed the other way, with 46 percent saying they are Republicans and 30 percent saying they are Democrats. Here too, however, there are no differences between men and women, a recurring pattern that may well reflect the sheer strength of their common occupational interests.

The patterns for ideology are quite similar. College-educated Americans in 2003 tended to rate themselves as conservative rather than liberal, by 46 to 31 percent, and, again, this gap within the general population is strongly influenced by gender differences: educated women are about equally split between conservative and liberal, but educated men are lopsidedly conservative, by 52 to 25 percent. *For teachers, the pattern is strikingly different.* Among teachers as a whole, the tilt is toward liberalism: 43 percent of teachers rated themselves as liberal and 35 percent as conservative. There are only slight differences, moreover, between men and women. As with partisanship, the liberal tilt of the teacher population is due to the ideological orientations of the teachers who are union members. Within this group, liberals heavily outnumber conservatives by 48 to 31 percent, with men and women looking very much the same. Teachers who are not union members, in contrast, are heavily conservative, by 46 to 30 percent, and this conservative tilt is present among women as well as men (although it is especially marked among the latter).

Voting behavior conforms to the same pattern.[29] In the 2000 election, college-educated Americans split their vote equally between George W. Bush and Al Gore, with women favoring Gore over Bush 53 to 43 percent and men favoring Bush over Gore 52 to 42 percent. Teachers, by contrast, voted overwhelmingly for Gore by 55 to 41 percent, and women and men teachers favored Gore by almost identical margins. This Gore advantage is entirely due to the disproportionate support he received from teachers who are union members: they voted 61 percent for Gore and just 34 percent for Bush, with women and men voting along the same lines. Teachers who are *not* union members, in contrast, voted overwhelmingly for Bush by 60 to 36 percent, again with no appreciable differences between women and men.

In sum, then, there is obviously a good deal of coherence in this political profile of teachers. The evidence shows that teachers are in no sense a cross section of the American public. On the whole, they are much more liberal and Democratic, and their approach to politics is virtually uninfluenced by gender. The evidence also shows, however, that the larger teacher constituency is divided into two strikingly different groups: teachers who are union members are heavily liberal and Democratic, while teachers who are not union members are heavily conservative and Republican.

Why are union members so different from nonmembers? An obvious reason is selective attraction: Republicans and conservatives are simply less likely to join unions. If we look at teachers in districts with collective bargaining, for example, 24 percent of Republicans choose not to join, compared to just 10 percent of Democrats. Another reason is that almost three-fourths of all nonmembers are located in the sixteen states that don't have collective bargaining laws, and these are the most conservative areas of the country. Teachers in these states are still more Democratic than their fellow college-educated citizens (by 39 to 26 percent), but as befits their local culture they are also more Republican (by 39 to 27 percent) than teachers elsewhere.

Finally, there may be another explanation at work here as well. Whatever teachers' political views happen to be when they become members, they may be socialized through their ongoing experiences within the unions—through newsletters, the appeals of leaders, discussions with colleagues, political campaigns—to embrace liberal political ideas and the Democratic Party. The unions themselves, therefore, may produce a more politically homogeneous (and supportive) membership by making liberals out of moderates and conservatives and Democrats out of Independents and Republicans. We don't have over-time data on members, so we can't explore this in a satisfactory way. But it is reasonable to suspect that socialization is playing a role, as it would in almost any organization.[30]

Political Support and Alienation

Union members are disproportionately liberal and Democratic. The unions they belong to are liberal-Democratic political organizations. There is a basic political congruence, then, between the unions and their members, and, as seen earlier, most union members *do* feel satisfied with the political representation they are getting.

These points are worth emphasizing, given the familiar stereotypes about "union bosses" taking teachers in directions they don't want to go. In order to understand the unions as organizations, though, we need to recognize that not all members are happy with union politics, and that the unions are not free from the internal stresses that go along with having an alienated minority.

A simple way to explore this is by comparing union members who are Democrats to union members who are Republicans. Let's begin with the issue of voluntarism. We know that the vast majority of teachers said they belong of their own free will. As table 3-5 shows, this is true for Republicans as well as Democrats: big majorities in both parties said they belong because they want to, not because they have to. But a sizable chunk of Republican members—a third of them—said they belong because they have to, and they are twice as likely as Democrats to give this response.

If we break these results down by state context, moreover, we find that agency fees make a difference: Republicans are more likely to feel coerced when agency fees are permitted (38 percent) than when they are not permitted (23 percent). Indeed, a finer breakdown of the data would reveal that, when agency fees are legally required, fully 49 percent of Republicans reported that their membership is involuntary. Thus, while the earlier analysis does not show agency fees as having much effect on teacher voluntarism in the aggregate, these data tend to suggest otherwise. In agency-fee states, then, the unions are able to gain additional members—but members who are inclined to be politically disgruntled.

The middle portion of table 3-5 deals with voluntarism at the local, state, and national levels. It shows that Republicans (like Democrats) were almost unanimous in saying that they would voluntarily join their *local* union—a telling statement about just how popular these organizations are with teachers generally. But 35 percent of Republicans said they would *not* join their state union if given a choice (compared with just 13 percent of Democrats), and a whopping 59 percent said they would not join the national union (compared with 21 percent for Democrats). It would appear, then, that when Republicans complain about belonging to the union because they have to, *they are referring to their membership in the state and (especially) the national unions, not the locals.* And given everything we already know about how the state and national unions are viewed, the reason is straightforward: these unions are regarded as highly political, and Republican members object to the brand of politics they are being "forced" to support.

Republicans, then, are conflicted. They support their local unions, but they frequently oppose the politics of the state and national unions and feel that their membership at those levels is involuntary. So what do they think about forced membership as a matter of public policy? Should teachers be forced to join a union or pay agency fees when the union represents them in collective bargaining, or should they be free to choose? Interestingly, while Republicans are more likely than Democrats to say that teachers should be free to choose, the flip side is that 66 percent of Republican union members *do* support a policy of forcing

Table 3-5. *Voluntarism of Union Membership, by Party Affiliation and Type of State*[a]

Percent unless otherwise noted

Indicator of voluntarism	Agency fees permitted			No agency fees			All states		
	Demo-crat	Repub-lican	Total	Demo-crat	Repub-lican	Total	Demo-crat	Repub-lican	Total
Reasons for joining union									
I belong because I really want to	83	62	76	82	77	82	83	66	77
I belong because I feel I have to or feel pressure to	17	38	24	18	23	18	17	34	23
N	791	367	1,551	253	134	476	1,042	498	2,027
If allowed, would member voluntarily join local union?									
Yes	97	89	94	93	94	94	96	90	94
No	3	11	6	7	6	6	4	10	6
N	757	341	1,466	242	127	453	998	466	1,919
If allowed, would member voluntarily join state union?									
Yes	89	60	80	79	80	82	87	65	80
No	11	40	20	21	20	18	13	35	20
N	689	301	1,317	219	111	408	907	410	1,725
If allowed, would member voluntarily join national union?									
Yes	80	42	67	76	39	65	79	41	66
No	20	58	33	24	61	35	21	59	34
N	597	271	1,160	208	103	377	804	372	1,537
Should union membership be voluntary?									
All teachers must belong to union	27	21	25	9	10	7	23	18	21
All teachers must pay fees to union	57	54	56	41	30	39	53	48	53
Teachers should have free choice	16	26	19	51	60	54	23	34	26
N	791	367	1,551	253	134	476	1,042	498	2,027

Source: Harris Interactive survey conducted online between April 24 and May 20, 2003.

a. Figures in body of table are percentages, with columns adding to 100 percent for each item. The number of responses, *N,* is the weighted number of observations. Population is union members in districts with collective bargaining.

Figure 3-2. *Reasons for Joining the Union, by Party Affiliation*[a]

Percent

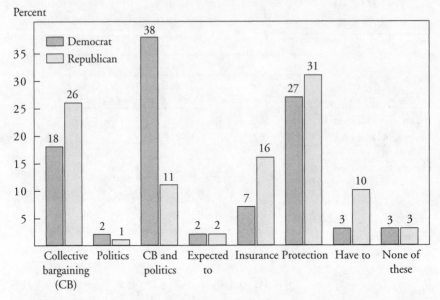

Source: Harris Interactive survey conducted online between April 24 and May 20, 2003.

a. Figures represent the percentage of union members identifying with each party who said that this particular benefit or rationale is their main reason for joining the union. Only union members in districts with collective bargaining are included here.

all teachers to either join or contribute. Their focus, presumably, is on the local union—which they support—and in that setting *they are perfectly willing to force everyone into the fold.* If we look across state contexts, the real divisions are not between Republicans and Democrats, but between teachers in different states: in states that allow agency fees, big majorities in both parties support the policy of forced membership or contributions, while in states that do not allow agency fees most members in both parties are opposed to such a policy.

When it comes to voluntarism, therefore, Republicans are not high-minded supporters of free choice as a matter of principle. They are more than happy to force other teachers to join or contribute to the local union. Their real concern, it appears, is the political liberalism of the state and national organizations, and many of them would like to be free to drop out of *those* parts of the union hierarchy—which, of course, the unions make it impossible for them to do.

Legally, Republicans do not have to join their unions at all. They could stay out and, if required, pay agency fees. So when they choose to join unions, why do they do it? The answers are displayed in figure 3-2. Here we can see that politics is almost never a positive inducement for them: just 12 percent said that politics, or the combination of politics and collective bargaining, is their reason for joining, whereas 40 percent of Democrats said this is mainly what attracts them to the union. The main reasons Republicans gave for joining usually have to do not with the unions' broader activities, even collective bargaining, but rather with the direct benefits of membership: some 47 percent said they join simply for protection or insurance. Thus the typical Democrat and the typical Republican are tied into the unions for very different reasons.

Even so, this mix of inducements generates high levels of satisfaction among members of *both* parties.[31] When teachers were asked how satisfied they are with their unions overall, 79 percent of Democrats said that they are either very or somewhat satisfied, but so did 72 percent of Republicans. Moreover, while Republicans usually did not single out collective bargaining as their prime reason for joining, pointing much more frequently to insurance or protection, the fact is that 81 percent of them said they are satisfied with how the unions represent their interests in collective bargaining. For Democrats, the figure is just slightly higher, at 84 percent. Clearly, then, Republicans like what they are getting from their local unions—valued services and collective bargaining—and when politics is not involved, they seem to be roughly as happy with their unions as Democrats are.

It is union politics that divides the two groups. Among Democrats, 82 percent are satisfied with how the unions are representing their interests in politics. They are just as satisfied with politics as they are with collective bargaining. But Republicans see things very differently: 66 percent of them are *dissatisfied* with union politics—the mirror opposite of how they feel about collective bargaining. This is a big number and well worth appreciating. *Fully two-thirds of Republican members are politically alienated from their unions.*

Yet we also need to put this in perspective. We know from the data on voluntarism that Republican dissatisfaction is centered mainly on the national unions and, to a lesser extent, the state unions. Not the locals. We also know, from their high overall levels of satisfaction, that their positive bonds with the local unions win out and cement them to the organizations. Yes, Republicans are dissatisfied with union politics. But, on balance, considering the mix of services and benefits they get from their local organizations, they recognize that they are better off belonging than not belonging.

Unity and Division

Now let's take a closer look at the collective bargaining side of the equation. Nationwide, of course, the Republican Party is known for its opposition to collective bargaining. So it would be interesting to know if Republican teachers—whose occupational interests are on the line—take a different view when it comes to their own lives.

Consider the Republicans who are union members in districts with collective bargaining. As table 3-6 shows, when these Republicans were asked how collective bargaining affects public education, *the vast majority said they see its consequences as either positive or neutral.* Only 6 percent of them think collective bargaining leads to lower academic performance, just 8 percent think it leads to worse teaching, and just 15 percent think it leads to less professionalism. Their negative assessments are appreciably higher on a few dimensions—37 percent think that it leads to more conflict, for example, and 34 percent think it leads to more rigid organization—but the same is true of Democrats, and the negatives are still heavily outweighed by the positives and neutrals. Members in *both* parties see collective bargaining as a benign influence on schools and children and believe that they face no moral dilemma in pursuing their own interests.

The more specific items on collective bargaining lead to the same conclusion. A full 73 percent of Republicans believe that contract-imposed rules and regulations help schools to promote learning, 65 percent said that seniority-based transfer rights make schools more effective, and 54 percent said that principals can abuse their discretion and need to be constrained. Here, Democrats are somewhat more likely to give positive responses than Republicans are, but the basic theme is the same for both groups: collective bargaining is a benign force within public education.

Collective bargaining brings Republicans and Democrats together. Politics pushes them apart. Let's turn to the political side of the ledger, then, and take a deeper look at what divides the union membership and, more generally, how teachers view union politics. We know that most Democrats are satisfied with how the unions represent their interests in politics, and we know that most Republicans are dissatisfied. But the survey tells us a good bit more.

In the middle of the survey, for example, teachers were asked to place their *national* unions on a seven-point ideology scale that varies from very liberal to very conservative. Much later in the survey, they were asked to place themselves on the same scale. Note that these two items were separated by many other items and that teachers had no indication the two would be compared. By subtracting the union score from the teacher score, then, we get a useful measure of the distance each teacher perceives between herself and the national union on politics—without asking about the issue directly. This is very different, obviously, from asking how satisfied they are with union politics, and it provides an independent source of information on the political congruence between members and their unions.

On a seven-point scale, the conceptual differences between adjacent categories—between "slightly liberal" and "liberal," say—are not that great, so it makes sense to code the union as being representative of a given member (in the member's eyes) if the scores are within one category of one another, and to code the

Table 3-6. *Teacher Attitudes toward Collective Bargaining,*
by Party Affiliation[a]

Percent unless otherwise noted

Attitude	Democrat	Republican	Total
Perceived impact of collective bargaining on			
Costs			
Higher costs	21	26	22
No difference	73	71	72
Lower costs	6	3	6
Academic performance			
Lower academic performance	2	6	3
No difference	44	50	47
Better academic performance	54	45	50
Organization			
More rigid	18	34	23
No difference	54	44	52
More flexible	28	23	26
Conflict			
More conflict	24	37	29
No difference	36	34	35
More cooperation	41	30	37
Professionalism			
Less professionalism	6	15	10
No difference	34	39	34
More professionalism	60	46	57
Teaching			
Worse teaching	3	8	5
No difference	44	52	47
Better teaching	53	39	48
Contending arguments			
Collective bargaining contracts			
Produce so many rules and restrictions that they make schools difficult to manage and lead	13	27	17
Produce reasonable rules and regulations that help schools promote learning	87	73	83
Transfer rights and seniority preferences			
Make schools less effective because they make it difficult to put the right person in the right job	28	35	30
Make schools more effective because they give teachers more options and prevent favoritism	72	65	70
Principals			
Need lots of discretion in order to manage their schools and promote learning most effectively	36	46	38
Can abuse their discretion and it needs to be restricted in order to protect teacher rights	64	54	62
N	1,042	498	2,027

Source: Harris Interactive survey conducted online between April 24 and May 20, 2003.

a. Figures in body of table are percentages, with columns adding to 100 percent for each item. The number of respondents, *N,* is the weighted number of observations. Political Independents are included in "Total." Population is union members in districts with collective bargaining.

Figure 3-3. *How Members Compare Their Union's Ideology to Their Own Ideology*[a]

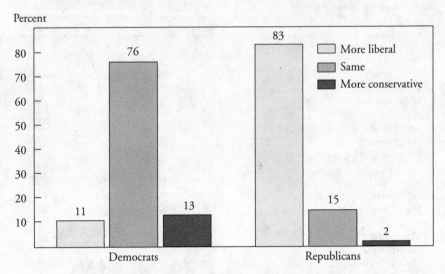

Percent

Source: Harris Interactive survey conducted online between April 24 and May 20, 2003.

a. These comparisons were calculated as follows. Members were asked to score their union on a seven-point ideology scale and to score themselves on the same scale. The two scores were then compared to calculate whether the union was "more conservative," "more liberal," or "the same" as the member, with the scores being counted as "the same" if they are within one level of one another. Population is union members in districts with collective bargaining.

union as more liberal or more conservative if the scores are more than one category apart in the relevant direction. The findings displayed in figure 3-3 show that the overwhelming majority of Republicans, a striking 83 percent, see their national unions as more liberal than they are and politically out of step with them. Among Democrats, in contrast, the story is one of near-universal ideological congruence: a remarkable 76 percent see the national unions as ideologically representative of them, with just 11 percent seeing them as more liberal and 13 percent as more conservative—a clear indication that *the national unions are operating precisely at the center of their internal Democratic constituency*.

This is graphic evidence that union leaders are not "bosses" who have little regard for member preferences. Within union organizations, Democrats outnumber Republicans by two to one. They are the dominant political constituency. And union leaders are right at the center of it, engaging in political activities that members regard as representative of their own views and beliefs.

Member Participation

As Albert O. Hirshman noted long ago, members can bring their preferences to bear on leaders in two ways: they can use "exit" or they can use "voice."[32]

The power of exit seems simple enough. If leaders make unpopular decisions, members can quit the organization. Or threaten to. And because leaders don't want to lose members (or money), they have incentives to heed what members want. The hitch is that exit may not be a rational strategy for many members. Even if they disagree with their leaders' decisions, the direct benefits of membership—insurance, protection—may easily be substantial enough to keep them in the group. Collective bargaining, which is often the focus of their membership, tends to bind them as well.

This doesn't mean that exit has no impact on member influence. Research has long shown, for example, that even though many consumers are poorly informed and don't exit in response to low quality, business firms are highly sensitive to the "marginal" consumers who are well informed and inclined to exit—and these consumers play key roles in keeping firms conscious of quality.[33] Similarly, leaders of the teachers unions may well be sensitive to the marginal members who are willing to exit when dissatisfied.

Members can also try to influence their leaders, however, without threatening to leave, for unions have internal decision processes—meetings, committees, votes, conventions, and other modes of participation—that allow them to express their preferences through voice. Indeed, this path to influence would seem especially relevant for *all* teachers, as they are highly educated and skilled (at public speaking, for example) compared to most citizens and meeting places tend to be conveniently located in the schools where they work.

Why would leaders pay attention to member voice, especially if the threat of exit is not credible for most of them? The answer, as I've discussed, is that leaders need member support if they are to succeed in collective bargaining and politics. In collective bargaining, leaders need to convince management that the rank and file will follow their lead, by engaging in strikes or work actions (if asked) or by accepting or rejecting contract proposals; and they can only do that if members are behind them and feel they are being represented. In politics, leaders must be able to draw on members to carry out the political work—making phone calls, ringing doorbells, getting out the vote, contributing money to the union political action committee—that translates into union power in elections and policymaking. Needless to say, leaders also need member support if they are to keep their elected positions of leadership—for competition and turnover are not at all uncommon when members are dissatisfied. All told, ignoring member preferences is simply unwise and self-defeating.

What can be said about the relative importance of exit and voice? And with regard to voice in particular, what can be said about who is participating, how much they participate, and what their political leanings are? A good place to begin is with a survey item that asks, "What would you do if your state or national organization often took political positions that you disagreed with or supported candidates that you disagreed with?" The possible responses were "(1) Realistically, I wouldn't do much of anything. (2) I would speak up at meetings and work to change their policies. (3) I would drop my membership in the local organization."

This is a strongly worded item, and if there is any bias in the way members respond, we might expect them to say they are willing to take some sort of decisive action—even if in reality they aren't. Voting researchers often run into this problem when asking people whether they voted in the last election: many people who didn't vote routinely report that they did, and thus that they behaved as good citizens.

Even so, most teachers clearly do *not* portray themselves as vigilant, politically demanding members.[34] Just 6 percent said that, if they were in frequent political disagreement with their union, they would drop out. This doesn't mean that leaders can ignore the threat of exit. They don't want to lose anyone, and they are surely sensitive to these marginal members. Still, the exit option is less a basis for member influence than it might otherwise be. For the vast majority of members, it is simply unavailable: they are tightly bound to their unions because of collective bargaining and direct benefits, and political disagreement (if it happens) is not enough to dislodge them.

Their preferred mode of influence is voice: some 41 percent of members said that, if disaffected, they would speak up in meetings to try to change union policies. While this figure may well be inflated—an attempt by teachers to look like good citizens—their reliance on voice makes good sense. If the benefits of membership are substantial, the *only* way to make political preferences felt is to remain in the group and participate.

A corollary finding, however, is that even though teachers are well educated, adept at public speaking, and quite capable of participating effectively at meetings, 51 percent of union members said they would *do nothing* if they often disagreed with union politics. This is a remarkable number, given the implicit social pressures to say the opposite. But it is also consistent with what social scientists know about member participation in unions generally, as well as most voluntary associations (and, for that matter, voting): while everyone has the right and the opportunity to participate, large percentages choose not to do so.[35]

Now consider how partisanship enters into the mix. Democrats are somewhat more likely (in percentage terms) to say they would exit their unions in response to political disagreement. But because Democrats far outnumber Republicans among members generally, the pool of marginal members willing to exit in response to politics is a heavily Democratic group; indeed, Democrats outnumber Republicans by almost three to one. To the extent that leaders are especially sensitive to these marginal members, then, their incentives are to tilt Democratic.

When it comes to the exercise of voice, the party differences are also striking. By 45 to 29 percent, Democrats are more likely than Republicans to say they would seek change by participating and speaking up. The great majority of Republicans, in fact, said they would *do nothing* to express their political disagreement—65 percent portrayed their "participation" in this way compared to 48 percent of Democrats. Republicans tend to respond to political disagreement by sitting on the sidelines. Thus when the Democrats' higher *rate* of participation is combined with their numerical advantage within the membership as a whole, the result is an internal voice process that they essentially own, outvoicing Republicans by more than three to one. To the extent that leaders have incentives to respond to the voices of ordinary members, then, these voices are heavily Democratic.

We need to take a closer look at participation, however, because some participants are clearly more important—and likely to be more influential—than others. It is the genuine activists who stand to be the most influential, in part because they are simply more involved and better informed, but also because they are enormously valuable to leaders for all the functions they perform. They must be listened to. Indeed, for many activists, being listened to and having an influence on union policy may be the main way they are "compensated" for their participation. These are the "payments" that keep them active, and thus doing the things that leaders find so valuable.[36]

Who, then, are the activists? One survey item gets at this by simply asking members how active they are within their unions.[37] On the whole, about half the members said they are "not at all active" or "not very active," and about half said they are "active" or "very active." As this is a purely subjective judgment, members are probably being rather charitable toward themselves. The research literature shows that the typical union member (across all types of unions) participates very little or not at all, although it is possible, of course, that teachers are more active than most because they are especially well educated.[38]

Whether these subjective figures are a bit inflated or not, the partisan breakdowns are instructive.[39] As the findings on voice would lead us to expect, Democrats are much more likely to be activists than Republicans are, with 15 percent of Democrats saying they are "very active" in their unions compared to 6 percent of Republicans. Again, when the difference in rates is combined with the Democrats' numerical dominance overall, the result is a partisan avalanche. If we look just at the top stratum of activists—the 12 percent of members who said they are "very active"—we find that 66 percent are Democrats, 13 percent are

Republicans, and 22 percent are Independents. By this measure, then, there are *five times as many* Democrats as Republicans among the top activists.

This measure of activism is subjective. Also, it is quite general: it may have to do with politics, but it may include some of the nonpolitical things that unions do, from collective bargaining to the various services that unions provide, as well as simple attendance at meetings and speaking up. The survey also offers a completely different measure of activism, however, that is tied to specific political behaviors and is less subjective. Members were asked whether they have engaged in the following campaign activities to support their union's political efforts: making phone calls, campaigning door-to-door, distributing leaflets, contributing money to favored candidates, or attending candidate meetings or rallies.[40] These activities are quite common during elections, and many types of campaigns—for school board, for state office, for national office—attract union involvement. If members are at all politically active, this measure should pick it up.

Fully 60 percent of union members said they have not engaged in *any* of these political activities.[41] They appear to be uninvolved in union efforts to influence electoral outcomes. Another 18 percent claimed to have participated in just one of these political activities—ever, presumably—while another 15 percent said they have participated in two or three of them, and 7 percent said they have participated in four or five. The muted activism among union members is hardly surprising, given the discouragingly low levels of voting and political participation among Americans generally.[42] But even so, it is important to recognize that the teachers unions, which are among the most electorally active interest groups in the country, depend upon a distinct minority of their members to do the heavy lifting during political campaigns. They cannot count on the general membership.

For obvious reasons, the relationship between partisanship and activism is even stronger in the political realm than in the realm of union activities generally. It is one thing for Republicans to go to meetings or to help out in union internal affairs and quite another for them to ring door bells for the unions' favorite Democratic candidates. No surprise, then, that 74 percent of Republicans said they engage in none of the listed political activities, compared to 52 percent of Democrats. And a trivial 2 percent of Republicans are in the top stratum of political activists compared to 10 percent of the Democrats.

This Democratic advantage in participation rates, moreover, translates into a much greater Democratic advantage within the pool of union political activists—because, again, it is magnified by the Democrats' two-to-one advantage in members overall. If we look just within the top stratum of political activists (the top 7 percent of all members), the distribution of partisanship is 69 percent Democrat, 7 percent Republican, and 24 percent Independent. This means that, among the union members who are the most politically active—and thus, by all odds, the most listened to, the most influential, and the most valued by leaders—Democrats outnumber Republicans by *ten to one*. If we drop the bar and regard as activists any member who has participated in just two or more of the listed activities, we get an activist corps comprising 22 percent of the membership. But even in this much larger group, Democrats outnumber Republicans by almost six to one.

The bottom line, then, is that union leaders face a coherent set of incentives that line up quite nicely. Externally, they must operate in a political world that strongly encourages their alliance with the Democratic Party and their leading role in the liberal coalition. From the standpoint of power politics—and getting the policies they want—these strategies make good sense. But do they make sense internally, within their own organizations? The answer is yes. Teachers are overwhelmingly Democratic, by two to one over Republicans, and see their unions as being politically representative of their own beliefs. The "marginal" teachers—those who are so sensitive to politics that they claim they would exit their unions if politically dissatisfied—are even more Democratic, by three to one over Republicans. And the teachers who exercise voice by participating most actively within their unions—and whose extremely valuable activities must be compensated by leaders though political responsiveness and attractive political positions—are still more extreme in their Democratic composition, with an advantage that ranges up to ten to one. Union leaders, therefore, can respond to their *internal* incentives—and build strong organizations—by doing precisely what their *external* environment calls for: being aggressively liberal and Democratic in the political process.

Education Policy

Conservative critics excoriate the NEA and the AFT for supporting gay rights, gun control, abortion, and other liberal policy positions that have nothing to do with education. Republican and conservative teachers no doubt feel the same. The unions go down this political path for reasons that make organizational sense, but these forays into liberal politics are not the essence of what the unions devote their time, attention, and money to. They are in the business of protecting and advancing the occupational interests of teachers. That is what they do in collective bargaining—and, except at the margins, that is what they do in politics too.

As we have seen, there are good reasons why union leaders want to engage in political actions—and win policy victories—that are consistent with what members want (or will support) in the realm of public education. If we look at the policies unions pursue in politics, then, and also look at the policies members say they favor, we should find a good deal of *congruence*.

In important respects, this congruence is rooted in perceptions of common interests. Each teacher is a unique individual, of course, with a unique perspective on society and politics; and individual partisanship and ideology certainly affect how the unions and their activities are viewed. Still, all teachers have something fundamental in common: *their jobs.* And because this is so, they tend to share basic interests. When education reform is debated and fought out in politics, therefore, these interests can be expected to shape their issue positions in similar ways and thus to generate a good deal of consensus inside the unions. Indeed, they should often generate consensus across the entire population of public school teachers, unionized or not.

Union leaders have incentives to support policies that are popular with their members. For many issues—tenure, for instance—the connections between policy and teacher interests are clear. But this is not always the case. And when the connections are more ambiguous—as they are, for example, with charter schools (in some respects)—union leaders can play a role in *framing* the issue (through newsletters, meetings, public statements, and the like) and getting their members to see the world in a common, coherent way that crystallizes the connection to their interests. Teacher interests become clear because union leaders *make* them clear and provide a focal point.[43]

The survey asked teachers about their positions on the following public policy issues, all of them central to the union's political agenda and to the nation's public schools.[44]

—The right of teachers to strike,

—Teacher tenure,

—Raising taxes to allow for higher school spending,

—Vouchers for disadvantaged children,

—Charter schools,

—Holding teachers accountable for student learning,

—Using standardized tests to measure learning.

In the realm of public debate, various arguments are made about each of these issues, pro and con, and reasonable people may disagree. Consider the strike issue, for instance. The unions and their supporters say that teachers need the right to strike if collective bargaining is to be meaningful and successful, for without the threat of walking off the job their bargaining position would be weak. Critics argue that teacher strikes should not be permitted—and in most states they are not—because they shut down the schools, create conflict and antagonism, and disrupt the lives of children and parents. Children should get top priority, they say, not the special interests of employees.

What do teachers think? Although the argument against strikes is certainly reasonable, teachers are not persuaded. The right to strike is in their interest, and they support it overwhelmingly. As table 3-7 shows, a resounding 85 percent of

Table 3-7. *Teacher Opinions on Policy Issues, by Union Membership, Party Affiliation, and Type of District*[a]

Percent unless otherwise noted

Issue	Union members					Nonmembers					All teachers
	District		Party			District		Party			
	CB	No CB	Dem	Rep	Total	CB	No CB	Dem	Rep	Total	
Right of teachers to strike											
Support	90	84	92	84	89	79	68	86	66	72	85
Oppose	10	16	8	16	11	21	32	14	34	28	15
N	1,989	337	1,229	605	2,326	311	483	234	369	794	3,120
Eliminate teacher tenure											
Support	16	21	13	22	17	48	37	39	41	42	23
Oppose	84	79	87	78	83	52	63	61	59	58	77
N	1,911	308	1,119	551	2,219	290	450	233	331	740	2,959
Vouchers for dis-advantaged kids											
Support	21	23	13	41	21	45	32	25	46	37	25
Oppose	79	77	87	59	79	55	68	75	55	63	75
N	1,961	321	1,146	559	2,282	291	480	240	355	771	3,053
Raise taxes for schools											
Support	74	80	80	63	74	61	66	78	54	64	72
Oppose	26	20	20	37	26	39	34	22	46	36	28
N	1,894	320	1,131	531	2,215	296	477	237	355	773	2,988
Hold teachers accountable											
Support	39	48	39	43	40	50	54	51	50	52	44
Oppose	61	52	61	57	60	50	46	49	50	48	56
N	1,888	319	1,109	536	2,208	302	488	246	361	790	2,998
Use tests to measure achievement											
Support	19	20	15	27	19	30	29	26	33	29	22
Oppose	81	80	85	73	81	70	71	74	67	71	78
N	2,051	337	1,205	585	2,388	329	533	260	389	862	3,250
Charter schools											
Support	37	33	31	45	36	67	54	55	63	59	42
Oppose	63	67	69	55	64	33	46	45	37	41	58
N	1,836	295	1,066	517	2,104	295	453	230	337	748	2,879

Source: Harris Interactive survey conducted online between April 24 and May 20, 2003.

a. Figures in body of table are percentages, with columns adding to 100 percent for each item. The number of respondents, *N*, is the weighted number of observations. Political Independents are included in "total." CB = collective bargaining. Population is union members in districts with collective bargaining.

all teachers favor the right to strike. Union members are more supportive of the right to strike than nonmembers are, and Democrats are more supportive than Republicans, so individual values and circumstances do matter at the margins. But even Republicans and teachers who are not union members (most of them from conservative states) support the right to strike by lopsided majorities—which says a lot, given that these are constituencies normally associated with antiunion political attitudes.[45]

Teachers tend to favor education policies that are good for *them*. As shown earlier in this chapter, most teachers see no conflict between collective bargaining and what is best for schools and children. They see a happy congruence. It is likely that a similar congruence—a reduction of cognitive dissonance—takes place for the right to strike and for other political issues as well. Teachers can favor self-interested policies because, in their own minds, those policies do no harm to society generally and may even be positive in their broader consequences. When teachers go out on strike, they see themselves as struggling for good schools and quality teaching, not just for bigger paychecks and retirement benefits for themselves.

The tenure issue is much the same. The existence of tenure makes it very difficult to remove mediocre teachers from the classroom, and studies have shown that many teachers are well aware of the problem.[46] Indeed, when my own survey asked teachers, "Do you think tenure and teacher organizations make it too difficult to weed out mediocre and incompetent teachers?" 55 percent of teachers said yes, including 47 percent of union members. Common sense would suggest that this situation can hardly be good for children and quality education. But tenure is also enormously beneficial for teachers, essentially guaranteeing them a job for life. Who wouldn't want that, if they were thinking only of themselves?

This, it appears, is precisely what teachers do. As the table indicates, when asked whether they would support a move to eliminate tenure, 77 percent of teachers said they are opposed. Again, while the opposition is stronger among Democrats and union members than among Republicans and nonmembers, all are opposed by big majorities. Teacher tenure, like the right to strike, is supported by a broadly based consensus—a consensus rooted in common interests.[47]

The tenure and strike issues are both about whether teachers should have specific rights that clearly work to their own advantage. What about more general issues? One of the most basic is taxation, a transcendent issue that has long been at the center of partisan political debate for the nation as a whole. Everyone has views on taxes, and people differ. But within public education, taxes are the revenue stream that teachers rely upon for wages, health benefits, retirement benefits, and full employment. It is in their self-interest to support higher taxes—and they do. When teachers were asked whether "taxes should be raised so that more money can be spent on the public schools," 72 percent said they support higher taxes. Here too, big majorities favor higher taxes regardless of their partisanship or union membership. Despite their party's staunch opposition to taxes, for example, Republican union members favor higher taxes—for the schools (and thus for themselves)—by almost two to one.[48]

The survey also asked teachers about school choice and school accountability, the two lines of reform that have defined the modern era. The choice issue most animating the unions is the issue of vouchers, which allow parents—virtually all of them low income and located in troubled urban school districts—to send their kids to private schools with the aid of government-funded scholarships. There are arguments on both sides, of course, with supporters arguing that these families are in desperate need of new educational opportunities, and opponents arguing that vouchers would drain money out of the public schools. But for teachers, this is not simply a matter of social principle. Vouchers would allow kids, money, and jobs to leave the public schools—where they work—and would thus threaten their security and livelihoods. Their opinions follow their self-interest, with 75 percent of all teachers saying they oppose vouchers for disadvantaged families. Republicans and nonmembers are less ardent in their opposition, but they are still overwhelmingly opposed.[49]

The charter schools variant of choice is more interesting, because it affects teachers differently than vouchers do. Like vouchers, charter schools are a way of giving disadvantaged families new educational opportunities, and they do take money, kids, and jobs away from the regular public schools. On the other hand, charters remain in the public sector, offer wages and benefits comparable to those in the regular public schools, and are an option for public teachers should they wish to transition out of their current jobs and into a "close" but more flexible, more collegial public alternative. The unions, despite periodic statements of "support," have seen charters as threats to public schools and teacher jobs and have fought their expansion.[50] Some 58 percent of all teachers likewise oppose charter schools. Among union members, opposition is almost two to one, with 64 percent opposed. Even most Republican union members are opposed. But among teachers who don't belong to unions, 59 percent actually support charter schools, with support reasonably high among Democrats (55 percent) as well as Republicans (63 percent).[51]

Why the difference? We can't definitively know, but a reasonable explanation is that the connection between charter schools and teacher interests is somewhat ambiguous; charters are a threat, yes, but they also offer attractive alternatives for teachers themselves. This being so, teachers need to sort this through and get a sense of where the balance lies, and the unions help them do that by framing the issue in a distinctive way: by emphasizing that charters are a serious threat to the public schools (and teachers). Teachers who belong to unions, then, whether they are Democrat or Republican, come to see charters as contrary to their own interests. Teachers outside unions, who are largely free of this negative framing, often see charters in a much more positive light. In any event, whatever the explanation, teachers are clearly split on this issue—along union lines.

Accountability is another interesting case, although it is interesting for a different reason. The general idea of accountability has certain motherhood aspects to it. It is only reasonable (and in the business world, a universally accepted principle of effective organization) that anyone with a job to do should be held accountable for doing it well. The obvious implication is that schools and teachers, whose job is to promote student learning, should be held accountable too. Who would disagree? But the deep background for public education is that schools and teachers have traditionally *not* been held accountable. And it is clear that, when people *are* held accountable, jobs are going to be less secure and performance pressures are going to be greater—impacts that most teachers are likely to see as contrary to their interests. Indeed, in the Public Agenda survey, teachers claimed that "unreasonable pressure to raise student achievement" is the single most difficult thing about being a teacher.[52] The unions, not surprisingly, are not keen on accountability either. They claim to favor accountability in concept, but in practice they are opposed to policies that would actually hold teachers accountable by measuring their performance and attaching genuine, enforceable consequences to it.[53]

The survey asked teachers a general question on accountability: "Do you think individual teachers should be held accountable for how much their own students learn during the school year?" This wording probably has a slight motherhood bias, because it does not say *how* they should be held accountable and makes no mention of any *consequences* for poor performance. What parent, for example, would say that teachers should not be accountable for how much their students learn? Even so, 56 percent of all teachers expressed opposition to even this conceptual version of accountability. Within unions, opposition is still greater, at 60 percent, including majorities of Republicans as well as Democrats. Outside the unions, things are somewhat different: some 52 percent of teachers said they support accountability, with even Democrats slightly favoring it—suggesting, again, that union framing may be playing a role here.[54]

When the discussion moves from the general to the specific, however, the battle lines begin to harden, and basic occupational interests become clearer and more determining. The survey asks teachers, "Do you think standardized testing is a good way to measure how much students are learning in school?" This is a telling question, because the most direct way of measuring a teacher's performance—and holding a teacher accountable (in conjunction, of course, with other measures and criteria)—is through the test scores of the students in her classroom. Reformers have long proposed as much. The unions, however, have long resisted the use of standardized tests in evaluating teachers, and have even gotten laws passed that (until reversed in response to Race to the Top in 2009–10) prohibited states from using them in this way.[55] Test scores are concrete, objective information on how much students are learning; they are the best information social science has been able to provide; and the American public certainly believes that they are good measures that need to be systematically employed.[56] For unions, however, they are a threat—because low scores provide objective grounds for removing mediocre teachers from the classroom, and job security is the unions' number one concern. It is clearly high on the list for teachers as well: low scores would (or could) threaten their jobs and bring pressure on them to perform.

On this issue, teachers are united: test scores are *bad* measures of student learning, and they should *not* be used to hold teachers accountable. Among all teachers, 78 percent reject the use of standardized tests as measures of student learning. Although union members are more opposed to them than non-members are (81 percent compared with 71 percent), both are overwhelmingly opposed. The same is true, moreover, for Republicans and Democrats in both groups. Thus, all teachers—even the nonmembers among them, who, on average, are willing to say that teachers *should* be held accountable for how much their own students learn—are opposed to the most direct, most obvious, most sophisticated measure of student learning itself.[57] Without that measure, what is left of accountability? Not much. And that, really, is the point.

These are just some of the educational issues that the teachers unions fight for and against in the political process. But the evidence does a good job of highlighting two basic features of teacher politics. The first is the considerable uniformity of opinion on educational issues—a uniformity that reflects the common occupational interests that prompt teachers to see these issues in much the same way. When teachers approach public policy in their own educational realm, whether they are Democrats or Republicans, they tend to ask, "How is this policy going to affect *me* as an employee? How does it affect my job, my security, my income, my work life?" And their answers are often much the same.

The second basic feature is that there is substantial congruence between the positions that the teachers unions take in politics and the positions their members support. Yes, there are ideological differences among teachers. Republicans are an alienated political minority. But their alienation is *not* due to the educational objectives that the unions pursue in politics. On these issues, which represent almost the entirety of what the unions do in politics, ideology takes a back seat to occupational interests, and Republicans and Democrats find themselves on the same side—the unions' side.

This is not to suggest that teachers are in total lockstep with their unions, or one another, on education policy. On the issues I've discussed, which are quite basic, agreement is substantial, but it is obviously not perfect. And if we explored member opinion on a broader range of issues, diversity would not be difficult to find. The fact is, the educational issues that arise in the political process—often due to pressure from reformers—do not all have simple, clear connections to the occupational interests of teachers. Many do. But some may affect different teachers differently or create opportunities and threats whose balance teachers don't agree on. They may also prompt different interpretations from leaders than from members, because leaders are responsible for the whole—for building strong organizations—and members are typically thinking just about themselves.

Charter schools provide one example of this: teachers are rather divided, with union leaders seeing charters as a threat to be opposed and union members falling in line behind their leaders. Consider another example: pay for performance. The notion here is that teachers should be paid, at least in part, on the basis of their classroom performance. This is an important issue in American education reform. It is also an issue on which different teachers may well have very different interests. Not everyone is going to be regarded as a high performer, and some are clearly more talented and successful at teaching than others. Also, some teachers are more risk-averse and suspicious than others and don't want a portion of their pay to be left uncertain and in someone else's hands.

Teacher opinion is a mixed bag. On the surface, teachers seem to favor pay for performance at a conceptual level, perhaps because (like accountability and many other issues) it has a motherhood appeal in the abstract. In the Public Agenda survey, for instance, teachers were asked whether they would support giving "financial incentives to . . . teachers who consistently receive outstanding evaluations from their principals," and they said that they favor it by two to one. These same teachers, however, also agreed by two to one that principals would "play favorites" rather than rewarding those who are truly meritorious; and they agreed by two to one that merit pay would lead to "unhealthy competition and jealousy among teachers" rather than better incentives. They also said, by wide margins, that they do not want teachers rewarded based on how their kids score on standardized tests.[58] What's wrong with this picture? They "support" pay for performance, but they don't trust principals to evaluate merit, they don't want test scores to be used, and they fear the internal divisions that would result among members. How, then, is their performance to be evaluated?

These ambiguities arise for a simple reason: there is no clear connection between pay for performance and the occupational interests of each individual teacher. Importantly, though, the unions have long taken stands *against* pay for performance (except in a few rare districts and, more recently, under the pressures of Race to the Top, which I discuss in chapter 10). Typically, they have framed the issue very negatively, in terms of precisely the sorts of fears and suspicions that concern many members. Why would they do that? The answer is not that they are "bosses" or somehow "against change." Rather, it is that a key job of union leaders is to figure out how to nurture member *solidarity*: because solidarity is crucial if their organizations are to be successful at pursuing their members' occupational interests—not just on this issue, but on *all* issues. Pay for performance is a threat to solidarity. So even if some members may find it attractive, it needs to be opposed.

Leaders, then, can sometimes seem to be out of step with their members (or at least a fair number of them). But this doesn't mean they are "bosses." In fact, departures of this kind are what leadership is about. Everything is connected to everything else, and union leaders need to think about the whole, about the bigger picture. On any given issue, then, this is how they think about the occupational interests of teachers. They don't think about it in isolation. They think about its broader consequences, especially as they bear on the foundations of their organizations. The organizations come first. And this, when push comes to shove, is usually how it should be: because the organizations are tools for making members better off, and what strengthens the organizations strengthens the ability of teachers to get the things they really care about.

The kind of congruence that characterizes the connection between members and leaders, then, is not a simple one-to-one correspondence between member issue positions and leader issue positions. It is more complicated than that, and it has to be. But the guiding theme is that member interests are a major constraint on what leaders do.

Are Young Teachers Different?

A common claim, even among union leaders, is that the unions have a problem with today's younger teachers, who are purported to be less interested in joining and, if they do join, less involved in their organizations. Here, for example, is what George Parker, president of the Washington Teachers Union, had to say recently in reflecting on his electoral defeat by an internal challenger. "We have a younger segment of our union membership that does not see unions as having meaning or purpose . . . We have to find a way to get more of our younger teachers active in the union and move the union in a direction that it understands that younger teachers have different goals and objectives."[59]

This concern about a generation gap is only reinforced by the rise of Teach for America—which has fought against union constraints and opposition in trying to forge new paths to teacher excellence, and has clearly captured the hearts and minds of the nation's reformers (and the media as well). Its young, enthusiastic, reform-minded teachers are a growing presence in urban districts, and they often seem to be quite out of step with their local unions. To many, this sort of rebellion of the young is the wave of the future.[60]

If so, it could obviously spell big trouble for the unions. Union-oriented older teachers will be retiring, and if the teaching ranks are filled by people who are markedly less prounion, membership and funding will drop off and activism will weaken. The unions will lose power and go into decline.

Two separate issues are involved in assessing this situation. The first is whether today's younger teachers are in fact different from today's older teachers. But the second has to do with what happens over time if the answer happens to be yes. The survey cannot address this second issue, of course, because it only gathers evidence from one point in time. Nonetheless, the time dynamics stand to be quite important—and there are good reasons for thinking that they will work in the unions' favor to mitigate whatever generation gap might seem to be a problem.

Consider. The turnover among young teachers is typically substantial—over a third leave the profession within the first five years[61]—and it is reasonable to think that, on average, those who stay are likely to be those who feel happier with the job and the school system, and thus happier with unions, than those who leave. Those who stay, moreover, will be subject to heavy socialization by their union leaders and colleagues over the years, which is likely to solidify and strengthen their prounion attitudes. And they will also undergo life-cycle effects: they will simply get older year by year, and as they do they are likely to get more risk averse, more concerned about pensions and retiree health benefits, and still more supportive of their unions. So, all in all, even if today's younger teachers *are* less prounion than their older colleagues, the time dynamics would seem to work in the unions' favor—and there may be no Waterloo awaiting them down the road.

We cannot explore these matters with the evidence at hand. But keeping in mind the limitations of what the survey can tell us, there is surely something to be gained from seeing if younger teachers are as different as they are made out to be. The details of the analysis—which revisits all the issues covered in prior sections, but this time controlling for age—are described in appendix C. What the analysis shows is that young teachers, which I've defined as those under thirty-five years of age,

—Are less likely than older teachers to join unions, but not by much,

—Are almost universal in seeing their own membership as entirely voluntary,

—Are even more satisfied with their locals than older members are,

—Are highly satisfied with collective bargaining, and indeed, in districts that don't have it, are even more likely to say they want it than older teachers are,

—Overwhelmingly believe that collective bargaining has benign effects on schools and kids,

—Have policy positions very similar to those of their older colleagues,

—Are much less active in union affairs and union politics.

Aside from the participation gap, which is likely to correct itself over time as these teachers age and continue their membership, there doesn't seem to be a major problem here for the unions. It may very well be that Teach for America recruits are very different from their senior colleagues on union issues; but TFA only accounts for a tiny portion of the nation's teachers—8,200 (in 2010) out of more than 3 million.[62] If we look across the vast population of young teachers as a whole, their attitudes toward unions and related issues turn out to be very similar to those of older teachers. And this shouldn't come as a great shock, because they all have the same basic interests.

Conclusion

Teachers are connected to unions in a host of ways. This chapter is about the nature of those connections—which ultimately make the unions what they are.

The locals are the bedrock of union organization. Virtually all union members, whether Democrat or Republican, see their membership in the local as entirely voluntary and are highly satisfied with what they are getting. It is what happens at the local level that securely binds teachers to their unions: tying them into state and national organizations that they might not otherwise be willing to join and dominating their perspective on what the union is and how satisfied they are with it. The locals are the key to union power and success.

Collective bargaining, in turn, is the basis for strong locals and the unions' major source of unity among the members. In overwhelming numbers, collective bargaining is supported by Democrats and Republicans alike, attracting them to their unions and knitting them together into cohesive units based on common occupational interests. It is also supported by teachers who don't already have it, and is enormously popular even in the southern and border states.

Especially among union members, moreover, collective bargaining is an exercise in self-interest that teachers embrace without moral qualms. They see it as benign in its larger consequences for schools and the quality of education, and they believe, as their leaders constantly claim, that what is good for teachers is good for kids.

Politics is more divisive. But teachers do not associate it with their locals. They associate it with the state and (especially) national organizations, which are the sources of almost all the internal political dissatisfaction among members—particularly Republican members, most of whom say they would drop out of the national unions if they could. The unions cannot do much about this disunity. If they want to achieve their education policy objectives—which include, I should emphasize, protecting their collective bargaining rights—they are wise to support Democratic political candidates and participate actively in the liberal coalition. Without these allies, they would be much weaker in the political process.

Internally, moreover, the center of political gravity among the membership is Democratic and liberal, and this is true in the extreme for the activist members who carry most of the participatory load and are so enormously valuable to leaders. The deck is stacked: leaders have strong incentives to craft their organizations in a liberal Democratic mold, and Republicans just aren't going to like it.

Yet it doesn't really matter. Republicans may often be politically dissatisfied, but their dissatisfaction only attaches to higher levels of their unions. The fact is, they love their locals, they love collective bargaining, and, on the whole, they are satisfied with their membership. What binds them to the unions, at the end of the day, is that they have interests in common with other teachers; and as they see it, the unions are doing a good job of representing those interests—which means, above all else, protecting their jobs. Partisanship is a secondary concern. It becomes relevant around the edges, when the unions support liberal candidates or come out in favor of abortion or gay marriage. But these really *are* the edges.

At the center are *common interests*—in job security, wages and benefits, working conditions—and here, partisanship and ideology are largely irrelevant. This is easily observed on collective bargaining, which fuses teachers together at the local level. But it also applies to basic issues of public policy. Extraneous political issues—abortion rights, gay rights, and other planks of the liberal agenda—stand to excite partisan passions precisely because they are *not* about education. But when policies bear on education and its reform, which are the unions' main concerns by orders of magnitude, the common interests of teachers take hold—clarified and deepened by the framing of union leaders—and political division often gives way to political unity. On the issues that matter most for their occupational lives and are related most directly to the public schools, teachers are largely in agreement. They agree with one another—Democrat or Republican, liberal or conservative—and they agree with their unions. When ambiguities arise, moreover, and teachers are unclear or divided on certain policy issues, leaders have incentives to take positions that promote solidarity and are conducive to the long-term strength of their organizations.

There is a larger story here as well, a story that is usually *not* told about teachers. Observers of American public education are typically very careful to distinguish teachers from their unions—and to treat teachers with kid gloves. Although everyone is aware that some are failing in the classroom, teachers in general are portrayed very positively: as caring, devoted, other-oriented, public-spirited, and doing their best against great odds to get the nation's children educated. Americans speak highly of teachers, and public officials go out of their way to extol their virtues and hail their contributions. Such accolades are rarely bestowed on the teachers unions. Their conservative critics never have a nice word, of course. But even their liberal allies are muted (if that) in their praise, for they are well aware that the unions often get in the way of reform and quality education. Whether from the right or the left, then, teachers tend to come off as blessed souls, while the unions loom as powerful special interests whose souls are decidedly in question.

This is the wrong way to think about teachers and their unions. It is true that the teachers unions are special interest organizations. And like the National Rifle Association, the trial attorneys, and all other interest groups, they pursue those special interests with a laser-like focus. But the kicker is that *this is what teachers want them to do,* because those special interests are *their* interests. If the unions are taking actions at variance with the best interests of kids and effective schools, the ultimate explanation—the real story—is not simply that the unions are special interest groups. It is that they are acting on behalf of the special interests of the teachers themselves—and doing precisely what the great majority of teachers want.

4

Unions and School Boards

Collective bargaining is the bedrock of union well-being. And for that reason, success in collective bargaining—doing what it takes to satisfy members locally—is a burning requirement of union leadership. How, then, can local leaders succeed in bringing home the bacon?

Part of the answer is that, like union leaders in the private sector, they need to be able to threaten strikes, work stoppages, and other unpleasantries that might force management into concessions. This is standard fare for all unions. But precisely because the teachers unions operate in the public sector, they are fortunate to have another avenue of influence that is typically not available to private sector unions at all. Indeed, to say that they are fortunate only begins to convey just how profoundly beneficial this avenue stands to be.

Here is why. The school board members who hold authority over district policy—and over the entire collective bargaining process—are elected by the public at-large.[1] By participating actively in electoral campaigns, then, and by using their members, money, and organizations to get favored candidates elected to office, the unions can play a role in *selecting the very people they will be bargaining with*. This is nothing like collective bargaining in the private sector, where labor unions must square off against management teams they can't control. If the teachers unions can exercise political power in elections, they will wind up bargaining with management teams in which some of the officials, and possibly all of them, are their political allies—and can give them the collective bargaining successes they need to satisfy their members.[2]

The teachers unions, needless to say, are well aware of the enormous opportunities that local elections open up for them, and they have strong incentives to develop a capacity for local political power—and to use it. The Michigan Education Association, for example, distributes a forty-page instructional (and hortatory) document to its local leaders, filled with operational details about how to evaluate and screen school board candidates, recruit friendly ones, run entire campaigns, set up phone banks, engage in door-to-door canvassing, get out the vote, and more. Its title: "Electing Your Own Employer, It's as Easy as 1, 2, 3."[3]

As we've seen, the average member cares much more about collective bargaining than politics. But what makes local politics more palatable—and barely "political"—from the members' standpoint is that, unlike the partisan politics that divides members when they assess their state and national unions, there is nothing essentially partisan about school board politics. It is straightforwardly about their jobs, their work rules, and their occupational interests. Almost all these elections, in any event, are formally nonpartisan anyway.

To understand collective bargaining, then, it is not enough simply to look at negotiations and labor contracts. We need to step back from these things and be fully aware of the political context in which they take place—and of the unions' strong incentives to take political action. The most fundamental question to be asked and answered is, how have they acted on these incentives? How have the teachers unions participated in school board elections, and how successful have they been at getting their allies into office? That is what this chapter is about.

Before I begin, though, I want to underline a simple fact: in southern and border states, whose districts typically do *not* have collective bargaining, democracy is similarly turned on its head. In those districts too, the teachers unions can use their political power to help choose the very people who will be running their districts and making all the authoritative decisions about money, personnel, and policy. Just like their counterparts elsewhere, these unions have compelling incentives to mobilize for political action—and to use democracy to make the governance of schooling their own. Indeed, because they have no collective bargaining to advance their interests, their incentives are even stronger to make politics a priority.

Although my focus in this chapter is on districts with collective bargaining, then, the underlying dilemma of democracy is quite general and applies to *all* districts. Whenever and wherever district employees get organized, they are driven to try to control the people who, in a democratic system, *are supposed to be controlling them* in the name of ordinary citizens.[4]

The Unions' Advantage

There are some 14,000 school districts in this country, almost all of them governed by elected school boards. These boards are not entirely free to run the schools as they see fit. Over the last half century or so, the state and federal governments have expanded their roles in funding, programs, and regulation, and the autonomy of the locals has declined along the way. Nonetheless, school boards are still responsible for much of what happens on the ground in American education. They build schools, select textbooks, design curricula, recruit teachers, award diplomas, set rules for discipline, and oversee a vast array of operations, plans, and policies that shape the educational experiences of some 90 percent of the nation's children.[5]

Americans seem to like it that way. They have long been big believers in local democracy, as de Tocqueville famously observed more than a century ago; and in more modern times, poll after poll has shown that they prefer to have the control of their schools lodged in locally elected school boards.[6] Indeed, the equation of school boards with government by the people is one of the enduring myths of public education.[7]

But myth it is. During the early years of the twentieth century, school boards were often under the thumb of party machines. Later, as Progressive reforms weakened the parties, local governance of the schools shifted to newly powerful groups—business, middle-class activists, education administrators—with their own special interests to pursue.[8] Then came the 1960s and 1970s, when the unionization of teachers led to yet another shift in the balance of power, and school boards found themselves under strong, special interest pressures from their own employees. The history of American school boards has never been a history of grassroots democracy. It has always been a history of special interests.

This is not good for children or schools, but there is nothing surprising about it. Ordinary citizens have largely abandoned the playing field. School board elections are often held at odd times, when no other offices—particularly major ones, like president or governor—are being voted on to help stimulate participation. Moreover, roughly two-thirds of registered voters are not parents of school-age children and so have only weak incentives to pay attention or get involved. Citizen apathy is the norm, and turnout in most districts is abysmal, often in the 10 to 20 percent range. To make matters worse, because these elections are almost always nonpartisan—thanks to Progressive reformers during the early decades of the twentieth century, who thought that nonpartisan elections would promote good government—voters lack the party cues that would provide them with much-needed information on the multiple candidates running for office. Many, as a result, may often be confused about and disinterested in their choices.[9]

Political scientists have studied these off-cycle, low-turnout elections to see if they tend to give special interest groups greater influence. Three very recent studies, two by Sarah Anzia and one by Christopher Berry and Jacob Gerson, focus on school districts and examine whether the teachers unions—the special interests of note—are able to win bigger salaries in districts that have elections at off times (controlling for other factors), compared to districts that don't. The answer in all three studies is *yes*.[10]

These studies provide important evidence, then, of union influence over local school boards, and they show that the unions' own influence appears to be greater in low-turnout electoral settings. Revealing as this evidence is, however, it gets at but one aspect of a much larger phenomenon: which has to do with how the unions' influence compares to that of *other* groups. It is this larger phenomenon that I highlight and explore in this chapter. The essence of it—which is simple, but exceedingly profound in its implications—is that the teachers unions *stand out* from all other interest groups in the local politics of education and have inherent advantages that are quite general. As this chapter shows, various aspects of the local context seem to condition their influence. But the take-away point is that, overall, they are distinctly and heavily advantaged.

Apathy stops at the schoolhouse door. Teachers and other employees of the school district are not just average citizens or even "concerned" citizens who care about the schools. They have a deeply rooted material interest in everything the district does: how much money it spends, how the money is allocated, how hiring and firing are handled, what work rules are adopted, how the curriculum is determined, which schools are opened and closed, you name it. Their livelihoods are fully invested in the schools, and they have a far greater and more enduring stake in the system than any other members of the community do. Given their interests, it is only rational for them to be especially concerned about wielding influence over their local school boards.

This is true in all districts, large and small, and in states throughout the country. Consider, for example, the 10,000-student Anderson school district in the red state of Indiana. Nothing unusual about it. Just a very ordinary school district in the nation's heartland. In 2004 Anderson's school board and the local teachers union (an affiliate of the AFT) were at loggerheads, unable to reach an agreement satisfactory to teachers. The union responded at the next election by launching a political campaign to defeat its opponents and put sympathetic members on the board. And it succeeded—in spades. Its foray into local democracy yielded not only a prounion majority, but also a new board president who was a retired teacher and a former president of the teachers union itself. The fox was now in charge of the chicken coop—and democratically elected to the job, no less. Needless to say, the relationship between the board and the union dramatically improved, to the great benefit of teachers.[11]

As individuals, district employees have strong incentives to get involved in school board politics. The things they want are simple and straightforward and need have nothing to do, at least directly or intentionally, with what is best for children or quality education. They want job security. They want better wages and fringe benefits. They want better retirement packages. They want work rules that restrict managerial control. They want policies (like smaller classes) that make their jobs easier and increase the demand for employees. They want higher taxes. And so on. But unlike parents and other citizens, who are typically atomized and ineffectual as political forces, most school employees have the advantage of being organized into unions. The teachers unions are the most powerful and active of the employee unions (by far), and in the political arena they are the ones that take the lead in championing the cause of employee interests.

They have the resources to do just that. While they are nominally collective bargaining organizations, they can readily turn their organizations toward political ends. They have guaranteed sources of money (member dues) for financing campaigns, paid staff (in the larger unions) to coordinate political activities, and activist members to do the invaluable trench work of campaigning. These are resources that, in most districts most of the time, are not available to other groups to nearly the same extent, giving the unions extraordinary advantages in getting sympathetic candidates elected to office. Just as they did in Anderson, Indiana.

To be sure, these advantages are not guaranteed, and they are not always sufficient to produce victory. In urban areas, for instance, the teachers unions are typically large, well financed, and politically active, but they are also faced with pluralistic environments that harbor competitors for power: groups representing business, minorities, religions, and other segments of urban society that care about education too and, like the unions, are organized and have the capacity for political action. Under certain circumstances, these sorts of groups do get actively involved in school board elections, and they sometimes take on the teachers unions directly. When this happens, the unions can find themselves on the defensive and even on the losing end.

In Los Angeles, for example, Mayor Richard Riordan made reform of the 750,000-student Los Angeles Unified School District a top priority, calling the district "a total disaster."[12] "There are a zillion reforms out there that could be done," he said, "but it won't happen with this school board," which was under the political sway of the union.[13] He formed a coalition of business and community groups in support of his efforts, and in the 1999 school board election, with four of the seven incumbents up for reelection, went to war with the powerful United Teachers Los Angeles to try to win majority control. Riordan's Coalition for Kids ran its own slate of reform candidates. The union pulled out all the stops to keep the incumbents in office.[14] In the words of the union president, "If God himself ran a candidate against them, we'd defend them."[15] But Riordan's coalition—spending more than $2 million on the campaign ($270,000 of it from Riordan's own pockets)—won all four seats up for election and gained majority control.[16]

In San Diego, business groups got actively involved in school issues during the late 1990s in response to continuing low performance and an unpopular teachers

strike. Backed by a thin 3-2 majority on the school board, they were able to engineer the appointment of attorney Alan Bersin as superintendent in 1998. Bersin
went on to launch "one of the nation's most ambitious efforts at urban school
reform," much to the chagrin of the local teachers union.[17] Suddenly in trouble,
the union furiously tried to capture control of the board—and get Bersin fired—
while business groups targeted union supporters on the board for defeat and
pushed hard to increase Bersin's majority. The elections of 2000 and 2002 were
fraught with conflict and vitriol, and enormous amounts of money were spent on
both sides. In 2002 alone, the San Diego Education Association spent more than
$600,000, and the California Teachers Association (supporting its local affiliate)
spent another $300,000.[18] The two sides essentially fought to a draw, enabling
business and the forces for change to maintain the pro-Bersin majority, keep Bersin in office, and keep the San Diego reforms on track.

In urban settings, then, the teachers unions can sometimes find themselves up
against powerful opponents. They can lose elections, and they can wind up with
reformist administrations that try to change the system in ways that threaten
their interests. It is of more than passing relevance, however, that in both San
Diego and Los Angeles the unions were down but by no means out. Riordan's
term as mayor of Los Angeles ended in 2001, taking much of the steam out of
his coalition's reform efforts; and the election of 2003 then saw the union—
whose term is never over—beat out the coalition and win its majority back.[19] In
San Diego, the teachers union kept bashing away at Bersin and in 2005 finally
succeeded in gaining a majority on the board. The new majority wasted no time
in getting rid of Bersin and then watering down and redirecting his reforms.[20]

In the years since, San Diego has not reemerged as a hotbed of innovation.
Los Angeles is another story. In May of 2005, the city elected as its mayor Antonio Villaraigosa, who, as a former organizer for the teachers union, appeared to
be very bad news for reformers. But in assuming his new job, his incentives and
constituency had radically changed—and the ex-union man became an ardent
reformer himself. After trying and failing to get control of the district through
new legislation, he ran his own slate of candidates for school board in 2007
(backed by some $3 million in campaign contributions), successfully wrested
control of the board from the teachers unions—and, backed by civic and newly
resurgent parent groups, proceeded to champion a proliferation of new schools,
run by charters and nonprofits, that is challenging the entrenched system and
attracting national attention.[21] How successful he will be remains to be seen. But
in a recent, high-profile address to state education leaders, Villaraigosa spoke out
clearly and bluntly—for the first time in a public setting—about why reform
in his city is so hard. "The most powerful defenders of the status quo are the
teachers unions," he said. "They intimidated people, especially Democrats, from
doing anything about reform. At every step of the way, when Los Angeles was

coming together to effect real change in our public schools, UTLA was there to fight against the change."[22]

The conflicts in Los Angeles and San Diego are well known to those who follow public education closely. They are well known because, as examples of school board politics, they are rather unusual—for they are cases in which reformers amassed enough power (backed by political contributions in the millions of dollars) to present a serious challenge to the unions. We shouldn't expect this to be the norm. It is quite true that American cities are home to many organized groups that *could* throw themselves into school board politics and, if the opportunity exists, could lend power to reformist mayors. But they usually don't do it, or don't do it with all their might, or don't have the opportunity to do it, or don't maintain their fervor and political involvement for very long. Their power, if exerted at all, inevitably wanes.

There is a reason for that. These other groups, whatever their economic or social constituencies, almost always have agendas that reflect a wide spectrum of public issues and concerns, *not* just education, and they allocate their resources accordingly. It is simply not in their best interests, given their goals, to focus their resources on education all the time. The teachers unions, by contrast, have a vested interest in public education—and *only* in public education—and that is where they focus *all* their resources and attention. Over the long haul, then, there is a mismatch that favors the unions. Even in urban settings with lots of urban competitors, they have an advantage.

Some of the most potent organizations in the ecology of urban politics, moreover, are not really competitors anyway. They are allies. Here I am talking above all about civil rights and other groups that represent minorities. Urban school districts are typically among the largest employers in their cities—indeed, often they are the single largest employer—and as American cities became increasingly concentrated with minorities during the middle decades of the twentieth century, and as school districts increasingly fell under the political control of minorities, public school systems came to represent a major source of jobs, upward mobility, and social status for minority employees. In recent decades, of course, minorities have criticized urban school systems for failing to educate their children. But their interest groups—the NAACP most notable among them—have at the same time been staunch defenders of minority jobs, and have often allied themselves with the teachers unions against reforms that are unsettling or threatening to employees. For minority groups as well as for the unions, the school system is an employment regime. This is the bond that cements their alliance—allowing the unions to turn a potential opponent into an active supporter, and to protect and strengthen their role as the leading power in public education.[23]

In the local arena, the greatest challenge to the teachers unions comes not from other social groups (at least not usually or directly), but from *mayors*. In a number of cities—among them, New York, Chicago, Cleveland, Boston, and Washington, D.C.—mayors have taken on more central and formal roles in the governance of the public schools, often with explicit authorization from the state legislature. Although their powers vary from city to city, in general they have moved to take public authority away from local school boards and to exercise some or all of that authority themselves, thus reducing or eliminating the importance of school board elections as determinants of local education policy.

If the teachers unions want to wield influence in districts controlled by mayors, therefore, they have to influence the mayors themselves, and this is typically more difficult than influencing school board members. Mayors have larger, more heterogeneous constituencies than school board members do. They have a broader range of public concerns. They operate much more in the public eye. They are more likely to be held personally responsible for the success or failure of the schools. For all these reasons, they may well be less susceptible to the special interest appeals of the unions, and their electoral prospects may be more difficult for the unions to engineer. This is probably why the school conflicts in Los Angeles and San Diego have played out so differently. In Los Angeles, even though the mayors don't have formal control of the schools, Riordan and Villaraigosa have chosen to get directly involved and put their political careers on the line in pursuing reform. And as mayors, they are big trouble for the unions. In San Diego, mayors haven't taken the lead role, and the unions don't face the same kind of institutional opposition. They just face reformers—and can beat them.

Mayoral control, in its various forms, is a rather recent development, and whether it will eventually bring better outcomes for inner city schools and children remains to be seen. Although useful case studies have been carried out, and although the evidence thus far does suggest that mayors are much more likely to stand up to the teachers unions—two high-profile cases, Mayor Michael Bloomberg in New York City and Mayor Adrian Fenty in Washington, D.C., are discussed later in the book—it is far from clear that mayors can succeed in bringing major reforms that will stick and truly transform the system. In the end, after all, a strong mayor eventually leaves office. The union never leaves.[24]

In any event, control of the schools by mayors is not the norm. Control by school boards is. And the more broadly relevant point is that, even though schools boards have been with us from the beginning of the public school system, there is very little evidence about *their* control of the schools either. School boards are among the most common and familiar of all the governmental institutions in America, but they are surely among the least studied.

If the arguments I have made here are correct, one of the key features of school board politics is that the teachers unions tend to have basic advantages. There is good reason to expect them to be influential—indeed, more influential than any other groups with an interest in public education. If these expectations are on the mark, then, by learning about union power in school board elections we are learning about something that is central to how America's public schools are governed and to the likelihood that they can be organized and operated in the best interests of children.

But are these expectations on the mark? What roles do teachers unions actually play in school board elections, how do they compare to other groups, and how successful are they in selecting the very people they will be bargaining with? In the sections that follow, I present the results of three studies of my own that shed light on these issues.

Teachers Unions and School Board Elections

The first study is drawn from interviews with school board candidates in the state of California—526 candidates (equally balanced between winners and losers) from 253 different school districts. The interviews were carried out over a period of several years, beginning in 2000 and continuing through 2003, with districts and candidates chosen randomly from their larger populations.[25]

Why study California? One reason is that states and localities around the country often don't publish election information for school boards—making a national sample very difficult to collect—while information on California elections is readily available through the League of Women Voters. California is an attractive subject of study anyway. It is the nation's most populous state, enrolling more than 10 percent of the nation's schoolchildren. It is large and demographically diverse, yielding a population of school districts that is enormously varied—urban and rural, big and small, conservative and liberal, white and minority.

The California Teachers Association is noted for being a very powerful union. But the teachers unions in virtually all states are noted for being quite powerful relative to other groups in their own states—power is always relative to context—and there is no reason to think that local politics in California is much different than anywhere else. Indeed, if there are unique factors that set California apart, they may well weaken the unions' incentives for local political activity. One of these factors is Proposition 13, adopted in 1978, which drastically limits local property taxes and thus the financial discretion of local school districts. Another is the radical equalization of spending across school districts required by the state supreme court's Serrano decisions, which limit local financial discretion still further. If anything, then, school boards may be less attractive targets of union influence in California than elsewhere, and the unions may be less locally involved in politics. On the whole, though, I expect the basic political patterns in California to be fairly indicative of what happens nationwide.

A guiding principle of this study is that any effort to understand union politics must recognize that what the unions do—and the power they exercise—is not going to be the same in every local district, but will vary with local conditions. Some conditions are more favorable to union power than others. The timing of elections seems to be one of these. But this factor has been studied by others; and because there is so much interesting ground to cover, I organize the analysis here around four additional aspects of the local context that also help us to understand district politics and union power. They are the size of the district (and therefore the union), political pluralism, political culture, and the incumbency of candidates.

District (and Union) Size

Larger unions should typically have more money, more paid staff, and more activists than smaller unions—and thus a greater organizational capacity for political action. So it makes sense to think, at least as a starting point, that union activity and power will be at their height in the largest districts and will drop off as districts and unions become smaller.

The survey asked candidates whether their local unions engage in certain electoral activities: supporting candidates, giving them money, recruiting people to run, mobilizing members to vote, mobilizing other citizens to vote, making phone calls, campaigning door-to-door, and providing mailings and publicity. The results are described in table 4-1.[26]

The relationship between union political activity and the size of the district (and thus the union) is quite dramatic. In districts with enrollments of less than 5,000, teachers unions often seem to play little or no role in school board elections. They regularly support candidates for office in 34 percent of these smaller districts, and most other political activities are even less common. They make campaign-related phone calls in just 21 percent of the cases, for example, they engage in door-to-door campaigning in 18 percent, and they provide mailings and other publicity in 20 percent.

As districts get larger, however, the unions themselves become larger and more politically capable as organizations. They become much more active along all dimensions, to the point that, in the biggest districts with the biggest unions, every mode of political action (except perhaps recruiting candidates) is common. The unions support candidates for office in 92 percent of these districts. They make phone calls in 97 percent, they campaign door-to-door in 68 percent, and they provide mailings and publicity in 94 percent.

These differences are certainly consistent with the notion that union power is greater in the larger districts, and thus that they are more successful there in getting sympathetic candidates elected to office. So let's take a look at (perceived) union influence and see what the data suggest.

As one way of measuring influence, the survey asked candidates a simple question: "In general, how important would you say the teachers union is in

Table 4-1. *Union Activity and Influence, by District Size*[a]

Percent of districts

	District size			
Type of activity	Less than 5,000	5,000 to 10,000	10,000 to 25,000	More than 25,000
Supporting candidates				
Yes	34	78	90	92
Mixed	10	7	5	3
No	56	15	5	5
Giving money				
Yes	22	55	72	94
Mixed	7	7	7	6
No	72	39	21	0
Recruiting candidates				
Yes	13	14	27	52
Mixed	11	14	14	15
No	76	73	59	33
Mobilizing members				
Yes	45	76	85	100
Mixed	17	2	7	0
No	37	21	8	0
Mobilizing other voters				
Yes	34	55	73	86
Mixed	17	12	11	9
No	49	33	16	6
Making phone calls				
Yes	21	50	64	97
Mixed	10	16	12	3
No	68	34	24	0
Door-to-door campaigning				
Yes	18	37	38	68
Mixed	6	15	15	15
No	76	49	47	18
Mailings and publicity				
Yes	20	69	75	94
Mixed	6	5	7	3
No	74	26	19	3
Number of districts	104	43	59	36

Source: Author's data as reported in Terry M. Moe, "Teachers Unions and School Board Elections," in *Besieged: School Boards and the Future of Education Politics,* edited by William G. Howell (Brookings, 2005).

a. Figures represent the percentage of districts falling into each category, based on the average scores of its respondents. District size is the number of students enrolled. A district is scored as a "Yes" if more than half the respondents in that district said that the local union engaged in the activity in question. A district is scored as a "No" if less than half said the local union engaged in the activity. A district is scored as "Mixed" if exactly half said the union engaged in the activity.

Figure 4-1. *Union Importance in School Board Elections, by District Size*[a]

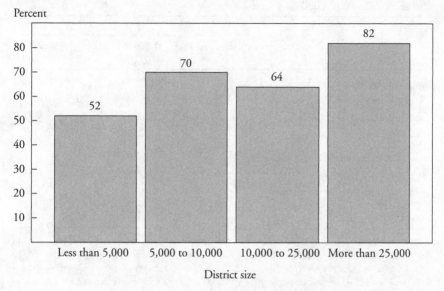

Percent

Source: Author's data as reported in Terry M. Moe, "Teachers Unions and School Board Elections," in *Besieged: School Boards and the Future of Education Politics,* edited by William G. Howell (Brookings, 2005).

a. Figures represent the percentage of districts in each size category reporting that teachers unions are important in school board elections. District size is the number of students enrolled.

your district's school board elections?" Their responses are set out in figure 4-1. According to candidates, the teachers unions are often electorally important *even in the smaller districts, where we know they are not very active.* In districts with less than 5,000 students, unions are regarded as important in 52 percent of the districts—a rather high level of importance given the unions' starkly low level of activity. Something is happening in these districts, it would seem, that is not being picked up by activity levels alone. This said, however, it is also true that assessments of union importance *do* grow with the size of the district. And in the largest districts, the unions are almost always regarded as important (82 percent). Big districts have powerful unions. Or so it appears.

It is worth pausing here to give special attention to the one resource that, in journalistic accounts and the public mind, is most often associated with interest group power: campaign contributions. How important is money in these elections, and how does its importance seem to vary with district (and union) size? As a baseline, let's consider the total amounts of money raised by "good" candidates: those who won their races, were incumbents, or were endorsed by the unions. We know, at least, that these were serious candidates.

Table 4-2. *Campaign Contributions to Candidates, by District Size*[a]

Median candidate totals, in dollars

| Contribution Information | District size | | | |
	Less than 5,000	5,000 to 10,000	10,000 to 25,000	More than 25,000
Campaign contributions to "good" candidates				
All "good" candidates	0	900	7,000	10,000
Endorsed	100	2,000	8,000	10,000
Unendorsed	0	250	6,250	10,000
Union contributions to endorsed candidates				
From teachers unions	0	188	1,000	3,000
From all district employee unions	0	400	2,200	3,500
Number of districts	87	35	32	13

Source: Author's data as reported in Terry M. Moe, "Teachers Unions and School Board Elections," in *Besieged: School Boards and the Future of Education Politics,* edited by William G. Howell (Brookings, 2005).

a. Data in first panel are for "good" candidates, meaning candidates who were incumbents, candidates who were endorsed by the teacher union, or any candidate who won his or her election. Data in second panel under "From all district employee unions" include contributions from teacher unions. The figures were calculated by first finding the median amount of money raised by the relevant set of candidates within each district and then taking the median of the district medians.

The data in table 4-2 show that the typical good candidate in the smaller districts spends *nothing* to run for school board.[27] The median amount of campaign money increases to the $500 to $1,000 range—still a minimal sum—as district size approaches 10,000 students. Then it jumps sharply to much more serious levels: $7,000 for districts with 10,000 to 20,000 students and $10,000 for the largest districts. Obviously, we are talking about very different types of elections here—ones in which candidates probably have to raise money rather than take it out of their own pockets, and in which money is necessary for appealing to (and becoming known by) a much larger constituency. Even in these contexts, however, the amounts of money are rather modest by this country's usual political standards. And they can't hold a candle to the millions of dollars that were spent during the pitched battles between unions and reformers in Los Angeles and San Diego, which were clearly *not* typical of school board politics.

If we break these good candidates into two groups, those who are endorsed by the unions and those who are not (see the table), we find that, in the small- and medium-size districts, the union-endorsed candidates tend to raise much more money than their unendorsed counterparts, but the dollar amounts are so small it's hard to believe they make much difference. In districts with between

10,000 and 20,000 students, the money differences narrow considerably, and in the largest districts there is no money difference at all: a first indication that these bigger districts are more competitive. The union-supported candidates do not appear to have any real money advantage, because other groups are able to match them.

The money raised by union-endorsed candidates, moreover, does not come mainly from the teachers unions themselves. As the table shows, the unions typically contribute nothing to endorsed candidates in the smaller districts; and although the median contribution increases with district (and union) size, it tops out at $3,000—30 percent of the total—in the largest districts. Even if we add in contributions by the unions' allies within the school district—notably, unions representing other district employees—as well as contributions made (as individuals) by teachers and other employees, the total percentage of candidate money coming from employee sources remains in the 25 to 35 percent range for districts of any size.

If the unions have strong incentives to control their local school boards, why do the amounts of money look so weak? The answer, I believe, is that the unions emphasize *other* kinds of political activities—making phone calls, getting out the vote, distributing literature—that in the context of local elections turn out to be more effective at influencing outcomes (except in unusual cases, like Los Angeles and San Diego and other huge cities). These are the sorts of things that, as a practical matter, money really can't buy, but that are tremendously valuable in producing support at the polls, particularly in elections where voters are often poorly informed about the candidates and (in off years) not inclined to turn out.

The candidates essentially say as much. They were asked, "To the extent that the teachers union is important in school board campaigns, is it mainly because of the money it can provide candidates or mainly because of these other support activities?" They overwhelmingly said that union power stems from these other activities, and thus from the coordinated human effort that the organization can offer during a campaign. In only 9 percent of the districts did candidates say that money is the most important factor. The role of money increases with union and district size, as expected, but even in the largest districts, it dominates these other support activities in only 19 percent of the cases. Most of the time what really matters in these local elections is the manpower, not the money.[28]

Political Pluralism

The other side of the coin, however, is that big districts may also present the teachers unions with certain problems that make it more difficult for them to wield power. If the moderating dynamics of pluralist politics are ever important, they are most likely to emerge in these larger districts. They should tend to have a greater number and variety of social groups than smaller districts, and it is reasonable to argue that this social pluralism should often generate more competition for the teachers unions and thus limit their power.

As I suggest earlier, we can't get carried away with this argument. Many broad constituencies are unlikely to achieve effective political organization due to collective action problems. Parents are typically only organized through the local parent-teacher association (PTA), if then, but the PTA is not solely a parent organization, and research shows that it rarely opposes the teachers unions.[29] Virtually all other groups that manage to get organized—business groups, community groups, ethnic groups, religious groups—are not focused on education. They have broader social and political concerns and allocate their attention and resources accordingly. The unions, meantime, are not just any old group in an apparently pluralist system. They have vested interests in public education, they have strong incentives to be politically active, and they are totally focused on education. In some districts at some times—times of crisis, scandal, or deep frustration, say—other groups may decide to invest in educational politics. But under most conditions, only the unions are likely to have both the motivation and the resources to do so.

Even so, competition may moderate their power, especially in the larger districts. This means that district size may be capturing two very different—and countervailing—effects. First, because there is an almost perfect correlation between district and union size, the unions' organizational capacity should grow with district size and so should their power. But second, because political pluralism is also more common in larger districts, the unions should find it more difficult to wield power as districts get bigger. If both effects are indeed operating, this could explain why the small unions in small districts seem to be more politically potent than their miniscule organizational capacity would lead us to expect. Yes, they don't have much capacity for political action. But they also don't have much competition.

The survey allows us to explore these issues in a bit more depth. Let's begin by looking at the competitiveness of elections. Candidates were asked to characterize their districts' school board elections in one of two ways: "Usually they are vigorously contested with a lot of campaign activity," or "There is usually little competition or campaign activity." Their responses, displayed in table 4-3, suggest that the electoral context changes radically as the districts increase in size. Elections are seldom vigorously contested in the smaller districts. Of districts with less than 5,000 students, only 15 percent are regarded as having competitive elections. As district size increases, however, the level of competition and campaigning increases dramatically—to the point that, in the largest districts, 61 percent are regarded as having highly competitive elections.[30]

This is evidence that the unions in larger districts do indeed face more competition than they do in smaller districts, as we should expect. But does this

Table 4-3. *Competition and Union Influence, by District Size*[a]

Percent of districts

	District size			
Nature of district elections	Less than 5,000	5,000 to 10,000	10,000 to 25,000	More than 25,000
How much competition do elections involve?				
Much	15	24	44	61
Mixed	29	28	26	21
Little	56	48	30	18
Number of districts	110	46	61	38
Are unions the most influential group?				
Yes	40	49	42	50
Mixed	14	18	19	21
No	45	33	39	29
Number of districts	104	45	59	38
Are unions the most influential group? (adjusted)				
Yes	66	70	61	68
Mixed	8	9	13	13
No	26	22	26	18
Number of districts	110	46	61	38

Source: Author's data as reported in Terry M. Moe, "Teachers Unions and School Board Elections," in *Besieged: School Boards and the Future of Education Politics,* edited by William G. Howell (Brookings, 2005).

a. Figures represent the percentage of districts falling into each category, based on the average scores of its respondents. District size is the number of students enrolled.

competition really limit union power very much? And what about the smaller districts? Does the lack of competition mean that all groups, including the unions, are without influence? Or does it mean that there are fewer obstacles in the way of union control?

The survey cannot answer these questions with certainty, but it does shed some additional light on them. For instance, it asked candidates whether, compared to all other organized groups in their districts, the teachers unions are the *most* influential. The district-level results, set out in the middle of table 4-3, are interesting on two counts. First, union influence does not vary in a consistent way with district size, and the unions show surprising strength in the smaller districts, where they play little overt role in campaigns. Second, the teachers unions in the larger districts do not come across as a dominant political force. They are rated as the single most influential group in 50 percent of the largest districts

Figure 4-2. *Influence of Groups Other Than Teachers Unions,*
by District Size[a]

Percent

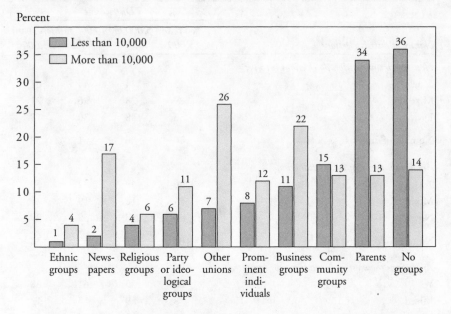

Source: Author's data as reported in Terry M. Moe, "Teachers Unions and School Board Elections," in
Besieged: School Boards and the Future of Education Politics, edited by William G. Howell (Brookings, 2005).
    a. Responses are from candidates who, after saying that the teachers union is not the most influential
group in the district, were asked to indicate what other groups are more influential. Figures represent the
percentage of districts in which the relevant group was mentioned by at least half of the respondents in the
district. District size is the number of students enrolled.

and in 42 percent of the next largest. These figures hardly support the brand of
pluralistic politics that education scholars seem to envision, for even at these levels the system is clearly tilted in the unions' favor. Nonetheless, the data indicate
that, in at least half the larger districts, *other* groups are regarded either as being
more powerful or as competing with them on an equal footing.

Figure 4-2 provides more detail. Candidates who said the unions are not the
most influential group in district politics were asked to indicate what other organized groups are more influential, and their responses are enlightening. As the
figure shows, large districts are clearly more pluralistic than small districts (aside
from the role of parents), as we would expect, with more groups of different
types regarded as influential. But this said, the one group that knowledgeable
observers would surely expect to rise to the top here—business—is singled out
for its influence in just 22 percent of the large districts and 11 percent of the
smaller districts. Remember, we are dealing here solely with districts in which

the unions are said *not* to be dominant, so these figures are especially telling about the weak role of business.

With perhaps one exception (parents in small districts), the other types of possible competitors—party and ideological groups, religious groups, newspapers, other unions, prominent individuals, community groups, ethnic groups—do no better than business and usually do worse. If the teachers unions are being effectively counterbalanced, it is happening through the action of different types of groups in different districts. In some districts, community groups may be especially influential. In others, prominent individuals. In still others, religious groups. This is quite plausible, and perhaps very important. But still, there is no consistent counterweight to union power. In small districts, parents come closest to providing such a counterweight. But they trump the teachers unions in just 34 percent of these districts, which hardly means that they can be counted upon. And "parents" may often refer to the PTA, which is typically not a counterbalancing force at all.

A closer look at these numbers raises additional questions about the potency of pluralism. In the first place, the groups most often singled out in large districts (and sometimes in small districts) as more influential than the teachers unions are *other unions*—meaning, most often, the unions representing classified (nonteaching) employees of the school districts. These unions are allies of the teachers unions. In the second place, many candidates were not able to name *any* group that is more influential than the teachers unions, so there is reason to think that the teachers unions are in fact the most influential organized group in those districts.

If we reclassify the districts in which these responses were given—the ones in which no other group was mentioned or in which only other unions were mentioned—then things look quite different. As the adjusted figures at the bottom of table 4-3 show, the unions emerge as the major political force in 68 percent of districts overall, with other groups more important in just 18 percent, and, interestingly, roughly the same ratio prevails for districts of all sizes.

This reclassification makes some assumptions and may err on the side of attributing too much power to the unions. (Later analysis speaks to this issue.) I offer it here for purposes of comparison, knowing that the truth may lie somewhere in-between the two classifications. Even so, there is good reason for doubting that the diversity often observed in school politics is providing a genuinely pluralistic politics. This is not to claim that the teachers unions always get their way or that other groups don't count. But it does appear that the kind of pluralism operating in local elections is heavily tilted in favor of the teachers unions and that this is the case for *both* small and large districts.

Before moving on, I want to add one more finding of relevance to the pluralism issue. Conventional accounts of school board politics have highlighted the key role of business—which suggests that, if there is an effective counterweight

Table 4-4. *Occupations of Winners and Incumbents, by District Size*
Percent of winners and incumbents

Occupation or sector	Small districts	Large districts
Public schools	11	16
Other education	3	8
No job, retired, and so forth	20	28
Ordinary employee	23	18
Professional	6	10
Small business or self-employed	13	5
Business (general)	2	2
Business (managerial)	6	4
Construction	7	3
Real estate	3	0
Consultant	6	4
Total	100	100
Number of districts	124	92

Source: Author's data from survey of California school board candidates, carried out 2000–03.
a. Small districts are those with student enrollments of less than 10,000. Large districts have enrollments of 10,000 or above.

to the unions, this is the most reasonable place to look for it. We already know that, in these data, business is usually not mentioned as an influential force in board elections. But we might also ask, who are the people who actually get elected to the board—and in particular, are they important business people who would provide a counterweight to the unions, and perhaps give a business tilt to board decisionmaking?

Consider the information in table 4-4, which describes the occupations of candidates who were either incumbents or won their elections. For the issue at hand, the findings are roughly the same for large and small districts, so I simply focus on the former. In the larger districts, 24 percent of board members either work for the public schools or are employees of other educational institutions (for example, community colleges). Another 28 percent have no job at all. Usually they are retired or are housewives. So some 52 percent of all board members, then, are clearly not prominent business people (except possibly retired ones). The remaining 48 percent might plausibly be categorized as coming from the business community—but this would be quite misleading. In a market economy, it is inevitable that most people in any school district, and probably most board members, will work in the private sector and thus for "business." But if we look at the actual jobs of the people who get elected, it becomes clear that any conclusion that they somehow represent business interests, or serve as some sort of coherent group or pluralistic counterweight, would be a big mistake.

In the larger districts, 18 percent of all board members—who constitute well over a third of all alleged business members—hold ordinary jobs and cannot be considered business leaders. A sample: auto mechanic, forester, radiologist, insurance broker, postal worker. Almost none of the other categories of business members can be regarded as representatives of the business community either: 10 percent have professional occupations and, although there are some attorneys who may fit the bill, most professionals are psychologists, optometrists, ministers, and the like, and they don't fit the bill at all; 5 percent are self-employed (beauty salon owner, craftsman, merchant); 3 percent are from the construction industry (mainly engineers and contractors, who probably care about getting a share of building contracts, but not about representing business interests generally); and 4 percent are consultants of one type or another (possibly interested in getting consulting business and making contacts within the district).

The board members who seem to come closest to the stereotype are those who have managerial-level jobs of one kind or another. But there are precious few of these, just 4 percent of the total, and most of them are hardly what we can consider leaders of the business community. They hold jobs like supervisor in a hospital, human relations director, purchasing manager, and director of accounting. There may possibly be a few business leaders in the category labeled general business—people who gave "businessman" as their occupation, or some such thing—but there aren't many of these (2 percent), and there is no reason to think they are prominent business types. So far as I can tell, in fact, there appear to be no true corporate executives in the lot.

All in all, business makes a very poor showing here. There is no evidence that business is a coherent, organized force in school board politics, except perhaps in unusual cases, and no evidence that its longtime reputation for local power is well deserved. Any notion that it serves as an effective pluralistic counterweight to the unions is probably overstated, at least most of the time.[31]

A Closer Look: Small Districts, Pluralism, and Union Satisfaction

Let's go back and look more closely at the smaller districts. There is clear evidence that the unions are not very active in these contexts, yet there is also evidence that they are surprisingly influential. How can they be influential if they aren't doing much of anything? Part of the answer may be that they face little competition from opponents, and we now know that their elections are often not competitive. Let me elaborate on this theme a bit.

Here is one possibility. When California's teachers unions first came on the scene in the 1960s and early 1970s, they entered a system controlled by other social interests; and they had strong incentives to take control for themselves by getting sympathetic people elected to local school boards and keeping them there. Acting on these incentives presumably brought them into conflict with the established interests, a period of upheaval ensued, and a new equilibrium emerged that reflected the newcomers' power.

If this theory is roughly correct, then what we are witnessing today is an outgrowth of political battles that were fought thirty years ago. In districts where the unions were largely successful, there may be no political battles at all in today's world. The districts are simply in an equilibrium satisfactory to the unions, everyone recognizes the new reality, and politics is peaceful. This could be what has happened in many of the smaller districts, whose environments—because they are relatively homogeneous, stable, and noncompetitive—may help to support such a political equilibrium. In the larger districts, in contrast, political environments are inherently more diverse, competitive, and subject to change; and the unions—even if powerful—may be threatened more often by opposition and political battles that require high levels of union political activity to maintain control. The serenity that prevails in many smaller districts, then, may often hide the fact that teachers unions are satisfied with what they are getting and simply have no need to be more active than they are. In many cases their inactivity may be a sign of power, not weakness.

The data suggest as much. Candidates were asked whether, in their own districts, the teachers unions tend to be satisfied with the school boards or would prefer to see members elected that are more prounion. Their responses indicate that the unions are satisfied with their school boards in some 39 percent of the districts statewide—and the percentage varies inversely with the size of the district. It is in the *small* districts that unions are most likely to be satisfied. In districts with less than 5,000 students, the unions are satisfied 45 percent of the time. By contrast, they are satisfied 32 percent of the time in the largest districts.[32]

The more general finding is that, over the entire population of districts—including districts of all sizes—unions tend to be *more satisfied* in districts with *little competition* and where they are *not very active*. It is not just a phenomenon due to small districts. Indeed, if we look *just* at small districts—which, of course, vary in their levels of competitiveness and union activity from one to another—we get an even closer look at how this phenomenon plays out. The teachers unions in these small districts tend to be

—More satisfied when they are *not* very active. They are satisfied in 50 percent of the small districts with little union political activity, but in 33 percent of the small districts with relatively high levels of union political activity.

—More satisfied when they are *not* regarded as important players in electoral politics. They are satisfied in 54 percent of the small districts where they are regarded as unimportant, but in 42 percent of the small districts where they are regarded as important.

—More satisfied when there is *little* competition or campaigning on anyone's part. They are satisfied in 55 percent of the small districts that are noncompetitive, but in 36 percent of the small districts that are competitive.

The evidence suggests, then, that the peace and serenity so characteristic of small districts are not indications that the unions are weak or that they aren't getting what they want. Indeed, there may very well be nothing happening in many of these districts, and no overt union activity, precisely because the unions are happy with the status quo there—a status quo that was essentially determined years ago.

Political Culture

Different districts may have different political cultures, as measured by a variety of social characteristics: party and ideology, ethnicity, income and education, religion, and perhaps others. Group competition aside, if the electoral system is reasonably democratic in responding to the public and reflecting its popular culture—a big "if" that I leave open to question here—these differences in public values should affect the kinds of platforms that attract public support, the kinds of people who get elected, and thus the ability of unions to get what they want. Three implications for union power stand out, which I illustrate with reference to the dimension of political culture on which I have information: party and ideology.

The first implication is that some districts—those that are Democratic and liberal, in this case—will have cultures that are more sympathetic to what the unions want and will be more likely to elect union sympathizers to office. Union power should be easier to exercise in culturally friendly environments.

The second is that, in environments that are relatively unfriendly—Republican and conservative ones—the unions do not have to sit by while hostile candidates are elected and their own candidates go down in flames. They can adapt by supporting candidates who are sufficiently reflective of the local culture to be electable—sufficiently Republican and conservative, in some sense—but who, on the specific issues that unions care about, are more sympathetic to union positions than the other candidates are. In this way, the unions can gain as much as possible—and be as powerful as possible—under difficult circumstances.

The third is that the content of union power will be very different across these contexts. In friendly contexts, the unions may have high win rates and very sympathetic boards. In unfriendly contexts, however, their win rates may also be high due to the compromises they have made in endorsing culturally electable candidates, but their victories may generate school boards that are less sympathetic to their cause. They can be powerful, in the sense of winning elections, yet

Table 4-5. *Party and Ideology of Union-Endorsed Candidates,*
by District Political Culture

Percent of candidates

Party or ideology	Democratic district	Mixed district	Republican district
Party of endorsed candidate			
Democratic	53	44	34
Independent	13	11	11
Republican	33	46	55
Number of districts	75	46	47
Ideology of endorsed candidate			
Liberal	49	33	31
Moderate	14	20	13
Conservative	38	48	56
Number of districts	74	46	48

Source: Author's data as reported in Terry M. Moe, "Teachers Unions and School Board Elections," in *Besieged: School Boards and the Future of Education Politics,* edited by William G. Howell (Brookings, 2005).

not highly successful at getting everything they want. This is the constraint of political culture.

Now let's take a look at the data. If we categorize districts as Republican, mixed-partisan, or Democrat based on the party registration of the citizens who live there, we find that union endorsements do indeed vary in a systematic way across political cultures.[33] See table 4-5. In school districts that are Republican and (presumably) conservative, 55 percent of the candidates endorsed by the teachers unions are Republicans and 56 percent are conservatives—figures that would otherwise be something of a shock, given the teachers unions' almost exclusive support of Democrats in state and national politics (see chapter 9). As the school district populations get more liberal and Democratic, so do the candidates the unions endorse—although the unions continue to endorse fair numbers of Republicans (33 percent) and conservatives (38 percent) even in heavily Democratic environments. (Keep in mind that these elections are nonpartisan, so the party labels do not appear on the ballot.)

These findings are a sign that party and ideology may not say as much about what candidates are likely to believe and stand for in local politics as compared to state and national politics. In any event, what ultimately counts for the unions are not the labels, but how sympathetic these candidates are to union interests. To get at this, the survey asked candidates a number of specific questions about the effects of union influence on various aspects of public education—costs, academic performance, school organization, conflict, teacher professionalism, and teacher quality.[34] As a follow-up, it then asked them for a summary evaluation: "In general, what is your attitude toward collective bargaining in public education?" The results, set out in table 4-6, have a lot to say about unions and their political environments.

First, the vast majority of school board candidates, 66 percent, have positive overall attitudes toward collective bargaining. Even among Republicans—indeed, even among Republicans who are not endorsed by the unions—the majority take a positive approach to this most crucial of union concerns. Thus districts that are heavily Republican and conservative may well be less friendly territory for unions relative to districts that are heavily Democratic and liberal, but they are not necessarily unfriendly in an absolute sense.

Second, candidates are more critical of union influence when assessing its specific effects. Almost two-thirds think union influence leads to higher costs, 42 percent think it leads to greater conflict, and 40 percent think it leads to more rigid organizations. But these aspects of schooling are several steps removed from what happens in the classroom, and, in any event, strong majorities still see the effects of collective bargaining on conflict and organization as being either positive or neutral, and thus benign. The more telling finding is that overwhelming majorities of candidates have benign views on the two items that are most directly related to how much kids learn—namely, academic performance and teacher quality. Only 22 percent think that union influence has negative consequences for academic performance, and only 20 percent think it threatens teacher quality.

Third, party does make a difference for candidate attitudes. If we compare all Republicans to all Democrats, disregarding endorsements, Republicans are consistently less supportive of collective bargaining than Democrats are. This is true for their general evaluations—57 percent positive for Republicans, 75 percent positive for Democrats—but it is also true for each of the more specific items. Just 36 percent of Republicans think union influence leads to better academic performance, for example, but 50 percent of Democrats do. Similarly, 32 percent of Republicans think union influence leads to less conflict within the district, but 41 percent of Democrats see it this way. These and other differences are not huge—a reflection of the fact that most candidates for school board are supportive of collective bargaining. But still, party does matter. (If these results were broken down by ideology instead of party, all of the same patterns would emerge.)

Fourth, and most important, the unions *do* appear to use endorsements strategically to promote the candidacies of people who are sympathetic to union interests. Endorsed Republicans are consistently more favorable toward union interests than unendorsed Republicans, and endorsed Democrats are consistently more favorable than unendorsed Democrats. Moreover, the endorsed Republicans tend to be more positive toward union interests than the unendorsed Democrats.

Table 4-6. *Candidate Attitudes toward Collective Bargaining,
by Party and Union Endorsement*

Percent of candidates

Attitudes toward collective bargaining	Democratic			Republican			
	Not endorsed	Endorsed	Total	Not endorsed	Endorsed	Total	All
General effects							
Positive	67	81	75	51	65	57	66
Neutral	2	0	1	3	4	3	2
Negative	32	19	25	46	31	40	32
Specific effects							
Effect on cost							
Lower	3	3	3	0	9	4	4
No effect	29	47	38	18	36	26	31
Higher	68	50	59	82	55	70	65
Effect on academic performance							
Higher	41	60	50	26	50	36	42
No effect	41	31	37	32	36	35	35
Lower	17	9	13	42	14	29	22
Effect on organization							
Flexible	24	39	32	29	40	33	34
No effect	35	27	31	18	24	21	25
Rigid	42	33	37	53	36	46	40
Effect on conflict							
Less	39	44	41	24	43	32	38
No effect	21	27	25	11	21	16	20
More	40	29	34	65	36	52	42
Effect on professionalism							
More	34	46	40	20	49	32	36
No effect	32	35	33	33	32	33	33
Less	34	18	27	47	19	35	32
Effect on teaching							
Better	28	54	41	19	45	30	35
No effect	50	40	46	40	47	43	44
Worse	22	6	14	41	9	27	20
Number of districts	60	67	127	76	54	130	257

Source: Author's data as reported in Terry M. Moe, "Teachers Unions and School Board Elections," in *Besieged: School Boards and the Future of Education Politics,* edited by William G. Howell (Brookings, 2005).

Figure 4-3. *Win Rates for Endorsed and Unendorsed Candidates,*
by District Political Culture

Percent

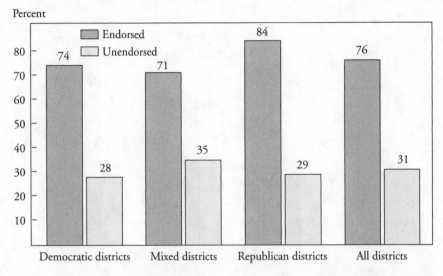

Source: Author's data as reported in Terry M. Moe, "Teachers Unions and School Board Elections" in *Besieged: School Boards and the Future of Education Politics,* edited by William G. Howell (Brookings, 2005).

Indeed, the endorsed Republicans are in some ways (on issues of organization, conflict, professionalism) just as positive as the endorsed Democrats. By using endorsements to support candidates who are at once compatible with the local culture (electable) and relatively sympathetic to union interests, then, the unions can take significant steps—especially in districts filled with Republicans and conservatives—toward loosening the constraints of political culture.

If this assessment is basically correct and if the unions are strategically adapting to their constraining environments, then even in relatively unfriendly districts they may well win elections just as often as they do in friendly districts. That, after all, is the reason that they are adapting. The downside, though, is that the content of their victories should tend to be less beneficial. What the constraints ultimately boil down to is not that the unions lose elections, but that in order to win elections they must accept candidates—and school board members—who are less sympathetic than the unions would like.

Evidence on these scores is set out in figure 4-3, which shows the rates at which endorsed and unendorsed candidates win and how these rates vary across types of districts. We have to remember, in interpreting these outcomes, that the sample was designed to include roughly equal numbers of winners and losers; so whatever the true win rate is across all these elections, the probability that a random candidate in the data set turns out to be a winner is about one half. That

Figure 4-4. *Percentage of Endorsed Winners Who Say That Collective Bargaining Has Positive Effects, by District Political Culture*

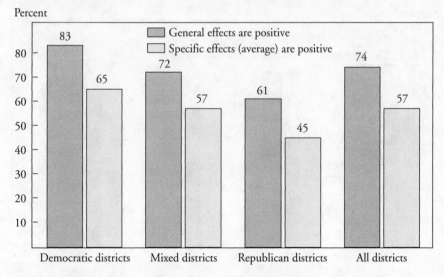

Percent

Legend:
- General effects are positive
- Specific effects (average) are positive

Democratic districts: 83, 65
Mixed districts: 72, 57
Republican districts: 61, 45
All districts: 74, 57

Source: Author's data as reported in Terry M. Moe, "Teachers Unions and School Board Elections" in *Besieged: School Boards and the Future of Education Politics,* edited by William G. Howell (Brookings, 2005).

said, it is clear from the data that the unions' candidates do quite well indeed. On average, 76 percent of endorsed candidates win their elections, compared to just 31 percent of the unendorsed candidates. Even more important, given our concerns here, the unions do *not* tend to lose more often in districts that are heavily Republican. In our sample, in fact, union candidates do somewhat better in heavily Republican districts (84 percent winners) than in mixed-partisan districts (71 percent) or even in heavily Democratic districts (74 percent). A more finely grained look at the data—not included in the figure—shows that the unions are more often regarded as electorally important in these Republican districts (85 percent compared to 70 percent for the Democratic districts), and they are more often seen as the single most influential group in school board politics (62 percent compared to 52 percent for the Democratic districts).

In these respects, the unions are adapting with great success. But what is the content of their victories? As figure 4-4 reveals, their wins clearly do not gain them as much in the districts where they need to make adaptive trade-offs. Despite their high win rates in Republican districts, their own winning candidates are *less* positive toward union interests than their winning candidates in mixed and Democratic districts. In terms of general attitudes, 61 percent of endorsed winners are positive toward collective bargaining in the Republican districts, compared to 72 percent in the mixed districts and 83 percent in the

Democratic districts. Similarly, if we categorize candidates based on the average of their responses to the specific-effects items, the pattern is exactly the same: 45 percent of endorsed winners in Republican districts come across as having positive views on the specific effects of union influence, compared to 57 percent in mixed districts and 65 percent in Democratic districts. Finally, if we look at all winners, endorsed and unendorsed—and thus at all candidates who wind up taking seats on their local school boards—the results are again the same: the unions are faced with less sympathetic school boards in less friendly political environments.

So the evidence suggests that the unions *are* constrained by political culture. The teachers unions can loosen these constraints by adapting endorsements to fit local circumstances. But they cannot avoid making trade-offs, and in the more conservative districts they are likely to be less successful as a result.

The Incumbency of Candidates

Whatever the level of government, incumbents tend to win elections at very high rates.[35] One reason is that they have name recognition—which, in an electorate poorly informed about politics, counts heavily. Another reason is that, as office holders, they have had a chance to serve their constituencies, build coalitions, and raise money. Yet another is that groups that might otherwise support challengers have to worry that incumbents will win their races anyway and, having won, will wreak vengeance on opponents. So groups that want access in the future may be wise to support incumbents even when they don't like them very much.

For these reasons and more, incumbents have their own sources of electoral power, and the teachers unions may have to make trade-offs in dealing with them. In particular, they may find themselves endorsing incumbents who are not especially sympathetic to collective bargaining or other union concerns. To the extent this is so, the unions may be quite successful at getting their endorsed incumbents into office, but less successful at getting what they want from them. The content of their power would suffer, constrained by the power of incumbency.

The data in figure 4-5 suggest that the unions do indeed make these sorts of trade-offs. As we would expect, the incumbents they endorse are more sympathetic to union interests than the incumbents they don't endorse. But it is also true that the incumbents they endorse are considerably *less* sympathetic to union interests than the *non*incumbents they endorse: 64 percent of endorsed incumbents have positive general attitudes toward collective bargaining, but the comparable figure for the nonincumbents they endorse is 84 percent. The results are precisely the same when it comes to candidate attitudes on the specific effects of union influence in collective bargaining: 47 percent of the endorsed incumbents are positive, compared to 70 percent of the endorsed nonincumbents. It appears that the unions do not have the free hand in dealing with incumbents that they

Figure 4-5. *Election Outcomes and Candidate Attitudes toward Collective Bargaining, by Incumbency and Union Endorsement*

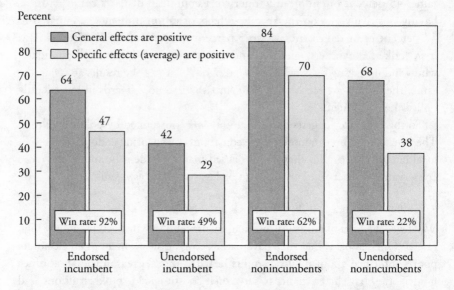

Percent

Source: Author's data as reported in Terry M. Moe, "Teachers Unions and School Board Elections" in *Besieged: School Boards and the Future of Education Politics,* edited by William G. Howell (Brookings, 2005).

have in dealing with nonincumbents, and are constrained to accept candidates less to their liking.

Despite being constrained, the data on win rates suggest that they are still able to come out ahead. In our sample, which has a baseline win rate of 0.51, a phenomenal 92 percent of the endorsed incumbents win their races, compared to just 49 percent of the unendorsed incumbents. The latter figure is nothing to sneeze at, because it means that half of these incumbents have been able to win even when the unions opposed them. Nonetheless, there is a weeding out process going on here: incumbents who are especially negative toward union interests are systematically being removed from office, while incumbents who are more sympathetic are being kept. In addition, the losers are often being replaced by union-endorsed nonincumbents, who win 62 percent of their elections and are considerably more positive toward union interests. Nonincumbents who are not endorsed by the unions—and who are less sympathetic toward union interests than those who are endorsed—win at a much lower rate, 22 percent.

The unions may be more successful than these figures indicate. We only have data on the incumbents who choose to run for reelection; and it is quite possible, especially in view of the big effect of union endorsements on win rates, that

Figure 4-6. *Candidate Attitudes toward Collective Bargaining,*
by Election Outcome and Incumbency

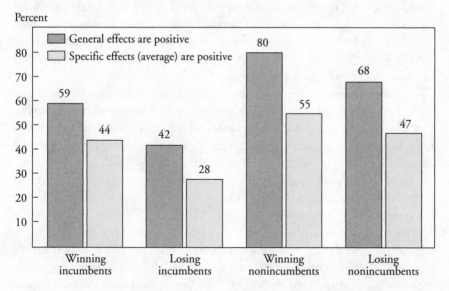

Percent

Source: Author's data as reported in Terry M. Moe, "Teachers Unions and School Board Elections" in
Besieged: School Boards and the Future of Education Politics, edited by William G. Howell (Brookings, 2005).

the incumbents who don't run for reelection are disproportionately those who are unsympathetic to union interests and wouldn't have received union support. Thus the unions may exercise power not only by ensuring that the (endorsed) candidates who win are more prounion than the (unendorsed) incumbents who lose, but also by scaring the antiunion incumbents out of running for reelection. The data used here can't measure this effect.

But they can suggest what the turnover looks like among the candidates who do run. See figure 4-6. Overall, the incumbents who win their elections—a mix of endorsed and unendorsed candidates—are more positive toward union interests than the incumbents who lose. In terms of general attitudes toward collective bargaining, 59 percent of the winners are positive, compared to 42 percent of the losers. And in terms of attitudes about the specific effects of union influence, 44 percent of the winners are positive, compared to 28 percent of the losers. Electoral attrition in the ranks of incumbents clearly favors the unions. Moreover, the new recruits coming onto the school boards are considerably more prounion than the incumbents who lose. Fully 80 percent of these nonincumbents have positive general attitudes, and 55 percent have positive attitudes on specific effects. Even ignoring the incumbents who don't seek reelection, then, the direction of turnover here is very much prounion.

It seems obvious that such results should be expected if the teachers unions are genuinely powerful. Yet this can't be the whole story. For the unions have been powerful for more than two decades; and if they had been racking up incremental gains all this time, the school boards would long ago have become totally prounion. We know this is not the case, so we are faced with a conundrum. How can the unions produce prolabor turnover year after year and yet fail in the end to create totally prolabor school boards?

A plausible answer arises from a fascinating pattern in the data that observant readers may already have noticed. As figures 4-5 and 4-6 show, incumbents in general—whether endorsed or unendorsed, winners or losers—tend to be much less sympathetic to collective bargaining than nonincumbents. This is true even though all incumbents were at one time nonincumbents, which suggests, assuming there is continuity to these patterns over time, that something happens to nonincumbents after they take office that *changes* their attitudes and makes them less sympathetic to collective bargaining.

That such a thing might happen makes perfect sense. When nonincumbents take office—and thereby become incumbents—their new jobs require that they represent management and deal with the unions across the bargaining table, experiencing firsthand (and probably for the first time) what collective bargaining is all about, and how the interests of unions and teachers can come into conflict with the interests of districts and children. If this process of socialization does occur—and I suspect it does—then it would resolve our conundrum: the unions could continually win elections, and nonincumbents could continually be more prounion than the incumbents they replace, yet the process would not lead inexorably to union control.

All this suggests that the unions are doubly constrained by incumbency. First, they find themselves having to endorse certain incumbents who are not as sympathetic as they would like. And second, because there is a sympathy gap between incumbents and nonincumbents, the unions tend to take an even bigger hit when they are constrained to support an incumbent. For both reasons, the impressive frequency of union electoral victories—especially the 92 percent victory rate (in our sample) of endorsed incumbents—overstates the true content of their victories. But victories they are, nonetheless. The unions are consistently able to shape the outcomes of school board elections, ensuring that candidates sympathetic to union interests are more likely to take office—and to be the "management" they bargain with.

Overview

This discussion is based on simple tables, usually showing how two variables—district size and union political activity, for example—are related to one another. This is the easiest way to make findings accessible to a broad audience. Yet simple tables can sometimes be misleading, because they don't control for other variables that might be relevant. In the more extensive study from which these data are taken, therefore, I provide a multivariate analysis that does so. In all important respects, it confirms and further refines the conclusions highlighted above. Here, to summarize briefly, is what the totality of the evidence seems to suggest.

District size is both a plus and a minus for union influence. Large unions in large districts have greater organizational capacity than small unions in small districts, and they are much more active in school board politics. The multivariate analysis shows, moreover, that union activism has a big impact on the kinds of candidates who get endorsed and who win elections: they are more prounion. Yet if electoral activism is held constant, it is in the smaller districts that unions do especially well in securing sympathetic endorsements and winners, because they benefit from having fewer competing groups. Large unions, while advantaged by their greater capacity and activism, are disadvantaged by their more pluralistic environments. Given these countervailing factors, it is probably wrong to think that the teachers unions are enormously powerful in the large districts and have little power in the small districts. They appear to be powerful in *both* settings— but their power is also somewhat moderated in both, for different reasons.

Union power is also affected by the local political culture. In Republican districts, as compared to Democratic districts, the teachers unions endorse candidates who are less sympathetic to union interests, and they wind up with school boards that are less sympathetic as well. It appears, then, that local democracy is operating—to some degree, anyway—to give weight to the preferences of ordinary citizens. The unions are clearly the dominant power, but the local political culture constrains what they can do, how they do it, and what they can achieve.

Finally, union power is moderated by incumbency. Incumbents have their own electoral advantages, and the unions make trade-offs by endorsing incumbents who are less sympathetic toward labor interests than the unions would like. While they do take steps (successfully) to get rid of incumbents who are especially antiunion, and while the incumbents they endorse are more sympathetic than the ones they don't, the unions are still settling for people they would not support if they had a free hand. It appears, moreover, that the experience of serving on school boards tends to make board members less sympathetic to union interests than when they were first elected. This means that the unions cannot count on locking up school boards by simply getting their supporters into office, and that they are forced to make even bigger trade-offs in agreeing to endorse incumbents.

Union power in school board elections, then, is hardly a matter of pure dominance. There are forces at work that constrain their influence and prevent them (usually) from gaining all-out control. We need to be aware of this if we want to understand the dynamics of local politics. Nonetheless, it does not change the core democratic problem: the teachers unions are by far the most powerful groups in these elections—and school boards, as a result, tend to be tilted in their favor.

The Voting Power—and Self-Interest—of Teachers

The study I describe above provides a broad overview of union power in school board elections. In this section, I present the findings of another study.[36] This one goes into greater depth by taking a close look at just one of the ways—but a particularly important and interesting one—that the unions can shape electoral outcomes to their own advantage: by relying upon the voting power of teachers themselves, together with their employee allies. The evidence sheds light on two basic issues.

The first has to do with voting behavior and its impacts. Do teachers and other district employees vote at higher rates than other citizens? If so, are the turnout differentials big enough to boost the unions' chances of victory in school board elections?

The second is more fundamental. It has to do with *why* teachers are voting in the first place. What are they trying to achieve? Are they (and other employees) turning out for reasons that are essentially public-spirited—because they want what is best for children, say, or want to promote public education? Or are they turning out to promote their own occupational self-interest—and thus doing what is best for *them*?

Background

The data from this study come from a larger project carried out in 2002, in which I collected the names and zip codes of school district employees in a stratified sample of seventy California school districts, all of them unionized, and matched the names to county voter files to get each employee's voting history. In the study I describe here, I restrict my attention to nine of these districts, all located in Los Angeles and Orange counties. These nine are analytically useful because, as they are clustered in close proximity to one another, teachers who don't live in the district where they work often show up as residents of one of the other districts. As I show, being able to compare these two types of teachers— those who live and work in a district and those who live in one district but work in another—is quite helpful for understanding the basics of teacher turnout, as well as its connection to power.

In national and state elections, interest groups of all types try to get their members out to vote, and member turnout is a measure of their potential influence. In school board elections, however, there is an important wrinkle that affects the teachers unions in a big way. The wrinkle is that if teachers don't live in the districts where they work, they aren't eligible to vote in those districts' school board elections. The unions' ability to turn member votes into electoral power, therefore, depends on exactly where their members live.

In the sample I'm examining here, the percentage of teachers who live in their own districts varies a great deal—from 8 to 55 percent—and tends to increase with the affluence of the district. Even in the more affluent ones, however, a strikingly large percentage of teachers do not live where they work, and thus cannot vote. Other district employees are much more likely to live where they work, regardless of the district's affluence. This enhances their value to the teachers unions as political allies.

There are no available data on what the residency figures look like for the nation's school districts. Living outside the district is presumably common when multiple districts are packed into an urban area, as they are in Los Angeles County and Orange County. In districts that are suburban, rural, or geographically spread out, far fewer employees may live outside their own districts. Still, some degree of nonresidency is a fact of life in most districts. And as that degree increases, teachers and their allies should have a harder time translating their own turnout into power.

The Turnout Gap

I include bond elections along with school board elections here, as they provide additional evidence on turnout, and they are surely relevant to the unions. For school board elections, I focus entirely on those that are held during odd years, when there are no general elections for federal and state offices. These elections offer the best opportunity for studying how teachers and other district employees act on their job-related incentives, because little else is being voted on. For bond elections, I focus on those that are not held at the same time as general elections or school board elections.[37]

For both types of elections, turnout among the local population is downright abysmal, even in the more affluent districts. In the off-year school board elections for which I have data, 1997 and 1999, the median turnout of registered voters is 9 percent. This percentage would be even lower, obviously, if the denominator were the voting-age population as a whole, because many people in the electorate—about a quarter—are not even registered. For bond elections, the turnout is 23 percent. In both cases, low turnout gives the unions an opportunity to mobilize support and tip the scale toward candidates they favor.

Do teachers vote at higher rates than average citizens? The answer is clearly yes, as illustrated in figures 4-7 and 4-8, which, to keep things simple, summarize the data across districts rather than providing the details for each.[38]

If we compute the turnout gap between teachers and average citizens in each district, the median gap over all districts and elections (both school board and bond) is 36.5 percent, which is a huge number given the very low turnout

Figure 4-7. *Voter Turnout for School Board Elections in Select Los Angeles County School Districts, 1997 and 1999*

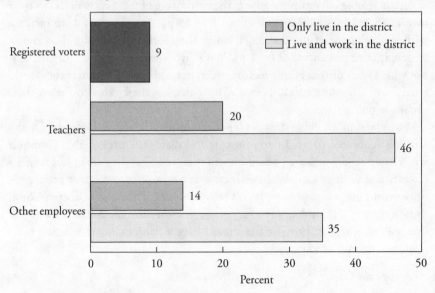

Source: Author's data as reported in Terry M. Moe, "Political Control and the Power of the Agent," *Journal of Law, Economics, and Organization* 22, no. 1 (2006): 1–29; Terry M. Moe, "The Union Label on the Ballot Box," *Education Next* 6, no. 3 (2006): 58–66. For each category, percentage represents the median turnout for such voters over the 14 board elections that occurred, in the aggregate, across the following districts: Charter Oak Unified, Claremont Unified, Covina Valley Unified, Garvey Elementary, Montebello Unified, Norwalk–La Mirada Unified, and Torrance Unified.

overall. In 1997, for instance, only 7 percent of registered voters in the Charter Oak school district voted in their school board election, but 46 percent of the teachers who live there did. In Claremont, 18 percent of registered voters went to the polls, but 57 percent of the teachers who live there did. Similar figures can be recited for *every* district, and the conclusion is the same whether we look at 1997, 1999, or bond elections. Teachers who live in their districts are from *two to seven times* more likely to vote than other citizens are.

Why do teachers turn out at such high rates? The answer may well be that they have an occupational self-interest that other citizens don't have. But this claim needs to be tested, for there is clearly a plausible alternative: that because teachers are better educated and more middle class than the average citizen, and possibly more public-spirited and more committed to public education, they are more likely to vote in school board elections anyway, *regardless* of their personal stakes. Can the evidence show that occupational self-interest, and not these other motivations, accounts for the turnout gap?

Figure 4-8. *Voter Turnout for School Bond Elections in Select Los Angeles and Orange County School Districts, 1998–2000*

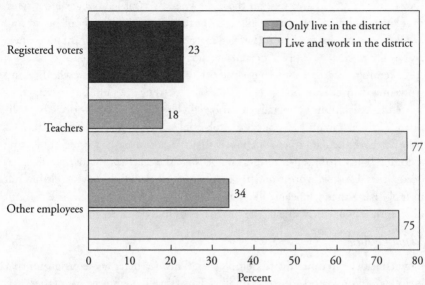

Source: Author's data as reported in Terry M. Moe, "Political Control and the Power of the Agent," *Journal of Law, Economics,* and Organization 22, no. 1 (2006): 1–29; Terry M. Moe, "The Union Label on the Ballot Box," Education Next 6, no. 3 (2006): 58–66. For each category, percentage represents the median turnout for such voters over the five special school bond elections that occurred in the following districts: Claremont Unified (2000), Montebello Unified (1998), Torrance Unified (1998), Huntington Beach City Elementary (1999), and Santa Ana Unified (1999).

The data offer a revealing test. Many teachers in the sample live in one school district but work in another. These teachers are presumably just as middle class, public-spirited, and committed to education as other teachers are, but, because they don't work in the district where they live, they do *not* have an occupational stake in their local school board elections. Do these teachers vote at the same high levels as teachers who *do* have such an occupational stake?

Whether we look at the 1997 elections, the 1999 elections, or the various bond elections, the answer is the same: in *every* case that allows a comparison, the teachers who live in a district but don't work there vote at lower rates than the teachers who both live and work there. The size of the difference is almost always substantial (and statistically significant). In Claremont, to take a rather typical example, 57 percent of the teachers who both live and work there voted in the 1997 election, but only 23 percent of the teachers who live but don't work there voted.

A corollary issue is whether the teachers who merely live in a district vote at higher rates than ordinary citizens do. Here the answer is less clear, and the low numbers advise caution. Statistical significance aside, these teachers turned out at higher rates than ordinary citizens in twelve of eighteen elections, but in five they turned out at lower rates. Of the cases when they turned out at higher rates, moreover, only six are statistically significant. Over all the school board and bond elections, the median difference in turnout rates between these teachers and ordinary citizens is just 7 percent, which could simply be due to social class.

Taken together, these findings contradict the idea that teachers who live and work in a district turn out at high rates because they are public-spirited, committed to education, or socially advantaged. They bolster the notion that self-interest is in fact mainly responsible. A plausible addendum, however—although I do not have the data to explore it—is that teacher turnout is probably getting a double boost from self-interest: one because the teachers themselves have an occupational stake in voting and another because their unions have a self-interest in mobilizing them. It seems likely that both are at work and that the turnout differential is not solely due to the incentives of individual teachers.

Valuable Allies

Now consider the other district employees. This is a heterogeneous group that includes administrators, nurses, and librarians as well as janitors, secretaries, cafeteria workers, and bus drivers. The latter types of rather low-paid workers, however, far outnumber the former types, and some 40 percent are Hispanic. On grounds of social class alone, therefore, we would expect this group to vote at much lower rates than teachers. In more affluent contexts (and perhaps others), they should also vote at lower rates than ordinary citizens.

These class-based expectations are quite wrong. In *every* district with available data, and for all three sets of elections, other district employees who live and work in their districts vote at substantially higher rates than ordinary citizens do—rates that, on average, are just a shade lower than those of teachers who live and work in the district (figures 4-7 and 4-8). If we look *within* each district at the difference in turnout rates between these employees and the teachers who also live and work in their own districts, the median of these differences is just 4 percent—which is stunningly small given the underlying differences in social class.[39] Clearly, something else is going on here. And that something is probably that these other employees, just like teachers, approach elections with their own self-interest in mind, and their unions mobilize them on those grounds.

This interpretation is bolstered by the fact that, when we look at other employees who live in a district but don't work there, and thus do *not* have an occupational stake in the elections, their turnout is decidedly lower on average than that of other employees who both work and live there. The former turn out at lower rates in *all* of the sixteen cases for which there are data, and thirteen of these are statistically significant. If we simply compare the median turnout rates for these groups across districts, the differential is 21 percent for school board elections and a whopping 41 percent for bond elections.

As is true for teachers, the other employees who live but don't work in the district tend to look pretty much like ordinary citizens in their turnout rates. The median difference is 8 percent across all elections, which is virtually the same advantage we find for teachers. In this case, though, social class obviously does *not* explain the turnout gap. And because this is so, it is reasonable to suspect that it doesn't explain the differential between teachers and ordinary citizens either. Some other common factor probably accounts for both differentials.

What these teachers and other employees have in common is that they both take a self-interested approach to elections and they both belong to unions. Because they don't work where they live, they have less incentive to vote and they are not mobilized by the local union (to which they don't belong). But they may also recognize—with reminding by their own unions—that they are all enmeshed in a big collective action problem, and that they should vote in their home districts to protect one another's jobs and interests. Because voting is not a very costly act, this could easily account for a turnout rate that is 7 to 8 percent above that of ordinary citizens.

This analysis reveals that turnout can be an important resource for teachers and their unions. Teachers turn out at much higher rates than other citizens do, they act on their occupational self-interest, and exactly the same is true of the other district employees—which makes them key political allies and allows the teachers unions to more than *double* their voting strength. There is also a downside, however, that weakens their ability to convert these advantages into electoral power. This is the problem of residency. The high turnout rates and driving force of self-interest are only of political value in school board elections to the extent that teachers and other employees live in their districts. And many (in this sample) do not.

Because of the residency problem, turnout is unlikely to be as potent a resource as money or political activists in producing electoral victory. But it can contribute in a positive way to the larger union effort, and in some cases—when elections are close—it can even be pivotal. These cases may be fairly common, in fact, because the margin of victory in school board elections is often rather small. By my own estimate (based on a separate sample of 245 districts for another study), the median gap between the best-off losing candidate and the worst-off winner is about 3 percent. Thus in many of these low-turnout elections it doesn't take much of a vote swing to change the outcome.

Consider some rough calculations for the Charter Oak school district. In the 1997 election, three candidates competed for two seats. The total number of votes cast (two by each voter) was 3,506, and the margin of victory was 2.54 percent, or eighty-nine votes. Are the turnout differentials in Charter Oak large enough to overcome an eighty-nine-vote gap and bring victory to a union-backed candidate? The answer is yes. The district had a total of 350 teachers, only 22 percent living in the district and voting at a rate of 46 percent. Thus there were thirty-five teacher-voters. The district also had 354 other employees, 50 percent living in the district and voting at a rate of 41 percent. This means that there were seventy-three voters among the other district employees and, when the teachers are added in, 108 total votes by school personnel. This figure alone exceeds the eighty-nine votes needed for victory, and it makes no allowance for other sources of prounion votes (for example, relatives, friends, neighbors). Similar calculations could be carried out for the other districts, showing that the turnout differential alone is often sufficient to overcome the margin of victory or, at least, comes close.

As I said, these are indications of what can happen in elections that are close, as many are. Not all elections are this close, of course. And we can't really expect all employees to vote as a bloc (although the prime role of occupational self-interest promotes such an outcome). Yet these sorts of calculations help to show that high employee turnout rates can indeed boost the prospects for union victory, even when considerably diluted by the residency problem. And even when turnout is not pivotal to the outcome, it is clearly a resource that works to the unions' advantage, and—as one of *many* weapons in the union political arsenal—contributes to their larger effort to shape electoral outcomes.

Electoral Impact

The bottom line, of course, has to do with exactly this effort to shape electoral outcomes: to what extent do the unions succeed in getting their favored candidates elected to office? This is the impact that ultimately counts. The studies just discussed shed light on this issue. But they were designed for other purposes—to tell us about important aspects of the politics of school board elections—and were not intended to be studies of electoral impact per se.

To explore the question of impact head-on, I carried out a separate study of union success in school board elections. The evidence comes from a sample of 245 California school district elections and the 1,228 candidates who competed in them during the years 1998–2001. This study is published elsewhere, and I simply summarize the results very briefly.[40]

A multivariate statistical analysis shows that, for candidates who are not incumbents, teachers union support substantially increases their probability of winning—indeed, it is roughly equal to, and may well exceed, the impact of incumbency itself. The comparison to incumbency is instructive. These are low-information, low-interest elections; and because incumbents tend to be well known and relatively well funded, there is every reason to expect the power of incumbency to be considerable. My statistical estimates show that it is. They also show that, when incumbents are endorsed by teachers unions, they are even more likely to win (by a good bit). For nonincumbents—who often do poorly in these elections—the impact of union endorsements is much more dramatic: it essentially transforms them into candidates who can compete *just as effectively as incumbents*. This is saying a lot about the lofty level at which the unions are playing the political game. They are heavy hitters, and they turn candidates into heavy hitters.

The unions' total influence is even greater than this might suggest. When they succeed in getting nonincumbents elected to school boards, these people *become* incumbents the next time around—and then their probability of victory is boosted not just by their union support, but also by the power of incumbency. When the two factors are combined, and thus when union winners run for reelection as incumbents, the candidates are virtually *unbeatable*.

As shown earlier, union success in local elections does not necessarily translate into complete control over school boards, because once candidates take office—and have to deal firsthand with union demands—they seem to become less prounion. This may well be why, in the current study, fully 46 percent of the incumbents running in contested elections were *not* endorsed by the unions: a clear indication that the unions were not happy with their performance in office. There is a continuing need, then, for the unions to stay active in school board elections. They need to defeat incumbents who aren't sufficiently sympathetic, and they need to replace them with new candidates who are. Although the unions are impressively powerful and have big impacts on local electoral outcomes, their control is imperfect—and they need to keep playing the political game in order to maintain their influence.

Conclusion

There is little research on the politics of school board elections and even less on the role of teachers unions. This is unfortunate, because what happens on these scores is fundamental to an understanding of America's public schools. The studies presented here are helpful, but much more work needs to be done before we can know, in detail, how local elections play out in school districts all across the nation.

That said, there is good reason to think that the themes emerging from this evidence are on the money. For one, California offers a broad array of districts, from urban to rural and liberal to conservative, and the patterns prevailing there should be indicative of what is happening elsewhere. For another, these patterns are wholly consistent with what we ought to expect, based on a deeper understanding of how politics and power generally operate.

The expectations are straightforward. To understand school board elections, we need to think about which groups have the *incentives* to get actively involved in them and, of these, which have the *resources* to do it with real power. In both respects, the teachers unions clearly stand out from all other groups.

Their incentives to get involved in local elections are strong indeed. Teachers, after all, work in the school districts, and their material interests are deeply rooted in how the districts operate, how they are organized, how they spend their money, and, in general, how they are governed. This is true whether or not the districts have collective bargaining. Even in states like Texas, Virginia, and North Carolina, where collective bargaining is prohibited, the teachers unions have every reason to get actively involved in school board elections—and they regularly do.[41] Indeed, in these places it is even *more* imperative for the unions to flex their political muscles, because, lacking the power of collective bargaining, it is their only avenue of influence. Fortunately for them, it couldn't be more available: democracy literally invites them to choose the very public leaders who will be making the personnel, financial, and policy decisions they care about.

The focus here, however, has been on districts that do have collective bargaining. The unions in these districts also have compelling incentives to elect district leaders, needless to say, but with a profoundly consequential twist. Collective bargaining is the primal base of union organization: the source of members and money and the economic means by which power is exercised over management—just as it is in the private sector. But then, this isn't the private sector. And precisely because it isn't, collective bargaining is a wholly different phenomenon. It is *not* just a matter of negotiations between two independent sides, one representing labor and one representing management, because the "management" sitting on the other side of the table is chosen through the electoral process—and can literally be *chosen by the unions themselves* if they have sufficient political power. Although "management" is supposed to represent the interests of ordinary people, democracy gives the unions every opportunity to see that this doesn't happen and that their own interests take priority.

By their nature, the teachers unions come into existence with organizations equipped for collective bargaining. But the symbiotic connection between collective bargaining and politics means that they can't just be collective bargaining organizations. They have to be *political* organizations too, and to amass and coordinate the resources—from campaign contributions to political activists to publicity campaigns—that enable them to bring victory to their favored candidates. They are well situated, moreover, for doing all these things: they are already organized, they enroll all (or virtually all) the teachers in their districts, they have a guaranteed inflow of money (member dues), and some portion of their members will be inclined to become activists. The elements of power are all at hand.

In both respects, incentives and resources, the most reasonable expectation—on simple, obvious, purely objective grounds—is that the teachers unions will normally be the most powerful of all groups that might care about public education. Parents certainly have strong incentives, but in most districts they are not organized (outside the PTA), not funded, not active—and not powerful. Business groups, ethnic groups, and other community organizations have resources they might employ in school board elections and, especially in cities, are potential competitors to the unions. But their social agendas are broad and diverse, and this gives the unions a huge incentive advantage—for the unions *only* care about public education. This incentive advantage, in turn, should ultimately translate into a huge resource advantage: because they not only have massive resources to begin with (compared to most other groups), but also incentives to invest *more* of their resources in education-related politics and to do it more regularly.

These expectations apply to school board politics in California. But they apply just as well to school board politics in Illinois or Florida or Tennessee. Wherever teachers unions engage in collective bargaining—and in many places where they don't—they should have advantages over other groups; and these advantages should show up in electoral outcomes and in the types of people who win office and exercise local authority over the schools. The evidence from California, then, simply confirms what we should *expect* for states and districts all across the country. In brief, what it shows is that

—The teachers unions are indeed more active and involved in school board elections than other social groups, and they are more powerful.

—They are powerful in both large and small districts.

—They use these elections to advance their own interests: by endorsing candidates who are especially sympathetic toward collective bargaining and by getting these favored candidates elected.

—Teachers are self-interested about these elections too, and they vote at much higher rates than other citizens do because they have a direct material stake in the outcomes.

This is not the entire story, of course. We should expect the teachers unions to be extraordinarily powerful in school board elections—but we need to recognize as well that there are basic forces at work that constrain what they can do. One is the presence of pluralism, which, particularly in large urban districts, may sometimes generate group competitors. Another is political culture, which prompts the unions to endorse less sympathetic candidates in conservative districts. A third is incumbency, which also compels them to endorse candidates that they are less than enthusiastic about.

The bottom line is not that the teachers unions consistently dominate their local school boards. They are constrained. Things don't always go their way. Nonetheless, they are by far the most powerful groups in the local politics of

American education. And they are quite successful at tilting the "democratic" governance of the local schools in favor of their own special interests.

It is no accident, then, that school boards have been pushed aside in a number of major American cities and that mayors have stepped in. The fact is, school boards have often been weak and ineffective at bringing real improvement to local school systems. They cannot make change. They cannot lead. And a big reason is that they are beholden to powerful interest groups—especially the teachers unions—that *don't want* them to make change and *don't want* them to lead. Mayors have bigger, more diverse constituencies, are able to act with greater independence and strength, and are simply better suited and thus a better bet for doing what is necessary in the face of union opposition.

I explore two prominent cases of mayor-led reform—those of New York City and Washington, D.C.—in chapter 7. It is important to remember, however, that mayoral control is the exception. Almost all of this nation's school districts are governed by school boards. That is the reality, and the implications for kids and schools are hardly inspiring.

5

Are Teachers Underpaid?

At the local level, teachers unions amass power for a reason: they want to win favorable contracts for their members. So what is the result? What do these collective bargaining contracts look like, and what do they mean for the organization and performance of the public schools?[1]

It would be natural to explore these questions right now. But before I turn to them, I want to give separate attention to a familiar claim that is always front and center in these negotiations, and that the unions have used to great advantage in the larger arena of public opinion to gain support for their efforts. This is the claim that teachers are underpaid.

Over the years, this notion has become woven into the warp and woof of modern American society, so much so that, in circles of reasonably well-educated people—including, in my experience, policymakers, journalists, business leaders, and most reformers—it is regarded as strange and some sort of heresy for anyone to argue the contrary. Of course teachers are underpaid! This is one of the taken for granteds of American public education: a "fact" that is widely bemoaned and regularly pointed to as evidence that the nation isn't doing enough to support and reward its teachers.

Needless to say, this kind of shared belief permeates the political atmosphere when school boards—and state legislatures and the U.S. Congress—are making decisions about how much money to spend on education, how funds should be allocated across competing uses, and what kinds of reforms are likely to improve student achievement. If teachers are underpaid, then fairness requires that they be paid more and that union demands be met. If teachers are underpaid, then surely we are not doing our best to attract and keep high-quality people, and we should do whatever we can—raise taxes, divert money from other educational uses (like textbooks, buildings, and technology)—to see that they are better compensated.

But are teachers really underpaid? No book on the teachers unions, it seems to me, can ignore this question. And so I deal with it here. The fact is, in the final analysis, I don't have a strong argument to make one way or the other. This is in part because the question itself does not have an objective answer. Underpaid compared to what? What does underpaid even mean? I do think, however, that this is an issue that—precisely because so many people have prejudged it, and because it has long played a central role in the policymaking process—deserves to be separately examined so that it can be more clearly understood.

Public Opinion and Teacher Pay

For decades, the unions have been arguing that teachers are underpaid and schools are underfunded, and they have waged an ongoing public relations campaign to convince the American public and its leaders that more money needs to be spent—not just for the good of teachers, but for the good of kids and public education.

In one of his many statements on the topic, for example, NEA president (at the time) Reg Weaver put it this way. "Low teacher pay comes at a very high cost. How can we expect educators to be focused, committed, and at their best on a daily basis when they are fearful of the consequences of not earning enough to support their families? Each year we lose excellent teachers because they can't afford to make ends meet. Low teacher pay shortchanges the teaching profession, and students end up paying the price."[2] The AFT's Ed McElroy, reflecting on his own union's survey of teacher salaries, could barely contain his anguish. "Even as teachers are being asked to do more, compensation packages are nothing short of insulting . . . States and school districts are crying poverty when it comes to teachers' pay, yet somehow find money for extravagant administrator salaries. Strong leadership without a quality teaching force won't improve education."[3]

The impact of these efforts cannot be known, but opinion surveys show that most Americans now see issues of teacher pay and school spending pretty much as the unions want them to. The 2003 Gallup/Phi Delta Kappa poll, for example, showed that the percentage of Americans thinking that teachers are underpaid hovered around 33 percent from the late 1960s until the middle 1980s and then jumped to 50 percent in 1990 and 59 percent in 2003—as compared, in that year, to just 33 percent who thought teacher salaries are "about right" and a miniscule 6 percent who thought they are "too high."[4] A 2010 survey by Howell, Peterson, and West showed that 59 percent of Americans think teachers should be paid more, while 37 percent think their pay should stay about the same, and just 4 percent think they should be paid less.[5] Among young college graduates—the pool of possible recruits for teaching positions—a 2000 Public Agenda survey showed that a whopping 78 percent believe that teachers are "seriously underpaid."[6]

Similar opinions apply for school spending as a whole. In the General Social Survey, the percentage of Americans believing that too little money is being spent on "improving the nation's education system" has been on an upward trajectory over the decades, increasing from 51.3 percent in 1973 to 70.8 percent in 2008.[7] As this would suggest, there is a clear connection in their minds between spending and the quality of education. In the 2003 Gallup/Phi Delta Kappa poll, 45 percent said that lack of funding has a "great deal" of effect on the failure of students to learn, and another 33 percent said it has a "fair amount" of effect.[8]

The union argument for more money resonates with the American people. Part of the reason, however, is that they are often grossly misinformed about how much teachers actually get paid and how much districts actually spend. In a fascinating recent survey, Howell and West explore how much the public knows on these counts and find that people *vastly underestimate* the true salary and spending levels in their own districts.[9] More than 90 percent of Americans underestimate how much their own districts spend. With the average district in the U.S. spending more than $10,000 a year (in 2007), "more than 40 percent of the sample claimed that annual spending was $1,000 per pupil or less."[10] This is an astounding misperception of how much money is being spent on the schools. A thousand dollars per pupil per year? No wonder they think more money needs to be spent. Their perceptions are more accurate for teacher salaries, but not by a lot. On average, they underestimate how much their local teachers are being paid by some 30 percent. Here too, it is little wonder they think teachers need to be paid more. Somehow, Americans have gotten the idea that districts are spending next to nothing and that teachers are being paid much less than they really are.[11]

How well are teachers actually compensated? The place to start is by recognizing that *teachers are compensated in several different ways*. Salary is one of them. But the others are quite valuable, add considerably to total teacher compensation, and are often easier and more desirable forms of payment from the school boards' standpoint. The unions are well aware of this, and they consciously make trade-offs. What they cannot get in salary, they can sometimes get in these other forms of compensation. In the end, *salary alone is not what matters*. What matters is the compensation package in its entirety.

Trade-Offs

Let's take a moment to understand the trade-offs that are involved here. The unions typically pursue two key goals that are in tension with one another: they want more compensation for their members, but they also want the districts to hire more teachers.[12] The latter is hugely to their advantage because it adds to their membership rolls, their finances, their legions of political activists, and their political power. And they have been very successful on this dimension—aided by the popularity of smaller class sizes. One of the most important historical trends in public education is that the number of teachers has risen relentlessly over the years relative to the number of students. In 1955 there were 26.9 students for every teacher, but that number has dropped steadily over the decades, and the latest hard count has it at 14.2 in 2007–08. Indeed, the number of teachers even went up during the 1970s and early 1980s, when the number of students *fell* by 15 percent.[13]

The hitch, of course, is that teachers are the single greatest expense of the public school system, and the hiring of more teachers per student inevitably means that there is less money to go around for paying each teacher. Although the unions complain about low teacher pay, they have essentially made a rational trade-off: more teachers, less compensation per teacher. *With a lower ratio of teachers to students, teachers could easily be paid considerably higher salaries.* Michael Podgursky calculates that, if the staffing ratio had remained constant from 1980 to 2007, teacher compensation could have grown by 78 percent during this period, yielding a 2007 average salary of $78,574. But because the staffing ratio rose dramatically during those years and the money had to be spread among more teachers, the average salary actually grew by only 7 percent, to $52,578. In important measure, then, the "problem" of teacher pay is a problem of the unions' own making.[14]

Trade-offs also need to be made because of budget constraints. Districts are chronically strapped for money, and the option of raising taxes (if they have that power) is hardly an attractive way out. The same is true at higher levels. States, which over the decades have supplied a growing percentage of local education funding, are strapped for money as well; they also have many competing functions that must be funded (and many interest groups wielding influence in these other domains), and they already devote a far greater portion of their total budgets—some 35 percent of their general funds, on average—to public education than to any other social function.[15]

The real costs of public education, moreover, are actually *much higher* than those that get reported. According to an eye-opening, detailed investigation recently carried out by Adam Schaeffer, the total per-pupil costs—which include expenditures for capital (like buildings), transportation, debt service, and more—are actually 44 percent higher than the official spending numbers reported by major school districts.[16] And Schaeffer's calculations don't even include the staggering costs of unfunded liabilities for teacher pensions and retiree health care benefits (to be discussed), which the districts (and states) should be paying but are not.

In view of how much is already being spent, plus how much is obligated (pensions, retiree health benefits) and must eventually be paid for, the idea that teacher salaries and benefits, which make up roughly half of all K–12 education spending, can somehow be substantially increased across-the-board for all public school teachers is sheer folly. As long as staffing ratios remain at anywhere near their current levels, it's not going to happen. The states and districts literally can't afford it.

Research shows that, even in the face of high staffing ratios and ever-present budget constraints, the unions seem to have been successful over the decades at raising teacher salaries. That is, teachers appear to make higher salaries in union-ized as compared to nonunionized districts, all else equal.[17] But the estimated impacts are not large, and thorny methodological issues make it difficult to even arrive at good estimates. The most sophisticated study thus far, by Caroline Hoxby, specifically addresses these confounding effects, and its estimate puts the impact of collective bargaining on teacher salaries at about 5 percent.[18] Even though the unions have been the most powerful force in public education for some thirty years, then, they have not been able to win major salary gains for their members. With high staffing ratios—*which the unions want*—the money just isn't there.

But other trade-offs can help out considerably. With money tight, school board members are in the best position to make concessions on matters that don't cost them much extra money—or any extra money at all—and don't press up against their budget constraint. This simple axiom points immediately to two important conclusions about collective bargaining. The first is that school boards are much more inclined to accede to union demands on work rules than on pay and benefits, because most work rules can be adopted with little or no financial cost. Work rules—requiring seniority-based transfers, for example, or free periods for prep time—are valuable to teachers and represent a form of com-pensation over and above salary. I deal with these aspects of the union contract in the next chapter. For now it is enough to observe that, when unions make trade-offs that allow districts to "pay" teachers in the form of work rules rather than salary, teachers are still being compensated. It just doesn't show up as salary.

The second conclusion is that, when it comes to teacher pay and benefits, school board members have incentives to favor benefits over pay. Or at least they did until recently. The rationale is that teacher pay not only is a far bigger budget item than benefits, but also shows up in its entirety as a *current* expense in the schools' operating budget. Much of the true expense of teacher *benefits,* on the other hand, can be put off until the future—making them strategically attractive.

This incentive advantage has been reduced in recent years as the costs of health care benefits have skyrocketed. As one labor expert recently put it, "Back in the day when health insurance cost absolute peanuts, it was very easy to give it away at the negotiating table, at very little cost to the employer and at no cost to the employee. Unfortunately, in today's environment, health insurance typically represents the second-largest expense to the employer, right behind payroll. Therefore, negotiating health insurance really requires a shift in negotiating strategy."[19] Recent accounting changes (to be discussed) may reduce this advantage further or even eliminate it in the years to come. But since collective bargaining became the norm in public education some thirty years ago, school boards have had plenty of opportunity to use benefits to sweeten the pot in ways that cushion the blow to their current operating budgets, and this has made increases in benefits—in the past, anyway—an attractive alternative to increases in teacher pay. This historical fact has shaped the current structure of teacher compensation, which unions are dedicated to protecting.

As part of this emphasis on benefits, many school boards (and other governments) have agreed to generous health care benefits for *retirees*, sometimes including their spouses and children—a major union demand, because so many teachers (and other public employees) retire in their fifties, well before they are eligible for Medicare. As concessions go, this is an attractive one for school board members to make, as most of the costs will be paid in future years after school board members have moved on. Today's politicians get the advantages—happy unions, happy teachers, labor peace—and tomorrow's politicians are stuck with the bill. And the bill for retiree health care is enormous, as we'll see.[20]

The same sort of maneuver applies to something as apparently straightforward as sick leave. Pressed by their unions, school boards are often quite generous in the number of days they give teachers for paid sick leave. Teachers are typically allowed to accumulate unused sick leave from year to year, usually up to some maximum amount. And when they retire they are often allowed to convert unused sick leave into lump-sum payments, which may amount to many thousands of dollars. When school boards make concessions by increasing the limits on accumulated leave or by favorably adjusting the conversion formulas, the additional costs are pushed off into in the future—to be paid by other politicians.[21]

The same logic applies to teacher pensions, to the extent that school districts have control over the costs and benefits of these programs. But for the most part, pensions are governed by state statute, with less local flexibility than for other benefits, and the politicians who make the concessions are often state legislators and governors rather than school board members. They are all doing the same thing, though, by responding to the incentives of their jobs, which prompt them to see many employee benefits as virtually free goods to be paid for later by someone else.[22]

The free lunch is probably over. In part, this is because the growth in health care costs has been so substantial in recent years that school districts—having already agreed to provide teachers with hugely beneficial heath care plans at bargain prices (often involving no co-pays at all)—are now demanding give-backs in the form of partial premium payments, co-pays, and deductibles. In addition, new accounting changes by the Government Accounting Standards Board (GASB), the independent nonprofit that sets accounting standards for state and local governments, are *for the first time* forcing school districts to calculate and publicize all of their future financial obligations and indicate how they intend to pay for them.

The impact of GASB 45, as the new accounting rule is called, is destined to be revolutionary. The financial obligations of state and local governments, including school districts, have long been obscured by political trickery, creative accounting, and flat-out secrecy. But as governments slowly come into compliance with GASB 45, the public is finding out just how devastating the financial picture really is. Early audits revealed, for example, that *for retiree health benefits alone* the Los Angeles Unified School District has incurred future obligations of $5 billion, equal to 80 percent of its annual operating budget, and that the Fresno Unified School District has incurred obligations of $1.1 billion, equal to almost twice its annual budget.[23] For New York City as a whole, audits have revealed the unfunded obligations to be a whopping $59 billion.[24]

States and other local governments all over the country find themselves in the same situation: they have promised future benefits, they have not funded them, and now they are in hock for billions of dollars that must ultimately be paid. A 2010 study by the Pew Center on the States estimates that the states alone have unfunded obligations for retiree health benefits (and other nonpension benefits) of more than $550 billion.[25] The Government Accounting Office, in a 2009 study, puts the figure at $405 billion.[26] And although these are shocking figures as they stand, neither fully reflects the aggravating effects of the Great Recession, and neither includes the much larger unfunded obligations of many thousands of local governments (including school districts)—which employ almost three times as many workers as the states, but are much harder to study and summarize.[27] A 2006 study by Edwards and Gokhale estimates that the total state and local unfunded obligations for retiree health benefits are $1.4 trillion, which seems in the right ball park—although again, this is based on financials prior to the nation's economic meltdown.[28]

When pensions are taken into account, the situation goes from bad to horrible. The 2010 Pew study estimates that, even without factoring in the full effects of the recession (their financial data are from 2008), state-run pension programs—which typically include teachers—are underfunded to the tune of $452 billion.[29] A 2010 study by Barro and Buck argues that the situation is still worse. It points out, quite correctly, that even under the new GASB rules state-run pension funds are allowed to make much rosier assumptions—for example, about their expected rate of return on investments—than privately run pension plans are legally allowed to make; and it shows that, when more appropriate assumptions are employed, these state pension funds turn out to have unfunded liabilities of $933 billion.[30]

The secret is out. And with such jaw-dropping information publicly available in the years to come, school districts (and other governments) will have to get serious about actually *funding* these obligations—and thus about eating into their operating budgets or augmenting them with painful new taxes to make the necessary payments. If they don't, their credit ratings will be destroyed, and they will be unable to borrow money. Many governments, including school districts, may have to declare bankruptcy.[31]

This new reality will surely put the squeeze on union financial gains. It will affect how much money districts have available for pay increases. It will affect how much money they have available for benefits. And because it limits the ability of politicians to bestow benefits on public employees without paying for them, it makes the provision of those benefits much less attractive. In the years to come, unions will have a far more difficult time winning new benefits and even holding onto the ones they've gained in the past. The chickens have come home to roost.

These troubles and constraints are mainly relevant for the future. Because of them, the *mix* of teacher compensation will change as time goes on. But the point to be appreciated is precisely that teacher compensation *is* a mix. It is partly a matter of the salaries that teachers make, but it also contains a range of *other* payments, rights, and privileges that are quite valuable in themselves and are traded off against salaries precisely because teachers *do* value them. What matters, in the end, is the totality of *all* these forms of compensation, not salary alone.

The following sections take a closer look at the basic components of teacher compensation. I begin with salary, which is itself more nuanced than generally thought, and then move on to the others.

Salary

According to one widely accepted estimate, the average teacher salary for the 2008–09 school year was $53,910.[32] Whether this figure is considered to be high or low, and thus whether it constitutes evidence that teachers are underpaid, depends in part on what it is compared to. But let's put that aside for the moment and begin by recognizing what the number itself represents: teachers are paid this "annual" salary for working much less than a full year. Indeed, their work year averages just thirty-eight weeks—because, unlike almost all other professionals, teachers have their summers off. Many people go into teaching precisely because they *want* to have free time during the summer. They like it, they value it.

In my 2003 survey of teachers (reported on in chapter 3), respondents were asked, "Which of the following situations would you prefer: a twelve-month job with twelve months of pay or a nine- or ten-month job with summers off?" and 77 percent of unionized teachers said they *preferred* the job with summers off and correspondingly *less pay*. This is no surprise. All teachers are well aware from the outset that the job comes with summers off and correspondingly less pay so we shouldn't be shocked to find that they actually prefer the package they have chosen. They are a self-selected group. The job comes with certain characteristics, and it attracts certain types of people: those who place high value on having summers off. This is a plus for them, a form of compensation over and above their salaries. The value they place on it, moreover, is greater than the value they attach to the extra money they could be earning for a twelve-month job.

Another form of compensation arises from the nature of their formally scheduled work day: it is shorter than that of other professionals, roughly 34.9 hours a week as contrasted to thirty-five to forty hours for comparable occupations.[33] This is not to say that teachers ultimately work less than other professionals do, for people in all these occupations may do some of their work at home, and it is unclear (and a matter of dispute) how many hours teachers and other professionals actually work.[34] But in general teachers tend to have more freedom and flexibility during the work day, which they can use for their families, leisure, or whatever they want. This too is a valuable aspect of the job, one that clearly has something to do with why so many women go into teaching. (They currently make up about three-fourths of the public school workforce.[35]) It allows them to juggle career and family in a far more manageable way than other workers can. This is a clear benefit of the job, an additional form of compensation.

And then there is the magnitude of the salary itself. The Department of Education does not collect systematic data on teacher pay, but the NEA and the AFT do, and they publish the information in annual surveys that give them regular opportunities to publicize and document their claims that teachers are underpaid.[36] Remarkably, the Department of Education relies heavily on the unions in compiling and publishing its own information on the nation's schools—for example, in the *Digest of Education Statistics*, a widely used source of objective information on America's public schools. This is unfortunate, as the unions clearly have a stake in making the numbers look as bad as possible. Among other things, they focus attention on *annual* teacher salaries, and they make comparisons to occupations—such as engineers, computer system analysts, full professors, and attorneys—that are not plausibly comparable to elementary or secondary school teachers and that one would expect to be more highly paid anyway.

In recent years, issues of teacher pay have given rise to a small but lively research literature, the findings from which have been conflicting and controversial. Among the researchers are Michael Podgursky, who is a professor of economics at the University of Missouri, and Sylvia A. Allegretto, Sean P. Corcoran, and Lawrence Mishel, who are associated with the Economic Policy Institute. (I should note that the Economic Policy Institute is heavily funded by the teachers unions, although this in itself does not discount the researchers' analysis and findings, which must be assessed on their merits.)[37]

Podgursky argues that, when teacher pay is adjusted for the number of weeks that teachers actually work, teachers are well paid relative to reasonably comparable occupations—about 33 percent better paid than police officers, for example, 21 percent better paid than registered nurses, and 21 percent better paid than computer programmers.[38] He also shows that, when teachers leave the profession for other employment options, the men who do so tend to earn slightly less than they did as teachers, and the women who leave tend to earn a lot less. This is another indication that teachers are not underpaid in their current jobs—for given the actual value of their skills and talent in the marketplace, they usually can't earn more elsewhere. It also provides another reason why teaching is especially rewarding to women.[39] In addition, Podgursky points to the one comparison group that ought to be the most obvious and telling, but that the unions never mention: private school teachers, whose salaries are set in a more competitive marketplace, and who make quite a bit less than teachers in the public sector. This is true even when factors like religion and student demographics are controlled.[40]

Allegretto, Corcoran, and Mishel carry out an extensively detailed analysis of teacher pay issues that responds to these claims, criticize the data and methods that Podgursky and others have used, and argue the need for alternative approaches, which lead them to very different conclusions.[41] Their bottom line is that teachers are paid a good bit less (also in terms of weekly pay) than comparable occupations—about 15 percent less, on average—and that this is true even when fringe benefits are taken into account, which takes the gap down to 12 percent.

The underlying debate here is over methodological issues: problems that plague the available data sets, whether and to what extent those data can be relied upon, what adjustments must be made to arrive at appropriate measures for weekly or hourly teacher pay, what occupations are truly comparable, how these occupations' weekly or hourly pay can be measured, and so on. That there is debate over these issues is entirely understandable, for there are no easy answers, and even the most objective and best intentioned researchers can disagree.[42] This being so, it is unavoidable that specific estimates of how teachers are paid relative to other occupations remain open to question. For now, as a result, I think it is best not to embrace any of these estimates with great confidence and instead to wait for researchers to continue refining and advancing their work.

Yet despite all this ambiguity, we do know something quite important about teacher salaries, and it speaks volumes. What we know is that the *annual* salaries of teachers are misleading. They are inappropriate measures of—and tend to understate—how well teachers are doing compared to other groups. In the media, among educators, and within most policy circles, the belief that teachers are underpaid is strong and well entrenched; yet it is almost singularly focused on the annual salaries of teachers, without any recognition that these salaries apply to just thirty-eight weeks of work and to shorter, more flexible work days, and without any attempt to factor in the other forms of "payment" that add considerably to the total compensation package. From a special interest standpoint, this is good for unions and good for teachers. But it is hardly the basis for good public policy.

Pension Benefits

The vast majority of American workers do not receive any sort of pension when they retire, aside from Social Security. And Social Security is not a very potent retirement program. Workers pay into the system throughout their working lives—the current rate for typical employees is 5.3 percent of their paychecks—and receive fairly small annuities once they retire.[43] In 2009 the average monthly annuity for a retired worker was $1,153.[44] More than 60 percent of American workers have some sort of "defined-contribution" retirement program as well—an individual retirement account or a Keogh plan, for instance—either through their employers or through their own initiative. But the median amount they have saved in this way is small, less than $30,000 per family.[45] As a result, most Americans face a very insecure retirement. Their future is fraught with risk.

Not so for teachers. Teachers are members of the pension elite. Some 96 percent of them have access to "defined-benefit" retirement programs, which provide them with pensions of specified amounts—much larger than Social Security—for the rest of their lives, usually with adjustments for inflation and often with provisions that extend payments to the spouse when the employee dies. In the private sector, only 21 percent of all workers have access to defined-benefit retirement programs (usually with much smaller annuities), and even among professionals, just 29 percent do.[46] Outside of government, these sorts of plans are rare—and getting rarer—because they are so expensive.

Teacher retirement programs, unlike salaries and other benefits, are largely set up and controlled at the state level, although certain details can often be negotiated locally through collective bargaining. The plans are typically designed around formulas—which are periodically changed, often in response to political pressure from the unions—that determine the size of teacher pensions as a function of three main factors: age, years of service, and final salary (or some enhanced version of it). In Ohio, for instance, a teacher qualifies for a full pension if she is sixty-five years old or if she has taught for thirty years. The latter requirement is what really counts, because many start teaching at twenty-five or before, and they have thirty years of service by their mid-fifties. If a qualifying teacher with thirty years of service has a final salary of $70,000, say, the state formula would yield a retirement annuity of $46,200. If such a teacher had thirty-five years of service, however, the retirement annuity would jump by a whopping 45.4 percent, to $61,950. And if she had thirty-nine years of service, it would increase another 13 percent to a full $70,000. Someone who started teaching at twenty-five, then, could retire at the age of sixty-four and receive *100 percent of her salary for the rest of her life,* with protections for inflation.[47] The vast majority of America's workers can only dream of such a thing.

In almost all these teacher retirement programs, including Ohio's, the formulas produce uneven jumps in benefits as a function of years served—in Ohio, the big jump comes at year thirty-five—and as a result, there are strong, built-in incentives for teachers to retire early (usually right after they qualify for the big jump). Teachers often retire in their middle to late fifties. In Ohio the average retirement age is fifty-eight. This in itself is a major form of compensation: teachers can retire at a relatively young age, look forward to many years of active retirement, and have a healthy annuity to support them. Forever.[48]

In addition—and this cannot be emphasized enough—*they do not have to shoulder any of the financial risk.* This too is a hugely valuable form of compensation. The elimination of risk is a key feature of defined-benefit programs and a key reason unions insist on them rather than accepting defined-contribution programs as alternatives. With defined-contribution plans—which most workers have, if they have any retirement plan at all beyond Social Security—the value of their retirement fund fluctuates with the stock market and the larger economy and can decline considerably during economic downturns. During the economic meltdown that began (roughly) in 2008, these retirement funds plummeted in value, threatening the security of millions of American workers. But that didn't happen to teachers. They have defined-benefit programs. With defined-benefit programs, the amount of the retirement annuity (usually with inflation safeguards) is "defined": it is *guaranteed.* It does *not* fluctuate with the stock market or the economy and can be counted upon as future income. All the financial risk is borne by state and local governments. If the money these governments place in pension funds is inadequate or if the investments they make are unwise or victims of downturns in the stock market, they are responsible for making good on the annuities anyway.

As we've seen, the money provided for these pension funds *is* inadequate. Politicians have awarded handsome pension benefits and then failed to ensure that the programs are fully paid for, creating a true financial crisis for governments and taxpayers. This is a disaster on many dimensions. But it also means, regarding the issue at hand, that the full costs of teacher pensions are not reflected in the contributions that teachers and their employers are making into the pension funds. They are paying less than they should for what they are receiving. This too is part of the compensation package. And it is an aspect of compensation that researchers mistakenly ignore. The economists who study teacher compensation—Podgursky and his colleaagues, Allegretto and her colleagues, and others—routinely measure the *value* of teacher pension benefits in terms of the contributions made to provide them. But these contributions are much lower than the actual cost, and do not reflect the benefits teachers are actually getting. Teachers are benefiting more from their pension benefits—and when the absence of risk is taken into account (which the economists also don't do), quite a bit more—than the usual calculations show.

With pensions, therefore, teachers benefit in three crucial ways. The retirement payments are substantial compared to what most Americans receive. The payments are guaranteed to them, forever, entirely without risk. And no one is paying the true costs.

Health Care Benefits

While states are the providers of pension programs, health care benefits are almost always a matter of local determination, and in unionized districts they are a key subject of collective bargaining. In the past, with costs low, teachers were easily able to win gold-plated benefit packages. But with costs increasing at such a fast clip over the past decade and with district budgets under serious pressure, the districts have been reluctant (and unable) to expand their health care offerings, and have pushed hard to get teachers to share the load—by making (partial) premium payments, for example, and by agreeing to co-pays and deductibles. The unions have been fighting a defensive action to keep what they have and avoid give-backs. Exactly the same reality, of course, has plagued the private sector, where large businesses have demanded more cost-sharing from their employees, and many small businesses have dropped health care benefits entirely.

Despite it all, teachers are still among the most advantaged American workers when it comes to health insurance. If we look at teachers generally, not just those from districts with collective bargaining, we find that 95 percent of them are provided with medical coverage, compared to 71 percent of all private workers and 85 percent of private sector professionals. Some 43 percent of teachers pay no monthly premium at all for these benefits, a bonus that is much less common among private sector workers (24 percent) and professionals (21 percent). The health services that teachers are receiving, moreover, are considerably more costly to provide—and thus are likely to be more extensive and valuable—than those in the private sector. For example, the average single-coverage monthly premium for teacher health care (which the district pays, in whole or in large part) is $458, which is 40 percent more expensive than the health care package for private sector workers ($328) and 29 percent more expensive than the health care package for private professionals ($355).[49]

These figures on teacher benefits, moreover, are for *all* teachers, and some 35 percent of them (mainly in southern and border states) do not have collective bargaining. It is reasonable to suspect that teachers in states and districts with collective bargaining do even better. Consider Pennsylvania—where formal bargaining is the norm and, thanks to a 2004 legislative report, there is good evidence on teacher benefits. In this state, 79 percent of all districts pay the entire cost of teacher health insurance. Although the data tell us what percentage of districts offer such benefits and not what percentage of teachers have them, it seems quite likely that a far higher percentage of Pennsylvania teachers get their entire premium paid by the district than is true for teachers generally (43 percent, as reported above). Other benefits show the same differential. A full 99 percent of Pennsylvania districts offer their employees a dental plan, for example—which means, obviously, that virtually every teacher receives this benefit, compared to a much lower 57 percent of all teachers who are provided with dental plans by their districts nationwide. Similarly, 82 percent of Pennsylvania districts provide vision care, but just 37 percent of all teachers receive this benefit nationwide.[50]

There is no comprehensive national data set on collective bargaining contracts, so there are no definitive figures to compare benefits across states and districts. The National Council on Teacher Quality, however, has gathered and coded the labor agreements from the nation's seventy-five largest districts. Of these, forty-nine have collective bargaining and twenty-six do not (because they are in states that prohibit it) but often have "agreements" nonetheless.[51] Even in nonbargaining states and districts, the teachers unions are often strong, especially in the larger districts—Houston, Dallas, Phoenix, and the like—and something that looks like collective bargaining takes place, but isn't called that.

In these seventy-five largest districts, health care benefits are universal, and virtually every single district—whether there is formal collective bargaining or not—offers teachers dental care and vision care. When it comes to how much teachers have to pay in premiums, however, there are clear differences: in 50 percent of the districts with collective bargaining, versus 32 percent of the districts without, teachers pay nothing for individual health care benefits, and in 82 percent of the collective bargaining districts, versus 64 percent of the districts without, teachers pay less than $50 a month.[52] Overall, then, data from the nation's largest districts suggest two conclusions. One, teachers in districts with collective bargaining do appear to have better benefits than teachers in districts without collective bargaining—and thus the national data on teachers as a group, which make no distinction between the two, tend to understate how well teachers are actually doing in collective bargaining districts. And two, even teachers in districts without collective bargaining—the large districts, anyway—tend to get better health benefits than other American workers and professionals.

In addition to these advantages, it is worth noting that the health care benefits specified in collective bargaining contracts sometimes carry "buy-back" provisions. As is rather common in two-career households, teachers whose spouses have jobs with attractive health care benefits may decide to participate in their spouses' plans rather than their own districts' plans, which saves the districts money. This being so, unions in many districts have negotiated "buy-back" provisions, in which the district pays teachers bonuses for *not using* the district health plan. In Rhode Island, for instance, a 2007 newspaper investigation found that thirty-three of the state's thirty-six school districts offered buy-backs. "Twenty-two districts offer buyouts of up to $3,500. But a handful of districts give teachers half the cost of a family plan—about $7,000."[53] Needless to say, this is a lot of money and gives these teachers a significant boost in their overall compensation. The percentage of districts offering buy-backs nationwide is unknown, but it is not an unusual practice. It does, after all, save the districts money, and they have incentives to do it. The important point, given our concerns here, is that it is an additional form of compensation that needs to be taken into account in assessing how well teachers are paid.

Finally, there is the huge issue of retiree health benefits. As discussed, school boards have followed in the footsteps of governors and state legislators in providing health benefits for retirees. The political incentives have been too tantalizing to resist: they can provide (or promise) benefits today, make their constituents happy, and push the costs off into the future for other politicians to pay. Public employees, meantime, are the big winners from these massively underfunded programs. They get great benefits. But they do not pay the true costs of those benefits and neither do the school districts. The free ride is coming to an end, as GASB 45 forces governments to begin revealing their financial obligations, but the ride has been extraordinarily beneficial.

Retiree health benefits are not common in the private sector, and they are getting less common all the time due to the skyrocketing expense. According to a recent study by the Kaiser Family Foundation, 65 percent of large businesses (those with more than 200 employees) provided retiree health care in 1988, but the percentage fell to 46 percent in 1991, to 40 percent in 1999, and to 35 percent in 2006. Governments have not been much affected. In recent decades, retiree health benefits have become a staple of the employee compensation package, and this remains true today. The same Kaiser study, for example, shows that retiree health benefits were offered by 82 percent of large state and local governments (those with more than 200 employees) in 2006.[54] A 2003 American Association of Retired Persons study shows that all fifty of the state governments were then offering health benefits to their retirees and that sixteen of the states were paying the entire premium.[55] Comparable statistics that focus specifically on school districts are harder to come by, but the numbers are clearly way beyond what is being offered in the private sector. A recent study of school districts throughout the state of New York, for instance, showed that 96 percent of them provided health benefits to retirees.[56]

These benefits are major components of the total package of teacher compensation. Along with defined-benefit pension programs, they allow teachers to retire in their fifties, receive a yearly "salary" comparable to what they received as an active employee, and know that their health care needs will be taken care of—for the rest of their lives. The value of these benefits is partly monetary, and obviously quite large when calculated over the teacher's entire post-employment lifetime. But it is also measured in *security*. Teachers *know* they will have a stable income and health benefits they can count on in future years. In this respect they are quite special: they do not have to endure the retirement risks that confront most other Americans.

Tenure

Pensions and health benefits provide valuable types of security for teachers after they retire. But the ultimate security is that, during the years when they are actively teaching, they essentially cannot be fired. They have "tenure" and—assuming they don't murder someone or molest a child or stop showing up for work—they are assured of being able to continue in their job for as long as they want. This is the case, moreover, regardless of how they perform in the classroom and regardless of how much their students learn. Here again, America's private sector workers can only dream of such a thing: a guaranteed, totally secure job.

State governments began to pass teacher tenure laws during the early to middle 1900s (New Jersey was the first, in 1909), when governments at all levels were reacting against the patronage system and its correlates—nepotism, corruption, favoritism, incompetence—and moving toward a civil service approach to public employment. The idea was to hire people on merit and then, through various procedural protections, make it difficult to remove them for reasons other than their objective performance in the job. Civil service ultimately swept the country, and it was and remains clearly superior to the patronage system it replaced. But in practice, the procedures that protect government workers from dismissal are written by legislators, are subject to powerful organized pressure from the workers themselves, and have evolved to the point where they make it virtually impossible to fire a public employee for poor performance.[57]

It is the same for tenure laws. On the books these laws come across as benign; indeed, they are often framed as granting teachers "due process" rights and don't even mention the word tenure at all, as though they are simply offering teachers protection against arbitrary dismissal. Often, the wording explicitly allows for the removal of teachers from their jobs in cases of poor performance. But even though it is technically possible for a teacher to get fired for poor performance, the reality is—for reasons the next chapter lays out in detail—that almost no one (literally) actually gets fired for incompetence or mediocrity in the classroom.

This has all sorts of bad consequences for schools, needless to say. But what I'm concerned about here is getting a handle on teacher compensation, and the point to be made is that teachers have much more than a job that comes with a salary, benefits, and a pension. They have a job that, once they get beyond the probationary period (which is usually three years) and are granted tenure, cannot in practice be taken away from them. They can count on having steady employment and a steady income—and this certainty, this avoidance of risk, is worth a great deal. All else equal, a job with tenure is clearly a lot more valuable than a job without tenure.

The debate over whether teachers are underpaid, as well as the economic research that goes along with it, consistently ignores the value of tenure in arriving at estimates of teacher compensation. This is a big mistake. Tenure is a highly valuable form of compensation, and ignoring it can only lead to an underestimate of the true magnitude of the total compensation package. How much is tenure worth, then? It is presumably worth different amounts to different people. But to get a sense, in my 2003 survey I presented teachers with a series of questions about tenure designed to probe the value they attach to it. I present the results here for unionized teachers from districts with collective bargaining.

The first survey item asked, "Would you support or oppose a policy proposal that would eliminate teacher tenure, but in return provide teachers a 20 percent increase in salary?" Faced with this trade-off—which puts an explicit monetary value (20 percent of salary) on tenure—33.1 percent agreed to go along with the deal. Those who did not agree were then sequentially offered trade-offs with greater and greater monetary values attached to tenure. When this was done, an additional 5 percent of teachers agreed to give up tenure for a 30 percent salary hike; an additional 6.6 percent agreed to do it for a 40 percent increase, and an additional 8.4 percent agreed to do it for a 50 percent increase. The upshot is that it took a salary increase of 50 percent to entice more than a majority (53 percent) of unionized teachers in collective bargaining districts to agree to give up tenure. Many were willing to do it for less, but 47 percent were not willing to give up tenure even for a 50 percent increase in pay.

This is just one survey, one way of getting at the value teachers attach to tenure. But what it suggests—recalling that the average teacher salary is well over $50,000 a year—is that most teachers see the security of tenure as being worth *tens of thousands of dollars a year*. This should come as no surprise. Job security *is* enormously valuable, and is something that employees in any industry would surely want if they could get it. For teachers, it comes as part of the compensation package—and adds considerably to the total value they receive as payment for their work.[58]

The Bottom Line

"Teachers are underpaid." Union leaders and their public relations experts have been hammering the point home, working it into stump speeches, and enshrining it as among the most serious problems of American education for several decades now. Most Americans—including those in influential positions—seem to have gotten the message, making it part of the conventional wisdom of modern American culture.

But the salary numbers the unions roll out are invariably based on *annual* salaries, and they conveniently ignore the *other* components of the compensation package. The fact is, teachers are compensated in many ways: through salaries, yes, but also through defined-benefit pension programs, health care insurance for active employees, health care insurance for retirees, tenure, summers off, flexible work schedules, health care buy-outs, and more. Taken together, these components add up to a compensation package that is clearly very valuable. While exact estimates of its monetary value are not currently possible, it is surely *much* higher than annual salary figures suggest. It is higher than most academic studies suggest as well, for the research on the subject ignores or understates important aspects of how teachers really get "paid." The value of tenure, for instance, which is clearly substantial, is never taken into account at all, nor is the underfunding of pensions and retiree health benefits, nor is the insulation from risk that defined-benefit pensions and retiree health benefits provide.

I am not saying that teachers are rich. The thrust of my argument is simply this: teachers are much better compensated than people tend to think. Most aspects of teacher compensation are overlooked, and they need to be recognized if citizens and policymakers are to have a good sense of how well teachers are actually "paid."

Whether teachers *should* be better compensated is another question. It does no good to stare at salary levels, or even estimates of total compensation, and complain that they are "too low"— because there are no criteria or standards of comparison to allow for such a conclusion. Too low compared to what? And if we put the focus on how teachers compare to other professionals, not much is really gained. These professions involve different skills and educational backgrounds from teaching and are typically occupations that few teachers could transfer into anyway. Moreover, it is well documented that, over the last few decades, the people going into teaching have increasingly been drawn from the lower strata of college graduates—as measured, for instance, by scores on the Scholastic Assessment Test—and thus, in terms of intelligence and academic achievement, they lag behind the people who go into many of these other fields (on average).[59] Why should a teacher get paid the same as a computer programmer? There is little rationale for claiming that she should.

The appropriate way to approach compensation is in terms of productivity. In economic analysis, an organization allocates its resources efficiently by paying its workers based on their productivity—that is, based on how much they contribute to the organization's goals (in the case of business firms, profit). The greater an employee's value added, the greater the pay. If the same reasoning were applied to schools—and it should be—then the proper level of teacher compensation, taking all of its components into account, would depend on how much individual teachers contribute to student learning and other educational goals. It is difficult to monetize these goals, of course, but the principle is clear: compensation needs to be hooked to productivity if schools are to use their resources efficiently in the best interests of children. Highly productive teachers should be better compensated than less productive teachers (many of whom should be dismissed). And overall spending on compensation needs to be assessed in terms of other ways the money could be spent (on buildings, computers, books, distance learning opportunities, and so on) and the relative contributions these options might make to productivity. More compensation for teachers may have positive outcomes for children—research on the subject is in fact mixed and suggests that the connection is weak[60]—but spending the money in *other* ways may be more productive still. The idea is not to single-mindedly pour money into salaries and benefits. It is to find the right balance, so that school resources are allocated across alternative uses to yield the most efficient outcomes for kids.

This kind of reasoning, however, is foreign to the way teacher compensation is actually handled. In the real world of public education, it is handled through power. The unions use their power in collective bargaining and legislatures to push for as much teacher compensation—in all its forms—as they can get. And they try to see to it that resources are not used in other ways. Productivity has nothing to do with it. For any type of organization, this is a formula for poor performance.

6

Collective Bargaining

Every few years, the teachers unions in most of the nation's school districts engage in collective bargaining on behalf of their members. To judge from news accounts, these events are mainly struggles over wages and benefits. Yet the real story is usually more complicated than that, and a good bit more consequential for schools and kids.

The unions *do* want higher salaries and benefits, of course. But they also want to protect jobs, expand the rights and prerogatives of teachers in the workplace, and restrict the discretion of management. To accomplish these aims, they demand specific *rules* that, in one way or another, cover virtually every aspect of what happens in the schools, their operation, and their governance. In a typical collective bargaining contract, in fact, there are so many rules about so many subjects, and the rules themselves can be so dense and complicated, that it often takes more than 100 pages to spell them all out. The contract for the Miami (Dade County) school system is 314 pages long. Cleveland's is 277 pages.[1]

It's too bad all Americans can't just sit down and read the collective bargaining contracts their school districts have to live by. Many people, I hazard to guess, would be stunned.[2] I know that, when my Stanford students—who are quite educated and mostly liberal—first take a look at some of these contracts, they can't believe what they are seeing. Here are some of the many rules that these documents tend to include:[3]

—Rules that allow teachers to make voluntary transfers to other schools, and to avoid being transferred away from their existing schools, based on seniority,

—Rules that allow senior teachers to take the jobs of junior teachers,

—Rules that require junior teachers to be laid off before senior teachers,

—Rules that require principals to give advance notice to teachers before visiting their classrooms to evaluate their performance,

—Rules that prohibit the use of standardized student tests for evaluating teacher performance,

—Rules that specify all the procedures that must be followed—in setting up an "improvement program," monitoring, reporting, mentoring, and so forth—if a teacher is evaluated as unsatisfactory,

—Rules that specify all the procedures to be followed in any effort to dismiss a teacher,

—Rules that give teachers guaranteed preparation times of a specified number of minutes a day,

—Rules that limit the number of faculty meetings and their duration,

—Rules that limit the number of parent conferences and other forums in which teachers meet with parents,

—Rules that limit how many minutes teachers can be required to be on campus before and after school,

—Rules that limit class size,

—Rules that limit the number of courses, periods, or students a teacher must teach,

—Rules that limit the nonteaching duties that teachers can be asked to perform, such as yard duty, hall duty, or lunch duty,

—Rules that allow teachers to take paid sabbaticals,

—Rules that give teachers liberal options for time off with pay (such as "personal" leave days),

—Rules that put important decisions—about school policy, assignments, transfers, noninstructional duties—in the hands of committees on which teachers participate and may have a majority,

—Rules that allow teachers to accumulate unused sick leave for years and eventually to convert it into cash windfalls,

—Rules that provide for complicated, time-consuming grievance procedures that teachers can invoke if they feel their job rights have somehow been violated.

—Rules that give teachers who are union officials time off to perform union duties (which means their classes must be taught by substitutes),

—Rules that give the union access to school mailboxes, bulletin boards, classrooms, and other facilities to use for its own purposes.

Exhausting, I know. But the fact is, collective bargaining contracts are essentially just books of rules, countless numbers of them. And getting these rules embedded in legally binding contracts is a big part of what unions are trying to do in these negotiations. They are quite successful at it. In no small measure, this is because most rules don't cost the districts anything, and, in a world where money is often scarce and wages and benefits cannot be increased to the unions' satisfaction, districts can rather easily make concessions on rules—and win agreement and peace.

However inexpensive these rules may be in purely financial terms, though, they are far-reaching in their importance for the schools. And for kids. The reason is simply this: the rules embedded in any collective bargaining contract are an integral part—usually a very big and consequential part—of how the schools in any school district are *organized*. They literally define, in large measure, the organization of schooling. They tell the district how it must operate, how it must spend its money, how it must allocate its resources—particularly its teachers, who are the most critical resource of all—and in general, what it can and cannot do in providing children with a quality education. So as collective bargaining has played out over several decades and over many thousands of school districts, it has heavily shaped the organization of the nation's entire public school system.

The problem is obvious. If America's schools are to provide the best possible education for the nation's children, they need to be organized for that precise purpose. This can't happen, however, unless the formal rules that define and fill out each school's organization are specifically designed on the basis of what works best for children and student achievement—and that is clearly *not* how the organization of the public schools is determined. It is determined, in large measure, through the exercise of union power in collective bargaining. The rules that emerge from this exercise of power are designed to protect and promote the job-related interests of teachers, not to create the most effective organization for children and learning. There is a *disconnect* between what the public schools are supposed to do and how they are organized to do it.

In this chapter, I take a closer look at some of the basic rules that make up collective bargaining contracts, and at the problems they create for the organization of schools. I should point out, before we begin, that collective bargaining is not the only avenue of union influence. Unions can also shape the schools through the political process—an approach that, when they succeed, is hugely advantageous to their cause because any new work rules enacted via state law (the feds are rarely involved in this realm) automatically apply to every district in their state.

So the unions are constantly operating at both levels to engineer the organization of schools. All states have laws about teacher tenure, for example, often accompanied by onerous, multistep procedures for dismissal. Many states also have laws that impose seniority rules when—due to economic downturns or declining enrollments, say—teachers must be laid off. Not surprisingly, when these and other issues are dealt with at the state level, they sometimes go unmentioned in collective bargaining contracts. But mentioned or not, they are just as binding on the districts.[4]

As we move ahead in this chapter to discuss work rules and collective bargaining, then, we need to keep in mind that it is the combination of local labor contracts and state laws that really counts. The contracts themselves are the main source of work rules, and they are often very heavily constraining, especially in the nation's larger districts. But the full set of work rules is often even more extensive—and more constraining—than the contracts alone let on.

The Bias of Collective Bargaining

It would be nice to think that collective bargaining simply allows districts and teachers to arrive at better decisions about how to make schooling more effective for children. But nice is one thing, and real is another. Any realistic assessment of collective bargaining has to recognize that, at least for most districts most of the time, it is destined to produce many key decisions that depart from—and are systematically biased against—what is best for kids and effective organization. This does not happen because the people are bad or ill-intentioned. It happens because of the structure of the situation and the incentives that are built into it.

The sources of bias are easy to see. They are discussed at some length in earlier chapters, so I just hit the highlights here as a bit of a reminder. For starters, the teachers unions are special interest advocates for their members. Their job in contract negotiations is to push hard for these special interests, and that is what they do.[5] Well-informed participants and observers of collective bargaining recognize as much. Here, for example, is an account from a basic practitioner-oriented text on the subject:[6]

> The bargaining agent representing teachers exists solely to articulate and try to achieve the goals determined to be in the self-interest of its members. The welfare of the school as an institution may, in fact, be advanced by teacher organizations seeking to achieve the interests of teachers. But that is a by-product. The bargaining agent represents teachers and their interests. The collective bargaining process is predicated upon the union or association being an advocate of a special interest group—the members of the bargaining unit.

Even if the districts were to push equally hard for outcomes that strictly reflect the best interests of children, the compromises of the negotiation process—which are required because the unions are genuinely powerful—would guarantee that final outcomes would be somewhere *in-between* what the districts demand and what the unions demand, and thus that they would *depart* from what is best for children.

This departure, moreover, is the best-case scenario. For the fact is, the district side of the table cannot be counted upon to push for what is best for children. As detailed in chapter 4, school board members—who have authority over the entire collective bargaining process—are elected, and the teachers unions are typically the most powerful force in local elections. As a result, many board members are union allies, others are reliably sympathetic to collective bargaining, and those who are unsympathetic have good reason to fear that, if they cross the unions, their jobs are at stake. This does not mean that school boards are happy to give the unions anything they want. Nor does it mean that they could even if they wanted to, because they operate under budget constraints that limit the concessions they can make. It means, rather, that school boards are likely to be weak representatives of children and overly inclined to give in (if budgets allow) to the special interest demands of the unions.

In the private sector, this kind of weakness is penalized. A weak management that allows its unions to impose heavy wage-and-benefit costs and inefficient work rules would find itself at a competitive disadvantage in the marketplace. Customers would take their business elsewhere, and the firm would ultimately be threatened with extinction. Knowing this from the outset, managers have clear incentives not to give in to the special interest demands of their unions— indeed, they have incentives not to be unionized at all—and to be vigilant in protecting the best interests of their firm.

In the public sector, these incentives are largely absent, giving rise to yet another bias in collective bargaining. School districts are essentially public monopolies, funded by taxes; and if the management caves in to union demands that increase costs and create inefficiencies, the districts don't lose students or money—for families have nowhere to go (unless they want to move or charter schools are available). Unlike in the private sector, managerial weakness is not penalized. Instead, the managers—elected school board members—retain their positions atop the hierarchy as long as they please the groups that hold political power. The system is geared to reward power, not performance, and this allows the unions to win concessions even if what they do is bad for schools.

Over the last decade or so, several developments have worked to reduce the prounion bias somewhat, at least in some districts. One development is that, in a relatively small number of urban districts—New York City, Chicago, Boston, Cleveland, Washington, D.C., and a few others—mayors have assumed a measure of control over local school districts, and their singular responsibility and larger constituencies give them greater incentives to stand up to the unions. A second is that, in some cities (but not most), charter schools have proliferated, and they offer a safety valve for families who want to escape from the local public schools, giving the districts greater reason to resist union demands. And third, the rise of the accountability movement has put districts under real pressure to raise student test scores, and has prompted leaders to take a more jaundiced view of contract restrictions that undermine effective organization.

These are promising developments, but they don't come close to compensating for the serious problems just discussed. Collective bargaining is fundamentally biased. It is biased because the unions are special interest advocates, and their demands—which drive the process—are not aligned with what is best for kids and schools. It is biased because school boards are weak representatives of children, weak bargainers, and politically influenced by the unions. And it is biased because the public sector lacks the discipline of the private marketplace, allowing school boards and unions to impose costs and inefficiencies on the schools without having to worry much about the consequences for performance. All of these biases work together and in the same direction, creating a context in which collective bargaining can be expected to function quite nicely for most of the adults involved—but not for the kids who are supposed to be getting educated.

The Single Salary Schedule and Weak Incentives

Now let's take a look at some of the common rules that find their way into collective bargaining contracts—and into the organization of American schools. I begin with a brief discussion of salaries. In part, I start here because salaries are salient to the negotiations in any district. I also do it to emphasize that, in one crucial respect, salaries are just like any other issue that gets formalized in the labor contract: they are dealt with by means of rules. With some exceptions, which I discuss later, this is the way the unions seek to deal with all issues that bear on how the schools will be governed and operated.[7] They want rules for every contingency. It is through rules that they tell administrators what they can and cannot do, limit their discretion, and constrain them to make official decisions that conform to what the union wants. For management, discretion is power. For the unions, rules are power.

When it comes to salary, the unions do not want administrators to have discretion. Above all, they don't want them to have discretion in paying good teachers more than mediocre ones and thus in making judgments about performance and productivity. Their arguments are familiar ones. To give managers this power, they say, would open the door to unfairness and favoritism. They also fear that it would stir envy and competition among their members, undermine group solidarity, and generate unwanted performance pressures in the workplace. As they frame the salary issue: all teachers do the same job (they teach), they are all competent (as documented by their formal teaching credentials), and they all deserve to get the "same" salaries based on simple criteria that anyone can meet.[8]

From the unions' standpoint, the "single salary schedule" is just what the doctor ordered, and virtually every collective bargaining contract has one. The typical salary schedule is a grid, with rows ("steps") representing a teacher's seniority within the district, and columns ("lanes") representing the teacher's educational degrees and extra educational credits (for example, from college courses or professional development classes). Any given teacher can easily and automatically be placed somewhere within the grid, in a box that specifies—by rule—exactly what the teacher's salary is.[9]

In the Prince George's County contract that took effect in 2007–08, for example, there are twenty steps to give teachers salary increments for seniority and seven lanes to give them salary increments for additional degrees and course taking. A teacher with a bachelor's degree in her tenth year of teaching would qualify—by rule—for a salary of $54,863. A teacher with ten years' seniority and a master's degree would receive a larger salary—by rule—of $60,143. Each of these teachers would automatically increase her salary by about 3 percent with an additional step in seniority.[10] Data from the Schools and Staffing Survey show that virtually all American school districts have salary schedules with similar sorts of rules.[11]

From the standpoint of what is best for children, these salary rules *make no sense at all*. Research has long shown that, beyond the first several years, a teacher's seniority makes no difference for student achievement. In particular, teachers are *not* more effective at promoting student achievement as they gain additional experience. Similarly, research has consistently shown that simply having a master's degree, or accumulating additional course or professional development credits, does not make teachers more effective in the classroom.[12] As a result, districts are saddled with compensation systems that are literally not designed to promote student achievement—and they are wasting millions of dollars that could be productively spent in other ways. The Seattle school system, for example, which is often regarded as progressive, spends some $48 million a year—a full 22 percent of its total payroll—just to reward teachers for their additional degrees and coursework.[13] Boston, another progressive district, spends $33 million a year on extra pay for these irrelevancies.[14] According to researchers Roza and Miller, the unnecessary salary bump that school districts dole out for master's degrees alone cumulates to some $8.6 billion a year across the nation as a whole.[15]

The single salary schedule is a formula for stagnation. It guarantees that good, mediocre, and bad teachers are all paid the same, and it ensures that this prime source of incentives—which plays such a key role throughout the private sector—is almost entirely absent in the public schools. The compensation system gives teachers no incentive whatever to become better teachers, but instead gives them strong, compelling incentives to spend their precious time and money pursuing credentials that, while unnecessary for better performance, are the keys to getting higher salaries. This is bad for the organization as a whole. But it is especially bad for teachers who are truly talented. A study by Hoxby and Leigh has shown that the system's failure to reward talent has been a major factor over the years in pushing talented women out of public education and into other professions where their talent is rewarded.[16]

Most generally, the single salary schedule weakens the prospects for effective management, making it impossible for administrators to reward productive behavior, to attract high-quality teachers—especially in shortage subjects like math and science—and to make sure that good teachers can be induced to teach (and stay) at disadvantaged schools, where they are clearly needed most (and are least likely to be found). District leaders *must* be able to do these things if they are to organize their districts for student achievement. The functions are absolutely basic, having to do with their control over the district's single most important resource: its teachers. Yet because of the restrictions built into labor contracts, they are purposely denied these essential tools of leadership. They are expected to lead with their hands tied behind their backs.

Over the last decade or so, as the pressures of accountability have steadily mounted, things have begun to change a bit. There is much talk of allowing extra pay for teachers in shortage subjects or in hard-to-staff schools. There is much talk as well of moving toward pay for performance. But talk far outpaces genuine reform. Many labor contracts now allow districts to give signing bonuses or salary increments to teachers in shortage subjects—but most don't, and in those that do the amounts tend to be rather small. In San Francisco, for example, shortage teachers are given an additional $1,000 a year as a salary increment. Much the same is true for hard-to-staff schools: most districts can't do it, and the amounts are fairly small when they can. In Anne Arundel, Maryland, for example, the hardship stipend is $1,500.[17] These amounts don't give the districts much flexibility in trying to get the right teachers in the right classrooms. Pay for performance, meantime, is even less common. There are a few well-known programs—Denver's in particular—but these are rare and tend to be based only loosely, if at all, on actual measures of student achievement. A major exception is Houston, which, not coincidentally, is located in a state that prohibits collective bargaining. (I discuss pay for performance in chapters 8 and 9.)[18]

The upshot is that, while there is change at the margins and perhaps much more to come, the single salary schedule still reigns supreme—formalizing the fiction that all teachers are the same, deflating incentives, distorting the allocation of resources, and imposing a compensation system that is entirely out of sync with the requirements of effective organization.

Generous Leave Benefits and Teacher Absences

Almost all collective bargaining contracts have long, elaborate sections dealing with various kinds of leave, which allow teachers to take time off from their jobs. These sections are long and elaborate for a reason: teachers get lots of leave time.

Some types of leave are unpaid—leave for military duty, for example—but many allow teachers to take time off from their classrooms with pay. These include sick leave, personal leave (which can typically be taken for any reason), bereavement leave (for attending funerals of relatives and perhaps acquaintances), professional development leave (for attending classes and workshops related to their jobs), sabbatical leave (which gives teachers, say, half of an entire school year off with pay), and more.

Winning big salary increases for teachers is difficult, because they are extremely expensive and districts just don't have the money. But leave time is far less expensive, and the unions have been quite successful at securing contract rules that give teachers generous leave benefits. As with other contract rules, this is an area in which districts can offer concessions—and win labor peace—at a modest financial price. The problem is that, like many other contract rules, it takes a toll on the organization of schooling. There *is* a price to be paid, and it's much bigger than it might seem on the surface.

The most basic types of leave are sick leave and personal leave. Of the fifty-one states (including the District of Columbia), thirty-two have laws specifying minimum amounts of sick leave for public school teachers—most often, ten days per school year. But unions are sometimes able to win more than ten days in the collective bargaining contract. And then there is personal leave, which the states rarely deal with, but the districts often do. Indeed, 92 percent of the nation's largest districts have contracts that grant teachers personal leave. This kind of leave is sometimes a substitute for sick leave—in effect, a way of allowing teachers to use sick leave when they are not sick. But it is sometimes an add-on that gives teachers more days of leave time as well as more freedom in when to take it.[19]

The nation's teachers often get well over ten days of leave per year in just these two types of leave alone. In Detroit, an abysmally low-performing district, teachers are granted a full twenty days of leave in these two categories. In Cleveland and Newark, two other districts famous for their rock-bottom achievement, teachers get eighteen days.[20]

The real problem is not just that unions have won generous leave policies for their members, but that teachers tend to *take* their numerous leave days—and are often missing from the classroom. When this happens, their students are dumped into the hands of substitutes, who, try as they may, cannot possibly provide a continuous learning experience for them. When teachers don't show up, students and learning suffer.

This is not some sort of fantasy complaint. Teacher absences have been studied by researchers, and here is what the evidence shows:[21]

—On average, public school teachers are absent 5 to 6 percent of all school days.

—Teacher absence rates are nearly three times those of managerial and professional employees in the economy at-large.

—These absence rates are higher the more generous the leave provisions written into their contracts.

—Teachers are absent most often on Mondays and Fridays.

—Tenured teachers have a higher rate of absenteeism than junior teachers.

—Teacher absenteeism has a negative impact on student achievement.

A detailed case study of the Seattle school system underlines these points. It finds, "Seattle's teachers are away from the classroom too often, approximately 9 percent of the school year . . . Teachers use, on average, almost all their ten days of sick leave, their two personal days per year, as well as three days for professional development purposes."[22] It also finds, "Teacher absences for personal reasons are twice as high on Fridays compared to other days of the week."[23] Because of this high rate of teacher absenteeism, the district is forced to rely heavily on substitutes, which means that "from the standpoint of students and the district, that's 56,000 instructional days largely lost over a single year."[24]

The leave policies written into collective bargaining contracts (and state laws), therefore, are not just benign fringe benefits for teachers. They are *rules* that tie the hands of district leaders, give teachers a license to be absent, and create an organization that is not suited to providing children with the best possible education. If leave policies were adopted with the best interests of children in mind, teachers would not have this embarrassment of riches. And they wouldn't be absent so often.[25]

Tenure, (Non)Evaluation, (Non)Dismissal, and the Protection of Mediocrity

The states leave most personnel issues to the locals to decide. Seniority transfers, within-school assignments, parent conferences, faculty meetings, labor-management policy committees, and all sorts of other employee issues are basically matters for local negotiation and are usually not specified in state law. Leave policy is one area where states have been active, putting floors under what teachers are offered. Job security is another.

Needless to say, job security is the unions' number one mission (aside from protecting collective bargaining itself). It is a sign of the premier status of this mission that the unions have not simply relied on collective bargaining contracts to bind the hands of district leaders. They have also pushed hard for extensive and detailed provisions in state law, and the states have largely complied. As a result, on matters related to protecting teacher jobs, the unions have been able to construct—partly through collective bargaining, partly through state law—a dense, multilevel network of formal rules.

The most basic rules are state laws allowing for teacher tenure. These laws, as noted in chapter 5, often do not even use the word "tenure." They are couched in such terms as "continuing contracts" and "due process" and "permanent status," and they set out procedures that must be followed if a teacher on a continuing contract is to be dismissed. These procedures tend to be complicated, involve multiple steps and appeals—to arbitrators, for example, or the courts—and entail a great deal of time and expense for any district leader who tries to dismiss someone. None of which is an accident. Moreover, because attempts to dismiss a teacher are based on evaluations of the teacher's performance, the states have also passed laws that deal in depth with the local evaluation process—often specifying what forms and criteria are to be used, who is to do the evaluating, how often, what other participants must be involved, whether a remediation program must be set up pursuant to an unsatisfactory rating, what the remediation program must consist of, what steps must be followed if the unsatisfactory performance continues, and so on.

With the unions so successful at getting the states to act on these security issues, collective bargaining contracts are sometimes silent on these things, or nearly so. But many local contracts do deal with them head-on, adding long sections on procedures for teacher evaluation and steps for dismissal that incorporate sundry details not dealt with by the state as well as all sorts of other restrictions: having to do, for instance, with what can be grieved and how grievances can be pursued, how parent complaints are handled, what goes into a teacher's personnel file, what specific roles the union will play in every type of personnel matter, and much more. When it comes to the security of teacher jobs—more than any other area of union concern—it is the combination of state law and local collective bargaining that determines the nexus of binding rules.

But are there enough bad teachers in the classroom, so that rules of this sort actually create problems for schools and kids? The answer is yes. Indeed, teachers themselves are quick to say as much. In one Public Agenda survey, 58 percent of teachers said that, in their districts, tenure does not necessarily mean that a teacher has worked hard and proved herself to be good (only 28 percent said the opposite), and a full 79 percent indicated that at least a few teachers in their own schools fail to do a good job and are just going through the motions.[26] In another Public Agenda survey, superintendents and principals were asked to rate various ideas for improving the nation's schools, and both gave their *top* rating to reforms "making it much easier to remove bad teachers—even those who have tenure."[27]

There is plenty of other evidence, as well, that the "bad teacher" problem is a serious one. In 2004, for instance, Pennsylvania gave many of its veteran teachers basic tests of competence in the subject matters they were teaching. Half of the middle-school teachers in Philadelphia—and a stunning two-thirds of the middle-school math teachers—failed their competency test. How are the kids in Philadelphia supposed to learn math if their own teachers don't know math?[28] More generally, even if we assume that only 5 percent of the nation's public school teachers are not sufficiently competent to be in the classroom—which is probably a very conservative estimate in light of the Philadelphia data—this means that more than 2.5 million American kids are stuck in classrooms with teachers who are incapable of teaching them. Clearly, this *is* a problem, and that's why superintendents and principals are so concerned about their lack of tools for addressing it.

Yet any administrators who attempt to dismiss a teacher are embarking on a process that is destined to be extremely costly and time-consuming. And even if they make the investment, they may well lose: for a minor departure from the labyrinth of procedural requirements can result in a legal judgment in the teacher's favor, regardless of the teacher's competence. The unions ensure that. Having laid the groundwork with a thicket of procedures, they provide teachers with expert legal defense by an army of labor lawyers who know the system inside and out and who aggressively represent anyone whose performance has been questioned, even the most obviously incompetent. One expert in labor law sizes it up this way: "When you try to fire a bad teacher, it's all about procedure. Rarely will the union lawyer argue that a particular teacher facing dismissal was good at his or her job. They will argue that not all the procedures were followed correctly."[29] And they will often win, leaving bad teachers in the classroom. As one union lawyer wryly observes, "If I'm representing them, it's impossible to get them out. It's impossible. Unless they commit a lewd act. Not that I want them on the job, as a private citizen, but as an advocate . . . I will give it my absolute best defense, and I will save the job."[30]

The lesson is not lost on school principals. They know that, if they give a teacher an unsatisfactory rating, they are setting themselves up for a formal grievance by the teacher and the union and entering a path of endless hassles. Even if they survive the grievance, the rules will probably require a remediation program—and thus monitoring, reports, additional evaluations, the involvement of other participants, and so on, leading to still more hassles. And these are just the beginning of a long, costly, conflictual process. Leading where? To the teacher very likely being let off the hook.

Here is one principal's candid view of the situation, expressed during a Public Agenda survey: "We don't get rid of those people [who] shouldn't be in our profession anymore, because we're afraid that we might get a grievance or a teachers union might gang up on us." In describing his own attempt to fire a bad teacher, he said, "The teacher tried to turn the tables and claimed that I was creating a hostile work environment. Both the local union and the state union jumped on board. So now the issue changed from addressing a teacher who should have been out of the classroom years ago to how I dealt with that teacher through that process, making sure I dotted every 'i,' making sure I crossed every 't.' Any mistake I made, that's where the focus of the conversation shifted to."[31]

Writ large, the logic of the situation is inescapable: for administrators throughout the public school system, as it is currently organized, there is no point in even *trying* to get bad teachers out of the classroom. As the New Teacher Project observes, based on its own research, "School administrators appear to be deterred from pursuing remediation and dismissal because they view the dismissal process as overly time consuming and cumbersome, and the outcome for those who do invest the time in the process is uncertain."[32] The rational solution for school principals, given the enormous costs and hassles involved, is clearly *not to go down that path at all.* One consequence, of course, is that bad teachers are almost never dismissed. Another is that, in order to avoid getting on the path from the outset, principals have strong incentives to make a mockery of the teacher evaluation process by giving virtually all teachers—including the incompetent and mediocre ones—satisfactory evaluations. This simply guarantees that virtually all junior teachers ultimately get tenure and that, once tenured, almost no one ever gets fired. Everyone is doing a "good job." Even in schools that are demonstrably horrible.

Data on teacher evaluations and dismissals have traditionally been very hard to come by, and until recently the whole subject had been shrouded by a conspiracy of silence among educators and policymakers. But a few years ago an Illinois news reporter, Scott Reeder, broke new ground by launching a massive research project in which he reviewed every dismissal case of an Illinois tenured teacher over an eighteen-year period, filed 1,500 Freedom of Information Act requests with various government agencies, conducted hundreds of interviews, and collected data from every one of Illinois' 876 school districts. This research now stands as the single most in-depth study of teacher dismissals yet conducted. Here are its major findings:[33]

—The average cost of a dismissal case during this time period was at least $219,000, a forbidding figure that nonetheless understates the actual cost, because 44 percent of the cases were still pending at the time.

—Over the eighteen years, fully 93 percent of Illinois school districts never even attempted to fire a teacher with tenure. Of the sixty-one districts that tried, only thirty-eight were successful.

—In their formal teacher evaluations over the last decade, 83 percent of Illinois school districts never gave a tenured teacher an unsatisfactory rating.

—More specifically, Illinois principals spent well over 1 million hours during the last decade carrying out some 477,000 evaluations, just 513 of which resulted in unsatisfactory ratings. This means that 99.9 percent of all tenured teachers in the state received satisfactory evaluations, and an infinitesimally small one-tenth of 1 percent received unsatisfactory evaluations.

—Out of roughly 95,000 tenured teachers throughout the state, an average of only seven a year were dismissed over the entire eighteen-year period, and of the seven only two were dismissed for poor performance. (The rest were due to misconduct.)

In 2009 the New Teacher Project came out with its own study, "The Widget Effect," which got far greater attention in the national media and hit like a bombshell. The title, which has now become ingrained in the lexicon of American reformers, "describes the tendency of school districts to assume classroom effectiveness is the same from teacher to teacher. This decades-old fallacy fosters an environment in which teachers cease to be understood as individual professionals, but rather as interchangeable parts."[34] What their research reveals is entirely in line with Reeder's findings:[35]

In districts that use binary evaluation ratings (generally "satisfactory" or "unsatisfactory"), more than 99 percent of teachers receive the satisfactory rating. Districts that use a broader range of rating options do little better . . . 94 percent of teachers receive one of the top two ratings and less than 1 percent are rated unsatisfactory . . . At least half of the districts studied have not dismissed a single nonprobationary teacher for poor performance in the past five years.

Other recent studies provide additional evidence and tell the same story. An inquiry into personnel decisions in the New York City schools, for example, shows that just eight teachers out of a total teaching force of 55,000 were dismissed for poor performance in 2006–07: a dismissal rate of about one one-hundredth of 1 percent. Each case, on average, required twenty-five days of hearings and 150 hours of principal time and cost $225,000—hardly an incentive for administrators to take action.[36] A 2009 study of Seattle finds that only sixteen teachers out of 3,300 received unsatisfactory evaluations, less than 1 percent. A 2009 study of Hartford finds the same thing, with less than 1 percent of all teachers rated as unsatisfactory.[37] A 2009 *Los Angeles Times* study finds that 99 percent of city teachers received satisfactory evaluations in 2003–04 and that the district fires fewer than one in 1,000 teachers (one-tenth of 1 percent) in any given year for *any* reason, not just performance.[38]

This book began with a brief tour of New York City's Rubber Rooms, where district leaders chose to warehouse bad teachers—with full pay and benefits—because they were unable to dismiss them. It should now be clear that the problem plaguing New York City is hardly unique to that one district. The problem is quite general and plagues the public schools all across the United States: excessive restrictions written into state laws and local collective bargaining contracts make it virtually impossible to get rid of even the most obviously incompetent teachers. Forget those who are merely mediocre. Or who are malicious or sexual predators or profoundly dishonest or otherwise unsuited to the classroom. However bad the teachers, their jobs are secure. Indeed, however bad the teachers, they are assured of getting satisfactory ratings—in a massive nationwide charade that has nothing to do with true teacher competence and that wastes millions upon millions of administrator hours in meaningless evaluations.

By any stretch of the imagination, is this the kind of personnel system that well-intentioned people would design to provide kids with the best education possible? I don't think so.

Seniority Rules and the Misallocation of Teachers

Teachers are the most potent resource in public education, the key to student learning. So it is a no-brainer that, if the public schools are to be organized effectively, teachers must be allocated to their most productive uses. For any given classroom in any given school, not just any teacher will do. The right teachers must be placed in the right jobs—throughout the system—and these judgments have to be made (and remade and adjusted over time) based on each teacher's performance and contributions in those settings. By any telling, this task is absolutely central to what district leaders *must* do if they are to create schools that provide children with the best education possible. Yet in most districts, this is precisely what they *cannot* do—because their collective bargaining contracts, backed by state laws, force them to allocate teachers in ways that they *know* are ineffective.

The main culprits are seniority rules, which the unions justify as fair and objective and as necessary insurance against arbitrary treatment on the part of management. As a Seattle union leader observes in explaining seniority rules for layoffs, "We don't want to go back to the '50s or '60s, when people were laid off because of the color of their skin or because a woman was pregnant." Says a Minneapolis union president, preferring more general language, "Seniority gives us a way of saying how do we lay people off in a way that's equitable."[39] Yet the fact is, all states have laws against the arbitrary and discriminatory treatment of all workers, public and private, and firing someone because they are a minority or because they are pregnant is illegal. So these fears can hardly justify having special seniority-based layoff rules for teachers. And what is "fair" or "equitable" about firing someone who is a great worker and protecting someone who is abysmally bad, based purely on their seniority? Nothing.

Union leaders may or may not believe their own arguments. What counts is that they have traditionally pushed hard for seniority rules, and these rules have major organizational consequences: severely limiting the discretion of district leaders, imposing job criteria that *any* teacher can readily meet if she just continues to show up, and putting control over the allocation of jobs into the hands of teachers themselves (and their unions). The big picture is that seniority rules *shift power* from district leaders to teachers and unions—and ensure that teachers and unions, not district leaders, will ultimately decide how most teachers get allocated across schools and classrooms.[40]

Many school jobs, for instance, are filled through a process of "voluntary transfers." When jobs open up in particular schools, teachers already employed by the district may apply for the vacant positions. In some districts, the contract simply says that the most senior teacher gets the job or that, if all teachers who apply are "equally qualified"—which they typically have to be (on paper), because all teachers get satisfactory evaluations—then the most senior teacher gets the job. In other districts, seniority is listed as just one of several criteria, along with (say) satisfactory evaluations, experience teaching the subject, and appropriate credentials—giving the appearance that seniority doesn't determine the job placement. But the problem, again, is that all teachers get satisfactory ratings, all tenured teachers are credentialed, experience is just another label for seniority, and so on, making it difficult for administrators to (legally) justify, based on objective criteria, the choice of a less senior teacher; and were they to go that route, they would be begging for the most senior teacher to file a grievance that could enmesh them in costly, time-consuming proceedings. The upshot is that, even when contracts seem to allow choices on other grounds, the most senior teacher tends to get the job—and it is the *teacher* who essentially makes the job choice, not district leaders. The interests of effective organization take a back seat. As Hess and West observe, "In practice, there is an overwhelming tendency to give senior teachers the plum assignments, with little regard for their skills, the needs of their students, or the implications for recruiting and retaining new teachers."[41]

Important job decisions also get made when teachers are "excessed"—as occurs, for example, when a school has falling enrollments and some of its excess teachers must be moved to other schools that have vacancies (which usually exist, because there is a good deal of turnover in the typical district, year to year). In many districts, seniority determines how the process works: teachers are removed from their jobs, one by one, in order of reverse seniority—even if the teachers being removed are the best in their schools and enormously valued by their principals. The same sort of logic tends to govern on the other end: these excessed teachers must be placed in new schools, and seniority often governs those placements—whether or not the teachers are good fits for the vacancies they are filling and whether or not the principals want them. Indeed, forcing excessed teachers on schools is an essential part of the process, because most teachers have legal rights to a job in the district. They need to land somewhere.[42]

Young teachers, even if fantastic in the classroom, lose out in the voluntary transfer process, and they lose out as well when their schools are subject to excessing. But it gets worse. It is sometimes the case—thanks to seniority rules written into the collective bargaining contract—that senior teachers are able to "bump" young teachers out of their jobs and take the positions for themselves. This can happen as part of the excessing process, when a more senior teacher finds herself excessed, wants to move to a particular school, and simply "bumps" a junior teacher from one of the jobs there—leaving the junior teacher looking for a new job somewhere else. But it can also happen because, in some districts, jobs held by young teachers are routinely "reposted" every year—and senior teachers can simply take them if they so desire, setting the junior teachers adrift. None of this, of course, has anything to do with the quality of anyone's teaching or with who is the best fit for the school in question. The junior teachers may be among the most talented in their districts and just the right match for their schools, and the senior teachers may be little more than deadwood. It doesn't matter.[43]

These common job practices—seniority, voluntary transfers, excessing, and bumping—are the targets of a recent study by the New Teacher Project, which conducted an intensive analysis of five urban school districts. Its findings are worth quoting at length:

> Urban schools are forced to hire large numbers of teachers they do not want and who may not be a good fit for the job and their school. The most detrimental impact of the transfer and excess rules is the widespread forcing of incumbent teachers on schools regardless of students' needs. Voluntary transfer rules often give senior teachers the right to . . . fill jobs in other schools even if those schools do not consider them a good fit. In addition, schools generally are required to hire excessed teachers without any selection process at all. As a result, across the five districts, in one hiring season: 40 percent of school-level vacancies, on average, were filled by voluntary transfers or excessed teachers over whom schools had either no choice at all or limited choice . . . 64 percent of [principals] who hired such teachers in 2004–05 said that they did not wish to have one or more of them in their school.[44]

All of these restrictions put principals in a tough spot. Principals are responsible for the performance of their schools, yet they cannot dismiss bad teachers, they cannot hire the teachers they want, and they have unwanted teachers thrust upon them. What can they do? A standard strategy is to threaten low-performing teachers with an unsatisfactory evaluation, and tell them that they will be given a satisfactory evaluation if they agree to transfer voluntarily to another school. This is entirely rational for each principal. And precisely because it is, bad teachers are routinely given satisfactory evaluations and passed around from school to school, in what has come to be called the "dance of the lemons." While some principals may be especially talented at this, as a group they are not better off. All the bad teachers remain in the district. And for each school, what goes out the front door often winds up coming in the back door. The "dance of the lemons" is a vivid illustration of just how perverse the organization of public education really is. It would be funny if it weren't so profoundly consequential and damaging.

There is more. Seniority also has a big role to play in teacher layoffs. This has always been true, but in the past layoffs weren't widespread enough to attract serious attention. Now they are. With the economic meltdown that began in 2008, government revenues have taken a nosedive and many districts across the country have had to lay off teachers. Although teacher jobs are protected by tenure and all its complex procedures, and although districts cannot (in practice) terminate teachers simply for being incompetent, they *can* lay them off when there are "reductions in force" due to declining enrollments and revenues.[45]

These actions are being taken out of necessity, and no one takes joy in it. Nonetheless, there are clearly better and worse ways of handling layoffs. Organizations that aim to enhance their own effectiveness would surely seek to lay off the least productive of their workers and retain the most productive. To put it in more strategic terms: they would view the necessity of layoffs as an *opportunity* to rid their organization of unproductive employees and thus to upgrade the average quality of their staff. But that is not how it works in the public schools at all. In collective bargaining contracts and state laws, the unions have pushed hard to see that teacher layoffs are based on seniority—and that teacher performance has nothing to do with it.[46]

These seniority rules have two basic consequences, both of them devastating. The first is that many excellent young teachers are the first to get laid off, while older teachers remain on the payroll even if they are downright awful in the classroom. It all happens automatically, without any effort to put a premium on performance or to upgrade the average quality of the district. The second is that, because the less senior teachers get paid a good bit less than the more senior teachers do, on average, *more teachers need to be laid off* in order to meet any given budget constraint. Marguerite Roza has calculated, for example, that if school budgets had to be cut 10 percent nationwide, "seniority neutral" rules would lead to layoffs of 612,000 teachers, but adherence to seniority rules—rules that apply in the vast majority of districts—would require the layoffs of 262,000 additional teachers: a huge difference that is clearly detrimental to children.[47]

To compound the problems, labor contracts typically give the laid-off teachers "recall" rights—based, of course, on seniority. This means that, when districts have job vacancies in the future, these teachers have legal rights to those jobs— even if other applicants are extremely talented and far better qualified—and the jobs go first to the laid-off teachers with the most seniority. Are they good in the classroom? Are they good fits with their schools and colleagues? It doesn't matter.

I should add, finally, that the problems unleashed by seniority are likely to have important impacts on equity, not "just" on school effectiveness and student achievement. Research shows that, when transferring within districts, teachers tend to avoid schools whose students are disproportionately minorities, economically disadvantaged, and low academic achievers, and they tend to seek out schools with more advantaged student bodies.[48] Research also shows that teachers who are new or have just a year or two of experience are not as good at their jobs (on average) as their more experienced colleagues—and disadvantaged schools have disproportionate numbers of these newer, less able teachers.[49] It is easy to see that seniority rules stand to make this serious problem even *worse*: because it gives senior teachers the right to transfer out of disadvantaged schools (or to avoid going there in the first place), leaving the "difficult" jobs to those with little experience.

In a recent study, I investigate this issue directly, using quantitative data from a large sample of California districts and schools, and find that this expectation is borne out: the stronger the seniority rights in a district, the more its disadvantaged schools will tend to be burdened with disproportionate numbers of highly inexperienced teachers. This can't be good for the kids in those schools—and they are precisely the kids who need the very best teachers a district can provide. But then, seniority was never intended to help needy kids. It was designed by adults, for adults. Any effects on kids are unintended.[50]

For the teachers unions, seniority is the Holy Grail of labor contracts. It is simple. It is objective. It is a criterion anyone can meet. And it ensures that management has no discretion—and cannot, in particular, use assessments of performance to make key decisions about jobs. But from the standpoint of effective organization, seniority rules make no sense at all. Leaders are literally prevented from allocating their single most important resource—teachers—to its most productive uses. They cannot do what they need to do to provide kids with the best education possible. And children are the ultimate losers.

Data on Large Districts across the Nation

The provisions just discussed only begin to describe what a full-blown labor contract looks like. There are many other rules as well, from grievance procedures to parent conferences to nonteaching assignments to the number of minutes that teachers are required to be on campus. The contract rules are never-ending. But each one makes its own bureaucratic contribution—and this is how the nation's schools get organized to do their work.

Until recently, it was very difficult to get a detailed national perspective on what the contract rules actually are and how they vary across districts. School districts and unions conducted their negotiations in secret (and still do), their contracts were essentially treated as in-house documents not for public consumption (unless someone had the temerity to demand access), and state and national governments did nothing to systematically collect the contracts and make the information public.

Today, many districts seem to be more open about their labor issues, perhaps due to accountability and budget pressures; and it is not uncommon for them to post their contracts on the Internet for all to see. And while governments are still unwilling to collect the contracts and make them available—because the unions don't want them to[51]—there is now a national data set that brings together the contracts of the largest districts in the country. Collected and compiled by the National Council on Teacher Quality (NCTQ), it provides citizens and researchers alike with a handy, centralized source of information.

We can use this NCTQ data set to shed light on three basic questions that bear on the bigger picture of collective bargaining nationwide.[52] First, how common are particular types of rules in the collective bargaining contracts of the nation's largest districts? Second, how often do the states enact their own laws on these issues, and thus give unions an alternative—and much more efficient— way of putting their favored work rules on the books? And third, how restrictive are these labor contracts compared to the "contracts"—the meet-and-confer agreements, or simply the district policies (whichever prevail)—in school districts that don't have collective bargaining?

To keep things simple, I focus here on fifteen types of contract provisions that cover a range of job-related issues. Some are issues that I have just discussed. Some are issues that I haven't had space to cover, but are worth recognizing as fairly typical of the work rules that districts and unions negotiate about and organize the schools around.

The findings are summarized in table 6-1. For most of these issues, a district's labor contract can either say nothing about it—be "silent"—or adopt a rule. We need to recognize, however, that when a state enacts its own rule (a law) on an issue, the districts in that state may sometimes choose not to mention that rule in their contracts. Their silence does not mean that there is no restriction affecting the organization of schools. There *is* a restriction. It's just contained in state law and not in the local labor contracts. In table 6-1, then, I provide two sets of results. The "local" columns indicate how often various types of rules are explicitly dealt with in the local contracts. The "combined" columns adjust the local figures to take into account state laws.

Now let's take a look at the findings, beginning with the various seniority rules. On the issue of voluntary transfers, which allow senior teachers to move into more desirable jobs within a district, the states almost never get involved. They are much more likely to take action when teachers' *job security* is on the line: nine states legislate on excessing, fifteen on layoffs, and seventeen on giving laid-off teachers priority in rehiring. Except in rare cases, they do so by requiring districts to follow seniority when teacher jobs are at stake. Even so, the vast majority of states do not do this. These most primal of job issues are decided mainly at the local level, through collective bargaining.

Table 6-1. *Contract Rules in Large Districts*
Percent of districts unless otherwise noted

Restriction	Local rules only		Combined local and state rules		Number of states with laws
	No collective bargaining	Collective bargaining	No collective bargaining	Collective bargaining	
Seniority, voluntary transfers					2
Silent	42	25	38	23	
No	42	17	46	19	
Yes	15	58	15	58	
Seniority, excessing					9
Silent	50	16	23	14	
No	4	5	4	5	
Yes	46	80	73	81	
Seniority, layoffs					15
Silent	8	13	8	9	
No	12	3	12	3	
Yes	81	84	81	88	
Seniority, rehire					17
Silent	50	17	50	9	
Yes	50	83	50	91	
Evaluation: prior notice					13
Silent	19	53	12	52	
No	54	11	62	11	
Yes	27	36	27	38	
Evaluation: remediation					24
Silent	12	19	8	8	
No	35	13	0	13	
Yes	54	69	92	80	
Prep time (minutes per week)					6
Silent	62	20	27	17	
150–225	23	16	58	19	
226–250	15	52	15	52	
251+	0	13	0	13	

Restriction	Local rules only		Combined local and state rules		Number of states with laws
	No collective bargaining	Collective bargaining	No collective bargaining	Collective bargaining	
Prep time, compensation					2
Silent	92	31	92	31	
None	0	2	0	2	
Time	0	11	0	11	
Money	8	41	8	41	
Time or money	0	16	0	16	
Faculty meeting cap					0
Silent	88	34	88	34	
No	8	5	8	5	
Yes	4	61	4	61	
Leave for union activities					0
Silent	92	38	92	38	
Yes	8	63	8	63	
Class size, grades 9–12					19
Silent	81	52	58	27	
No	8	2	23	2	
Yes	12	47	19	72	
Sick plus personal leave					32
10 days	38	36	38	36	
10.5–14.5 days	54	39	54	39	
15 days or more	8	25	8	25	
Salary, number of lanes					51
1–3	48	6	48	6	
4–5	28	48	28	48	
6–7	20	30	20	30	
8 or more	4	16	4	16	
Number of districts	26	64	26	64	

Source: National Council on Teacher Quality.

a. Note that sick leave and salary lanes are issues that districts universally deal with in some way; and when the states get involved, their laws tend to prescribe minimums that all districts meet and usually exceed.

How common are seniority rules? The "combined" figures show that they are nearly universal in collective bargaining districts when job security is at issue: 81 percent of these large districts have seniority rules for excessing, 88 percent have them for layoffs, and 91 percent have them for rehiring. They are not as dominant on the less primal issue of voluntary transfers, although even here they are quite common, with 58 percent of the districts giving preference based on seniority. On all these dimensions, however, it is important to realize that districts may often follow seniority *even when the rules don't explicitly require them to*—because seniority may be mentioned as one criterion of many, and administrators know that by following seniority they can avoid the discretionary judgments that invite teacher and union grievances. Seniority is safe, and it tends to be the norm. If anything, then, these figures understate the extent to which seniority governs the allocation of teachers to jobs.[53]

Note that districts without collective bargaining are not wholly free of restrictive rules.[54] As chapter 2's data showed, many teachers belong to unions in these (southern) states. In the large districts especially, the unions are very active in school board elections and regularly bring their power to bear on board decisions. And the unions are active, and almost always major players, in the politics of education at the state level. So while the stereotype is that the teachers unions are "weak" in the states without collective bargaining, this is usually far from true. In any absolute sense, the unions tend to be quite powerful—just not *as* powerful as their counterparts in collective bargaining states. When it comes to restrictive work rules, then, we shouldn't expect the unions in these nonbargaining states to be entirely unsuccessful at tying the hands of management. We should just expect them to be *less* successful than unions are elsewhere, and thus for their "contracts" to be less restrictive.

That is what we find. On some issues, though, differences across the two types of districts are surprisingly small once state laws are taken into account. As table 6-1 shows, seniority rules for voluntary transfers are much less likely to show up in nonbargaining districts (15 percent) than in bargaining districts (58 percent). District leaders in the former have far greater flexibility in allocating teachers across jobs, just as we might expect. Yet on matters directly related to *job security*, seniority is exceedingly common even in these "weak" union contexts—with 73 percent following seniority when teachers are excessed, 81 percent following seniority when teachers are laid off, and 50 percent following seniority when teachers are rehired after layoffs have occurred. These figures are all lower (especially on rehiring) than those for bargaining districts. But it is clear that, even in unfriendly contexts, the unions are often powerful enough to see that district leaders have little or no discretion when teacher jobs are at stake—and thus little or no authority to ensure that jobs are filled with the most competent people.

Now let's move to the realm of teacher evaluations. Contracts and state laws are often filled with rules about how teachers must be evaluated—rules that, as we've discussed, the unions care about a great deal because of the close connection between evaluations and (potential) dismissal. The unions, of course, want their members to get satisfactory evaluations. So they sometimes push for a requirement that, when principals visit teacher classrooms to observe performance, the teachers *must be told in advance when the visits will occur*—which allows them to prepare, and possibly even to arrange for, activities that look nothing like what normally happens in their classes. As table 6-1 shows, this early-warning evaluation rule is imposed on principals in 38 percent of the bargaining districts and 27 percent of the nonbargaining districts, and thirteen states have relevant laws on the books.

This kind of protection is not pervasive, and we might suspect that it's because 99 percent of teachers get satisfactory evaluations anyway. Teachers probably don't need an early-warning system to sail through. But then there are the occasional teachers who do get rated as unsatisfactory—or the many more who would if such a rating were easy for principals to do. *These* are the teachers who really need protection, and one way the unions can do that is through rules that make it as onerous and as costly as possible for principals to give teachers unsatisfactory ratings. In particular, they can push for rules that require a remediation process for any teachers who are actually given such ratings—a process that involves all sorts of bureaucratic procedures, formal observations, reports, consultations, and other hassles for school principals. On paper, this looks like a way to get teachers to improve. And sometimes it may do that. But it is also a way to scare principals into giving all teachers satisfactory evaluations.

The figures in table 6-1 show that remediation rules—and the constraints they place on principals and districts—are nearly universal: they apply in 80 percent of bargaining districts and 92 percent of nonbargaining districts and are required by legislation in a whopping twenty-four states. Why is so much emphasis placed on remediation as part of the evaluation process? The answer, I suggest, is that this component of the process is *really about job security*, and thus is a matter of great salience to the unions. It protects low-performing teachers from dismissal by guaranteeing that they have extensive opportunities to improve and by creating bureaucratic burdens that prevent principals from giving them bad ratings in the first place. Remediation is nominally about evaluation and improvement. But it is unavoidably, and quite predictably, a means of job protection. Which makes it a union favorite.

Another domain of work rules has to do with teacher "preparation time." The union argument here is that teachers need time outside the classroom to prepare their lessons, to do their grading, and so on, and that they will be better teachers as a result. This is not unreasonable as far as it goes. But teachers do not have an eight-hour workday to begin with (often it is not even seven hours). And in practice, prep time is treated as guaranteed time that teachers have a legal right to, and can spend any way they want, behind closed doors. It is *time away from students* during the workday. One of the unions' goals in collective bargaining is to give teachers as much time away from students as possible.

This is a local matter that the states rarely get involved in: only six have relevant laws. As table 6-1 indicates, however, overwhelming numbers of districts do provide teachers with guaranteed prep time, by rule, in amounts that are literally calibrated down to the minute. Across districts, prep time is typically in the range of 150 to 250 minutes a week, but teachers in bargaining districts clearly tend to get more time away from students than teachers in nonbargaining districts do. About a quarter of the nonbargaining districts have no rules on the subject, and of those that do, the median amount of prep time is 225 minutes. In the bargaining districts, just 17 percent are silent, and the median prep time for those with rules is 250 minutes. District leaders in these settings are more constrained, once again, in how they can allocate their teaching resources.

The kicker, though, is that prep time is treated as a *property right* by the unions and their members. It is not just time off to prepare, so that teachers can do their jobs well. The time they are allowed to spend away from students is a valuable benefit in and of itself, just as leave time is, or vacations. And if for some reason—because, for instance, they have to fill in for an absent colleague—they don't get to take their prep time on any given day, the contract often stipulates that, by law, *they must be compensated for the loss*. As table 6-1 shows, this rarely happens in nonbargaining districts, where 92 percent of contracts are silent on the matter. But compensation rules are written into the contracts in two-thirds of the bargaining districts. When they are, the standard requirement is not simply that teachers be given additional time, but that they actually be given *money*. Any notion that prep time is really about quality teaching, then, is a bit difficult to take seriously. It is about time off—and if teachers are denied their rightful time off, the unions want them to be paid.

Now let's turn to the more familiar way that teachers are given time off: through paid leaves. The two major forms are sick leave and personal leave (where the latter can usually be taken for any reason whatever), and thirty-two states have laws requiring a minimum amount of sick leave—usually ten days—which the districts are free to add to. As table 6-1 indicates, teachers in almost two-thirds of the NCTQ districts receive more than ten days of sick and personal leave a year, and teachers in bargaining districts tend to receive more days of leave than teachers in nonbargaining districts do. Indeed, 25 percent of the bargaining districts provide their teachers with fifteen days or more of such leave, while just 8 percent of the nonbargaining districts provide this much. The problem with all this leave time, as emphasized earlier, is that it gives teachers a legal right to take extensive time away from their students, with pay—which is precisely what they often do. Teachers are absent at very high rates. District leaders can do little or nothing about this. Their hands are tied, by rule.

Teachers are often granted many other types of leave as well. Table 6-1 includes just one of these (for reasons of space), but it is an especially interesting one: paid leave for teachers to attend official union activities. This is usually most relevant for union officials or activists at the school level; but what it means is that, for many hours a year, students are left with substitutes while their real teachers are off engaging in union activities—all of it paid for by the district. Such arrangements might seem surprising, and indeed, they are quite rare in nonbargaining districts, where they show up in only 8 percent of the "contracts." But they are very common in bargaining districts. In those settings, almost *two-thirds* have provisions that pay teachers to leave their classrooms and participate in union affairs while the district foots the bill and students put up with substitutes. Here, district leaders not only find their hands tied in allocating their resources—teachers, money—most effectively, but they are forced to "support" the union.

Some of the issues that find their way into labor contracts are surprising for another reason: they seem like such small matters, and such natural components of any professional organization, that attaching formal rules to them is downright odd. Take faculty meetings, for instance. Why in the world should there be a formal limit on the number of times a school can have faculty meetings? Doesn't it make sense to have them when, in the judgment of principals, they are useful or necessary? Yet this is not the way unions view the situation. Faculty meetings are "extra work" that takes place after normal school hours, and all such work time is to be minimized—unless teachers are paid extra for it. In nonbargaining districts, the unions have made little headway on this issue: only 4 percent have rules putting caps on faculty meetings. But in the bargaining districts, 61 percent do (by, for example, limiting the number of meetings to once a month). From an organizational or professional standpoint, there is no justification for this. But there it is. And it can't help but affect the way schools operate.

Another issue often dealt with in labor negotiations is class size. The conventional wisdom is that smaller classes are good, so union efforts to get rules limiting class size might seem to be pro-student. Yet research shows that there are only modest benefits to reduced class size in the very early grades, and there is no evidence that it helps after that (within the ranges we normally see in schools).[55] Also, it is enormously expensive—and therefore, when classes must be reduced, resources cannot be spent on many other things that could better promote quality education, and district leaders are constrained (perhaps severely) in how they can allocate their teachers.

The unions, however, have their own reasons for demanding restrictions on class size. Smaller classes mean less work for teachers, and they mean that more teachers must be hired—both of which are hugely beneficial (quite aside from any effects on students) in the unions' scheme of things. As table 6-1 shows, nineteen states have enacted legal limits on class size: a level of activity that, in itself, testifies to how much the unions have pushed for these rules.[56] Their success, however, has varied markedly across bargaining and nonbargaining contexts. Only 19 percent of the nonbargaining districts are burdened by formal rules (or laws) that limit class size, while in bargaining districts these restrictions are the norm, with a full 72 percent constrained by them. This is yet another way, and a particularly important one, in which district leaders' hands are tied.

Finally, let's take a closer look at salary rules. The unions push hard for salary schedules that—via their formal "lanes"—require extra pay for master's degrees and other coursework and credentials that are unrelated to student achievement, but translate into enormous additional costs for districts. One measure of union success is the sheer number of lanes—for the greater their number, the more opportunities teachers have to increase their pay simply by accumulating new credentials (which anyone can do, good teacher or no). As table 6-1 reveals, the differences in lane structure across districts are dramatic. In nonbargaining contexts, almost half the districts have just one to three lanes. In bargaining contexts, by contrast, almost half the districts have either four or five lanes, another 30 percent have six or seven lanes, and 16 percent have eight or more lanes. This would suggest, then, that where collective bargaining prevails unions are much better able to get districts to reward teachers based on credentials—and (although more detailed data would be necessary to nail it down) that these districts are required to waste much more of their money on these irrelevant pay criteria.

The formal rules discussed in this section are only illustrative. They merely scratch the surface of what this nation's collective bargaining contracts look like—because most contracts, in districts of any size, are thick documents that contain so many rules it's difficult to count them all, much less discuss and present them in a simple way. It should be apparent from these examples, though, that district leaders are heavily constrained in how they can spend their money, allocate their resources, find and keep the best employees, and otherwise operate their schools. These constraints are not absent in districts that lack collective bargaining, because the unions are still powerful in these contexts and are still able to write restrictive work rules into local policies. But in collective bargaining districts, the unions tend to have more leverage, there are more restrictive rules, and district leaders are more constrained.

Throughout the nation, districts of all types and sizes have collective bargaining and are burdened by these sorts of organizational restrictions. The conventional wisdom, however, is that labor contracts are especially restrictive in the nation's larger districts, as well as in districts with high percentages of minority students—and the conventional wisdom is essentially on target. The NCTQ

Figure 6-1. *Contract Restrictiveness, by District Size*

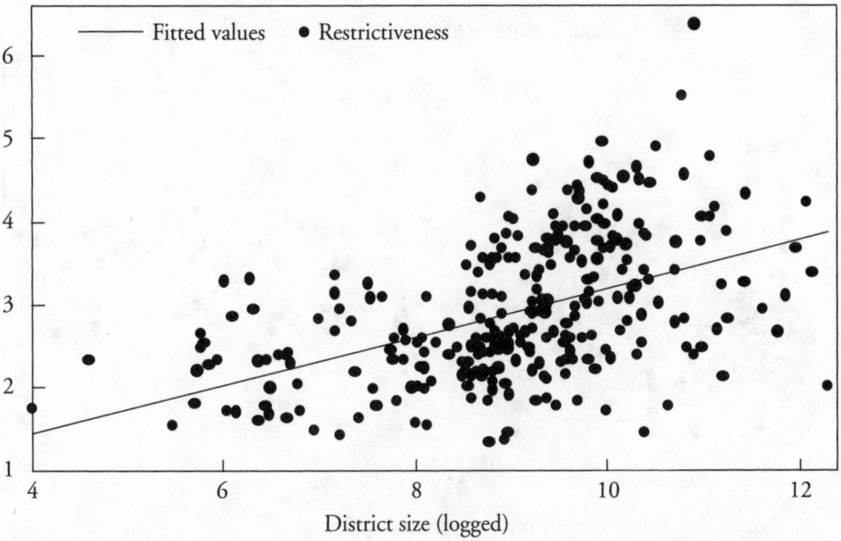

Source: Author's calculations based on a coding of 288 labor contracts drawn randomly (stratified by size) from the National Center for Education Statistics, Schools and Staffing Survey, 1999–2000. The vertical axis represents an index of contract restrictiveness.

data set is limited to the nation's largest districts and therefore isn't particularly helpful. But in my own research several years ago, I had occasion to code a set of 288 contracts from a cross section of districts nationwide.[57] These were contracts in force during the year 2000, but there is good evidence (which I discuss later) that things haven't changed much in the interim.

When these contracts are coded for the restrictiveness of their formal rules, the results are very much as we should expect when we look at the connections to district size and minority enrollment. As figures 6-1 and 6-2 clearly illustrate, labor contracts *do* tend to become more restrictive as the districts get larger in size, and they *do* tend to get more restrictive as districts enroll higher percentages of minority students. It is precisely in the nation's most troubled school districts, then—large districts filled with minority kids—that district leaders tend to be *most constrained* in their efforts to build effective organizations and promote student achievement.[58]

Do the Positives Outweigh the Negatives?

Union leaders say that what is good for teachers is good for kids. Yet as we've seen in gory detail by looking at one contract provision after another, this claim

Figure 6-2. *Contract Restrictiveness, by Percent Minority in District*

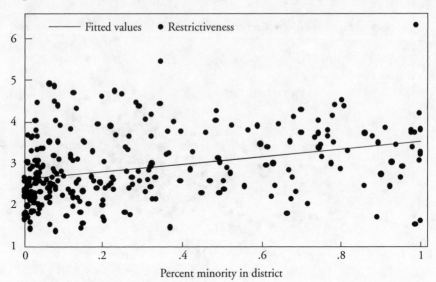

Source: Author's calculations based on a coding of 288 labor contracts drawn randomly (stratified by size) from the National Center for Education Statistics, Schools and Staffing Survey, 1999–2000. The vertical axis represents an index of contract restrictiveness.

simply isn't true. The unions regularly pressure for—and get—work rules that are *not* good for kids. Although there are surely some issues on which the interests of children and unions overlap, the ultimate outcome is that schools get organized in ways that undermine effective education.

But maybe this cloud has a silver lining. Maybe, at the same time that unions are imposing unwarranted work rules, they are doing other things—very beneficial things—that more than make up for these negatives. Perhaps the bottom line, when all the effects are added together, is actually positive, and the unions are a net plus for the system.

There is something specious about this line of thinking, on its face. Because even if the unions do make valuable contributions to public education, the net effect would be much *more* valuable—and children would be much better off—if the unions would *stop* doing the things that have negative consequences. It would be helpful to know, of course, if unions produce more pluses than minuses. But there is no justification for the minuses—for seniority rules, for rules protecting bad teachers, for spending huge sums on master's degrees, and so on. And whether there are pluses to unionization or not, doing what's best for children requires that the negatives that go along with unionization be eliminated.

That said, let's take a look at the positive side of the ledger. What are the big positives that unions might be contributing? The usual arguments for unionization—that teachers need job protection, that they need powerful representation to get better salaries and wages, and so on—are not of the essence here, because they are about the special interests of teachers, not about what is best for children and schools. The simplest, most direct question that needs to be answered is, how do unions contribute to making the public schools more effective? What are their positives for effective organization?

In the final analysis, there are two notable ways that unions might contribute to making the public schools more effective. Both are familiar grounds on which union leaders—and many Democrats, liberals, and moderates—tend to justify unionization as a positive and necessary component of the education system.

The first is that unions provide teachers with a "voice" that needs to be heard if the education system is to perform well. It is through voice, of course, that the unions represent the (special) interests of teachers. But voice can also serve as an organized means of injecting the knowledge, expertise, experience, and judgment of teachers into the educational decision process—thus providing policymakers with a vast storehouse of expert information about how schools can be better organized, kids better taught, money better spent, and reforms better designed.[59]

There is an important truth at work here. Teachers *are* experts on many aspects of schooling, and it is clear that, if decisionmakers wanted to organize schools as effectively as possible, the information provided by teachers would be enormously valuable—and if put to serious, systematic, objective use, would make the schools better. Any effort to design a well-functioning system of teacher evaluation, for example—one that accurately identifies good and bad teachers, with gradations in-between—would benefit tremendously from the in-depth knowledge of teachers about their own craft and how it can be observed and measured. The same is true for performance pay, which will only work well if it is based on measures that reward the right teachers and are designed to give all teachers strong incentives to do a good job. The examples are endless, the conclusion straightforward: to design an effective organization, the designers need the best possible information—and that means they need to have systematic input from teachers.[60]

But here is the hitch. When the unions deal with management negotiators or participate on school committees or collaborate on education reforms, they are *not* just providing objective information from teachers about how schooling can be made more effective for children. *The unions are special interest advocates.* They are advocates for the best interests of teachers, not for the best interests of children—and they use their power in all decision forums to see that outcomes reflect those special interests. Along the way, they use information strategically.

They use it in the way defense lawyers use it: to make the best possible case for achieving their own objectives.

This problem is built-in. It is rooted in the unions' organizational DNA, and it isn't going to change. The result is an unfortunate dilemma for the education system as a whole. On the one hand, the system would surely benefit from regular input conveying the expertise that teachers possess. Schools could be made more effective. On the other hand, teachers are unionized, and unions are *not* wired to provide the kind of objective, useful information the system needs. They are wired to do something very different.

The upshot is that the positives associated with teacher voice and input, while attractive in theory, are diluted and corrupted in practice. The usual references to voice and input have a nice sound to them, and so does all the related talk about collaboration, joint decisionmaking, and cooperation. But the reality is that, in all these processes, the unions are acting as special interest advocates, and much of what they do takes a toll on the effective organization of schools.

So voice and input don't provide the significant positives that might balance off the negatives of union power. There is, however, another major way that the unions are often claimed to promote better schools. Among supporters, a common refrain is that the unions are the vanguard of professionalism in public education. The notion here is that unions try to secure better salaries and working conditions for teachers, expand teacher rights and autonomy in the workplace, and push for higher levels of teacher training—all of which are hallmarks of professionalism. In so doing, supporters argue, they help to make teaching a more desirable job, attract higher-quality people, increase the quality of those already in the field, and ultimately boost the productivity of the schools.[61]

These are familiar claims. In fact, almost everything the teachers unions say and do in presenting themselves to the public (and their own members, for that matter) is framed in terms of professionalism.[62] Yet the claims on these scores are strikingly contradicted by what happens on the ground. The reality is that the teachers unions do *not* promote professionalism in public education. They do the *opposite*—ensuring that, in the formal structure of schooling, teachers are treated like blue-collar workers, and that the value of their professionalism cannot be fully realized.

Yes, the unions do try to raise teacher salaries, but that is hardly germane. Accountants are paid far less than brain surgeons, but both are professionals, and their relative salaries have nothing to do with how professional they are. More important is how the unions approach the whole subject of salary setting. Their ideal is the single salary schedule, in which every teacher's salary is strictly determined by seniority and credentials—and thus is entirely rule-governed and has zero to do with their performance. They also try to see to it that teachers are paid for *every minute* that they work. They want rules that specify exactly how many minutes teachers need to be in the classroom, how many minutes of preparation time they are guaranteed, and how much time they need to stay on campus. And they seek rules that minimize all work activities outside the classroom (meetings with parents, faculty meetings, after-school meetings with kids) for which teachers are not explicitly paid extra.[63]

This is an industrial approach characteristic of what blue-collar unions insist upon for unskilled workers. It bears no resemblance to the way doctors, lawyers, business managers, and other professionals are paid, as their compensation typically *does* depend on their performance (and the satisfaction of their clients), and they work *as long as they need to work* in order to do their jobs well. It undermines the productivity of schools: by paying good teachers and bad teachers the same, wasting huge amounts of money on criteria that are irrelevant to student performance, and restricting what teachers do in the workplace. And it discourages high-quality people from entering teaching (and staying), because these people know that, unlike in a truly professional setting, their talent and success will not be rewarded.

A similar story can be told for autonomy. All professionals need considerable autonomy if their expertise and judgment are to be put to productive use. But the incentives also have to be right. Doctors and lawyers have autonomy in their work, but they also know that, if they don't do a good job, they will lose patients and clients. There will be consequences. This is not the case for teachers, and the unions have tried to keep it that way. They have long opposed efforts to link pay to performance or even to *measure* teacher performance, and they make it virtually impossible to get bad teachers out of the classroom. Aside from a teacher's internal motivation, then, the incentives for productive behavior are as weak as they can be. What the unions push for is autonomy *without* incentives, which has some of the trappings of professionalism, but is a formula for poor performance and ineffective organization.[64]

The mark of a workplace filled with autonomous professionals is that the basic structure of organization is highly flexible, cooperative, and informal.[65] But this is precisely what the unions don't want. For them, the workplace is an adversarial system in which the union's job is to protect teachers from their adversaries, the administrators. They do that through formal rules that specify precisely what must happen, when, where, and how in excruciating detail. Every minute of the day is accounted for and anchored in bureaucratic concrete. The purpose is to give teachers specific rights and to limit the discretion of administrators, not to harness the expertise and judgment of teachers toward the goal of more effective schooling. This, again, is blue collar unionism. It has nothing to do with genuine professionalism.

Another characteristic of professionalism is rigorous training. Good professionals are well trained, and they continue their educations to keep their skills at the highest levels. The teachers unions are all in favor of "training," push hard for more training money and programs, and laud their value in professionalizing the teaching force. But much of this is not what it seems.

It is well known that America's education schools have done a poor job of training the nation's new teachers.[66] But the teachers unions have done little of consequence over the years to speak out against their inadequacies or to support alternative paths to teaching. The fact is, there is no justification for the ed school monopoly on new-teacher training. Teaching does not have anything like the core of technical knowledge that must be acquired, say, in medicine, law, engineering, or accounting, and does not call for the same model of training and legal restrictions on entry. It probably makes much more sense to rely on brief summer training schools, followed by mentoring and on-the-job training—as, for example, Teach for America does—and to get away from ed school requirements altogether.[67]

Experts may differ about the best approach to training. But the teachers unions have approached training in the same way they approach everything else: in terms of their self-interest. They support the ed schools not because the training provided there is any good, but because the ed schools are their close friends and allies, because the existing system of laborious, time-consuming, formal certification and ed school training has all the *symbolic* trappings of professionalism (making education look like law and medicine), and because the system and its formal hoops and hurdles create barriers to entry that operate to restrict supply and bolster the security (and prestige) of existing job holders. All professions, I should note, have incentives to erect barriers to entry to limit and control their own supply—and they are famous for it.[68]

When it comes to on-the-job training for veteran teachers—often referred to as professional development—the unions are again big supporters. The idea sounds good: teachers engage in continual training throughout their careers to maintain and enhance their classroom skills. But the fact is, the unions do not have a stake in *high-quality* training that really pays off in student performance. Thanks to the single salary schedule, they have a stake instead in supporting various types of professional development programs—however shoddy and irrelevant they may be—that teachers can use to get formal credits that qualify them for higher levels of pay, whether or not they become better classroom teachers. Not surprisingly, there is little evidence that most of what passes for professional development is effective.[69]

Finally, the unions also have incentives to be enthusiastic supporters of teacher training because it gives them a crucial alternative to the dismissal of teachers for poor performance. They do not want anyone to be dismissed. So their argument

COLLECTIVE BARGAINING   207

is always that, when teachers are doing a bad job in the classroom, these teachers need additional training. This is firmly embedded in the unions' ethos: every
teacher can be trained, so no teacher needs to be fired. And if a teacher seems
not to be doing a decent job, the blame falls on management for not giving her
the right kinds of training.[70]

The bottom line is that the standard arguments in favor of union power—
that the unions advance teacher professionalism and offer valuable teacher
input—are exceedingly weak. The overarching reality is that the unions' interests are simply *not aligned* with the interests of children. And because that is so,
when they use their considerable power to pursue those interests in collective
bargaining, they often create organizational arrangements for the schools that
diverge from those that are best for students.

There is one more consideration to keep in mind. To the extent that the
unions do anything that—through the pursuit of their *own* interests—happens
to be *good* for kids and schools, we have to ask: why would the districts need
to be forced into doing these things? In a hypothetical world without powerful unions, any modes of organization that promote effective schools—having
to do with teacher pay, class size, work rules, overall spending levels, or anything else—could be adopted by school districts *on their own*. And indeed, in the
modern era of accountability, they would have incentives to do just that. They
would only have to be *forced* to do things that make the schools *less* effective—
and much of collective bargaining involves exactly that.

Quantitative Studies of the Impact of Collective Bargaining

It is easy to see, from a simple perusal of the contracts, that many of their formal rules come into conflict with effective organization. And as we've discussed,
there are a growing number of case studies—by the New Teacher Project, for
example, and the National Council on Teacher Quality—that clearly show as
much, by examining what happens on the ground in real school districts.

It's important not to make this more complicated than it needs to be. If bad
teachers can't be removed from the classroom, that is definitely bad for children. If, due to seniority rules, teachers cannot be assigned to the schools and
classes where they are needed most, or great young teachers are laid off while
mediocre senior teachers are kept, these things are bad for kids too. This is not
rocket science.

Even so, it would be valuable to demonstrate through definitive quantitative
research how these problems ultimately affect student achievement and, more
generally, how collective bargaining affects student achievement. We have good
reason to expect, of course, that the effects will be negative. But demonstrating
that, and doing it thoroughly and convincingly, turns out to be very difficult.

Among other things, there are a great many factors that affect student achievement—some of which are also tangled up with (and probably causes of) collective bargaining—and unless all these variables and their effects can be measured, disentangled, and controlled, it is difficult to separate out and estimate the one thing we really care about: the impact of collective bargaining on student achievement.

That it is difficult doesn't change the underlying reality. Whether the exact effects of collective bargaining on achievement can be well estimated or not, rules that keep bad teachers in the classroom are still bad for kids. But if possible, social scientists should try to estimate the effects—and eventually, ideally, sometime way down the road, to map out the entire "causal structure" that links unions to student achievement. This is a challenge that social scientists have taken on, and there is a small research literature on the subject. But it has yet to make a lot of headway.

Before I discuss this research, warts and all, I want to emphasize that the kind of causal *thinking* involved here is important—and often gets completely lost in the fog of politics, when arguments get made that have no logical or scientific foundation at all. Throughout American politics, interest group leaders of various stripes, across all policy arenas, are constantly doing this to cobble together plausible-sounding cases for favored positions. And the teachers unions do it too. They do it on many issues, but one of them is the connection between collective bargaining and student achievement.

Randi Weingarten, for example, trades on the fact—and it is a fact—that the southern and border states tend to have less collective bargaining *and* lower academic achievement than other states do. It is a fact, then, that the states *with* collective bargaining tend to do better academically than the states without it. But she goes on to assert—quite publicly and quite often—that *therefore* collective bargaining is *not* having negative effects on achievement. As she puts it, "The states that actually have lots of teachers in teacher unions tend to be the states that have done the best in terms of academic success. And the states that don't tend to be the worst. The issue is not a teacher union contract."[71] She executes the same sort of logical maneuver in making comparisons across nations, noting that, because Finland, Singapore, and other high-scoring nations have collective bargaining, this "debunks the myth" that collective bargaining has negative consequences for achievement.[72]

There is no logical basis for this kind of causal inference. Finland has collective bargaining and also has high levels of student achievement, but that says *nothing* about the causal impact of collective bargaining on achievement. Countless other factors that affect achievement—Finland's small size, homogeneity, culture, investment in education, recruitment of teachers, family structure, virtual absence of poverty, and so on—are simply being ignored.[73] It is entirely possible that, if Finland had *no* collective bargaining at all, its schools would do *even better*. Moreover, the very nature of collective bargaining is starkly different in Finland, where labor relations are founded on broad national agreements among national organizations and look nothing like the U.S. system of district-level bargaining and detailed local contracts; indeed, the hallmark of Finnish schools is their *autonomy* from detailed formal rules specifying what they must do and how. To talk about the impact of "collective bargaining" on student achievement in Finland and the United States, then, is to be talking about two very different things.[74]

A similar logic applies to Weingarten's spurious comparisons across the American states. While it is true that the southern and border states have less collective bargaining (of the U.S. type) than the remaining states, they are also quite different from these states in all sorts of other ways too: their educational histories (segregation and low funding, among other things), the minority composition of their students, their political cultures (which help explain why they don't have collective bargaining in the first place), and much more. Simple comparisons can tell us nothing about the impact of collective bargaining on achievement unless these other factors and their various effects are taken fully into account.

Ideally, the social science of education would be well enough developed that spurious arguments like Weingarten's wouldn't even get made. Unfortunately, this ideal isn't close to being met. The shortfall has less to do with the peculiarities of collective bargaining, or of education generally, than with the complexities of society and the methodological requirements of good science: requirements that are much more difficult to meet in social science than in the natural sciences. Natural scientists are often able to carry out controlled experiments, for example, while social scientists (outside psychology) rarely are. Partly due to these inherent difficulties, much of social science—almost regardless of the topic—is made up of mixed findings. Underlying this mixture, there are often quantitative studies of varying quality, many of them using questionable data or relying on methods that are weak or flawed or second-best. Pick a topic in social science, as a result, and there will almost always be room for disagreement as to what the studies supposedly say.

This does *not* mean that social scientists don't "know" anything. There are many sources of evidence (including case studies and everyday experience), and the basic theories, observations, and common sense that guide ideas are often well founded. It simply means that, at least as things now stand, quantitative studies may not always help very much. Such is social science.

A rather small quantitative research literature explores the impact of collective bargaining on student outcomes. It should come as no surprise that it has generated mixed findings (so far) and doesn't provide definitive answers. One reason for the mixed findings is that the various studies often use different methods and measures, are not always studying the same thing, and are not of equal quality, all of which make coherent or uniform findings very unlikely. I don't review these studies individually here, but a brief look at their characteristics suggests how extensive the heterogeneity is and why it can easily lead to disparate results.[75]

—Many studies are carried out at the state level and are thus based on heavily aggregated data: average student achievement scores for entire states, for example, or the overall percentage of teachers unionized for entire states. This super-aggregation makes it very difficult to discover causes and effects at the *district* level, where collective bargaining actually takes place.

—Collective bargaining is measured differently in different studies. Some simply use a dummy variable that takes on a value of 1 or 0 to indicate whether a state or district does or does not have collective bargaining; if the analysis is at the state level, the dummy hides the fact that many individual districts may not actually have collective bargaining and that the prevalence of such districts can vary quite a bit from state to state; if the analysis is at the district level, the dummy simply indicates the presence or absence of collective bargaining, without saying anything about the substance of the labor contract—notably, how restrictive it is. In some studies, collective bargaining isn't measured at all. Rather, the percentage of teachers belonging to unions is used as a proxy.

—Student achievement is typically measured in one of two ways: mathematics test scores or scores on the SAT or the ACT exams.[76] Yet the SAT and ACT are only taken by college-bound seniors, who are unrepresentative of students generally, and math scores capture just a small part of the curriculum and are narrow measures of achievement. The populations whose math scores are featured, moreover, vary dramatically from study to study. Eberts and Stone, for example, focus on fourth graders, Argyris and Rees target tenth graders, and Milkman studies twelfth graders.[77]

—Some studies are based on student-level data and thus on very large samples. Eberts and Stone, for instance, analyze a sample of approximately 14,000 students in 328 elementary schools, and other studies also have samples in the thousands.[78] Ordinarily, large samples would be a good thing. But in these studies, many students are drawn from the same schools and districts and thus should not be treated as independent observations. Yet none of these studies adjusts for such "clustering." If they did, their findings would be weakened.

—As noted, states with low union density and little or no collective bargaining are almost all in the South or along its borders, where school systems have historically been low performers. The same applies to school districts, with the added fact that, in states where collective bargaining is common but not universal, the smaller, more rural districts are the ones that tend not to have it, and these districts too have historically been low performers. Again, the de facto association between low performance and low collective bargaining need have nothing to do with causality, but it does create problems when researchers try to estimate union impacts on student achievement. Most analyses essentially just compare jurisdictions in southern, border, and rural areas with jurisdictions elsewhere, so it is all too easy to get spurious results "showing" that weak unions cause low school performance, and thus that strong unions and collective bargaining make schools better. Part of the problem is the lack of adequate statistical controls. But "endogeneity" issues are also involved here. They arise because some of the same factors that explain why unions are weak in these jurisdictions may also explain why the school systems do not perform well; their political cultures, for instance, tend to be characterized by attitudes and laws hostile to unions, but also by low spending on public goods (like schools), low taxing, and less educated populations. To disentangle these effects, and thus to get estimates of union impact on school performance that are not spurious, these endogeneity problems must be recognized and dealt with. Most studies in the literature ignore these problems entirely. Others address them merely by adding a dummy variable for the South, which doesn't do the job.[79]

In view of how different these research efforts are and how many questions are raised by their methods, there can be little surprise that this literature has not led to a coherent set of findings or even, in some cases, to findings that can be believed at all. Few have been published in top-level academic journals. If we focus on studies at the district or school level, however—the level at which this sort of analysis is best carried out, rather than at the state level—there are two studies that *have* been published in top-level academic journals. One is a detailed empirical analysis by Caroline Hoxby, published in the *Quarterly Journal of Economics*. The other is a detailed empirical study of my own, published in the *American Journal of Political Science*. It is of some significance that these two studies are in agreement: both find that collective bargaining has a negative impact on performance.

Hoxby explores the impact of collective bargaining by looking at changes in school districts over time. She includes all of the nation's districts in her analysis and employs a methodological design—entirely novel for this literature—that allows her to determine (while correcting for endogeneity problems) what difference it makes when districts become unionized and engage in collective bargaining. In the literature's most sophisticated statistical analysis, she shows that collective bargaining leads to increases in total spending, teacher salaries, and teacher-student ratios. That is to say, unions are able to use their power in collective bargaining to get more of the inputs they care about most, money and jobs. She also shows that, although collective bargaining increases school inputs, it also decreases their productivity, so that the unions' overall impact on school performance is actually *negative*, as measured by the student drop-out rate.[80]

My own study, carried out on a large sample of California school districts, approaches the subject from a different angle. I explore the actual contents of the labor contracts themselves, coding them according to how restrictive their rules are. Because all districts in the sample regularly engage in collective bargaining, I avoid the problem of comparing the "normal" districts that have it with the unusual districts that don't. My focus is on the "normal" districts themselves and on whether their contract rules have consequences for student learning.

The baseline finding is that, controlling for a long list of variables that account for student backgrounds and the characteristics of schools and districts, the restrictiveness of the contract has a *large negative impact*: the more restrictive the contract, the lower the gains in student achievement. The size of the impact, moreover, is *greater than that of any other organizational aspect* of schools and districts. Collective bargaining matters for the effectiveness of schooling, and it matters a lot.[81]

I go on to ask whether the magnitude of its impact might be different under different circumstances, and in particular, whether it might vary depending on the size of the district and the minority composition of the schools. It is a reasonable conjecture, for instance—it is only a conjecture—that because school personnel in smaller districts are more likely to know one another and function as a community, they are also more likely to bend formal rules when the best interests of kids are threatened. Larger districts, by this logic, would tend to be more impersonal and rule governed, and their contract rules would tend to be adhered to more often even when the consequences for children are clearly not good. The upshot is that the impacts of collective bargaining may vary with district size—and be *more* negative the larger the district.

There is also reason to think they could be more negative for schools with high percentages of minority students. In part, this is because seniority rules (and other restrictions, like the single salary schedule) hit these schools especially hard, ensuring that they will wind up with teachers who are lower in quality, inexperienced, and imposed via the "dance of the lemons."[82] These problems are only reinforced by the fact that minority parents are likely to have less political clout than more advantaged parents in fighting back against these perverse arrangements. The negative impacts of collective bargaining, then, may be especially large for high-minority schools, and thus take an especially big toll on how much minority kids learn.[83]

These are reasonable arguments, and they are supported by the data. Regarding district size, the findings show that contract restrictiveness does indeed have more negative effects on student achievement in the larger districts. There is, however, a surprising twist: the estimated impact for the smaller districts, those with less than 20,000 students, is essentially zero. In principle, this could mean that the "community" aspects of small districts operate quite effectively to ensure that contract restrictions aren't enforced—at all—when they conflict with what is good for kids. But all things considered, I think this is quite unlikely. Unions bargain for work rules for a reason, and it makes little sense that they would simply allow these rules to become inconsequential. The more likely explanation is that this statistical estimate is simply a bit wide of the mark, an odd product of this particular sample. Such results are hardly uncommon in social science research. I would expect future research to show that collective bargaining does have an impact in these smaller districts—but still one that is lesser in magnitude than for the larger districts.

The other side of the coin is that the negative impact of contract restrictiveness within the larger districts—which enroll 47 percent of the students in California and 40 percent of students nationwide—appears to be *huge*. Indeed, the restrictiveness of the labor contract proves to be such a powerful influence on student achievement in these districts that its effects are comparable in magnitude to those of student background characteristics: which, as education researchers well know, are the prime determinants of how much students learn. And they tower over those associated with other aspects of school and district organization.

The analysis also shows that collective bargaining has different effects depending on the minority composition of schools. These effects, as the above results imply, tend to show up in the larger districts. In these settings, contract restrictiveness has negative consequences for schools generally, but the consequences are considerably more negative for schools that have high percentages of minority students. This lends credibility to the arguments that restrictive rules (like seniority preferences) put high-minority schools at a disadvantage in the competition for teachers and resources within districts, and that minority parents are less influential than white parents at protecting their kids from these perversities.

If these empirical findings are on the mark, their substantive implications are important. They tell us that collective bargaining does have negative consequences for student achievement and that the effects are greatest for precisely those districts and schools—large districts, high-minority schools—that, over the years, have been the worst performers and most difficult to improve. It follows that efforts to boost achievement in these contexts, as well as to reduce the achievement gap between whites and minorities, need to recognize that collective bargaining is part of the problem—and that it deserves to be taken seriously as a target of reform.

Conclusion

In assessing collective bargaining and its impact on schools and kids, it is easy to get lost in the weeds. Quantitative research on the topic is inherently complicated and messy, as it is in any area of social science, largely for reasons of methodology and measurement. And although the studies I've discussed are surely helpful, many more studies and many more years of work are needed to create a literature that can nail down all the details with scientific confidence.

That said, we don't need to know every last detail to have a good sense of what is happening here. We have a great deal of evidence to go on, from a variety of sources, and when we step back from it all and take in the bigger picture, the basic themes that come through are exceedingly straightforward.

It is a simple fact that, in American public education, labor contracts are filled with rules that are adopted for reasons that have *nothing to do with what is best for children.* Whether the provisions establish a single salary schedule, seniority rights in transfers and layoffs, caps on faculty meetings, prep time requirements, expansive sick leave, or whatever, they are clearly intended to advance the occupational interests of teachers, and it is easy to see that they often come into conflict with what is best for kids.

These rules, moreover, are not something separate from the organization of schooling. They *are* the organization of schooling. And to the extent that unions are successful in collective bargaining, the public schools have organizations imposed on them that are simply *not designed* to promote the academic achievement of students and that make it *more difficult* for the schools to be effective.

Ask yourself these questions. If it were possible to go back to square one and design schools from scratch, aiming to build organizations that are maximally effective at getting students to learn, would well-intentioned designers choose to adopt seniority rules that give senior teachers their choice of jobs, regardless of their competence? Would they adopt seniority rules that, in layoff situations, force talented junior teachers to be fired while mediocre senior teachers remain in the schools? Would they adopt rules making it impossible to dismiss bad teachers? Would they adopt onerous evaluation (and dismissal) procedures that give principals incentives to give all teachers, however incompetent, satisfactory ratings? Would they pay teachers on the basis of educational credentials that are irrelevant to student achievement? Would they pay good teachers exactly the same as bad teachers?

The answer in all these cases—and many, many more—is obviously no. *No one who wants what is best for children would organize the schools as they are currently organized.* The schools are only organized as they are because *other* interests have been in the driver's seat: the interests of adult employees. And these interests are brought to bear through the exercise of union power in collective bargaining.

So, yes, the details can get very complicated. But the bottom line is straightforward indeed.

7

Small Victories for Sanity

Since the 1970s, restrictive labor contracts have been common in American education, especially in large urban districts. Until recently, very little has been done or even said about them. The unions, after all, have been tremendously powerful throughout the modern era, and the districts—led by elected school boards often beholden to the unions themselves—have been weak bargainers not fully able to resist.

The past decade has seen signs of change. The most radical departure from the norm has occurred in New Orleans, which, in terms of reforms to the basic structure of public education, is surely the nation's standout case of path-breaking innovation. Yet New Orleans is not an example that other districts can emulate, because its own situation is historically unique: the entire school system—a miserable performer, immune to change, riddled with corruption—was physically destroyed by Hurricane Katrina in 2005, all its teachers were dismissed, and the *local union and its formidable power were essentially wiped out.* When state and local officials began to reconstruct the schools in the following years, they were largely free from the usual constraints of union power—and they consciously chose *not* to embrace unionization and collective bargaining, and more generally, *not* to rebuild their system along traditional lines. Instead, they moved toward a full-blown choice system filled with autonomous charter schools, where virtually all important decisions—about hiring, firing, evaluations, the allocation of resources, and more—are made at the school level, and stifling union restrictions are a thing of the past. As of late 2010, all children in New Orleans choose their schools, 61 percent of them are in charters, and the plan is to increase that percentage considerably in the years ahead. This is a city overflowing with new and unorthodox ideas, with young, energetic teachers and principals (many of them products of Teach for America), and with a sense that something big and important is happening there. And it is.[1]

Although other districts cannot emulate New Orleans—they cannot, of course, wipe out the power of their local unions, wipe out their labor contracts, and start with a clean slate—its experience still conveys an important lesson. The lesson is that stunning innovations are possible, and boundless entrepreneurial energy can be unleashed, when local school districts are liberated from the stifling constraints of union power. It is profoundly telling that the resurgent New Orleans school system does not look like any other big-city school system. The experience of that district allows us to "see," in effect, what is *not* happening in other districts—because they are not free to act. While the local union may eventually regenerate itself and, with support from its state and national parent organizations, exert its power once again, for now New Orleans *is* free. And it is letting a thousand flowers bloom.

No other American school districts have that kind of freedom. They are locked into the traditional system, and any effort to break out is guaranteed to be met by fierce resistance. Even so, recent developments have given reform a much-needed boost. Accountability systems, imperfect though they are, have shone a spotlight on poor performance, aroused the public and its opinion leaders, and ramped up the pressure on district officials to get serious about effective organization—and thus to resist debilitating union rules that have long gotten in the way. At the same time, charter schools have proliferated in many urban areas—enrolling, for example, a whopping 38 percent of the kids in Washington, D.C., 36 percent in Detroit, and 32 percent in Kansas City during the 2009–10 school year—and forcing district officials to confront an unsettling new reality: if the local schools don't improve, kids will leave for the competition.[2] Here too they have reason to fight for effective organization, and against the restrictive work rules that weigh their organizations down.

As a driver of reform, this new environment has been more than just an environment of pressures. It has also been an environment of *opportunities*. For as education has grown in salience, and as the public has demanded better schools, it has become an attractive realm of political action for the more intrepid public officials who *want* to take on the hard challenges, prove themselves as leaders, and leave a lasting legacy. Traditionally, needless to say, most district officials have not been cut from this mold. They are the ones who need to be pressured into action. But there are others—including some big city mayors—who approach their jobs and career trajectories very differently, and who are looking for a way to make their mark as leaders. These days, the fight for better schools gives them a prime opportunity to do that.

So the context seems ripe for America's school districts, or at least some of them, to rise up and challenge the power of their unions. But the question is, have they actually done that? And if so, how successful have they been? In this chapter, I provide some answers, offering views from two very different angles. First, I present some simple data on how the labor contracts have changed—or not changed—over the last decade in our nation's large districts. Having done that, I spend the bulk of this chapter on two districts that, New Orleans aside, stand out from all the others in their insistence on effective organization and their commitment to bringing radical reform to the labor contract.

These districts are New York City and Washington, D.C. Not coincidentally, they have been led by strong, committed mayors—Michael Bloomberg and Adrian Fenty, respectively—who made education reform the centerpiece of their leadership agendas. And they pursued it by appointing school chancellors—Joel Klein in New York City, Michelle Rhee in Washington, D.C.—who were tough, skilled, and courageous. These two districts are the nation's best-case scenarios for confronting union power and doing away with senseless restrictive rules. Their experiences have a lot to tell us about how much progress can be made when all the reformist stars seem to be lined up just right.[3]

Contract Change in Large Districts

To get a handle on how labor contracts have changed over the past decade, I took advantage of the fact that thirty-five of the districts in my own national data set (described in chapter 6), whose contracts were in force in 2000, are also present in the more recent National Council on Teacher Quality (NCTQ) data set, whose contracts are in force for 2010. I then selected a set of eight labor issues from table 6-1 in chapter 6 that are included in both data sets, and—to ensure consistency in coding—recoded the NCTQ contracts so that they could be compared to my own.

Although the districts in both samples were chosen randomly, the thirty-five districts we'll be looking at here constitute a fairly small sample, and all are large districts (with enrollments greater, often much greater, than 20,000). Nonetheless, I believe that, if we are going to see major change, we should see it here: because the nation's largest districts have been the ones most savagely criticized for low performance, they are the ones most in danger of losing their students to charter schools, and their contracts have most often been the targets of critical public scrutiny. They are also, because of their sheer size, of real importance to the nation: they are its major districts, responsible for educating a big chunk of its kids.

So the data on contract changes are worth examining. Set out in table 7-1, they are quite fascinating. If we look at the overall sample, the evidence clearly shows that *there has been no tendency over the last ten years for labor contracts to become less restrictive.* Across all eight issues, the contract rules in virtually every

Table 7-1. *Changes in the Restrictiveness of Contract Rules in Thirty-five Large Districts, 2000–10*

Number of districts meeting the criteria

Type of rule	Less restrictive	Unchanged	More restrictive
Seniority, voluntary transfers	0	33	2
Seniority, excessing	1	33	1
Seniority, layoffs	0	31	4
Seniority, rehire	0	32	3
Evaluation, prior notice	0	34	1
Guaranteed prep time	0	35	0
Faculty meeting cap	0	32	3
Class size limits	0	35	0

Source: Author's calculations based on a comparison of contracts from 2000 and 2010. The 2000 contracts were obtained directly from the districts. The 2010 contracts were accessed on the website of the National Council on Teacher Quality (www.nctq.org/tr3/home.jsp).

district *have remained exactly the same*—and on those rare occasions when the contract has changed, it has almost always become *more* restrictive.

On seniority-based transfers, for example, thirty-three of the contracts remained the same over this ten-year period, none became less restrictive, and two became more restrictive. On faculty meeting caps, thirty-two contracts remained the same, none became less restrictive, and three became more restrictive. On the teachers' right to receive advanced notice before principals visit their classrooms, thirty-four districts remained the same, none became less restrictive, and one became more restrictive. Overall, out of 280 possible changes to these union contracts (thirty-five districts times eight issues), there were fourteen instances of greater restrictiveness, one instance of less restrictiveness, and 265 instances of no change at all. The norm has been profound, unshakeable stability. The work rules that prevailed in the past—when union contracts were far less often in the public spotlight—are virtually the same work rules that prevail now.

To the extent that these figures are at all representative, then, they challenge the notion that the nation's largest districts have been successfully fighting back against the formal constraints of their contracts. If observers of American education think that America's public schools are making substantial progress in creating leaner, more flexible, more effective organizations by paring down their labor contracts, they need to think again.

Yet this is not the whole story. Some districts *are* fighting back. They may not be representative of districts generally, but they are public arenas in which fierce struggles are taking place—struggles that are very much in the news, and could serve as models for the rest of the country.

The key to these rare, high-profile struggles is that, in a number of major U.S. cities, mayors have recently taken control of the schools—beginning with Boston in 1992 and followed by Chicago in 1995 and a host of others, including New York City, Cleveland, Washington, D.C., Providence, and Hartford.[4] Where it has happened, mayors have stepped in because they see an education system that is fundamental to their cities' well being, but clearly failing and in desperate need of strong leadership. Not all mayors seek out such challenges. Most don't. But those who do are often the type of people—Michael Bloomberg of New York City, Richard Daley of Chicago, Adrian Fenty of Washington, D.C.—who mean business, who see challenges as opportunities, and who know (because they have chosen to make it so) that their own success in office turns on their ability to improve the schools and bring real change.

Where mayors have taken control, the shift in governance is usually not good for unions. Compared to school board members, mayors have constituencies that are bigger and more diverse, and they have many more political, administrative, and informational resources at their disposal for wielding power. All of this makes them less dependent on the unions and less vulnerable to their influence. Of course, mayors are elected too and are not beyond the unions' reach. Moreover, any intrepid mayors who seek out control of the schools will eventually be out of office, to be succeeded by other people who may well have very different priorities and aspirations—and perhaps stronger connections to the unions, if the latter have boosted their efforts in city elections. But it's all relative: the unions are likely to be worse off with mayors than with school boards.

It is in the few systems run by mayors that districts have been on the offensive: railing against perverse work rules, demanding "thinner" contracts, and pushing for new provisions that give them more control over hiring, dismissal, evaluation, and the organization of work. These districts (or some of them) are trying hard to create what they've never had before—effective organizations—and they see restrictive union contracts as the biggest obstacle.

While it is hardly a groundswell, this is a historic development, one that—if it is ultimately successful—points to a more productive future for American public education. But success won't come easily. To get a better sense of what the districts are up against, let's take a closer look at two districts—New York City and Washington, D.C.—that have been at the cutting edge of this new movement, and whose efforts have attracted high-profile national attention.

New York City

New York City is the largest school district in the nation, enrolling a mind-boggling 1.1 million students in 2010–11. For most of its modern history, it has been the poster district for dysfunctional public schooling in America's big cities:

famous for its massive bureaucracy, its mismanagement, its patronage and cor-ruption, and its legion of low-performing schools.[5]

That the district needed deep, fundamental change was obvious, and mayors in the modern era finally stepped up to do something about it by trying to take control of the school system. To do that, though, they needed new legislation from Albany—and the city's United Federation of Teachers (UFT), probably the most powerful teachers union in the country, was opposed. It wanted to keep things as they were, and it had plenty of allies in the state legislature. So when David Dinkins tried to win mayoral control of the schools in the early 1990s, he failed. When Rudolph Giuliani tried to gain control in the middle and late 1990s, he failed too. The saga continued with Michael Bloomberg, who cam-paigned in 2001 by putting education reform at the top of his political agenda and arguing the need for mayoral control. This time, there was a difference. Very soon after winning office, he also won control of the city's schools. Albany came through for him.[6]

How did that happen? It didn't happen because the union suddenly became less powerful or because state legislators had a dramatic reawakening. It hap-pened because, in June 2002, after nineteen months of stalled labor negotia-tions (stretching back to the Giuliani administration), the union and the new mayor struck a deal: the mayor would get control of the schools (for awhile), and the union and its members would get money. Lots of it. Specifically, the new contract—described as the union's "biggest contract ever"—gave teachers huge raises of 16 to 22 percent.[7] In return, the union *supported* new legislation autho-rizing mayoral control of education in New York City (with a seven-year sunset provision), and the state legislature dutifully turned the deal into law.[8]

From Bloomberg's standpoint, this was the price that had to be paid if he was to have a shot at turning this school district around, which he aimed to do by creating—for the first time—an organizational system that is accountable, per-formance-driven, and designed to boost student achievement. From the union's standpoint, giving Bloomberg control was an obvious risk. But most of the deal was actually not risky at all. Teachers were guaranteed to get big money in their pockets. And as for reform—the potentially risky part of the deal—the union was essentially betting that, as reform efforts unfolded over time, they could use their power to block major change. They also had a back-up: after seven years, if things went badly, they could let mayoral control permanently lapse.[9]

Bloomberg quickly chose Joel Klein to be his schools chancellor. Klein, a former Clinton administration antitrust lawyer, came to the job with no expe-rience running a school system. He was also unwedded to the past, commit-ted to reform, and willing to make waves if necessary in forging the building blocks of effective organization. Bloomberg and Klein made a formidable team. In the early going they moved aggressively to implement their Children First plan, which involved replacing the central district's thirty-two local districts—known for corruption and incompetence—with ten instructional divisions, radically paring back the district bureaucracy, giving principals more authority over budgets, and imposing a mandatory curriculum in reading and math. They also began closing large, impersonal high schools and replacing them with many smaller ones, in a move that had substantial financial backing from the Bill and Melinda Gates Foundation.[10]

The unions were not pleased, but these first attempts to transform the organization of schooling did not focus on jobs or personnel rules, so their core interests were affected only tangentially. But as reforms moved forward in 2003, the existing union contract expired at the end of May with no serious movement toward a new one. Something had to be done, eventually. And then, in November, a dramatic event captured the city's attention and brought collective bargaining to center stage.

What happened was that the head of the City Council's education committee, Eva Moskowitz, broke the norms of labor secrecy in this heavily unionized, heavily Democratic city by holding open hearings on the school district's labor contracts. The details of these contracts had always been negotiated behind closed doors (as is true in virtually all school districts); and once negotiated, they had never been subjected to open public scrutiny and discussion. As the New York Times observed, "Union work rules are the third rail of city education policy,"[11] meaning that politicians regarded them as too dangerous to talk about in public. The obvious reason was that, if ordinary people knew what these rules actually were, many would be outraged. And once the secrecy broke down, this is precisely what happened. Just as the politicians—and the unions—had feared.

Moskowitz was under intense pressure to back off. But she didn't. She used the council hearings to shine a bright light on the education system's collective bargaining contracts. Her rationale, as the New York Observer summarized it, was that the rules in these contracts "stand in the way of everything from firing incompetent teachers to making sure kids aren't reading in the dark. They contribute to chaos in the schools by barring teachers from monitoring hallways and lunchrooms and exacerbate the teacher shortage by preventing schools from offering competitive salaries to attract experienced math and science instructors."[12] And as the Observer went on to note, "These subjects were all but taboo until the education committee's hearings.[13]

The result was a media extravaganza, and a bad dream come true for the unions. The newspapers and television news shows were filled with stories about mediocre teachers who couldn't be fired, principals without authority over their own staff, school custodians who couldn't be asked to vacuum, and on and on—all because of rules written into collective bargaining contracts. There was surprise and outrage, and journalists were having a field day. As one aide to the mayor commented, "What we are seeing are all the contractual things that make it very difficult to improve the way children are taught . . . You'd think she was releasing atomic secrets to the Russians."[14]

To heighten the drama, there were also stories about witnesses being afraid to testify before the committee, worried that they would suffer retaliation and have their careers ruined. "They felt they would be blacklisted," Moskowitz said, and "that the UFT chapter leader at their school would never forget this and make their lives miserable."[15] Two principals agreed to testify only if they could do so anonymously, with their voices disguised by computer, conjuring up images of Serpico-like exposés fraught with danger and intrigue. That there was political danger for Moskowitz and (possibly) her colleagues was apparent too—because the union, which "[hadn't] been reluctant to remind Ms. Moskowitz that politicians fooled with the UFT at their peril,"[16] went out of its way to drive the threat home very publicly. As the *New York Daily News* described the situation,

> Politics and education always have been closely linked in New York, but rarely has that connection been clearer than at yesterday's City Council hearing on the teachers' contract. There in the back row, his arms crossed, was Howard Wolfson, the Democratic powerhouse who revealed he is now on the payroll of the United Federation of Teachers. In the front row, sitting next to UFT president Randi Weingarten, was Brian McLaughlin, head of the New York City Central Labor Council and a man many believe will run for mayor in 2005. The show of muscle demonstrated how unnerved the unions are by the hearings.[17]

Moskowitz didn't flinch. The hearings ran their course, produced an avalanche of public information, and were a debacle for the UFT. The union, however, ultimately got its pound of flesh. Moskowitz was an ambitious Democratic politician and had intended to run for the Manhattan borough presidency in 2005 as a stepping stone to the mayor's office sometime down the line. The UFT marshaled its political weapons to have her defeated in the borough presidency bid—and thereby ended her political career.[18] The union made it clear that her defeat was indeed payback for misbehavior, calling her a "slow learner" for failing to anticipate the political consequences of her actions.[19]

Yet the 2003 hearings were a watershed—not just for the city, but for the country as a whole. The *New York Times,* hardly a voice of antiunion sentiment, editorialized about "what reasonable people know to be true: that work rules need to change for schools to work better."[20] And while Bloomberg and Klein had not been shy, in prior months, about saying that they wanted to cut back on restrictive work rules, their reform strategy now became much more focused on the labor contract and much more assertive in demanding radical change.

In February 2004, several months after the hearings had ended, Bloomberg proposed that the entire 200-page labor contract be scrapped and replaced with a "thin" eight-page contract that would wipe out almost all the existing work rules. Klein too spoke out strongly for a total transformation, zeroing in on work rules as key obstacles to school improvement. "At the heart of the problem are . . . lockstep pay, seniority, and life tenure," he said. "Together they act as handcuffs and prevent us from making the changes that will encourage and support excellence in our system."[21]

The union called the thin contract proposal "insulting," and the idea went nowhere. But the district stuck to its guns in demanding major changes in work rules. Among them: no seniority in hiring and transfers, pay bonuses for exemplary performance, signing bonuses for hard-to-staff fields (like math and science), more flexibility in assigning teachers to noninstructional duties, and new rules to ease the dismissals of mediocre teachers. The union countered by demanding higher wages and more job protection through a no-layoff provision, smaller classes (which require more teachers), and a "peer intervention" program for poorly performing teachers (to avoid their dismissal).[22]

The two sides were at loggerheads, and months passed. But in October 2005, more than two years after the prior contract had expired—and shortly before Bloomberg would stand for reelection—a new contract was finally settled. The timing was not coincidental. The UFT had threatened to strike or to endorse the mayor's Democratic challenger if it didn't get a contract by early October.[23]

Despite the political pressure to settle, Bloomberg and Klein achieved a genuine breakthrough in the new contract. They paid a price, of course. The union was not about to relax its protective rules for nothing. So teachers won a healthy pay raise of 15 percent over four years, and, because most of the contract was by now retroactive, this meant that all teachers would be receiving (as under the prior contract) big lump-sum payments. Those at the top of the pay scale, for example, would get checks of $5,771 by Christmas: a nice inducement and an expensive one for the district. In return, however, the administration won a more rational organization. It lost on most of its demands for more flexible work rules, but it succeeded—dramatically—by eliminating seniority in hiring and transfers and by giving principals the right to determine who works at their schools. No longer would senior teachers be able to transfer from one job to another, regardless of whether the receiving principal wanted them and regardless of their performance. And although excessing decisions—in situations when schools are closed or downsized—would still be made according to seniority, the excessed teachers would no longer be allowed to bump their more junior colleagues and take their jobs. Principals would have to give their consent before excessed teachers could be placed in their schools, and they had the right to say no.[24]

The 2005 contract was a watershed event. For the first time since the district became unionized decades earlier, it had taken major steps toward *retaking control of its own organization*. Ridiculous as that sounds as something to cheer about—journalist Sol Stern referred to it as a "small victory for sanity"[25]—the shift in rules represented a transformative reversal of direction that clearly needed to happen. Much more needs to happen, obviously, if true effectiveness is ever to be remotely approximated; and in subsequent years, knowing this full well, Bloomberg and Klein continued to build upon their early, hard-won success and refused to let up. They continued to push against union restrictions. They continued to insist on more productive forms of organization. Predictably, their efforts generated almost perpetual resistance and turmoil, making progress very difficult. Still, they made progress.

Two departures from the ancien régime stand out. The first has to do with the way teachers are compensated. Both Bloomberg and Klein have long believed that the pay of individual teachers should depend, at least in part, on their classroom performance; good teachers should be rewarded, all teachers should have incentives to do their best, and no one should get paid just for showing up. The only way to change the pay system, however, was through bargaining with the UFT, which refused to go along. In late 2007, however, the mayor ponied up an enormous amount of money to get the UFT to accept a compromise, and it did. As journalist Stern observed, "Weingarten took the city to the cleaners in the negotiations over bonus pay. To get her to 'concede' to the fat, pensionable bonuses, New York gave teachers a long-sought change in their already munificent retirement plan: thousands achieved the right to retire with full pension benefits at fifty-five with a minimum of twenty-five years of service, putting even greater strain on the city's future pension obligations."[26] In addition, the city agreed to pay $160 million to settle a dispute over its contribution toward health benefits for teachers and retirees.[27]

In return, Bloomberg got performance pay, but a much weaker version of it than he wanted. Under the compromise plan, performance would *not* be linked to pay for individual teachers. Instead, bonuses would go to *whole schools* based on their success in raising average test scores; only high-poverty schools would be included; and "compensation committees" at each school would distribute the money to individuals as they saw fit.[28] This approach may encourage more team effort in the participating schools, but it is otherwise problematic. A pay system that rewards large groups rather than individuals is sure to provide weak incentive effects. This is especially so because the "compensation committees" are controlled in practice by the union itself and can be expected to distribute the bonuses equally, ensuring that good teachers and bad teachers within any given school will actually be paid the same. Most of the district's teachers, at any rate, are not affected.

Subsequent experience with the program has been less than inspiring. Test scores have been rising throughout the district—a very good thing—but as a result, performance bonuses went out in 2009 to more than 90 percent of the high-poverty schools in the program, whose compensation committees typically distributed them equally. The city wound up paying a hefty $27 million in bonus payments, and *virtually every teacher in every participating school got the bonuses, whether they were good teachers or not.* This is hardly what a true pay-for-performance system is supposed to look like. So far, it is functioning as just another way of distributing more money to teachers. The union got a good deal.[29]

Whether it was a good deal for Bloomberg remains to be seen. All the evidence is not in. Perhaps the program is stimulating enough team effort to justify the enormous expense, and perhaps this will ultimately be demonstrated. But even if the team effects are minimal, there is still a big upside here. For the first time, performance at least makes a difference for how teachers are paid in the participating schools, and everyone knows it. This is another "small victory for sanity," and if nothing else, it succeeds in getting the camel's nose inside the tent. The question is whether the rest of the camel will follow.

The pay-for-performance program is a small step compared to Bloomberg's efforts along a second major front in the battle for effective organization. This one has to do with the quest for teacher quality—and thus with issues of tenure, evaluation, dismissal, hiring and firing, and seniority. The stage was set in January 2007, when Bloomberg announced a reorganization plan that the *New York Times* called "the most sweeping changes to the system since the mayor reorganized it after gaining control of the schools in 2002."[30] At its heart was a call for more rigorous evaluation of teachers and a decentralization of authority that put money and control in the hands of principals. These were changes he could pursue unilaterally, outside the straightjacket of collective bargaining and union veto.

Shortly thereafter, Bloomberg announced the creation of a Teacher Performance Unit, consisting of five lawyers, along with a team of five consultants. Their job was to work with principals in identifying low-performing tenured teachers, to assist with efforts to improve the latter's performance, and in cases where performance could not be improved, to help principals deal with the necessary paperwork and legal proceedings to see that these tenured teachers are removed from the classroom and ultimately dismissed. If tenure laws and collective bargaining could not be changed, then Bloomberg would mount a serious, sustained effort—unprecedented in district history—*within* these constraints to take action against problem teachers.[31]

He also announced an effort to get serious about tenure. Up to then, tenure in New York City—as everywhere else—was essentially automatic. During the 2006–07 school year, for example, only half of 1 percent of all eligible teachers were denied tenure: which means, in effect, that anyone who could walk and chew gum at the same time was getting tenure, and the district would be saddled with them for the rest of their working lives regardless of whether they were any good at their jobs.[32] Bloomberg sought to change all this by making the tenure review much more systematic and rigorous. To that end, he and Klein set in motion an ambitious new program, to be piloted on some 2,500 teachers, using student test score gains to measure teacher success in the classroom. The idea was that this objective information on student learning, together with other information on teacher performance—subjective evaluations by the principal, for example—would be used in assessing a junior teacher's case for tenure.[33] In Klein's words, tenure should be a "well-deserved honor, not a routine right."[34]

The UFT was strongly opposed to all this. It could not stop Bloomberg and Klein from giving principals better assistance on dismissal cases nor from taking the tenure process more seriously. But it did go after what is surely the most game-changing aspect of the administration's new approach: the move to use test score data in evaluating teachers for tenure. In an awesome display of raw political power, it went to the state legislature in the spring of 2008 and got it to *pass a law* prohibiting any district, anywhere in the state, from using test score data as even one part of the tenure evaluation process.[35]

The new law was a roadblock, needless to say, but Bloomberg and Klein didn't end their measurement program. They changed and expanded it. In the fall of 2008 the district announced that test score measures would be used on a much broader scale to generate "teacher data reports" on every math and English teacher in the fourth through eighth grades, tenured and untenured alike, some 18,000 of them. The data would not be used for formal evaluations nor for pay or promotion.[36] But the implication was clear: the development of such a system would give Bloomberg and Klein the *capacity* to use student test score data in these ways in the future, should the opportunity present itself.

It didn't take long. In November 2009, following a new legal interpretation of the legislature's ban on test score usage, Bloomberg argued that teachers hired in 2007 (before the ban took effect) were not covered by the law—and therefore that student test scores could be used in evaluating them for tenure. He instructed Klein to do exactly that.[37] Very clearly, then, this is a capacity that *will* be applied to evaluation, pay, and promotions in future years—as long as Bloomberg remains mayor, at any rate.

The battle over teacher quality took place on another important front as well. Because of the 2005 contract breakthrough, the thousands of teachers who had been excessed in the years since—due to downsizing and school closures—were not guaranteed of finding jobs in other schools. Seniority was of no help to them anymore. Principals now had to *consent* to any new hires, and they were being selective about whom they took on—which, of course, was precisely what

Bloomberg and Klein wanted. Principals were under pressure to raise student achievement and so had incentives to hire the best teachers they could find. Plus, as a result of Bloomberg's 2007 decentralization of school finance, principals controlled their own budgets and had incentives to hire younger teachers with lower salaries if they were effective in the classroom. Performance and efficiency were now guiding decisions as never before. And the result was that many excessed teachers—between 1,000 and 2,000 a year—could not find a school to hire them. These were the teachers who, in the view of principals and based on the teachers' track records and reputations, were simply not good enough to justify their cost.[38]

The opportunity for Bloomberg and Klein was obvious: large numbers of low-performing teachers were being automatically identified every year, they had no jobs, and they should be moved out of the system. In the private sector, this would be straightforward. But in the New York City schools, these teachers were protected under the union contract and could not be fired. Instead, *they had to be paid their full salary, plus benefits, even though no one would hire them.* Given the situation, they were placed in what was called the Absent Teacher Reserve, where they were available to serve as substitute teachers—albeit very expensive ones who were not considered good in the classroom. The cost to the district was enormous: somewhere in the range of $100 million a year and possibly much more.[39]

Controversy over this well-paid army of the unemployed first erupted in the spring of 2008, when a report by the New Teacher Project drew attention to the situation.[40] Bloomberg and Klein pressed for changes in the union contract that would allow excessed teachers four months to find a new job, after which they would be removed from the payroll. The union was totally opposed and tried to ensure—by demanding a freeze on new hires, which would constrain principals to fill more of their slots from candidates in the Absent Teacher Reserve—that *all* these teachers would be placed somewhere and no one would lose a job.[41] More than two years later, the standoff continues. And throughout this time, the union has essentially been the winner: all excessed teachers have received full pay and benefits for as long as they have been unemployed, and the district has been forced to waste enormous sums of money.

The Absent Teacher Reserve has a lot in common with the city's Rubber Rooms, which we toured in the opening pages of this book. Both are vivid illustrations of how stunningly perverse the organization of schooling can be. Both are shocking examples of the rampant waste of scarce resources. Yet both are also outgrowths of Bloomberg's and Klein's efforts to get serious about teacher quality, and there is a method to the madness. Special interest rules make it nearly impossible to dismiss bad teachers, but Bloomberg and Klein, as strong leaders, refuse to let bad teachers stay in the classroom. So for years they took direct action to remove the most egregious cases—those believed to be violent or sex offenders, for example, or sometimes just strikingly incompetent—and put them in Rubber Rooms (until the 2010 agreement with the UFT that ended the "program"[42]). They also took action to get bad teachers out of the classroom by simply allowing principals not to hire them, which then led to the Absent Teacher Reserve, a pool that contains more than twice as many unwanted teachers as the Rubber Rooms ever did and is far more expensive. Both are organizationally ridiculous. But in the grander scheme of things, they may well be functional as way stations along the path to a more effective system.

So let's take stock here. As I finish up this book, the organization of the New York City schools is a work in progress. The district is fighting hard to create the building blocks of effective organization: accountability, quality teachers, performance-based incentives, and a rational allocation of resources. But the only way to do these things is by overhauling the Byzantine maze of restrictive work rules that, for so long, have made the city's school system an organizational nightmare, and these rules are powerfully protected by the United Federation of Teachers, whose mission has nothing to do with effective organization. The result has been eight years of conflict and struggle.

The story hasn't been pretty. But truth be told, next to Washington, D.C., New York City is the premier case of a school district that is well situated for challenging its union.[43] The district is controlled by a powerful mayor. The mayor is unafraid of the union, truly committed to eliminating restrictive work rules, and willing to pursue ground-breaking reforms that would transform the system in the best interests of children. He chose a strong chancellor who shared his values and goals and was willing to fight for them in the face of stiff resistance from the union. In these key respects, New York City is truly unusual among districts nationwide. And fortunate.

In November of 2010, New York City lost its dynamic duo—and possibly its mojo—when Joel Klein announced that he was retiring after two terms as schools chancellor and moving on to an executive position with News Corporation in the private sector. Bloomberg announced that he would be replacing Klein with Cathleen Black, chair of the Hearst Corporation—who, like Klein, comes to the job with no previous experience in public education, but with a deep background in management and an abiding concern for effective organization.[44]

Whether Black will be able to fill Klein's shoes remains to be seen. But what is clear is that Bloomberg and Klein made a very good team and succeeded in moving the ball downfield during their time together. Most important, they eliminated seniority in hiring and transfers and introduced a new process that is more flexible, is more performance-based, and gives principals the authority to build their own teams at the school site. They also made progress in connecting teacher pay to improvements in student achievement, carrying out more rigorous evaluations of teachers, and getting bad teachers out of the classroom—efforts that are surely necessary if the district is to upgrade the quality of its teaching force and instill the right incentives. They managed to achieve these things against what is probably the most powerful teachers union in the country. Given the opposition, what they have done is remarkable.

Yet precisely because the union is so powerful, their achievements have been limited. Seniority continues to control decisions in other areas of schooling—in excessing, in layoffs, and in the ways teachers are assigned to grades, classes, and subject matter within their schools.[45] The pay-for-performance plan, based as it is on rewards that go to whole schools rather than exemplary individuals, makes only a weak connection between pay and performance. Teachers are being evaluated more seriously, but as of 2010 data on how much students are actually learning are not being put to use in these evaluations and are not part of the tenure decision (although state-level reforms adopted during Race to the Top will presumably change that—see chapter 10). And while the Absent Teacher Reserve is keeping more than a thousand unwanted teachers out of the classroom, it is still true that a sky-high 98.2 percent of all teachers get satisfactory evaluations and that virtually all junior teachers (93 percent for 2009) are granted tenure.[46]

Meantime, these partial victories have been gained at enormous financial expense. To the extent that the union has agreed to relax the rules—notably, in the 2005 contract changes—and to keep the peace (important to Bloomberg during election years), it has essentially been bought off. Teacher salaries have gone up an astounding 43 percent on Bloomberg's brief watch, and district spending has soared.[47] Sol Stern calls this boost in spending, which increased the education budget from $12.7 billion in 2003 to $21 billion in 2009, "probably the greatest increase by a school district in the history of American education."[48] This avalanche of spending is more than just a positive indication of how much the mayor cares about improving the public schools. It is what happens when a reformer is dedicated to change but, because change is being held hostage by a powerful adversary, he is forced to pay dearly for it. The logic is simple. Over the decades, the union has succeeded in getting restrictive work rules written into legal concrete, rules that make effective organization impossible. If the mayor—or anyone—wants to lift even some of these rules in order to create a more effective system, then the union will demand to be compensated for it. It will demand to be paid. This is the price of reform. And while the price is extraordinarily high at every step along the way, the steps themselves are small and don't really do the job.

As 2010 comes to a close, Bloomberg finds himself without Klein—a huge loss for the mayor, and for the school reform movement as a whole—and the New York City school district still has a long, long way to go before the tangle of union restrictions is truly cleared away and the schools can be organized in ways that best improve student achievement. Breathing over his shoulder, moreover, is a cold, hard truth: *he doesn't have forever to do this.* In 2009 Bloomberg's authority over the city schools came to an end, and he managed to get it renewed. He also managed to get the City Council to change its rules and let him run for a third term. Yet he won't be in office for much longer, and there is no guarantee whatever that mayoral control will remain in place either. Even if it does, the next mayor may not be—indeed, almost surely *will not be*—nearly as committed to challenging the union as Bloomberg has been. In fact, the next mayor could well be a union supporter—and the UFT will clearly try to use its electoral clout to make that happen. In any event, *the UFT will be around well after Bloomberg is gone.* Its interests will be the same. It will still be hugely powerful. And it will be in a position not only to resist further change, but to reverse the gains that Bloomberg and Klein have achieved. This is the sobering reality of "reform"— and the real meaning of power.[49]

Washington, D.C.

The nation's capital has long been known for having one of the worst, most incompetently run school systems in the country. Its problems aren't due to a lack of money. In fiscal 2009 its self-reported current spending was $17,542 per child, roughly 80 percent more than the average American school district is laying out. Other estimates suggest that, when the costs of school construction, other capital expenditures, and a vast array of other items outside the "current" budget are included, it actually spends in the neighborhood of $28,000 per student.[50] Yet in the 2007 National Assessment of Educational Progress (before the reforms we discuss here began), the District of Columbia came in dead last behind all fifty American states, with just 8 percent of its eighth graders proficient in math and 12 percent proficient in reading.[51] Only 43 percent of its ninth graders manage to graduate from high school within five years.[52] Parents have reacted by fleeing to charter schools—which in 2010 claimed a stunning 38 percent of all public school kids in the district—producing an enrollment free-fall within the traditional schools at the core of the system.[53] This is a district in crisis.

Recent mayors have stepped up to meet the challenge. Mayor Anthony Williams, elected in 1998 to bring fiscal responsibility to the District of Columbia's city government, aimed to take on the public school system as well. He tried to wrest control from the local school board in 2000, but won only a partial victory from the D.C. City Council, which authorized him to appoint just four of the nine board members—not a majority. He tried a second time to gain control in 2004, but the council refused.[54]

In 2007 Williams was succeeded by Adrian Fenty, who made reforming the school system his number one mission and got the council to give him control of the schools. In June of that year, he surprised everyone by appointing Michelle Rhee, a thirty-seven-year-old Korean American, as chancellor of the D.C. schools. Rhee had formerly served as chief executive of the New Teacher Project, known for its innovative approaches to teacher recruitment and for its eye-opening studies of seniority and other obstacles to effective organization. She had never run a school district before.[55]

What was Fenty thinking? He was thinking big, about what he called "wholesale changes" of the education system.[56] In Rhee he had found someone with vision, courage, boundless energy, and no attachments to the traditional structure. As befits her background, Rhee's focus was squarely on personnel. The key to rejuvenating the schools, she believed, was to get rid of low-performing employees and to attract new people who are talented, energetic, motivated, and eager to be part of a "culture of accountability" in which employees are expected to perform at high levels and are held to that standard.[57]

Rhee took immediate aim at tenure and seniority, the formal rules that had long protected even the worst-performing district employees from dismissal. She quickly proposed that more than 700 nonunion central office employees be shifted to "at will" contracts, allowing her to proceed with dismissal in cases of inadequate performance. She wanted the same authority to fire underperforming teachers. She announced plans to shut down twenty-three schools with declining enrollments and to overhaul another twenty-seven that had consistently failed to make "adequate yearly progress" under No Child Left Behind's accountability objectives—plans that would (and did) lead to the excessing of many veteran teachers. She signed an agreement with the union president that allowed her to circumvent seniority and bumping rights in reassigning them to new schools. She offered buyouts to as many as 700 teachers who were either near retirement or from the schools being closed or overhauled, attempting to get them off the employment rolls to make room for a new crop of talented recruits. And she was just getting going.[58]

The teachers union was not happy, but at least in the early going it did not launch an all-out attack on Rhee or her proposals. The fact that it didn't is clear evidence of the way competition (due to charters, in this case) can affect union incentives and strategy. George Parker, president of the Washington Teachers Union, was open to new approaches because he felt he had to be. "We have lost 1,500 members in ten years, all because of charter schools," he said. "Our very survival is dependent on having students remain in [traditional] public schools. If we don't get on the ball in terms of improving our schools, the charters will have the majority of our students."[59] It was in the best interests of the union, he believed, to support reforms that could bring back kids and jobs.

So Rhee was fortunate. She faced a teachers union that had been weakened over the years, and it was led by a president who—precisely for that reason—was open to change. Yet Parker continued to believe that the improvements should *not* come about through the dismissal of teachers. "You can't fire your way into a successful school system," he argued, and he continued to feel strongly about maintaining rule-based job protections.[60] Moreover, he faced serious opposition within his own ranks, from many teachers concerned about their jobs and from other union leaders who saw him as caving in to management. Parker was "leading" an organization in turmoil, and it wasn't clear how many followers he had.

Rhee, meantime, was relentless. In the summer of 2008, after a year of break-the-mold reforms and performance-based personnel shake-ups—which included the firing of 15 percent of the central office staff, twenty-four principals, twenty-two assistant principals, 500 teaching aides, and 250 teachers who failed to meet the requirements of No Child Left Behind, along with the buyouts of more than 200 other veteran teachers[61]—she upped the ante yet again. She proposed a revolutionary new labor contract. Veteran teachers would be given a choice between two compensation plans: a "green" plan that linked pay to performance and a "red" plan that did not. New teachers first entering the district would automatically be part of the green, performance-based plan—which would eventually become standard, therefore—and all teachers would lose their seniority transfer and bumping rights, giving Rhee and her principals much greater control over assignments.[62]

Under the red plan, veteran teachers would keep their tenure and get regular raises in pay based (as before) on their credentials and seniority. Under the green plan, teachers would get smaller guaranteed raises, but they would stand to make much more money if they performed well, with top performers able to move well beyond $100,000 in just a few years. To qualify for this track, they would be required to give up tenure for a year, go on probation, and either gain a permanent position by getting the recommendation of their principals (all of whom served at Rhee's discretion) or be dismissed. New hires would be on probation for four years, instead of the traditional two, before being considered for tenure.

The idea was not just to weed out the incompetents, because most of the low-performing teachers would presumably seek safe haven by choosing the red plan. The idea, rather, was to build a new personnel system around performance: rewarding good teachers for their success, creating strong incentives to promote student achievement, and—just as important—attracting a new breed of teachers who are confident in their own talent and *want* to be evaluated on that basis. Rhee's purpose was to bring about a total transformation of the District of Columbia teacher corps and through it to transform the quality of its schools.

Under the collective bargaining law, however, Rhee's path-breaker could only become reality if the contract were ratified by a vote of union members. Knowing this from the outset, she was essentially offering all existing teachers a trade-off they might find attractive and giving them choice. Teachers who were more risk averse could opt to protect their jobs and still receive a big raise in pay by simply choosing the red plan. Teachers who were more confident in their own performance could opt for the green plan and willingly accept certain risks in return for potentially huge economic gains and opportunities. There was something for both types.

The key to making this trade-off attractive was money, lots of it—millions of dollars in extra cash that, from the very beginning of her term, Rhee had been busily raising from outside foundations, which saw the District of Columbia as a model for spurring major change throughout the nation. In a crude sense, the teachers were simply being bought off: if they gave up formal protections and granted Rhee more discretion, they would be rewarded with much higher salaries. In the old days, collective bargaining used to work the other way around: districts couldn't afford big pay raises, so they gave teachers formal protections instead of money. Now the shoe was on the other foot. The district wanted the protections relaxed, but it had to pay if the teachers were to go along. This was an expensive proposition, and it was unclear where the funding would come from if the foundation money were eventually to dry up. But first things first: Rhee's goal was to make the revolution happen.[63]

That was not George Parker's goal. He was sitting atop a volcano. Although the internal battle lines formed a generational divide, with younger teachers apparently more open to performance-based pay and older teachers more resistant to change and risk, a union survey showed that teachers overall opposed it by three to one.[64] The union's vice president, Nathan Saunders, called the plan "a tremendous step backwards for teachers as dignified professionals," denounced it as "the purchase of valuable rights for cash," and portrayed Parker as a sell-out.[65] Yet Parker himself was hardly rushing into anything, emphasizing that the new plan lacked "adequate due process protections"—an opaque way of saying that too many teachers could be dismissed for poor performance. He refused to take the proposed contract to his membership for a vote. Nothing was happening.

This refusal was a potent strategy. Rhee needed the union's consent to put the new contract in place, and by doing nothing Parker was preventing change and raising the specter that she could ultimately fail as a reform chancellor. Parker could not stall forever, because his members would be denied any raises at all until some sort of new contract was ultimately signed. But in the meantime he was putting enormous pressure on Rhee and signaling that he was quite willing to use his veto if she didn't pay more attention to union concerns.

Rhee could have reacted to this blocking strategy by watering down her reforms, as Parker wanted. Instead she came out swinging, announcing in September 2008 that she was moving to "plan B." Negotiations over the two-tier pay plan would continue, but as they did she intended to use authority already on the books that, via procedures so cumbersome they had rarely been used, allowed her to partner with principals in evaluating targeted teachers under ninety-day improvement plans and dismissing them if their performance was determined inadequate. She also said the district would be moving forward with a new teacher licensing procedure in which teachers would be required to get an "advanced teaching credential" in order to keep their license—and to get that credential, they would need to demonstrate effectiveness in the classroom. The upshot was that low-performing teachers could be denied credentials and thus dismissed. [66]

Shortly thereafter, Rhee appeared on the cover of *Time* magazine—posing (now famously) with a broom, symbolic of her efforts to sweep out the old, inefficient ways of American schooling. Inside was a long, very favorable story on her fight against the union to bring change to the abysmal D.C. school system. [67] She had become, by any account, the human face of American school reform.

The union was not cowed by her growing fame and popularity. It simply hunkered down and continued to do its job—receiving reinforcements now from the national AFT, which joined the struggle on all fronts and could offer reserves of money and legal talent dwarfing those of the struggling local. Parker, backed (and monitored) by the AFT, indicated that any teachers targeted for dismissal by Rhee under her new strategy would receive all necessary support, and that the union would "legally challenge any such process that is unfair to our members,"[68] threatening the same sort of bureaucratic nightmare that had prevented dismissals in the past. He also worked jointly with the AFT to formulate a contract counterproposal: one that put the emphasis on greater job protections and on training low-performing teachers rather than dismissing them. Rhee wasn't just up against George Parker anymore. She was up against Randi Weingarten, who controlled enormous resources and was thinking about the national implications. And what Weingarten did *not* want was a precedent-setting victory by Rhee that might put unions on the defensive everywhere in the country. As the *Washington Post* noted at the time,

> If Rhee succeeds in ending tenure and seniority as we know them while introducing merit pay into one of the country's most expensive and underperforming school systems, it would be a watershed event in U.S. labor history . . . It would trigger a national debate on why public employees continue to enjoy what amounts to ironclad job security without accountability while the taxpayers who fund their salaries have long since been forced to accept the realities of a performance-based global economy.[69]

Months passed without a breakthrough. But Rhee kept moving ahead, using what flexibility she had to advance her goals. In the spring of 2009, she announced that she would end-run the union by developing a new evaluation system to assess teacher performance (a system that, when subsequently implemented for the 2009–10 school year under the acronym IMPACT, was partly based on student test scores and involved five evaluations a year for each teacher).[70] During the 2008–09 school year, she and her principals put roughly 150 teachers on probationary ninety-day plans and dismissed eighty of them. During the fall of 2009, she dismissed another 266 teachers (along with more than 100 support staff), citing a looming budget deficit that allowed her to engage in a reduction in force.[71] The mass firings quickly led to a union lawsuit demanding a preliminary injunction and reinstatement of the teachers, but it was turned down by the court.[72] More lawsuits followed.

The months continued to pass. As 2009 gave way—agonizingly—to 2010, pressures for some sort of solution mounted. Teachers hadn't received a pay raise for almost three years. Parker was facing a May reelection challenge from his (and Rhee's) arch enemy Nathan Saunders; and coming up empty handed for his members—no contract, no pay raise—was hardly the basis for a winning campaign. Mayor Adrian Fenty was looking toward his own reelection campaign in September against political rival Vincent Gray, a city councilman and critic of reform supported by the unions; and Fenty too needed results.[73]

The breakthrough came in early April, and it was a huge victory for Michelle Rhee.[74] Although Weingarten sought to portray the "agreement" as yet another indication of her own support for reform—a ploy that worked well in the media and among many in education circles—the fact is that she had resisted Rhee's revolutionary proposals and, while managing to soften them about the edges, ultimately failed to stop them. They had engaged in battle, and Rhee had simply won.[75] After the dust cleared, Weingarten did her best to argue that, much as she supported reform in D.C., her union had actually gained important concessions and protections from Rhee, while the latter had gained few new powers in return: face-saving claims that were completely unfounded. She went on to say that the contract was a reflection of the district's own uniqueness and peculiarities and should not be regarded as a model or precedent for other districts. Quite a balancing act.[76]

Rhee succeeded in getting a new pay-for-performance system. Compensation would be based on a two-track system: one a traditional track in which pay would be based on seniority and credentials, the other a performance track in which teachers could earn up to $20,000 in bonuses for promoting student learning. This win, of course, was huge. She also succeeded in purging the contract of seniority and bumping rights. When teachers want to transfer from one school to another, there must be "mutual consent" between the teacher and the principal—which means that principals can choose their teachers on performance grounds and need not take the most senior candidate. When teachers are excessed due to closures or downsizing, decisions about which teachers lose their jobs are also to be made on performance grounds, not seniority. And if excessed teachers are unable to find another school willing to take them, they are to be ushered out of the system (through, for example, early retirement or a buyout). Finally, when there are layoffs, decisions about who gets laid off are to be made in the same way that excessing decisions are made: on the basis of performance, not seniority. Clearly, getting rid of seniority was another huge win.

Rhee didn't get exactly the contract she wanted. No teachers would have to give up tenure. And the performance track would be entirely voluntary, even for new teachers, which means that performance pay would not automatically become the norm over time as older teachers leave and new teachers arrive. Indeed, the union could well use its muscle with members to try to see that it doesn't and that the single salary schedule remains dominant.

Even so, there was yet another major victory lurking in the contract that attracted little media attention, but actually gave Rhee enormous new leverage in controlling teacher quality and removing bad teachers from the payroll— regardless of which pay track they happened to choose. This one had to do with provisions stipulating that teachers who are rated "ineffective" for one year or "minimally effective" for two can be dismissed even if they are tenured. And here is the kicker: the criteria for determining these ratings are *not* subject to negotiation with the union and are entirely within the district's discretion. The district now has ample tools for removing bad teachers. Another huge win.[77]

These victories were not free, of course. They were part of a gigantic trade-off, in which the union agreed to make big concessions on work rules in return for huge new district expenditures that would ultimately wind up in teachers' pockets. Rhee wanted new, more favorable work rules; but if she wanted them, she would have to spend big bucks to get them. And she did. The cost of the new contract was estimated at $140 million. Teachers would get an across-the-board 21.6 percent raise over five years, but the raises would be retroactive to 2007, which meant that a big chunk of money would be handed out to teachers almost immediately. The district also agreed to make "significant increases" in teacher benefit programs, such as vision, dental, and legal services.[78] And the pay-for-performance plan, of course, called for millions of dollars in additional spending to fund its substantial pay bonuses. Add it all up and the amount of money being shoveled at teachers was enormous—at a time of national economic scarcity when most districts were suffering major budget problems, cutting back on staff, holding the line on salaries, and pushing more of the costs of health plans onto teachers themselves.[79]

It is unclear, at the end of the day, if the district can actually afford this contract. Rhee was counting on some $65 million in foundation grants to help finance it, and these amounts cannot be guaranteed in future years—indeed, some of the grantors made their money contingent on Rhee staying in office. So the contract may well be beyond the financial capacity of the district itself.[80]

But even though the story of Rhee's new contract remains unfinished, there are important lessons to be learned from her Herculean efforts to transform the Washington, D.C., school district.

Looking back, there can be no doubt that Washington was an ideal setting for radical reform. Academic performance was abysmal, charter schools were attracting huge numbers of kids, the local union was relatively weak, the mayor was firmly committed to transforming the system, and he appointed a chancellor who was dedicated to reform and entirely unafraid of taking on the union. There can also be no doubt that Rhee succeeded in bringing about major change. She took this moribund district by storm: putting the focus on children rather than jobs and seniority, closing down failing schools, dismissing hundreds of low-performing teachers and central office employees, instituting serious teacher evaluations, and winning a contract that takes bold new steps toward a more effective organization of the district's schools. These are stunning achievements, and they show what can happen when the stars line up just right.

But much as Michelle Rhee and Adrian Fenty deserve accolades for what they accomplished, their saga is also sobering in the extreme—and this is part of the lesson we need to learn as well. To begin with, Rhee spent *nearly three years* bashing her head against a wall of union power, and for what? To bring about changes that are simply *common sense* and *should never have been needed in the first place.* They were needed because, over the decades, the teachers unions in D.C. and elsewhere have used their power to impose a labyrinth of onerous work rules that prevent the schools from being effectively organized, and because, when anyone has tried to change those rules to benefit children, the unions have fought to prevent commonsense reform, giving ground on only some issues and only when they have to. Yes, Rhee made real progress—after three years of continual struggle, under the best possible political circumstances—in moving a dysfunctional system toward a more rational organization. But dysfunctional organization is still the norm throughout the nation, and it is still well protected by union power. The glass may now be half full, but it is also half empty, and children are not getting what they need.

Oh, there's one other thing. This perfect lineup of the political stars was critically dependent on Adrian Fenty (or someone just like him) being mayor of Washington, D.C., and in September 2010 he lost the Democratic primary to Vincent Gray. So for the next four years and possibly longer, Vincent Gray—a critic of Rhee and an ally of the teachers unions—will be Washington's mayor. He will be in charge of the schools. He will be in charge of its new labor contract. The AFT, led by Randi Weingarten, spent $1 million on Gray's behalf to see Fenty defeated. It was joined in the campaign by the AFL-CIO and AFSCME, two other union behemoths that wanted Fenty—and more important, Rhee—out. They got what they wanted. Within a month, Michelle Rhee announced her resignation.[81] (To complete the sweep, union leader George Parker was thrown out of office by his members shortly thereafter, defeated by Nathan Sanders—a staunch opponent of the contract who thought Parker had betrayed the District's teachers.[82])

The election was a disaster for the reform movement. It was also a warning shot by the teachers unions to remind mayors everywhere that their heads are on the line if they think path-breaking reform is a good idea. The Fenty-Rhee years were exciting while they lasted, and they surely served as an instructive model for the nation. But given the logic of electoral politics, it was always in the cards that Fenty and Rhee would eventually be gone—and that the union would remain.[83]

Conclusion

The teachers unions are playing a lot of defense these days. Among people in the public arena who follow education closely—journalists, policymakers, think tank types—their popularity has sunk to an all-time low. New York City and Washington, D.C., are more than just districts whose leaders have aggressively taken on the unions. They are districts whose leaders have become *famous* and *widely admired* for taking them on.

Read the education coverage of some of the nation's major publications: *Time*, *Newsweek*, the *Washington Post*, and many more.[84] Or watch the kinds of high-profile television shows on education reform that are shown regularly on national television: specials by John Stossel, for example, on NBC's *Dateline*, or by John Merrow for PBS's *Jim Lehrer News Hour*. The themes (when they touch on labor issues) are almost always the same: the reformers in these cities are fighting valiantly to clear away contract restrictions that are archaic, unreasonable, and debilitating to effective organization, and the unions are using their power to stand in the way. Among the nation's opinion leaders, the teachers unions are not faring well.

But does it really matter? The brute fact is that the teachers unions are powerful. And whether they are popular or not among people in the know, they can still use their power to resist change, protect jobs, and maintain labor contracts that make a joke of effective organization. There has been no stampede at the district level to make collective bargaining contracts less restrictive over the last ten years. As we will see in chapter 10, Race to the Top has generated new policies (for now) at the *state* level that could, in some states, lead to changes in local labor contracts down the road. It is also true, as the next chapter shows, that some districts—among them, Denver, New Haven, Memphis, Pittsburgh—have recently made noteworthy changes on their own, especially in moving toward performance-based systems of teacher evaluation and pay.

These are very new developments, and they are not the norm. In general, the local picture for the last decade has been one of *stability*, not innovation and change. This has been so, moreover, despite all the pressures—from accountability and charter schools—for districts to be more aggressive in pressuring their unions for major changes in their labor contracts. The lesson to be drawn, it would seem, is simple but grim: this is what happens when the defenders *really are* powerful and have a vested interest in maintaining the status quo. The districts may well know what they need to do to create more effective organizations. But they are often controlled by school boards that are under the sway of the unions. And even if they aren't, they know what they are up against, and they are unlikely to want to tilt at windmills.

Yet there is more to it than that, as New York City and Washington, D.C., bear witness. In those cities, the stars lined up to provide a best-case scenario for real reform: with mayors and school chancellors totally committed to change, unafraid of challenging their unions, and willing to do whatever was necessary in pursuit of effective organization. These districts marshaled their own power to get results and were simply not going to take no for an answer. So what happened?

Well, that depends on how you look at it. Michelle Rhee and Joel Klein became rock stars because, unlike almost all other superintendents in the country, they were courageous enough to launch all-out assaults on restrictive work rules, and they won important victories on seniority, performance pay, and teacher evaluations. In the normal context of American public education, a context of restrictive union contracts and formidable union power, these victories are remarkable. And that is why Rhee and Klein (and Bloomberg and Fenty) have received so much media attention. They pushed the envelope and showed the rest of the nation what is possible when a district is truly committed to effective organization and student achievement. For what they've done and accomplished, they are models for other district leaders. And their cities are models of reform.

But we shouldn't get carried away here. The baseline was defined by organizations so heavily burdened by nonsensical rules that they were not even remotely well suited for the effective education of children. Because district leaders were fighting against powerful unions, the best they could do was to chip away at these massive, special interest structures to create organizations more capable of providing quality education. Their victories were indeed remarkable under the circumstances—circumstances of powerful resistance and grossly bad starting points. But they were victories that took many agonizing years of perpetual struggle to achieve. They were also incredibly expensive, because "reform" is really a process in which the unions hold a near veto and only agree to make work rule changes if they receive enormous financial payments for doing it. And even after all this, they left the districts a very long way from effective organization—still burdened by tenure, the single salary schedule, and countless rules having to do with faculty meetings, prep time, class size, time off, and other basic aspects of schooling.

Sol Stern had it right. These reforms were "small victories for sanity." They were small because they could not fully jettison the accumulated weight of their organizational past, which remains debilitating. And they struck a blow for sanity because they were establishing organizational practices that are simply common sense and that should have been in place a long time ago if the system were actually run to benefit children and deliver quality education. In this respect, the new victories were remarkable *because they simply did what makes sense*. The stunning thing about modern times is that everyone is now cheering about this, seeing it as a radical new development. Doing what makes sense has become a revolutionary act.

Is this exciting or is it pathetic? We probably ought to see it as both. In any event, we also need to recognize that the exciting part is under constant threat. Remember, the key players here—Bloomberg and Klein, Fenty and Rhee—have won their victories precisely because they and their situations are so unusual. But their situations are not long for this world. Fenty and Rhee are already gone— and in Washington, D.C., there is a real danger that the fox is now in charge of the chicken coop. The District of Columbia's revolutionary labor contract will only be revolutionary in practice if the discretion embedded within it is purposely used in revolutionary ways; and there is no indication at this point that Vincent Gray and his union allies intend for that to happen. In New York City, Klein has stepped down after fighting the good fight for eight years. Bloomberg is still in place and pressing hard for effective organization, but his days are numbered by the electoral clock, and he will eventually be replaced. When he is, there may well be a head-spinning "regression toward the mean" in which the mayor who takes his place is much closer to the norm: less committed to radical reform, less willing to take on the union, more concerned with getting along and going along. The union, meantime, will remain. It will be the same, and it will use its still-considerable political power to try to regain the ground it has lost— and return the district to normal.

New York City and Washington, D.C., are the best-case scenarios. In almost all other districts around the country, things *are* normal. District leaders have their hands bound by work rules that make no sense. Effective organization is an impossible dream. And the status quo, however poor its performance, is well protected.

8

Reform Unionism

It is fair to say that many who are directly involved in school reform—elected and appointed policymakers, think tank experts, leaders of foundations, advocates for the disadvantaged, opinion leaders, and commentators from major news outlets—recognize that the teachers unions are standing in the way of effective schools. But recognizing the problem is one thing. Doing something about it is quite another. What do they think can be done?

That's the rub. Many of these same movers and shakers also see the unions as legitimate "stakeholders" in the system. They believe that teachers need representation, that unions in general are a good thing, and that, at any rate, the teachers unions are permanent fixtures in the institutional makeup of American education. If the nation's schools are to be successfully reformed, so the conventional wisdom goes, the key to progress is not to try to do away with the unions or even to diminish their power, but rather to encourage what is sometimes called "reform unionism"—a new, more enlightened approach in which the teachers unions would get genuinely involved in the reform movement itself and voluntarily begin doing what is best for children and effective schools. Productive collaboration would become the new order.

To skeptics, this may sound like a joke. It isn't. The ideas behind reform unionism are widely embraced and influential. This is clearly true among Democrats and liberals, whose ideologies, values, and political commitments have long bound them to unionism in general, and who can't bring themselves to believe that perhaps American education would be better off without unions, or that the teachers unions should be rendered far less powerful—notions that smack of a dreaded "antiunionism" of which they want no part. A belief in reform unionism allows them to have their cake and eat it too: the nation *can* have powerful unions as long as the unions can be persuaded to do *good* things with their power.

Similar ideas appeal to many pragmatists: people who are not ideologically wedded to unionism, but who recognize that the unions are too powerful to be done away with and thus need to be dealt with. For the pragmatists, reform unionism is the only port in the storm. America's schools can't be reformed in the face of major union opposition, and the unions aren't going to disappear, so they need to be brought on board. Reform unionism provides a way for this to happen.

As a prescription for change, reform unionism has become a staple of mainstream thinking on education reform. It is also a card that union leaders—especially leaders within the AFT, which portrays itself as pro-reform—have repeatedly played over the years to burnish their public image and deflect criticism.

For these reasons, I devote this chapter to reform unionism. Its ideas are completely wrong-headed, but anyone who seeks to understand the role of unions in American education—and how reformers think about, and try to come to grips with, union power—needs to recognize the key ideas that have gained currency over time. And these, unfortunately, are very influential ideas indeed.

What Is Reform Unionism?

Over the years, much ink has been spilled on the topic of reform unionism (although it is not always called that), and many speeches given. The basic notion is that, while the teachers unions have long followed the industrial model of blue-collar unionism, with its bread-and-butter focus on material benefits, contract rules, and conflict with management, this model is inappropriate for teachers and public education. A well-functioning education system—built around the professionalism of its teachers, organized for effectiveness, and capable of preparing children for the demands of the twenty-first century—calls for a *new* brand of unionism. Under the new model, the teachers unions would make students their top priority. They would take a cooperative approach to the governance of schools. They would swear off onerous work rules that get in the way of effective organization. They would actively promote teacher quality and stop protecting bad teachers. They would support productive reforms rather than blocking them.[1]

The obvious question that arises is, *why would the unions ever agree to this*? The answer, so the thinking goes, is that they will voluntarily move toward the new model if—through a process of enlightenment—they can arrive at a new understanding of their own best interests. How this process of enlightenment is supposed to happen is rather mysterious, but the basic notion is that, if union leaders are properly tuned in to modern reality, they will begin to see their own interests in a different light. And to be properly tuned in, they need to recognize two fundamental aspects of the educational world.

First, they need to recognize that teachers are not factory workers, but *professionals* who value knowledge, seek to perform at the highest levels, demand excellence from their colleagues, and aspire to promote the well being of their clients (students). What teachers want and need are unions that act on these professional concerns and give much less centrality to the narrow goals of wages, benefits, and working conditions.

Second, union leaders need to recognize that it is in their own interest to improve the public schools and to put children first. In the extreme: if the schools don't improve, reformers may seek out radical options—like private school vouchers—and the entire public school enterprise may go down in flames. If the system goes down, the unions will go down with it. More generally, if the unions are regarded as self-interested and obstructionist, they will be doomed to watch from the outside as other players make the key decisions about schools. They are best off dropping their adversarial approach, supporting reforms that are good for schools and kids, and being welcomed into the governance process, where they could have more influence on reform than they could as outsiders. The same rationale applies to collective bargaining. They need to stop thinking of administrators as the enemy and instead pursue collaboration in school governance as trusted contributors. This approach too will actually yield them more influence, and it will be good for kids and schools.

The prevailing idea, then, is that the problem of union power can eventually be solved through enlightened thinking about the realities of modern-day education—and voluntary adaptation to it. The unions will remain powerful, on this account, but they will no longer *use* their power simply to promote the job security and work-related interests of their members. With enlightenment, they will use it to promote student achievement, teacher professionalism, effective schooling, and the best interests of kids generally. The problem of union power will go away.

Many smart, well-intentioned people buy into the logic of reform unionism. It has attracted major funding grants (for example, to the Teachers Union Reform Network, which I discuss later) from prominent supporters of educational change, among them the Broad Foundation, the MacArthur Foundation, and the Pew Charitable Trusts.[2] It has been written about glowingly in influential books.[3] It has attracted copious headlines and continuing journalistic attention. And it prompts otherwise sophisticated reformers to hang on every word that union leaders utter in their public pronouncements on issues of the day, looking for signs that maybe—just maybe—enlightened unionism is about to take hold, and the unions are going to jump on board the reform train and make children their top priority.[4]

From the standpoint of American education reform, this kind of thinking gets in the way of progress—because it is fanciful and misguided and prompts reformers to look for solutions where they don't exist. Reform unionism is not rooted in a genuine understanding of union leadership and organization. Nor is it rooted in a genuine understanding of teachers and what they want and expect from their unions. There is simply no compelling intellectual basis for it.

Its fatal flaw is that it assumes union leaders can be persuaded to ignore, or give short shrift to, the bedrock occupational interests on which their organizations are based—notably, teachers' most primal concerns for job security, wages, benefits, and rights and prerogatives in the workplace—and leaders are never going to do that. This is worth repeating: *union leaders are never going to do that.* If they did, they wouldn't be leaders very long. This is true even if they believe that, over the long haul, their obstruction of reform could lead to pressure for more radical change in the system. Their incentives are heavily front-loaded and short term: their members want them to bring home the bacon right away, and that's what leaders try to do.[5]

Proponents might find it inspiring to wax eloquent about teachers as "united mind workers" and about the lofty professional values that teachers presumably care most about.[6] But these are flights of wishful thinking. The brute fact is that teachers are wildly supportive of their local unions precisely because their bread-and-butter interests as employees are being forcefully represented.

The one thing that reform unionism gets right is that union leaders are wise to be pragmatic in their approach to reform. When power is ranged against them on an issue, they may well have incentives to "support" reform, to compromise, and to give greater weight—in that instance, at that time—to what is best for kids. More generally, leaders may follow a collaborationist strategy of influence, accepting decisionmaking arrangements (like joint governance of schools) that allow them to play roles as insiders rather than belligerent outsiders. But pragmatism does not mean that the unions are somehow in the business of representing children. They are still in the business of representing the job-related interests of teachers. They are just doing it *differently,* and in the most potent ways they can under the circumstances.

When union leaders are pressed to compromise, for example, and there is a trade-off between what is good for teachers and what is good for kids—as is often true, for example, with seniority rights, teacher tenure, teacher evaluations, leave time, and many other work issues—the unions will try to strike compromises that are as close to the teacher end of the continuum as possible. Similarly, when they engage in collaborative arrangements that allow them to participate as insiders, the whole point of their participation is to use their insider status to promote the job-related interests of teachers. They may do it in a more collaborative way. But when faced with trade-offs between the interests of teachers and the interests of kids, they will still side with teachers. That is their business. Everything else is just a strategy for being good at it.

Teachers unions are special interest groups. Given the pressures of modern-day politics and collective bargaining, their leaders often have strong incentives to *say* they are reformers and to *say* they are interested in what is best for kids. This is the public relations side of their jobs, and it has little bearing on what they actually *do* when real decisions of consequence are being made. What they *do* is represent the special interests of their members. And that is something you can count on.

Al Shanker: The Icon of Reform Unionism

The history of reform unionism has largely been a history of words, not deeds. Its most visible proponent in years past was Al Shanker, the longtime president of the AFT (1974–97), who was surely the most revered of all teachers union leaders during his reign and whose exalted status in education circles has only grown since his death in 1997.

Shanker began his rise to fame as the firebrand leader of New York City's United Federation of Teachers (UFT), where he was known during the 1960s for relentlessly pushing the occupational interests of his members (and among other things, being jailed twice for leading illegal strikes). As his power and visibility grew over the years and as the teachers unions increasingly came under criticism, Shanker began talking the talk of reform unionism and positioning himself as a national statesman. In a regular column in the *New York Times* and in countless speeches and interviews, he lamented the inadequate performance of the public schools and outlined his public-spirited visions about the need for teacher professionalism, national standards, accountability, innovative arrangements for differential pay, school choice, getting bad teachers out of the classroom, giving priority to the needs of children, and other innovative breaks from the past. He also argued that it was in the unions' own best interests to improve student achievement, and thus to demonstrate through high performance that the public system deserved to win out over privatized alternatives (vouchers). "It doesn't do you much good being a strong man on a sinking ship," he soberly observed.[7]

The rhetoric of reform unionism made Shanker a statesman in the public eye, something he clearly wanted. But the rhetoric was not accompanied by serious, effective action. When the chips were down and his members' self-interests were at stake—and in the gritty reality of collective bargaining and education politics, they always were—Shanker *behaved* as a traditional union president would. In no meaningful sense did he transform the AFT into a fundamentally different kind of union. Under his leadership, its state affiliates throughout the country continued (with rare exceptions) to oppose school choice, to resist serious accountability, to oppose pay for performance, to protect bad teachers from dismissal, and in general to obstruct fundamental reform of the education system. At the local level, in major urban areas like Detroit, Philadelphia, Washington, D.C., and New York City, AFT unions used their power to win highly restrictive labor contracts, filled with seniority rights and every other protective, self-interested provision imaginable, that burdened schools and districts so heavily that effective organization was an impossible dream. Shanker's soaring rhetoric had almost nothing to do with how the AFT's state and local organizations were actually using their power.[8]

Consider a simple but obvious question: why did Michelle Rhee even *need* to take on the Washington Teachers Union and the local labor contract in her efforts to turn around that city's deplorable schools? The answer is that the union had used its power over the years—*years when Shanker was in charge of the AFT*—to bury the D.C. schools in an avalanche of restrictive work rules that made effective organization impossible. Shanker was president of the AFT for more than twenty years, yet he did nothing to stop the organizational mess that was being created in Washington. The same thing was happening all over the country, in one AFT city after another. His AFT locals continued to do what they had always done: they behaved like bread-and-butter unions and did everything they could to protect and promote the job-related interests of their members. All the while, Shanker was regarded as a visionary.

This is not to say that Shanker was being disingenuous in arguing for reform and endorsing innovative ideas. He may well have been stating his honest personal views. What counts with all leaders, however, is not what they say as human beings but what they actually *do* in their institutional roles. And in the case of union leaders in particular, there are strong incentives—if they want to stay union leaders and maintain their internal popularity and influence—to pay close attention to the bread-and-butter interests of their members and represent those interests faithfully and forcefully. These are the built-in constraints of the job: the constraints that determine their behavior. As human beings, they may care deeply about kids, want the best for the public schools, and see the benefits of school choice, school accountability, and other reforms. Talking publicly about these beliefs, moreover, is likely to bring them attention and accolades in policymaking circles, enhance their reputations, and give their unions a more positive image. Seriously acting on these beliefs to push for true organizational reform, however, would quickly bring them into conflict with the occupational interests of their members and put their leadership at risk. The deck is stacked in favor of all talk and little action.

Today, more than a decade after his death, Shanker is treated as an icon, as the essence of what a progressive, forward-looking union leader should be. But the brute fact is that the AFT was a bread-and-butter union when he took over the presidency in 1974, and it was a bread-and-butter union when he died in 1997. Were the state affiliates somehow enlightened in their approach to reform? No. Were the local AFT unions creating enlightened, flexible, organizationally sensible contracts? No. At bottom, in terms of its basic interests and how it used its power, the AFT was the same union at the end of his reign as it was at the beginning. Shanker talked a good game, but he did *not* transform the AFT into a "reform union" that somehow made children and effective schools its top priority. Its top priority has always been to protect jobs—and more than ten years after his death, it still is.

Bob Chase and the New Unionism

Shanker was one of a kind. But many other union leaders have embraced the ideas of reform unionism over the years, and they have done much to give these ideas continuing currency, publicity, and influence among those who closely follow public education. Two developments are of special significance.

The first is a much-celebrated speech given by NEA president Bob Chase at the National Press Club in Washington, D.C., in 1997.[9] In part, the speech was a surprising mea culpa, in which Chase uttered words that rarely cross a union leader's lips, at least in public. Among other things, he acknowledged, "In some instances, we have used our power to block uncomfortable changes, to protect the narrow interests of our members, and not to advance the interests of students and schools." He also said, "There are indeed some bad teachers in America's schools. And it is our job to improve those teachers or—that failing—to get them out of the classroom." Admitting to the errors of the past, he declared his support for a new unionism (a label he coined) and his intention to lead a "reinvention" of the NEA around new principles that would embrace professionalism and collaboration and put "issues of school quality front and center at the bargaining table" as top union priorities. If the union didn't begin taking the lead in pushing for better schools, he warned, its own survival would be at stake: for with voucher proponents pushing to give kids alternatives in the private sector, "We must revitalize the public schools from within or they will be dismantled from without."

Chase's embrace of the new unionism was a media bombshell, and was fully intended to be. It came just three weeks after the NEA board of directors was presented with a report from the Kamber Group, a public relations firm "with strong ties to organized labor and the Democratic Party" hired to study the organization's external relations.[10] Titled "An Institution at Risk," the report argued that the NEA was deeply distrusted as a self-interested, obstructionist force in public education and that it needed to "shift to a crisis mode of operation" aimed at building a new, reform-friendly reputation. How could it do that?[11]

The campaign should be launched in a speech by President Chase in which he acknowledges the crisis, says some things for their shock value to open up the audience's minds (e.g., there are bad teachers and our job is to make them good or show the way to another career), and then details the Association's substantive programs to improve public schools . . . It should be supplemented by a full-court press blitz, television advertising, and a host of other outreach efforts.

It is difficult to avoid the conclusion that Chase's words, and the "reinvention" of the NEA that they called for, were little more than a self-interested strategy designed by a public relations firm. Still, Chase—like Shanker before him—may well have believed much of what he said, for he did continue to sing a reformist tune, if in much-moderated form, for the rest of his term in office (which ended in 2002).[12]

Whatever the truth may be, two basic facts are clear. The first is that he received considerable blowback from leaders and activists at the lower levels of his organization—the very people he was supposed to be leading. Officers from Milwaukee, Madison, Racine, and Green Bay, for example, accused him of "capitulation to the agenda of the enemies of public education."[13] Activists from Los Angeles lampooned him for being "naïve," saying, "The most successful means of improving the schools is precisely through massive, militant pressure on school boards and the district bureaucracy, not reliance on a 'collaborative, non-adversarial process.'"[14]

The second basic fact is that, during the years when Chase was president, no reinvention of the NEA actually took place, and nothing of the sort has occurred in the years since. It was Shanker and the AFT all over again: the NEA was a traditional, bread-and-butter union in 1997 when Chase gave his big speech, and it remains a traditional, bread-and-butter union today. Thus, whether Chase was really serious about his reform agenda or not, the agenda itself has been a monumental failure. His successors to the NEA presidency, Reg Weaver and Dennis Van Roekel, have essentially dropped it. Their agendas have been as traditional as they could be.

The Teachers Union Reform Network

Chase's exploits received plenty of attention over a period of years. But another development, probably of greater long-term importance in bringing credence to the notion of reform unionism, began a bit earlier and received far less attention at the time from the media and the public. This was the founding in 1995 of the Teachers Union Reform Network (TURN), which brought together the representatives of twenty-one "progressive" unions for ongoing discussions about how to reform the larger movement and remake the role of unions. The guiding spirit behind TURN was Adam Urbanski, president of the Rochester Teachers Association, and he remains at its helm today some fifteen years later.[15]

Although the "new unionism" of the NEA borders on farce, the TURN movement does not. Its members genuinely see themselves as reformers dedicated to changing the teachers unions from the inside. Some of them, in their own ways, have taken concrete steps within their local districts to make reform a reality. But the operative phrase here is "in their own ways." The reforms they have pursued may look progressive to them, as clear departures from union tradition. But the fact is, the fundamentals of bread-and-butter unionism have been left entirely intact, and little has really changed. To see why, let's take a brief look at three prominent reforms that (some) TURN unions have pursued in their break from tradition: peer review, differential pay, and cooperative governance.

Peer Review

Peer review is an evaluation system in which teachers are relied upon to assess other teachers. The idea is that, as professionals, teachers are especially knowledgeable about what constitutes good teaching, desirous of having high-quality colleagues, capable of coaching and training those who have problems, and insistent on weeding out the ones who (after receiving coaching and training) aren't able to make the grade.

Teacher input is surely valuable. As I discussed in chapter 6, teachers know more about teaching than anyone else. Teachers who are good at their jobs and have considerable experience at it are well equipped to be perceptive judges of competence—and its absence—in others, and they can provide expert guidance in helping to train and upgrade the skills of colleagues who need to improve. They are the experts, and building an evaluation system around their regular input and involvement makes eminently good sense—all else equal.

The caveat is that, in practice, peer review is *not* just about expertise and information. Teachers are members of unions, unions are powerful, and—because peer review involves members judging members, and because it directly affects the job security of those being judged—the unions will inevitably be centrally involved in making sure that these systems work in ways compatible with their interests. What sounds like a great idea—and in concept *is* a good idea, in the realm of expertise and information—may not work out so smoothly in the real world of unionized school districts, and indeed may even add to union control over personnel and undermine the effective management of schools.[16]

Toledo is the pioneer in peer review, having begun its program in 1981, and it has long been the national model touted by union progressives. There are also peer review programs in some twenty to sixty other districts—no good count is available—including Cincinnati, Columbus, and Rochester. The AFT has endorsed peer review since 1984. The NEA opposed it until Chase launched the "new unionism" and then came around. But as we'll see, what the nationals say is not necessarily what the locals do. Or believe.[17]

In embracing peer review, TURN unions say that they are acting to ensure that teachers are seriously evaluated, given opportunities to improve, and dismissed if they can't—and thus that the unions are acting on the side of reform, in the best interests of kids. They say that the districts using it have weeded out more beginning teachers on grounds of low performance, increased the retention rate of young teachers who are good performers, and dismissed more poorly performing tenured teachers by comparison to the previous, administrator-controlled evaluation systems. But the data for these claims are fairly thin and mostly provided by the districts themselves or by program proponents.[18] Peer review systems have not been subjected to rigorous quantitative study by independent researchers, with attention to teacher quality, dismissal rates, and student outcomes.[19]

It is worth noting, though, that in "The Widget Effect," the New Teacher Project's study of teacher evaluation and dismissal in twelve urban districts, Toledo was one of the districts in the sample. And its basic teacher outcomes looked just as dismal as those for the other districts. While all its untenured teachers are required to participate in the district's intern program as part of peer review, less than 1 percent of them failed to get their contracts renewed over a five-year period. Toledo also has an intervention program for tenured teachers who aren't performing well. But the data show that more than 99 percent of its tenured teachers got satisfactory evaluations over this same five-year period and a miniscule 0.01 percent (that's one one-hundredth of 1 percent) were actually dismissed for performance reasons.[20]

In practice, then, peer review has yet to demonstrate an impressive upside, especially in identifying poor teachers and getting them out of the classroom. But the downside is very real, and can't be ignored. Peer review gives the unions substantial new decisionmaking and operational roles in the organization of schooling. It gives them new power, moreover, in precisely the area they care about most—jobs—and pushes management (and thus elected officials, who appoint management) to the periphery.

These new union roles are fraught with conflicts of interest. Teachers join unions to protect their jobs. Yet by taking on these new personnel powers, the unions are supposed to be in the business of recommending that certain teachers be fired. How can they do both? How can they fire low-performing teachers and yet stand up for them, argue for them, and ensure that they get the most forceful protection possible? This conflict of interest is a legitimate reason to worry that the unions won't be serious about firing poor performers—especially veterans, who hold most of the power within the unions themselves. On the other side of the equation, many teachers are worried about the conflict of interest for their own reasons. It is no accident that peer review has only been adopted by a tiny number of districts nationwide, while some 14,000 districts have chosen not to do so. Peer review is not popular with the overwhelming majority of local union leaders and their rank-and-file members. They don't want teachers (unions) evaluating and firing teachers. They want managers to be responsible (and blamable) for these things and unions to be 100 percent on the teachers' side.[21]

Finally, peer review comes with costs that supporters rarely acknowledge. It is expensive on monetary grounds alone, because the teachers who do the evaluating and coaching—experienced teachers who are considered excellent in the classroom—are paid up to 20 percent of their salaries in bonuses for doing this supervisory work. In the meantime, *they are not teaching their own classes.* Someone else is, either a substitute (as in Toledo) or a full-time replacement (as in Hillsborough County, Florida), and these people must be paid too. The shifting of personnel also threatens to take an academic toll (nonmonetary but very real) on children: because excellent teachers are literally being moved *out* of classrooms, and they are being replaced by teachers who, on average, aren't as good—especially if they are just substitutes who are not in the same classrooms on a continuing basis.[22]

The bottom line is therefore mixed. Peer review is embraced by TURN members as a path-breaking innovation in which "reform unions" take aggressive action to promote teacher quality and student learning, but the reality is more complicated than that. Teachers *are* the best judges of good (and bad) teaching, and it makes sense to use peer review in some fashion. But how to do that is not so straightforward. There is no good evidence that, as currently designed, it is yielding major benefits in the (unionized) districts where it has been adopted; it flies in the face of what most local unions and their members think unions ought to be doing to protect each and every job; it is costly to implement; and although it surely *can* (in principle) make important contributions to teacher evaluations and ultimately to teacher quality, it also stands to give unions still more control over the operation of schools. Because the unions' interests are what they are—and because peer review doesn't change that—there is every reason to worry that, in practice, most peer review systems will not even be able to get bad teachers out of the classroom and will generally fall far short of realizing their potential.

Departures from the Single Salary Schedule

In some districts, TURN leaders have also supported departures from the single salary schedule, reflecting what Urbanski characterized—a full decade ago—as their "willingness to break the mold."[23] Movement in this direction is surely called for, because the single salary schedule is so dismally inappropriate and stifling.

But until Race to the Top dramatically ramped up the pressures for change, Urbanski's hyperbole was matched by only small and unimpressive steps forward.

The inhibitions at work are no mystery. Unions must represent all their members, and they thrive on sameness and solidarity. Differential pay can easily threaten these fundamentals. What TURN reformers have done over the years, essentially, is to "support" differential pay by pursuing muted forms of it that cause the fewest internal problems among members. In some TURN districts, as a result, reforms have allowed teachers to qualify for additional pay by getting certified by the National Board for Professional Teaching Standards, by serving as "mentors" or "master teachers" who help to train younger colleagues, by demonstrating (via formal course taking) valued knowledge or skills, or by taking a job at a disadvantaged or troubled school. Note that these opportunities are readily available to all teachers, and that most involve extra pay for extra (or more difficult) work or education—making them more acceptable to the rank and file. Note also what is missing: *they do not depend on what students are actually learning.*[24]

From a union standpoint, this makes perfect sense. The use of student test scores to measure teacher effectiveness in the classroom is highly unpopular among teachers: they don't think test scores are good measures of learning or of their performance. The same is true of evaluations based on the subjective assessments of principals: teachers worry that principals will be arbitrary and show favoritism.[25] TURN leaders, like other union leaders, have strong incentives to be sensitive to these views. They talk about differential pay as though it offers pay for "performance," but actual performance in the classroom, as measured by student test scores, typically has little or nothing to do with their vision of a good plan. They are also wary of having teacher pay based on the professional evaluations of school principals. In the end, their inclination is to fall back on formal criteria that virtually any teacher can eventually satisfy: credentials, training, course taking, and mentoring.

TURN leaders are reformers, then, in the sense that they are more open to departures from the single salary schedule than other union leaders are. But they also face similar constraints, and the kinds of reforms they favor are *limited*. Consider, for example, the Denver ProComp Plan, which went into effect in 2006 and was designed over a period of years through collaboration between the district and the local union—a TURN union. This pay-for-performance plan is widely hailed as a national model and an example of what can be achieved when districts and their unions work together on reform. It is also indicative of the limitations that come along with union buy-in.

In the first place, the union only agreed to go along with the plan if Denver voters would raise taxes by $25 million a year (with future adjustments for inflation). This allowed the district to give teachers their "first really substantial increase in more than two decades," which meant, for the typical teacher, up to an additional 20 percent in raises and bonuses.[26] Despite the lofty talk of collaboration, the district essentially bought off the union by devoting considerably more money to teacher pay than in the past, making it possible for *all* teachers to benefit—including those who don't perform well. Second, while all new teachers were required to join, veteran teachers were not. They could opt to remain under the single salary schedule, and as of late 2009 that is what a majority of them had chosen to do. As is almost always true in education reform, then, veteran teachers were treated with kid gloves and allowed to escape scrutiny. Third, student test scores play almost no role in evaluations of teacher performance; they are relevant for only about 30 percent of Denver's teachers, and even for them the impact of test scores on raises is tiny compared to other criteria.[27] And finally, the other criteria—the factors that together almost totally determine the "performance" pay that teachers receive—are the types that unions tend to favor, and are (or can turn out to be, in practice) only loosely connected to what happens in the classroom. They involve: obtaining formal upgrades through professional development classes, national certification, and graduate degrees; receiving "satisfactory" evaluations by school principals; meeting student growth objectives (goals that are proposed by teachers and agreed to by principals); being part of a school that achieves "distinguished" status, based on multiple measures; and teaching in hard-to-serve schools or occupying a hard-to-staff assignment.[28]

The Denver plan is probably better than the single salary schedule.[29] But it is still a pale version of what a serious, well-designed pay-for-performance plan might look like if the sole concern were to make the schools as effective as possible. The reason is simply that, with the unions heavily involved in its design, it is built to protect the occupational interests of teachers—ensuring that all teachers are rewarded, that no one loses a job, that actual classroom performance is not very important, and that they have countless ways to increase their salaries *without* improving the achievement of their students.[30]

Prior to Race to the Top, only a few states (such as Florida, Minnesota, and Texas) and districts (such as Houston, Denver, and Minneapolis) had taken steps toward even limited forms of pay for performance. Race to the Top changed that dramatically. President Obama's secretary of education, Arne Duncan, made it clear that new, performance-based systems of evaluation and pay—particularly those that give substantial weight to student test scores—would be highly valued and likely to be rewarded. With more than $4 billion at stake during a time of economic downturn, the states competed frenetically to be among the anointed winners of the race, and a number of them came up with new legislation, or new proposals, calling for innovations along these lines. Union leaders, under strong pressure to "buy in" (lest their states lose out), sometimes went along with these reforms or were directly involved in their design.[31] I discuss this in more detail in chapter 10.

Another game-changer is that, over the last few years, the Bill and Melinda Gates Foundation has made performance-based evaluation and pay the centerpiece of its education reform efforts. It has offered huge grants to three districts—translating into huge pay increases for their teachers—for launching major innovations along these lines. Two of these districts—Memphis (which got $90 million) and Pittsburgh ($40 million)—are TURN districts. One isn't: Hillsborough County, Florida ($100 million).[32]

At this writing, all of the evaluation and pay reforms stimulated by Race to the Top and the Gates Foundation grants are in their formative stages. By comparison to the past, of course, they are exciting developments. But we are wise to keep our heads and stay focused on the fundamentals. The fact is, the innovations of the past few years only came about because, during a very bad economic time, enormous amounts of money were used as an inducement—and states, districts, unions, and teachers desperately wanted the money. In particular, the innovations were not adopted because TURN leaders were out there pushing for new forms of evaluation and pay centered on student test scores. Had it been solely up to them and had there been no pots of gold (and no pressure from Race to the Top), *these reforms would not have happened.*

At this point, it is unclear what these reforms really *are.* The details of these plans have yet to be determined—and as time goes on and as decisions are made in the trenches about how performance will actually be measured, how it will actually affect pay, and whether anyone will actually be fired for poor teaching, the unions can be expected to use their ongoing power to ensure that their members and their interests are protected. If the fundamentals are our guide, what looks like path-breaking innovation now is likely to look a lot less exciting later on, when reality takes hold.

Collaborative Governance

Peer review and pay for performance are two specific departures from traditional unionism associated with TURN. A third departure is much more general and is perhaps the defining feature of TURN's approach to the new unionism. This is the emphasis on collaborative governance.

It is natural, when we think of collaboration, to think of cooperation and productive interaction and, in the case of schools, to think of teachers being involved in the decisionmaking process, having a voice, and contributing their expertise. These are surely good things. Teachers are experts about what they do, they have hands-on experience in virtually all aspects of schooling, and, if well designed, a collaborative process that welcomes their contributions could obviously give a great boost to effective organization.

But when TURN leaders talk about collaboration, they have much more in mind. To them, collaboration is a *power-sharing arrangement between districts and unions*: an arrangement in which they jointly make the *all* the important education decisions—not just about wages, benefits, and working conditions, but also about curriculum, instruction, budgets, resource allocation, and the full range of policy and organizational matters that affect the operation of schools. The scope of bargaining, in effect, would be expanded to include virtually everything. In Urbanski's words, the districts and unions would be "equal partners" in governing public education.[33]

Collaborative governance has not been studied in a rigorous way, so there is no definitive evidence on how its pursuit in TURN districts over the years has affected student achievement. An instructive case to consider, however, is Rochester—because it is Urbanski's own district, and because it is regarded as the nation's pioneer in union-district collaboration, having adopted a path-breaking reform contract in 1987 that thrust it into the media limelight as a presumed hotbed of innovation.

The deal that attracted all the attention was, as we should expect, very much about money. The district raised teacher salaries a whopping 42.5 percent over three years, making them among the best paid in the country, and created career ladders that allowed teachers to move up the salary scale through new responsibilities (as "lead" teachers). In return, there was to be more accountability for performance, pursued through "school-based planning committees" in all schools and other forms of active union involvement in school governance. Formal collaboration was now built into the very structure of the district.[34]

In the years since, however, Rochester's experiment in collaborative governance has had little success in bringing about true labor-management cooperation or in improving the quality of education for students. In 1993, some seven years after the reforms were first initiated, the *New York Times* reported:[35]

> The city still awaits the transformation of its school system. Student performance has barely budged, the district is desperate for money, and those who remember headlines about "the Rochester experiment" have cooled to Mr. Urbanski's vision of the teacher as creative professional and agent of change . . . "One on one, he's the epitome of reason, very enlightened, informed, a bold thinker," said William A. Johnson Jr., president of the Urban League . . . "But in front of his members, the smell of bacon overpowers everything. The teachers say, 'Where's my contract?' and he becomes a different person. He's become less of a citizen and more of a union leader.

Johnson's point about Urbanski is precisely the one I've made in reference to Shanker, Chase, and other reform unionists. What they say—and may well believe—as human beings is one thing. But what counts is their actual behavior as union leaders, and their behavior is heavily shaped by the organizational incentives of their jobs, and thus by the job-based concerns of their members. They can talk until the cows come home about collaboration, professionalism, cooperation, and all the rest. But in the end, they use their power to promote bread-and-butter objectives and to bring home the bacon.

In 1995 a panel representing higher education, business, and civil rights groups concluded, "Rochester has suffered from a surplus of educational rhetoric and a scarcity of . . . educational change." Its spokesman, a vice president at the University of Rochester, said, "There has been no discernible progress in the decade since we began here . . . There has been no improvement in drop-out rates, graduation rates, or test scores."[36]

Meantime, there was plenty of conflict. The district was pushing for change and accountability, and the union—as all unions do—was protecting jobs, pushing for more money, and responding to its members' concerns. The dynamics were volatile, to say the least. Indeed, in 1997 "a raucous teachers meeting nearly turned into a melee, with Janey [the superintendent] calling the police to try to have the union's president, Adam Urbanski, arrested. Urbanski, in turn, prepared for a vote of no confidence against Janey."[37] Is this what collaboration looks like? A 1997 study summarizes Rochester's labor-management relations in the postreform era as follows:[38]

> By 1990–91 the alliance between the teachers and the district had been fractured during extended negotiations over the subsequent contract, a conflict that was repeated again in contract negotiations during 1992–93 and 1996–97. A central question in the disputes was the process for establishing teacher accountability, with the board of education pushing for a pay-for-performance model, which teachers have repeatedly rejected . . . The fragile collaboration begun by Urbanski and McWalters [the superintendent in 1987] has been destroyed.

Urbanski himself was quite explicit about just how conflictual the relationship was. In the run-up to negotiations in 2000, he offered the following overview: "If past experiences tell us what to expect, we should brace ourselves for the acrimony and adversarial relationships that characterized virtually all prior negotiations. It's like that for some understandable reasons. We negotiate every three or four years, trying in a few months to resolve all the problems that have accumulated in the interim. By then, some are no longer solvable, some are moot, and most have festered so long that the damage has already been done."[39] The real question is, why were these things happening? The whole point of collaboration—if it is real and meaningful—is to *solve* problems and to ensure that they do *not* fester. This is precisely what was not happening in Rochester.

It still isn't happening. As of 2009 the Rochester school district continues to be mired in serious academic woes, with a graduation rate that "has steadily declined to one of the lowest in the state."[40] Labor-management conflict continues to be described as "acrimonious," and, despite all the TURN rhetoric about doing what is best for students, "the 152-page Rochester Teachers Association contract is cited more often than any other labor agreement in debates over the ills of public education in Rochester."[41] When an issue arose over how to handle student suspensions, informal collaboration utterly failed and the union filed a class-action grievance against the district. Similarly, when the union objected to how the district was planning to spend the 2009 federal stimulus money—saying that the district was not doing enough to save teachers' jobs—the union lodged a formal complaint with the state Department of Education and threatened to sue the district in court. A recent newspaper account reported Urbanski as saying "that current Superintendent Jean-Claude Brizard has imported a culture of fear and intimidation toward teachers that reminds him of the Communist state he left as a child."[42]

Rochester's experiment in collaborative governance is no longer an experiment. It is more than twenty years old, firmly entrenched—and hardly a beacon of progress. It has not delivered on its promise to boost student achievement. It has not delivered on its promise to bring cooperation. The district remains troubled and conflictual and in most outward respects is virtually indistinguishable from other urban districts around the country.

None of this is surprising. The district's leaders are centrally concerned with boosting student achievement, a goal that has become ever more salient as the forces of accountability, magnified by No Child Left Behind, have increased the pressure to perform. The union, however, is centrally concerned with the occupational interests of its members, special interests that inevitably bring it into conflict with the district. Collaborative governance doesn't change that. It provides new structures and new modes of decisionmaking, but the union's interests are the same as ever—and the problem of union power remains.

As with peer review, there is a real dilemma here. Teachers are the experts, they are the key ingredients in making schools effective, and it only makes sense, in the interests of quality education—and children—to give them a voice, invite their participation, and put their vast knowledge and experience to productive, systematic use. In this form, collaboration would be a very good thing. Yet when teachers are represented by unions, collaboration morphs into something else. It becomes a vehicle by which the unions seek to gain greater control over the schools and additional leverage in pursuing their special interests.

Even if collaborative governance could somehow lead to a more peaceful relationship between labor and management—which it has not done in Rochester—peace would come at an onerous price. Let's be clear. *The unions are not elected to run the schools.* As a matter of democratic governance, *they are not supposed to be "equal partners."* Public officials and their appointed administrators are properly in charge of the schools: *they* are the people's representatives. If they don't do their jobs well and don't represent the interests of their communities, they can (in principle) be thrown out of office. The unions can't be. They are special interest groups, and collaborative governance—of the kind TURN leaders have in mind—simply gives them extraordinary new powers to pursue their own interests more fully and effectively.

New Haven and Green Dot

In recent years, reform unionism has gotten its greatest boost from Race to the Top, which has caused states to embrace innovations they never would have embraced in times past and pressured unions to "buy in" to new legislation and proposals. There is less here than meets the eye, as we'll see in chapter 10. But at the very least, this historically unusual reformist environment, while creating thorny problems for the unions, has also handed their leaders countless opportunities to talk the reformist talk, to make a virtue out of necessity (by "buying in" to reforms they don't like and will try to weaken later on), and to give the impression that reform unionism is on its way.

More on that in chapter 10. Here I want to briefly discuss two recent developments that are not part of Race to the Top, but have captured a good deal of attention among reformers as examples of the compatibility of strong unions and effective schools. The first is the "progressive" labor contract adopted in the New Haven school district in 2009. The second has to do with Green Dot, a successful charter organization that has welcomed unionization and collective bargaining with open arms.

The New Haven contract was widely hailed as a break-the-mold labor agreement that should serve as a model for other unions and districts.[43] What it did, in general terms, was to call for a new system of teacher evaluation based on student achievement, a new system of performance pay, and new powers for turning around failing schools by reconstituting them (with a new principal and staff) or converting them into charters. U.S. Secretary of Education Arne Duncan, watching closely, praised it as a "really important progressive labor agreement" that showed "real courage on the union's part."[44] Said Randi Weingarten, whose local affiliate had inked the contract, "I rarely say that something is a model or a template for something else, but this is both."[45]

New Haven's mayor, John DeStefano, is an education reformer who means business, and he and his allies pushed hard for a truly progressive contract. And they surely had some success. But as is often the case, the devil is in the details. The contract preserves tenure and seniority rights, preserves grievance procedures, guarantees no layoffs (when schools are reconstituted, say), and leaves almost all the important decisions—regarding, for example, exactly how teachers are to be evaluated, how test scores are to be taken into account, and whether low-performing schools will actually be reconstituted or turned into charters—to committees that will make the ultimate determinations in a process that will unfold over time. So it is simply unclear, from the contract itself, what the policies really are and what is going to happen. And there's more. If schools are converted to charters, the charters must be unionized and follow restrictions in the union contract. And the pay-for-performance plan just gives bonuses to high-performing schools; it does not pay good teachers more than bad teachers.[46]

So the New Haven contract is not a "model" that warrants adulation or boundless optimism. Said the *Washington Post*, "We assumed it contained bold reforms. In fact, there's little that's remarkable about the contract . . . It hardly contains the innovations needed for serious reform."[47] The *New York Times* saw it similarly:[48]

The accolades seem premature given that crucial details have yet to be worked out . . . School reformers were excited to hear that New Haven planned to take student performance into account in its teacher evaluations. But they uttered a collective "uh-oh" upon hearing that the details—including how much weight would be given to student performance—would be hashed out by a committee that includes teachers and administrators. To be taken seriously, the evaluation must be based on a clear formula in which the student achievement component carries the preponderance of the weight. It must also include a fine-grained analysis that tells teachers where they stand. The New Haven contract represents a promising first step. But there is still a lot of room for politicking and shenanigans.

Green Dot is something of a man-bites-dog story. One of the key advantages of charter schools is that that they are able to operate with substantial autonomy from state and district regulations as well as from the immense burdens of collective bargaining contracts. Almost all charters seek out as much autonomy as they can get, and they stay nonunion. Green Dot clearly prizes its autonomy too. It has opened nineteen charter schools since 1999, eighteen in Los Angeles and one (most recently) in New York City. It specializes in taking large, failed high schools in low-income areas, replacing each with several small charters, and—although each follows the same educational model—emphasizes flexibility, autonomy, and decentralized decisionmaking within each school. In one key respect, however, Green Dot doesn't fit the charter mold at all. It wants its employees to be unionized and to engage in collective bargaining, and it has actively arranged for these things to happen.[49]

What's going on here? The explanation is that Steve Barr, the founder and guiding spirit of Green Dot, is a lifelong social democrat and activist (and former fundraiser for the California Democratic Party). He deeply believes in unions, and he is convinced not only that his own teachers ought to be unionized and covered by collective bargaining, but also that Green Dot will be more effective because of it. He is a believer in reform unionism.[50]

Green Dot has indeed been very successful. It has significantly raised student achievement and, it appears, transformed the lives of its kids and families.[51] In the process, Barr has made quite a reputation for himself, attracted grants from Gates and Broad (and others), and is in high demand across the country to replicate his model in other districts. He also has a higher acceptability quotient among Democrats and union leaders, because his schools are all unionized, and he is a wedge by which, as some see it, the entire charter sector might go union.

The fact is, however, that Green Dot's experience with unions looks nothing like the experience of the typical public school (at least for now). Barr's teachers are not represented by the powerful United Teachers Los Angeles (UTLA), which is at war with Green Dot and with all charters. The teachers at Green Dot have their own special union, the Asociación de Maestros Unidos, which technically has an affiliation with the California Teachers Association but is actually a tiny independent union that came into existence with Barr's encouragement purely to represent Green Dot teachers. [52]

From the beginning, Barr no doubt wanted the best for his employees and wanted them to have an independent voice, but he also held all the cards. The contract—just thirty pages long the first time around, fifty-three pages long the second—bears little resemblance to the normal labor contract in public education. Teachers do not have tenure. They have no right to strike. They have no seniority rights in transfers or assignments. They are required to work a "professional" day (as long as the work takes) rather than a specific number of minutes. And so on.[53]

This kind of "thin" contract is misleading as a model of what is possible for America's schools. The union is weak and new. Green Dot, moreover, is a new and successful organization, its teachers are enthusiastic and happy, and their union is not driven to be assertive at this point. But what if, five or ten years from now, these teachers decide they want tenure? Or the right to strike? Or seniority rights? Or any number of other rights and prerogatives that other teachers have and that other unions regularly fight for and win? Then what? And what if they choose to become an active part of UTLA, so that its power can be employed on their behalf? Then what? As things now stand, the AFT and the NEA have every reason to go easy on Green Dot. It is their Trojan horse for bringing unionization to the charter sector. Indeed, Randi Weingarten and Steve Barr recently agreed to open a Green Dot in New York City, following the same model as in Los Angeles, and there will doubtless be more Weingarten-Barr partnerships down the road and in other cities.[54] In general, the two established unions are happy to see *any* union—however weak, however independent, however thin and inconsequential its contract—make inroads into the charter sector. For that would pave the way for the union giants to organize the entire sector in future years, turning weak unions into powerful ones and replacing thin contracts with much more restrictive documents that provide teachers with the kinds of rights and protections unions regularly seek.

The fly in the ointment, from the unions' standpoint, is that a competitive environment is not good for them and not good for restrictive contracts. When families have choice, as they do in the charter sector, they can leave ineffective schools for effective ones. And because this is so, unions that impose restrictive contracts on their own schools—making it more difficult for them to be effective—may find that they are losing clients to their less-restricted competitors. Faced with competition, they are also faced with consequences. In the end, therefore, the unions cannot simply rest content with trying to organize the charter sector. They are only putting up with charters because they happen to exist. They are best off in a world with as little choice and as little competition as possible—a world in which all schools are uniformly regulated, there are no consequences for poor performance, and kids and money are nicely and peacefully divided among them, guaranteed.

The Green Dot story, then, does not demonstrate that powerful unions are compatible with effective organization. Its own union is weak and benign, and its own experience with unions is artificial. The larger problem is that other reformers may draw the wrong lesson, and that the union giants may pull more and more charters into their web—where real power is exercised and dynamism extinguished.

Randi Weingarten

Last but not least there is Randi Weingarten herself, today's embodiment of reform unionism. In any objective sense, these are the worst of times for the teachers unions: criticized by liberals for obstructing change, pummeled by high-profile opponents within the Democratic Party, and under severe pressure from President Obama, Arne Duncan, and Race to the Top to go along with major reforms that they have long fought against. But even so—indeed, precisely *because* it is so—Weingarten is in her element.

When the unions are criticized, Weingarten is the one who speaks out forcefully in their defense and receives wall-to-wall media coverage. When the unions are pressured to embrace reform, Weingarten is the one on camera, arguing her openness to change and tantalizing a reform community desperate to see the unions become partners in progress.

The bad times, then, have been very good to Randi Weingarten. She has positioned herself as the "most visible, powerful leader of unionized teachers."[55] And by singing a tune of reform unionism—beautiful music indeed to the ears of most reformers—she has made all good things seem possible. This is a sophisticated crowd, and they are aware that the unions have been blocking reform for a quarter century. But they want to believe that this might change, and she has convinced many of them that she is a reformer too and that she wants to stop the blocking. So all eyes are on her. And reformers are anxiously asking themselves, almost day to day, will she or won't she? What will Randi do next?

As I've argued from the first pages of this book, it is a mistake to personalize politics. We do not know what truly motivates Randi Weingarten as a human being, in her heart of hearts. When she says, "I have always thought of myself as a school reformer"[56] or "There's a much more important purpose here, which is the love of children,"[57] we do not know if these are honest reflections of her deeply felt values and beliefs or if they are all for public consumption.

But we *do* know something very important: we know that she is a union president. As such, whatever her personal values and beliefs may be, she is *heavily constrained* in what she can actually do in her official capacity, and she has strong institutional *incentives* to make jobs and the occupational interests of union members her number one concern. Due to the environment in which she operates, these constraints and incentives give her strong and eminently rational reasons to *say* that she is a reformer and to follow a strategy of convincing people it is true. They also prompt her to *behave* in ways that protect and promote the special interests of her members, even when they come into conflict with what is best for kids. *She is a special interest advocate for teachers.* If we want to understand what she says and does, this is the key.

Different leaders design their special interest strategies in different ways, depending on their circumstances. As Weingarten has plotted her own strategies, two circumstances have surely proved of great relevance.

The first is that she heads the smaller and weaker of the nation's two teachers unions. As discussed in chapter 2, the NEA and the AFT engaged in an all-out struggle to organize the nation's teachers during the 1960s and 1970s, and the NEA came out on top. It is a much larger union than the AFT, has a lot more money, is a truly national organization (the AFT is highly concentrated in New York), and is arguably a much more consequential force in American education. So the AFT is the Avis of the teachers union movement. And like Avis, it has to try harder—to gain prominence and recognition, and to wrest center stage from the NEA. Aside from exercising power in numerous big-city districts, the chief way it has done that over the years is by carving out a distinctive niche for itself. It is the "reform" union.

Al Shanker was the pioneer in creating this reformist niche, and other leaders within the AFT—those associated with TURN, mainly—have consciously built on his legacy by continuing to make reform a *brand* that wins them positive attention and creates a sharp contrast to the curmudgeonly NEA. This perpetual branding campaign has been successful. The stereotype among those who follow American education is that the AFT is the nation's reform-friendly union.

Like almost all stereotypes, there is an element of truth to it. On the whole, AFT unions are more open to change—albeit modest, incremental change—than NEA unions are. But like almost all stereotypes, this one is also false at its core. Throughout the modern era, the AFT has used its political power to block and eviscerate serious education reforms, just as the NEA has. And like the NEA, it has used its power in collective bargaining to impose self-interested work rules that make it impossible for the public schools to be organized effectively. Although AFT unions have sometimes gone along with changes about the edges, and in rare cases (New Haven, for instance) have gone somewhat further, this cannot be allowed to distract from the essence of their behavior. On the whole, AFT unions have been enormous obstacles to the nation's pursuit of effective schools. *That* is what lies at the core.[58]

When Randi Weingarten assumed the AFT presidency in July 2008, its brand was suffering. The prior president, Ed McElroy, had been a lackluster "labor man" not given to the usual reformist rhetoric; and this absence of dynamism at the top, combined with the hostility of the Bush administration—which kept both the AFT and the NEA on the outside looking in (at the national level only) for eight long years—prompted an *Education Week* article with the headline, "AFT No Longer a Major Player in Reform Arena."[59] Before long, however, this was old news. The AFT very much needed someone who would respond more forcefully to the incentives of the job—someone who could build the brand and take advantage of it—and Randi Weingarten was just what the doctor ordered. As her tenure in New York City vividly demonstrated, she was tough as nails in defending the rights and privileges of her members, yet she was also a master at the AFT branding game. Very much in the Shanker tradition, she could sing the praises of education reform, and big audiences would listen—and hope and believe.

So this is the first circumstance of great relevance to Weingarten's strategy of leadership: the AFT's reform-friendly image has enormous strategic value, and if used wisely it can bring legitimacy, attention, and even accolades to an organization that is ever-vulnerable to the charge of obstructionism (for good reason)—and doesn't want to play second fiddle to the NEA. Whatever she believes in her heart of hearts, then, Weingarten has strong incentives to portray herself as a reformer and to excel at singing precisely the songs—whatever the words, whatever the melody—that the American reform community wants to hear.

The second circumstance is that, by comparison to the past, the political environment is a very difficult one for the teachers unions, and they are up against the wall like never before. Never have they been so unpopular with the nation's opinion leaders, and never have they been under so much pressure to go along with reforms that they have long opposed.[60] Chris Cerf, former assistant to Joel Klein in New York City, recently observed, "The earth [has] moved in a really dramatic way, to the point that a very successful strategist like Randi Weingarten has to know that teacher unionism itself is in jeopardy, perhaps even mortal jeopardy."[61] This paints the situation in direr terms than I think is warranted given the enormous power of the unions, which is rooted in millions of members and tons of money and won't just go away. But you get the picture.

For an AFT leader, a strategy of "reform" is a smart, rational way to deal with this kind of highly threatening environment. Indeed, the two are a perfect fit. A bad environment means that the unions are ultimately going to have to make concessions. Weingarten surely knows that; and were she to follow a purely oppositional strategy, not only would she lose ground anyway, but her reputation (and the AFT's) would also suffer. The strategy she has followed instead is a much more attractive way of dealing with adversity. A big part of it is that she has fought to keep the concessions to a minimum—and thus, as she must, fought to protect the job interests of her members—but she has also made a virtue out of necessity by claiming reformist *credit* for whatever concessions she has had to make. The concessions are reframed, via revisionist history, as desirable reformist moves that she has embraced. They become her reforms, her ideas, and she points to them as evidence that she is indeed a reformer.

Examples are easy to come by. In a major speech to the National Press Club in 2008, for instance, shortly after assuming the AFT presidency, she talked about issues like seniority and merit pay that have prompted critics to see the unions as impediments to change, and she challenged that image. As the *New York Times* reported, "On teacher assignments, she pointed to new contract rules the union negotiated with New York City that no longer require principals to accept teachers, or teachers to take jobs, in schools that are not a good fit for them . . . On merit pay, she pointed to a system she negotiated in New York that allows all teachers in a participating school to receive extra pay when that school excels."[62]

Perhaps Weingarten really does care, first and foremost, about "the love of children" and making reform a reality. But her storyline here was clearly a reconstruction of history. As we saw in chapter 7, she vigorously defended a perverse labor contract filled with more than 200 pages of restrictive rules, and she stridently resisted the efforts of Bloomberg and Klein to eliminate the more egregious of these rules and bring a more effective organization to that city's schools. Weingarten resisted the elimination of seniority in assignments. She also resisted the introduction of merit pay. She only gave way—and then only partially—because Bloomberg and Klein were themselves powerful, were pushing hard for these reforms, and in the end were willing to pay huge sums of money for her to make concessions. By holding the rules hostage, she was able to win an enormous ransom in the form of astronomical raises for her members.

While Weingarten now trumpets these reforms as desirable innovations that "she negotiated," she is simply putting a strategic spin on her concessions. These reforms were *not* her reforms, and indeed, if she had had her way—absent the money—*they would not have happened at all.* They only happened because of the dedicated efforts and genuine power of Bloomberg and Klein. The credit is theirs, not hers. She was an obstacle to change, and her "contribution" was to get out of the way when they paid her enough money to do it.

The same thing is true in spades for the revolutionary labor contract engineered in Washington, which was entirely due to the courage and stamina of Michelle Rhee and her strong backing by Mayor Adrian Fenty. The difference in this case, though, is that Weingarten (and the weak Washington Teachers Union) had to make such huge concessions that—so far, anyway—she hasn't been eager to claim credit for it, and has been doing some fancy footwork to argue that it should not be regarded as a precedent for other districts.[63] These concessions were hard to swallow and hard to dress up as anything but what they were: a major defeat.

In any event, her leadership strategy is not limited to claiming credit for the concessions she's had to make. It is not just backward-looking and reactive. It is also adaptive, forward-looking, and realistic about the actual power that she is up against. If she is going to convince people that she is a reformer, that she is a leader of the reform movement rather than a staunch opponent, then she has to do more than reconstruct history. She has to be proactive and *make* the history that she and the AFT will ultimately have to live with.

Take charter schools, for example. Charters are popular with parents, with reformers, and with President Obama and Arne Duncan. They are also well established and here to stay. So Weingarten, ever the realist, recognizes as much and gives the impression that she supports charter schools too—under the right conditions. She also takes proactive steps, by entering into the charter movement itself and trying to shape its development going forward, so as to render it less threatening.

In a 2009 debate with Eva Moskowitz, who operates the stunningly effective Harlem Success charters in New York City, Weingarten said that "she welcomes charters as 'incubators' and she looks forward to 'exporting to public schools' anything 'good going on' there."[64] Under her leadership, the UFT began operating two charter schools of its own in New York City, which she regularly points to as evidence that charter schools can do just fine if they are unionized.[65] Plus, as we've seen, she has enthusiastically and very publicly joined arms with Steve Barr and the Green Dot charters—which are unionized—and has portrayed them as the future of the movement.

If we explore Weingarten's "support" for charters, however, the facts are revealing. She fought hard to prevent New York from even *adopting* a charter law in the first place. When the state finally did so in December 1998 (because Republican Governor George Pataki threatened to deny legislators a salary increase if it didn't pass), thirty-three other states already had such laws.[66] By no accident, New York came very late to the party. In the process, Weingarten won restrictions that made the new law pathetically weak, with a tight 100-school cap on the number of charters allowed statewide (in a state with some 4,500 public schools) and a requirement that charter schools enrolling more than 250 kids in their first two years had to be unionized and engage in collective bargaining.[67] The whole point of charters, of course, is to provide families with as many attractive alternatives as possible, and to have the kind of autonomy and flexibility that union restrictions have made impossible for most public schools.

In subsequent years, Weingarten fought attempts by proponents to increase the cap even slightly. Even during Race to the Top, when she and state policymakers were under immense pressure to raise the cap in order to meet Arne Duncan's criteria for innovation, Weingarten and her New York union leaders were so opposed to an expansion of charters, so demanding of further restrictions—and so powerful with legislators—that the state was simply unable to pass a bill at all. The state did abysmally in the first round of the competition. For the second round, legislators finally raised the cap (to a mere 460 schools statewide) to get the state back in contention, but over strong union opposition. These, moreover, are just the charter highlights at the state level.[68]

On her home turf in New York City, Weingarten fought throughout her tenure to prevent Bloomberg and Klein from setting up new charter schools and, among other things, filed a lawsuit against them when they announced plans in the spring of 2009 to close two public schools in Harlem and replace them with charters. The schools Weingarten aimed to keep open were PS 194 and 241, notorious low performers that had both received Ds on their district report cards and, of course, were operated by members of Weingarten's union. Parents, voting with their feet, were *avoiding* these two schools in droves. PS 194 had space for 628 students, but enrolled only 288. PS 241 had space for 1,007 students, but enrolled only 310. *Most parents clearly did not want their kids in those schools.* The district's plan was to replace them with new charters run by Harlem Success, whose existing, nearby charters had achieved spectacular academic results. Parents desperately *wanted* to get their kids into these Harlem Success schools: the previous year, some 6,000 students applied for just 500 available seats. On objective grounds, the idea here was a no-brainer: the district aimed to replace unpopular, low-performing schools with hugely popular, high-performing schools. Who could object to that? Weingarten did—and went to court to stop it. This is Weingarten the reformer, out in the trenches. Weingarten the supporter of charter schools.[69]

How about accountability and related issues, like tenure and teacher evaluations? Here too reforms on these scores are popular and on the front burner of American education, and Weingarten says she's on board. More than on board: she says that she's a progressive who wants to *lead* the charge for fundamental change.

This has been so for years. In 2004, for example, she said in a high-profile speech, "If a teacher doesn't belong in the classroom, my members want that teacher out . . . The fact is that even one incompetent teacher in our schools is one too many."[70] In her 2008 National Press Club speech, she announced her openness to new approaches to issues like teacher tenure and merit pay, and dramatically intoned, "No issue should be off the table, provided it is good for children and fair for teachers."[71] As Andrew Rotherham and Richard Whitmire observed in the *New Republic*, Weingarten "received a hero's welcome . . . she vowed to give ear to almost any tough-minded school reform and, in a line that thrilled many reformers, promised that the AFT will not protect incompetent teachers. 'Teachers are the first to say, let's get the incompetents out of the classroom.'"[72] In June 2009, at her farewell address before union members in New York City, she proclaimed, "We have not been defensive when so-called reformers wanted to see our profession change. Rather than resist change, we have led it."[73]

But what about Weingarten's actual *behavior* on these key reform issues? In New York City, she and the UFT's lawyers used the labor contract and state law to aggressively protect the jobs of all teachers thought to be incompetent, dangerous, or unsuited to the classroom.[74] When Bloomberg and Klein removed the problem teachers anyway and put them in Rubber Rooms, Weingarten furiously protested—and her contract required that they be fully paid, with all benefits and vacations. When, due to relentless pressure from Bloomberg and Klein, seniority transfer rights were dropped from the contract (in 2005) and principals were given control over hiring in their schools, the result was a pool of teachers (the Absent Teacher Reserve) who could not find jobs because they were so undesirable that no one wanted to hire them, and Weingarten refused to allow these teachers to be moved off the payroll. The district was then on the hook for some $100 million a year—money properly used for children—to pay for teachers no one wanted in the classroom.[75] When, in 2008, Bloomberg and Klein tried to use student test scores as one factor among many in evaluating teachers for tenure, Weingarten went to the state legislature and won a new law prohibiting the use of test scores in such evaluations anywhere in the state.[76]

Upon becoming president of the AFT in 2008, she expanded her scope. In her acceptance speech at the union's national convention, she immediately took out after the country's watershed accountability law, No Child Left Behind. Supporters of bringing true accountability to the public schools agreed at the time that the act has its flaws and needs to be modified. Well-intentioned lawmakers could surely do that and do it well, given the chance. But Weingarten's goal was not to modify it so that it could work more effectively. Her goal was to kill it, saying that it was "too badly broken to be fixed."[77] The headline in *Education Week:* "New AFT Leader Vows to Bring down NCLB Law."[78]

That same year, Weingarten and the AFT supported Hillary Clinton in the Democratic presidential primaries and pointedly did not support Barack Obama. Clinton was a vocal opponent of No Child Left Behind, testing, and serious attempts to hold schools and teachers accountable for student achievement. Obama wasn't playing ball. On the contrary, he made it clear that, rather than kill No Child Left Behind, he intended to preserve its positive features and move toward a better, more effective system for holding schools and teachers accountable; he also favored pay for performance and charter schools. Weingarten's choice of candidates revealed where she really stood on these issues. She touted herself as a reformer, but she opposed the one Democratic candidate who stood strongly and clearly for genuine reform.[79]

I could go on. But this, basically, is Weingarten's *behavioral* track record as a reformer. Most of the time—unless she's talking to her own members—she talks the talk of reform, and her strategy is designed to make her look like one. But there is a gigantic gulf between what she says and what she does. In a 2010 panel discussion, held after a screening of the movie *Waiting for Superman,* Michelle Rhee put it to Randi Weingarten face-to-face: "You cannot say you support effective teachers and then send me lawsuits when I fire teachers. You cannot say you support good schools and then work to cap the number of charter schools."[80] But this is exactly what Weingarten does. It is her strategy of leadership.

This strategy has been put to the acid test in recent years. When Obama became president, Weingarten got just what she tried to prevent: a president who really was committed to reform, or at least to a much stronger version of it than she could accept. His Race to the Top put union leaders under tremendous pressure to "buy into" reform, and thus to "embrace" innovations they had long fought against, lest their states lose out. The pressure was especially great to replace the time-honored charade of teacher evaluation—in which everyone is rated satisfactory—with new systems that base evaluations (in part) on how much students are actually learning.

As the Race to the Top gained momentum, Weingarten was in the midst of a perfect storm. Power had shifted. And as a realist, she could surely see where politics was headed: there would soon be major reforms of teacher evaluation, and student test scores were going to be part of it. She could have complained and moaned about it. She could have stood her ground, continued her denunciation of test scores, and gone down in flames. But then she would have been left behind, very obviously and very publicly, and her reformist image would have suffered a serious blow.

In January 2010, amid the uncontrolled frenzy occasioned by Race to the Top, Weingarten gave another speech to the National Press Club that electrified the reform community and sent hopes through the roof. She "called for sweeping changes in how school districts evaluate teachers and work with teachers unions" via collaboration; she also said that she was "receptive" to the use of standardized test scores in evaluating teachers, as long as many other factors are taken into account too; and she said she favored new due process procedures that would make it easier to get bad teachers out of the classroom. The headline in the *New York Times* screamed out the breaking news: "Union Chief Seeks to Overhaul Teacher Evaluation Process."[81]

Weingarten could have written this headline herself. Yet, given her track record, there was no credible basis for saying that she was *seeking* anything of the sort and every reason to think she was rationally—strategically—*adapting* to a bad situation. She had long fought to protect teacher jobs, to resist accountability, to eliminate student test scores from teacher evaluations, and indeed to make their use *illegal*. But she had precious few allies anymore on accountability issues—even the *New York Times* favored linking teacher evaluations to student test scores—and she could see that, unavoidably, she would need to make important concessions down the road.[82] Better to commit to them now, confound her critics, and call the reforms *hers*.

Whitney Tilson, a founding member of Teach for America and an acute observer of American education reform, hit the nail on the head: "You know the saying, When you're being run out of town, get out in front? Make it look like a parade? Well, that is what she's doing."[83] She was also doing more than that. She was putting her unions in a position—as "supporters" that were ostensibly "buying in" to these reforms—to demand collaboration, and thus participate as insiders in designing what the reforms would actually look like in practice.

So let's take a step back and ask a simple question here. When Weingarten commits to a new system of teacher evaluation, what is she really committing to? The answer is, nothing in particular. This is what makes a strategy of lofty language and tantalizing promises so attractive. For it happens that, by its nature, accountability reforms are easy to endorse at the level of ideas and then to weaken considerably when the ideas are translated into substance. It is one thing, after years of bashing test scores as "the most unreliable measure of student learning,"[84] for Weingarten to concede that, yes, test scores can be taken into account in evaluating teachers. But this says nothing about exactly how those scores will come into play, how they will be qualified by an array of other factors, or exactly what they will do (if anything) to get bad teachers out of the classroom—because all of these decisions, and more, can be *left unspecified* in any agreement.

How are the all-important "details" to be filled in? As Weingarten sees it, "These systems should be negotiated with the collective bargaining representatives or exclusive recognized representatives of teachers."[85] This is one way of saying that, with the AFT buying into the reform, it expects to participate in writing the details. It is also just another version of the long-standing TURN emphasis on *collaboration*. The details of policy are not to be determined by elected officials in the writing of law. They are to be determined through a *process* that happens later: a process of formal collaboration with the unions.

As I've said, collaboration can be a very good thing if it simply involves getting valuable input from teachers, who clearly have much to contribute and whose voices need to be heard if innovations are to be well designed. But Weingarten's idea of collaboration is really about power sharing and joint governance. In practice, it would simply allow the unions to use their power and tenacity—once the spotlights have been turned off and the frenzy has died down—to shape the details to their own advantage and to turn a bold-sounding reform into something much weaker, less consequential, and less threatening. This, in substantive terms, is what she is really endorsing. It may sound like revolutionary reform. But if her vision of collaboration is adhered to, the outcome will not be revolutionary at all. Indeed, Weingarten's job is to see that it isn't.

Since her National Press Club speech, Weingarten has continued to champion the cause of teacher evaluation reform. This is her parade, and she is out front. During Race to the Top, the AFT leadership in New York—with whom, obviously, she is very close as national president—entered into a widely hailed agreement with state education leaders to move toward a new, performance-based teacher evaluation system. Several other AFT unions around the country agreed to move in similar directions.[86] Weingarten also made a big media hit by parachuting into Colorado just as its reform legislation on teacher evaluation was about to pass and giving it her public support (after proponents agreed to beef up seniority and due-process protections in their bill). Not coincidentally, the NEA affiliate—which organizes more than ten times as many Colorado teachers as the AFT and dwarfs the latter in political clout there—was totally *opposed* to the reform. So this was a perfect opportunity. On a bill that already had enough support to pass, and in a state where the AFT is a bit player, Weingarten swooped in out of nowhere to take center stage, brighten her reformer's halo, and make the NEA look like Neanderthals. For an AFT president, life doesn't get much better than that.[87]

It is important to note that both the Colorado and New York reforms, and a number of other state reforms as well, did indeed leave the key details unspecified. (Recall that the contract in New Haven did exactly the same thing.) True to form, they set up collaborative processes in which the unions would participate as key decisionmakers and thus be in a position to shape—and weaken—the real guts of the policies later on.[88] With the political environment so difficult to navigate and with reformers suddenly so influential, these were good outcomes for Weingarten. Yes, she made concessions. But they were concessions that allowed the unions to maintain a measure of control and to *limit* the extent of true reform.

By the time this book is published and sits on the shelf for awhile, a good deal more will have happened in the American education arena, and the details recounted here will have been superseded by newer developments. Whatever happens, though, it is a good bet that Randi Weingarten will maintain her hold on the spotlight. If reform is on the march—whether it deals with teacher evaluations or something else—she will continue to make it her parade. And because she's good and convincing at what she does, reformers will continue to be mesmerized by her every move, and they will continue to cheer her "courage" and say that she deserves credit for the progress that is being made.[89]

Too many reformers, as well as too many in the media, have never fully understood what Randi Weingarten is doing. They believe—or at least they hope and want to believe—that she is an enlightened leader who wants to do what is best for children, who aims to bring about changes in policies and labor contracts to make schools effective, and who intends to use her power and position to bring the unions wholeheartedly into the reformist movement.

The reality is that, whatever Weingarten's personal values might be, she is severely constrained by her official position as union president, and she has compelling incentives—unless she wants to be thrown out on her ear—to give first priority to the jobs and occupational interests of her members. This does not mean that she will never go along with reform. Indeed, in the current political environment, it is a rational strategy for her to portray herself as a champion of reform and to make various kinds of concessions and forward-looking proposals. But in the trenches, when the details are actually hashed out, she will only go as far as she has to—and she will ultimately weaken, limit, and dissipate reform when the job-related interests of her members call for it. From her standpoint, as a special interest advocate for teachers, the purpose of collaboration with reformers is not to adopt solutions that are best for children. It is to protect the interests of her members and prevent reforms from going too far.

Conclusion

Reform unionism is among the most influential and seductive forces in American education. It is also one of the most misleading.

Many reformers and policymakers want to believe that union power is not, in the end, going to be a problem for the nation's public school system or for its kids. They do recognize, at least—in a way they didn't in the past—that union power *has* been a problem. A big one. But they also tend to believe that it won't be a problem in the future, or doesn't need to be, because through enlightened leadership the unions will someday evolve into very different kinds of professional organizations that voluntarily use their power to do what's right for children. On this account, then, it is fine for the unions to *remain* powerful because they can be expected to *use* their power—eventually—to good ends.

These ideas are doubtless comforting to people who, for reasons of ideology or partisanship or career or personal values, believe that unions *should* be an integral part of public education and welcome them as legitimate "stakeholders" in the public education system. The same is true for people who are not wedded to unions per se, but are pragmatists who believe that the unions are too powerful to be dislodged and must be worked with and encouraged to change. For both, powerful unions are a given, and reform unionism provides them with a tidy belief system that makes everything come out all right. As reform unionism tells the story, the unions can stay right where they are, hugely, powerfully, and deeply embedded in the school system, and the nation can still have schools that are organized in the best interests of kids. How? Enlightened unions will agree to go along. They will agree because, as (evolving) organizations rooted in professional values, they will see it as the right thing to do. And they will agree because, as Shanker warned decades ago, they play into the hands of critics—and thus threaten their own existence and that of the public school system—by *not* supporting reform.

This line of reasoning, however, is filled with holes and has little basis in reality. Shanker, other "progressive" union leaders (like Adam Urbanski), and influential academics were saying these things back in the late 1980s and early 1990s—and what happened? The AFT unions continued to impose stifling, highly restrictive contracts on their school districts, and they continued to block or weaken major reforms (serious accountability systems, serious choice programs) in state and national policy processes. Why did Bloomberg and Klein have to fight so hard in New York City against onerous contract rules that made effective organization impossible? Why did Michelle Rhee have to do the same thing in Washington? Both these districts had AFT unions. Yet while Al Shanker was president of the AFT—and singing the sweet songs of reform unionism—both these unions were burying their districts in self-interested rules that clearly were not good for kids. Bloomberg, Klein, and Rhee were dedicated to building truly effective public schools, but in order to do that they had to fight pitched battles to try to clean up the organizational messes created by their AFT unions.

What's wrong with this picture? If we take a realistic view of unions—not an ideological or emotional view, but simply a view that recognizes their essential nature as organizations—then nothing is wrong with it. It's exactly what we ought to expect: these are unions acting like unions. But if we allow our thinking to be guided by reform unionism, we immediately run into trouble: because reform unionism is a feel-good characterization of the unions that is simply not supported by the facts and leads to fantastical expectations that are not borne out. Al Shanker talked a good game, and he is revered for it. Even the unions' severest critics put him up on a pedestal as a shining exemplar of what a good, public-spirited leader should look like. But the AFT unions behaved like bread-and-butter unions when he was president. They regularly used their power in ways that were not good for kids and undermined the effective organization of schools.

This is not to say that all talk of reform by union leaders is disingenuous. It is to say that, beneath all the talk, important fundamentals are at work—and the fundamentals drive most of the action. Teachers fully expect that their leaders will protect their jobs, promote their economic well being, and win work rules that give them valuable rights and prerogatives. Leaders who are perceived as departing from these basic occupational interests, even if only marginally, do so at their own peril. Some TURN leaders have found this out the hard way, when their members rose up against unpopular reforms—seeing certain efforts at collaboration, for instance, as getting "too close to district management" and seeing pay for performance as a threat to their security—and threw them out at election time. Louise Sundin in Minneapolis. Edwin Vargas in Hartford. John Perez in Los Angeles. Deborah Lynch in Chicago. Rick Beck in Cincinnati All were defeated by members who wanted their leaders to champion a more traditional style of unionism that sticks closely to hard-core job interests.[90]

It is tempting to think that things have changed radically in recent years and that the vision of reform unionism is somehow being realized. But much of this is misleading. What has changed is that the political environment has become more hostile and pressure-filled for the unions, that reformers have gained in power, and that union leaders have had to adjust their strategies accordingly—by making concessions, by claiming reformist credit for them, and by claiming that they too are reformers and share the reformist goals of the larger movement. This is only rational under the circumstances, and by following this strategy and crafting it to a fine art, Randi Weingarten has thrust herself into the national spotlight as the second coming of Al Shanker.

With so many believers in reform unionism out there, reformers and policymakers are jumping out of their skins with excitement—and with hope. Now, finally, the unions seem to be getting on board, and the nation can make enormous progress. But this is the great danger of reform unionism: as a set of ideas, it seduces smart people into misperceiving what is really happening. The fact is, the fundamentals are the same. The unions are still unions. Their leaders—including Randi Weingarten—are still heavily constrained in what they can do, and they still have strong incentives to give top priority to the occupational interests of their members. Self-interest is still in the driver's seat, determining what they do in collective bargaining, in politics, and in their collaboration with reformers and policymakers.

If, after all the sobering ground covered in this chapter, you still wonder what the unions really want, ask yourself a simple question: why did the AFT, under Weingarten's enlightened leadership, spend $1 million to defeat Mayor Adrian Fenty in Washington, D.C.—and get rid of Michelle Rhee? Michelle Rhee is the number one symbol of education reform in this country and rightly so. Through sheer courage and dedication, she persevered through years of attacks and struggle, and she made more progress in the pursuit of effective organization than any other superintendent in modern history. *Yet the AFT wanted her out.* And she is out. The lesson is not lost, moreover, on other superintendents who might have their own visions of revolutionary reform—and the AFT was surely aware of that from the outset. This is what reform unionism looks like in reality. This is what Randi Weingarten's "support" for reform amounts to, when push comes to shove.

I conclude with one final point. The pragmatists might say, yes, Weingarten and almost all other union leaders aren't fully on board—but because the environment is so bad for them right now, they are willing to go along with important reforms (linking teacher evaluations to student performance, for example), and these are positive steps forward. We should link arms with the unions, bring them into the decision process, and move forward together.

This has a nice sound to it. Cooperation always does. And it makes a certain sense, because positive steps, especially when achieved without pitched battles, are surely better than no steps at all. But it is important to maintain perspective and see this for what it is. The unions are not in the business of representing children. It is not their goal to create a school system that is organized for truly effective performance. They are driven by their own interests, and those special interests are in the driver's seat even when the unions engage in "reform." They have strategic reasons, in this current environment, for making concessions and "embracing" change—but they will do everything they can to put their own special interest stamp on reforms, to protect jobs, and to minimize any changes that might be threatening.

If, as Weingarten insists, "collaboration must be the byword of education policy"[91] and if reformers happily link arms with her and walk down the garden path, the reform movement in this country will make some progress. But as long as the unions remain powerful, that progress will inevitably be limited. And the reform movement *will never get where it aims to go.* It will never be able to build a school system that is organized for effective performance. It will never be able to simply do what's best for children. It will be caught up in a grand compromise— and in the end, children and effective schools will be short-changed.

9

The Politics of Blocking

The teachers unions exercise power over America's schools in two ways. They do it through collective bargaining. And they do it through politics. So far, we've devoted a good deal of attention to collective bargaining and very little to politics. It's time to change that.

In the grander scheme of things, the power they wield in politics may be even *more* consequential than the power they wield in collective bargaining. That may be hard to imagine, but it's probably true. Politics is simply more fundamental. The public schools, after all, are government agencies. Virtually everything about them is subject to the authority of local, state, and national governments—and public officials in all of these governments make their decisions through the political process. The public schools are therefore the *products* of politics. This means that, because politics is driven by power, the schools are inevitably the products of political power.

By law and tradition, the public schools are governed mainly by the states. The enduring American myth is one of "local control" through school districts. But the school districts are actually state creations, and all of their essential features—their boundaries, their organizations, their funding, their programs, their involvement (or not) in collective bargaining—are subject to state authority. So while it is quite true that local decisions are important to what happens in the schools, state governments are in a position to set the basic structure of public education, and all the local players are constrained to act within that structure. The states are also able to fill in as many of the operational details as they might want—including, as we've seen, the work rules normally found in labor contracts. Any group that hopes to wield power over the public schools, therefore, needs to wield power in state politics. This is where the fundamentals are decided. This is where the real action is.[1]

From the late 1800s until the mid-1900s, the states allowed much schooling to be locally controlled. But this was simply a choice, and over the last half century they have asserted their authority. In part, they were responding to court pressures for funding equalization, which called for shifts away from local property taxes toward more centralized (state) finance. It was also a response to the modern reform era, which put the public spotlight on academic performance and motivated states to take responsibility for improving the quality of their schools. The states are now very active in controlling what the locals do. And state politics is where the powerful need to go—and win.

The national government has also gotten much more involved since midcentury. Its main vehicle has been the Elementary and Secondary Education Act (ESEA), first adopted in 1965, which authorizes a variety of programs—particularly for disadvantaged children—and funnels billions of dollars through the states to the districts. In 2001 the feds moved aggressively into the reform era with No Child Left Behind (NCLB): a ground-breaking revision of ESEA that created a nationwide system of school accountability (although the design left much discretion to the states). To this day, the states continue to reign as the key governing authorities in public education. But national politics is more relevant than ever.[2]

For the teachers unions, politics can be enormously advantageous—but it can also be enormously threatening. Governments (especially state governments) are in a position to adopt virtually *any* work rules, education programs, or funding arrangements they want for the public schools, and the decisions automatically apply to *all* the districts and schools in the relevant jurisdictions. When the unions are able to exercise political power, then, all these wonders can be made theirs—and so can the schools. But the downside is that reformers can do the same thing: by pushing for greater accountability, more school choice, pay for performance, and other reforms the unions find threatening—and turning them into the law of the land.

In either case, the stakes are huge. Because the unions know this, getting thoroughly involved in state and national politics is more than just an attractive option for them. They really don't have any choice. They need to invest in political resources and organization and to be active and powerful in the political process. And that is exactly what they've done.

In this chapter, I discuss how the unions have put their political power to use. But I have a specific focus. For the last quarter century, the politics of American education has been consumed by the continuing efforts of state and national governments (but especially state governments) to improve the public schools. Reform has been the defining educational mission of the modern era, and it is the center of attention in the pages that follow. To understand its politics is to understand a great deal about why this era—our era—has been such a disappointment, and what reformers are up against as they try to create a school system that is organized to be truly effective for kids.

What they are up against is the politics of blocking: the power of the teachers unions to stifle true reform and to preserve an ill-constructed system that is simply not built to provide children with the best education possible. When all is said and done, the power of the unions to block change is the single most important thing that anyone needs to know about the politics of American education.[3]

The Structure of Education Politics

As discussed in the opening chapters, the teachers unions were not always powerful. In fact, for the first half of the twentieth century they barely existed, and administrators ruled the roost as the acknowledged leaders of public education. But that all changed during the 1960s and 1970s, when most states enacted new labor laws to promote public sector unionism. By the early 1980s, the teachers unions had become a formidable presence from coast to coast and had established themselves as the new leaders of the nation's education system. From here on out, they would be the ones leading the charge when the system made demands on government. And they would be the ones leading the defense when the system came under attack. They became the political face—and the political force—of public education.[4]

The result was essentially a new kind of education system: very similar in structure to the older one handed down by the Progressives, but different in its leadership and distribution of power. Today, this system defines the status quo of modern American education. Born of teacher revolution, it has been in equilibrium now for some thirty years and is eminently stable, well entrenched, and well protected.[5]

Within this second-generation education system, the teachers unions are more powerful than the administrators ever were, because the sources of their power are perfectly suited to the hardball world of electoral politics. As I discuss in the next section, they have money, they have manpower, they have legions of activists, and they are superbly organized, giving them an arsenal of weapons that boost them into the stratosphere of America's political interest groups. They don't just outgun the administrators (by orders of magnitude) and other groups that have a stake in public education. They outgun virtually all other interest groups of *any* kind.

Since their meteoric rise, the teachers unions have exercised their political power in two basic ways: to pressure for the policies they want and to block the policies they don't want. In the first role, they take the lead in pushing policymakers to spend more money on the schools, adopt new programs, lower class size, increase teacher pay, protect teacher jobs, and take all sorts of related actions—for there is no end to what governments can do in the realm of public education. It is worth noting, moreover, that almost anything that adds money and programs to the system is also good for teachers and unions. At least half of all spending on the schools, whatever its purpose, tends to find its way into teacher compensation; new programs tend to require more teachers and more money; and all of this tends to increase the membership and dues revenues of the unions. By promoting a bigger, better funded education system, the teachers unions are promoting their own interests.

Their second leadership role is negative. Or to put it somewhat differently: it is defensive, and it provides support for the system—and for teachers and unions—in a wholly different way. In this role, they use their political power to oppose serious education reforms. They don't do this because they want to prevent the schools from improving, as they surely would like to see the schools perform at higher levels. And they don't do it because they don't care about kids, as they surely want kids to learn and thrive and prosper. They do it because almost any change of real consequence is likely to unsettle the jobs, security, autonomy, and working conditions of teachers—prospects that are fundamentally threatening to their members—and as unions it is the essence of their own job to protect their members' basic occupational interests. There is nothing unusual about this sort of thing, needless to say. It is what makes the American political world go 'round. In *all* areas of politics and policy, not just in public education, special interest groups are active and powerful in pushing for policies that advance their interests and opposing policies that threaten them. When the teachers unions oppose reform, then, they are simply behaving normally. They are doing what all interest groups do when their interests are threatened.[6]

And here is something else the teachers unions have in common with all other interest groups: they all have to operate within the distinctive structures of the American political system, and this system is built in such a way that the two applications of interest group power—the positive and the defensive—are not equally attractive as strategic options. This is a system famously filled with checks and balances, and the effect of these checks and balances is to make new legislation—and thus any group's positive agenda for new policies—very difficult to achieve.

Typically, whether we are talking about the state or national governments, a proposed bill must make it past subcommittees, committees, and floor votes in each house of the legislature; it must be approved in identical form by each; it may be threatened along the way by various parliamentary roadblocks and maneuvers (such as the filibusters and holds that often immobilize the U.S. Senate); and if it makes it past all these hurdles, it can still be vetoed by the executive.

For a group to get a favored policy enacted into law, then, it must win political victories at *each and every step along the way,* which is quite difficult. For a group to block a policy it opposes, in contrast, it needs to succeed at *just one* of the many veto points in order to win, which is a much easier challenge to meet. The American political system is literally designed, therefore, to make blocking—and thus defending the status quo—far easier than taking positive action. The advantage always goes to interest groups that want to keep things as they are.[7]

That the American political system favors the politics of blocking is well known. Here, for example, is an observation from a widely used text on interest groups about how the political process works in Congress:[8]

> For most organized interests in Washington, having nothing happen is a winning proposition. Most organized interests are in Washington to protect the status quo . . . The legislative process is chock full of opportunities for organized interests to mobilize a relatively small group of members or staff to kill a piece of legislation. The deck is stacked severely against those interests who wish to change public policy.

This observation is about politics in Washington, but it could just as well have been about politics in any of the state capitals. The same status quo bias is at work throughout American government, in every nook and cranny of the country. And it is at work in all areas of public policy, including education.

Because this is so, the teachers unions have a difficult time getting their own policy agendas enacted even though they are extraordinarily powerful. More often than not, especially when the policies they seek are consequential to opposing groups—which is always the case when large amounts of money are involved (because all groups want it, including groups in other realms of public policy, and there is only so much money to go around)—the unions will either lose or find that much of what they want has to be compromised away. These other interest groups will use the system's checks and balances to stop them. The teachers unions' power is likely to be stunningly effective, though, when the shoe is on the other foot and all they want to do is block the policy initiatives they dislike. Because not only do all blockers have a decided advantage, but the unions' massive political power magnifies that advantage many times over, making it quite likely that they can stop or thoroughly water down any reform proposals that threaten their interests.

Considered as a whole, these basic elements coalesce to give a distinctive structure to the modern politics of education. For the first time in its history, the American education system has a powerful protector capable of shielding it from the unsettling forces of democratic politics. The teachers unions, now the unchallenged leaders of the education establishment, have amassed formidable power rooted in collective bargaining and electoral politics. They have fundamental interests that drive them to oppose almost all consequential changes in the educational status quo. And they operate in a political system that, by favoring groups that seek to block change, makes it relatively easy to ensure that genuine reform doesn't happen.

Union Power and Union Money

By comparison to other interest groups, and certainly to those with a direct stake in public education—parents, taxpayers, even administrators—the teachers unions are unusually well equipped to wield power. The NEA and the AFT enlist more than 4 million members between them, and they blanket the entire country—including virtually every political district where public officials are running for office. Both unions have immense organizational apparatuses for communicating with their members, influencing their political perceptions of issues and candidates, and mobilizing them for coordinated action. Both can count on a zealous cadre of political activists to ring door bells, man phone banks, and do all the things that candidates love, need, and fear. Both have massive lobbying organizations for bringing their views to bear on policymakers. Both have public relations machines that can conduct media campaigns on a wide range of educational issues, and are designed with the intention of shaping public opinion and influencing elections.[9]

In addition to all this, the teachers unions are fabulously wealthy. Do the math. If some 4.5 million members are paying about $600 per person per year in dues, the total comes to $2.7 billion annually. And that's just their dues money. The unions don't spend all of it on politics, of course, but their capacity for converting money into power is way beyond what almost all interest groups can even dream of.

Most aspects of the union power formula—the role of its activists, for example—are difficult to document. But thanks to modern computer technology, excellent information is available on political contributions, and we can put this information to good use in exploring what the teachers unions are doing in politics and how they stack up against other groups. Money is not the be-all and end-all of union power, but it is certainly a major component of it—and as the data show, an impressive one by almost any standard.[10]

Candidates and Parties

For starters we need to recognize that, because public education is controlled primarily by the states, the teachers unions have good reason to invest more money in state elections than federal elections. This is only heightened by some basic facts: there are tight legal limits on campaign contributions in federal elections, whereas this is less so in most states; there are fifty state governments with

Table 9-1. *Contributions by Teachers Unions to Federal and State Campaigns*[a]

Dollars unless otherwise noted

Level and year	Contributions to candidates and parties	Contributions to ballot measures	Total contributions	Percent of contributions to Democrats[b]
Federal				
1989–90	3,793,281	...	3,793,281	94.8
1991–92	4,769,153	...	4,769,153	96.2
1993–94	5,178,006	...	5,178,006	98.8
1995–96	5,859,486	...	5,859,486	97.3
1997–98	5,854,528	...	5,854,528	96.3
1999–2000	6,724,868	...	6,724,868	95.2
2001–02	8,694,953	...	8,694,953	98.0
2003–04	4,207,343	...	4,207,343	94.1
2005–06	4,987,350	...	4,987,350	93.5
2007–08	5,396,070	...	5,396,070	95.0
Local				
2002	29,257,450	n.a.	29,969,625	85.0
2003	915,031	n.a.	1,909,381	75.0
2004	18,383,529	15,711,434	34,094,963	82.2
2005	911,141	61,009,010	61,920,151	79.0
2006	34,464,967	28,561,458	63,026,425	88.0
2007	1,414,197	5,333,371	6,747,568	79.1
2008	24,333,826	37,462,927	61,796,753	87.2

Sources: Federal data are from the Center for Responsive Politics at www.opensecrets.org. State data are from the National Institute on Money in State Politics at www.followthemoney.org.

a. All figures are combined contributions of the NEA and the AFT.

b. For state campaigns, the percentage of contributions going to Democrats is based on the money given to candidates and parties, and the calculation excludes the amounts going to third parties or to nonpartisan campaigns (which are small).

. . . Not applicable. There are no ballot measures in federal elections.

n.a. Not available. Followthemoney.org does not have complete contributions data for ballot measures for 2002 or 2003.

their own separate elections, each requiring money and attention; and there are twenty-seven states that allow citizens to vote on ballot measures (either through initiatives or referenda, usually both), and these campaigns are often extraordinarily expensive.[11]

Table 9-1 shows that the teachers unions do indeed invest much more of their money in state elections than in federal elections. At this writing, the most recent complete funding figures are from 2008. In that electoral cycle, the teachers unions contributed about $5.4 million to national campaigns. By contrast, they contributed a whopping $61.8 million at the state level: $24.3 million of it to candidates and parties and another $37.5 million to ballot measures. The states are where the action is.[12] (Here and throughout, the figures I report do not include the "independent" expenditures of unions and other groups during election cycles, only the contributions specifically made to candidates, parties, and ballot measures.[13])

Let's take a closer look at the national money. It might seem that, as contributors, the teachers unions would be dwarfed by some of the other players on the national scene, for countless interest groups and corporations are involved in national politics, including the most powerful political groups in the country, and they pony up enormous contributions to politics. Yet it turns out that the teachers unions, even in this biggest of political ponds, are still gargantuan compared to the other fish.

As shown in table 9-2, when the contributions of the NEA and AFT are combined (and as representatives of "teacher interests" it makes sense to do that: for there is only one association of real estate agents, one union of autoworkers, one association of bankers, and so on), the teachers unions are revealed to be the *number one* political contributor to national campaigns over the entire time period from 1989 through 2009, spending $59.4 million. In second place, and rather far behind, is AT&T ($45.7 million), followed by ActBlue, a Democratic political action committee (PAC, $44.7 million), the American Federation of State, County, and Municipal Employees (AFSCME, $43.0 million), the National Association of Realtors ($37.6 million), and other familiar political groups.[14]

It is notable that the teachers unions, despite their much greater interest in state politics, still topped all other groups in the country as a source of money for national candidates and parties. But two other facts are essential to note here. The first is that *not one* of the other interest groups in this list of the twenty-five top contributors has a special interest in public education. There is no group representing parents. No group representing taxpayers. Not even a group representing administrators or school boards. The unions are the biggest of the big contributors for the nation as a whole, besting interest groups of all types—but they are also the *only* group that is intensely focused on education. In important respects, then, it is misleading to compare them to the other heavy hitters—which they beat anyway. They should really be compared to groups that aren't even on the list, and that can't hold a candle to them when it comes to political money. *As education interest groups, the unions are in a league of their own.*

The second basic fact, as table 9-2 indicates, is that the teachers unions contribute overwhelmingly to Democrats, typically more than 95 percent of their totals. As a further refinement would show, at the national level the AFT has directed at least 98 percent of its contributions to Democrats in every election

Table 9-2. *Top Twenty-Five All-Time Donors in Federal Elections, 1989–2010*

Rank	Organization	Total contributions (dollars)	Percent of contributions going to Democrats
1	NEA plus AFT	59,354,731	95
2	AT&T	45,728,859	44
3	ActBlue	44,681,701	99
4	AFSCME	43,028,411	98
5	National Association of Realtors	37,629,299	48
6	Goldman Sachs	33,035,202	62
7	International Brotherhood of Electrical Workers	32,686,566	97
8	American Association for Justice	32,685,029	90
9	Laborers Union	29,834,300	92
10	Carpenters and Joiners Union	28,945,308	89
11	SEIU	28,895,482	95
12	Teamsters Union	28,877,009	93
13	Communications Workers of America	27,999,606	98
14	Citigroup	27,723,481	50
15	American Medical Association	26,865,020	39
16	United Auto Workers	26,510,252	98
17	Machinists and Aerospace Workers Union	26,151,277	98
18	National Auto Dealers Association	26,004,258	32
19	United Parcel Service	25,119,404	36
20	United Food and Commercial Workers Union	24,975,233	98
21	Altria Group	24,416,516	27
22	American Bankers Association	23,804,070	40
23	National Association of Home Builders	23,299,405	35
24	EMILY's List	22,801,244	99
25	National Beer Wholesalers Association	22,309,765	33

Source: Center for Responsive Politics at www.opensecrets.org/orgs/list.php?order=A.

since 1990, and the NEA's contributions have varied from 88 percent Democratic (in 2006) to 99 percent Democratic (in 1994). At the state level, the teachers unions are less inclined to shut out the Republicans, but the Democrats still get between 80 and 90 percent of union dollars.[15]

The unions' overwhelming support for Democrats is an instructive indicator of how they have chosen to play the political game. It would be easy to argue that, when political offices—legislatures, executives, chairs of education committees—are controlled by Republicans, the teachers unions would do well to cross party lines and provide them financial support. They may not convert the Republicans to their side, but they may gain some friends, win a degree of access, and get some help on key issues—especially if it "just" means blocking, or controlling the agenda, so that certain matters never make it out of committee or come up for a vote.

Yet they don't usually play it this way. At the federal level, the Republicans controlled the House of Representatives from 1995 through 2006 and the Senate for much of that time as well; yet, as table 9-1 shows, the teachers unions continued to contribute almost all their money to Democrats. More detail would show that the NEA slightly increased its support for Republicans during this period, raising its portion from about 5 percent to about 10 percent—still pretty measly—while the AFT never budged, continuing to put 99 percent of its money into Democratic coffers despite the Republicans' control of Congress.

This one-sided partisanship is even more intriguing as it applies to the states. Many states are reliably Republican, year after year; and even in some of the more competitive states, the Republicans often have control of the legislature. Nonetheless, as we've seen, the teachers unions contribute more than four of every five campaign dollars to Democrats in state elections overall, and this hasn't changed much over the last decade. If we look at their contributions state by state, moreover (see table 9-3, which I discuss in the next section), we see that, even in staunchly Republican states like Utah, Idaho, Kansas, and Arizona, the teachers unions are giving the lion's share of their contributions to Democrats. The proportion is usually lower than in other, less red states. But they still overwhelmingly put their money behind Democrats even when the Republicans control the state government and pervade the political culture.

That said, the teachers unions don't ignore Republicans entirely. In Pennsylvania, for instance, Republicans have consistently controlled the state Senate for the last twenty years, and although the Pennsylvania Teachers Association has spent the great bulk of its campaign money on Democrats anyway, it has also made an effort to build bridges to key Senate Republicans. During the 2008 electoral season, 84 percent of its money went to Democratic candidates, but it also gave its three largest senatorial contributions to Republicans.[16] And not just any Republicans. They were James Rhoades, chair of the Senate education committee; Joseph Scarnati, president pro tempore of the Senate (its top leadership position); and Dominic Pileggi, Senate majority leader. This kind of selective treatment makes political sense, and the unions in many other states do the same thing.[17]

Another commonality is that, when they do give money to Republicans, they almost always give to incumbents—who, of course, are going to win anyway and are a force to be dealt with in the state legislature. Consider the red state of Utah. Even in this bastion of Republican dominance, the teachers union gave 79 percent of its campaign money to Democrats in 2008, and that was pretty typical.[18] The Utah Education Association supported thirty-seven Democrats in

2008 for the state legislature, and twenty-one of them lost. It only supported ten Republicans. Of these, however, seven were incumbents who went on to win; two were nonincumbents who ran for open seats and trounced their Democratic opponents (a result that was presumably predictable from the outset); and one was a candidate who lost in the Republican nomination process, but to another Republican. Thus, while the state teachers union was willing to back many Democratic candidates who eventually lost—in its effort, presumably, to make Democratic and policy gains in the legislature—*it never backed a Republican candidate who lost in the general election.*

Which brings up another strategy that the unions sometimes follow when they (rarely) support Republicans: they occasionally pick out key primary races on the Republican side and try to get "more sympathetic" Republicans nominated. This is especially attractive in districts that are overwhelmingly Republican, where the Democrats don't stand much chance in the general election anyway.

Consider Kansas, one of the most Republican states in the country. There, in 2008, the Kansas National Education Association followed the national norm and contributed 80 percent of its campaign money to the Democrats.[19] It contributed to 102 Democratic candidates for the state legislature that year, fifty of whom lost and one of whom withdrew. It also contributed to thirty-eight Republican candidates: thirty-four of these were incumbents, and they all went on to win. Three ran for open seats, and they all went on to win as well. One was a Republican challenger, who went on to take out the Republican incumbent and win the seat. And nine others were Republican challengers who tried to get their party's nomination and lost. In Kansas, then, nine of the thirty-eight Republicans supported by the teachers union actually lost, but every one of them was a challenger in a primary election and not running against a Democrat. As in Utah, *every one of the Republicans it supported in the general election was a winner*—and presumably, fully expected to win from the get-go.

So here are a few basic patterns at work when the teachers unions invest their money in political candidates. One, they are overwhelmingly inclined to support Democrats. Two, when they do support Republicans, they are selective about it—bestowing contributions on leaders who are well positioned to do them some good in the legislative process and on incumbents (also carefully selected) who are sure to win anyway. And three, they are not shy about getting involved in Republican primaries, which gives them an opportunity to replace unfavorable incumbents with more sympathetic challengers (although this strategy often seems to fail).

To round out this picture, we need to recognize that the teachers unions do not simply devote their campaign money to individual candidates. Ballot measures aside (I get to them below), they also make contributions—sometimes enormous contributions—to party organizations: most often to the state

Democratic Party, but also, in many cases, to the party's campaign committees in the state senate and the state house of representatives. The decision about how to divide up the money between individuals and parties is a strategic one, of course. The teachers unions lose control of their money once it goes to the parties, because the parties then dole the money out to their candidates—and get the credit for it. Yet the unions and the Democrats are on the same team. And because of campaign finance laws—which in most states limit how much money PACs, individuals, and organizations can give to candidates—the parties can almost always give much more money to candidates than the unions can give on their own. So it makes good sense for them to contribute to the party. Moreover, the party campaign organizations are overseen by party leaders, and they look very favorably on groups that help them out. This is just another way that the teachers unions keep the Democrats as strong allies. They support Democratic candidates *and* they support the state Democratic Party campaign committees.

Pick any state, look at the top interest group contributors to the Democratic Party, and the teachers unions are almost always at or near the top. They are major contributors to the party—core supporters—but how they divide up their money between candidates and parties varies quite a bit from state to state, often depending on the campaign finance laws and on just how strictly limiting those laws are.

I won't go into the details. But to illustrate, consider California, New York, and Washington. All have contribution limits, as is common. In 2008 the California Teachers Association (CTA) spent $812,000 on Democratic candidates, but it also contributed an astounding $1.8 million to the state Democratic Party. New York State United Teachers contributed $447,000 to Democratic candidates, but $841,000 to the party. The corresponding figures for the Washington Education Association are $129,000 and $287,000, respectively. Now consider four states (of thirteen) where contributions to candidates were unlimited in 2008: Illinois, Indiana, Oregon, and Pennsylvania. The Illinois Education Association contributed $1.1 million in that year to Democratic candidates, but *nothing* to the state Democratic Party. The Indiana State Teachers Association contributed $1.2 million to Democratic candidates and $15,000 to the Democratic Party. The relevant figures for the Oregon Education Association are $645,000 and $57,000; and for the Pennsylvania State Teachers Association, $850,000 and $314,000.[20]

In almost all states, the teachers unions make some sort of contribution to the Republican Party as well. This contribution is usually small by comparison, but it is not always a trivial amount. In New York, for example, the state teachers union contributed $254,000 to Republican Party organizations in 2008, and in Pennsylvania the state union contributed $125,000 to the Republicans—nothing to sneeze at and an indication, once again, that they don't want to turn away from the Republicans entirely (although the California Teachers Association actually did, giving the Democratic Party a cool $1.8 million and the Republican Party zero).[21]

All in all, these are instructive patterns. They tell us something about how the teachers unions are playing the political game and strategizing the investment of their political money. But the bottom line is simple: the teachers unions overwhelmingly support Democratic candidates, and they are key supporters of the Democratic Party organization.

Comparing Teachers Unions to Other Interest Groups

Now let's take a closer look at how the teachers unions spend their political money in state-level campaigns and how they stack up against other interest groups. Comparisons across states can be tricky, because the absolute amounts spent by the unions (and other groups) in any given year depend on the size of the state, its campaign finance laws, whether education-related initiatives are on the ballot, and so on. In 2008, for example, the teachers unions contributed more than $1 million to political candidates and parties in Texas, whereas they "only" contributed about $146,000 in South Dakota. This doesn't tell us much, however, because Texas is a much more populous state than South Dakota, and we would expect campaigns to cost more there and major interest groups (which tend to have more members and more money) to contribute more. The rankings of groups *within* each state are more revealing. When we look at spending in these relative terms, we find that the teachers unions' $146,000 in South Dakota made them the top-contributing interest group in the state, while in Texas the unions' $1 million put them sixth on the list.[22]

Table 9-3 sets out within-state rankings for all fifty states, showing how the teachers unions compare to other interest groups in their contributions to candidates and parties. To help ensure an apples to apples comparison, I have only included actors that would normally be considered interest groups (including corporations and Indian tribes) and have omitted party committees, candidate PACs, and individuals. I have also excluded interest group spending on ballot measures because half the states don't have them and, in any event, the issues involved can vary quite a bit from election to election. The focus here is on the kind of campaign politics that is universal across all states: contributions to candidates (mainly governors and state legislators) and to parties.[23]

The rankings in table 9-3 are provided for two election cycles, labeled 2006 and 2008. (At this writing, the data for 2010 are still incomplete.) I have adjusted for the fact that several states have their elections in odd numbered years. In these cases, the 2005 election is listed under 2006, and the 2007 election is listed under 2008. It is worth noting, moreover, that in most states the two election cycles are not equally important. One typically involves the selection of

Table 9-3. *State-Level Contributions by Teachers Unions to Candidates and Parties, 2006 and 2008*

State and stance on collective bargaining and agency fees	2006 Contributions (dollars)	Rank	Percent going to Democrats	2008 Contributions (dollars)	Rank	Percent going to Democrats
States that have collective bargaining laws and allow agency fees						
Alaska	$41,861	14	82	$44,025	7	87
California	7,561,976	1	99	3,431,097	2	99
Connecticut	207,475	1	91	42,304	1	100
Delaware	54,975	2	67	46,232	2	65
Hawaii	212,350	1	87	167,215	1	93
Illinois	5,047,898	1	75	3,595,378	1	74
Maine[a]	58,650	4	100	24,125	21	99
Maryland	232,116	4	97	133,180	2	99
Massachusetts	141,062	1	100	176,325	1	100
Michigan	1,603,206	2	90	722,665	1	88
Minnesota	1,097,967	1	95	401,505	1	93
Montana	36,837	3	97	126,625	1	100
New Hampshire[a]	40,500	1	100	38,535	9	100
New Jersey	561,997	1	76	676,365	2	73
New Mexico[a]	216,995	3	99	127,117	6	97
New York	1,958,589	1	69	1,825,252	1	73
Ohio	1,495,748	1	88	1,241,555	1	92
Oregon	1,202,978	1	97	917,364	2	97
Pennsylvania	2,365,550	1	74	2,305,701	1	73
Rhode Island	181,430	1	99	118,280	1	99
Vermont[a]	3,375	21	100	3,140	21	100
Washington	265,727	2	97	518,448	2	96
Wisconsin	476,271	1	99	369,399	1	99
States that have collective bargaining laws but prohibit agency fees						
Florida	776,100	12	94	784,866	7	95
Idaho	110,350	1	78	124,450	1	88
Indiana	1,007,552	1	90	1,562,915	1	95
Iowa	479,602	2	100	564,890	1	100

State and stance on collective bargaining and agency fees	2006			2008		
	Contributions (dollars)	Rank	Percent going to Democrats	Contributions (dollars)	Rank	Percent going to Democrats
Kansas	150,976	1	79	185,030	1	79
Nebraska	238,328	1	n.a.	167,630	1	n.a.
Nevada	501,580	2	92	743,126	1	96
North Dakota	45,025	2	84	29,000	21	70
Oklahoma	109,277	15	93	139,981	8	77
South Dakota	131,425	1	89	85,250	1	84
Tennessee	196,750	7	89	222,600	6	90
States that do not have collective bargaining laws						
Alabama	3,316,062	1	96	523,716	2	96
Arkansas	54,300	21	97	43,357	21	98
Colorado	326,631	1	94	374,964	1	99
Kentucky	155,800	1	73	152,350	1	80
Louisiana	96,904	6	88	237,975	8	79
Missouri	193,475	10	86	194,145	21	82
Utah	121,961	3	66	98,588	7	81
West Virginia	194,750	1	96	229,575	1	96
Wyoming	35,195	2	67	38,810	2	69
States that prohibit collective bargaining						
Arizona	66,051	21	95	62,612	12	98
Georgia	247,384	21	75	104,750	21	81
Mississippi	2,750	21	100	67,000	21	98
North Carolina	459,350	4	98	595,929	3	98
South Carolina	94,700	21	84	144,550	10	89
Texas	977,271	5	71	1,053,339	6	76
Virginia	214,608	21	81	199,215	21	81

Source: Data on contributions were provided to the author by the National Institute on Money in State Politics.

a. States that have recently changed their laws to allow for agency fees and are therefore new to the strong-law category.

n.a. Not available. Because Nebraska elections are formally nonpartisan, contributions cannot be broken down by party.

just state legislators, while the other involves the selection of state legislators and governors (and other statewide offices) and thus attracts higher levels of spending. These and other details, such as the issue content of campaigns, could shed further light on how much the teachers unions and other groups are contributing and why, but I don't want to get into all the complexities here. I just want to provide a general overview—and the pattern of contributions, it turns out, is quite similar across the two years.

As table 9-3 indicates, the teachers unions are big-time contributors compared to other interest groups. Whether we look at either 2006 or 2008, they are the number one contributors to candidates and parties in well over 40 percent of the states, and they are either the number one or number two contributors in 60 percent. There is, however, some interesting variation across the states, and the pattern is just as we would expect. In the twenty-three states with collective bargaining laws that allow for agency fees—a category that includes many of the more industrial, urban states with more liberal political cultures—the teachers unions are almost always among the very top spenders in political campaigns. Indeed, if we set aside the states that only *recently* moved into this strong-law category (Maine, New Hampshire, New Mexico, and Vermont—recall the discussion in chapter 2), we find that the teachers unions were either the number one or number two contributors in 84 percent of these states in 2006, and the corresponding figure for 2008 is a whopping 95 percent. If we look at the states that lack collective bargaining laws but still permit collective bargaining, the unions' ranking relative to other interest groups is a good bit less dominant; but it is still remarkably high under the (conservative) circumstances, as they maintain their number one or two ranking in 56 percent of the states in both 2006 and 2008. In the seven most conservative states where collective bargaining is prohibited, the teachers unions are never among the top two contributors and, in most cases, are not even in the top ten.

If money is any guide to union power, then, the teachers unions appear to be more powerful—or less—in precisely the places we'd expect. But the pattern is not ironclad, and we need to be careful about over-generalizing. Alabama, for instance, is a conservative southern state with no collective bargaining law, yet its teachers union has long been a major powerhouse—indeed, its president, Paul Hubbert, was the Democratic candidate for governor in 1990—and it is among the top two contributors in both 2006 and 2008. This is not at all typical for the South. Similarly, the teachers unions are the number one contributors in Kentucky, South Dakota, Nebraska, and Idaho, all known for their conservative politics. The teachers unions are sometimes electoral powerhouses in states where all the signs would seem to point in the other direction.

Whatever the state, however, here is a generality that clearly holds. A look inside the rankings would reveal that, as we see at the federal level, the other high-spending political groups almost never have any direct stake in education. Groups representing administrators, school boards, or parents simply never show up. The groups that do show up tend to be highly specialized business groups (or companies) whose types vary considerably across states—from oil interests to real estate interests to Indian gaming interests to construction interests. But they have one crucial thing in common: their political concerns have nothing to do with public education. Sometimes the other top spenders include other public sector unions, notably the AFSCME or the Service Employees International Union (SEIU). But as we'll see, these unions aren't in the same league with the teachers unions, and on virtually all policy issues of joint interest—government spending and taxing, for example—they are allies rather than competitors.

The rankings in table 9-3 show quite vividly that the teachers unions are often among the very top contributors to politics. What they don't reveal is that, even when the unions are, say, in fifth or tenth or even twentieth place, they are probably being out-contributed only by interest groups that are unconcerned with public education and entirely uninterested in opposing them in the political process. That being so, it is perhaps useful to take a look at the unions' political contributions from another angle to get a different perspective on how much they are spending compared to other groups that are known to be active and important.

As I've said, many of the business contributors are highly specialized. But the groups that play *leadership* roles in the business community as a whole, and that tend to speak and act for it in politics, are different. They are general business associations, such as the Business Roundtable, the Chamber of Commerce, and various associations representing small business. These groups are usually important in state and local politics, and it stands to reason that, of all types of business groups, they are the most likely to take an active interest in public education. Since *A Nation at Risk*, business leadership groups of various sorts have provided much of the political power behind the movement to reform American education, acting on the business community's deeply felt concern about the connection between the quality of public education and the quality of the nation's workforce. They have, in particular, been strong political supporters of school accountability.

As one way of sizing up the monetary might of the teachers unions, then, let's compare their political contributions to those of business associations. And to make it a tough comparison, let's include *all* business associations of *all* kinds (chambers of commerce, international, small business, and so on) under the same umbrella. Thus, we are comparing the teachers unions not to specific groups, as is done in table 9-3, but rather to an entire *category* that is likely to include all the leading business groups in each state. To simplify the presentation, contributions are aggregated over the entire period from 2000 through 2009.

The results are set out in table 9-4. Rather than present dollar figures, which are not very meaningful across states, I present the ratios of teachers unions contributions to business association contributions. Any number greater than 1 means that the teachers unions are contributing more than business associations are and vice versa.

Even though business associations are legendary for their political spending and even though we are combining all business associations into one "group," *the teachers unions are typically outgunning them.* Overall, the unions are the bigger spenders in thirty-six of the fifty states. It turns out, moreover, that there is a strong regional pattern at work here: the same pattern we have witnessed time and again. The states where business associations have the upper hand are almost all southern or border states. In the rest of the country, the teachers unions out-contribute business in almost every single state. Of the twenty-three states that have collective bargaining laws with agency fees—the states where we would expect the unions to be the best organized and financed—they out-contribute business in twenty-one.[24]

Again, we need to keep in mind that these business associations have policy goals that span the full spectrum of issues that might affect the business community. Education is just one of their many political concerns. Their agendas are diverse, and their power is essentially parceled out and divided. The teachers unions, in contrast, focus *all* of their power on educational issues, and their political money is devoted entirely to those causes. In their special niche of the political world, then, they don't have much competition from other big spenders.

Finally, let's use another, very different benchmark for assessing the teachers unions' contributions to politics. As I discuss in chapter 2, the labor movement has changed dramatically over the last half century, with private sector unions experiencing massive losses in members, money, and political power and public sector unions coming on strong to become the key political power brokers. At the top of the heap, along with the teachers unions, are AFSCME and the SEIU: formidable organizations that unionize public sector workers throughout the country and whose political clout is widely recognized.[25]

The SEIU, for example, spent more than $60 million in 2008 to help elect Barack Obama. After the election, SEIU President Andy Stern was the most frequent of all visitors to the White House (twenty-one times in the first six months) and was widely touted as the most influential of all laborites with the new administration. More tangible evidence: a political director from a giant SEIU local in New York (Patrick Gaspard) was appointed White House political director, and a top SEIU lawyer (Craig Becker) was appointed to the National Labor Relations Board. These successes just begin to convey the breadth of the SEIU's political clout—for much of it is exercised not at the national level, but at the state and local levels where member jobs are located.[26]

Table 9-4. *Ratio of Campaign Contributions by Teachers Unions to Those by Business Groups, AFSCME, and the SEIU, 2000–09*[a]

State and stance on collective bargaining and agency fees	Ratio of teachers unions contributions to those of		
	Business	AFSCME	SEIU
States that have collective bargaining laws and allow agency fees			
Alaska	1.62	0.30	n.a.
California	7.50	3.18	0.88
Connecticut	2.02	2.36	1.50
Delaware	0.58	1.06	5.07
Hawaii	35.45	2.65	inf.
Illinois	2.26	5.55	3.56
Maine[b]	2.21	6.45	0.55
Maryland	4.23	1.09	0.75
Massachusetts	2.70	1.19	0.76
Michigan	2.16	10.63	15.09
Minnesota	8.63	1.79	1.96
Montana	19.98	4.28	1.22
New Hampshire[b]	2.81	9.93	4.75
New Jersey	1.26	3.12	2.47
New Mexico[b]	2.13	0.59	8.43
New York	5.01	1.00	1.02
Ohio	3.63	1.19	0.76
Oregon	2.49	4.63	1.22
Pennsylvania	4.31	2.60	4.10
Rhode Island	4.40	6.05	11.24
Vermont[b]	0.35	1.47	1.71
Washington	2.96	0.62	0.54
Wisconsin	8.87	4.37	7.53
States that have collective bargaining laws but prohibit agency fees			
Florida	0.68	3.19	3.27
Idaho	1.89	61.19	61.8
Indiana	1.71	3.62	5.83
Iowa	2.67	0.70	1.27
Kansas	1.28	7.11	7.95

(*continued*)

Table 9-4 (*continued*)

State and stance on collective bargaining and agency fees	Ratio of teachers unions contributions to those of		
	Business	AFSCME	SEIU
Nebraska	1.13	10.19	17.31
Nevada	2.81	5.71	8.32
North Dakota	0.42	2.08	20.02
Oklahoma	0.40	4.30	103.35
South Dakota	7.85	4.66	864.44
Tennessee	3.94	32.86	1.62
States that do not have collective bargaining laws			
Alabama	0.20	1,509.80	186.67
Arkansas	0.92	3.00	2.02
Colorado	3.81	4.11	1.85
Kentucky	47.74	9.10	41.56
Louisiana	0.42	3.57	19.22
Missouri	0.69	0.24	0.42
Utah	24.55	3.58	inf.
West Virginia	5.02	5.68	24.08
Wyoming	354.90	inf.	3.04
States that prohibit collective bargaining			
Arizona	5.03	0.38	0.87
Georgia	0.64	2.45	0.79
Mississippi	0.32	8.87	0.96
North Carolina	5.95	469.43	0.89
South Carolina	0.26	inf.	149.10
Texas	0.35	7.09	35.61
Virginia	0.57	0.54	0.81

Source: Data on contributions are from the National Institute on Money in State Politics at www.followthemoney.org.

a. "Business" aggregates all contributions from organizations coded by the National Institute on Money in State Politics under the broad heading of "business associations." For each group—teachers unions, business associations, AFSCME, and the SEIU—contributions include those made by local, state, and national affiliates.

b. States that have recently changed their laws to allow for agency fees and are therefore new to the strong-law category.

inf. = infinite. The ratio is infinite because the nonteacher organization made zero contributions.

And AFSCME? It is a political powerhouse too. Although it is active all over the country and at all levels of government, just as the SEIU is, one indicator of its political muscle is the flood of money it unleashed during the 2010 federal election—at a time when Democrats and their allies were frenetically trying to avoid losing their majorities in Congress, and the Supreme Court's decision in *Citizens United* had blown the lid off "independent" campaign spending.[27] The U.S. Chamber of Commerce and other conservative groups were spending a fortune for Republican candidates. Who would counter that spending for the Democrats? The big dog turned out to be AFSCME. As the *Wall Street Journal* observed at the time,[28]

> The American Federation of State, County, and Municipal Employees is now the biggest outside spender of the 2010 elections, thanks to an 11th hour effort to boost Democrats that has vaulted the public sector union ahead of the U.S. Chamber of Commerce, the AFL-CIO, and a flock of new Republican groups in campaign spending.
>
> The 1.6 million-member AFSCME is spending a total of $87.5 million on the elections . . . to help fortify the Democrats' hold on Congress . . . The group is spending money on television advertisements, phone calls, campaign mailings, and other political efforts, helped by a Supreme Court decision that loosened restrictions on campaign spending . . .
>
> AFSCME's campaign push accounts for an estimated 30 percent of what pro-Democratic groups, including unions, plan to spend on independent campaigns to elect Democrats.

The $87.5 million figure is an aggregation of all types of campaign spending (independent expenditures, spending on candidates and parties, spending on ballot measures) at all levels of government. But you get the idea: AFSCME is a monster political force and one of the leading contributors to American electoral campaigns.

So now let's get back to the teachers unions. How do they compare to these other, obviously quite formidable public sector unions, AFSCME and the SEIU? The answer is that, across the fifty states, *they almost always out-contribute them*. When we look at aggregate spending from 2000 to 2009, the teachers unions spent more on candidates and parties than AFSCME did in forty-two states (with a virtual tie in New York), and they spent more than the SEIU did in thirty-eight states (with five of the states favoring the SEIU, interestingly enough, being southern or border states). As the ratios in the table indicate, moreover, the teachers unions are often out-contributing them by huge amounts—spending, on average, two or three times as much in the typical state and often many times more.[29]

Of course, there isn't just one, definitive way to make these sorts of comparisons of group spending. And because that is so, reasonable people might come to somewhat different conclusions—were they to measure spending differently, choose their years differently, or make different comparisons—about what groups are truly "number one" and how the various groups stack up against one another. Whatever the finely grained details, however, it should be clear that the teachers unions are in the *highest stratum* of contributors to American electoral campaigns.

The Florida Election of 2002

They can be an imposing electoral force, moreover, even in states where they might appear relatively weak. Consider Florida, for example. Florida labor law does not allow agency fees, so the Florida Education Association (FEA) and its affiliates are lacking a major organizational (and money) advantage available to their brethren in many other states. Their role in campaigns would appear to reflect as much: as table 9-3 reveals, they only ranked twelfth among all Florida contributors in 2006 and seventh in 2008—unusually weak by comparison to the teachers unions in most other states. In addition, as table 9-4 shows, they were out-contributed during 2000–09 by the state's business associations—which, again, is unusual.

Yet consider what the "weak" Florida Education Association is capable of. In the Florida gubernatorial election of 2002, the incumbent running for reelection was Jeb Bush. During his first term in office, Bush had made education his number one priority, and had taken advantage of outsized Republican majorities in both houses of the state legislature to enact truly path-breaking reforms—in both accountability (via his A+ program, which required rigorous annual testing and the grading of individual schools) and school choice (via three new voucher programs and the expansion of charter schools). Bush was, even in his first term, the most successful "education governor" the nation had ever seen.[30]

From the FEA's standpoint, he was a nightmare come true—and with the 2002 election looming, the union had an opportunity to throw him out of office. But what could a "weak" union do? Plenty.

The front-runner in the Democratic primary was Janet Reno, fresh from an eight-year stint as attorney general in the Clinton administration, and thus a well-known public figure. But the FEA didn't like Reno as a candidate, and it took aggressive action to *deny her the nomination* and *install its own candidate* as the party's nominee. Its choice was a man named Bill McBride, who was a complete unknown and had never before run for office. Early on, Reno was some 30 points ahead of McBride in the polls. But the FEA sank some $3 million into a blitzkrieg of campaign ads, which eventually had the desired effect. On Election Day, McBride won the nomination.[31]

During the general election, the FEA literally *ran the McBride campaign*. The FEA's own director of government relations, Cathy Kelly, became the McBride organization's campaign director, and her salary was paid by the union. The union's own communications director, Tony Welch, was also loaned to the McBride organization, and his salary too was paid by the union. Education was McBride's number one issue, and his agenda—shaped by the FEA—was wholly predictable: he wanted to do away with the A+ accountability system, he wanted to dump the state's voucher programs, and as "reforms" he favored smaller classes and increases in teacher salaries. Said the *St. Petersburg Times*, "The union is involved in his campaign at every level, from strategy to communications. Not in recent history has a Florida candidate been so publicly entwined with a single interest group."[32]

How much the FEA ultimately spent to unseat Bush is unclear, because almost all of its money went into advertising and other independent expenditures that are difficult for anyone to track. But it spent millions. Indeed, there were media claims that it had even mortgaged its state headquarters building for more than $1.5 million in order to beef up its available cash.[33] For some time, all the FEA spending and advertising—with help from its friends in the Democratic Party, the AFL-CIO (whose state affiliate "it dominates"[34]), and AFSCME (which spent $1 million[35])—seemed to be making for a close election, and the Bush forces were worried.[36] But in the end, it was to no avail. Bush was popular, he had plenty of his own money, and he won the election by 13 points. (The FEA did, however, succeed in passing a phenomenally expensive and constraining class size requirement through a ballot measure.[37])

The lesson, however, is not that the FEA lost, especially to someone of Jeb Bush's stature. The lesson is that this "weak" state teachers union, which reasonable indicators would suggest is not in the same league with its counterparts in most other states, was nonetheless able to *hijack the entire Democratic campaign apparatus* in an all-out effort to defeat the nation's most prominent reformist governor. The FEA wasn't just another "important" interest group. It *took over* the Democratic side of the campaign. The election wasn't really between Bill McBride and Jeb Bush. It was between the Florida Education Association and Jeb Bush.

An addendum. In the 2010 general election, the Democratic nominee for governor—who ran with strong FEA support but lost by a hair—was Alex Sink. Alex Sink is Bill McBride's wife.

Ballot Measures

Union contributions to parties and candidates are intended to buy access and influence in the legislative process, which is where almost all the lawmaking action is. In twenty-seven states, however, laws can also get made through ballot measures that are decided by direct vote of the people.

Numerically, very few laws are adopted this way. Nonetheless, because ballot measures can deal with almost any type of policy—public education, health care, assisted suicide, taxes and spending, you name it—and because direct democracy blasts through all the usual checks and balances by allowing for a simple up or down vote, it can be extremely attractive for groups whose policy goals have been stifled in the legislative process. For the same reasons, it can be extremely threatening to groups that oppose these policies: they only have one opportunity to block, and if they fail they have no recourse (except the courts). The stakes on either side can be tremendous, and the result is often massive conflict and awesome levels of political spending.[38]

From a research standpoint, the nice thing about ballot measures is that they are specific policy proposals, and they allow us to see just what policies the teachers unions want, how much they are willing to contribute to get their way, and how their contributions compare to those of other groups. The results speak volumes.

The best-known ballot measures on public education have involved proposals for school vouchers, which would allow children to attend private schools with government assistance. (I discuss vouchers in more detail later on.) The teachers unions see vouchers as a survival issue. They don't want one child or one dollar to leave "their" schools for the private sector. And over the years they have spent a small fortune on ballot campaigns to defeat them: in California (twice), Utah, Michigan, Colorado, and elsewhere. While various groups have gone on record as opposing vouchers, from the NAACP to the PTA to the ACLU, *these groups have done virtually nothing to bankroll the ballot campaigns.* The unions have taken the lead and contributed virtually *all* the political money.[39]

The California voucher campaigns have been the most costly. Indeed, in that state's 2000 voucher battle, the teachers unions contributed a mind-boggling $21 million, dwarfing the contributions of others in their coalition.[40] Magnitude aside, the pattern has been exactly the same elsewhere. Take Utah's voucher battle in 2007, for example. There, opponents spent a grand total of $3.5 million in their successful campaign to defeat vouchers, an enormous amount for Utah politics. Virtually every penny of the money was contributed by the teachers unions. The NEA and the Utah Education Association together contributed $3.2 million (almost all of which, bookkeeping aside, was funneled into the state by the NEA). The rest came from teachers unions in other states—California, Washington, Colorado, Illinois, New Jersey, Kentucky, Wisconsin, Pennsylvania, and Ohio—that sought to help out. The name of their PAC was "Utahns for Public Schools," which had the sound of a diverse, public-spirited coalition. But from a financial standpoint, it wasn't a coalition at all, and it wasn't even funded by Utahns. It was simply a campaign by the NEA and its affiliates to stop vouchers.

California has an especially active tradition of ballot-measure politics and, vouchers aside, has been the scene of some of the most memorable campaigns. In 1988 the California Teachers Association (CTA) put a proposal on the ballot, known as Proposition 98, that would require the state to spend some 40 percent of its budget every year on public education, and the union spent $4.5 million (a tremendous sum in those days) in a successful effort to have it enshrined in law.[41] This was a political coup of the first order for the CTA. How often is a special interest group able to commandeer 40 percent of a state's entire budget for its own realm of policy? It was also a watershed in California political history, for it placed massive, debilitating restrictions on the state's policymakers, who to this day have been forced to deal with the full range of California's other problems and needs with just 60 percent of their revenues.

More recently, in 2005, California featured the most celebrated ballot campaign of the decade when Governor Arnold Schwarzenegger—stymied by a Democratic legislature—tried to bring about major reforms by taking them directly to the people. He proposed that redistricting be taken out of the legislature's hands and determined by an independent panel; that government spending be capped and Proposition 98 loosened; that teachers be evaluated for tenure after five years rather than just two; and that unions be required to get the consent of individual members before using their money for politics. These proposals excited the opposition of many groups in the Democratic coalition, particularly public sector unions—and above all the teachers unions. In the battle royal that ensued, the California Teachers Association assumed overall leadership of the opposition and became its biggest spender by far: laying out an unfathomable $54.7 million for the campaign. The total for all teachers unions was a cool $60.1 million.[42] All four ballot measures went down to defeat, and the governor was thoroughly humbled. Schwarzenegger eventually reinvented himself, winning reelection in 2006. But his governing style became much more consensual, and fundamental reform was essentially off the agenda for his entire second term.[43]

The magnitude of California ballot politics is extraordinary. But the basic patterns are the same all across the country. Here are but a few illustrations of what the education coalitions tend to look like when school-related issues are on the ballot.[44]

—The citizens of Idaho voted in 2006 on a statewide proposition that would add 1 percent to the state sales tax and dedicate the new funds to K–12 education. The supporting political action committee, which called itself the Invest in Our Kids Education Campaign, spent $2.2 million. Of this total, $1.1 million was contributed by the Idaho Education Association, and another $970,000 was contributed by the NEA national organization. Virtually all the rest was contributed by teachers unions from other states: California, New Jersey, Washington, and many others.

—In Washington, voters in 2007 were asked to decide whether school districts should be allowed to raise property taxes based on a simple majority of the votes cast (a change that would make it easier for districts to increase taxes). The PAC supporting this proposition, called People for Our Public Schools, spent $3.3 million on the campaign. More than 40 percent of its contributions came from the teachers unions, including the NEA, and the rest came in much smaller amounts from a variety of other educational employee groups.

—In 2004 Washington voters were presented with a ballot proposal that would have authorized charter schools in the state. The PAC opposing the proposition was called Protect Our Public Schools. It raised $1.3 million, with well over 90 percent of the money coming from the Washington Education Association, the NEA, and local teachers unions.

—Michigan voters in 2006 considered a proposition that would establish mandatory funding levels for the public schools. The support PAC, called Citizens for Education, spent a total of $4.5 million. Three-fourths of this money came from the NEA, 14 percent from the Michigan Education Association, and most of the rest from other teachers unions.

These illustrations are pretty typical. When propositions dealing with public education are on the ballot—which often happens because the unions have *put* them there—two basic patterns emerge. The first is that the teachers unions are regularly the *leaders* of their side of the coalition and its *number one spender*. Indeed, despite the lofty names associated with their PACs—which usually imply that they are representing children or citizens generally—it is a stretch to say that there is a coalition at all. Other groups rarely play a consequential role. The teachers unions *are* the coalition, and they are often funding the lion's share of the campaign.

The second pattern is that, although these are state-level elections involving contests over state propositions, active intervention by the NEA—the national parent—is quite common. The NEA does not view these elections as isolated events. It takes a national perspective, recognizing that success or failure in one state is likely to affect what happens elsewhere. It also recognizes that some state unions (unlike in California) don't have the money to launch formidable campaigns of their own; even if they did, they would not have incentives to take full account of the spillover effects on the nation at-large and would tend to spend less than a national perspective would warrant. So the NEA does not simply sit on the sidelines and provide advice and guidance. It often digs deep into its financial pockets to try to shape the outcomes of state elections. It orchestrates union politics from the center.

There is even more to be said about the unions' role in direct democracy than this, however. The fact is, they also get involved in ballot measures that are *not* specifically about education, but deal with much broader issues—spending and taxing authority, especially—that affect the entire operation of state government. The reason for their involvement is no mystery: public education usually claims a bigger share of state and local budgets than any other governmental function—health care, public welfare, prisons, police, fire, roads—and the teachers unions know that any significant change in how taxes are levied or revenues are spent can hugely affect the funding available for schools and thus teachers. They have a direct material stake in bigger budgets and higher taxes.[45]

They are hardly alone. Lots of groups benefit from bigger government. All public sector unions do, including huge organizations like AFSCME and the SEIU. So do construction firms, trial attorneys, minority groups, and more. The list is endless. They all are on the receiving end of government spending, and they all have something to gain from ballot measures that affect taxes or spending. This being so, it is perhaps natural to think that participation on these measures would be very broadly based, at least among organized interest groups. In particular, it is perhaps natural to think that campaign contributions would come from a vast array of sources and that the teachers unions would not play an especially prominent role.

This kind of thinking is not entirely wrong. Often, more groups *are* involved, and the contribution load is more widely shared. But the teachers unions, even on these most general of governmental issues, still stand out from all the other groups. They aren't just involved. They are clearly leaders of their coalition. Consider, for instance, some of the more recent ballot campaigns in which citizens were asked to pass new laws that would limit government spending (with increases allowed for inflation and population growth).[46]

—In Washington's election of 2009, a measure to cap government spending was opposed by a PAC called the No on I-1033 Committee, which raised $3.5 million. It attracted about half of its contributions from public sector unions, another 10 percent from private sector unions, and the rest from various business groups (associated with hospitals and nursing homes, for instance) that depend on government for income. Of all these groups, however, the teachers unions contributed the most—and the single largest contributor was the NEA.

—In the same year, Maine also considered a government spending cap. The PAC leading the charge against it was Citizens Unified for Maine's Future, which spent $2.4 million. That money came mainly from public sector unions, with assorted help from municipal associations and government-related business interests. But the teachers unions were the heavy hitters. Together, the NEA and the Maine Education Association provided roughly a third of the PAC's total funding. The NEA, which alone contributed 24 percent, was by far the single largest contributor.

—In 2006 Nebraska's voters were also presented with a spending cap proposal. The opposition was led by Nebraskans against 423, which spent $2.4 million.

Public sector unions (aside from teachers unions) are weaker in Nebraska than in Washington and Maine, and they shared much less of the contributions load, although they were certainly involved. The other contributors included school administrators, school boards, municipal associations, business interests, and the like, as well as the American Association of Retired People (AARP), which provided a surprising 20 percent of the PAC's total funds. Still, none of these groups could hold a candle to the teachers unions, which provided 58 percent. And the single largest contributor? The National Education Association, at 32 percent.

These examples are just illustrative and deal only with spending caps. We could easily take a look at many more issues, covering a much wider array of state taxing and spending issues. Here are a few more illustrations:[47]

—In 2008 Massachusetts voted on a proposal to end the state income tax, and the opposition coalition (Citizens for Our Communities) raised $7.6 million to defeat it. The teachers unions contributed 81 percent of the total, and the biggest single contributor was the Massachusetts Education Association. (The NEA came in second.)

—In the same year, North Dakota voted to reduce corporate and individual income taxes and also to create an oil tax trust fund. Partners to Protect North Dakota's Future raised $571,000 to defeat these measures, and the teachers unions contributed 70 percent of the total. The biggest single contributor was the NEA.

—In 2006 Washington voted on whether to repeal the estate tax. This proposition was opposed by No on 920, which raised $2.1 million to defeat it. The teachers unions contributed 58 percent of the total. The biggest single contributor was the Washington Education Association. (The NEA was number two.)

—In the same year, Minnesota considered a proposal to dedicate taxes from the sale of motor vehicles to public transit and highways. It was opposed by Education Minnesota, the state teachers union, which contributed $2.5 million to defeat the proposition—and was the only contributor on that side of the issue.

Union Money: An Overview

The teachers unions are a political money machine. In national elections, despite the enormous numbers and types of interest groups and their great diversity, they have doled out so much money to candidates and parties that they top the list as the number one contributors to campaigns over the last few decades. In state elections, especially outside the South, their dominance is even more clearcut: they are almost always among the very largest contributors to candidates and parties, they regularly out-contribute general business associations (even when the latter are aggregated into one giant "group"), and in ballot campaigns they are consistently the political leaders and top contributors on their side of the issue—even on matters of taxing and spending that have nothing directly to do with education.

Money is not all that matters in politics, and big contributors don't always get what they want. In ballot campaigns, for instance, getting propositions passed is often more difficult than defeating them; and when the unions try to use their electoral heft to increase taxes, they often lose. This is what happened in the Idaho 2006 campaign discussed earlier: Idaho is a very conservative state with a tradition of low taxes, and getting its citizens to raise taxes is a hard battle—one the unions lost despite all their money. The same thing happened in the Michigan 2006 election on mandatory school funding.

When it comes to candidates and parties, moreover, big contributors face another problem: almost all incumbents tend to win regardless of party. Union money is unlikely to unseat Republican incumbents. And it can't guarantee the unions great clout with every Democrat they support, because incumbents with safe seats may feel they can win without union money if they have to.

So money is no guarantee of power. But it surely gives top-spending interest groups real advantages in the political process. Politicians and parties clearly *do* want money. They aggressively seek it out, and they are in a position to use government decisions to reward their supporters. Meantime, the unions and other interest groups are not contributing out of the goodness of their hearts. They are spending huge sums precisely because they expect to get something in return for their investments. They get something in return if their political money helps to get "right thinking" politicians elected to office: people who share their views and can be counted upon for votes. And they get something in return, even in the absence of shared views, when the people they support are willing to grant them access—and be more responsive to their policy demands—in order to *keep* that support. This is what political influence is all about.[48]

We have to keep in mind, moreover, that money is just *one* dimension of power for the teachers unions. It only begins to indicate the full range of resources they can bring to bear. In the eyes of many candidates, the teachers unions loom large not simply because of their campaign contributions, but because they can unleash an army of political activists at election time. What other groups can do that? This is something that requires numbers, organization, experience, and leadership—all of which the unions have assiduously cultivated over the years and that almost all other groups lack. The near-universal role of teachers unions as big-time political contributors, then, is an important measure of their power in American politics, but their money also goes hand in hand with an awesome array of complementary resources that beef up their power quotient considerably—and set them apart from other interest groups. They really are in a league of their own.

Education Reform and the Politics of Blocking

Ballot measures aside, the teachers unions get involved in elections because, by exercising power in those settings, they can prepare the way for what they really want to do, which is to influence state and national education policy. So the key question we need to answer is, how well and in what ways are they actually able to do that?

This question is difficult for one book—far less, one chapter—to address in a comprehensive way. Virtually all aspects of the public schools, from budgets and programs to layoffs and excessing to whether teachers can be assigned to lunch duty—are subject to the authority of government officials and thus to political decision. *Everything* about the schools can be dragged into the political process and dealt with through policy. Decisions about policy, moreover, don't just happen in state legislatures or the halls of Congress or initiative elections. They also happen in state school boards, teacher certification boards, textbook adoption committees, state and federal courts, and a host of other arenas.

All of this affects the schools—and children—in one way or another. That said, some things are clearly more important than others. Over the last quarter century, policymakers throughout this country—at the national level, but especially at the state level—have been deeply engaged in an ongoing effort to significantly improve the schools and boost student achievement. This movement is the defining feature of the modern era of American education. Nothing is more central or more important. To understand this nation's schools, then, and to understand their politics, we can do no better than to focus our attention here.[49]

What we see, in the sections to follow, is that the teachers unions have been *the* pivotal players throughout the modern era. They are not all powerful. Sometimes they lose, and often they have to compromise. But their extraordinary power has allowed them to shape the nation's public schools in two fundamental ways, both of which involve the politics of blocking. First, they have purposely chosen not to block minor, mainstream "reforms": those that mean more jobs and money and that don't threaten their interests. And second, they have acted to block or weaken the more far-reaching reforms that are designed to bring profound change, and hopefully significant improvement, to the system. Over the decades, as a result, there has been a lot of costly, time-consuming, much-ballyhooed "reform" activity—but the unions have been quite successful at preventing true reform, and at protecting a status quo that continues to disappoint and underperform. The story of American education reform, then, is not mainly a story about what happened over the last several decades. It is mainly a story about what *didn't* happen.

As I finish this book, there is much buzz in the air about the prospects for major reform, due in large measure to Arne Duncan's Race to the Top. The teachers unions are on the defensive—and publicly criticized and pressured to make compromises and concessions—to a greater extent than ever before. I discuss these very recent developments, including Race to the Top, in chapter 10. I think it is important to emphasize first, however, that anyone who aims to understand the politics of reform and its true prospects needs to have perspective, and thus the ability to see these recent events in historical and institutional context. The present is a continuation of the past, shaped by the same fundamentals. To understand recent developments, exciting though they may seem, we need to understand the past. And we need to keep our eyes on the ball—looking to the fundamentals that explain behavior, strategy, and power. Buzz is just buzz, and likely to be misleading, unless it is rooted in something deeper.

Mainstream Reform

A good place to begin is the early 1980s, when two new forces burst onto the scene that would shape the contours of American education for decades to come. The first was the publication of *A Nation at Risk*, the 1983 report by the President's Commission on Excellence in Education that stoked the fires of reform and launched the reformist era. The second was the emergence of the teachers unions—after twenty-some years of furious organizing—as the de facto leader of public education, the most powerful force in its politics, and an immensely well-armed defender of the very system the reform movement sought to change. The battle lines were drawn.

At the time, the key drivers of reform were business groups and state governors. Deeply concerned about a faltering economy and the growing threat of international competition, business groups saw a mediocre education system as a big part of the problem. They demanded action and found allies in the nation's governors, who became the political leaders of the reform movement. Unlike legislators, governors have large, eclectic constituencies that prompt them to think about the broader interests of their states, and they are held responsible—as legislators are not—for their state economies. In a federal system that gives businesses plenty of choice in deciding where to locate, moreover, governors are unavoidably competing against each other: all want to create economic environments, and thus education reforms, that businesses find attractive.[50]

But what reforms would really work? Not experts themselves, governors turned to experts within the education community. They also set up countless commissions and task forces. All around them, moreover, were high-profile reports by prominent national organizations—the Carnegie Forum on Education and the Economy, the Holmes Group, the Twentieth Century Fund, the Education Commission of the States, and many more—arguing the need for specific lines of reform and urgent action.[51]

Early on, the ideas that gained the most traction were decidedly incremental: the schools could be improved by spending more money, adopting more rigorous curricula, boosting teacher quality, and making other incremental changes that fit comfortably within the existing system. As a result, the education tsunami that swept across America in the early years after *A Nation at Risk* involved little that was threatening to the teachers unions. When threatening ideas did emerge—this was, after all, a tumultuous time—the unions were largely successful at blocking them. But for the most part, mainstream reform was quite compatible with their interests, and they supported it.[52]

National spending on public education shot up dramatically, as politicians demonstrated their commitment to reform in the most obvious way. From 1982–83 through 1989–90, per-pupil spending increased a full 74 percent—providing the schools, after inflation, with 35 percent more money for every student. Over the following decade, per-pupil spending adjusted for inflation increased another 14 percent.[53] From the unions' standpoint, of course, this emphasis on spending was a dream come true and exactly what education reform should be about—for most of the money goes to hire more teachers, to pay them higher salaries and benefits, and, unavoidably, to make the unions themselves bigger, wealthier, and more powerful. As a means of improving the schools, however, there was never any credible basis for this spending strategy: there was no evidence that more money would lead to significant achievement gains, but every reason to believe that an unproductive system would take the additional money and spend it unproductively. Which, in the years since, is precisely what has happened.[54]

Strengthening the curriculum was a reform idea that made far better sense than simply spending more money. Clearly, students need challenging coursework if they are to achieve at high levels. But this line of reform didn't work either, at least as it was implemented at the time. What the political process yielded was not academic rigor, but the appearance of rigor: stricter formal requirements ensuring that more students would take higher-level courses. Over the 1982–83 to 1989–90 period, graduating seniors did indeed amass more credits in English, math, science, and foreign languages, and they took classes that were supposedly more advanced.[55] It is not enough, however, to give courses impressive-sounding titles or to force students to sit through more academic classes, unless there is an accountability system to assure that the content is actually being taught and learned—which, of course, there wasn't. Writing in 1991, in what is perhaps the best historical overview of the early period of reform, Thomas Toch observed, the "vast majority of high school students . . . are getting little more exposure to rigorous course work than they did previously. Despite the reformers' successful push for new graduation requirements, [students] are receiving an academic education in name only."[56]

Efforts to improve teacher quality were also a disappointment. The goal surely needs to be a national priority, as teacher quality is the single most important determinant of student achievement (aside from the social backgrounds of the students themselves). Yet efforts by reformers to improve the quality of teachers quickly got tangled up with issues of certification, evaluation, and job security—and came face to face with the teachers unions.

The unions were in favor of improving teacher quality too. But they wanted it pursued, and still do, in traditional ways that aren't threatening to their members—and, in particular, aren't threatening to members who may *not* be high in quality. In their view, the keys to better teaching are to be found in beefing up the existing system:

—Higher across-the-board salaries for *all* teachers, which, in addition to helping attract better candidates to the profession, would put more money in the pockets of all existing members,

—Stricter certification requirements, which would keep the supply of teachers down and only make life difficult for teacher wannabees who aren't yet members,

—Better education school training of teachers, which follows the same rationale,

—The ongoing training of veteran teachers during their careers, via professional development, college credits, and master's degrees, which would move them onto higher steps on the salary ladder.[57]

The evidence suggests that these approaches to teacher quality don't work very well. Across-the-board raises are unproductive: they throw money at bad teachers as well as good ones and would have to be astronomically expensive to deliver any impact. The education schools do a poor job of training teachers, and the formal certification they provide has been shown to have little positive effect on student achievement. The same can be said of professional development, college credits, and master's degrees.[58] Nonetheless, all these approaches to teacher quality proliferated during the 1980s—and remain nearly universal today—because they seem so sensible to policymakers and because the unions find them quite acceptable and have kept the political gates wide open to allow them through.

For other paths to teacher quality, the unions have shut the gates. It is painfully obvious, for instance, that teacher quality could be improved if the dismissal of mediocre and incompetent teachers were easier to accomplish instead of being virtually impossible. Such a policy is likely to have enormously beneficial payoffs. As I've noted before, the difference between having an excellent teacher and a bad teacher, for the typical student, translates into a year's worth of learning. Indeed, economist Eric Hanushek estimates that, were the bottom 5 percent of teachers permanently replaced, U.S. students would make huge achievement gains and would move from well below average in the international test-score ranking to somewhere near the top. Over a twenty-year period, the nation's GDP would increase an estimated 1.6 percent.[59]

Yet the unions are in the business of protecting the jobs of *all* their members, and they are strongly opposed to reforms that allow administrators to remove even the most poorly performing teachers from the classroom.[60] Their political success has been so great and so consistent that ideas for modifying the ironclad job security of teachers have rarely even made it onto the political agenda for discussion. The idea that bad teachers should be moved out of the classroom is obvious to any reasonable person, but for decades it has been a political nonstarter.

Things are beginning to change, as reformers have succeeded in making it a focus of public attention and outrage, aided immensely by Race to the Top and its emphasis—coming directly from Obama and Duncan—on rigorous teacher evaluations. As part of the surge of activity under Race to the Top, Colorado managed to adopt a bold reform, over strenuous union opposition, that tied teacher evaluations to student achievement and imposed new requirements that could lead low-performing tenured teachers to lose their tenure and, ultimately, to be dismissed. Several other states—Louisiana and Delaware, for instance—moved in the same general direction, although not as far as Colorado.[61] (We'll discuss all this in detail in chapter 10.)

Whether these reforms will last and how they will pan out in practice remains to be seen. The details—ominously—remain to be filled in via collaborative processes that the unions can still influence, and even the "breakthrough" bills have built-in obstacles. As *Education Week* says of the Colorado reform, for example, "Teachers won't be at risk of losing tenure until 2015 because lawmakers slowed down the process under political pressure from the teachers union. Teachers can appeal dismissal all the way to the state Supreme Court, and school districts have the burden of proving why they should be terminated."[62] And Colorado's reform is probably the boldest.

In any event, these efforts to relax tenure so that districts and states have a prayer of getting bad teachers out of the classroom are hardly the norm, and they are outgrowths of an unusual event whose reformist incentives are likely to go away. Modern history is better reflected in what happened several years ago when California's Governor Schwarzenegger tried to put tenure reform on the political agenda in the normal course of events—if only in a weak form that had nothing to do with dismissing anyone. What he proposed, in his 2005 ballot measure, was a simple modification of the state's teacher tenure law that would extend the probationary period from two years to five years. Even this was unacceptable to the California Teachers Association, which was furious at the suggestion. As we've seen, it unleashed a brutal political onslaught against him during the campaign, and he and his proposal went down to a crushing defeat.[63]

Or take what happened to Governor Ray Barnes of Georgia. A Democrat elected with union support in 1998, he got serious about tackling the state's low-performing education system and ultimately succeeded in passing a far-reaching school accountability reform, which included the elimination of tenure for incoming teachers. The Georgia Association of Educators refused to endorse him in 2002 (although it endorsed all other Democratic candidates for office), went on the warpath, and is widely credited with bringing about his defeat to Republican Sonny Perdue—who very quickly moved to rescind the offending tenure reform.[64] Fast forward to 2010. Perdue was set to leave office after two terms, and ex-governor Barnes was on the campaign trail trying to put together enough support to reoccupy his old job. At the top of the list: getting the teachers union back on his side by being very, very sorry for the bad things he did in the past.[65]

Roy Barnes' mea culpa tour has lasted more than a year, as he begs forgiveness from teachers who helped oust him from the governor's mansion in 2002 . . . "I apologize," one of his campaign videos starts out. "I should have slowed down, and I should have reached consensus better and listened better. I think it was the greatest failure of my administration." There's a reason he's making such a fuss. Georgia has more than 125,000 teachers. Throw in retired educators and hundreds of thousands of family members and friends they could influence, and they make a formidable constituency that could have a big impact on elections.

Tenure reform aside, another simple way to improve teacher quality is to test all veteran teachers for competence in the subjects they teach. This idea surely makes sense. Clearly, if a math teacher doesn't know math, she can't possibly be an effective teacher.[66] But the unions have stridently opposed such testing, arguing that all teachers with formal certification are competent to teach. During the mid-1980s, new laws requiring the testing of veteran teachers were adopted in Arkansas, Texas, and Georgia—states with relatively weak unions—but even in these cases, the tests were purposely pitched at such a low level that they barely weeded out the illiterate, if that, and quickly fell into disuse. North Carolina adopted a testing plan in 1997 for veteran teachers in its lowest-performing schools, and Pennsylvania adopted a plan in 2001 for testing all its veteran teachers; but within a few years, both were no longer operating. Everywhere else, the unions were successful at blocking even such pathetic attempts to assure substantive competence, and in most states the idea of testing has simply been kept off the agenda.[67]

As noted in chapter 7, any notion that all veteran teachers are competent, or nearly so, and thus that such tests are not needed, is egregiously wrong—because when serious tests are actually given to veteran teachers, appreciable numbers of them do quite badly. The Philadelphia case referred to earlier is a graphic example: recall that more than two-thirds of the middle school math teachers in that city failed the math test, and the failure rate for middle school teachers overall was about one half. Testing is a simple, straightforward means of identifying teachers who don't know their subject matter, which in turn is an obvious, necessary component of any strategy for improving the quality of teaching in the nation's schools. Yet the teachers unions have made it impossible to do the obvious.[68]

Another sensible reform is pay for performance. Teaching aside, performance pay is quite common among professionals. More generally, about three-fourths of all salaried workers in the private sector are covered by some sort of performance pay and are not simply placed on lockstep salary schedules.[69] Performance incentives are also often used in both private and charter schools, so there is nothing about education per se that makes them difficult to employ.[70] In fact, student learning can be directly measured, teacher behavior in the classroom can be directly observed, and research has shown that the variation in teacher effectiveness, even within individual schools, is often quite dramatic.[71]

If teacher pay were to depend (just in part) on performance in the classroom, good teachers could be paid more than bad ones. By rewarding productive behavior, such a system would then do two things: it would give teachers incentives to perform at high levels, and it would generate a dynamic of "selective attraction" in which high-quality people would be more attracted to teaching—knowing they will be rewarded for their productivity—and low-quality people would be less attracted and less likely to stay.

There are many ways of designing pay-for-performance systems. These days it is common for them to involve value added measures of student achievement (which are the changes in test scores over a given year, or perhaps averaged over two or three years), additional measures (such as classroom observation) that go beyond test scores, and adjustments for student background. Exactly how these things come into play can vary quite a bit from one design to another; and research will surely show that some are more effective than others. But it is only reasonable to think that, with well-intentioned designs that are modified over time with experience and new information, performance pay can help raise the quality of teaching.[72]

The teachers unions have traditionally been opposed to performance pay.[73] As a recent *New York Times* article observed, "Unions offer a range of arguments against linking pay to what goes on in the classroom—that it is unhealthy for teachers to compete with one another, that they will cheat, that it is impossible to quantify good teaching, that the benefit to students is not proven, that all teachers deserve equal reward, that it allows management to play favorites. The bottom line is solidarity."[74] What the teachers unions strive for is a world of professional sameness, in which all teachers with the same experience and educational credentials are paid the same and all teachers see themselves as doing the same job and having the same interests.

During the 1980s and 1990s, pay for performance was actively discussed as a policy option. Indeed, it was proposed in *A Nation at Risk* and a number of subsequent reports. But it went nowhere in the political process. The unions regularly used their power to block it. The political dynamics have been changing on this issue over the last decade. Political support for performance pay has picked up considerably among policymakers and reformers, and modest progress has actually been made. But "modest" is the key word here, because the unions continue to resist.[75]

Prior to Race to the Top, various states had adopted programs that encouraged districts to embrace some version of pay for performance. Most often, these departures from the single salary schedule didn't amount to much. But sometimes they did. The most innovative programs were in Florida, Texas, and Minnesota, states that, not coincidentally, were led at the time of adoption by Republican governors with substantial Republican support in the state legislatures (the Republicans controlled both houses in Florida and Texas and one house in Minnesota). Even in these three states, the pay plans that passed were essentially a foot in the door: the school districts were allowed to decide for themselves whether to participate, and most chose not to. In Florida, for example, just eight of sixty-seven districts participated. In Minnesota, moreover, the details of any pay plan had to be hammered out through bargaining with the local unions, which hardly favored serious innovation. Still, when districts did participate—induced, in many cases, by the extra money—each program required that performance be measured (at least in part) by student test score gains, and thus that there be a connection between a teacher's pay and how much students learn in the classroom.[76]

These plans were the result of state legislation. That is our focus in this chapter. But pay for performance has also been advanced, as discussed in chapters 7 and 8, through innovations at the district level. The most notable is in Washington, D.C., where Michelle Rhee engaged in a fierce battle for more than two years with her local union and eventually won the nation's boldest departure yet from the single salary schedule. Precisely because she was so successful, however, she also *lost her job,* and it's unclear what will happen to that pay plan going forward, now that the union's allies are in charge of the district. Other notable innovations in performance pay have been adopted (prior to Race to the Top) in Denver, Houston, Minneapolis, and New York City—and, with the inducement of enormous grants from the Bill and Melinda Gates Foundation, in Memphis, Pittsburgh, and Hillsborough County. Of these, the standouts are Houston, which has put strong emphasis on student gain scores (and does not have collective bargaining), and Memphis and Hillsborough County, which have done the same in collaboration with their unions in order to get the Gates money.[77]

Perspective is of the essence here. Yes, these are pioneering moves toward a more sensible system of teacher compensation. And some movement is much better than none. Even so, these are changes *at the margins*. Worse, and it's hard to emphasize this enough, *they have taken almost three decades to achieve*. When all the cheering dies down, the reality is that, in thousands upon thousands of districts throughout this country, salary schedules and across-the-board raises are the norm. The status quo prevails, and it is well protected. As a result, the American education system has been almost entirely unable to use pay as an effective tool for boosting teacher quality. Good teachers and bad teachers are paid the same. Performance incentives are weak. Selection effects work in exactly the wrong way, with high-quality people turned off by a profession that doesn't reward productivity and low-quality people finding it a good deal. And across-the-board pay raises—which are extraordinarily expensive and can't possibly be very large—do nothing to change any of this. They simply perpetuate the sameness. On this critical issue, as on so many others, the teachers unions have used their political power to block or weaken changes that simply make good sense.[78]

Still another teacher-quality reform that has attracted serious attention over the years is alternative certification. Unlike pay for performance, some version of this reform has been adopted in almost all states, beginning with New Jersey in 1983. While in the past virtually all new teachers had to be trained by education schools before districts could hire them, now roughly one in five new teachers comes into the profession through an alternative path, and the numbers are growing.[79]

The reason for this reform's political success, however, is precisely that it often does *not* do what it has the potential to do. The traditional, education school approach to teacher certification, which the states have long relied upon to ensure teacher quality, has never been shown to promote student learning.[80] It is costly, time-consuming, and adds little value. Because this is so, alternative approaches to certification have the potential to be transformative in boosting teacher quality. Properly designed, they could sweep away these needless barriers to entry, allow competent people to get certified quickly at little cost, and vastly increase the pool of candidates that districts have to choose from.[81]

Most alternative certification programs in the American states, however, are not intended to do these things. Yes, they help districts out by allowing them to hire people who initially lack formal certification. This expands their choices somewhat, which is good. But the people they hire are then typically required to *get* certified over time by fulfilling a vast array of traditional requirements, often by earning course credits comparable to those of a master's degree—and often by attending education schools. Thus, most of the old costs and hurdles are still there, dissuading potential candidates from entering the field, especially those who are high in quality and likely to have attractive opportunities in other lines of work.[82]

These half-a-loaf versions of alternative certification are the norm and have proliferated because they have not been blocked: the teachers unions have been willing to go along with them—grudgingly, in light of the districts' hiring problems—but they have opposed anything resembling the *full* loaf, which would dramatically open the profession to large numbers of new recruits. While putting up with weak alternative certification programs, then, the unions have remained staunch defenders of the teacher training status quo and all its unnecessary hurdles and obstacles.[83] They see it as a hallmark of professionalism, paralleling the systems in medicine and law, and a symbol of the stature (and pay) to which teachers aspire. As NEA President (at the time) Reg Weaver put it a few years ago, "The solution is not to develop alternative routes of entry into the profession or to increase the supply of recruits by allowing prospective teachers to skip 'burdensome' education courses or student teaching. The solution is to show a little R-E-S-P-E-C-T, and show us the money."[84]

Perhaps the most exciting development in the realm of alternative certification is not a governmental reform at all. It is the rise of Teach for America (TFA), a privately funded organization that, beginning in 1990 and growing like gangbusters ever since, has recruited, trained, and placed thousands of the nation's elite college students to teach in the most disadvantaged public schools.[85] For the 2009–10 school year TFA received some 35,000 applications from students at top universities, including—how remarkable is this?—fully 11 percent of all seniors at all Ivy League universities and 35 percent of all African American seniors at Harvard.[86] Anyone interested in resolving the teacher-quality problems of the public schools would have to see TFA as an obvious gold mine of talent. That's exactly what it is. Research has shown, moreover, that despite their lack of experience in the classroom, TFA teachers perform at least as well as their more experienced colleagues, especially in math and science.[87]

Yet for the teachers unions, Teach for America is not a gold mine at all. It is a threat, and it has been treated as one—in part because the success of TFA candidates is graphic evidence that education schools and all the other traditional barriers to entry are simply unnecessary, and in part because these new recruits may essentially be hired in place of more senior teachers in times of layoffs. So rather than welcoming TFA with open arms as a boon to better teaching, the unions have gone on the warpath, pressuring the districts not to hire TFA grads and taking every opportunity to talk it down and undermine its reputation. According to John Wilson, executive director of the NEA, Teach for America hurts children by bringing "the least prepared and the least experienced teachers" into the schools. "What they're doing to poor children," he says, "is malpractice."[88]

Whether these public relations tactics have worked is uncertain, for Teach for America is highly regarded these days among most of the movers and shakers in education circles. Nonetheless, the unions' power is very real, and they have been quite successful at keeping the TFA from operating at anywhere near its potential. In 2009–10 only about one-tenth of TFA applicants were placed in teaching jobs. As the *Wall Street Journal* observes, "Union and bureaucratic opposition is so strong that Teach for America is allotted a mere 3,800 teaching slots nationwide . . . Districts place a cap on the number of Teach for America teachers they will accept . . . In Chicago, former home of Secretary of Education Arne Duncan, it is an embarrassing 10 percent. This is a tragic lost opportunity."[89]

So let me sum up. A *Nation at Risk* set off a coast-to-coast blitzkrieg to improve the public schools, but notwithstanding all the hullabaloo about a revolutionary era of educational change, the reforms it triggered didn't amount to much. They didn't amount to much in the 1980s. They didn't amount to much in the 1990s. And they still don't amount to much.

It is no secret, and hardly a mystery, that Americans today are frustrated with the public schools and desperate for improvement. But the fact is, they were frustrated with the pace of reform even in the late 1980s. For by the end of that first decade of reform, there was widespread agreement that these early efforts had failed and that something much more fundamental needed to be done if the educational tanker were actually going to be turned around and headed in the right direction. More and more, the talk among reformers was about transforming the system. It was about fundamental change.[90]

The result at the time was a surge in support for two major movements that soon took on lives of their own: the choice movement and the accountability movement, both of which I discuss shortly. Even with the rise of these new political forces, however, governments throughout the country continued to invest heavily in mainstream reforms. Indeed, as parts of the above discussion suggest, the reforms they pursued during the 1990s—and to the present day—have often been the very same kinds of reforms they pursued during the 1980s. Over this entire period, the states have persisted in trying to improve their schools through more spending, higher across-the-board salaries, stricter academic requirements, more teacher training, and the like—all with great fanfare, as though this time around these recycled efforts would pay off.

A number of "new" mainstream reforms gained support and attention along the way. Of these, the most popular is class size reduction, which was heavily promoted by President Clinton via his effort to fund 100,000 new teachers for the public schools and aggressively pursued in a number of states as well: notably in California, which was the pioneer in 1996, and in Florida, where voters passed a statewide initiative in 2002 requiring drastic reductions in class size.[91] Needless to say, this is a reform the teachers unions strongly support. Teachers like the reduction in workload, and it can only be carried out by hiring lots more of them, which adds to union membership rolls (and power). But like all the other mainstream reforms, class size reduction is a disappointment. It does nothing to restructure the system, and there is no evidence that it works to bring about big improvements in student learning, especially beyond the first few years of school. Worse, it is among the most expensive of all possible reforms and cannot be justified in terms of bang for the buck.[92]

What is the problem here? Why, over the last quarter century, have the states invested so heavily in reforms that offer so little promise? The answer is quite simple: these reforms have a superficial appeal that makes them an easy sell to the broader public—and because they are not threatening to the teachers unions (nor, for that matter, to their usual allies like the school districts and the education schools), the unions don't use their political power to block. The political gates are swung open, and governments are allowed to take action in these particular ways—ways that are acceptable to the powers that be and don't upset the applecart.

From the standpoint of politics and power, then, mainstream reforms are all pluses and no minuses. The only downside is that they don't work.

School Accountability

The greatest achievement of *A Nation at Risk* is not that it generated countless education reforms. Most of them have been a waste of time and money. Its greatest achievement is that it directed attention to the problems of public education, put power behind the cause of reform, and gave impetus to the movements for accountability and choice, both of which have the capacity to transform American education for the better.

The ideas behind school accountability have obvious merit. If the school system is to promote academic excellence, it must have clear standards defining what students need to know. It must engage in testing to measure how well the standards are being met. And it must hold students, teachers, and administrators accountable for results—and give them incentives to do their very best—by attaching consequences to outcomes.[93] Writ large, these are simply the principles of effective management that business leaders live by every day: setting goals, measuring performance, attaching consequences, and creating strong incentives.

As the 1980s drew to a close, and as the first wave of incremental reforms proved impotent, accountability offered an approach that promised to get at fundamentals. Moreover, because it was a top-down approach—a demand for effective management that business leaders, governors, and the general public could readily understand—it came across as a natural extension of mainstream efforts to make the existing system work better. It was a reform that everyone could agree was desirable.[94]

Well, almost everyone. The teachers unions had a very different view. The point of this reform was to hold schools—and thus teachers—accountable for seeing to it that children learn what they are supposed to learn. And this they did not want. Historically, teachers had been granted substantial autonomy, and their pay and jobs had been almost totally secure regardless of what they did in their classrooms and regardless of how much their students learned. Why would they want to have new requirements thrust upon them, their performance seriously evaluated, real consequences attached to poor performance, and their jobs made less secure?

With accountability so broadly popular, however, and so much power arrayed behind it, the unions were in a political bind. Full-fledged opposition would have put them on the wrong side and pegged them as self-interested defenders of the status quo. This being so, they opted for a more sophisticated course of action: to "support" accountability, participate in its design, and try to block or water down any components they found threatening.

In the years since, the unions have largely displayed their "support" for accountability by embracing the need for curriculum standards. Indeed, the AFT has gone to great lengths to position itself as a strong proponent.[95] But the unions have little to fear from the standards themselves, as long as the latter are not accompanied by serious testing regimes and consequences for poor performance. So it is the tests and the consequences that the unions have tried to block, or at least weaken and render ineffectual.

Standardized tests have been used for many decades in American education to measure what students are learning, and they do a fine job of that. The science of student testing is by far the best developed, most sophisticated component of the academic field of education.[96] Traditionally, however, test results were not used to evaluate schools or teachers, were not made public, and usually did not even have consequences for students. The accountability movement has tried to change all this—against union opposition. Publicly, the unions say they "support" testing, but the reality is that they rarely come across an actual test that they like. When Massachusetts instituted a high-stakes accountability test for high school graduation, for example, the Massachusetts Teachers Association launched a $600,000 advertising campaign to undermine its public support, calling it "flawed and unfair" and encouraging citizens to "Say No to the MCAS graduation requirement."[97]

This is but a dramatic version of what has been happening all across the country for years. In general, teachers unions disparage standardized tests as inadequate measures of student performance and call instead for broader criteria—course grades, portfolios of student work, graduation rates, parental involvement, and more—that would make assessments far more flexible, complicated, and subjective, and much less dependent on hard, specific measures of how much students are actually learning.[98]

The teachers unions are not alone in these views. There are (some) academics, researchers, and activists who agree with them, and (some) parents, too, who think that kids are over-tested.[99] As is true in virtually all areas of education reform, the unions have allies to boost their cause and make their arguments. But what makes the unions different is that, whatever their leaders may truly believe about the validity of standardized tests, they have a *self-interest* in opposing them and in making the arguments they do.

From the standpoint of union interests, the problem with standardized tests is that they don't just measure the performance of students. They also provide concrete evidence on the performance of schools—and *teachers*—and threaten to generate all sorts of problems that the unions are keen to avoid. If the scores show that kids aren't learning, the publicity will inevitably give rise to public complaints and pressures to improve, and the accountability system may require consequences of various kinds. Test scores are especially threatening, moreover, because any system that puts them to rigorous use would quickly reveal (after appropriate controls for student background characteristics and the like) that some teachers are much better than others and some are very bad. Indeed, that is precisely what the research literature does reveal.[100] Were such information routinely collected and readily available, it would be much more difficult for policymakers to embrace the myth that somehow all teachers are the same, that they all have a right to be in the classroom, and that they should all be paid equally. There would be objective grounds for removing bad teachers from classrooms. There would be objective grounds for giving better teachers higher pay. Accountability would begin to have real teeth.

The unions want to make sure that these things don't happen, and they have traditionally taken strong action to try to prevent student test scores from being put to use in evaluating teacher (and school) performance.[101] The New York City example speaks volumes. Recall that Mayor Michael Bloomberg and Chancellor Joel Klein, both strong proponents of accountability, attempted to improve teacher quality by reforming the tenure process. Their idea was to use student test scores as one measure of teacher performance in the classroom and then to bring this information to bear—along with much other relevant information—when new teachers were being evaluated for tenure. The idea that data on student learning should be relevant to teacher tenure seems woefully obvious. Who could disagree? The United Federation of Teachers could, and did. The union took its case to the state legislature and succeeded in getting a new law passed that *prohibited* any district in the state from using student test scores in the tenure evaluations of teachers. The information was available on how much students were actually learning in their classes. But in New York, the teachers unions—with a little help from their allies in the state legislature—made it illegal to take the information into account.[102]

New York City is but a microcosm of the information challenge that unions are increasingly up against—and fighting—nationwide. The rise of information technology has dramatically enhanced the ability of state governments to collect data on students, schools, teachers, finances, and other aspects of the education system; to store all this information in "data warehouses"; and to employ it in better managing their schools and promoting student achievement. Virtually all states are doing these things as part of their overall accountability efforts. Nothing could be more basic to school improvement than good information. Yet the unions see good information as a serious threat, because these modern data systems can readily be designed to *link* teachers to the students in their classes and thus to provide objective and continually updated measures of teacher performance. With this kind of information, states and districts would have the potential to transform the fundamentals of teacher evaluation, teacher pay, and the entire personnel system—tying these things much more closely to student learning. So however innocuous the topic of "data systems" might sound, the political stakes are incredibly high.[103]

The unions cannot stop the rise of technology more generally, of course, as this is a social transformation that is beyond their control. But they are well aware of its disruptive potential, and they have used their political power to stifle its contributions to public education. In legislatures around the country—Texas, Colorado, California, and elsewhere—they have fought these data battles over and over again. They have pressured policymakers not to authorize teacher identifiers that can be linked to student identifiers, arguing that teacher and student data sets need to be kept entirely separate. If they have lost on that score, they have pushed for laws that (as in New York) simply prohibit the use of student test score data in the evaluation or compensation of teachers. For a long time, they were quite successful. Until Arne Duncan's Race to the Top intervened to change the landscape, only eighteen states even had systems that were capable of linking the student data to teacher data.[104]

Consider what happened in California. There, the teachers unions defeated a 2005 bill that would simply have added teacher identifiers to the state data system—a unique number for each teacher, allowing for the collection of data over time. The California Federation of Teachers testified about what it called the "hidden danger in creating a teacher identifier"—namely, that "it could easily be linked to student databases and thus student performance."[105] How much clearer could the conflict of interest be? To the state, school districts, and citizens at-large, this database offered a wealth of information for the management and improvement of the public schools. To the teachers union, it was a "danger."

In 2006 a teacher identifier provision did pass the state legislature. But the unions were able to win language in the new law that sharply limited how the data could be used. Here is what the law said: "Data in the system may not be used . . . for the purposes of pay, promotion, sanction, or personnel evaluation of an individual teacher or groups of teachers, or of any other employment decisions related to individual teachers. The system may not include the names, social security numbers, home addresses, telephone numbers, or e-mail addresses of individual teachers."[106] The battle, moreover, continued. Over the next few years, as Governor Schwarzenegger regularly requested some $30 million annually to fund the expanded data system, the Democratic legislature refused to provide the money. It was dead in the water.[107] Finally, during Race to the Top, California policymakers did take action to rescind the legal restrictions—over union opposition and with no guarantee of funding—in an attempt to win the Race.[108]

In the information age, the battle against data is a battle the unions are destined to lose (eventually). The brute fact is that technology makes it possible to collect performance-based information—and once the information exists, *it will be used* (someday). Another California event provides a nice illustration of what the unions are up against. In 2010 reporters from the *Los Angeles Times* obtained local test score data from the Los Angeles school district under the state's Public Records Act: data the district had collected but never revealed, analyzed, or put to any educational purpose. With expert help, the reporters created seven years' worth of value-added scores to arrive at measures of classroom effectiveness for each of some 6,000 school district elementary teachers. They then—amid great controversy, not just locally but nationwide, with the unions fervently protesting—published the ratings of individual teachers, by name, in the newspaper, along with a searchable database that ultimately got many hundreds of thousands of hits from parents and others *who wanted to know* the effectiveness of local teachers. For the first time in any district, anywhere, the public was being provided with information about the effectiveness of local teachers and being shown what researchers have long known: that some teachers are consistently much better than others, some are consistently much worse, and many children are being short-changed.[109]

Publishing teachers' names in the newspaper has its downsides, needless to say, and so does a reliance on any one measure of performance. Accountability is ultimately about putting data to valid, systematic use within a well-organized school system, and many proponents would be concerned about what the *Los Angeles Times* did if it became a regular thing.[110] Yet this event needs to be understood in context: information on teacher effectiveness has long been *suppressed,* and the unions have played a big role in that suppression. The *Los Angeles Times* was attempting to do something about that by taking action on its own. It published its ratings, it said, "because they bear on the performance of public employees who provide an important public service, and in the belief that parents and the public have a right to the information."[111] Had it not taken action, "this information might have remained uselessly locked away."[112]

The *Los Angeles Times* also explicitly recognized the role of United Teachers Los Angeles (UTLA) in keeping the data under cover. "The UTLA's position," it argued, "is understandable; it exists to protect teachers, including the bad ones. Fortunately for parents and the public, a newspaper exists to give them information that would otherwise be withheld."[113] Through no coincidence, shortly after the *Los Angeles Times* articles appeared, the L.A. Unified School District moved to begin negotiating with the UTLA on a new, performance-based system of teacher evaluation that would take student test score gains into account, a reform the union fiercely opposes.[114] Meantime, the nation was watching. Secretary of Education Arne Duncan, pressed by the media to comment on the *Los Angeles Times* articles, said, "In other fields, we talk about success constantly, with statistics and other measures to prove it. Why, in education, are we scared to talk about what success look like? What is there to hide?"[115]

The unions' fight against test scores may be a losing battle, but their resistance has for decades prevented the nation from simply putting objective information to reasonable use in trying to improve the public schools. For all this time, the unions have essentially won by delaying the inevitable—and along the way, ensuring that their members all get satisfactory evaluations and have safe, protected jobs.

As this suggests, the unions' ultimate goal is not to fight test scores. By challenging student test scores and how they can be used, they are pursuing a much larger mission at the same time. For with some form of accountability system unavoidable—all the states have them—what the unions aim for is a system that actually has *no negative consequences* for poor performance, and thus *does not really hold anyone accountable*. Above all else, they want to make sure that no one ever loses a job, that there is no weeding out process by which the school system rids itself of mediocre teachers, and that no one's pay ever suffers. Needless to say, other kinds of sanctions that are more far-reaching—such as closing down or reconstituting low-performing schools—are strongly opposed as well. The union attack on test scores is ultimately a means of trying to ensure that there is *no evidentiary basis* for such negative consequences. In the end, it is the negative consequences that are truly threatening, not the test scores themselves.

The unions are actually fine with having consequences for poor performance—as long as they are entirely positive consequences. Low-performing schools should get more money, more assistance, more support. As the unions argue it, these are the keys to turning such schools around. Similarly, low-performing teachers should get more training and professional development (which would often qualify them for higher salaries). These, they argue, are the keys to making teachers better in the classroom. Meantime, everyone's jobs would be safe. And everyone would stay right where they are.

This logic of positivity is fundamental to the unions' "support" for account-ability and pervades the way they talk about how it should operate in turning around problem schools. Here, for instance, is a typical statement of official NEA policy: "The paradigm must change from labeling and punishing to investing in proven programs and interventions . . . Hard-to-staff schools, especially those . . . that have consistently struggled to meet student achievement targets, need sig-nificant supports and resources, including additional targeted funding to attract and retain quality teachers, and induction programs with intensive mentoring components that will help teachers become successful."[116] Here and elsewhere, union positions are couched in terms of school improvement and doing what works, but the focus is exclusively on positive inducements and thus, ultimately, on spending more money—and spending it on the existing staff, all of whose jobs are totally safe. This is what "good" accountability comes down to, in the final analysis, and this is the kind of accountability they support. What they oppose is true accountability—which would, among other things, identify poorly perform-ing teachers and get them out of the classroom and off the payroll.

The teachers unions are not the only interest groups that fight against school accountability. They have allies among (some) school administrators, who see accountability—accurately—as a threat to their traditional autonomy and a source of considerable new performance pressures. They also have allies among (some) civil rights groups, concerned that testing may lead to high failure and drop-out rates for minority kids; among disaffected parents, who think their kids are being over-tested; among certain experts, who claim that tests are misleading and culturally biased; and ironically, among certain Republican policymakers, who believe strongly in local control and don't want to see the national govern-ment intrude on what has traditionally been a local prerogative.

This is not much of a coalition. In the first place, the unions' allies are not united at all. Many school administrators support the basic thrust of account-ability, because it gives them new managerial and informational tools for improv-ing their schools and being successful at their jobs. Many groups speaking for minorities and other disadvantaged kids—Education Trust, for example—have moved beyond the traditional minority-group distrust of testing and are now among the strongest, most adamant supporters of accountability. Most parents and citizens support accountability as well, as opinion surveys have consistently shown. Most experts firmly believe that test scores can be put to valid, reliable use in making accountability work effectively. And most Republicans—although ideologically resistant to national accountability (but not state accountability) efforts during the 1990s, and although a truly major force in impeding those early, national-level initiatives—have come around on this issue and are now more persuaded by the obvious need for school accountability than by the "costs" of violating local control.[117]

In the second place, the various members of today's anti-accountability coalition are grossly unequal in terms of numbers, organization, money, and political clout. As in the case of ballot measures, the teachers unions really *are* the present-day coalition. Without them, the whole thing would collapse in a heap, and there would essentially be no opposition to accountability with sufficient power to stand in the way of true reform.[118]

That the unions are largely fighting this alone is not so unusual. On many educational issues, they are the only power that really matters on their side of the battlefield, and their power has typically been more than enough to enable them to block or substantially weaken reform. Accountability, however, is probably the most difficult political challenge they have ever faced. Unlike with other lines of reform, the stars have lined up just right in this case—it has popularity with the public, powerful support from business, the leadership of political executives—and the unions and their allies have had a hard time stopping its progress. Accountability systems of some sort were adopted in most states during the 1990s. And these efforts were followed by the movement's single biggest victory—and the teachers unions' single biggest defeat—the watershed No Child Left Behind Act, adopted by Congress in 2001, which created an accountability framework for the nation as a whole.[119]

Yet even in what passes for victory, reformers have a long way to go in their pursuit of genuine accountability for the nation's schools. Part of the problem is that, with institutional reforms as far-reaching and complex as these, even the best-intentioned designers—and even if they faced no political opposition at all—would have found it difficult to create accountability systems that work smoothly and effectively from the get-go. Problems should be expected, and they need to be worked out over time as it becomes clearer what they are and what can be done to correct them. This has been the case with major reforms throughout American history—Medicare, the Clean Air Act, you name it—and it has also been true of No Child Left Behind. As originally designed, it contained a number of flaws that ultimately created problems as it was implemented across the country. Many supporters of accountability came to agree, for example, that it was probably a mistake to measure the performance of schools in terms of the proficiency levels of students rather than (say) their growth in achievement; that it labeled too many schools as low performers; that it put too much emphasis on math and reading at the expense of the rest of the curriculum; and that in certain other ways, too, it was off the mark. In basic respects, it needed a mid-course correction.[120]

But not all the flaws in NCLB can be explained as well-intentioned mistakes by reformers who were trying to build effective accountability systems. This goes for the various state accountability systems as well. Some of the most critical flaws in all these systems arose because their basic designs were influenced by the unions and their allies—which *do not want* educators held accountable and were using their power to purposely create a kind of "accountability" that would be weak and ineffective. The unions' ability to do this, of course, varies from state to state. They tend to be weaker in the South than in the rest of the country, for instance, which is why some of the pioneering efforts in accountability have come from states like Texas, North Carolina, and Kentucky. Their influence also tends to be weaker at the national level than at the state level because national politics attracts far more interest groups, politicians have larger, more diverse constituencies, and the unions have much more competition.

It was due to this relative disadvantage at the national level, plus the fact that the stars happened to line up just right for reformers—a very unusual event, with even top Democrats on board—that the unions lost control of the politics of No Child Left Behind. They were unable to block it. They also failed in their efforts to deflate many of its key features, such as its strict reliance on standardized test scores in evaluating the "adequate yearly progress" of schools. But even in a losing cause, they did not entirely lose out. Indeed, they scored important victories—notably, in stipulating that nothing in NCLB's requirements would take priority over the provisions written into local collective bargaining contracts, in eliminating private school vouchers as a means of providing options for kids in failing public schools, and in eviscerating the apparent NCLB requirement that veteran teachers need to demonstrate competence in their subject matters (an evisceration that led, years hence, to the charade of virtually every one of the nation's 3 million teachers being declared "highly qualified"). Perhaps most important of all, they used their power to ensure that NCLB was *almost devoid of serious consequences* when districts and schools failed to do their jobs.[121] As education journalist Joe Williams (now executive director of Democrats for Education Reform) rightly observed as the realities on the ground were becoming clear,[122]

> Improve your schools, or someone else will. That was supposed to be the bite in the federal No Child Left Behind Act that would leave teeth marks on underperforming school districts, ushering in long-resisted reforms and restructuring in the education systems where they were most needed . . . But nearly five years after No Child Left Behind was signed into law, not a single school district has undergone radical restructuring . . . as part of corrective actions for districts under the law. To date, NCLB has been relatively toothless in terms of holding districts accountable through the use of strong-arm sanctions . . . Underperforming districts have encountered little pain under NCLB other than the stigma that comes from being branded failing systems.

Almost ten years after NCLB went into effect, this nation has fifty-one different accountability systems, one for each state and the District of Columbia, which conform to national requirements but have their own standards, their own tests, and their own sets of (supposed) consequences and enforcement actions.[123] To call them "accountability systems," though, is more a matter of symbol—or habit or convenience—than a valid reflection of what they actually do. For once we get beyond the standards and tests and all the commotion about who gets labeled a low performer, these systems have a hollow core. When it comes to basic components that are obviously necessary—that anyone can see are fundamental to a true system of accountability—there's simply nothing there. Among other things,

—There are no mechanisms for weeding out mediocre teachers. Teachers stay in the classroom year after year even if their children learn absolutely nothing.

—Data on student performance are regularly collected, but they are not put to use in measuring the performance of teachers. Teacher performance is quite purposely *not* being measured.

—Teacher pay continues to follow the traditional salary schedule and is not linked in any way to how much students learn.

—Schools rarely suffer any sanctions (reconstitution, leadership or staff changes, choice options for students, and the like) for continually failing to teach their children.

The list of weaknesses could go on. This is not to say there isn't an upside, for these accountability systems are surely much better than nothing at all: they put the focus on student achievement, provide objective measures of performance, encourage public discussion about how the schools are doing, and increase the incentives and pressures for improvement—and there is evidence that the schools have actually improved somewhat as a result.[124] But these systems are also inherently weak, because they fail to include mechanisms that are pivotal to their effective operation. A big reason they fail to include these mechanisms is that they were designed under the influence of their enemies—who "support" accountability systems that, at the end of the day, don't actually hold anyone accountable.[125]

Design is just the first, troublesome stage of a political battle that never ends. Soon after NCLB was adopted, for example, the NEA went to court in an attempt to have it declared illegal and thus to block it after the fact.[126] Both unions, meantime, launched public relations campaigns that loudly criticized accountability—claiming that students are over-tested, teachers are teaching to the test, pay for performance is "a blatant attack on collective bargaining,"[127] and so on—in efforts to convince the American public and its political representatives that NCLB was fatally flawed.[128] And throughout, both were attempting to poison the well and marshal their troops so that, when the bill came up for reauthorization (originally scheduled for 2008), it could be permanently defeated—or, if that weren't in the cards, substantially weakened by, for example, minimizing the role of student test scores and rendering the system even more toothless than it already was.

The unions' seriousness about killing NCLB, despite their avowed "support" for accountability, came into full political flower during the 2008 presidential primary season. The competition was frenzied on the Democratic side of the campaign, and the unions made NCLB a litmus test among the many Democratic candidates—who, in debate after debate on national television in front of untold millions of viewers, were tripping all over one another to denounce NCLB, excoriate student testing, and plead for a kinder, gentler approach to school improvement. The unions couldn't have said it better themselves.

I return to accountability in a bit. For now, the simplest point to be made is that, notwithstanding all the political fireworks, there is nothing radical about it. It is a reform that makes sense. Business leaders take accountability for granted as an essential component of *any* effective organization, and surely the same applies to the nation's school system. Indeed, the notion that our governments would hand over more than $600 billion a year to the public schools and *not* hold them accountable for teaching children what they are supposed to know is shockingly irresponsible and by almost any managerial standard, stupid. Yet the public schools have had free reign, and been virtually accountability free, for more than 100 years now. Reformers are trying to change that. The unions are trying to stop them—and despite their "defeats," they have been quite successful at seeing to it that the nation now has accountability systems that don't actually hold anyone accountable.

School Choice

School choice has provoked more conflict than any other education reform, accountability included. This might seem surprising. Who could object to letting parents choose where their kids go to school?

The benefits of choice are pretty obvious. When parents have the right to choose, they can seek out better options for their kids. This means, most importantly, that they can leave bad schools, and that children can no longer be trapped in schools that fail to educate them. The power to leave is especially valuable to children who are poor and minority, because they are disproportionately stuck in the nation's very worst schools—which, year by year, crush their opportunities for good careers and productive futures. In American society, affluent people are rarely in dire need of school choice, because they already have it: their money empowers them to seek out decent schools in the suburbs or in the private sector. It is mainly the poor and the disadvantaged who are denied the power to choose, and who find themselves stuck in schools that no one with money would ever allow their own kids to attend.

There is another key dimension to choice as well. When families are denied the right to choose, their public schools can take them for granted. The schools have a guaranteed clientele and a guaranteed pot of money; and if they do a bad job of educating children, nothing happens. The kids stay where they are, and the money keeps rolling in. When choice enters the equation, however, the guarantees evaporate. All schools are put on notice that, if they don't do their jobs well, they are likely to lose children and resources. Because of choice, then, there are consequences for bad behavior—just as there are (or would be) with a true system of accountability. These consequences give the schools greater incentives to perform and innovate. They also help to ensure that, if bad schools don't respond to those incentives and if they continue their unproductive ways, they are likely to wither on the vine for lack of support.[129]

The take-away is not that every "choice school" is guaranteed to be wonderful. Any system that encourages a proliferation of new alternatives will produce some that are mediocre along the way. This is the price of innovation and change, which are inherently unpredictable at the margins.[130] If we let a thousand flowers bloom, not all of them will be exquisite. Nor is the take-away that families will always be able to benefit from choice. Sometimes parents will make mistakes. Sometimes there won't be any good schools available to them. But if choice is carefully and appropriately designed by people who genuinely want it to work, and if it is adjusted over time in light of experience, what it *can* do stands to be enormously valuable. It can give families alternatives that they don't have now, and these alternatives can literally be lifesavers when kids are stuck in terrible schools. It can give schools—*all* schools, not just schools of choice—strong incentives to perform, to be responsive, and to provide kids with a quality education. And it can initiate a dynamic that, over the long haul, discriminates against bad schools and in favor of good ones.[131]

To the teachers unions, however, choice is deeply threatening. In fact, it is much *more* threatening than accountability is. When families are able to seek out new options—charter schools, for example, or possibly (with the help of vouchers or tax credits) private schools—the regular public schools lose children and money, and thus jobs. From a societal standpoint, this is not a problem at all. There would simply be more kids getting educated in charters and private schools, and the money and jobs would follow the kids. As they should. The regular public schools would lose money and jobs, but they would also have fewer kids to educate.

Yet this kind of sensible shift is the last thing the unions want to see happen—because the regular public schools are unionized, and charters and private schools (with rare exceptions) are not. When families are given the right to choose, unionized teachers lose jobs and nonunion teachers gain them. So choice, while not threatening to teachers per se, is threatening to union members—and the unions are dedicated to protecting those jobs. To make matters worse, were choice adopted on a grand scale, it would also threaten the unions' very survival: for if families actually had lots of attractive options to choose from, the unions could well suffer a devastating plunge in membership, resources, and power. This is their greatest fear.

When it comes to school choice, then, the unions are deadly serious about keeping the lid on. They do *not* want families to have alternatives to the schools where their members teach. This is true regardless of who the families and kids are. It is even true if the families are the poorest in the nation, if the kids are trapped in public schools that are abysmally bad, and if they would obviously benefit from a wider array of choices. The teachers unions portray themselves as champions of the disadvantaged, dedicated to providing poor kids with the best educations possible. And in terms of the personal values of union leaders and activists, this may well be true. But when poor kids want to leave the regular public schools—and thus, when they threaten jobs—the unions' fundamental interests take priority, and they do everything they can to prevent the exodus. What this means, in the reality of politics, is that when reformers try to expand school choice, the unions will marshal their political power to try to stop them. This, in fact, is what they have been doing for decades. And because their power is very real, they have done it with considerable success. That is why true school choice remains so limited within the American public school system.

The teachers unions are its main political opponents. As in other matters of reform, they are the ones that spend most of the money and mobilize most of the troops. But they also have important allies. The NAACP has little faith in school choice (and market mechanisms generally) and has long seen it as a veiled opportunity for whites to flee blacks; it is also concerned about job protection, for urban school systems are a prime source of minority jobs, and these jobs would be threatened if kids were given the freedom to leave. The ACLU and the People for the American Way are mainly vexed about the separation of church and state, seeing vouchers for private schools (many of them religious) as a dangerous breach in the "wall of separation." Liberals in general tend to be supportive of government, suspicious of markets (and their conservative supporters), and worried that the poor cannot make good choices for themselves. Last but hardly least, Democratic elected officials—who play the pivotal roles in the politics of blocking—tend to be liberal, electorally dependent on union power, and willing to support them on key issues.[132]

Choice was first proposed in the mid-1950s by economist Milton Friedman. He pioneered the idea of a voucher system, in which governments would provide families with vouchers that would pay for their kids to attend the private schools of their choice. While this idea attracted attention over the next few decades and while other, less radical ideas for *public* school choice—magnet schools, for instance—made their appearance during the 1970s, the movement didn't pick up steam until the 1980s, when *A Nation at Risk* set the stage for coast-to-coast reform.[133]

Other factors were at work too. This was a time when top-down approaches to government were falling into disrepute worldwide for their heavy bureaucracy and inefficiency and when policymakers everywhere—from the United States to Western and Eastern Europe to South America to China—began turning to more market-based approaches to economic and social policy. Meantime, the Reagan administration held power in Washington, and its commitment to market-based reforms—along with its willingness in politics to cross swords with the teachers unions—led it to champion school choice and to nurture a nationwide network of activists for the cause.

But conservatism and an appreciation of markets were not enough to overcome the blocking power of the union-led coalition. Nor, stereotypes aside, could the political clout of business be counted upon to even the balance. Although well-heeled individuals sometimes played prominent roles in the choice movement (and still do), most business leaders tend to think about education reform in terms of *management* problems, because management is essentially what they do for a living and what they see as the key to effective organization. They are naturally inclined to be ardent supporters of accountability—which is simply a top-down approach to better management—but *not* to be ardent supporters of choice (or markets and competition more generally). Throughout the 1980s, as a result, the choice movement was fueled by conservative activists, churches, private schools, parent groups, and the like—an enthusiastic lot, but hardly the kind of institutional power base necessary to take on the teachers unions and make progress. To do that, the movement needed to broaden its constituency and its agenda.[134]

Which it did, by taking a left-hand turn from its libertarian roots. The signal event came in 1990, when parents in inner city Milwaukee—where the public schools were abominable—rose up to demand vouchers as a means of escaping to better options in the private sector. They were vigorously opposed by the teachers unions and their allies, and the political lineup couldn't have been more potently symbolic: the unions unleashed their full arsenal of weapons to prevent poor parents from getting their kids out of failing schools. But the urban poor had effective grassroots leaders—notable among them Polly Williams and Howard Fuller—and by entering into a coalition with conservatives and the state's Republican governor, Tommy Thompson, they were able to achieve a surprising victory. It was a limited one: a pilot program in which no more than 1,000 disadvantaged kids could qualify for vouchers, and religious schools were disallowed. But the choice movement got a huge boost. And the nation got its first voucher program.[135]

Since 1990, choice advocates have focused most of their reform efforts on poor and minority families in the inner cities. The modern arguments for vouchers have less to do with free markets than with social equity. They also have less to do with theory than with the commonsense notion that disadvantaged kids should never be forced to attend failing schools and that they should be given as many attractive educational opportunities as possible.

This shift toward equity has expanded the constituency for choice, with public opinion polls consistently showing (then and now) that its greatest supporters are poor and minority parents.[136] The shift to equity has also put Democrats in an awkward position. They are the party of the poor and the disadvantaged, but in the realm of public education, unlike virtually every other area of public policy, they have found themselves fighting *against* their own constituents—and, in particular, fighting against poor parents who are simply trying to get their kids out of terrible schools. The contradiction is palpable. But it is something many Democrats do because they "must": the teachers unions are extraordinarily powerful and poor people aren't.

For the unions, it is all about protecting their fundamental interests, and they have been quite successful at it. When voucher proposals have appeared as ballot initiatives, as we've seen, the unions have poured millions of dollars into advertising campaigns to convince voters that vouchers will destroy the public schools, leading in each case (there have been ten of them, going back about twenty years) to defeats for choice.[137] The unions' bread and butter, however, has been in the state legislatures and the U.S. Congress, the main forums in which the nation's key education policies get designed and adopted. In these policymaking settings— where the Democrats have faithfully cast the official votes—the unions have done a masterful job, year after year, of preventing voucher proposals from becoming law. Even in a state like Texas, where the unions are weaker than in other states, they have been strong enough to ensure that nothing at all has ever passed.[138]

Despite all the blocking, choice advocates have managed to eke out victories here and there. They won major expansions of the original Milwaukee voucher program. They also won a number of new voucher programs (almost all of them quite small) in states and districts around the country—programs for low-income children in Cleveland and Washington, D.C.; programs for kids in low-performing schools in Florida, Ohio, and Colorado; programs for kids in special education in Florida, Arizona, Utah, Georgia, Ohio, and Oklahoma; and even a program for all kids statewide in Utah. In addition, they enacted voucher-like programs that, through tax credits and nonprofit foundations, provide scholarships for low-income children (Florida, Iowa, Pennsylvania, Rhode Island) and children generally (Arizona, Georgia).[139]

As with accountability, though, the battle is never over even in the rare cases of apparent victory. The unions target each newly minted program and doggedly try to overturn it. They overturned the Utah program, after its adoption by the state legislature, by putting it on the ballot and spending heavily (aided by $3 million from the NEA) to defeat it.[140] They also got state courts to invalidate the Colorado voucher program, one of the three Florida voucher programs, and the Arizona tax credit programs for special needs kids, foster kids, and children generally.[141] (The Arizona case is before the U.S. Supreme Court, at this writing). Most recently, their Democratic allies—having swept to victory in the 2008 elections and gained control of both Congress and the presidency—took swift action to kill the Washington, D.C., voucher program for disadvantaged kids.[142]

For many years, the unions pursued court challenges to the Milwaukee and Cleveland programs, but both eventually survived. The Cleveland case ultimately was heard by the U.S. Supreme Court, resulting in the landmark *Zelman* decision in 2002, which ruled that including religious schools in a voucher program is constitutional.[143] This case was a big victory for the choice side. But the unions barely lost, five to four, and one switched vote would have struck a serious blow to the entire voucher movement—for most private schools are religious schools, and excluding them would mean that voucher recipients have nowhere to go. Moreover, by simply launching these and other court actions (there have been many), the unions keep voucher programs in a continual state of uncertainty, making it difficult for the programs to attract parents and get established.

The voucher programs that remain deserve to be considered impressive victories, given the opposition. Even so, they are unimpressive as crucibles for a real transformation. There are roughly 50 million public school students in this country, and only 180,000 children are receiving publicly funded vouchers or tax-credit scholarships.[144] Most of the programs are quite small, moreover, and most of the total is due to just a few that are very large by comparison: the Milwaukee voucher program (20,328 in 2009–10), the Florida McKay scholarship program for special education kids (19,913 in 2009–10), the Arizona tax credit program (28,933 in 2009–10), the Florida tax credit program (26,987 in 2009–10), and the Pennsylvania tax credit program (44,839 in 2009–10).[145] Outside the larger programs, vouchers today provide little competition to the regular public schools in their states—their enrollments are a drop in the bucket—and they do little to change incentives or generate improvement. The bottom line is that, despite a smattering of programs that have managed to get by them, the teachers unions have been extremely successful at preventing vouchers (or tax credits) from getting a real toehold in American education.[146]

The idea of vouchers is an old one, having been floated by Milton Friedman almost thirty years before the larger movement for education reform got under way in the early 1980s. The other seminal idea for bringing choice to the American school system came along later and was very much a product of the reform movement itself. This was the idea of charter schools.

Ironically, the first person to bring charters to public attention was AFT President Al Shanker, in a 1988 speech before the National Press Club in Washington, D.C. Building on the work of educator Ray Budde, who had called for "chartering" as a means of freeing teachers to initiate new programs within their schools, Shanker extended the idea to the chartering of schools themselves, arguing that the creative potential of teachers, long stifled by bureaucracy, should be unleashed to drive education reform and improve education. He proposed that innovative teachers be granted charters by local districts to set up their own schools and that they be given the autonomy to do things differently and go their own ways. Parents, meantime, would be allowed to choose whether to send their kids to one of these new types of public schools and would thereby be provided with a system of *public school choice* that would substitute for, and indeed render unnecessary, vouchers for private schools.[147]

Shanker's vision of freeing schools and teachers to be innovative, however, was really a vision of freeing them from *district* control. They were *not* to be freed from union control. Quite the contrary, Shanker's charter schools would be run by teachers, who in turn would be unionized and covered by collective bargaining contracts, making the schools subject to the power and control of local unions. By offering his dramatic proposal for charter schools, then, Shanker was "embracing" choice and innovation—but in a distinctive, highly selective way that reflected his interests as a union president. Yes, he favored more parental choice, but parents would only be able to choose among unionized public schools. Yes, he sought to promote innovation, but the agents of innovation would be unionized public school teachers. Yes, he favored greater autonomy, but only the types agreed to by unions through collective bargaining contracts.

Reformers quickly picked up on the charter idea, but not on Shanker's version of it. Their emphasis was on true autonomy—from district control, from local and state regulations, *and* from union power and collective bargaining contracts. They also wanted to give parents as many attractive alternatives as possible to the regular public schools and to inject a measure of healthy competition into the system so that all schools felt the pressure to perform and improve. For some reformers, especially the more liberal and Democratic, there was another big attraction as well: charters offered a way to gain the advantages of choice and competition *within the public sector*, and thus to head off the movement for vouchers.[148]

Needless to say, the teachers unions wanted to head off vouchers too. But the reformers' embrace of autonomy, including autonomy from collective bargaining, meant that charters would be a direct threat to union interests. If charters were allowed to proliferate, money and students—and thus jobs—would leave the regular public schools for alternatives that would typically be nonunion and not covered by collective bargaining. So despite all the misplaced excitement generated by Shanker's charter proposal, the teachers unions were fundamentally *opposed* to the kinds of charters the reform movement aimed to create. And they still are, to this day. Nothing has changed. Their interests are the same. Still, because charters are part of the public sector and thus more vulnerable to legislative and district (and through them, union) efforts to control them than private schools are, the unions would much rather put up with charters than vouchers.

Before there were any charters at all, ground zero for charter reform was Minnesota. This state had already given students more choices within the public sector (by allowing them to choose public schools across district lines, for example), and its homegrown reformers included people like Ted Kolderie, Joe Nathan, and John Brandel—the true pioneers of the charter movement. These reformers, along with a few Democratic allies in the state legislature, began pushing for charter schools in the late 1980s—insisting on genuine autonomy, not the unionized version favored by Shanker—and by 1991 were on the verge of passing the nation's first charter legislation. But a big obstacle stood in their way: the state's teachers unions. They were opposed. Very opposed.[149]

The Minnesota Education Association called the whole idea "insulting" and "a hoax."[150] The Minnesota Federation of Teachers refused to go along unless the schools were covered by district collective bargaining contracts. Eventually, reformers did succeed in getting new legislation, but the unions used their power to water it down considerably. Under the new law, there would be a ceiling of just *eight* charter schools in the entire state. Charters would need approval from their local districts (which have incentives to say no, as they don't want the competition) *and* the state school board. And a majority of the governing board of each charter would consist of teachers. So this victory was a far cry from what reformers had in mind. It provided almost no choice for parents and no competition for the regular public schools, and it barely made a dent in the entrenched bureaucratic school system the movement was trying to change. As Joe Nathan observed, "Most charter reformers were deeply disappointed."[151]

Yet something revealing had happened here. This new charter bill had managed to pass a Democratic legislature, and its leading advocates had been Democrats. What was going on? The fact is, although charters are a relatively easy sell to most Republicans, they also have a special appeal to Democrats, and this appeal has been politically crucial to the movement as a whole, giving charters much broader support across the political spectrum—and brighter political prospects—than vouchers. Democrats have good political reason to support *some* form of meaningful school choice for their constituents. They are well aware that disadvantaged children are often stuck in terrible schools, and they do not want to be in the position of denying them desperately needed opportunities. Nor do they relish standing in the way of parents when they want to make choices for their kids. So charters offer Democrats an attractive middle ground: they can support more *public sector* choice for disadvantaged families (and other families too), and at the same time, they can appease the unions by opposing vouchers and going along with some of the restrictions the unions want to see imposed on charters. As a result, the choice movement has found it easier to pick up (some) Democratic allies in pushing for charter schools, and easier to win on that dimension of choice—although what they win is usually weak, because it is larded up with union-backed restrictions.[152]

In 1992 the nation's second charter school bill passed, this one in California. The state legislature was controlled by Democrats, and as in Minnesota, they were the lead actors. Here is what happened. The teachers unions—with a voucher initiative looming in 1993 and a stronger bill being written by reform-minded state Senator Gary Hart—"supported" a charter bill crafted by state Assemblywoman Delaine Eastin, one of their staunch Democratic allies (who later became, with their support, state superintendent of public schools). The Eastin bill authorized the creation of charter schools, but it contained a cap of just twenty-five total schools: a drop in the bucket for a state with some 5,000 schools at the time. Its charters had to be covered by collective bargaining and could only be authorized if the local teachers unions gave their consent. The alternative Hart bill, strongly opposed by the unions but still heavily influenced by them, was not much more expansive: it imposed a statewide ceiling of a mere 100 schools and no more than ten in any one district. It also contained other restrictions. But it did not require union consent or collective bargaining and so gave the schools more autonomy to operate as they saw fit. In a weird concatenation of events, both bills passed the legislature. Republican Governor Pete Wilson vetoed the Eastin bill and signed the Hart bill, which then became law. But it wasn't much of a bill. Like the one in Minnesota, it offered almost no choice and no competition. And it would have been even weaker if the unions had had their way.[153]

Baby steps though they were, the Minnesota and California reforms showed that the teachers unions had lost control of some of their Democratic friends in state legislatures and that the reformers' vision of autonomous charter schools—not Shanker's unionized vision—had become the focal point of charter politics. Similar dynamics were occurring almost everywhere in the country. As a result, within a few short years of his much-celebrated Press Club speech, Al Shanker stopped extolling the virtues of charter schools and, in an about-face, "repudiated them for what he saw as their anti-public education, anti-union biases."[154] His flirtation with charters was over. The fact is, of course, he never *had* a flirtation with the kinds of autonomous charters that reformers wanted to create. He was always opposed to them. And now they were beginning to spread.

The 1990s turned into America's charter decade. In 1990 charter schools didn't exist. But by 2000, thirty-seven states (including Washington, D.C.) had adopted charter legislation, and by 2003 the number had jumped to forty, where it has remained. As the dominoes were falling, charters became the most widely accepted approach to school choice in American education. They grew increasingly popular with parents and students, especially in urban areas with chronically underperforming public schools. They gained considerable attention in the media, often via inspiring news stories—and of late, widely seen films as well (*Waiting for Superman, The Lottery, The Cartel*)—about the successes that charter schools have had with disadvantaged kids. They attracted support from leading politicians, including prominent Democrats. President Bill Clinton and Vice President Al Gore, for example, were both vocal supporters of charter schools during the 1990s, when the early battles were being fought. And in recent years, President Barack Obama and his secretary of education, Arne Duncan, have been more than vocal—making charter reform a key part of their Race to the Top (as I discuss in chapter 10) and thus taking tangible steps to translate words into action.[155]

These are important developments. Yet throughout this time, the teachers unions didn't just climb under a rock and quit. They continued to oppose charters, they continued to weaken legislation, and they continued to exercise heavy (but not total) influence on Democrats—who, inevitably, talked a better game of charter "support" than they actually played.

For an eye-opening illustration of just how tight the Democrats often are with the teachers unions, consider what happened in California in 1998. As we've seen, that state had a legal cap of just 100 charters at the time, which did nothing to bring choice or competition to the school system. Reed Hastings, a Silicon Valley entrepreneur (who went on to found Netflix), wanted to change that. His idea was to put an initiative on the 1998 ballot that would remove the charter cap entirely. He let it be known that he was ready to spend $15 million to get this proposal on the ballot and approved by voters. His opponent, predictably, was the California Teachers Association, which knew it would have to spend many millions of dollars on the other side (money it would not be able to spend on candidates in the upcoming general election). To avoid a bank-draining blowout, Hastings and the CTA ultimately got together and struck a deal: Hastings would call off his dogs if the CTA would agree to a legal change that would increase the cap by 100 schools a year thereafter.

But wait, you might say: neither Hastings nor the CTA had the authority to make law! How could *they* agree to a new law—and bring it about—if neither had the authority to make it happen? The answer is that the legislature, controlled by Democrats, could be counted upon to dutifully follow the script. For years, Democrats in the state legislature had complied with the CTA's wishes and refused to raise the cap. Now the CTA signaled that it had agreed to an increase in the cap of 100 schools a year—and voilà, the legislature immediately produced a bill that exactly mirrored what the CTA had agreed to. It passed both houses with roughly 90 percent of the vote, 60-4 in the Assembly and 20-3 in the Senate. No controversy at all. The Democrats were happy to raise the cap once the CTA gave the go-ahead.[156]

The charter movement gained some ground here, but only because Reed Hastings was wealthy enough and dedicated enough to back the unions into a corner. Some variation on this theme—with situations arising that put the unions behind the eight ball, or that render them willing to compromise in return for concessions (like more money)—has often explained why charters have been able to make a modicum of progress, and when Democrats have been needed for passage, why sufficient numbers of them have been willing to give charters their votes. But it is important to recognize, as a political baseline, that the unions' ideal—if they can get it—is to have no charter schools at all, with the possible exception of unionized charter schools.

We've seen what happened in Minnesota and California, and examples are easy to come by throughout the rest of country.[157] Almost all states have had their charter battles, with the unions leading the opposition. If there is one case, however, that really speaks volumes about how deep the union opposition to charters runs, it is the imbroglio that played out recently in Detroit.

The Detroit public schools are among the worst in the nation. If any city's children are desperately in need of new educational alternatives, Detroit's are. Recognizing as much, a philanthropist offered in 2006 to put up $200 million of his own money to fund fifteen new charter high schools in that city. A gift of this magnitude would have been manna from heaven, and stood to be enormously beneficial to these inner city kids. Indeed, given what the future normally holds for these children, it may even have saved some of their lives— literally. But the local teachers union, rather than welcoming the gift with open arms, went ballistic. It shut down the Detroit schools for a day, sent its members to demonstrate outside the state capitol in Lansing, and convinced the politicians there to *turn down* the $200 million. The free money was lost. The fifteen charter schools were never built. Needless to say, had the philanthropist sought to build fifteen regular public schools, filled with unionized teachers and covered by collective bargaining, there would have been no controversy at all. His sin was to fund autonomous charter schools. And to threaten union jobs. That children might benefit was simply not part of the union's political equation.[158]

The unions' attack on charters is multipronged. Most directly, they try to prevent states from adopting charter laws or, as in Detroit, they try to prevent charters from being created within school districts. But now that most states have charter laws and now that charters are so popular, the unions have often followed a more accommodationist strategy: they express their "support" for charter schools in concept—and then "collaborate" with policymakers in the legislative process to ensure that any new bills are filled with restrictions that neuter the reforms.

This is a formula that has worked well for many Democrats, who have often been willing to enact legislation that is high on symbolism and weak on substance. Among the usual restrictions: stunningly low ceilings on the number of charters allowed statewide, lower per-pupil funding than the regular public schools, districts as the sole chartering authorities (because the districts don't want competition and have incentives to refuse), no charter access to district buildings, no seed money to fund initial organization, requirements that charters be covered by union contracts, and, in general, the imposition of as many of the usual state and district regulations as possible, to make charters just like the regular public schools. The unions don't always get every restriction they want, especially with regard to collective bargaining. Restrictive charter bills are nonetheless the norm—and as a result, almost all charter systems have been designed, quite purposely, to provide families with very little choice and the public schools with very little competition.[159]

Restrictive legislation is just the beginning of the unions' strategy of keeping charters weak. Once these programs are in place, the unions try to unsettle them and bring them down. One line of attack is through public relations: they generate a stream of claims, reports, and studies arguing that charter schools do not improve student achievement and aiming to shrink the popularity of charters and defuse the movement. One of the most "successful" of these studies, which wound up on the front page of the *New York Times,* was actually conducted by the AFT's own staff.[160] When independent researchers come out with studies that reflect poorly on charter school performance (or can be interpreted that way), the unions publicize those studies relentlessly and systematically ignore other studies—however sophisticated and well done—that show most charters to be performing well.[161]

Another standard line of attack is through the courts. The unions have gone this route in many states that have enacted charter legislation—New York, New Jersey, Minnesota, Ohio, and others—usually arguing that charter schools violate state constitutions and that the new legislation should be annulled. Ohio is perhaps the most telling example, because the charge there was led by Tom Mooney, who was not only the president of the Ohio Federation of Teachers (OFT), but also a founding member the Teachers Union Reform Network (TURN) and an icon of progressive union leadership.[162]

Notwithstanding TURN's mission of bringing about a more enlightened unionism and forsaking traditional job interests, Mooney and the OFT went to state court in 2001 *to have Ohio's entire charter school system declared unconstitutional,* and they accompanied their court case with a public relations campaign to discredit charters as poor performers. Ultimately they lost, as the Ohio Supreme Court ruled against them in 2006.[163] But this was hardly the end of charters' legal troubles in that state. Well before this case was decided, the Ohio Education Association (OEA)—the other state teachers union—filed suit in federal court, claiming that charter funding was unfair and violated the due process clause of the fourteenth amendment to the U.S. Constitution. Then, in 2007, the OEA filed suit in state court seeking to end the diversion of funds away from traditional public schools to charters.[164] This suit was later dropped when the state's Democratic attorney general announced he would launch his own legal attack on charters.[165] Meantime, Democratic Governor Ted Strickland, an ally of the teachers unions who took office in 2007, made it clear that seeking drastic reductions in charter school funding would be a key part of his educational agenda throughout his term. And it was.[166]

As these examples can only illustrate, the road to progress for charter schools has been a rocky one indeed. After two full decades of reform and despite all the accolades heaped upon them by prominent public officials from President Obama on down, the charter movement has managed to generate a mere 5,000 schools or so (as of 2009–10): a pittance compared to the more than 90,000 regular public schools that populate the larger system. They enroll just 3.4 percent of the nation's public school students (1.7 million students out of some 50 million).[167]

The tiny enrollments, however, are no indication of what families want for their children. Most of the existing charters have long waiting lists of children eager to get in. In Harlem, for instance, charter schools are enormously popular, enrolling 20 percent of public school kids, but many more are clamoring to get in and can't, because there aren't nearly enough charters to take them. In the spring of 2010, some 14,000 Harlem children submitted applications for just 2,700 open slots, and more than 11,000 were turned away.[168] Nationwide, about 420,000 children are on wait lists, hoping to get into schools that don't have room to take them.[169] The demand for charters far outstrips the supply.

The simple reason is that, while charters have in some sense swept the nation, the unions have been using their political power to keep the supply of charters down. As far down as they can get it. In some contexts, the situation has gotten away from them, and charters have made truly impressive gains. In New Orleans, where the traditional school system was destroyed by Katrina and reformers gained the upper hand, charters now enroll a stunning 61 percent of students. This is obviously an unusual situation. The charters' "market share" is also quite high, however, in Washington, D.C. (38 percent), Detroit (36 percent), Kansas City (32 percent), Dayton (29 percent), Flint (29 percent), Gary (28 percent), St. Louis (27 percent), and a number of other urban districts, where they are clearly offering families many new choices and creating meaningful competition for the regular public schools. The trajectory in many urban areas is upward—and shows that, in some places, unions are having a difficult time keeping the pressure for charters under control.[170]

But remember, reformers have been at this *for twenty years*. That's a long time for children and families to wait and a long time for the regular public schools to avoid competition. And while reformers have managed to eke out progress in certain urban areas—charters are, by and large, an urban phenomenon—they have been far less successful in the rest of the country. In many of the states that *have* charter laws, there are actually very few charter schools and only small percentages of kids actually attend them. Here, for example, are a few "charter states" and their enrollment percentages: Connecticut (0.9 percent), Illinois (1.7 percent), Indiana (1.8 percent), Iowa (0.1 percent), Kansas (1.1 percent), New Hampshire (0.4 percent), New Jersey (1.4 percent), New York (1.6 percent), Oklahoma (1.0 percent), and Tennessee (0.5 percent). When we hear that forty states have adopted charter laws, it is natural to think that charters must be making great progress almost everywhere, but this is very far from the truth. Most charter laws are filled with restrictions that are designed to limit the spread of charters and to keep enrollments down. And that's exactly what they do. The real winner here is not the charter movement or the countless families who desperately want new alternatives for their kids. The real winner is the politics of blocking.[171]

Finally, I want to pay at least brief attention to yet another line of market-based reform that the unions have been fighting against for years: the reliance on private, for-profit firms to carry out some of the core functions of public education. Private firms have been actively involved in the charter sector from the beginning—managing some charter schools and providing specialized services to many others—and the unions have tried their best to prevent it; but they haven't been able to do that, in large part because the entities holding charters can make their own independent decisions to hire private firms if they want, and they often do. But private firms can also get involved in public education much more directly: school districts can contract with them to operate regular public schools—most obviously, schools that are persistently failing. In this way, districts can take advantage of the expertise, efficiency, and innovation of the marketplace in trying to transform schools that have long shown themselves incapable of improvement. Contracting with private firms is surely reasonable under the circumstances. If it succeeds, great—the schools are improved, and the students are better off. If it doesn't, the contracts can be terminated.

But here again, what is reasonable for kids and schools is nonetheless threatening to the unions. They have virtually no control over the actions of private firms, whose approaches to education—longer hours, different teaching methods, different personnel procedures—may force changes that unions and teachers don't want. And most important, small experiments with private firms could actually show them to be successful, which could lead to a greater role for them in the future and thus to a flow of jobs and money to the private sector. In the end, the teachers unions oppose "contracting out" for the same reason that all unions in all industries, throughout the entire economy, oppose it: they want to keep control over the jobs and the money. It has nothing to do with whether enlisting the help of private firms might actually be good for kids and schools.[172]

With the unions so opposed, these innovative arrangements have been blocked in all but a small percentage of the nation's school districts. They are adopted only when the schools in question are failing miserably and the district (or the state) has a determined, outside-the-box leader willing to put up with fierce resistance. This is what happened, for example, in Baltimore and Hartford during the early 1990s, when those districts entered into path-breaking contracts with Education Alternatives, which was to run nine failing schools in Baltimore and all of Hartford's thirty-two schools.[173] These were the nation's first major experiments with school privatization. It also happened more recently in Philadelphia, whose troubled school system was taken over by the state in 2002, and private firms and nonprofits were invited in—by the state School Reform Commission (under a Republican governor)—to help run thirty-six of the very worst schools in the district: twenty by the for-profits, sixteen by the nonprofits.[174]

These breakthroughs are rare. Even in these best-case scenarios, moreover, the firms are walking into a firestorm. The local unions, having lost the fight to prevent contracting out, just keep on fighting: making ceaseless claims in the local press about the firms' "poor" performance, inciting teacher and parent opposition, accusing firms of doctoring test scores, pursuing court cases to challenge the firms' authority and decisions, and otherwise making privatization a miserable, costly, and politically tumultuous experience for all concerned. This was the fate of Education Alternatives in both Baltimore and Hartford: the unions were able to have it fired within a few years.[175] And much the same has been going on more recently in Philadelphia. The unions and their allies went on the warpath after 2002, trying to rid their district of outside management groups; and in this atmosphere of hostility, district leaders (who have changed over the years) and the School Reform Commission (which shifted composition under a Democratic governor) began looking for other ways to turn around their low-performing schools. By mid-2010, the accretion of decisions left the for-profit firms with just six of their original twenty schools.[176]

In their crusade against private firms, the teachers unions have done everything they can to see that the practice of contracting out is discredited, that contracts are terminated, and that firms are too scared to enter—because they will be so tormented that they cannot succeed and will lose money. While the unions haven't put a complete end to these arrangements, they have minimized them to the point of trivializing their overall role in American education. In principle, it makes perfect sense for districts to try to take advantage of whatever the marketplace has to offer for its schools and kids. In practice, districts aren't allowed to do that. Powerful interests are threatened—and in the end, power calls the shots.

Conclusion

The politics of education is hardly a shining example of democracy in action. On the surface, it may seem vibrant and pluralistic. Countless groups and public officials are involved, and there is lots of flowery rhetoric about solving education problems and doing what's best "for the kids." But most of this is misleading, for beneath the complex action and soaring symbolism a very simple structure is at work: the politics of blocking.

The building blocks of this structure are rooted in a few basic facts of political life. It is a fact that the teachers unions have vested interests in preserving the existing education system, regardless of how poorly it performs. It is a fact that they are more powerful—by far—than any other groups involved in the politics of education. And it is a fact that, in a government of checks and balances, they can use their power to block or weaken most reforms they do not like. To recognize as much is not to launch ideological attacks against the unions. It is simply to recognize the political world as it is.

Because the politics of blocking is very real and because it has long kept the lid on American education reform, the challenge of *A Nation at Risk* has gone unmet. Major reforms that attempt to address the fundamentals of poor performance and inject strong, performance-based incentives into the heart of the system have been resisted and undermined at every turn. Even the simplest, most straightforward attempts to target the school-level determinants of student achievement—efforts to get bad teachers out of the classroom, for example—have run into a wall of obstruction.

After a quarter century of reform, the nation has made scant progress. Indeed, most of its reforms are not worthy of the name. Its accountability and choice systems are too weak to do their jobs well and are under constant attacks intended to weaken them further. And the mainstream reforms that make up most of what the policy process actually produces—more spending, across-the-board pay raises, more teacher training, reductions in class size—have little to do with student achievement, but a lot to do with why the American school system gets more and more expensive without gaining in productivity.

Thankfully, this is not the end of the story. The downside is that the fundamentals that have driven it—the ever-present logic of power and self-interest, the uniquely American political system that favors blocking over reform—are not going to go away. They help us to understand the past, they will help us to understand our present and our future, and they are surely sobering. But the story, as it continues to unfold, is about to change considerably—because new forces are beginning to enter the equation, and they are destined over a period of years to break the unions' iron grip on America's public schools. And to make education reform a reality.

10

A Critical Juncture

The chapters in this book cover a lot of ground. If we step back from it all and take in the broad panorama of American education reform over the last three decades, what do we see? We see a nation whose leaders fully agree that improving the public schools is absolutely critical to the economic and social well being of the country, and who are willing to invest heavily to bring that improvement about. But we also see an education system that is protected from change—protected by a special interest group that has a deep stake in the status quo and has used its formidable power on all fronts to prevent real reform.

Even under the best of circumstances, improving the nation's schools would be a complicated business. No knowledgeable person would suggest otherwise. Yet the basic requirements of success are easy enough to understand. The first is that, at the local level, schools need to be organized in the most effective ways possible to promote student learning. The second is that, when higher-level policy decisions are made about the structure and operation of the larger school system—and thus about accountability, choice, pay for performance, credentialing, tenure, or anything else—these decisions too need to based on what is best for children and effective organization.

It is a central theme of this book that, as long as the teachers unions remain powerful, *these basic requirements cannot be met.* At the local level, the unions use their power in collective bargaining to impose their own organization on the public schools, burying them in restrictive, special interest work rules that make no sense from the standpoint of effective schooling. In the policymaking process, where higher-level reform ideas are battled out, the unions use their power to block or weaken anything that threatens their own interests, making it impossible for governments to correct for the system's pathologies and create organizations that are built for top-flight performance.

These are abstract points. But consider what they mean in reality. We have a public school system that can't even get bad teachers out of the classroom. Does that make sense? Is that good for children? Obviously not. But there it is: a fundamental component of the organization of America's schools. Anyone can see that it's ridiculous and that it prevents literally millions of children from getting a quality education. *But the nation has been unable to do anything about it.*

And this just scratches the surface. Seniority rules for teacher transfers, excessing, and layoffs ensure that the schools' teaching resources get allocated in ways that have nothing to do with productivity or quality. The single salary schedule ensures that good teachers get paid exactly the same as bad teachers and that the criteria on which they are paid—seniority, formal credentials—have nothing to do with how much children actually learn. We have accountability systems that don't actually hold anyone accountable, in which no one ever loses a job regardless of how poor the performance, in which teachers are not even evaluated in terms of whether their students learn anything, and in which more than 99 percent of teachers are rated as doing a satisfactory job. And so it goes, on and on. The American public school system is hobbling along with an organization that any reasonable person can see is horribly suited to effective education. Yet its perversities are protected by an entrenched power, the power of the teachers unions.

This protection of perversity has been the norm for many decades, since the unions first took center stage in the 1960s and 1970s. The modern American education system has thereafter been defined, structured—and stifled—by union power, and incapable of meeting the needs of the nation and its children. The modern era of education reform, which has been going full tilt since *A Nation at Risk* first raised the red flag in the early 1980s, has failed to make much of a dent in any of this. As of today the system remains a profound disappointment. And its power structure remains intact—and doing its job to prevent change.

So what now? Is there any hope that, going forward, the nation's public schools—and the policymakers who govern them—can somehow overcome the problem of union power and successfully organize for effective performance? Under normal conditions, the answer would be no. The American political system is filled with veto points that make major reforms difficult to achieve, render blocking relatively easy, and allow any group with serious power to stand in the way of change. This is normal throughout American government. It is also the basic structure of the situation in public education—a structure that has been in place for many decades and is not simply going to melt away because Americans want better schools.

How, then, can it change? If we assume that the veto-filled features of American government are destined to continue (and of course they are) and if we assume that the unions are not suddenly going to forgo their special interests and begin representing children (a fanciful "reform unionism" that is never going to happen), then there are only two basic ways to move forward.

The first is hard-headed pragmatism. Union power can simply be accepted as one of the givens of modern American education, and reformers can try to make as much progress as possible under the circumstances. They can do it by fighting against the unions and trying to win valued reforms that the unions oppose. But they can also do it by working *with* the unions—notably, through collaboration in the policy process or in collective bargaining—to find common ground: an approach that may have genuine payoffs during times when the unions are under great public pressure to make concessions and get out of the way of change.

Pragmatism always seems reasonable, and it is surely a means to incremental progress. But it also has a fundamental flaw: it accepts union power as a continuing reality, and in so doing it ensures that progress will be inherently limited and heavily shaped by the unions and their special interests. Ultimately, pragmatism takes what it can get. It does not really expect the schools to be organized in the best interests of children, and it puts the nation on a path that virtually guarantees that *they never will be*. Pragmatism is a very good way of taking small steps forward. But it is a very bad way of getting the nation where it ought to be going.

If reformers want to stand up for children—and win for children—there is only one way out of the current bind. The power of the teachers unions must somehow be *drastically reduced*, so that the interests of children and effective schooling can take priority among the nation's policymakers and real reform can go forward. This is the goal. Baby steps won't get us there.

In normal times, a drastic reduction in union power would be very unlikely to happen. The teachers unions have been enormously powerful for decades; they are powerful now; and aided by the checks and balances built into the political system, they are in a position to *use* that power to combat any attempts to take their power away. This is the Catch-22 of power: if you try to take away the power of powerful groups, they will normally be able to use their power to stop you.

The most potent and direct way to undermine the teachers unions' power, for example, is to pass new laws prohibiting collective bargaining in the public schools. Conservatives have long wanted to do that, but they usually don't even bother proposing this kind of legislation because under normal circumstances it doesn't stand a chance. Other, less Draconian methods of reducing union power—laws that prohibit agency fees, for example, or "paycheck protection" laws that prohibit unions from using member dues for political purposes unless members explicitly agree—are almost always doomed to failure as well. The unions and their Democratic allies can typically block. They can *use* their power to *protect* their power, and that's what they've been doing for decades.

All sorts of interesting ideas for the future would fall into the same trap. It is perfectly reasonable, for example, to suggest that reformers might pursue (through legislation, say) a new, much more limited kind of unionism whose main purpose would be to provide teachers with some form of representation, give them a means of exercising voice and having input, and allow them to contribute important information and expertise to the policy process. But the conundrum is: how could such organizations be created without their also *becoming powerful* and *using* that power to pursue their special interests? And even if that conundrum could be solved, today's unions would never go along with it, and would use their existing power to try to prevent any such ideas from becoming reality.

Despite all the grounds for pessimism, this cloud has a silver lining. The public school system is entering an abnormal time—a time that, because of two recent developments that the unions (and the rest of us) have never confronted before, is set to unleash forces for change that ultimately can't be blocked. Political scientists might put it this way: the American education system has long been stable and well protected by union power, but now, because of a unique confluence of events, it stands at a critical juncture that eventually will undermine the unions, put the system on a new and radically different path, and make reform a reality.[1]

The two developments driving change have little to do with one another. Their confluence is accidental, but fantastically powerful. This is not unusual for critical junctures that bring about big institutional change. Our nation didn't get the New Deal, for example, in the normal course of events. It happened because the stable "good times" of the Roaring '20s were disrupted by a calamitous economic depression, which was followed by Herbert Hoover's traditional and wholly ineffective response and a realigning election that brought massive majorities to the Democrats—and gave rise to the presidency of Franklin Roosevelt, who turned out to be (and it could easily have been otherwise) a remarkable leader hell-bent on innovating his way out of disaster. A confluence of events. A lining up of the stars. In normal times, the New Deal wouldn't have become the centerpiece of modern American government. But the 1930s were not normal times, and this allowed an improbable institutional upheaval to become reality and to happen when it did.

This final chapter, then, is about American education's critical juncture and the two developments that define it. One is an "endogenous" development, arising from *within* the education system itself. The Race to the Top of 2009 and 2010, engineered by President Obama and his secretary of education, Arne Duncan, is part and parcel of this dynamic of change. But it is more an expression of it rather than the causal force itself. What is happening, most fundamentally, is that the political alliances that have buttressed union power over the decades are coming unhinged—and the unions are increasingly isolated, blamed for the system's poor performance, and forced to make compromises they would never have made in the past. As a result, reforms are gaining greater traction, and there is a growing sense (not entirely justified, for now) that the nation is on the verge of a spectacular breakthrough.

This first development is profoundly important, and it will grow in future years. But for reasons I discuss in this chapter, it is only equipped to bring about modest changes and, by itself, would leave the unions with enough power to continue standing in the way of effective organization. This is where the second development comes in. It has nothing to do with the first. It is an "exogenous" development, arising from *outside* the system—specifically, from the revolution in information technology that has been sweeping the entire world. This revolution is only just beginning to invade public education. But the invasion is happening. And as it continues, it will bring powerful forces for change that will dovetail with, and magnify, the endogenous political developments. The combination will be impossible for the unions to hold back, and will ultimately overwhelm them and vitiate their power.

The nation, in effect, is lucky. The political tides that are now moving in the reformers' favor—and generating exuberant optimism—are actually not strong enough to win the war for effective schools. But they are a big help. And it so happens, by an accident of history, that they are about to be aided by an external force of staggering magnitude that will put them over the top.

The Shifting Political Tides

Accountability and choice have been only minimally successful as education reforms. We've already seen a key reason why: the teachers unions have used their power to ensure that they have been kept weak, and that they are pale reflections of what they could be. Both these reforms have been around and struggling for roughly twenty years, and their stories are sagas of deep frustration and continuing disappointment.

But when the history of our era is ultimately written, decades from now, one of its themes may well be that the most consequential impacts of accountability and choice during their first twenty years were not their impacts on the schools themselves, but rather their impacts on the *politics* of American education—and in particular, on the political alliances that determine the prospects for reform. Both accountability and choice, weak though they are, have set in motion forces that are disruptive to the traditional political alliance—the unions' political alliance—that has protected the educational status quo. And they have propelled both the emergence of a new alliance on the other side and a new balance of power far more conducive to change.

Consider accountability. Throughout almost the entire history of the public school system, Americans had little objective data on which to judge the performance of their schools. In the 1970s and 1980s, international tests of student achievement began to show that the nation's children didn't stack up to children in other nations—that the schools, in other words, weren't teaching them what they needed to know—and during the 1990s, information provided by the National Assessment of Educational Progress (NAEP) and state-level tests reinforced concerns that the schools needed improvement. But this information was highly aggregated, giving scores for the nation as a whole or for entire states. There was precious little information for parents and citizens on how their own schools and districts were performing or how they compared to those in other communities.

The accountability movement has not succeeded in holding schools and teachers accountable. But it has succeeded in testing kids regularly, evaluating local schools, and *making the information about schools and districts public.* This information—concrete, objective information on performance—has changed the politics of education. Above all else, it has put the spotlight on schools and districts that are performing poorly, making it clear just how abysmally bad many urban schools are and how egregiously they are short-changing the disadvantaged, often minority kids who are stuck in them. In so doing, it has awakened many parents and citizens to the brute facts of educational life, giving them a well-grounded basis for making demands and taking action. Above all else, it has shocked and mobilized the leaders and political groups that represent disadvantaged constituencies. During the 1990s, as accountability was just getting a foothold, these groups tended to resist out of concern that disadvantaged kids would score badly on tests, that urban schools would do poorly, that graduation rates and resources and reputations would suffer, and that their kids would be held back. But as time went on and as evidence piled up about just how bad their kids' schools are, they did an about-face. They became outraged and insistent that policymakers get serious about accountability. They changed sides.[2]

The symbolic turning point was the politics of No Child Left Behind (NCLB) in 2001. That this was also the teachers unions' biggest defeat of the reform era is no coincidence: for their usual allies in national politics—the representatives of the disadvantaged, along with key Democrats—largely abandoned them. The groups speaking for disadvantaged kids, led by Education Trust—often singled out as the key driver of support for the bill—increasingly saw what accountability could do *for them* by laying bare what was really going on in their schools, providing a basis for genuine improvement, and focusing national attention on the achievement gap (a centerpiece of NCLB). With these advocacy groups behind the bill—and business groups too—it was much easier for many Democrats to support it. (They were also worried that George W. Bush and the Republicans would steal their thunder on public education, traditionally a Democratic issue, and believed that they needed to get out front and be active players on this bill.)[3]

Accountability also affected political alignments by putting the unions themselves on the hot seat. Once systems were in place for measuring performance and publicizing the results, the unions were headed for trouble; for many of the things they regularly do—from protecting mediocre teachers in the classroom to imposing restrictive work rules (like seniority) on the schools—are obvious impediments to effective organization, and it was only a matter of time before everyone else began to connect the dots. Increasingly, as accountability has advanced, the unions have become subjects of scrutiny and been put on the political defensive, and other political constituencies have mobilized against them, leaving them more and more isolated. Ironically, then, the unions have bitten accountability by making it weak and relatively ineffective, but even a weakened accountability has bitten the unions right back, putting the spotlight on poor performance and casting the unions as enemies of reform, causes of ineffective organization, and in general, *part of the problem.*

Something similar has happened with school choice. The unions have stalled and weakened and tried to kill it, but even in its limited forms it has given rise to new political pressures that are bad indeed for the unions. Choice too has bitten back.

For the last two decades, virtually all the nation's choice programs have been designed to provide new options for the kids in American society who clearly need them most: those who are poor, ethnic minorities, disabled, and disproportionately trapped in the worst schools in the country. Opinion polls, not surprisingly, have consistently shown that the parents of these kids are the strongest supporters of school choice.[4] As choice has expanded, this constituency of the disadvantaged has grown and so has its political footprint. Increasingly, not only do disadvantaged families support the idea of choice, but they also have a direct stake in it—their kids attend a local charter or voucher school, and they tell their friends, their neighbors, and their local politicians how important these options are to them. Go to Harlem nowadays and try to convince the people there that school choice is a bad idea. See what kind of reception you get. The idea of choice is popular. But the reality of choice is even more popular—and politically powerful.

From the first choice-based uprising in Milwaukee, Democrats have been faced with a dilemma: genuinely wanting to do what's best for their disadvantaged constituents, but being held back by union power. Until recently, their political balancing act has been to oppose vouchers and tax credits and to provide tepid support for charters—(often) going along with charter laws, but then favoring all sorts of restrictions that limit choice and competition. That kind of resistance-masquerading-as-support, however, is no longer quite so rational. The power equation is changing.

It is changing, in part, because the Democratic constituency for choice is bigger, more vocal, and more demanding than ever before. It is also changing because of accountability. As accountability has provided concrete evidence of just how deplorable the performance problems are in many districts, particularly urban districts filled with disadvantaged kids, it has fueled the argument that these kids absolutely need to have new options—and that school choice is an essential component of any comprehensive plan to provide them with a quality education. Today, the pressure on Democrats to support choice—really support it, not just give it lip service—is greater than ever before, because accountability has helped to demonstrate and drive home the need for it.

Interestingly, the synergy between accountability and choice works the other way around as well. Accountability generates forces, via evidence on poor performance, that give Democrats stronger reasons to support choice. But choice also generates forces, by allowing kids to leave the regular public schools, that give Democrats stronger reasons to take accountability more seriously. For a true system of accountability is intended to make the regular public schools more effective—and such a system would help prevent the hemorrhage of kids to outside choice options. For Democrats who increasingly have a difficult time denying choice to kids trapped in bad schools, then, accountability becomes a way of *saving* the public schools—saving them by improving them.

Here is a telling comment on the politics of NCLB from Amy Wilkins, of Education Trust, that nicely illustrates this last point and suggests how accountability, choice, the teachers unions, and minority groups all fit together in the Democrats' political calculus and encourage a new orientation toward reform:[5]

> The Democrats didn't really evolve much on education until [the Bush administration] . . . As [they] saw minority—especially African American and Latino—support for vouchers increasing it began to pit two important voting blocs within the Democratic Party against one another. The teachers unions were saying, "Everything is fine, just give us more money," but increasing numbers of African Americans and Latinos were saying, "We want out of these schools." This was forcing Democrats into a place where they had to deal—they had to do something on [accountability].

In the years since NCLB was adopted, reformist pressures within the Democratic Party have grown considerably. Although, throughout the decade of the 2000s, the Democrats continued to be the party of resistance and blocking, they were also a party in turmoil and under stress when education was at issue. Liberal-leaning opinion leaders—from the *Washington Post* to *Newsweek* and *Time* to the *New Republic* and many others—came around to strongly embrace both accountability and choice (always in the form of charter schools, sometimes even vouchers) and to speak out explicitly against the special interest obstructionism of the teachers unions.[6]

In the past, speaking out against the unions was simply off limits for political liberals, a violation of the faith. But no more. Nicholas Kristof, in an opinion piece for the *New York Times*, puts the new view of unions quite bluntly: "The Democratic Party has been too close to the unions for too long, and their interest is not precisely the same as the students' . . . Education reform is going to mean challenging the unions."[7] Says Joe Klein in *Time* magazine, "The unions, and their minions in the Democratic Party, have been a reactionary force in education reform for too long."[8] This sort of heresy is entirely new. On education, we are witnessing a new liberalism.

In the meantime, groups representing the disadvantaged have gotten even more forcefully organized to push for change within the Democratic Party on matters of education. This is not the case, I hasten to point out, for some of the old-line civil rights groups, particularly the NAACP, which seem permanently stuck in the past and entirely without vision. Their hearts are in the right place, but their solutions amount to little more than pumping tons of additional money into high-poverty districts, and they have maintained their long-time suspicion of bold structural changes (and threats to jobs).[9] For their stodginess, they have paid a price: other groups are taking their place as dynamic, respected advocates for disadvantaged kids.

I have already mentioned Education Trust. Two even newer organizations stand out as well: the Democrats for Education Reform (formed in 2007) and the Education Equality Project (formed in 2008). Their mastheads read like a who's who of progressive Democratic leadership in the realm of public education. Both are committed to accountability. Both are committed to choice. And both see the teachers unions as obstructionist forces that have prevented the Democratic Party from doing right by its neediest constituents. Here, for instance, are the opening lines from the mission statement of the Democrats for Education Reform:[10]

A first-rate system of public education is the cornerstone of a prosperous, free, and just society, yet millions of American children today—particularly low-income and children of color—are trapped in persistently failing schools that are part of deeply dysfunctional school systems. These systems, once viewed romantically as avenues of opportunity for all, have become captive to powerful, entrenched interests that too often put the demands of adults before the educational needs of children . . .

Both political parties have failed to address the tragic decline of our system of public education, but it is the Democratic Party—our party—which must question how we allowed ourselves to drift so far from our mission. Fighting on behalf of our nation's most vulnerable individuals is what our party is supposed to stand for.

Democrats for Education Reform aims to return the Democratic Party to its rightful place as a champion of children, first and foremost, in America's public education systems.

Who do you suppose are the "powerful, entrenched interests that too often put the demands of adults before the educational needs of children"? The central goal of these new groups is clear: to stand up to the teachers unions, put an end to their control of the Democratic Party on matters of education, and make children the party's number one priority. Such efforts by high-profile Democrats to reorient their party are truly historic and a striking departure from the past. Ten years ago, such a thing would never have happened.

In what may be the single most symbolic event in the modern politics of education—even more important than No Child Left Behind, because it signals the rise of a new and truly progressive educational coalition within the Democratic Party—these groups held a much-publicized and heavily attended forum at the party's 2008 presidential convention in Denver. All the party's luminaries and power holders were at the convention, of course. And the leaders of the teachers unions were active and ever-present: treated as celebrities and granted the massive respect that is regularly accorded massive power. As has been true for years, moreover, their members made up roughly 10 percent of all delegates—a stunning and sobering fact of political life. It was a convention of teachers almost as much as a convention of Democrats. Yet the reformers chose this place and this time to make a dramatic public statement—to their party, to the nation.

Here is one media account of what happened. It gives a good sense of just how sharply the tables seem to have turned on the Democrats' home ground.[11]

The evening provided a truly unusual spectacle at the convention: A megawatt group of Democrats, including Mayor Cory Booker of Newark, Mayor Adrian Fenty of Washington, D.C., and former Gov. Roy Romer of Colorado, bashed teachers' unions for an hour . . . "Ten years ago when I talked about school choice, I was literally tarred and feathered," said Booker, whose celebrity at this convention, as a young African American politician said to have the ear of Barack Obama, cannot be overstated. "I was literally brought into a broom closet by a union and told I would never win office if I kept talking about charters." . . . Moderator John Merrow, a reporter on *The News Hour,* asked Fenty what interests benefited from reactionary education policies that hurt children. The mayor took the bait. "Definitely the unions." . . . Summing up the panel's feelings,

Roy Romer said, "In the Democratic Party, you have to be realistic about some coalitions that are wedded to the past on education." He intoned, "Let's not be wedded to somebody's union rules . . . An adult agenda wins too often in our present union situation."

As Democrats, it took courage for these people to do what they did. Cory Booker could well have found himself being dragged into another closet, only this time to listen to a much more ominous message. But he is not without his own power base, and the reformers as a group are far more powerful still—they are organized, they have money, they have positions of authority and responsibility, and they have the public spotlight and can get their message out. Together, they are a force to be reckoned with. Since the Democratic national convention, the teachers unions have been put on notice that their control of the party on education is no longer acceptable to others with power. They are being challenged. Seriously. Openly.

Reformers at the Periphery of Power

Before we move on, I want to mention one other endogenous development that is important to the future trajectory of reform. This one is at the periphery of politics and is more about ideas and social activism than about the exercise of sheer political power. It stands to have major consequences, however, for how the power struggle is likely to play out.

I'm talking about two dynamics, really. One has been driven largely by Teach for America, which, after twenty years in operation, can now claim some 17,000 alumni, two-thirds of whom have remained within the education system—as teachers, but also as principals, superintendents, operators of charter schools, and much more, sometimes at much higher levels and in more pivotal positions. These are some of the nation's top college graduates, and as a group they tend to be committed to genuine reform of the public schools—supporters of accountability, choice, rigorous teacher evaluation, pay for performance, ridding classrooms of bad teachers, and all the rest. They are no friends of teachers unions. Michelle Rhee came out of Teach for America. So did Mike Feinberg and Dave Levin, the founders of KIPP, the spectacularly successful network of charter schools for disadvantaged kids. So did a large percentage of the principals and teachers who make up the huge new population of charter schools in post-Katrina New Orleans, which is now, thanks to the influx of talent and enthusiasm (which followed the destruction of the local union), the most innovative school district in the country. The list goes on and on.[12]

These people are young, smart, unwedded to the past, in positions to engineer change, and motivated to do just that. And they form an informal social network: they communicate with one another and see themselves as a movement for change. This network, which contains more reformers than just Teach for America alumni, has spawned a number of organizations that are now active in the reform movement. Among them are the New Teacher Project (begun by Michelle Rhee) and New Leaders for New Schools (run by Jon Schnur, now an adviser to President Obama), which have been crusaders for novel ways to recruit new talent into the public schools and opponents of the restrictive formalisms (including the collective bargaining rules) that bind the traditional system.[13]

The second development at the periphery involves the role of nonprofit foundations in pushing for education reform. Their great advantage is that they are not held back (at least explicitly) by politics or government: they can decide what projects and aims they want to support, they can allocate their own money to promote them, and they can use that money as a carrot—a very desirable carrot indeed—to get districts around the country to get on board and do things they wouldn't otherwise do.

During the 1990s, much of the foundation money for K–12 education came from philanthropies like the Ford Foundation, the Carnegie Foundation for the Advancement of Teaching, the Rockefeller Foundation, and the Annenberg Foundation—which wanted to improve the public schools, but were not subversives looking to shake up the system. But that has changed. Since the turn of the century, the biggest givers have been the Bill and Melinda Gates Foundation and the Walton Family Foundation, and the Broad Foundation has been quite prominent as well.[14]

The Walton Family Foundation has been a huge funder of school choice, in the form of both charter schools and vouchers (including tax credits), and has long been a major force in propelling and organizing the entire choice movement. The Broad Foundation has been extremely active on a much broader front, supporting a vast assortment of innovative projects that range from identifying and training new leaders to creating new data systems to constructing SchoolMatters.com, a website that collects and publicizes performance information on all schools nationwide.

By any standard, however, Bill Gates has emerged as the single most influential philanthropic force in American public education. His foundation, with a $35 billion endowment, is the largest private contributor to reform, spending its largesse selectively on the specific innovations that Gates and his educational advisers and staffers believe are most promising. In the early part of the decade, their focus was on breaking up big schools and replacing them with smaller, more personal ones—an inside-the-box agenda that, however reasonable, did not prove especially successful. By the latter 2000s, they had moved away from small schools and embraced a much more transformative agenda that put them at the forefront of the reform movement—by directing their financial support to charter schools, data systems linking student and teacher data, new performance-based systems of teacher evaluation and pay, and national standards.

Much of this agenda, needless to say, rubs the unions the wrong way and potentially brings the foundation into conflict with them. But Gates has adapted by arguing that productive change needs to be brought about through collaboration with the unions, and he has made some of his biggest grants—for new performance-based systems of evaluation and pay in Memphis, Pittsburgh, and Hillsborough County, for example—contingent on districts working with their unions and getting buy-in for their proposed reforms.[15]

There is considerable overlap between these philanthropic foundations and the network of young, enthusiastic reformers just described, and it is an overlap that goes beyond personnel to include ideas and agenda. The overlap is not perfect, of course. But still, many of the movers and shakers in the larger education community who are outside the halls of government, and who don't occupy positions of public authority or wield political power directly, are increasingly committed to bold reform. They *want* to transform this education system. They think outside the box and are willing to act outside the box. They have access to money and expertise. They are well connected.

As power alignments begin to change within the political system, then, and particularly within the Democratic Party, the people who are in positions of authority and policymaking responsibility—presidents, governors, legislators, superintendents, mayors—now have access to a large pool of talented innovators, and often seed money, for making things happen. This is a reformist basis for change that, for the most part, simply didn't exist ten years ago.

In almost all respects, this is a good thing. For more than a quarter century, education reform has been stifled by the politics of blocking, and these new entrants—energized, talented, committed, and well financed—are making changes happen that never would have happened without them. Yet there is a downside that needs to be recognized: these people may sometimes put their substantial clout behind ideas that send the reform movement off in unproductive directions. The Gates Foundation's pursuit of small schools is one example, but a fairly minor one: the money could have been better spent, but the exercise didn't hurt or derail the reform movement. But now that Bill Gates has decided that reform needs to be carried out through collaboration with the unions, the implications are not minor at all. They are potentially profound. He may be successful at engineering beneficial reforms—but he may also do it in such a way that the reforms are inherently limited in what they can accomplish and that sets other reformers, and indeed governments, off on a path that simply can't take them very far.

Getting Perspective

So these are the political fundamentals. Accountability and choice, weak though they are as policies, have unleashed forces with major consequences for politics—heightening the dissatisfaction of low-income and minority constituencies, enhancing their political power, magnifying their demands for reform, and prompting them (and the liberals who support them) to distance themselves from the teachers unions, which they now see as obstacles to quality education. The Democratic Party used to know where it stood on public education. Whatever its spinmeisters might have said and however lofty their rhetoric about children and schools, the party stood with the teachers unions. But throughout the 2000s that stand was being contested. On education, a fight was under way for the soul of the Democratic Party; and it was a struggle, inevitably, for power. It was also a fight whose main policy goal—transforming the public schools for the benefit of children—was attracting a small army of young reformers, along with innovation-oriented foundations, who were infiltrating the educational terrain on their own and providing a base that the politically powerful could tap into for support, ideas, and progress.

Pretty impressive. If we want to understand this thing, however, we can't get carried away. We need, as always, to maintain perspective. The decade of the 2000s was not some sort of conversion period during which Democrats changed their political spots. They were still Democrats, union friendly and union dependent. The teachers unions were still absolutely central players in the larger Democratic coalition, much needed for their money, their activists, and their vast organizational contributions to electoral campaigns. They remained enormously powerful—and the Democrats, true to form, spent the 2000s opposing most serious reforms. They were the party of weak accountability. They were the party of limited choice. They were the party of employee protections.

Bigger picture, then, the way to think about these developments is not in terms of a cataclysmic political shift, but rather in terms of incremental changes in political alliances, which in turn have generated incremental changes in the balance of power within the Democratic Party. These changes are important and surely brighten the prospects for meaningful reform. But they are not enough, in and of themselves—even as they continue to grow in the years ahead—to bring about a radical transformation of America's schools in the best interests of children. They leave the unions too powerful. They leave the Democrats too weak and conflicted.

Barack Obama and Race to the Top

With these considerations in mind, let's pick up the political story again and take a look at how the alignments have continued to change in recent years.

During the 2008 presidential nomination season, a stampede of candidates vied for the Democratic nod: Barack Obama, Hillary Clinton, John Edwards, Joe Biden, Christopher Dodd, and others—and all but Obama had education platforms that were built on traditional, high-spending, system-preserving Democratic ideas. Education was not a salient issue during the campaign. But when it came up, the subject was almost always NCLB, which the teachers unions had spent years denouncing and undermining. Excoriating NCLB—and with it, serious reforms aimed at holding schools and teachers accountable—became the unions' litmus test for Democratic candidates. All but Obama passed with flying colors.[16]

Remember, this was 2008, near the end of the 2000s. These were some of the top leaders of the Democratic Party—and, Obama aside, they were doing *absolutely nothing* to express the reformist sentiment that for years had been building up within their own constituencies. This should tell us something about just how powerful the reformers actually were within the party. They were an enthusiastic new presence, chafing for recognition and change. But in a savvy group of professional Democratic politicians, they carried little clout.

On education, Obama stood apart from the crowd. He made it clear that, even if NCLB had its flaws, he supported the basic principles of accountability. He talked openly about getting bad teachers out of the classroom. He supported some form of pay for performance. He wanted more charter schools. And he was loudly booed at an NEA conference for laying out his ideas. But he was no radical reformer. His agenda was essentially one of innovation at the margins rather than thoroughgoing transformation. Needless to say, he left unions and collective bargaining entirely alone and tried not to take sides in battles between reformers and unions. Like all Democrats running for president in years past, he portrayed himself more generally as a good union man—it would be political suicide to do anything else.[17]

Obama managed to eke out the Democratic nomination and then win the presidency, in campaigns that were mainly about the economy, the Iraq war, and health care. Not education. So in no way did he take office with a mandate to reform the public schools, and in no way was his victory a triumph for education reformers over the traditionalists within the Democratic Party. Once the primaries were over, the traditionalists and the unions—which had previously supported Hillary Clinton—swung behind Obama to help him defeat John McCain during the general election campaign, and they were all now on the Obama team. They were core power holders in the Democratic coalition, and he was to be "their" Democratic president.

Obama's first order of business as president was to respond aggressively to the economic meltdown. His main legislative thrust was the "stimulus bill," the American Recovery and Reinvestment Act, which passed Congress in February

2009, less than a month after he took office. It authorized $789 billion in new spending to prop up the economy and included some $100 billion (depending on how you count) for public education and colleges, $45 billion of which went to local school districts to prevent the layoffs of teachers.[18] The educational emphasis was clearly on saving jobs, and the teachers unions could only be thrilled.

Tucked inside the bill, however, was a relatively tiny fund of $5 billion, set aside for the discretionary use of Obama's secretary of education, Arne Duncan, in carrying out a new program he labeled Race to the Top. The idea was that Duncan would use this money as an incentive to encourage innovative reforms in the states. How the program would work was left to Duncan to decide. Never had any secretary of education had this much money to spend at his own discretion. The question was, what would he do with it?[19]

That spring, the reformist signals coming out of the new administration were hardly uniform. In February and March, Senator Dick Durbin (D-Ill.) and Representative David Obey (D-Wis.) led a successful move by congressional Democrats to kill the Washington, D.C., voucher program for disadvantaged children, and Obama and Arne Duncan did nothing to stop it. Nor did they say anything in its defense. The teachers unions had wanted to kill this program for years; and now that the Democrats were in power, they got their wish. Many reformers were dismayed, including many liberals. Here is what the *Washington Post* had to say in an editorial as the legislation advanced:[20]

> Congressional Democrats should spare us their phony concern about the children participating in the District's school voucher program. If they cared for the future of these students, they wouldn't be so quick as to try to kill the program that affords low-income, minority children a chance at a better education . . . The debate unfolding on Capitol Hill isn't about facts. It's about politics and the stranglehold the teachers unions have on the Democratic Party.

So far, this was hardly the dawning of a new era. Yet Obama was clearly more willing to challenge the unions than most of his fellow Democrats were. In a high-profile speech on education, delivered that same month to the Hispanic Chamber of Commerce, he reinforced his commitment to the basic reformist ideas he had embraced during the campaign. And he was blunt about it, saying, among other things, "States and school districts [need to take] steps to move bad teachers out of the classroom . . . If a teacher is given a chance or two chances or three chances but still does not improve, there's no excuse for that person to continue teaching. I reject a system that rewards failure and protects a person from its consequences."[21] Strong stuff for a Democrat.

This speech laid the groundwork for Obama's education agenda. As meat was put on its bones in the weeks ahead, emphasis was placed on high academic standards that would be uniform across the states; sophisticated new data systems that would promote accountability by, among other things, allowing student test scores to be used in evaluating teacher performance; new compensation systems that would tie teacher pay to measures of student learning; serious efforts, via detailed evaluations and streamlined procedures, to get bad teachers out of the classroom; new laws to encourage the proliferation of charter schools—by, most obviously, lifting existing state caps on their numbers; and major interventions to turn around low-performing schools, including reconstitution (a new principal and staff) and conversion to charters.

These objectives found their first tangible expression in Arne Duncan's Race to the Top, which became the administration's prime vehicle for reform. The idea of Race to the Top took shape as a genuine competition: only the most innovative states, by these specific criteria, would get grants. To be considered favorably, moreover, states needed to go beyond simply proposing new approaches. Once they had the money, after all, there was no guarantee that they would actually do what they proposed to do. The states, Duncan said, needed to show actual policy innovations that met the Race to the Top criteria. What this meant, of course, was that they could boost their own chances by enacting new reform laws prior to the application deadlines. A clever prod to immediate action.[22]

But Duncan also added a stipulation whose cleverness—or motivation, anyway—is very much in doubt. This was that states would win extra points by getting union "buy-in" for their proposals. The rationale he gave was much the same: he wanted evidence that innovative ideas would actually be put into practice—and because union opposition made that much more difficult, it was best to have them on board from the beginning. The innovations most likely to work would be the ones with union support.

Critics soon jumped all over the union buy-in provision, for good reason. It clearly put the unions—again—in the position of being able to block genuine innovation. But Duncan stood firm, and in the first round of the competition drove his position home by giving awards to two states—Delaware and Tennessee—that, although certainly near the forefront of innovation, were *not* the most innovative. That distinction went to Florida and Louisiana, particularly Florida, which has been the hands-down leader in education reform for more than a decade now: in accountability, in school choice, in virtual schooling. But Florida only had 8 percent buy-in from its unions, and Louisiana had very low levels as well (for obvious reasons), while in Delaware and Tennessee all the stakeholders had joined hands and sung "Kumbaya": union buy-in was universal in Delaware and 93 percent in Tennessee.[23] This was what Duncan seemed to be focusing on. "The biggest distinguishing thing for me," he said, "is that the two state winners were touching 100 percent of their students."[24] The lesson to all the other states: if you want the money, get union buy-in.[25]

Criteria aside, the big question from the outset of Race to the Top was whether the money would be enough to attract serious state interest. Although the size of Duncan's discretionary pot (now a modified $4.35 billion) was huge beyond precedent, the amount going to any given state was destined to be fairly small. California, for example, stood to pick up $700 million with a winning application, but this would be less than 2 percent of its annual education budget, which was in the range of $50 billion.[26] Worse, the grant would be a one-shot deal. Would the states really be motivated by such small potatoes? The answer, in most cases, was a resounding yes. The economy had melted down, and state governments were melting down too, faced with enormous deficits and massive layoffs. Even if Race to the Top could offer just a 2 percent boost, *the states wanted the money.*

So the race was on. And the media loves a race. The media spotlight was intense in virtually every state, as "thousands of local news stories across the country speculated about how particular states were faring, some of them breathlessly referring to the 'March Madness'."[27] And government leaders now had even stronger reason to win: everyone was watching. The pressure was on for them to make their state a winner. The teachers unions were feeling the pressure too. Yes, they were possibly in a position to veto state innovations. But by following their usual blocking strategy, they risked a public relations debacle in which—with everyone watching—they would be loudly *blamed* for torpedoing their states' chances of winning money that was desperately needed in a time of unprecedented scarcity. Their usual Democratic allies, moreover, were no longer so reliable, because they didn't want to get blamed either—and they wanted the money.

From the unions' standpoint, this was a very bad situation. But it was bad in degree, not in kind. For in most respects, it was just a more extreme version of situations they had been facing for some two decades in dealing with accountability and charter schools. Both reforms were popular, and the unions did not want to get blamed for defeating them. So what was their standard, time-tested way of dealing with such sticky situations?

Step one: as a matter of public relations, they would openly declare their "support" for the general concepts. Step two: they would use their power in the legislative process to weaken and undermine the actual reform proposals. Sometimes this would mean going all-out to defeat them ("supporting" the concept, while objecting to key provisions). Sometimes, when the votes were harder to come by, it would mean embracing compromises that watered down what the reforms were trying to accomplish ("supporting," for example, accountability programs with no consequences for poor performance or charter programs with tight ceilings on the number of schools allowed). Step three: if any reform legislation did pass, they would continue the fight—in the courts, in the implementation process, in collective bargaining—to weaken the programs further.

This last step is crucial. The unions are in it for the long haul, and for them the struggle never ends. Any compromises they make in the legislative process can often be reversed or neutered somewhere down the line.

So Race to the Top did put the teachers unions in a tough spot. But they also knew how to deal with these situations, and they would continue to do what they had always done—protect their interests, resist total reform—in whatever ways were good strategic fits to the new context. Arne Duncan's buy-in stipulation, moreover, had handed them a trump card. They could use it to try to keep state leaders from adopting overly bold reforms. They could also use it, if they chose, to "support" weaker, compromise reforms that they did *not* actually support at all—allowing them to escape blame, to burnish their reformist credentials, and then to use other venues at other times to keep the reforms weak, contained, and as nonthreatening as possible.

Consider the case of Tennessee, where the unions were presumed to be on board and the state was rewarded for it. Here is a contemporaneous account from *Education Week* on why the unions did what they did:[28]

> Political realities influenced the Tennessee union's participation, said Earl Witman, the past president of the Tennessee Education Association. "We saw the legislative call sheets, and this became a runaway train," he said about a state law passed to position the state to compete in the Race to the Top program. Rather than oppose the legislation, the union worked to reduce the percentage of a teacher's evaluation based on test-score growth and to add provisions to the state code allowing teachers to "grieve," or formally protest, procedural aspects of their evaluations, Mr. Witman said.

Not coincidentally, while Tennessee was also touted for linking pay to performance, the actual legislative translation made such an alternative pay system optional for school districts and required the agreement of local unions.[29] The long and the short of it is that the union knew it was going to be unable to stop this reform train in its tracks; rather than simply go down in ignominious defeat, it chose to get involved and to use its collaborative influence to water down the legislation, add new formal appeal rights for teachers, and make the details contingent on union approval down the road. It did not do this because it supports the reform. This was a *strategy* to minimize the damage, get credit for buying in, and win money for the state.

Buy-in is an odd term. The fact is, when the unions buy in to a reform proposal, it does not mean that they support it. It does not mean that they are really committed to do anything. There is no enforcement mechanism, no sanction for noncompliance. They are just signing on to the proposal for purposes of the application process—and they are entirely free, later on, to resist the reform's implementation, to try to weaken or change its provisions, or even to have it overturned. Union leaders may choose not to buy into some reforms; they might not want to go on record as supporting certain specifics, for example, or they might fear a reaction among their members. Different unions may play the buy-in card rather differently, as a matter of strategy. But if they choose to buy in, it certainly does not mean they can be counted upon later to actually support the faithful, effective implementation of the reform. Their interests are what they are, and they can be expected to pursue them.[30]

So why did Arne Duncan emphasize union buy-in? It may, of course, have been a nakedly political move intended to mollify a powerful Democratic constituency, pure and simple. But there may have been more to Duncan's thinking than that. As I discussed in chapter 8, many Democrats are heavily influenced by the ideas of "reform unionism," and they believe that, with enlightenment and sufficient pressure, the unions can be brought around to do the right thing by children and to support reforms that would make the schools more effective. Whatever the underlying motivation, Duncan has consistently made collaboration with the unions one of his political themes. As he said in a 2009 speech to the NEA, "The president and I have both repeatedly said that we are not going to impose reform but rather work with teachers, principals, and unions to find what works."[31]

As I write, Race to the Top has recently come to an end with the much-awaited announcement of the second-round winners. Ten states joined Tennessee and Delaware in the winner's circle: the District of Columbia, Florida, Georgia, Hawaii, Massachusetts, Maryland, North Carolina, New York, Ohio, and Rhode Island. Policymakers and educators in the winning states were, of course, joyous, proud, and eager to get their money. Arne Duncan, standing at the finish line, waxed eloquent about how deserving the winners were, saying, "The creativity and innovation in each of these winning applications is breathtaking."[32]

But many experts didn't see it that way. The final decisions struck them as a mixed bag and as a stunningly inappropriate and disappointing end to Race to the Top. The District of Columbia and Florida were obviously good choices. But some states with tepid, unimpressive reform agendas—Hawaii, Maryland, Ohio—were being singled out as path-breakers. And two states that truly *were* path-breakers—Colorado and Louisiana—didn't make the list at all.[33]

What happened? Politics could have had something to do with it. Both Maryland and Ohio, for example, had Democratic governors facing close electoral contests in November, and the Race to the Top wins in September were surely pluses for them. There is some evidence, moreover, based on a quantitative study of first-round scoring, that the official reviewers of state applications—outside experts selected by Duncan's team at the Department of Education—were indeed sensitive to political considerations (a close senatorial race, a close gubernatorial race) in arriving at their scores.[34]

Yet any such notions have to be regarded as tentative at this point. It may turn out, when all the facts are in, that politics didn't influence the scoring at all. Whatever the case, two things seem clear. One is that, in picking the winners, Duncan simply went along with his reviewers, who were not necessarily outside-the-box thinkers themselves or even sympathetic to real innovation, and whose differing inclinations and abilities (with different reviewers scoring different states) doubtless worked in favor of some states and against others. When their scores gave results that sometimes flew in the face of reason, he did not use his own discretion—his leadership—to ensure that merit won out. He played it safe by making the decisions automatic. The second is that the union buy-in provision was taken very seriously in the reviewers' scoring. As a result, states like Colorado and Louisiana were heavily penalized precisely because their reforms were so big that the unions fought them tooth and nail and refused to buy in. Meantime, states like Ohio and Hawaii, which were hardly pushing the envelope, got union buy-in—and extra points—for not doing much.[35]

If Race to the Top was supposed to reward and recognize innovation, which of course it was, then this was not the most effective way to do it. The Fordham Foundation's Michael Petrilli, an incisive observer of American education, succinctly expressed what many others were thinking as the content and meaning of the grand finale began to sink in:[36]

> This is a disastrous outcome for the administration . . . At the end of the day, Secretary Duncan could have funded Louisiana and Colorado regardless of their scores. He might even have nixed Maryland, which nobody in their right mind regards as an incubator of serious education reform. Yes, he would have taken much heat . . . for mucking around with reviewer recommendations. But it would have been worth it, just to demonstrate that Race to the Top's—and Duncan's—focus on results and reform was for real. Instead . . . he and his team chose the path of least resistance.

In some respects, then, Race to the Top fell short. That is unfortunate. Yet the picking of the winners is not really the proper endpoint on which an overall assessment should be based. What we really want to know is how all the reform proposals and reform bills that Race to the Top unleashed—many of them in states that didn't win—will pan out in the trenches of American education, and what the consequences will prove to be for schools and kids. There is no way to determine these things in the short term. It will take several years, at least, for the evidence to become clear.

That said, and disappointments notwithstanding, Race to the Top has been genuinely historic: a unique national experience that succeeded in setting off the biggest explosion of reformist activity since the years immediately following *A Nation at Risk* a quarter century ago. Most of this activity has *not* been break-the-mold reform. But some of it has, and in general there has been much more reform—and much more public attention to the need for it—than the nation has experienced in a very long time. That is a huge accomplishment.

Four states did not participate in Race to the Top at all, and nine dropped out after the first round—some because they felt they had no chance (and no stomach for the reforms needed to compete) and some (Minnesota, Indiana, Oregon, West Virginia) because union opposition made progress impossible. But most states did take steps, or at least proposed to take steps, compatible with the Obama reform agenda. The level of union buy-in was uncommonly high overall, with 62 percent of local unions signing on.[37]

The administration was quite successful in using Race to the Top to energize the movement toward national curriculum standards—which, if finally agreed to by all the states, would replace the wide-ranging diversity of separate state standards with a common set of standards that would bring greater coherence and uniformity to the system as a whole and promote accountability. The Common Core State Standards Initiative—a project undertaken (with federal encouragement) by the National Governors Association and the Council of Chief State School Officers—yielded its first set of common standards in 2010 on math and English (with more subjects to follow). Race to the Top gave the states extra points for agreeing to adopt the common standards, and the great majority of them did. By the time the final winners were picked, thirty-six states plus the District of Columbia had signed up, and the foundation had been laid for a comprehensive set of national standards. This was a major achievement for Duncan. I should add that, while some of the states were not happy about this—because they lost a measure of local control and in some cases (California and Massachusetts, for example) because the existing state standards were more rigorous than the national standards—there was little of the usual political conflict that surrounded the other types of reforms. The reason? National standards do nothing to threaten the teachers unions or their members, so they have no incentive to stand in the way.[38]

Charter schools, of course, are another matter. Although Duncan surely wanted to encourage more charter schools, the states had little to offer on that score because the unions *did* stand in the way. Of the ten states lacking a charter law going into Race to the Top, *not one* enacted new legislation to authorize charters.[39] Of the states that already had charter laws, several passed laws raising their caps on the number of schools allowed—but the changes were pitiful. Tennessee, supposedly at the cutting edge of innovation, raised its cap on charters from a mere fifty to a still-mere ninety statewide, and even added restrictions on where they could be located. New York raised its cap from 200 to 460, which, in a populous state with roughly 4,500 public schools, is really nothing of consequence and a simple continuation of the long-standing effort of New York unions to keep choice alternatives to a minimum. That same legislation, more-over, explicitly prohibited for-profit companies from operating charters, which added a new restriction on the dynamism of the state's charter sector. Iowa lifted its cap on charters entirely, but independent organizations are not even allowed to operate charters—only districts can do that—so Iowa doesn't actually have a true charter system at all.[40]

Duncan had also made it clear that states needed to get serious about devel-oping sophisticated data systems and, to be a winner, needed to eliminate any legal firewalls that prevented student test score data from being used in teacher evaluations. In California, Wisconsin, Nevada, and Maine, the firewalls did come down. This was an impressive achievement, entirely due to Race to the Top, and absolutely necessary if state data systems are to be put to effective use. But the removal of firewalls merely makes the data *available* should the districts decide to *use* student test scores in evaluating their teachers or creating pay-for-performance systems. In none of these states did the new firewall-removal laws require these things. The new laws left them as matters to be dealt with in collec-tive bargaining, which simply ensured that, except in rare cases (think Michelle Rhee, Washington, D.C.) and absent further legislation, test scores would *not* be put to serious, systematic use in those states.[41]

Even so, if Race to the Top gave a big boost to any single line of reform, it was in the realm of teacher evaluation—setting off a flurry of action in which, at least rhetorically and on paper, numerous states embraced the new-age concept that teachers actually need to be seriously evaluated in terms of their effectiveness in the classroom and that student test scores need to be part of the evaluation. Nine states passed new laws linking teacher evaluation to student test scores. Others stated their intentions to do so in their proposals. Often, the teachers unions had signed on to the Race to the Top applications.

In a few states—Colorado, Louisiana, Florida—the reform legislation on teacher evaluation was especially bold; in Colorado and Florida, it included pro-visions that dramatically altered teacher tenure and made it much easier to dis-miss mediocre teachers. In all three of these most-innovative states, however, the reforms were *opposed* by the state teachers unions.[42] Florida's reform bill was ulti-mately vetoed by Governor Charlie Crist, who was looking to run as an Inde-pendent in the upcoming race for U.S. Senate and was under heavy pressure from the Florida Education Association. Crist's veto left the state's Race to the Top application in the lurch, but it also won him the union's endorsement in the Senate election.[43]

In most states that somehow moved to connect teacher evaluations to student achievement, the exact nature of the connection—and thus of the reform—remains unclear. The main reason is that many of the key details—what role test scores will truly play, what other factors will be taken into account, whether significant numbers of teachers will actually be rated as ineffective, whether incompetent teachers will be dismissed as a result of these ratings—have yet to be decided or acted upon. The typical reform plan, whether specified in law or in a proposal, calls for various kinds of consultation with stakeholder groups— notably the unions—and often leaves critical details to collective bargaining.[44]

The winning plan from Tennessee, for instance, sets up a fifteen-member Teacher Evaluation Advisory Committee (with heavy teacher representation) to make the key decisions later on. The winning plan from Delaware says that the state's secretary of education will fill in the details "after consulting with stake-holders, including the teachers union."[45] As *Education Week* observes of that state, "One of the biggest tasks will be defining exactly what student achieve-ment measures will be used in evaluating teachers. How well students perform on state exams will be one piece . . . but how much of a teacher's annual evalu-ation will be based on those test scores and other indicators of student perfor-mance must be hammered out between state officials and the statewide teachers union."[46] No one really knows what the details in these and other states' reforms will turn out to be.

Even in Colorado, where reformers had their greatest success, the details are left to a fifteen-member council. As the *Denver Post* puts it, "By March 1 [of 2011], the council must define what makes an effective teacher and principal, develop a high-quality statewide evaluation system for both teachers and princi-pals, and create performance standards for each category of licensed educator— among a host of other duties."[47] After that, their decisions must be approved by the state board of education before they can go into effect. The Colorado Education Association, which opposed this reform bill "every step of the way," will of course be well represented in these forums. So will Democrats, and most Democrats voted against it.[48] So any notion that this reform is a done deal is highly premature. The unions still have ample opportunity to shape the details of this law and to weaken its potential.

And, then, consider New York, where AFT leaders created a stir by agree-ing to a new system of teacher evaluation based in part on student test scores. It seems clear that this was their only attractive strategy. Race to the Top and the frenzy surrounding it had boxed them in: all eyes were on them to see if New York would be denied federal money because of the union's intransigence. Moreover, with Obama so fully on board, the issue of (somehow) linking teacher evaluation to student achievement had largely become a matter of common agreement among liberal opinion leaders, including the *New York Times*.[49] No more allies. Better to make a virtue out of necessity, make the compromise, and call yourself a reformer.

The new agreement, which quickly became law, is a significant step forward for New York, but not as significant as it appears. Only 20 percent of a teacher's evaluation is definitely based on student test scores (when such tests are available for any given subject, and they often aren't). Another 20 percent is based on local measures of student growth, but what these measures *are* is to be determined via negotiations with the teachers unions in local collective bargaining, and the measures need *not* take the form of test scores. The remaining 60 percent of the evaluation is to be determined through local collective bargaining and may be based on such things as observations and peer review. So the role of test scores could well be quite small. Moreover, the legislation does *not* require that these evaluations be used as a basis for teacher compensation. They are required to be taken into account in tenure and other employment decisions, but exactly *how* they are taken into account must—again—be determined through collective bargaining. And while two successive "ineffective" ratings can be grounds for dismissal, how teachers will get such ratings—and how many who deserve to get them will actually get them—remains totally unclear. Plus the law baldly states that there must be "very significant evidence of incompetence" for dismissal to be legally justified. The UFT's own explanation to its members says, "Does the new agreement make it easier for schools to fire teachers deemed ineffective? Absolutely not. The new agreement safeguards the due process rights of our members."[50] These are ominous words, backed by an army of union lawyers. Given the UFT's militant protection of teacher jobs in the past and the fact that the percentage of New York City teachers dismissed for incompetence has long been near zero (despite Bloomberg's and Klein's best efforts), it is hard to believe that this new evaluation system—heavily shaped by the state union and its locals—will suddenly make it possible to get bad teachers out of the classroom.

These cases help to illustrate how intricately the unions are woven into the fabric of the reform process and how many future opportunities they will have—as the details are ultimately filled in—to weaken the actual content and consequences of reform. The unions' strategy is to make the reform process as collaborative and as dependent on collective bargaining as possible. Which is just another variation on the politics of blocking.

Yet another example of the same thing has to do with the way the unions actually signed on to their states' reform proposals. During the first round of applications, the unions in many states—not knowing how the department might react—gave their buy-in (which state officials desperately wanted) without actually signing the department's official memoranda of understanding (MOU); instead, they signed modified ones, hidden away in appendixes. The modified MOUs made their buy-in to certain aspects of the proposals—new teacher evaluation systems, for example—conditional on collective bargaining and thus on each local union's approval. For obvious reasons, the proposals themselves didn't make this conditionality explicit.[51]

The Department of Education was not fooled (or happy), so this strategy gave way the second time around. But as the next-round applications were submitted, a newspaper exposé revealed that, in Florida, some of the largest districts had again entered into side agreements—which were not made public and were not part of the state's application at all—that made their formal buy-ins conditional. "Several of the side agreements clarify that, if unions object, districts will not impose changes to things like teacher pay and evaluations. Others suggest any such changes will end when the grant money runs out—which would appear to counter the Obama administration's goal of using Race to the Top to sow long-term reform."[52] The same incentives are present in other states, needless to say, so many similar agreements may well have been made elsewhere, although we may never know for sure.

This sort of thing is hardly surprising, as it fits hand-in-glove with every other aspect of Race to the Top and how the states have responded. The fact is, Race to the Top was an effort by Obama and Duncan to get the states to do things they wouldn't otherwise do, using money as the inducement. The underlying problem is that, because of the political fundamentals in the states, there are good reasons why state leaders didn't embrace the Obama education agenda on their own. *They didn't want to.* If they did, they would have done it earlier, prior to Race to the Top. The money inducement changed the equation a bit, especially during a time of budgetary crisis, because it gave the states a reason to try to please Obama and Duncan—and get the money. But the goal was to get the money, not to reform the schools. And because that was so—and because, for that matter, Duncan and Obama are themselves Democrats and sensitive to keeping the teachers unions at the table—Race to the Top was inherently limited in what it could hope to accomplish.

Since 2009, when Race to the Top began, the states have engaged in an enormous amount of reformist activity. But there is a big difference between the activity of reform and the substance of reform—which has been far less impressive than all the hoopla would suggest, and contingent on future collaborative processes that give the unions myriad opportunities to shape the details and keep the reforms contained. The American education system is almost surely better off, and the cause of education reform has been advanced, because Obama and Duncan have done this. But the progress it will spur over the next several years is likely to prove modest by comparison to what is needed to bring about effective organization.

The limited progress is in part because the content of the reforms themselves, as collaboratively developed, is likely to be modest. But it is also because, once the money is doled out, the states' incentives will change and so will the politics of reform. The losers can simply drop their reform plans and go back to business as usual. The winners, money in hand, can "pursue" their reforms in ways that accommodate the powerful. And the unions and their allies can marshal their forces to keep the reforms weak and limited and, if possible, to roll them back and reverse them. Andy Smarick, a close observer of Race to the Top and American education more generally, offers some wise words:[53]

> This may be a short romance. We should not be surprised to see many of the officials who warmly embraced reform because of tough budgets and fed largesse turn cold when political conditions return to normal. Charter caps could resurface, data firewalls could be rebuilt, performance pay plans could be defunded, and meek interventions for failing schools could return . . . Reformers might well expect a vigorous counteroffensive when Race to the Top funds expire; at that point, unions and other reform opponents may find themselves rejuvenated, mobilized, and positioned on more favorable terrain.

Looking Ahead: Reform and Its Politics

What lies ahead for American education? To understand that, we need to avoid a fixation on Race to the Top. It was an unusually influential event—on the order, I'd say, of *A Nation at Risk*. But what did *A Nation at Risk* lead to? Decades of disappointment. We are well advised to remember that.

Race to the Top was genuinely important for a few reasons. One, it moved the ball downfield. Several years from now, the schools may be on the forty yard line instead of the thirty yard line. That's hardly great success, for the goal line is still far away. But it is progress. Two, it set in motion certain institutional changes—in data collection, in teacher evaluation, in charters—that may well develop roots and provide a basis for additional progress. And three, it helped to legitimize key reform concepts—for example, that teachers need to be evaluated with attention to how much their students learn and that bad teachers need to be removed from the classroom—and these ideas may ultimately become an accepted part of American culture and expectations.

Obama and Duncan deserve credit for all this. And they continue to press ahead. At this writing, they have requested additional money to extend Race to the Top into next year. And in their plans for reauthorizing No Child Left Behind, they have asked that considerable funding to school districts be made on a competitive basis, rather than (as it has always been) by formula. Many members of Congress will no doubt object, as they have political incentives to favor formulas; they want their share of the money, and they want it guaranteed. The unions will surely play on that. So Obama and Duncan will have their hands full, and they may not get their way. But they are trying to move the ball downfield.[54]

The prospects, at best, are for incremental gains. But reformers should consider themselves lucky. Just consider this sobering question: *What if Hillary Clinton had been elected president?* She missed the Democratic nomination by a hair; and had she gotten it, she almost surely would have won the presidency. How would education reform have fared—genuine reform intended to transform the system—under President Clinton? Would anything like Race to the Top have occurred? The obvious answer is no. Not even remotely. Hillary Clinton was the unions' candidate right down the line, and the presidential thrust behind American education reform would have come to a quick and unceremonious end. Indeed, the presidency would have become a source of *opposition* to education reform. And history would have played out very differently.

This counterfactual is worth dwelling on, because it could easily have happened. History is not linear. It is readily shaped and redirected by accidental confluences of events. Obama won the election. And he won at a time of great economic hardship, when the federal government was able to dole out stimulus money in unprecedented amounts and when states were so desperate for it that something like Race to the Top could get them to dance on their hind legs. So education reformers were able to make a modicum of progress. But if the times had been better, there would have been no stimulus money and no Race to the Top. And we could easily have been governed by Clinton instead of Obama and gotten no reform at all or even a period of serious backsliding. Today, reformers could be licking their wounds instead of cheering about their gains.

To keep our perspective, we need to separate ourselves from the confusing blur of reformist activities and get back to basics. Since their organizational success in the 1960s and 1970s, the teachers unions have been the single most powerful force in American education, and the Democrats have been their strong political allies. This is *still* true today, and it is not going to change anytime soon: for the unions are firmly entrenched at the local level, where collective bargaining gives them a guaranteed hold on members and money—and power. This power allows them to shape the organization of America's schools from the bottom up, through intricately detailed labor contracts. And it allows them to shape the schools from the top down, through the political process—where they block, weaken, and eviscerate reform. They do all these things with the active support of Democrats, who are there to cast the official votes and make the official decisions. As politicians, they willingly play these supporting roles because they benefit from what the unions can provide them. The unions *are* extraordinarily powerful. That is the simple reality.

Over the last decade or so, however, the political tide has begun to move against them. This is the big educational story of our time. The unions have been blocking reform and undermining the organization of the nation's schools for well over a quarter century now, but they will be less able to do that in the future. Not *un*able, *less* able. I've already discussed the reason for it: although reformers have had little success since *A Nation at Risk,* their two major movements for change—the movement for accountability, the movement for choice—are beginning to take a toll on the teachers unions. They are doing it not by directly transforming the education system (at which they have largely failed), but rather by transforming the politics of education—driving minorities, the disadvantaged, and many influential liberals to distance themselves from the teachers unions and to join the ranks of reformers. This shift in alliances is largely taking place inside the Democratic Party, creating an internal ferment that is loosening the unions' iron grip and allowing more Democrats to vote against them.

For the teachers unions, then, the political fundamentals are changing in a bad way, and their power is slowly being eroded. Race to the Top was a reflection of that. The teachers unions were not powerful enough to stop it from happening, because the reformers had the upper hand in the Obama administration—even though it is filled with Democrats. And as the Race to the Top played out, many states adopted reforms that the unions opposed, even though the amounts of money dangled in front of the states were rather small and even though there were usually enough Democratic votes to block reform. In many cases, too many Democrats bailed. The unions couldn't hold them.

But Race to the Top was an extreme situation. And even then, the reforms it generated were not very bold or impressive and left us on the forty yard line. Why didn't the reformers go farther? The answer is that, even in the hostile environment they had been forced to navigate over the last three decades, the unions were still powerful enough to defend their turf. Their power had slipped, and so in a relative sense they were hurting. But in an *absolute* sense, they remained the 800-pound gorillas of the education reform process, and everyone recognized it. Indeed, Race to the Top put the spotlight on union power more than any other educational event in American history. It was no accident that union buy-in was the center of attention.

Obama and Duncan are the heroes of this saga for being Democrats who didn't toe the union line. But there is another side to their story. They are not revolutionaries, and the aim of their leadership strategy is not to do whatever is necessary to bring effective organization to the public schools. Why? Because as Democrats, even though they are not playing by the Democratic rulebook, they are politically entangled with the teachers unions, concerned about antagonizing them, and willing to make trade-offs that leave the unions with a powerful, self-interested say in how America's schools are organized. Obama and Duncan genuinely want to make progress. But they intend to do it within an education system filled with powerful unions that must somehow be accommodated. Given that constraint—which, for Democrats, is very real—they can only go so far. Obama and Duncan, moreover, are the reformers' Democratic dream team. Most other Democratic officials are far less enthusiastic about reform and don't even like being at the forty yard line.

This is why the political dynamic we are now witnessing in American education—an "endogenous" development that has emerged within the system itself—is not equipped to do the job. It is exciting. It is unprecedented. It is a very positive force that propels the education system in the right direction. But it is inherently limited, because it does very little to *reduce the power* of the teachers unions—and they will continue to use their power to prevent the schools from being effectively organized.

Something more is needed. Something that *does* reduce union power and that reduces it significantly, so that real reform can flow through and the goal line can ultimately be reached.

Exogenous Change and the Decimation of Established Power

To get a sense of what that something might be and how it might work, let's take a step back and consider two instructive examples.

The first is New Orleans, whose remarkable story we've already discussed (chapter 7). Recall that the school district in that city was for many years among the worst in the nation, and showed no signs of being able to reform its way out. But then, in 2005, a cataclysm occurred: the entire education system and its protective power structure—including its powerful local union—were literally destroyed by an immense force from the outside. The origin and timing of this force had *nothing to do* with education. It just happened.

Hurricane Katrina was an *exogenous* development. It was an extremely costly one in terms of life and property, and a horrific turn of events. But it also had a good side. Precisely because it was *beyond anyone's control,* it overwhelmed the educational status quo and the powers that protected it, and thereby accomplished what nothing *within* the education system had ever been able to accomplish before. In doing that, it freed the forces of innovation and change that had long been completely stifled, and it allowed dedicated reformers—people like state schools superintendent Paul Pastorek, local superintendent Paul Vallas, and Senator Mary Landrieu—to open the gates and transform New Orleans into a hotbed of reform.[55]

In *The Rise and Decline of Nations,* one of the great books of modern political economy, Mancur Olson argues (and marshals evidence to show) that political systems frequently become ossified over time by entrenched interest groups—and that wars and other disasters, by destroying these established power structures, can be *liberating* and can lead to the creation of dramatically new and improved institutions. The salient examples are Germany and Japan. Both were destroyed by World War II; and as they were destroyed, so were their old author-itarian institutions and established groups. Institution builders were then much freer to depart from the institutional past, and both countries rose from the ashes to become democratic nations and market-based economies.[56]

Katrina was an exogenous development of the same type that ravaged Ger-many and Japan. It was like a war. It physically devastated New Orleans, its school system, and its local teachers union—and that physical devastation led to liberation and to new institutions. Important though the story is, however, in showing the burst of reform that can happen when the educational power struc-ture is destroyed, New Orleans is clearly not an example that other American school districts can somehow follow. Katrina was a random, highly unusual act of nature. Nothing comparable is likely to happen to other districts. Nor would anyone want it to.

So consider, then, a second example of how an exogenous development can bring about fundamental change to an established system. This example, although it comes from the private sector and is not about public schools, is in fact much more indicative of what lies ahead for American education and the power of its unions. It is the story of one of the great unions in modern Ameri-can history, the United Auto Workers (UAW).

During the middle decades of the 1900s, life was good for the UAW. It was a true powerhouse in American politics, a major force in the Democratic Party, and so successful in collective bargaining that it was able to make autoworkers the elite of the working class, with sky-high wages and platinum benefit pack-ages. Led for most of that time by Walter Reuther—then one of the best-known figures in American society and literally a household name—the UAW had more than a million members in the aftermath of World War II. Its membership grew to 1.5 million in 1979, and the union seemed a permanent fixture in the Ameri-can power structure.[57]

But in the 1980s, the UAW's organizational base began to crumble in a slow, steady decline that has continued to the present day. The proximate cause: com-petition from Toyota, Honda, and other carmakers, exacerbated by the inability of company management to respond with vision and effective strategy, and by the UAW's refusal to yield on wages, benefits, and work rules, which put the companies at a severe cost disadvantage.[58]

There was also, however, a larger force at work. The world economy was becoming globalized and thus more highly integrated and interconnected. The competition being thrust on the auto industry was but one aspect of a world-changing development, affecting virtually all aspects of the economy, over which the unions and the auto companies had no control. Nor could they pressure the government for protective tariffs to keep out foreign cars, because globalization brought with it international trade agreements that largely prevented such responses.[59]

More generally, then, the UAW's environment had radically changed and was much more hostile to the industry's traditional mode of organization. And to the UAW's power. Car sales fell. Employment fell. And the results have been devastating. General Motors and Chrysler have gone bankrupt (and reemerged in leaner form), and the UAW has seen its membership fall to roughly 355,000 in 2009, a drop of about 75 percent from its 1979 zenith.[60] The union is no longer a major power in American politics and no longer a major force in the Democratic Party. It is a pale reflection of its former self.

Unlike Katrina, then, globalization is a development that has occurred slowly over a long period of time; and although it surely has its downsides, it brings tremendous benefits as well. In most respects, it is not like a war. It is an incrementally emerging *shift in the environment,* one so dramatic and profound that it affects and often threatens the power and survival prospects of major institutional actors. In the context of American education, *this* is the kind of exogenous development that—when coupled with the endogenous political ferment in favor of reform—is destined to produce a drastic reduction in the power of the NEA and the AFT.

I don't mean to push the analogy too far. The NEA and the AFT are not the UAW, the public school system is not the auto industry (and won't go bankrupt), and globalization is not the issue here. But both stories, in the end, are about seemingly invincible organizations going into decline, and about the exogenous shifts in the environment that make it happen. For the UAW the exogenous shift has already largely occurred, and the consequences for its organization have been shattering. For the NEA and the AFT, the shift is only just beginning—and the education watchers who live in its midst, and who focus on the here and now of America's schools, have barely recognized its transformative potential. There is a revolution in the making. But it is slow and silent and almost no one sees it for what it is.

What education watchers see and recognize, for the most part, are the recent—and genuinely exciting—developments within the Democratic Party and American politics more generally: the early stirrings of a revolutionary dynamic propelled by the two great reform movements of our era, the movements for accountability and choice. Important though they are, these political developments are not sufficient to bring about a revolution. But they are about to be turbocharged by a social force from the outside so massively powerful and irrepressible that it will eventually overwhelm the teachers unions and make real reform possible. The UAW was brought down by one such social force—the globalization of the international economy—that it couldn't control and couldn't adapt to. Something similar is about to happen to the teachers unions. But for them, the agent of doom is not globalization. It is the worldwide revolution in information technology.

Technology and Transformation

Accountability and choice are education reforms. As such, from the time they made their first halting gains, they have been stifled by the political process and had much of their revolutionary potential wrung out of them. They are threatening to the unions, and the threat is growing. But they can't resolve the Catch-22 of union power on their own.

Help, however, is on the way. Or rather, it is already here and is all around us. I'm speaking of the worldwide revolution in information technology, which is one of the most profoundly influential forces ever to sweep the planet and is fast transforming the fundamentals of human society. Computers and their progeny have made communication and social networking—among anyone, anywhere—virtually instantaneous and costless, put vast storehouses of information and research within reach of everyone, dramatically boosted the prospects of cooperation and collective action, internationalized the cultures of insulated nations, and in countless other ways transformed how human beings interact with one another and gain information.[61]

There can be little doubt that technology has the capacity to revolutionize the way students learn. It could hardly be otherwise. Information and knowledge are fundamental to what education is all about—to what it means, in fact, for people to become educated—and it would be impossible for the information revolution to unfold and *not* have profound implications for how children can be educated and how schools and teachers can more productively do their jobs.

In a recent book, *Liberating Learning: Technology, Politics, and the Future of American Education,* John Chubb and I argue in some detail that the revolution in information technology is destined to transform the nation's schools in the coming decades and that, as an integral part of this transformation, it is also destined to undermine the power of the teachers unions and open up the political process to innovation and change. Rather than recount the details of that analysis here, I briefly summarize some of its central points and themes.[62]

At the level of students and schools, what technology has to offer is astounding. Even today, with education technology in its early stages, curricula can be customized to the learning styles and life situations of individual students, giving them instant feedback on how well they are doing, providing them with remedial work when they need it, allowing them to move at their own pace (and thus move ahead quickly if they are able), and giving them access—whether they live in Appalachia or downtown Detroit or anywhere—to a vast range of courses their own schools don't offer, and ultimately to the best the world can provide. Education can be freed from geography and from social class: wherever students are and whoever they are, they can have access to these riches. And they can do it through programs that—whether all-virtual or (as will surely be the norm) hybrids of traditional schooling and online learning—allow for intensive interaction with teachers and other students, allow parents to be much more fully involved and informed, generate reams of data on how students are actually doing, and are much more cost-effective and far less labor-intensive than the way education is traditionally organized.[63]

Precisely because technology has the capacity to transform the core components of schooling, it is disruptive to the jobs, routines, and resources that define the status quo. When children take some or all of their courses online, for example, their teachers and schools can (in principle) be anywhere—outside the district, outside the state, even outside the country. The clear prospect is that, if more and more kids are allowed to do this, jobs and money will flow out of the regular public schools. Moreover, computer-based learning requires many fewer teachers per student, because technology can be substituted for labor in the learning process, and this too translates into a reduction in jobs and money for the regular public schools and the people who work in them.

When technology is fully harnessed to do what it can do, then, it is deeply threatening to the teachers unions as well as to most school districts. They are fine with computer labs in the regular public schools. They are fine with kids doing research on the Internet. They are even fine with online coursework—if they control and staff it. But the full advantages of technology can barely be tapped within these institutional constraints. And as innovators push out the boundaries of what is possible, offering students and families a dazzling array of exciting new options in the cybersphere, the unions' tolerance of the information age evaporates. They are not fine with these things. They want to stop them—and keep the genie in the bottle.

Which brings us back, once again, to the politics of blocking. In basic respects, the political story is the same-old-same-old. Technology is but the latest threat to union interests and the traditional system, the latest source of reform whose fires they seek to put out. As such, it faces the same political obstacles that education reforms of all types have been up against, and largely defeated by, for decades. The obvious expectation—other things being equal—is that technology, like choice and accountability before it, should have the wind taken out of its sails in the political process. Why should technology be any different?

But that is the remarkable thing. Technology *is* different. Unlike accountability or choice, it is much more than an education reform. It is a social force more profound and pervasive in its worldwide influence than almost any other in human history. Its origins are entirely *outside* the education system, it is transforming virtually every aspect of social life in the United States and around the world, and it is basically *beyond anyone's control*. What it brings is a true social revolution: one that is already happening, but will continue to generate wave upon wave of change over the coming decades in all facets of human behavior, interaction, and knowledge.

The American school system is unavoidably caught up in all this. Whether the unions like it or not, the education system lives in this larger social environment, depends on it for survival, and cannot avoid being affected. Through the usual political protections, erected via the politics of blocking, the unions can partially insulate the public schools from the social changes going on around them—but only partially. Because this social revolution is too big. And it is everywhere.

How, then, will technology bring change to the public schools, and to the unions themselves? Part of the answer is that, with the traditional system so powerfully defended, change will happen gradually over time, much of it coming a decade or two (or three) from now. For many years in the early going, technology will be seeping in around the edges and slowly injecting the ingredients for the transformation to come.

How Technology Seeps In

The seepage will take various forms, but it is useful to think of them in terms of supply and demand. The demand for technology-based education can only grow. As parents and other citizens become aware of these boundless new opportunities, especially as some schools start adopting them, many will want them for themselves. They will want their own schools to be up to date. They will want their own kids to have the best. Students, for their part, are already technology natives, frustrated with traditional schooling and eager for online alternatives. Ten or twenty years from now, these students will themselves be parents and voters—and a massive constituency. This evolution of social opinion and educational demand is in its early stages. But the long-term trend is inexorable, and the unions cannot stop it from happening.[64]

The supply side, meantime, is dynamic and largely out of control. Even within government itself, where the pressure to preserve the existing system is obviously strong, many public officials have incentives to "go virtual"—at least at the margins. These officials, unlike union leaders, are broadly responsible for providing quality education and for meeting the needs of all the various constituencies of students. When kids in rural or inner city areas need advanced placement courses (some 40 percent of America's high schools don't even offer them) or instruction in foreign languages, or when dropouts need additional credits to graduate, or when gifted students need to move ahead more quickly—situations that only begin to describe the underserved population of students in this nation and the huge demand for more customized offerings—the regular public schools often don't have the money or staff to accommodate them. By outsourcing to online providers, which are numerous and even now can readily meet these kids' needs at a reasonable cost, legislators and superintendents can move beyond the constraints of anemic budgets and curricula to see that underserved kids get the courses they need and that constituents are happy. By "going virtual" for courses the public schools are *not* actually providing and thus by simply supplementing their core activities, they can serve constituents in ways that aren't immediately competitive or threatening. These are strong inducements to embrace at least some of what technology can do. And to allow it to seep into the system.[65]

Districts all across the country are beginning to contract with online providers to meet these curricular needs of the underserved, usually by allowing students to take one or more courses (but rarely a whole curriculum) online while staying formally enrolled in their local schools. The International Association for K–12 Online Learning estimated in 2010 that 1.5 million students in the United States are taking one or more courses online.[66] In Michigan and Alabama, all high school students are required to take at least one online course in order to graduate. In Florida—the nation's technology trailblazer—all school districts are required to make online classes available to their students, who have been given the legal right to pursue online options. More states and districts will follow. We can only expect that today's numbers will increase exponentially in the years ahead, as "parts" of more and more students are allowed to go virtual.[67]

The most easily observed response of governments to the new online technologies, however, is that some thirty-nine states (as of 2009–10) have set up state-level virtual schools or online learning initiatives that enroll students statewide. As products of the political process, these state-level virtual programs have been designed to supplement the school districts—not to threaten them—by providing courses they don't offer and getting funds from lump-sum appropriations that don't reduce their budgets. The national model is the Florida Virtual School, which currently has more than 220,000 course enrollments a year and is widely recognized for the quality of its offerings and organization. Other states are clearly paying attention, consulting with Florida and learning from its example. As the states move more aggressively in this direction—bolstered politically by the new support clienteles that are automatically created and strengthened along the way—these virtual schools will capture an increasing share of the student population (if only by enrolling "parts" of individual students). As they do, their budgets will ultimately be integrated into the overall education budget—as has already happened in Florida—and their success will mean less money and fewer jobs for the districts. But this is long term. For now, they are relatively nonthreatening and a great tool for public officials, which allows them to get established and grow.[68]

Important as these outsourcing incentives are within government, the incentives for innovation are far greater outside of government, where tech entrepreneurs are swarming all over the education sector. Some of these are for-profit companies—K12, Connections Academy, Insight Schools (owned by Apollo, which also owns and operates the University of Phoenix), Advanced Academics (owned by the major education firm DeVry), and EdisonLearning, among others—that are eager to make money through outsourcing arrangements with districts. But most of these same firms, and lots of other organizations as well, are also interested in going much further by creating new virtual schools that compete directly with the districts for students and thus for funding and jobs. These entrepreneurs, by taking advantage of state charter laws and school choice laws—and often acting hand in hand with the more entrepreneurial district authorizers (a small percentage of all districts)—are the driving force behind the modern movement for virtual charters, which are today the most powerful vehicle by far for bringing technological innovation and profound institutional disruption into the public education system.[69]

Virtual charter schools are now operating in twenty-seven states and the District of Columbia, enrolling some 200,000 students nationwide, and their numbers are growing rapidly. Some of the first-movers are now well established and providing graphic evidence of what is possible. Pennsylvania Cyber Charter School, which got under way in 2000, now enrolls more than 9,000 students throughout the state of Pennsylvania. The Electronic Classroom of Tomorrow, started in 2000, enrolls more than 8,000 kids throughout Ohio. Both have plenty of competition from virtual schools in their own states; as of 2009–10, there were eleven virtual charters operating statewide in Pennsylvania and seven operating statewide in Ohio (and many more operating more locally). There is extensive virtual charter activity in many other states as well. In the years ahead, virtual charter schools are destined to increase at a rapid rate. With fifty states, fifty different systems of laws (forty of which include charter laws), and differing party balances in state governments, not to mention all the diversity inherent in more than 14,000 school districts, tech entrepreneurs have plenty of legal and political variation to exploit in planting their innovative seeds. And that is what they are doing.[70]

At present, almost all virtual charters enroll students who take a full virtual curriculum and do their studying at home. But this is just the opening burst of growth that targets unmet needs at the margins of the public system: homeschoolers, kids in rural areas, dropouts, and so on. Most American parents want their kids to "go to school"—that is, to a physical place—and the modal virtual schools of the future will almost surely be hybrids of traditional and online learning: schools in which kids are surrounded by other students and teachers, receive the usual socialization, take art and music and physical education, but also take a good portion (I would guess 80 percent) of all their academic coursework online. Hybrids offer the best of both worlds, with technology strategically substituted for labor where it is most productive and strikes the kind of balance that most parents and kids are likely to want.[71]

Hybrids are just beginning to get established in public education as a self-conscious model of schooling, but a good place to look for early examples is in San Jose—where the Rocketship charter schools, under the pioneering leadership of John Danner and Preston Smith, are smoking the competition and (in serving a heavily disadvantaged student body) closing the achievement gap. By having students take a portion of their academics online, Rocketship schools have redesigned the role of teachers, saved money (some $500,000 per year, which is then used to pay Rocketship teachers higher salaries and to pay for one-on-one tutoring), and boosted student achievement to extraordinary levels. In 2009, the first Rocketship school (its other two schools are brand new) was ranked number three in the entire state among low-income schools.[72]

The teachers unions are not cheering. Throughout the nation, they are trying to block the advance of virtual schooling at every turn—trying to get the courts to declare virtual charters illegal, trying to get legislatures to disallow them or slash their funding or eviscerate them through disabling restrictions on how they can operate. Not surprisingly, they have had their successes. In Wisconsin, they got the legislature to put a temporary cap on statewide virtual enrollments at roughly 5,000 students, an artificial ceiling well below demand. In Oregon, they won a law requiring all virtual charters to enroll at least half their students from their authorizing districts, which puts severe limits on their ability to enroll students statewide. In California, virtual charters can only enroll students from counties that are contiguous to their home county, and they are required to have the same teacher-student ratios as the largest district in their county. And these are just a few examples.[73]

Yet there is simply too much action in too many places for the unions to snuff it all out. Cyber charters are growing at an astronomical rate, and they are clearly responding to a demand that is very real and spiraling upward; for many student needs are not being met by the core activities of the regular schools, technology offers access to a wide range of high-quality programs that are literally customized to each student's needs—and students and parents now see, as technology advances and real schools emerge to provide new educational options, what is possible for them in the information age.

The unions can slow the process down. But they can't stop it. Technology is seeping into the system already, even as the unions are at the height of their power. And it will continue to seep in, at increasing rates, as time goes by. The genie is out of the bottle and can't be put back in.

Seepage, Politics, and Union Power

And because it can't, the unions are in trouble. As technology seeps into the system, there will be consequences of great importance for schools and children. But this seepage will also unleash a whole range of associated forces that, without anyone's plan or intention, are destined to eat away relentlessly at the power of the unions, weaken their ability to block, and transform the *politics* of education well beyond the positive "endogenous" developments we are currently witnessing.

How can this be? What is the connection between technology and politics? In fact, the seepage of technology is destined to incrementally generate several important drivers of change over the years—each of them different from the others, but all of them pushing in the same direction to upend the traditional politics of blocking. I want to talk about four of these that are particularly consequential.

THE SUBSTITUTION OF TECHNOLOGY FOR LABOR. Public education has long been afflicted with "Baumol's disease," a syndrome first identified by economist William Baumol in the 1960s. The source of the problem is that, because certain industries—the service sector, the arts, the helping professions, and virtually all of government, including public education—are inherently labor intensive, they can't take advantage of the technological innovations that drive progress in the rest of the economy. As a result, they get more costly and less productive over time.[74] While this characterization of the public schools was probably quite valid for the entirety of the last century, it is no longer true. With the revolution in information technology, *technology can be substituted for labor:* with computers and software doing much (not all) of what teachers have traditionally done in the classroom. The new computer-based approaches to learning simply require *far fewer teachers per student*—perhaps half as many and possibly fewer than that. Schools can be made more productive, and—with technology growing cheaper and more sophisticated over time, and labor getting more and more expensive—the relentless increase in educational costs can be brought under control.[75]

These prospects augur well for education and learning, but they also have hugely important consequences for politics. For with the spread of technology—and with the obvious incentives that policymakers will have for reducing costs by putting technology to use—the demand for teachers will be smaller than it would otherwise have been, as will the numbers of teachers participating in the education system. While we cannot know the actual numbers, the deflation of demand spells serious trouble for the unions, because it points to future limits on the pool of potential union members. In the past, as the teacher-student ratio has soared from decade to decade, the unions have been in the catbird seat, easily expanding their memberships as the pool of teachers has grown seemingly without bound. But no more. They are moving into a period of hard times, with the demand for labor dropping and fewer teachers to grow their ranks.

The sheer size of the teachers unions is a crucial determinant of their political power. The more members they have, the more money they can wield for campaign contributions, lobbying, and advertising, the more activists they can unleash to influence election outcomes, and the more votes they can influence.

The advance of technology, by bringing about new combinations of inputs that are less labor-intensive, directly undermines their membership base and, as a result, tends to weaken virtually every one of the weapons that have traditionally been responsible for their power.[76]

THE TRANSCENDENCE OF GEOGRAPHY. Geographic concentration is one of the keys to union success in public education. When teachers work together in the same location and share the same local employer, union organizers have ready access to them, and they can generate a sense of solidarity and obligation based on personal connections and common occupational interests—all of which makes recruiting members (and their dues money) much easier. Geographic concentration also facilitates the coordinated actions—the willingness to strike, engage in work slowdowns, ring door bells, hand out campaign literature, and the like—that unions rely upon for success in collective bargaining and politics.

As virtual schools gain in prominence, and as more and more students take some (or all) of their academic coursework online, their teachers can increasingly be *anywhere*—in another county, in another state, or in India for that matter—and need not be employed by the local school district. When teachers are more dispersed and lack a common employer, the unions' job is far more difficult. We can already see as much by looking at how the unions have fared historically with private schools and (nonvirtual) charter schools. When these are the intended "bargaining units," teachers are fragmented into thousands of such units, each a small employer that must be organized separately, and unions have found the task exceedingly difficult. Their track record is not good. Only about 12 percent of charter schools are unionized, and the figure for private schools is just 4–5 percent.[77] In important respects, technology makes the union's situation even more difficult, for the teachers in private and (nonvirtual) charter schools are at least geographically concentrated at the school site. Not so for virtual schools and online learning programs, whose teachers can be totally dispersed.

The upshot is that, as virtual schooling expands over time, the geographic basis for union organization will break down. Teachers will be less and less concentrated in school districts, and their dispersion will make it increasingly difficult for the unions to attract and retain members, to amass dues money, to unleash armies of political activists, or to engage in coordinated job actions—all of which have been fundamental to their organizational success and political power. For decades, geographic concentration has been the unions' unheralded ally. But technology is going to create a new, more fragmented professional world that is far less friendly to what the unions have traditionally been able to do.

It is worth adding that the geography-shattering effects of technology are not just a problem for the teachers unions. They are a problem for unions generally (although the severity, of course, depends on the nature of the work involved). As one scholar of American labor relations puts it,[78]

[Traditionally, unionization in the United States] explicitly assumes that employees anticipate a continuing relationship with their employers and that union representation occurs at the workplace. The Internet defies these assumptions by creating a corps of workers with lowered physical and psychological attachments to their place of employment . . . Admittedly, any appraisal of the future impact of information technology must be speculative. But there is already enough evidence based on the present technology to see the contours of the threat to unions. Workers whose jobs have been reshaped by the Internet (e.g., sales representatives, professionals working on a contractual basis, home workers) are not approaching unions in large numbers and unions are not successfully recruiting them . . . All signs point to serious, perhaps unsolvable, problems for unions.

TRANSPARENCY AND RAMPED-UP ACCOUNTABILITY. As discussed earlier, the accountability movement has created real problems for the teachers unions. The key reason is simply, but profoundly, that it generates information on student achievement that provides a concrete basis for evaluating the performance of the public schools. By putting the spotlight on those that are chronic low performers—many of which are in high-minority urban areas—this information has mobilized traditionally Democratic groups, constituencies, and policymakers to demand fundamental change. And it has prompted them to take an increasingly jaundiced and intolerant view of the teachers unions, whose special interest proclivities are now widely regarded as a drag on school effectiveness.

This is ground we have already covered, but here is the point of revisiting it: accountability is itself rooted in technology and is destined to get a gigantic boost as technology becomes more sophisticated and widely employed. Even though accountability is already creating problems for the unions, the advance of technology is going to supercharge those problems and make the unions' lives much more difficult. As student testing gains in rigor and sensitivity (largely because of what computers and their interactive capabilities make possible), as measures of teacher performance are perfected (complete with more comprehensive methods for factoring out the effects of student background and other nonteacher influences), as states and districts construct sophisticated data warehouses for the effective management of schools and teachers, and, not least, as finely grained performance data on schools (and inevitably, teachers) become more readily available to parents, interest groups, policymakers, and the public at-large, inadequate performance will increasingly become common knowledge and won't be tolerated. Far more than now, the unions will find themselves faced with heated opposition. And with less power to stand in the way of change.

VIRTUAL SCHOOLING AND RAMPED-UP CHOICE. Choice, like accountability, is already making life difficult for the unions, as I've discussed. But just as technology is destined to supercharge school accountability, along with its effects on the unions, so it is also destined to supercharge school choice and its effects. Indeed, technology is going to generate the greatest expansion of school choice that this country's education system has ever seen and, with it, the greatest expansion of competition.

The fundamentals are already in place. The burst of new technology is generating powerful innovations for teaching and learning; countless entrepreneurs are eager to take advantage of them; there is a big demand for what they are offering; and despite the predictable union opposition, many new cyber schools and online options are being created that reflect the new technology and respond to the demand. Their numbers will grow explosively with time, and the result will be a dazzling array of new choices that offer students opportunities they do not now have, supplied by a variety of organizations outside the regular public schools (even, in many cases, when the latter are making online options available to their own students). And with choice comes competition. The consequences for politics are profound. As cyber schools and online options proliferate, they will attract students and money away from the regular public schools, the number of teaching jobs in those schools will decline, and so will membership in the teachers unions, the resources they control, and the political power they wield. The teachers unions have always seen school choice as public enemy number one, and they have vigorously resisted it. Now the threat is at their door, delivered by a force beyond their control.

Competition also has the effect of boosting the political power of the pro-choice side. With the revolution in technology, choice will create many new constituencies, as students in rural and inner city areas, advanced placement students, home schooling students, students needing credits to graduate, students needing flexibility in scheduling, and more stand to gain from the new opportunities that cyber schools have to offer. This will serve to broaden the political base of the choice movement, enhance its power, and allow it to press ahead against a weakened union opponent.

The Dynamics of Change

These changes are just beginning to take off, and reformers are just beginning to realize what technology can do for students, for schools, and for the larger cause of transforming the system. But as technology gets traction, it will prove to be power-packed, because *the changes it unleashes are mutually reinforcing*. Any one change, in and of itself, may not deflate the union base very much, but they all work together, in the same direction and at the same time. The rise of cyber schools and online options leads not only to the geographic dispersion of teachers, but also to the substitution of technology for labor and enhanced choice and competition—and all of them, in their own ways, weaken the fundamentals of union power. Similarly, the technological supercharging of accountability puts the spotlight on poor performance, mobilizes groups and policymakers to take action, and creates a hostile political environment for the unions when they try to block change and protect unproductive behavior. It is the combination of these changes, rather than any one of them alone, that is so consequential for union power over the long haul.

As these changes gain traction over the years, moreover, they will benefit from a positive feedback effect that makes additional change—and political gains by reformers—*easier* to achieve as time goes on. This may seem like wishful thinking, but it is inherent in the logic of the situation. For with the rise of technology over the next five or ten years, the unions' power can be expected to decline somewhat—and as it does, their ability to block reform in the political process will also decline. That being so, the political gates will open a little wider, allowing reformers to win a greater proliferation of technologically driven sources of change—and this in turn will corrode union power still further, reduce their blocking power still further, and open the gates still wider for even more change. Reform will thus become easier and easier over time, because technology and its by-products will increasingly eat away at the politics of blocking and free up the policy process to move in directions the unions have long been rejecting.

It is important to recognize that, with the politics of blocking substantially weakened, the door will be open to a *broad range* of reforms—not just those that involve cyber schooling or are somehow high tech. Without union obstruction, for instance, the way will be paved for the design of more effective accountability systems that actually attach serious consequences to poor performance and are purposely built to hold schools and teachers accountable for student learning. The way will also be paved for more expansive charter systems, backed by rules and financial arrangements designed to encourage (rather than undermine) their success. For additional voucher and tax credit programs that give new options and desperately needed financial assistance to disadvantaged kids. For sensible new pay systems that reward productive teachers and abandon the archaic single salary schedule. For new laws and personnel rules that make it easier to get mediocre teachers out of the classroom. And on and on.

So technology is much more than a source of promising innovations for kids and schools. In the grander scheme of things, technology's real importance is that it is literally a force of liberation. As its innovations seep into the education system, they are going to unhinge the politics of education. And it is this *political* impact that is destined to be truly transformative: undermining union power, eroding the barriers that have long protected the system from change, and allowing all manner of productive reforms to pass through the political gates, whether high tech or not.

The timing of all this is hard to predict. The transformation could play out rather quickly—within fifteen years, say. Or it could take several decades, and thus prove agonizingly slow for the millions of children and families who are desperately in need of better schools. It will be propelled by the incentives of districts and constituents to take advantage of its innovations and by the incentives of various suppliers, both private and public, to meet the demand with attractive and increasingly sophisticated offerings. But there will also be powerful resistance. And although the uncontrollable seepage of technology will inexorably weaken that resistance and allow it to be overcome, the speed with which that can happen will depend in large measure on how the reform movement responds to the challenge.

There is much for reformers to do. They have important roles to play, of course, in pushing technology-based education reforms through the political process, and thus in marshaling their power to meet and overcome the resistance. But along the way, they need to ensure that the fundamentals of the new system are put in place through appropriate governmental action: new forms of cyber education need to be authorized and encouraged, traditional rules—for funding, certification, accountability, teacher training—need to be overhauled and rewritten to accommodate these new forms, and new policies need to be adopted that take advantage of what technology and its emerging markets can contribute to student learning.

If the reform movement elevates technology to high priority and moves aggressively to put the right policies and legal frameworks in place, the transformation can come about rather quickly. If the reform movement is less effective— or just slow to realize that it has a tiger by the tail—then the transformation may take much longer. But whatever the timing, it *is* coming. The revolution in information technology is bigger than all of us. It is transforming the entire world. And it *will* transform America's public schools.

After a quarter century of disappointment, then, there is good reason to think the American education system can look forward to a much brighter future. It may take many years for the transformation to take hold, and real improvement may lie far in the future indeed. But powerful forces are even now beginning to loosen the unions' iron grip. And as these liberating effects are played out over time, policymakers should be much freer to put children first and to insist on a school system that is truly organized to provide them with the best education possible.

Back to the Present

I didn't write this book to offer a solution to the problem of union power. I wrote it to describe and document the problem—and to try to understand it. As it happens, there is solution, at least over the long haul. But it is only a solution because of an accident of history. The accident is that we live in a very special time: we are caught up in a historic revolution in information technology. This is a monster development, entirely beyond the realm of normal reform activity, that is being thrust upon the education system from the outside.

I think it is quite likely that, were it not for this bombshell from without, there would be no solution. As I've observed several times before, power is its own protection. Under normal conditions, the Catch-22 of union power would guarantee the stability of today's system, along with the stability of union power itself, well into the distant future. Reformist efforts to address the problem through new legislation would tend to fall short, because the unions would typically be able to block. The wistful hopes of reform unionism would fail too, because the unions are simply not going to set aside their fundamental interests and do what's best for kids and schools. And a pragmatic reliance on compromise, collaboration, and cooperation—while a reasonable path to incremental progress—is inherently quite limited and will never allow the nation to get where it needs to go.

If there is a nascent solution in the works, technology aside, it might possibly emerge from the accumulated effects of accountability and choice, Race to the Top, and the shifting political tides that have given reformers considerably more support and clout in the policy process. These are exciting developments, and they may well grow in strength and intensity. But they still leave the teachers unions with enormous power and, without a big boost from technology, are likely to prove insufficient over time to take education reform anywhere near the goal line. Small victories for sanity are beneficial and much-needed. But they are still small, and we shouldn't pretend otherwise.

In any event, the future is difficult to know with certainty. And in the long run, as Lord Keynes so famously put it, we are all dead. The fact is, we live in the present, and it is our current situation that we most need to understand. That is what I've tried to do in this book.

In the present, many children are sitting in classrooms and learning nothing. Or at least not nearly enough. These kids have only one opportunity to get a good education, and a good education is essential if they are to have productive careers, build promising futures, and contribute to the economic and social well being of the nation as a whole. As the minutes tick by and the years drag on, they are being denied the educations they so desperately need and have a right to. Lives are being ruined. Generations are being lost. In a globalized world of competition, high technology, and demanding work requirements—for independence, autonomy, creativity—kids without good educations are increasingly left behind. And their nations are left behind too. This was precisely the concern that motivated *A Nation at Risk* in 1983. The very same worry is at least as pressing today, despite decades of effort to do something about it.

Why are America's schools falling so short of the mark and failing so many of our kids? Why are they organized in perverse ways that are so clearly unsuited to effective education? Why have they proven so resistant to change and so difficult to improve? These are the kinds of questions, along with many others, that naturally arise when we try to comprehend the reality in which we live.

If one central thesis arises from this book, it is that the answers to these questions have a lot to do with the teachers unions. It is a fact that they are incredibly powerful, far more so than any other groups with a stake in public education. And it is abundantly clear that the job interests that drive their behavior, and are woven into the fabric of their organization and leadership, prompt them to *use* their power in ways that often come into conflict with what is best for kids and schools.

In collective bargaining, they impose bizarre forms of organization on the public schools that no one in their right mind would favor if they were simply concerned with what works best for children. The schools are organized mainly to benefit the adults who work there. In the political process, the unions block or weaken reforms they find threatening, however helpful those reforms might be for schools and kids. This is obviously true for major and eminently sensible reforms, such as accountability and choice, which, if seriously pursued, would bring fundamental change to the system. But it is also true for extremely simple, easy-to-accomplish reforms, such as getting bad teachers out of the classroom.

Think about this last point for a moment. Why is it, after decades and decades, that the nation has done almost nothing to get bad teachers out of the classroom? What possible excuse could there be for inaction on something so incredibly basic and obvious? There isn't any excuse. There is only a reason: the teachers unions are extraordinarily powerful, and they are in the business of protecting the jobs of their members. That kids lose out when bad teachers remain in the classroom is just collateral damage, a cost of doing business.

Children should always come first. But in America's system of public education, governed as it is by power and special interests, they simply do not. And in the near term, they will not. As things now stand, we have an education system that is not organized to be effective for children, can't be productively reformed in their best interests, and is powerfully protected to ensure that the interests of adults prevail. This is our reality. And in the realm of public education, it is the great dilemma of our time. Technology is likely to resolve this dilemma, many years down the road. But that is little comfort to the children of today—who deserve much more than they are getting, but don't have enough power to do anything about it.

Appendix A: Union Membership and State Labor Laws

A s I said earlier, we are fortunate to have two data sets to work with in exploring the impacts of state bargaining laws on union membership. One is based on aggregate, state-level data. The other is based on individual-level data, which are from a national survey of more than 3,000 teachers (discussed in chapter 3).

Let's begin with the aggregate, state-level data (whose membership percentages are set out in table 2-2) and ask, why does the level of union membership among teachers vary as it does from state to state? Table A-1 sets out the results of a simple regression analysis that explores, via several different models, the impacts of various factors we have reason to believe are relevant

Model 1 shows what happens when union membership is explained solely by reference to collective bargaining laws and the presence of agency fees. (Separate controls are included for Maine, New Hampshire, New Mexico, and Vermont because their legal status only recently changed, and their membership levels have not had much chance to adjust to what is "normal" for their groups.) The estimation shows that these legal variables alone explain 78 percent of the variance in union membership across states. It also indicates that membership is primarily affected not by collective bargaining laws themselves, but by the presence of agency fee provisions.

Specifically, in states that have collective bargaining laws *and* agency fee provisions, union membership is about 48 percent higher than in states that do not permit collective bargaining (which is the statistical baseline here). In states that *do* have a collective bargaining law but do *not* allow agency fees, in contrast, union membership is just 21 percent higher than in the baseline states—which is comparable to the impact, at 17 percent, associated with states that do not

Table A-1. *Union Membership, State-Level Analysis*[a]

Variables	Model 1	Model 2	Model 3	Model 4
Collective bargaining (CB) law, agency fees	47.65*** (4.14)			36.35*** (5.84)
CB law, no agency fees	20.82*** (4.56)			18.28*** (4.77)
No CB law, CB permitted	17.22*** (4.76)			14.69*** (5.01)
Maine	−16.65* (9.67)	0.74 (18.93)	12.25 (14.69)	−1.28 (10.81)
New Hampshire	−14.65 (9.67)	−14.24 (18.02)	4.02 (14.24)	−5.75 (10.41)
New Mexico	−54.65*** (9.67)	−25.87 (16.57)	−18.22 (12.80)	−40.78*** (10.22)
Vermont	−11.65 (9.67)	−5.78 (20.24)	16.48 (16.07)	5.36 (11.76)
Kerry vote		0.62** (0.28)	0.11 (0.23)	− 0.14 (0.19)
Log population, 2004		−2.02 (2.90)	−2.64 (2.23)	0.08 (1.75)
Log HH income, 2004		61.68*** (21.34)	34.16* (17.15)	13.19 (13.95)
Mfg, % of GSP, 2004		0.52 (0.52)	0.39 (0.40)	0.27 (0.29)
% Urban, 2000		0.08 (0.31)	0.22 (0.24)	0.19 (0.18)
Pvt., % unionized, 2004			3.11*** (0.57)	1.28** (0.51)
Constant	48.00*** (3.57)	−606.45*** (218.37)	−315.73* (175.97)	−107.98 (146.10)
N	51	51	51	51
Adjusted R^2	0.78	0.39	0.64	0.81

Source: State-level population, household income, Kerry vote, gross state product from manufacturing, and urbanization data are from the U.S. Census Bureau, *Statistical Abstract of the United States* (Washington: Census Bureau, 2007), available at www.census.gov/compendia/statab/2007. Data on private sector union membership are from www.unionstats.com.

a. Dependent variable is union membership of teachers in each state and the District of Columbia from 2004 to 2008, as presented in table 2-2. Data are from the National Center for Education Statistics, Schools and Staffing Survey. Regressions are carried out in Stata. Tests for collective bargaining and agency fees are one-tailed, as a one-sided hypothesis is being tested in each case. All other tests are two-tailed. Standard errors are in parentheses.

***$p < 0.01$.

**$p < 0.05$.

*$p < 0.10$.

have a collective bargaining law at all (nor agency fees) and simply permit collective bargaining. Indeed, these latter two impacts are not statistically different from one another. So the key factor—according to this simple aggregate analysis—is not the labor law itself, but the allowance for agency fees.

In model 2, the legal variables are omitted, and the focus is just on the other factors discussed in the text as possible influences. They are: the state's vote for John Kerry in the 2004 presidential election (a proxy for liberal political culture), the log of the state's population, the log of the state's average household income, manufacturing as a percentage of gross state product (a proxy for industrialization), and the percentage of the state population living in urban areas. As the estimation in table A-1 shows, these factors by themselves account for 39 percent of the variance in teachers union membership across states. The variables that stand out are the Kerry vote and household income, indicating that membership tends to be higher in the liberal, wealthier states.

Model 3 introduces one more variable of relevance: the percentage of the state's private labor force belonging to unions. The variance explained now jumps to 64 percent, but the reason isn't entirely clear. Membership in private unions may be another proxy (along with the Kerry vote) for the state's political culture and thus may reflect how open or sympathetic the state's citizens are to unions generally. But it may also reflect the background of state labor laws (and agency fee provisions) for private sector unions, which are often similar to those for public sector unions. If the latter is the case, this variable's impact—in this particular equation—could actually be capturing the legal effects estimated in model 1. What happens, then, when the laws from that model are added back into the equation?

Model 4 helps to disentangle these contending influences by putting all these variables into the model at the same time. The resulting model explains 81 percent of the total variance, so both sets of variables are contributing something. Most important, the effects of the state legal environment remain strong and statistically significant even when all the other factors are controlled—and again, it is the presence of agency fees that stands out. Among the nonlegal factors, only private sector union membership makes a difference, and its impact has been reduced by more than half now that the laws have been reintroduced into the equation. Political culture, as measured by the Kerry vote, does not demonstrate any independent impact—but its influence might also be reflected, indirectly, in the strength of private sector unions.

A simple analysis of the aggregate data, then, tends to support the claim that agency fees—which, to reiterate, are authorized by state labor laws—do indeed lead to significantly higher levels of membership in the teachers unions. To get another, completely independent test of the impacts of state labor laws, let's turn now to a different source of data: the national survey of American public school teachers that is discussed in chapter 3. With this data set, it is possible to conduct the analysis at the *individual* level and to take into account not only the state-level variables already considered, but also characteristics of each teacher that may plausibly be relevant to the decision to join. Here I include each teacher's party identification, gender, ethnicity (nonwhite), age, location (urban, suburban, rural), and the size of his or her school district.

The dependent variable is a dummy equal to 1 or 0, depending upon whether the teacher is a union member or not. Normally, it is preferable to use probit or logit in this situation rather than simple regression, but to ease the presentation and interpretation of results, I stick to regression here. Had I used probit or logit, the pattern and statistical significance of results would have been exactly the same (with one exception, which I'll discuss). The findings are set out in table A-2.[1]

Consider model 1 of table A-2. Here union membership is modeled solely by reference to the individual characteristics of each teacher, with no state-level factors at all. These individual characteristics explain only 8 percent of the variance in membership—but virtually every one of these factors has a statistically significant impact in the expected direction. Republicans, for instance, are 23 percent less likely to join teachers unions than Democrats are, males are 8 percent more likely to join than women are, young people under thirty are 13 percent less likely to join than senior teachers over fifty are, and urban teachers are 10 percent more likely to join than rural teachers are.

None of this takes into account the state-level factors that have concerned us all along. Model 2 begins to do that by introducing the state political culture, state wealth, and other nonlegal aspects of state context—which collectively yield a dramatic boost in the explained variance, from 0.08 to 0.24. When the private sector union variable is added to the equation, as reported in model 3, the explained variance moves up to 0.27—with political culture, private sector unionization, and industrialization all proving statistically significant and in the expected direction.

Model 4 puts these state-level variables aside for the moment and substitutes the state legal variables. When this is done we find that these labor laws, absent all the other state-level variables, boost the explained variance from 0.08 to 0.30—an indication that it is the labor laws, not the other state-level variables, that seem to be having the greater impact. As in the earlier analysis at the aggregate level, the biggest single effect on union membership comes when states have a collective bargaining law *and* legal provisions for agency fees. When agency fees are absent, and states differ simply in how their laws treat collective bargaining, these legal differences do make a difference—but the difference they make pales in comparison to the impact of agency fees.

Table A-2. *Union Membership, Individual-Level Analysis*[a]

Variables	Model 1	Model 2	Model 3	Model 4	Model 5	Model 6 (collective bargaining districts)
Party, Repub	–0.23***	–0.17***	–0.16***	–0.15***	–0.15***	–0.12***
	(0.04)	(0.03)	(0.03)	(0.03)	(0.03)	(0.03)
Party, Indep	–0.09***	–0.09***	–0.09***	–0.07***	–0.08***	–0.06***
	(0.03)	(0.02)	(0.02)	(0.02)	(0.02)	(0.02)
Male	0.08***	0.07***	0.05**	0.05***	0.05***	0.04*
	(0.02)	(0.02)	(0.02)	(0.02)	(0.02)	(0.02)
Nonwhite	–0.04	–0.00	0.02	0.02	0.03	0.04
	(0.06)	(0.04)	(0.04)	(0.04)	(0.04)	(0.03)
Age, under 30	–0.13***	–0.12***	–0.11***	–0.11***	–0.12***	–0.09**
	(0.03)	(0.03)	(0.03)	(0.03)	(0.03)	(0.04)
Age, 30–39	–0.11***	–0.09***	–0.08***	–0.07***	–0.07***	–0.07***
	(0.02)	(0.02)	(0.02)	(0.02)	(0.02)	(0.02)
Age, 40–49	–0.07***	–0.05**	–0.05**	–0.03*	–0.03*	–0.01
	(0.02)	(0.02)	(0.02)	(0.02)	(0.02)	(0.02)
Inner city	0.15***	0.02	–0.01	0.01	–0.01	–0.02
	(0.05)	(0.04)	(0.04)	(0.04)	(0.04)	(0.05)
Urban	0.10**	0.01	–0.01	–0.01	–0.02	–0.02
	(0.04)	(0.04)	(0.04)	(0.03)	(0.04)	(0.04)
Suburban	0.07**	–0.01	–0.01	–0.01	–0.01	–0.01
	(0.03)	(0.02)	(0.02)	(0.02)	(0.02)	(0.03)
Log district size	–0.01	0.00	0.01	0.01	0.01*	0.00
	(0.01)	(0.01)	(0.01)	(0.01)	(0.01)	(0.01)
Kerry vote		0.02***	0.01*		0.00	–0.00
		(0.01)	(0.00)		(0.00)	(0.00)
Log population, 2004		–0.06	–0.06		–0.03	–0.02
		(0.05)	(0.04)		(0.03)	(0.02)
Log HH income, 2004		0.33	0.23		0.12	–0.06
		(0.22)	(0.15)		(0.21)	(0.11)
Mfg % of GSP, 2004		0.01***	0.01***		0.01	0.00*
		(0.00)	(0.00)		(0.00)	(0.00)
% urban, 2000		0.00	0.00		–0.00	0.00
		(0.00)	(0.00)		(0.00)	(0.00)
Pvt., % unionized, 2004			0.03***		0.01	0.01***
			(0.01)		(0.01)	(0.00)
CB law, agency fees				0.52***	0.43***	0.22***
				(0.07)	(0.09)	(0.06)
CB law, no agency fees				0.26***	0.24***	0.02
				(0.08)	(0.06)	(0.05)

(continued)

Table A-2 (*continued*)

Variables	Model 1	Model 2	Model 3	Model 4	Model 5	Model 6 (collective bargaining districts)
No CB law, CB permitted				0.11* (0.09)	0.06 (0.09)	
Maine		–0.03 (0.15)	0.10 (0.11)	–0.16*** (0.02)	–0.17 (0.12)	0.04 (0.07)
New Hampshire		–0.35*** (0.10)	–0.20** (0.08)	–0.37*** (0.01)	–0.40*** (0.09)	0.27*** (0.06)
New Mexico		–0.28*** (0.10)	–0.18** (0.07)	–0.49*** (0.01)	–0.43*** (0.08)	0.38*** (0.04)
Vermont		–0.03 (0.17)	0.24* (0.14)	0.04 (0.04)	0.01 (0.14)	0.17* (0.09)
Constant	0.94*** (0.11)	–3.66 (.36)	–2.33 (.59)	0.44*** (0.11)	–0.80 (.25)	1.31 (1.15)
N teachers	3,181	3,181	3,181	3,181	3,181	2,263
N states	51	51	51	51	51	44
R^2	0.08	0.24	0.27	0.30	0.31	0.18

Source: State-level population, household income, Kerry vote, gross state product from manufacturing, and urbanization data are from the U.S. Census Bureau, *Statistical Abstract of the United States* (Washington: Census Bureau, 2007), available at www.census.gov/compendia/statab/2007. Data on private sector union membership are from www.unionstats.com.

a. Dependent variable is union membership of teachers, as measured by the individual responses to the question on union membership in the national teacher survey described in chapter 3. Regressions are carried out in Stata using robust standard errors with clustering on the state. Tests for collective bargaining and agency fees are one-tailed, as a one-sided hypothesis is being tested in each case. All other tests are two-tailed. Standard errors are in parentheses.

***$p < 0.01$.

**$p < 0.05$.

*$p < 0.10$.

Model 5 puts all the individual and state-level variables in the equation at the same time and forces them to compete for explanatory power. The individual-level variables hold up well: Republicans, women, and younger people are less inclined to join teachers unions than their counterparts are. Of the state-level variables—aside from those that represent the legal context—*not one* proves to have a significant effect on union membership. Political culture, private sector union membership, and industrialization, all of which show some promise in the earlier models, now fail to perform. When forced to compete with the legal environment, they lose their explanatory force entirely.

Again, it is the combination of collective bargaining laws and agency fees that has the greatest impact: teachers in these legal contexts are 43 percent more likely to join unions than are teachers in states where collective bargaining is prohibited. Unlike in the aggregate data analysis, though, collective bargaining laws seem to have a considerable effect here even in the absence of agency fees: teachers in states that have collective bargaining laws without agency fee provisions are 24 percent more likely to join unions than teachers in states that prohibit collective bargaining, while teachers in states that just permit collective bargaining but have no labor law are only 6 percent more likely to join (an estimate that is not statistically significant from 0).

Based on a completely separate data set, then, the statistical analysis indicates that agency fees are hugely consequential in boosting membership in the teachers unions—the same finding that follows from an analysis of the aggregated state-level data set. The main difference in findings between the two data sets is that the aggregate analysis suggests that the simple presence of collective bargaining laws, absent agency fees, has little impact on membership—whereas the individual-level analysis, in its most comprehensive (and thus the most valid) equation, suggests that this isn't so and that the impact is considerable. All else equal, we should be inclined to trust the individual-level analysis over the aggregate analysis, because the former gives us more finely grained information rooted in the characteristics of individual teachers.

If collective bargaining laws do give an appreciable boost to membership even in the absence of agency fees, why would that be? The obvious answer is that, in states with collective bargaining laws, local unions are much more likely to win collective bargaining rights in their districts; and when they do, and thus when they become the exclusive representative of all the district's teachers, more teachers may feel that they want to join (because the union is more relevant to their everyday work lives) or that they ought to join (to do their "fair share") or perhaps that they are expected to join by others. The simple *existence* of collective bargaining in a district is likely to make joining more attractive—and the laws have an impact on union membership only indirectly, by making collective bargaining more prevalent.

This is an idea we can test. If (agency fees aside) the impact of state laws on union membership is entirely due to their role in promoting local collective bargaining, then we should find *no* relationship between state laws and union membership if the existence of collective bargaining at the local level is controlled. We can do that, and still get an assessment of whether agency fees have their own separate impact, by looking just at school districts that *do* have collective bargaining. Some of these districts are in states that have collective bargaining laws, and some are in states that don't have such laws (but still permit collective bargaining). The question is, when we control for the full range of factors that might affect union membership in these "bargaining districts," are the levels of union membership higher when the state has a collective bargaining law than when it doesn't?

The findings are set out in model 6 of table A-3, which shows that, when the comprehensive model of model 5 is reestimated on just those districts that do have local-level collective bargaining, the impact of state collective bargaining laws (absent agency fees) disappears. The laws have no impact on union membership at all. Agency fees, meantime, continue to have a large impact. The evidence suggests, then, that the impact of collective bargaining laws (in the absence of agency fees)—as demonstrated in model 5 on the full sample of teachers across all states—is indeed due to their ability to promote collective bargaining. The simple existence of collective bargaining serves to stimulate higher levels of union membership. And agency fees add another, much bigger boost.

Finally, I'd like to briefly explore an issue that is too interesting to ignore and that the evidence can readily speak to. It has to do with the details of how agency fees affect the membership decision. What we know is that, in states with agency fees, teachers are much more likely to join unions. We also know that membership decisions are influenced by a teacher's partisanship, gender, and age—but it only makes sense to think that, when agency fees are involved, these factors are much less important. In Colorado, for instance, a Republican who is uncomfortable with unions can simply act on his ideology and refuse to join. But in Ohio, where agency fees are allowed, a Republican can be assessed agency fees if he refuses to join—whereas, by paying almost (or exactly) the same amount, he can join and gain entrée to a range of benefits. Partisanship should have a bigger impact on the decision to join in Colorado than it does in Ohio. Similar arguments could be made for gender and age. Agency fees, one would think, are great levelers: they give everyone much stronger incentives to join, and they reduce the impact of personal values and beliefs that, in a legally unconstrained setting, would have much freer rein.

We can test this notion by simply taking the comprehensive model 5 of table A-2 and adding interaction terms, which are designed to determine whether the impacts of partisanship, gender, and age are shifted as we would expect when agency fees prevail. I've also included an interaction for ethnicity, although the latter isn't significant in earlier models. The findings are set out in model 1 of table A-3. The pattern conforms exactly to our expectations. Republicans, for example, are 23 percent less likely than Democrats to join teachers unions when agency fees are not involved, but the gap shrinks to just 7 percent in the presence of agency fees.[2] Men are 8 percent more likely to join than women when agency fees are not involved, but the gap is 3 percent when agency fees are present. Young people are 17 percent less likely to join unions than teachers over fifty when there are no agency fees, but just 6 percent when agency fees are legal. A few of these coefficients don't quite reach statistical significance, but most do (five of the seven interaction terms)—and all of them are in the right direction. The pattern we'd expect is followed perfectly.

Table A-3. *Do Agency Fees Dilute the Effects of Personal Values and Beliefs on Union Membership?*[a]

Variables	Model 1 (regression)	Model 2 (probit)
Party, Repub	−0.23***	−0.61***
	(0.03)	(0.09)
Party, Indep	−0.12***	−0.34***
	(0.03)	(0.09)
Male	0.08**	0.22**
	(0.04)	(0.11)
Non-white	0.07	0.18
	(0.07)	(0.19)
Age, under 30	−0.17***	−0.49***
	(0.05)	(0.14)
Age, 30–39	−0.10***	−0.28***
	(0.03)	(0.09)
Age, 40–49	−0.04	−0.10
	(0.03)	(0.08)
Inner city	−0.01	−0.02
	(0.04)	(0.19)
Urban	−0.02	−0.10
	(0.03)	(0.14)
Suburban	−0.01	−0.07
	(0.02)	(0.09)
Log district size	0.01*	0.07**
	(0.01)	(0.03)
Kerry vote	0.00	0.01
	(0.00)	(0.01)
Log population, 2004	−0.03	−0.13
	(0.03)	(0.13)
Log HH income, 2004	0.11	0.22
	(0.20)	(0.81)
Mfg % of GSP, 2004	0.00	0.02
	(0.00)	(0.01)
% urban, 2000	−0.00	0.00
	(0.00)	(0.01)
Pvt., % unionized, 2004	0.01	0.04
	(0.01)	(0.03)
Maine	−0.19	−0.74*
	(0.12)	(0.42)
New Hampshire	−0.42***	−1.43***
	(0.09)	(0.38)
New Mexico	−0.43***	−1.59***
	(0.07)	(0.34)

(continued)

Table A-3 (*continued*)

Variables	Model 1 (regression)	Model 2 (probit)
Vermont	0.05	—[b]
	(0.14)	—[b]
CB law, agency fees	0.35***	1.52***
	(0.09)	(0.38)
CB law, no agency fees	0.23***	0.56***
	(0.06)	(0.19)
No CB law, CB permitted	0.06	0.02
	(0.08)	(0.26)
Agency fees*Repub	0.16***	0.11
	(0.04)	(0.20)
Agency fees*Independent	0.08**	0.01
	(0.04)	(0.21)
Agency fees*Male	–0.05	0.11
	(0.04)	(0.18)
Agency fees*Nonwhite	–0.09	–0.31
	(0.07)	(0.29)
Agency fees*Age<30	0.11**	–0.08
	(0.06)	(0.24)
Agency fees*Age 30–39	0.06*	–0.13
	(0.04)	(0.15)
Agency fees*Age 40–49	0.00	–0.26*
	(0.03)	(0.16)
Constant	–0.66	–2.29
	(2.16)	(8.44)
N teachers	3,181	3,177
N states	51	51
R^2	0.32	
Pseudo R^2		0.30

Source: State-level population, household income, Kerry vote, gross state product from manufacturing, and urbanization data are from the Census Bureau, *Statistical Abstract of the United States* (Washington: Census Bureau, 2007), available at www.census.gov/compendia/statab/2007. Data on private sector union membership are from www.unionstats.com.

a. Dependent variable is union membership of teachers, as measured by the individual responses to the question on union membership in the national teacher survey described in chapter 3. Regression and probit analyses are carried out in Stata using robust standard errors with clustering on the state. Tests for collective bargaining and agency fees are one-tailed, as a one-sided hypothesis is being tested in each case. All other tests are two-tailed. Standard errors are in parentheses.

b. Probit automatically dropped Vermont from the estimation because its four cases were perfectly predicted (all scored 0 on the dependent variable).

***$p < 0.01$.

**$p < 0.05$.

*$p < 0.10$.

This is reasonable evidence that agency fees do indeed mute the effects of personal values and beliefs that would otherwise keep some people out of unions. To my surprise, however, when I ran this same estimation using probit (and logit), which, as noted above, is more appropriate than regression for the analysis of dichotomous dependent variables (join/not join), these interaction results fell apart completely. As the findings in model 2 of table A-3 show, a probit analysis indicates that none of the interaction terms is statistically significant, and the pattern fails to show up as well. For all of the other models estimated in this appendix, probit yields results that are virtually identical to the regression results. In this one case, it doesn't.

I don't have an answer. My inclination is to think that, because there is excellent reason to expect agency fees to mute the impacts of these personal factors, the regression results are doing a good job of telling us what is actually going on—and the probit results are off track and misleading. But if so, I don't know why. The best I can say at this point is that there is *some* evidence to support the "muted effects" notion—a notion that makes good sense—and that we simply need more research to figure things out with greater confidence.

Appendix B: The Survey Sample: Comparisons to SASS

Teachers in this study were asked whether their school districts engage in collective bargaining and also whether they themselves belong to a teacher organization, defined as "a local affiliate of the National Education Association, the American Federation of Teachers, or some other similar organization that represents teachers."

Table B-1 presents a summary of teacher responses across the nation as a whole, broken down by the strength of state collective bargaining laws. These figures are very similar to those presented in chapter 2 from the Schools and Staffing Survey (SASS). There are differences—which we should expect, because both are just estimates—but the differences seem to make sense.

In the teacher survey, about 74 percent of the sampled teachers (when weighted) are unionized. This compares to a SASS figure of 79 percent. One reason for this difference may be that SASS asked teachers whether they are "a member of a teachers' union or an employee association similar to a union," without asking the name of the organization. Everyone who answered affirmatively is counted as a union member. My survey asked them to name the organization to which they belong; about 6 percent of the teachers, almost entirely in southern and border states, were members of independent teacher organizations that are not unions at all, but alternatives to unions that provide members with insurance and (usually) represent their interests in politics. I classify teachers who belong to such organizations as nonmembers.

Another difference between the two surveys is that 65 percent of the SASS teachers are categorized as being covered by collective bargaining, while in the

Table B-1. *Membership in Teachers Unions, by State Context*
Percent

Union membership	States that have collective bargaining laws and allow agency fees	States that have collective bargaining laws but prohibit agency fees	States that do not have collective bargaining laws	States that prohibit collective bargaining	Total
Collective bargaining district					
Member	92	62	35	0	63
Nonmember	8	31	17	0	11
Not a collective bargaining district					
Member	0	4	17	40	11
Nonmember	0	3	32	60	16
N	1,783	500	343	671	3,297

Source: Harris Interactive survey, commissioned and designed by Terry M. Moe and administered online between April 24 and May 20, 2003.

teacher survey it is a higher 74 percent. Here, SASS is probably the more accurate estimate on purely formal grounds, because it explicitly asks the districts about their formal arrangements for labor management relations, and they are likely to know whether they have what is formally called "collective bargaining" or not. The teacher survey relies on teachers themselves to know whether their districts have collective bargaining, and some of them may think they have it when they do not. This is especially likely if the district has a union and the union regularly "meets and confers" with district administrators on personnel and policy matters.

It must be recognized, however, that even well-informed participants may find their local labor relations difficult to describe. In some districts, for instance, meet-and-confer arrangements may in practice be much the same thing as collective bargaining. Indeed, in some states that legally prohibit collective bargaining—Arizona and Texas, for example—the larger districts often have meet-and-confer arrangements that are close substitutes, and are sometimes just ways of evading the law and responding to union pressure under another guise. Thus, what is and is not collective bargaining is fuzzy at the margins. It could be argued that SASS, rather than providing a more accurate measure of the extent of collective bargaining, is really just measuring a stricter, more formal version of it and that the additional districts coded as having collective bargaining in my own survey actually have much the same arrangements with their unions as some of the SASS districts coded (in that survey) as not having collective bargaining.[1]

The differences (and ambiguities) across surveys need to be kept in mind, of course. But when the data are broken down by groups of states, the teacher survey gives results that look exactly as we should expect given the SASS data presented in chapter 2. As table B-1 clearly shows, union membership declines with the strength of state bargaining laws. In states that have strong laws and allow agency fees for nonmembers, union membership is a nearly universal 92 percent. In states that have strong laws but prohibit agency fees, union membership falls to 66 percent. In states that have no labor law but allow collective bargaining (if the unions can get districts to agree to it), membership falls further to 52 percent. And in states that prohibit collective bargaining, union membership is just 40 percent.

As discussed in chapter 2 (and explored further in chapter 3), this pattern appears to be due not only to the laws themselves, but also to the political culture of the states in each category, for the weaker laws are found in the more conservative states. The point to be made here, however, is that the pattern emerging from the national teacher survey is the same as the pattern in the SASS data, and what we should expect.

Appendix C: Young Teachers

In comparing young teachers with their older colleagues, this appendix summarizes and briefly discusses the findings rather than presenting another round of tables and charts. Young teachers are defined as those who are under thirty-five years of age. The rest are divided into a middle group who are between thirty-five and fifty and an older group aged fifty-one and up. Of the total teacher population, the youngest teachers constitute 28 percent, the middle group 44 percent, and the oldest group 28 percent.

The evidence shows, first, that the younger teachers are in fact less inclined to join unions. But in districts with collective bargaining—the most common situation by far throughout the country—the main contrast is to the oldest cohort of teachers. In these districts, 19 percent of younger teachers don't join their unions. But 16 percent of teachers aged thirty-five to fifty also don't join. It is the oldest teachers who stand out, with just 9 percent deciding against union membership. They are the outliers. Moreover, consider the flip side: a full 86 percent of the young teachers in these districts *do* choose to join unions. They are hardly running the other way and are *not* an antiunion contingent within the profession.

In districts without collective bargaining, which are mainly in southern and border states, most teachers don't join their local unions, and this is true for teachers of all ages. In these contexts, the connection between age and membership is more linear and compelling: 70 percent of the young teachers don't join compared to 62 percent of the middle cohort and 51 percent of the oldest cohort. It is important to remember, though, that these districts are a distinct minority—and even there, young teachers do not look like a breed apart.

If young teachers are alienated from unions, it should show up in their attitudes toward voluntary membership. The evidence suggests as much, indicating that, at least when it comes to their policy attitudes, young teachers are more likely to support voluntarism than their older colleagues are. In states that allow agency fees, 31 percent of young teachers believe that, as a matter of policy, membership decisions should be entirely voluntary—compared to 22 percent of the middle cohort and 17 percent of the oldest cohort. In the (more conservative) states that don't allow agency fees, most teachers support voluntarism. But the same relationship holds: support is 85 percent among the young teachers, 74 percent among the middle group, and just 60 percent among the oldest group.[1]

Yet this (relative) embrace of voluntarism fits comfortably with their experiences as union members. When asked whether, if membership were purely voluntary, they would choose to remain members of their local, state, and national unions, young members gave the same positive responses as their older colleagues. Most important, some 94 percent of younger members said they would voluntarily remain in their local union—a resounding vote of support. They do not feel forced. They are, moreover, highly satisfied with what they are getting. Overall satisfaction with their unions is 80 percent for the young teachers, compared to 77 percent for the middle cohort and 75 percent for the oldest cohort.[2]

Do young teachers support collective bargaining, the unions' raison d'être? The answer is yes. Young union members are highly satisfied with their local unions' collective bargaining activities, at levels (greater than 80 percent) that are virtually identical to those of their older colleagues. And while their attitudes about collective bargaining, issue by issue—how it affects teaching, how it affects professionalism, and so on—are somewhat more critical than those of their colleagues, they are quite positive on the whole and, by overwhelming majorities, tend to see collective bargaining as a benign influence on the public schools.[3] The pursuit of teacher self-interest, in their eyes, does not come into conflict with the greater good and produces no moral dilemma. Finally, it is of great note that, in districts that do *not* have collective bargaining, fully 61 percent of young teachers said they *want* it, compared to 55 percent of teachers in the middle cohort and 59 percent of teachers in the oldest cohort.[4]

As for union politics, young teachers are a bit more dissatisfied than other members. But still, some 65 percent said they are satisfied. The real difference here comes with their activism—or lack of it—within their unions. Only 26 percent of them said they would speak up at meetings if their unions adopted political positions they disagree with, compared to 42 percent for the middle cohort and 52 percent for the oldest cohort. When asked to assess their participation, just 27 percent claimed to be "active," compared to 46 and 59 percent for the middle and oldest cohorts, respectively. And when asked to indicate what activities they had engaged in during electoral campaigns, only 1 percent of the young members said they had engaged in three or more activities, compared to 8 and 12 percent of the older two groups. Clearly, then, young members rarely participate in their unions' internal decision processes, and the population of union activists—doubtless the most influential of all members—is made up almost entirely of older teachers. If there is a sharp divide between younger and older teachers, this is it.

One consequence may be that, when it comes to how wage gains are distributed in collective bargaining, or to how much emphasis is placed on pensions and retiree health benefits, the greater influence of older teachers will affect union behavior. But as we've seen, young members are extremely well satisfied with what they are getting from collective bargaining and clearly do not feel that they are getting the short end of the stick. On the political side, moreover, the evidence suggests that their public policy positions are so similar to those of the older cohorts that whatever influence they may lack internally probably doesn't make much difference. On the right to strike, for instance, young members are at least as supportive as their colleagues are, and all are supportive at through-the-roof levels. Young members are also strongly opposed to vouchers, accountability, and the use of standardized tests, and strongly supportive of teacher tenure and higher taxes—just as their older colleagues are, and entirely congruent with the unions' positions. If there is an exception, it is that young union members are distinctly more supportive of charter schools, with 49 percent taking a positive view (contrary to their unions), compared to just 34 percent of the middle cohort and 31 percent of the oldest cohort. But even here, a majority of the young group still takes the union's side against charters.

All in all, then, the evidence seems to indicate that the "youth problem" is not much of a problem. Yes, young teachers are somewhat less inclined to join unions, and when they do join they are far less likely to participate in union affairs. But in other ways, young members are very much like their older colleagues. They love their locals. They are highly satisfied. They place great value on collective bargaining. And they support what the unions do in the political process. On the whole, their occupational interests prevail in shaping their views and beliefs.

As time goes on, moreover, their apathy in union affairs will likely give way to greater involvement and activism. After all, it is normal in most organizations for the older, established members to be more active; and as today's young teachers get older themselves, they will probably respond in the same way. In addition, as I note in chapter 3, the other time dynamics should tend to work in a prounion direction as well: due to self-selection (the more alienated choosing to leave teaching altogether), socialization (the acculturation that naturally occurs over the years), and life cycle effects (which, among other things, make members more risk averse and more concerned about what their unions can do for them).

As the unions look to the future, there is much on the horizon for them to fear. As I argue in the final chapter, major forces are being unleashed that are destined to undermine their membership, their money, and their power. There is no compelling reason, however, for thinking that the "youth problem" is one of them.

Notes

Chapter One

1. Steven Brill, "The Rubber Room: The Battle over New York City's Worst Teachers," *New Yorker*, August 31, 2009. Except where noted, my account follows Brill. To protect the confidentiality of individual teachers, I have substituted fictitious names for real names.

2. See, for example, Erin Einhorn, "Teachers in Trouble Spending Years in 'Rubber Room' Limbo that Costs $65M," *New York Daily News*, May 4, 2008; Angela Montefinise and Melissa Klein, "Why Is the City Paying 757 People to Do Nothing?" *New York Post*, September 30, 2007.

3. Quotes are from Brill, "The Rubber Room."

4. Quotes are from Brill, "The Rubber Room." For more details about New York City's Rubber Rooms, see, in addition to Brill's piece in the *New Yorker*, Karen Matthews, "700 NYC Teachers Are Paid to Do Nothing," *Associated Press Archive*, June 22, 2009; Einhorn, "Teachers in Trouble Spending Years in 'Rubber Room' Limbo That Costs $65M"; Montefinise and Klein, "Why Is the City Paying 757 People to Do Nothing?"; Samuel G. Freedman, "Where Teachers Sit, Awaiting Their Fates," *New York Times*, October 10, 2007.

5. See Joel Klein's Temporary Reassignment Center agreement with Michael Mulgrew, president of the United Federation of Teachers, April 15, 2010, available at wwwwww.uft. org/files/attachments/temporary-reassignment-centers-agreement-april-2010.pdf.

6. Jennifer Medina, "Teachers Set Deal with City on Discipline Process," *New York Times*, April 15, 2010.

7. Quoted in Medina, "Teachers Set Deal with City on Discipline Process."

8. New York City Department of Education, "About Our Schools" for 2010, available at schools.nyc.gov/AboutUs/schools/default.htm.

9. See, for example, Daniel Weisberg, Susan Sexton, Jennifer Mulhern, and David Keeling, "The Widget Effect: Our National Failure to Acknowledge and Act on Differences in Teacher Effectiveness" (New York: New Teacher Project, 2009), available at www.tntp.org.

10. See, for example, Frederick Hess and Martin West, "A Better Bargain: Overhauling Teacher Collective Bargaining for the 21st Century" (Harvard University, Program on Education Policy and Governance, 2006). See also Jessica Levin, Jennifer Mulhern, and Joan Schunck, "Unintended Consequences: The Case for Reforming the Staffing Rules in Urban Teachers Union Contracts" (New York: New Teacher Project, 2005), available at www.tntp.org/files/UnintendedConsequences.pdf.

11. See Eric A. Hanushek and Steven G. Rivkin, "Teacher Quality," in *Handbook of the Economics of Education*, edited by Eric A. Hanushek and Finis Welch (Amsterdam: Elsevier, 2006).

12. Eric A. Hanushek, "Teacher Deselection," in *Creating a New Teaching Profession*, edited by Dan Goldhaber and Jane Hannaway (Washington: Urban Institute, 2009). For the research, see Steven G. Rivkin, Eric A. Hanushek, and John F. Kain, "Teachers, Schools, and Academic Achievement," *Econometrica* 73, no. 2 (March 2005): 417–58.

13. Eric A. Hanushek, "There Is No War on Teachers," *Wall Street Journal*, October 19, 2010.

14. The $102 trillion figure is measured over the lifetime of the generation born in 2010. Quote is from Eric A. Hanushek, "Economic Aspects of Improving Teacher Quality," PEPG Working Paper 10-13, prepared for the Program on Education Policy and Governance (PEPG) conference Merit Pay: Will It Work? Is It Politically Viable? Harvard University, Kennedy School, Cambridge, Mass., June 3–4, 2010. Research referred to is Eric A. Hanushek and Ludgar Woessmann, "The High Cost of Low Educational Performance: The Long-Run Economic Impact of Improving PISA Outcomes" (Paris: Organization for Economic Cooperation and Development, 2010).

15. See, for example, "A Stagnant Nation: Why American Students Are Still at Risk" (ED in '08, the Strong American Schools Project, April 2008), available at media.heralddispatch.com/advertising/pdf/050908-Stagnant_Nation_Executive_ Summary.pdf; Paul E. Peterson, ed., *Our Schools and Our Future: Are We Still at Risk?* (Stanford, Calif.: Hoover Institution Press, 2003).

16. President's Commission on Excellence in Education, *A Nation at Risk: The Imperative for Educational Reform* (Washington: U.S. Department of Education, 1983). See also Thomas Toch, *In the Name of Excellence* (Oxford University Press, 1991).

17. See Terry M. Moe, "Teachers Unions and the Public Schools," in *A Primer on America's Schools*, edited by Terry M. Moe (Stanford, Calif.: Hoover Institution Press, 2001); Terry M. Moe, "The Politics of the Status Quo," in *Our Schools and Our Future*, edited by Peterson; Terry M. Moe, "Union Power and the Education of Children," in *Collective Bargaining in Education: Negotiating Change in Today's Schools*, edited by Jane Hannaway and Andrew Rotherham (Harvard Education Press, 2006); Myron Lieberman, *The Teacher Unions* (New York: Free Press, 1997); Peter Brimelow, *The Worm in the Apple* (New York: HarperCollins, 2003).

18. The history is discussed in chapter 2. But see, for example, Marjorie Murphy, *Blackboard Unions* (Cornell University Press, 1990); Maurice Berube, *Teacher Politics*

(New York: Greenwood Press, 1988); Lieberman, *Teacher Unions*; Stephen Cole, *The Unionization of Teachers: A Case Study of the UFT* (New York: Praeger Publishers, 1969).

19. The political side of union organization is well discussed and documented in Lieberman, *Teacher Unions*. But see also Murphy, *Blackboard Unions*, and a host of reference works cited in chapter 2.

20. David Tyack, *The One Best System* (Harvard University Press, 1974); also Murphy, *Blackboard Unions*.

21. For a prescient early statement about this transformation of the system, see William J. Grimshaw, *Union Rule in the Schools* (Lexington, Mass.: Lexington Books, 1979).

22. For data on their enormous political spending and how it compares to that of other political groups, see chapter 9. For an account of their political resources, see Lieberman, *The Teacher Unions*; Brimelow, *Worm in the Apple*; and Mike Antonucci, "The Long Reach of the Teachers Unions," *Education Next* 10, no. 4 (Fall 2010): 24–31.

23. Data on political spending are from the Center for Responsive Politics (www.open secrets.org). Spending amounts for the NEA and the AFT were added together to give a single total. The complete list of groups for 2009 is presented in chapter 9, table 9-2. As the discussion of chapter 9 shows, the teachers unions are also the biggest spenders in state campaigns.

24. A long-running study of state-level politics found the teachers unions to be the single most powerful interest group in the country throughout the 1990s and in 2002 ranked them a close second behind general business organizations (which rarely focus their total clout on education reform). See Clive S. Thomas and Ronald J. Hrebenar, "Interest Groups in the American States," in *Politics in the American States*, 8th ed., edited by Virginia Gray and Russell L. Hanson (Washington: CQ Press, 2004).

25. For a political science account of how veto points affect policymaking, see George Tsebelis, *Veto Players: How Political Institutions Work* (Princeton University Press, 2002).

26. For extensive evidence on how the unions have used the politics of blocking, see chapter 9. For early arguments and evidence on this point, see Moe, "Teachers Unions and the Public Schools," and Moe, "The Politics of the Status Quo." For detailed political accounts of the early days of reform and how the unions used their power to block, see Toch, *In the Name of Excellence*.

27. These points about the Democrats are well documented in chapters 9 and 10. But for an earlier extensive discussion, see Terry M. Moe, *Schools, Vouchers, and the American Public* (Brookings Institution, 2001).

28. See NCES, *NAEP 2008 Trends in Academic Progress: Reading 1971–2008, Mathematics 1973–2008* (Washington: National Center for Education Statistics, 2009, available on the NCES website at nces.ed.gov/nationsreportcard/pdf/main2008/2009479. pdf. For a deeper analysis of the trends with breakdowns by ethnic groups, see Terry M. Moe and John E. Chubb, *Liberating Learning: Technology, Politics, and the Future of American Education* (San Francisco: Jossey-Bass, 2009).

29. NCES, *Digest of Education Statistics: 2009* (Washington: National Center for Education Statistics, 2009). See table 182.

30. NCES, "The Nation's Report Card: Trial Urban District Assessment Reading 2009," available on the website of the NCES at nces.ed.gov/nationsreportcard/pubs/dst2009/2010459.asp.

31. "Graduation by the Numbers: Diplomas Count," *Education Week*, June 10, 2010.

32. The achievement data are available on the website of the NCES from various NAEP publications (nces.ed.gov/pubsearch/getpubcats.asp?sid=031#), but can be accessed directly using the NAEP "Data Explorer" tool (nces.ed.gov/nationsreportcard/naepdata/). It has been true in the past that black seventeen year olds also scored about the same as white thirteen year olds in math, but the math scores were recently rescaled for seventeen year olds, so a simple comparison across the two age groups is no longer possible.

33. See Trevor Williams and others, *Highlights from TIMSS 2007: Mathematics and Science Achievement of U.S. Fourth and Eighth Grade Students in an International Context* (Washington: Institute of Education Sciences, National Center for Education Statistics, 2009); OECD, *PISA 2009: What Students Know and Can Do* (Paris: OECD, Program for International Student Assessment, 2010), available on the OECD website at www.pisa.oecd.org/document/61/ 0,3343,en_32252351_32235731_46567613_1_1_1_1,00. html. American kids also do badly at the upper end of the continuum: compared to students in other nations, very few score at the "advanced" level in math. The international ranking of the United States, by this measure of achievement, is thirty-one out of fifty-six (including countries that are not in the OECD)—see the analysis in Eric A. Hanushek, Paul E. Peterson, and Ludgar Woessman, "Teaching Math to the Talented," *Education Next* 11, no. 1 (Winter 2011): 10–19. More generally, see Paul E. Peterson, "Little Gain in Student Achievement"; Eric A. Hanushek, "The Importance of School Quality," in *Our Schools and Our Future*, edited by Peterson.

34. See OECD, *Education at a Glance 2010* (Paris: OECD, 2010), table B1.1a. Only Luxembourg spends more at the primary level, and only Luxembourg, Norway, and Switzerland spend more at the secondary level.

35. Jill Casner-Lotto, Elyse Rosenblum, and Mary Wright, "The Ill-Prepared U.S. Workforce: Exploring the Challenges of Employer-Provided Workforce Readiness Training," Conference Board Research Report BED-09Workforce_RR (New York: Conference Board, August 2009).

36. See, for example, Claudia Goldin and Lawrence F. Katz, *The Race between Education and Technology* (Belknap Press of Harvard University Press, 2010); also Eric A. Hanushek and Ludgar Woessmann, "Education and Economic Growth," in *Economics of Education*, edited by Dominic J. Brewer and Patrick J. McEwan (Amsterdam: Elsevier, 2010).

37. See, for example, Richard Rothstein, *Class and Schools: Using Social, Economic, and Educational Reform to Close the Black-White Achievement Gap* (Washington: Economic Policy Institute, 2004); Jonathan Kozol, *The Shame of the Nation: The Restoration of Apartheid Schooling in America* (New York: Three Rivers Press, 2006). The classic, of course, is Jonathan Kozol, *Savage Inequalities: Children in America's Schools* (New York: Harper Perennial, 1992).

38. Eric A. Hanushek, "The Failure of Input-Based Schooling," *Economic Journal* 113, no. 485 (2003): 64–98.

39. This is what a coalition—among them, Randi Weingarten and other teachers union leaders—has recently called "The Broader, Bolder Approach to Education." This

coalition emerged at roughly the same time as two others, the Democrats for Education Reform and the Education Equality Project, which I discuss later in the book, that offer reform agendas focusing much more specifically on the challenge of fixing the public schools and on the special interests, notably the teachers unions, that get in the way of doing right by kids. Many genuine reformers (like Arne Duncan) have signed on to the "Broader, Bolder" plan, and there is overlap among the three groups. But the "Broader, Bolder" plan has also served, quite clearly, as a vehicle by which the teachers unions have sought to divert the education reform movement from putting the spotlight on schools and teachers. Their hope was that the Democrats would choose to put their eggs in the "Broader, Bolder" basket and not to follow the aggressively reformist agenda of Democrats for Education Reform and the Education Equality Project. When Obama won the presidency and he and Arne Duncan designed Race to the Top, it was clear that the latter two reform groups had won the better part of the battle for the party's educational soul—at least for awhile. I discuss the ferment within the Democratic Party in chapter 10. For background on the "Broader, Bolder" plan and its coalition, see, for example, Sam Dillon, "New Vision for Schools Proposes Broad Role," *New York Times*, July 15, 2008; Dana Goldstein, "Education Wars," *American Prospect*, March 23, 2009; and the plan's website (www.boldapproach.org/).

40. KIPP is an acronym for the Knowledge Is Power Program. For up-to-date information on KIPP, its students, and its organization, see the frequently asked questions section on its website at www.kipp.org/about-kipp/faq. See also KIPP's discussion of the Five Pillars.

41. Christina Clark Tuttle, Bing-ru Teh, Ira Nichols-Barrer, Brian P. Gill, and Phillip Gleason, "Student Characteristics and Achievement in 22 KIPP Middle Schools" (Mathematica Policy Research, June 2010), available at www.kipp.org/about-kipp/results/mathematica-study.

42. See KIPP Foundation, *KIPP Report Card 2009*, available at www.kipp.org/about-kipp/results/annual-report-card.

43. See the Aspire website (www.aspire.org) for information on achievement and other aspects of their schools. For a summary of some of the details, including this statement about their outperforming all large districts (defined as districts having more than twenty schools), see "Aspire Public Schools Outperforms Every Large School District in CA Serving Majority High-Poverty Students," press release, Aspire Public Schools, September 13, 2010, available at www.aspirepublicschools.org/sites/aspirepublicschools.org/files/2009-2010 API Press Release - Aspire Public Schools.pdf.

44. See, for example, Frederick Hess, *Common Sense School Reform* (New York: Palgrave Macmillan, 2004); Jay P. Greene, *Education Myths* (Lanham, Md.: Rowman and Littlefield, 2005); Hanushek, "The Failure of Input-Based Schooling."

45. Quoted in Gilbert Cruz, "Can Arne Duncan (and $5 Billion) Fix America's Schools?" *Time*, September 14, 2009.

46. On critical junctures and how they figure into analyses of institutional change, see, for example, Paul Pierson and Theda Skocpol, "Historical Institutionalism in Contemporary Political Science," in *Political Science: The State of the Discipline*, edited by Ira Katznelson and Helen V. Milner (New York: W. W. Norton, 2002); Paul Pierson, *Politics*

in Time: History, Institutions, and Social Analysis (Princeton University Press, 2004); Ruth Berins Collier and David Collier, *Shaping the Political Arena: Critical Junctures, the Labor Movement, and Regime Dynamics in Latin America* (Princeton University Press, 1991).

47. The quote is from Evan Thomas and Pat Wingert, "Why We Must Fire Bad Teachers," *Newsweek*, March 6, 2010. See also, for example, Amanda Ripley, "Rhee Tackles Classroom Challenge," *Time*, November 26, 2008; Amanda Ripley, "'Waiting for Superman': A Call to Action for Our Schools," *Time*, September 23, 2010; Steven Brill, "Teachers Unions' Last Stand," *New York Times Magazine*, May 17, 2010; Evan Thomas, "Schoolyard Brawl," *Newsweek*, March 6, 2010; Jonathan Alter, "How Congress Keeps Screwing Up Education," *Newsweek*, July 2, 2010; Joe Klein, "Why We're Failing Our Schools," *Time*, January 28, 2010; "'Potential Disruption?' Ending DC School Vouchers Would Dash the Best Hopes of Hundreds of Children," editorial, *Washington Post*, March 2, 2009.

48. Quote is from Greg Toppo, "Democrats, Teachers Unions Now Divided on Many Issues," *USA Today*, September 2, 2008.

49. For accounts of these political developments, with attention to the struggle taking place within the Democratic Party, see, for example, Dana Goldstein, "The Education Wars," *American Prospect*, March 23, 2009; Dana Goldstein, "The Democratic Divide," *American Prospect*, August 25, 2008. For a more detailed discussion of Race to the Top and the Obama agenda, see chapter 10; Brill, "Teachers Unions' Last Stand."

50. See, for instance, Lloyd Grove, "Superman's Villain Fights Back," *Daily Beast*, September 17, 2010, available at www.thedailybeast.com; Matthew Shaffer, "Rocking the Boat on Education: A Review of *Waiting for Superman*," *National Review Online*, September 27, 2010, available at www.nationalreview.com; John Heilemann, "Schools: The Disaster Movie," *New York Magazine*, September 5, 2010. For Randi Weingarten's response to the movie, see "Teachers Union v. Superman," *Huffington Post*, September 9, 2010, available at www.huffingtonpost.com. Two other movies with very similar themes were released during 2010, *The Cartel* and *The Lottery*. Both deserved much more attention than they received.

51. The most vocal and visible purveyors of reform unionism are the various members of the Teachers Union Reform Network (TURN), who see themselves as agents seeking to make the teachers unions less focused on bread-and-butter job issues and more oriented by what is necessary for quality schools and student achievement. For information on TURN—which I discuss at length in chapter 8—see their website (www. turnexchange.net/blog.html). The most prominent written work on reform unionism has been published by enthusiasts who have been influential in providing an intellectual foundation—albeit a very shaky one, in my view—for these ideas about how the teachers unions can and ultimately will transform themselves. See especially Charles Taylor Kerchner and Douglas E. Mitchell, *The Changing Idea of a Teachers Union* (New York: Falmer Press, 1988); Charles Taylor Kerchner and Julia E. Koppich, *A Union of Professionals: Labor Relations and Educational Reform* (Teachers College Press, 1993); Charles Taylor Kerchner, Julia E. Koppich, and Joseph E. Weeres, *United Mind Workers: Unions and Teaching in the Knowledge Society* (San Francisco: Jossey Bass, 1997).

52. Moe and Chubb, *Liberating Learning*.

53. For an extensive analysis of technology, its implications for learning and schools, and the political resistance to it, see Moe and Chubb, *Liberating Learning*, which is the basis for the argument I am making here as well as in chapter 10. See also Clay Christensen, Curtis W. Johnson, and Michael B. Horne, *Disrupting Class: How Disruptive Innovation Will Change the Way the World Learns* (New York: McGraw-Hill, 2008); Paul E. Peterson, *Saving Schools: From Horace Mann to Virtual Learning* (Harvard Education Press, 2010). Both these books have much to say about technology and its transformative potential, but they do not deal with the politics of technology, with the fact that the unions have strong incentives to fight and block it, or with why the unions are destined to lose and to have their power undermined in the process. That, in large measure, is what *Liberating Learning* is about.

54. For prominent early examples, see National Commission on Excellence in Education, *A Nation at Risk* (Washington: Government Printing Office, 1983); Twentieth Century Fund, *Making the Grade* (New York: The Fund, 1983); Carnegie Task Force on Teaching as a Profession, *A Nation Prepared* (Washington: Carnegie Forum on Education and the Economy, 1986).

55. See, for example, Weisberg and others, "The Widget Effect"; Levin, Mulhern, and Schunck, "Unintended Consequences"; Emily Cohen, Kate Walsh, and RiShawn Biddle, "The Invisible Ink in Collective Bargaining Agreements" (Washington: NCTQ, 2007); "Bumping HR: Giving Principals More Say over Staffing" (Washington: NCTQ, 2010); "Teacher Layoffs: Rethinking 'Last-Hired, First-Fired Policies" (Washington: NCTQ, February 2010); as well as a number of studies NCTQ has carried out of the personnel policies of urban districts, including Baltimore, Boston, Seattle, and Hartford. See its website for the reports (www.nctq.org/p/publications/reports.jsp). I should note that there is also a small quantitative literature in professional journals on the impact of collective bargaining on student achievement, most of it from the 1980s and 1990s, which I discuss in chapter 6.

56. To get a sense of what institutionalism consists of in political science, especially its rational choice component (which is its dominant variation), see, for example, Kenneth A. Shepsle and Mark S. Bonchek, *Analyzing Politics: Rationality, Behavior, and Institutions* (New York: W. W. Norton, 1997). Here are a few more specific examples. Keith Krehbiel, *Pivotal Politics: A Theory of U.S. Lawmaking* (University of Chicago Press, 1998); Barry R. Weingast, "Rational Choice Institutionalism," in *Political Science: The Science of Politics*, edited by Katznelson and Milner; and Terry M. Moe, "Power and Political Institutions," *Perspectives on Politics* 3, no. 2 (June 2005): 215–33.

57. See, for example, Shailagh Murray, "For a Senate Foe of Pork Barrel Spending, Two Bridges Too Far," *Washington Post*, October 21, 2005.

58. See, for example, Mary Whitley, "Earmark Reform? Stimulus Bill Contains 9,000." *Plain Dealer*, February 22, 2009; Michael Grabell and Christopher Weaver, "In Stimulus Bill, Earmarks by Any Other Name," *ProPublica*, available at www.propublica.org/article/welcome-in-the-stimulus-bill-an-earmark-by-any-other-name.

59. See, for example, Alan Fram, "Fact Check: Ban on Pet Projects Mostly Symbolic," *Real Clear Politics*, November 19, 2010, available at realclearpolitics.com; "The Empty Earmarks Pledge," editorial, *New York Times*, November 16, 2010; also A. G. Sulzberger,

"Defenders of Earmarks Point to Urgent Needs That Would Not Be Met," *New York Times*, November 22, 2010.

60. See, for example, Richard Rubin, "Tricks of the Tax Trade," *CQ Weekly*, September 6, 2010; TasVox, "New Bill Extends Special Interest Tax Breaks," *Christian Science Monitor*, May 26, 2010; C. Eugene Steuerle, *Contemporary U.S. Tax Policy* (Washington: Urban Institute Press, 2008); Jeffrey H. Birnbaum and Alan S. Murray, *Showdown and Gucci Gulch* (New York: Vintage, 1988). I should point out that the largest deductions in the aggregate are for employer-provided health care, pension contributions, and mortgages—but even with these, the beneficiaries are still properly regarded as special interests. And there are countless others that are targeted at much smaller, more specialized groups.

61. See, for example, Brian M. Riedl, "How Farm Subsidies Harm Taxpayers, Consumers, and Farmers, Too," Backgrounder 2043 (Washington: Heritage Foundation, June 19, 2007); Bruce Gardner, "Plowing Farm Subsidies Under," On the Issues (Washington: American Enterprise Institute, June 2007); John Mark Hansen, *Gaining Access: Congress and the Farm Lobby, 1919–1981* (University of Chicago Press, 1991). See also the website of the Environmental Working Group at www.ewg.org/farmsubsidies, which has extensive information on farm subsidies, including a searchable database.

62. See, for example, Peter Juul, "The Coming Battles over the Defense Budget" (Washington: Center for American Progress, November 22, 2010), available at www.americanprogress.org/issues/2010/11/defense_budget_politics.html; Bryan Bender, "A Dog Fight Obama Seems Bound to Lose," *Boston Globe*, July 12, 2009; Craig Whitlock and Dana Hedgpeth, "Congress Pursues F-35 Engine That Defense Secretary Robert Gates Doesn't Want," *Washington Post*, May 28, 2010; Barry S. Rundquist and Thomas M. Carsey, *Congress and Defense Spending: The Distributive Politics of Military Procurement* (University of Oklahoma Press, 2002); David C. Sorensen, *The Process and Politics of Defense Acquisition: A Reference Handbook* (New York: Praeger, 2008).

63. See e.g., David R. Mayhew, *Congress: The Electoral Connection*, 2d ed. (Yale University Press, 2004); Morris P. Fiorina, *Representatives, Roll Calls, and Constituencies* (Lexington, Mass.: Lexington Books, 1974); Barry R. Weingast, Kenneth A. Shepsle, and Christopher Johnsen, "The Political Economy Approach to Benefits and Costs: A Neo-Classical Approach to Distributive Politics," *Journal of Political Economy* 89, no. 4 (1981): 642–64; Glenn R. Parker, *Congress and the Rent-Seeking Society* (University of Michigan Press, 1996).

64. The organizational foundations of these leader incentives are discussed in more detail in chapter 3.

65. There are still local unions that call themselves Retail Clerks. But for the record, in 1979 the Retail Clerks International Union merged with the Amalgamated Meat Cutters Union to form the United Food and Commercial Workers International Union (UFCW). For a brief history, see the UFCW website (www.ufcw.org/about_ufcw/where_we_come_from/industries/retail_clerk_history.cfm).

66. For political science accounts of what interest groups do in politics and why, see, for example, David Lowery and Holly Brasher, *Organized Interests and American Government* (New York: McGraw-Hill, 2004); Paul S. Herrnson, Ronald G. Shaiko, and Clyde Wilcox, *The Interest Group Connection: Electioneering, Lobbying, and Policymaking*

in Washington (Washington: CQ Press, 2005); Scott H. Ainsworth, *Analyzing Interest Groups: Group Influence on People and Policies* (New York: W. W. Norton, 2002); Allan J. Ciglar and Burdette Loomis, editors, *Interest Group Politics,* 8th ed. (Washington: CQ Press, 2011); Frank R. Baumgartner and Beth L. Leech, *Basic Interests: The Importance of Groups in Politics and Political Science* (Princeton University Press, 1998).

67. Polls regularly ask Americans which professions they trust the most, and teachers always score near the top. In a 2006 HarrisInteractive Poll, for instance, teachers came in second, right behind doctors, on a list of twenty-two professions. For a rundown on the survey's results, see Harris Interactive, "Who Do You Trust?" *lexisONE,* September 2006 (www.lexisone.com/balancing/articles/090006i.html). In a recent Phi Delta Kappa survey (conducted by Gallup), to take another example, seven out of ten Americans said that they would like their child "to take up teaching in the public schools as a career." See William J. Bushaw and John A. McNee, "Americans Speak Out: Are Educators and Policy Makers Listening? The 41st Annual Phi Delta Kappa/Gallup Poll of the Public's Attitudes toward the Public Schools," *Phi Delta Kappan* 91, no. 1 (September 2009): 8–23.

68. See, for example, Dina Martin, "CTA Launches Ad Campaigns," available on the California Teachers Association's website at www.cta.org/Professional-Development/Publications/Educator-October-10/CTA-launches-campaign-ads.aspx; also "Concerned Educators and Parents for Jerry Brown/TV Ad," also available on the CTA's website at www.cta.org/About-CTA/News-Room/Media-Center/Video/2010/Parents-and-Teachers-For-Jerry-Brown.aspx.

69. Political science is filled with books and articles about special interest politics and influence. Here are a few classics. E. E. Schattschneider, *The Semi-Sovereign People: A Realist's View of Democracy in America* (New York: Holt, Rinehart, and Winston, 1960); Theodore Lowi, *The End of Liberalism: The Second Republic of the United States* (New York: W. W. Norton, 1979); Grant McConnel, *Private Power and American Democracy* (New York: Knopf, 1966). For overviews and assessments of the interest group literature, see, more recently, Herrnson, Shaiko, and Wilcox, *The Interest Group Connection*; Lowery and Brasher, *Organized Interests and American Government* ; Ainsworth, *Analyzing Interest Groups*; Ciglar and Loomis, *Interest Group Politics*; and Baumgartner and Leech, *Basic Interests.*

70. See, for example, Dan Eggen, "Industry Cash Flowed to Drafters of Reform," *Washington Post,* July 21, 2009; Jeffrey Young, "K Street's Heathcare Winners and Losers," *TheHill.com,* December 25, 2009, available at thehill.com/business-a-lobbying/73605-k-streets-healthcare-winners-and-losers; Joe Klein, "Will Special Interests Stymie Health Care Reform?" *Time,* July 30, 2009; Timothy P. Carney, "Obama Gives Sugar Plums to the Special Interests," *Washington Examiner,* March 24, 2010; David Catanese, "Interest Groups Play Health Care Hardball," *Politico,* March 19, 2010, available at www.politico.com/news/stories/0310/34653.html.

Chapter Two

1. The classic, most influential statement of the collective action problem as it applies to political interest groups—and "voluntary" organizations more generally—is by Mancur Olson Jr., *The Logic of Collective Action* (Harvard University Press, 1965).

2. The literature on collective action problems and their possible solutions is huge. I won't go into all the analytic subtleties here, which may involve, for instance, infinitely repeated play, various sorts of strategies (tit-for-tat, grim trigger), communication, imperfect information, fairness and altruism, and more. I am writing this book for a broad audience, and, in any event, many of the more sophisticated lines of theory are not of the essence here. I just want to make a few very basic points of relevance to unions. For some of the generic issues involved in collective action, see, in addition to Olson's *The Logic of Collective Action,* Russell Hardin, *Collective Action* (Johns Hopkins University Press, 1982); Elinor Ostrom, *Governing the Commons: The Evolution of Institutions for Collective Action* (Cambridge University Press, 1990); Robert Axelrod, *The Evolution of Cooperation* (New York: Basic Books, 1984). For discussions of more recent developments with regard to collective action, see Ernst Fehr and Klaus M. Schmidt, "The Economics of Fairness, Reciprocity, and Altruism: Experimental Evidence and New Theories," in *Handbook on the Economics of Giving, Reciprocity, and Altruism,* vol. 1, edited by Serge-Christophe Kolm and Jean Mercier Ythier, pp. 615–91 (Amsterdam: Elsevier, 2006); Louis Fernando Medina, *A Unified Theory of Collective Action and Social Change* (University of Michigan Press, 2007).

3. For discussions of how collective action problems apply to unions specifically, see, for example, Olson, *The Logic of Collective Action*; David Lowery and Holly Brasher, *Organized Interests and American Government* (Boston: McGraw-Hill, 2004); Casey Ichniowski and Jeffrey S. Zax, "Right-to-Work Laws, Free Riders, and Unionization in the Local Public Sector," *Journal of Labor Economics* 9, no. 3 (1991): 255–75; Medina, *A Unified Theory of Collective Action and Social Change.*

4. Olson's original statement of the collective action problem puts heavy emphasis on tangible selective incentives (such as insurance) as partial solutions. See Olson, *The Logic of Collective Action.* For an extensive discussion, see Terry M. Moe, *The Organization of Interests* (University of Chicago Press, 1980).

5. See, for example, Fehr and Schmidt, "The Economics of Fairness, Reciprocity, and Altruism"; also John O. Ledyard, "Public Goods: A Survey of Experimental Research," in *Handbook of Experimental Economics,* edited by J. H. Kagel and A. E. Roth, pp. 111–81 (Princeton University Press, 1995).

6. For a nice overview of the arguments and literature, see Leda Cosmides and John Tooby, "Evolutionary Psychology: A Primer," University of California, Santa Barbara, Center for Evolutionary Psychology, 1997.

7. See, for example, Bill Sammon, "Workers Report Union Violence," *Washington Times,* April 10, 1998; Samuel R. Friedman, *Teamster Rank and File: Power, Bureaucracy, and Rebellion at Work and in a Union* (Columbia University Press, 1982); U.S. Senate, Committee on Labor and Human Resources, *Labor Violence* (University of Michigan Library, 1985); John Arena, "Labor, Globalization, and African American Liberation: The Case of the Charleston 5 Dockworkers Struggle," paper presented at the annual meeting of the American Sociological Association, Atlanta, Ga., August 16, 2003.

8. See, for example, Richard Vedder, "Right-to-Work Laws: Liberty, Prosperity, and Quality of Life," *Cato Journal* 30, no.1 (Winter 2010): 171–80; Randall G. Holcombe

and James D. Gwartney, "Unions, Economic Freedom, and Growth," *Cato Journal* 30, no. 1 (Winter 2010): 1–22.

9. See Richard B. Freeman, "Unionism Comes to the Public Sector," *Journal of Economic Literature* 24, no. 1 (March 1986): 41–86.

10. On the early history of public sector unions, see Martin West, "Bargaining with Authority: The Political Origins of Public Sector Bargaining," paper presented at the 2008 Policy History conference, St. Louis, May 29–June 1, 2008; Joseph E. Slater, *Public Workers: Government Employee Unions, the Law, and the State, 1900–1962* (Cornell University Press, 2004); Sterling D. Spero, *Government as Employer* (New York: Remson, 1948).

11. See especially Slater, *Public Workers.*

12. Quoted in Spero, *Government as Employer*, p. 346.

13. See West, "Bargaining with Authority."

14. See, for example, Spero, *Government as Employer*; also Paul P. Van Riper, *History of the United States Civil Service* (Evanston, Ill.: Row, Peterson, 1958).

15. See Van Riper, *History of the United States Civil Service*; also Ronald N. Johnson and Gary D. Libecap, *The Federal Civil Service and the Problem of Bureaucracy* (University of Chicago Press, 1994); Stephen Skowronek, *Building a New American State* (Cambridge University Press, 1982).

16. On the tensions between public sector unionism and patronage and the unions' support for civil service, see, for example, West, "Bargaining with Authority"; Jack Steiber, *Public Employee Unionism: Structure, Growth, Policy* (Brookings, 1973); also Johnson and Libecap, *The Federal Civil Service*. On Gompers, the American Federation of Labor, and "pure and simple unionism," see, for example, Julie Greene, *Pure and Simple Politics: The American Federation of Labor and Political Activism, 1881–1917* (Cambridge University Press, 1998); also J. David Greenstone, *Labor in American Politics* (New York: Alfred A. Knopf, 1969).

17. West, "Bargaining with Authority"; Seymour Martin Lipset, "Labor Unions in the Public Mind," in *Unions in Transition,* edited by Seymour Martin Lipset (San Francisco: ICS Press, 1986); Taylor Dark, *The Unions and the Democrats: An Enduring Alliance* (Cornell University Press, 1999); Greenstone, *Labor in American Politics.*

18. See, for example, Nelson Lichtenstein, *State of the Union: A Century of American Labor* (Princeton University Press, 2002); William B. Gould IV, *A Primer on American Labor Law*, 4th ed. (MIT Press, 2004).

19. See Barry Hirsch, "Sluggish Institutions in a Dynamic World: Can Unions and Industrial Competition Coexist?" *Journal of Economic Perspectives* 22, no. 1 (Winter 2008): 153–76.

20. See Lichtenstein, *State of the Unions*; Dark, *The Unions and the Democrats*; and Greenstone, *Labor in American Politics.*

21. See especially West, "Bargaining with Authority."

22. Max Green, *Epitaph for American Labor: How Union Leaders Lost Touch with America* (Washington: AEI Press, 1996), p. 162; for the history, see, for example, Spero, *The Government as Employer*; West, "Bargaining with Authority."

23. On the AFSCME breakthroughs, see, for example, Leo Kramer, *Labor's Paradox: The American Federation of State, County, and Municipal Employees, AFL-CIO* (New York: John Wiley and Sons, 1962); Irving Bernstein, *Promises Kept: John F. Kennedy's New Frontier* (Oxford University Press, 1991); Francis Ryan, "Everyone Royalty: AFSCME, Municipal Workers, and Urban Power in Philadelphia, 1921–1983," Ph.D. dissertation, University of Pennsylvania, 2003. On events in New York City, see, for example, Bernstein, *Promises Kept*; and Jewel Bellush and Bernard Bellush, *Union Power and New York: Victor Gotbaum and District Council 37* (New York: Praeger Press, 1984).

24. See, for example, Stephen Cole, *The Unionization of Teachers: A Case Study of the UFT* (New York: Praeger, 1969).

25. For an overview of these developments in public sector unionism generally, see James L. Stern, "Unionism in the Public Sector," in *Public Sector Bargaining*, 2d ed., edited by Benjamin Aaron, Joyce M. Najita, and James L. Stern (Washington: Bureau of National Affairs, 1988).

26. See Freeman, "Unionism Comes to the Public Sector"; Leo Troy, *The New Unionism in the New Society: Public Sector Unions in Redistributive States* (George Mason University Press, 1994); Richard B. Freeman and Casey Ichniowski, eds., *When Public Sector Employees Unionize* (University of Chicago Press, 1988); Aaron, Majita, and Stern, eds., *Public Sector Bargaining*.

27. These figures are from www.unionstats.com, a widely used website constructed and maintained by Barry Hirsch and David Macpherson, whose data come from the Current Population Survey (CPS). The CPS data are not without their problems, as I discuss in a later note, but they are the best available for broad-sweep historical statistics on public and private sector unionization (although not for teachers). The most reliable CPS data are from 1983 to the present.

28. For data on state laws, see Henry S. Farber, "Union Membership in the United States: The Divergence between the Public and Private Sectors," in *Collective Bargaining in Education: Negotiating Change in Today's Schools*, edited by Jane Hannaway and Andrew J. Rotherham (Harvard Education Press, 2006); Richard B. Freeman and Robert G. Valletta, "The NBER Public Sector Collective Bargaining Law Data Set," in *When Public Sector Employees Unionize*, edited by Richard B. Freeman and Casey Ichniowski (University of Chicago Press, 1988); Donald S. Wasserman, "Collective Bargaining Rights in the Public Sector: Promises and Reality," in *Justice on the Job: Perspectives on the Erosion of Collective Bargaining in the United States*, edited by Richard N. Block, Sheldon Friedman, Michelle Kaminski, and Andy Levin (Kalamazoo, Mich.: W. E. Upjohn Institute, 2006).

29. See, for example, Hoyt N. Wheeler and John A. McClendon, "The Individual Decision to Join," in *The State of the Unions*, edited by George Strauss, Daniel G. Gallagher, and Jack Fiorito (Madison, Wis.: Industrial Relations Research Association, 1991); Gary N. Chaison and Dileep G. Dhavala, "The Choice between Union Membership and Free Rider Status," *Journal of Labor Research* 13, no. 4 (December 1992): 355–69.

30. Richard B. Freeman, "Unionism Comes to the Public Sector," *Journal of Economic Literature* 24 (March 1986): 41–86. Quote is from p. 45.

31. See especially Gregory M. Saltzman, "Bargaining Laws as a Cause and Consequence of the Growth of Teacher Unionism," *Industrial and Labor Relations Review* 38, no. 3 (April 1985): 335–51; Gregory M. Saltzman, "Public Sector Bargaining Laws Really Matter: Evidence from Ohio and Illinois," in *When Public Sector Employees Unionize*, edited by Freeman and Ichniowski. See also David T. Ellwood and Glenn Fine, "The Impact of Right-to-Work Laws on Union Organizing," *Journal of Political Economy* 95, no. 2 (1987): 250–73; Jeffrey S. Zax and Casey Ichniowski, "Bargaining Laws and Unionization in the Local Public Sector," *Industrial and Labor Relations Review* 43 (1990): 447–62; Casey Ichniowski, Richard Freeman, and Harrison Lauer, "Collective Bargaining Laws, Threat Effects, and the Determination of Police Compensation," *Journal of Labor Economics* 7, no. 2 (April 1989): 191–209; Ichniowski and Zax, "Right-to-Work Laws, Free Riders, and Unionization in the Local Public Sector"; Farber, "Union Membership in the United States."

32. Here and in the previous paragraph, figures on union membership are from www.unionstats.com, whose data are compiled by Barry Hirsch and David Macpherson from the Current Population Survey. For earlier data, see Leo Troy and Neil Sheflin, *Union Sourcebook: Membership, Structure, Finance, Directory* (West Orange, N.J.: Industrial Relations Data and Information Services, 1985).

33. See, for example, Troy, *The New Unionism in the New Society*; Farber, "Union Membership in the United States"; and Hirsch, "Sluggish Institutions in a Dynamic World."

34. In addition to Farber, "Union Membership in the United States," and Hirsch, "Sluggish Institutions in a Dynamic World," see, for example, Richard B. Freeman, "Why Are Unions Faring Poorly in NLRB Elections?" in *Challenges and Choices Facing American Labor*, edited by Thomas A. Kochan (MIT Press, 1985); John F. Burton Jr. and Terry Thomason, "The Extent of Collective Bargaining in the Public Sector," in *Public Sector Bargaining*, edited by Aaron, Najita, and Stern.

35. For discussions of why government environments are more conducive to unions than the private economy, see Troy, *The New Unionism in the New Society*.

36. For a list of right-to-work states, go to the Department of Labor's website at www.dol.gov/whd/state/righttowork.htm.

37. For an example of the unions' standard views on agency fees, free riding, and right to work, see, for example, what the AFL-CIO has to say in "Right to Work States Are Really Restricted Rights States," on its website at www.union1.org/badforindiana.

38. See, for example, the work and arguments of the National Right to Work Committee (nrtwc.org). See also Vedder, "Right-to-Work Laws."

39. *National Labor Relations Board* v. *General Motors*, 373 U.S. 734 (1963).

40. See, for example, Charles W. Baird, "Right to Work before and after 14(b)," *Journal of Labor Research* 19, no. 3 (Summer 1998): 471–93. Baird is a critic of forced unionism, but gives an informative historical account of court cases and legal background.

41. For overviews of American labor law and the issues surrounding forced unionism, see, for example, Derek Curtis Bok, Robert A. Gorman, Matthew W. Finkin, and Archibald Cox, *Labor Law: Cases and Materials*, 14th ed. (Eagan, Minn.: Foundation

Press, 2006); Douglas L. Leslie, *Labor Law in a Nutshell*, 5th ed. (Eagan, Minn.: Thompson West, 2008).

42. I discuss the impact of agency fees in much more detail later in the chapter. For now, it is perhaps worth simply noting that, in states that permit or require agency fees—where the great majority of districts (of any size) can be counted upon to have agency fee provisions written into their collective bargaining contracts—only 6 percent of teachers have chosen to remain nonmembers. These nonmember teachers are much more likely to be Republican (and conservative) than member teachers are. In agency-fee states, members are 51 percent Democrat and 24 percent Republican, while nonmembers are 31 percent Democrat and 42 percent Republican. The data are from my own national survey of teachers, discussed at length in chapter 3.

43. *Abood* v. *Detroit Board of Education*, 431 U.S. 209 (1977).

44. *Teachers* v. *Hudson*, 475 U.S. 292 (1986).

45. See especially Myron Lieberman, *The Teacher Unions* (New York: Free Press, 1997), ch. 10. For a discussion of the legal history and some of the issues it raises—about freedom, organizing rights, and the like—see, for example, Harry G. Hutchison, "Reclaiming First Amendment through Union Dues Restrictions?" *University of Pennsylvania Journal of Business and Employment Law* 10, no. 3 (2008): 663–716. For the basic law on work rights, see Bok and others, *Labor Law*; Leslie, *Labor Law in a Nutshell*.

46. Here and below, on the NEA's early history of organizing and "representing" teachers during the first half century of the American school system, see Marjorie Murphy, *Blackboard Unions: The AFT and the NEA, 1900–1980* (Cornell University Press, 1990); E. G. Westley, *NEA: The First Hundred Years* (New York: Harper, 1957); A. M. West, *The National Education Association: The Power Base for Education* (New York: Free Press, 1980); T. M. Stinnett, *Turmoil in Teaching: A History of the Organizational Struggle for America's Teachers* (New York: Macmillan, 1968); David Tyack, *The One Best System* (Harvard University Press, 1974); Lawrence A. Cremin, *The Transformation of the School: Progressivism in American Education, 1876–1957* (New York: Knopf, 1968); Wayne Urban, *Why Teachers Organized* (Wayne State University Press, 1982); Ronald D. Henderson, "Teacher Unions: Continuity and Change," in *Teacher Unions and Education Policy: Retrenchment or Reform?* edited by Ronald D. Henderson, Wayne J. Urban, and Paul Wolman (Amsterdam: Elsevier, 2004).

47. Figures are from Murphy, *Blackboard Unions*, p. 277.

48. Basic historical material on the rise of the teachers unions and specifics on both the NEA and AFT can be gleaned from many sources. In addition to the works cited earlier, see also Richard D. Kahlenberg, "The History of Collective Bargaining among Teachers," in *Collective Bargaining in Education*, edited by Hannaway and Rotherham; Cole, *The Unionization of Teachers*; Lieberman, *The Teacher Unions*; Maurice R. Berube, *Teacher Politics* (New York: Greenwood Press, 1988).

49. Figures are from Murphy, *Blackboard Union*, p. 277.

50. On the AFT, in addition to the works cited above, see Robert J. Braun, *Teachers and Power: The Story of the American Federation of Teachers* (New York: Simon and Schuster, 1972); David Selden, *The Teacher Rebellion* (Howard University Press, 1985); Philip

Taft, *United They Teach: The Story of the United Federation of Teachers* (Los Angeles: Nash Publishing, 1974).

51. Murphy, *Blackboard Unions*, p. 216.

52. The 20,000 figure is from Murphy, *Blackboard Unions*, p. 216. For details about the New York City strike, see, in addition to Murphy's book, Cole, *The Unionization of Teachers*; Braun, *Teachers and Power*; Selden, *The Teacher Rebellion*; Taft, *United They Teach*.

53. For overviews of the struggle between the NEA and the AFT and the NEA's conversion to a union, see West, *The National Education Association*; Henderson, "Teachers Unions: Continuity and Change"; Kahlenberg, "The History of Collective Bargaining among Teachers."

54. Saltzman, "Bargaining Laws as a Cause and Consequence of the Growth of Teacher Unionism."

55. The figure for 2008 is probably less reliable than the figures for other years, because the wording of the SASS survey was changed for 2008 in ways that introduced ambiguity and caused a number of districts that do have collective bargaining to say that they only engage in meet-and-confer arrangements. I have tried to adjust for this bias by recoding districts that, in years past, indicated that they did indeed have collective bargaining—for it is almost never the case that districts with collective bargaining slip back into meet-and-confer. (I verified that districts had indeed given erroneous responses to the ambiguous question by telephoning a number of them.) These adjustments don't make a big difference in the aggregate percentages one way or the other, however, because most of the affected districts are rather small and they aren't that numerous. A bigger issue, here and throughout this section, is how to code the Arizona districts that *say* they have collective bargaining, but, under Arizona law, don't. I discuss this later in the text.

56. Here and throughout this book, I use SASS when I report figures for teacher unionization and the percentage covered by collective bargaining. The other major source of information is the Current Population Survey (see www.unionstats.com), which yields estimates on both counts that are somewhat lower than those from SASS. In my view, the SASS data are the best available for the public schools and are more likely to be on target. One problem with the CPS is that it is based entirely on respondent self-reports of their true occupation, of whether they are full time or part time, and so on. But more important are two additional problems. One, it calculates unionization and coverage rates based on all employed workers—or, in this case, all people who say they are employed as teachers—rather than focusing just on full-time workers. To calculate reliable, meaningful unionization and coverage rates for public school teachers, these rates need to be based on people who really are teachers and who are employed full time. Two, CPS calculates coverage rates by assuming that all union members are covered by collective bargaining and then asking nonmembers whether they are covered. But for teachers in the seven states where collective bargaining is not permitted, rather large percentages of teachers are union members—yet no teachers are covered by collective bargaining in any of these states. This problem is present to a smaller degree in other states as well. Because CPS misses the mark on these counts, it is likely to come up with unionization

rates that are too low and coverage rates that are way too high in some states (notably, the seven that prohibit collective bargaining) and possibly too low in others (because unionization is underestimated). SASS, by contrast, asks school districts directly about whether they engage in collective bargaining with a union; it also has data on teachers who are actually employed by those districts and on whether each teacher is or is not full time. Ambiguities remain—see the note about the survey question that seems to have confused a small number of districts and affected their responses. Moreover, whatever survey is used, we still need to decide what to count as collective bargaining—see my discussion later on about Arizona, for instance. Nonetheless, all in all, SASS seems to provide the most reliable figures on unionization and coverage.

57. The figure on total membership is from the NEA website (nea.org). The figure on the number of teacher members is from NEA national headquarters (Ramona Parks).

58. The figures on NEA membership are from the *2009 NEA Handbook*, available online at www.nea.org. Figures on the total number of teachers in the public schools are from the National Center for Education Statistics, *Digest of Education Statistics 2009*.

59. This information was obtained in February 2010 from the AFT's website (www. aft.org) by following the "About AFT" link.

60. See Lieberman, *The Teacher Unions*. I carried out my estimation in early 2006. Because AFT membership is concentrated in the largest school districts in the country, I identified all AFT districts among the nation's largest 100 school districts. Although perhaps 5 to 10 percent of the teachers in these districts probably did not belong, I erred in the AFT's favor and assumed that all teachers in those districts were AFT members. I also assumed, for the three states in which the AFT and NEA had merged, that all unionized districts in those states were AFT districts, and I gave the AFT half credit for the total number of teachers in those states who were union members (according to SASS data). Finally, because New York is a bastion of AFT organization and because some 99 percent of New York teachers are unionized, I gave the AFT credit for 99 percent of all the teachers in that state as of 2006, minus the number that the NEA says belong to its own New York locals (in data they provided to me directly for 2000). The numbers are not exact. The estimates for particular districts and states are on the high side, but they are balanced by the omission of small AFT unions (which are not numerous). They show that the number of AFT teacher-members is about *half* of the total membership that they publicly claim—meaning that, if their membership figures are accurate, half are nonteachers.

61. This figure is from my national teacher survey, discussed in chapter 3.

62. See especially Saltzman, "Bargaining Laws as a Cause and Consequence of the Growth of Teacher Unionism"; Gregory M. Saltzman, "The Growth of Teacher Bargaining and the Enactment of Teacher Bargaining Laws," PhD dissertation, University of Wisconsin, 1981. See also Saltzman, "Public Sector Bargaining Laws Really Matter."

63. These data were sent to me by Saltzman personally—I thank him for that—and were taken from his doctoral dissertation, which was the basis for his subsequent articles. See Saltzman, "The Growth of Teacher Bargaining and the Enactment of Teacher Bargaining Laws."

64. Ohio and Illinois were politically odd cases, and neither got collective bargaining statutes until well after the other states did (in 1983, after which the percentage of

teachers covered by collective bargaining rose substantially). These cases are dealt with separately by Saltzman in "Public Sector Bargaining Laws Really Matter." For simplicity I have not included them here.

65. The pre-state-law figures for New York reflect the AFT victory in New York City, which was conducted under *local* rules that put electoral machinery for unionization in place. See, for example, Cole, *The Unionization of Teachers*; Braun, *Teachers and Power;* Selden, *The Teacher Rebellion;* Taft, *United They Teach.*

66. Here and throughout, the information on state collective bargaining laws is from the National Right to Work Legal Foundation, which I have found to be the most accurate source of comprehensive legal information on collective bargaining. The report is "Teacher Monopoly Bargaining, Compulsory Unionism, and Deduction Revocation Table," which was updated as of 2010.

67. This background was provided to me by the National Right to Work Legal Foundation. The key Arizona attorney general decision is AGO 74-11. For a key Arizona court decision on meet and confer, see *City of Phoenix* v. *Phoenix Employment Relations Board,* 145 Ariz. 92, 97-98 (Ariz. App. 1985). To read some actual agreements, go to the website of the National Council on Teacher Quality (www.nctq.org).

68. Lisa Fine Goldstein, "Collective Bargaining Gets New Life in New Mexico," *Education Week,* March 19, 2003.

Chapter Three

1. Julie Blair, "Miami Union Leader Pleads Guilty to Fraud," *Education Week*, September 3, 2003. "Tornillo Should Go," editorial, *St. Petersburg Times,* May 13, 2003; Joe Mozingo and Manny Garcia, "Union Paid Private Bills for Tornillo," *Miami Herald,* May 11, 2003.

2. Carol D. Leonnig, "Bullock Brazenly Recounts Embezzling," *Washington Post,* June 17, 2005.

3. Julie Blair, "D.C. Union Leader Admits to Bilking Funds," *Education Week*, October 15, 2003; Justin Blum, "Audit Says Union Lost $5 Million to Theft," *Washington Post*, January 17. 2003.

4. For a discussion of the constraints under which leaders operate and the incentives of leaders to make the organization's interests their own, see Miriam Golden, *Heroic Defeats: The Politics of Job Loss* (Cambridge University Press, 1996). Quote is from p. 18.

5. The literature on union democracy is very thin and uneven, and much of it is made up of work that was carried out from the mid-1950s through the 1980s, a time when there was much more scholarly interest in unions. For a recent discussion of this literature, an analysis of the internal organizational forces that give leaders incentives to be responsive to member interests, and a discussion of the long-standing debate about whether unions are oligarchic or democratic, see Margaret Levi, David Olson, Jon Agnone, and Devin Kelly, "Union Democracy Reexamined," *Politics and Society* 37, no. 2 (2009): 203–28. See also Julian Barling, Clive Fullager, and E. Kevin Kelloway, *The Union and Its Members: A Psychological Approach* (Oxford University Press, 1992); George Strauss, "What's Happening Inside U.S. Unions? Democracy and Union

424 NOTES TO PAGE 68

Politics," *Journal of Labor Research* 21, no. 2 (2000): 211–25; Samuel Estreicher, "Dereg-ulating Union Democracy," *Journal of Labor Research* 21, no. 2 (Spring 2000): 247–63; Richard B. Freeman and James L. Medoff, *What Do Unions Do?* (New York: Basic Books, 1984); and Samuel Estreicher, Harry C. Katz, and Bruce E. Kaufman, eds., *The Internal Governance and Organizational Effectiveness of Labor Unions: Essays in Honor of George Brooks* (New York: Kluwer International, 2001). My purpose here is not to develop a detailed theory of leadership or union democracy, nor is it to argue that unions are truly democratic. It is simply to introduce some basic—and, I think, fairly straightforward—ideas about how leaders are connected to, dependent upon, and constrained by their members. The implication is that we need to understand the membership if we are to understand what unions ultimately do in education and politics. The themes emphasized here might appear to depart from those developed in a book I wrote some thirty years ago, *The Organization of Interests* (University of Chicago Press, 1980). That book, how-ever, focused more narrowly on the decision to join (arising out of the logic of collective action) and its implications for the internal dynamics of groups, with little attention to the broader array of concerns that are brought into play here. Were it possible to go into depth about the various theoretical issues involved and to clarify and extend the elements of the earlier theory (with the broader concerns taken into account), the two perspectives would turn out to be similar. But that sort of exercise would take us far afield and distract from the more practical aims of this chapter.

6. Kathleen Kennedy Manzo, "Cincinnati Vote Obscures Pay Plan's Future," *Education Week*, April 25, 2001; Karla Scoon Reid, "Challenger Topples Chicago Teachers Union President," *Education Week*, June 6, 2001.

7. The survey was administered online between April 24 and May 20, 2003, to public school teachers who are part of the Harris Poll Online database. The survey was completed by 3,328 teachers. To correct for the self-selection biases that may result from using online polling, Harris researchers constructed "propensity scores" for weighting the data. In this case, the propensity scores were constructed by drawing an additional sample of 600 teachers who were administered a telephone survey for purposes of comparison to the online group. The final weights for the data also took into account standard demo-graphics for the population of U.S. public school teachers at the time: grade level taught, geographic region, district size, gender, age, and race or ethnicity. The target demograph-ics for the sample as a whole were based on data from the Schools and Staffing Survey (conducted by the National Center for Education Statistics) and the Bureau of Labor Statistics Occupation Survey. For details about the Harris approach to propensity scores, see George Terhanian, John Bremer, Renee Smith, and Randy Thomas, "Correcting Data from Online Surveys for the Effects of Nonrandom Selection and Nonrandom Assign-ment," Harris Interactive White Paper (New York: Harris Interactive, 2000); George Ter-hanian and John Bremer, "Confronting the Selection-Bias and Learning Effects Problems Associated with Internet Research," Harris Interactive White Paper (New York: Harris Interactive, August 16, 2000).

8. The unions themselves have carried out surveys of their members and asked probing questions, but these studies are not made available for public consumption. For surveys of teachers that are not specifically about unions, see, for example, a recent

study by the Gates Foundation of some 40,000 teachers: "Primary Sources: America's Teachers on America's Schools," a project of Scholastic and the Bill and Melinda Gates Foundation (www.scholastic.com/primarysources). See also "The Metlife Survey of the American Teacher: Collaborating for Student Success," carried out in 2009 and available on the MetLife website at www.metlife.com/assets/cao/contributions/foundation/ american-teacher/MetLife_ Teacher_Survey_2009.pdf. MetLife has conducted a series of such studies over the years. So has Phi Delta Kappa. The most recent of the Phi Delta Kappa teacher surveys, at this writing, is Carol A. Langdon and Nick Vesper, "The Sixth Phi Delta Kappa Poll of Teachers' Attitudes toward the Public Schools," *Phi Delta Kappan* 81, no. 8 (April 2000): 607–11. For Public Agenda surveys that include samples of teachers but don't focus on unions, see, for example, *Reality Check 2006, Issue No. 3: Is Support for Standards and Testing Fading?* (New York City: Public Agenda, 2006) and *A Sense of Calling: Who Teaches and Why* (New York City: Public Agenda, 2000). Some of Education Next's polls have also included samples of teachers. The most recent at this writing is William Howell, Paul E. Peterson, and Martin West, "Meeting of the Minds," *Education Next* 11, no. 1 (Winter 2011): 20–31.

9. See Steve Farkas, Jean Johnson, and Ann Duffett, with Leslie Moye and Jackie Vine, *Stand by Me: What Teachers Really Think about Unions, Merit Pay, and Other Professional Matters* (New York City: Public Agenda, 2003); Ann Duffett, Steve Farkas, Andrew J. Rotherham, and Elena Silva, *Waiting to Be Won Over: Teachers Speak on the Profession, Unions, and Reform* (Washington: Education Sector, 2008). Both of these are mail surveys with very low response rates. The Public Agenda survey had a response rate of 27 percent, with a final sample size of 1,345. The Education Sector survey had a response rate of 14 percent, with a final sample size of 1,010. It is unclear whether the findings they present are based on weighted data (with weights designed to ensure that their samples are representative).

10. The exact wording of the item is as follows: "Which of the following statements is more accurate about your membership in the teacher organization? (1) I belong because I really want to. (2) I belong because I feel I have to or feel pressure to."

11. The exact wording of the item is as follows: "Suppose you were free to make separate decisions about whether to join the local, state, or national teacher organization, and suppose that membership in each was purely voluntary. Would you (1) Voluntarily join and pay dues to the local organization? (2) Voluntarily join and pay dues to the state organization? (3) Voluntarily join and pay dues to the national organization?"

12. The lead-in wording is as follows: "When a district has collective bargaining, and when teachers are represented in collective bargaining by a particular union, which of the following approaches do you think is best?"

13. When a simple multivariate analysis is carried out, taking into account all the state-level and individual-level factors of the models discussed in appendix A, the differences shown in table 3-3 remain. Legal context and union membership continue to have big effects on attitudes toward coercion. An individual's party (or ideology) also makes a difference (the more Democrat or liberal, the more likely to favor coercive approaches), and, because teachers are much more Republican and conservative in the states without strong labor laws, culture does seem to play an important role here. Again, though, a

more detailed and sophisticated analysis is needed to pull the various factors apart, as the laws themselves are reflections of culture.

14. Duffett and others, *Waiting to Be Won Over*, p. 21. Their respondents were public school teachers generally, not just union members. The figures would doubtless be higher still if only union members were responding.

15. The lead-in wording is as follows: "Which of the following best describes why you are a member of your teacher organization?" The list of alternatives presented in the text is taken directly from the survey.

16. To the extent that members place great value on direct benefits, as I emphasize in *The Organization of Interests*, leaders are under less pressure to represent member interests in politics (and collective bargaining); if they don't, members will tend to remain in the group anyway. This is an "all else equal" statement about what will actually happen. It is important to recognize that these same members may *also* place high value on collective bargaining and politics, and they may react to unresponsive leaders through various kinds of disruptive behaviors that leaders want to avoid. At the extreme, these members might leave the group. But they also might refuse to cooperate with leader directives, refuse to provide support activities of various sorts, get active in opposition movements within the union, or simply vote the leaders out. Thus, while direct benefits—and, for that matter, forced membership—do help to lock certain members in and thus to give leaders more flexibility, there are still important forces at work that connect leaders to even those members who appear to be locked in.

17. As I and others have pointed out many times, there is no conflict between this finding and the logic of collective action. If people acted purely on the basis of their economic interest, they would usually not join (large) groups that seek to provide collective goods. But motivations are typically more complicated than that. For example, people often gain "expressive" benefits for supporting such causes—thinking, say, that it is only fair or right that they do their share to support a group that is working in their interest, and in the interests of people like them. When this happens, then it is quite rational for them to join in response to the kinds of collective goods that a group provides. Social norms—about cooperation, for example—can obviously have the same effect. The same result would follow if people felt that their contributions, in the form of dues, participation, or both had a consequential impact on outcomes. Political scientists have for years relied on this same basic logic to explain why people vote in democratic elections, even though the outcomes are collective goods and their own participation objectively makes no difference. The reality is that people get expressive benefits from voting (by fulfilling their civic duty, for example), respond to social norms about voting, and often feel that their vote "counts" and makes a difference. For discussions of these issues with regard to interest groups, see Moe, *The Organization of Interests*. With regard to voting, see David E. Campbell, *Why We Vote: How Schools and Communities Shape Our Civic Life* (Princeton University Press, 2006).

18. The teachers in this latter group may often be in districts that have meet-and-confer arrangements.

19. The Public Agenda survey also asked teachers about what union services they value most. The survey did not distinguish union members from nonmembers or districts that

do and do not have collective bargaining—all teachers, everywhere, were weighing in on the value of union services—so making sense of the findings is a bit difficult. Nonetheless, by far the greatest portion of teachers (47 percent) pointed to collective bargaining as the service they value most. When asked about the service they value least, by far the greatest portion (49 percent) pointed to politics. See Farkas, Johnson, and Duffett, *Stand by Me*, p. 49.

20. The question reads as follows: "In general, how satisfied are you with the teacher organization? Very satisfied, somewhat satisfied, somewhat dissatisfied, or very dissatisfied?" For this item and a few others throughout this chapter, the findings are straightforward, and I simplify the presentation by summarizing them rather than including additional tables or figures. The findings here are presented for union members in districts with collective bargaining, as I will later be exploring member satisfaction with collective bargaining and politics, as well as comparing the motivational salience of the two, and it is necessary to look at districts that provide both.

21. The wording is as follows: "How satisfied are you with how the teacher organization represents your interests in (1) Collective bargaining and (2) Politics?"

22. The dependent variable is overall satisfaction with the union, measured on a four-point scale. The independent variables are satisfaction with collective bargaining (a four-point scale), satisfaction with politics (a four-point scale), gender, age, nonwhite, elementary school, inner city, other urban, suburb, and small town. The estimated coefficient for the collective bargaining term is 0.53, compared to an estimate of 0.18 for the politics term. Both are significant at well beyond the 0.001 level. $N = 1,761$, adjusted R^2 = 0.38. Regression is used here, rather than ordered probit or logit, because the results are virtually identical and the coefficients are easier to report and interpret.

23. The dependent variable in each regression is the feeling thermometer for the relevant level of union organization (local, state, national), measured on a scale from 0 to 100. The independent variables are the same as those described in the previous note. In the local equation, the estimated coefficients for collective bargaining and politics are 16.6 and 3.6, respectively. (They are of a different magnitude than in the previous regression because the dependent variable has changed, and is measured from 0 to 100 rather than from 1 to 4). $N = 1,766$, adjusted R^2 = 0.49, and both coefficients are significant well beyond the 0.001 level. In the state equation, the coefficients for collective bargaining and politics are 7.7 and 10.4, respectively. $N = 1,766$, adjusted R^2 = 0.42, and both coefficients are significant well beyond the 0.001 level. In the national equation, the coefficients for collective bargaining and politics are 2.1 and 14.0, respectively. $N = 1,766$, adjusted R^2 = 0.32, and both coefficients are significant well beyond the 0.001 level.

24. Here the dependent variable is the same as in the first regression: overall satisfaction with the union, measured on a four-point scale. The independent variables are the separate local, state, and national feeling thermometers, each measured on a scale from 0 to 100, plus all the other control variables described earlier. The key estimated coefficients are 0.0185 on the local variable, 0.0039 on the state variable, and 0.0032 on the national variable. (Note that they are of a smaller order of magnitude than the coefficients in the other regressions only because the independent variables here are measured on a 0 to 100 scale, while the dependent variable goes from 1 to 4. The smaller

magnitudes are just a matter of scale and say nothing about their substantive significance. When the local thermometer, for example, shifts from one standard deviation below its mean to one standard deviation above, its impact on overall satisfaction with the union is 0.96 of a standard deviation, which is enormous.) $N = 2,057$, adjusted $R^2 = 0.35$, and the estimated coefficients are significant at the 0.001 level or beyond.

25. The lead-in wording is, "In your own judgment, how do you think collective bargaining affects public education? Does it seem to produce. . . ." The survey goes on to present teachers with alternatives for each of the dimensions mentioned in the text. Regarding professionalism, for example, the alternatives are "(1) Better academic performance, (2) Neither better nor lower academic performance, (3) Lower academic performance."

26. See their website at www.electionstudies.org.

27. Political scientists have long studied the impact of education, gender, and many other factors on political attitudes, party identification, and voting. See, for example, William H. Flanigan and Nancy H. Zingale, *Political Behavior of the American Electorate*, 12th ed. (Washington: CQ Press, 2009); Robert S. Erikson and Kent L. Tedin, *American Public Opinion: Its Origins, Content, and Impact*, 8th ed. (London: Longman, 2010); Virginia Sapiro and Shauna L. Shames, "The Gender Basis of Public Opinion," in *Understanding Public Opinion*, edited by Barbara Norrander and Clyde Wilcox (Washington: CQ Press, 2010).

28. Because virtually all teachers are older than twenty-five and younger than seventy, I have structured the comparison by including only those NES respondents who are between these ages.

29. In the voting data, only the NES 2000 data set is used, and thus the relevant figures in the table are based on a smaller number of respondents than the figures for party identification and ideology. The pattern is quite consistent with the others, however, so there does not appear to be problem.

30. See, for example, Michael Kramer, *Organizational Socialization: Joining and Leaving Organizations* (Cambridge, U.K.: Polity, 2010); David G. Allen, "Do Organizational Socialization Tactics Influence Newcomer Embeddedness and Turnover?" *Journal of Management* 32, no. 2 (April 2006): 237–56; Clive Fullagar, Don McCoy, and Carla Shull, "The Socialization of Union Loyalty," *Journal of Organizational Behavior* 13, no 1 (January 1992): 13–26; Gareth R. Jones, "Socialization Tactics, Self-Efficacy, and Newcomers' Adjustments to Organizations," *Academy of Management Journal* 29, no. 2 (June 1986): 262–79; Meryl Reis Louis, "Surprise and Sense Making: What Newcomers Experience in Entering Unfamiliar Organizational Settings," *Administrative Science Quarterly* 25, no. 2 (June 1980): 226–51.

31. Here, as earlier, I simply summarize the findings on satisfaction rather than presenting new tables. Findings are for union members in districts with collective bargaining.

32. Albert O. Hirschman, *Exit, Voice, and Loyalty: Responses to Decline in Firms, Organizations, and States* (Harvard University Press, 1970).

33. See, for example, Steven Rhoads, *The Economist's View of the World: Government, Markets, and Public Policy* (Cambridge University Press, 1985); Hans Thorelli and Jack Engledow, "Information Seekers and Information Systems: A Policy Perspective," *Journal of Marketing* 44 (Spring 1980): 9–27; Lawrence F. Feick and Linda L. Price, "The

Market Maven: A Diffuser of Marketplace Information," *Journal of Marketing* 51 (January 1987): 83–97; Mark E. Slama and Terrell G. Williams, "Generalization of the Market Maven's Information Provision Tendency across Product Categories," *Advances in Consumer Research* 17 (1990): 48–52. For a discussion in the context of education, see Mark Schneider, Paul Teske, and Melissa Marschall, *Choosing Schools: Consumer Choice and the Quality of American Schools* (Princeton University Press, 2000).

34. Again, I summarize the findings rather than adding a new table. The data are for union members in districts with collective bargaining.

35. See, for example, Barling, Fullagar, and Kelloway, *The Union and Its Members*; Daniel G. Gallagher and George Strauss, "Union Membership Attitudes and Participation," in *The State of the Unions,* edited by George Strauss, Daniel G. Gallagher, and Jack Fiorito (Madison, Wis.: Industrial Relations Research Association, 1991).

36. The literature gets at this in various ways. For one example, see David Knoke, "Commitment and Detachment in Voluntary Associations," *American Sociological Review* 46, no. 2 (April 1981): 141–58.

37. The wording is as follows: "How would you describe your role as a member of the teacher organization?" The alternatives are not at all active, not very active, active, very active.

38. Again, see Barling, Fullagar, and Kelloway, *The Union and Its Members.*

39. Again, I summarize the results here without adding a new table. The data are for union members in districts with collective bargaining.

40. The wording is as follows: "Have you engaged in any of the following campaign activities to support the organization's political efforts?"

41. Again, I describe the findings here rather than adding a new table.

42. See, for example, David Hill, *American Voter Turnout: An Institutional Perspective* (Boulder, Colo.: Westview Press, 2006); M. Margaret Conway, *Political Participation in the United States*, 3d ed. (Washington: CQ Press, 1999); Sidney Verba and Norman H. Nie, *Political Participation: Political Democracy and Social Equality* (University of Chicago Press, 1987).

43. See, for example, Amos Tversky and Daniel Kahneman, "The Framing of Decisions and the Psychology of Choice," *Science* 211, no. 4481 (1981): 453–58; Edgar H. Schein, *Organizational Culture and Leadership*, 3d ed. (San Francisco: Jossey-Bass, 2004), pp. 225–72.

44. These issues are taken from different survey items. One item asks, "What is your position on the following issues?" The subsequent list of issues includes the right of teachers to strike, private school vouchers for disadvantaged kids, and charter schools. The other issues are measured as follows. Tenure: "Do you think the policy of teacher tenure should be eliminated?" Taxes: "Do you think taxes should be raised so that more money can be spent on the public schools?" Teacher accountability: "Do you think individual teachers should be held accountable for how much their own students learn during the school year?" Testing: "Do you think standardized testing is a good way to measure how much students are learning in school?"

45. The figures in this table are based on teachers who took positions on the issues, and exclude those (usually few in number) who said, "don't know." There has been no

consistent polling over the years on how the American public feels about teacher strikes, but it appears that most Americans are very much opposed. A 1981 Phi Delta Kappa/ Gallup poll showed that 56 percent of Americans opposed the right of teachers to strike, 37 percent supported it, and 7 percent were unsure. By contrast, teachers surveyed in 1984 and 1989 (with union members and nonmembers grouped together) were overwhelmingly in support of the right to strike by more than two to one. For a review of these early surveys, see Stanley Elam, "The Second Gallup/Phi Delta Kappa Poll of Teachers' Attitudes toward the Public Schools," *Phi Delta Kappan* 70, no. 10 (June 1989): 785–98.

46. See Farkas, Johnson, and Duffett, *Stand by Me*; Duffett and others, *Waiting to Be Won Over*.

47. The American public is not very knowledgeable about tenure laws, and it appears that roughly half the citizenry is unclear about what tenure is and what it means for teacher employment. See the survey by the Gallup Organization, August 8–August 11, 2005, retrieved from the iPoll Databank, University of Connecticut, Roper Center for Public Opinion Research (www.ropercenter.uconn.edu/ipoll.html). When they are provided with more detailed information about what tenure means, however, Americans tend to be against it. A 2009 Phi Delta Kappa/Gallup survey, for instance, asked, "Most public school teachers have tenure; that is, after a two- or three-year period, they receive what amounts to a lifetime contract. Do you approve or disapprove of this policy?" 73 percent of Americans said they disapprove. See William J. Bushaw and John A McNee, "Americans Speak Out: Are Educators and Policy Makers Listening? The 41st Annual Phi Delta Kappa/Gallup Poll of the Public's Attitudes toward the Public Schools," *Phi Delta Kappan* 91, no. 1 (September 2009): 9–23. In a 2010 Education Next poll, Americans were provided with a brief definition of tenure, brief arguments pro and con, and asked what they think: 25 percent said they favor tenure for teachers, 47 percent said they oppose it, and 29 percent said they are neutral (another indication of their lack of familiarity with the issue). See Howell, Peterson, and West, "Meeting of the Minds." Earlier polls that ask Americans whether they favor changes in tenure laws that would make it easier to terminate teachers yielded overwhelmingly positive responses, in the 80 percent support range. See, for example, the survey by Zogby International, December 1998, retrieved from the iPoll Databank, University of Connecticut, Roper Center for Public Opinion Research (www.ropercenter.uconn.edu/ipoll.html).

48. Americans on the whole tend to give positive responses to survey items asking whether they would be willing to pay extra taxes to support the public schools, but the data aren't very good or convincing because they don't give people a sense of trade-offs. They appear to be responding in ways that indicate that they like the schools, want to support them, and want to see them improve. In a 2010 Education Next poll, for example, 63 percent of Americans said they think funding for the local public schools should be increased, but when they were asked about taxes, only 29 percent said taxes should be increased. See Howell, Peterson, and West, "Meeting of the Minds." To take another example, in a 2000 Gallup poll 67 percent of the public said that they would be willing to pay higher taxes "in order to improve the quality of education in [their] local school district"—which essentially offers them a pie-in-the-sky trade that isn't at all

real or practical—but in that same survey, people were asked whether the taxes they pay for the local schools are too high, too low, or about right, and only 9 percent said they are too low; 58 percent thought they are about right, and 26 percent thought they are too high. This poll was conducted by the Gallup Organization, August 24–August 27, 2000, and retrieved from the iPoll Databank, University of Connecticut, Roper Center for Public Opinion Research (www.ropercenter.uconn.edu/ipoll.html). See also, for example, "2003 Survey of Public Opinion: Demanding Quality Public Education in Tough Economic Times; What Voters Want from Elected Leaders" (Washington: Public Education Network and Education Week, 2003), available at www.publiceducation.org/pdf/Publications/national_poll/2003_poll_report.pdf.

49. Americans are not well informed about vouchers, and their responses to survey items can vary considerably depending on the precise wording of the items. If the items indicate that vouchers are available to all parents, including parents of *public* school children, and give them a *choice* of schools with government paying any tuition, then most Americans—especially black and Hispanic parents (by huge margins)—tend to be favorable. If the items make it appear that vouchers are for the parents of private school kids, and say they are being provided "at public expense"—a pejorative way of mentioning government assistance—then most Americans tend to be opposed. For a discussion of these issues, see Terry M. Moe, *Schools, Vouchers, and the American Public* (Brookings, 2001); Terry M. Moe, "Cooking the Questions?" *Education Next* 2, no. 1 (Spring 2002): 71–77; Terry M. Moe, "Dodging the Questions," *Education Next* 2, no. 3 (Fall 2002): 77–81; Howell, Peterson, and West, "Meeting of the Minds"; William G. Howell, Paul E. Peterson, and Martin West, "The Persuadable Public," *Education Next* 9, no. 4 (Fall 2009): 20–29.

50. See chapter 8.

51. Americans have long been poorly informed about charter schools, but in recent years, as charters have increased substantially in number, people seem to have become much more familiar with them. The Phi Delta Kappa/Gallup polls have regularly asked a survey item that defines charter schools in terms of their freedom from regulation, but does not mention that their purpose is to provide parents with additional choices. The findings on this item show that Americans were rather evenly split on (this definition of) charter schools during the early 2000s, but have become much more positive over time, and in 2010 gave charters their endorsement by a margin of 68 to 28 percent. See William J. Bushaw and Shane J. Lopez, "A Time for Change: the 42nd Annual Phi Delta Kappa/Gallup Poll of the Public's Attitudes toward the Public Schools," available at www.pdkintl.org/kappan/docs/2010_Poll_Report.pdf. Recent polls by Education Next (whose question wording also fails to mention choice) find big margins in favor of charters as well. See Howell, Peterson, and West, "Meeting of the Minds"; Howell, Peterson, and West, "The Persuadable Public." Although the positive trend over the past decade is surely accurate, the early findings are probably an artifact (to some extent) of question wording. A survey conducted by the Center for Education Reform in those early years, for instance, told respondents that charters "are freed from regulations except health and safety and discrimination and are open to parents by choice." In their 1997

poll, 55 percent of the public responded favorably to charter schools based on that item, with just 33 percent opposed. See Center for Education Reform, "1997 National Survey of Americans' Attitudes toward Education," press release, Center for Education Reform, September 23, 1997 (www.edreform.com/Resources/Polls_Surveys/?National_Survey_ Of_Americans_Attitudes_ Toward_Education). The general point to be made, however, is that Americans are much more favorable toward charter schools than teachers are.

52. Farkas, Johnson, and Duffett, *Stand by Me*, p. 41.

53. See the extended discussion and references in chapter 7.

54. Where Americans stand with regard to teacher accountability depends, as with other issues, on how the items are worded. This particular issue is almost always polled, if at all, with reference to teacher salaries (rather than accountability more generally), and whether salaries should be tied to student performance—almost always test scores. From these surveys, however, it seems clear that Americans do think teachers should be held accountable for how much their students learn. The 2010 Phi Delta/Gallup survey asked Americans, "How do you, yourself, feel about the idea of merit pay for teachers?" Merit pay was favored by a margin 72 to 21 percent. In 2009 the Phi Delta Kappa/Gallup survey asked, "Should each teacher be paid on the basis of the quality of his or her work, or should all teachers be paid on a standard-scale basis?" And Americans favored merit over the standard scale by 71 to 27 percent. For the 2010 survey, see Bushaw and Lopez, "A Time for Change." For the 2009 survey, see Bushaw and McNee, "The 41st Annual Phi Delta Kappa/Gallup Poll of the Public's Attitudes toward the Public Schools." The general point to be emphasized here is simply that Americans tend to think that teachers should be held accountable for how much their students learn, and teachers, especially unionized teachers, don't.

55. As a result of the pressures generated by Race to the Top, the unions have made some accommodations on this score and agreed to accept new forms of evaluation that rely (in part) on student test scores. They have done this for strategic reasons—because they had to, essentially, given the political power and expectations lined up against them—and not because they believe it is good policy or in the best interests of teachers. As a result of Race to the Top, the more egregious laws prohibiting the use of student data in evaluating teachers have been overturned. I review these developments in some depth in chapter 10—but they do not indicate that the unions have somehow changed their underlying views.

56. Americans have long been believers in using standardized tests to measure what students know. When asked about whether the government should or should not systematically test students for accountability purposes, Americans favor testing by huge margins. See Howell, Peterson, and West, "Meeting of the Minds." They also believe that, if there were a merit pay system for teachers, teacher pay should be based in part on student test scores. In the 2009 Phi Delta Kappa/Gallup poll, for example, respondents were asked whether merit pay should be based in part on student test scores, and 73 percent agreed. Just 26 percent disagreed. See Bushaw and McNee, "Americans Speak Out," from 2009. For additional evidence, see Howell, Peterson, and West, "Meeting of the Minds": Howell, Peterson, and West, "The Persuadable Public"; Lowell C. Rose and Alex M. Gallup, "The 37th Annual Phi Delta Kappa/Gallup Poll of the Public's

Attitudes toward the Public Schools," *Phi Delta Kappan* 87, no. 1 (September 2005): 41–57; and Jean Johnson and Ann Duffett, "An Assessment of Survey Data on Attitudes about Teaching, Including the Views of Parents, Administrators, Teachers, and the General Public" (Washington: Public Agenda, 2004). It is true that Americans do express worries about over-testing and "teaching to the test," and the numbers vary depending on how the survey is worded. In Gallup's surveys, about 60 percent of Americans said that the amount of testing is either "not enough" or "about right." See, for example, Bushaw and McNee, "Americans Speak Out"; Lowell C. Rose and Alex M. Gallup, "The 36th Annual Phi Delta Kappa/Gallup Poll of the Public's Attitudes toward the Public Schools," *Phi Delta Kappan* 86, no. 1 (September 2004): 41–56.

57. For other studies showing the same, see, for example, Farkas, Johnson, and Duffett, *Stand by Me*; and Duffett, Farkas, Rotherham, and Silva, *Waiting to Be Won Over*.

58. Farkas, Johnson, and Duffett, *Stand by Me*, pp. 54–57.

59. Bill Turque, "Washington Teachers Union President George Parker Loses Run-Off Election," *Washington Post*, November 30, 2010.

60. For perspectives on Teach for America and the unions, see, for example, Steven Brill, "The Teachers Unions' Last Stand," *New York Times Magazine*, May 17, 2010; Dana Goldstein, "Grading 'Waiting for Superman'," *The Nation*, September 23, 2010; (no author) "Teach for (Some of) America," *Wall Street Journal*, April 25, 2009; Evan Thomas and Pat Wingert, "Why We Must Fire Bad Teachers," *Newsweek*, March 6, 2010.

61. See, for example, Ashley Keigher and Freddie Cross, "Teacher Attrition and Mobility: Results from the 2008–09 Teacher Follow-up Survey, First Look" (Washington: National Center for Education Statistics, August 2010); Michael T. Luekens, Deanna M. Lyter, Erin E. Fox, and Kathryn Chandler, "Teacher Attrition and Mobility: Results from the Teacher Follow-up Survey, 2000–2001" (Washington: National Center for Education Statistics, August 2004); also Eric A. Hanushek, John F. Kain, and Steve G. Rivkin, "Why Public Schools Lose Teachers," *Journal of Human Resources* 39, no. 2 (2004): 326–54.

62. Information on the placements of Teach for America recruits in classroom jobs is available on the TFA website at www.teachforamerica.org/about-us/our-history/.

Chapter Four

1. More accurately, it usually takes place between unions and administrators hired by the board. However, because board members are the authorities and ultimately responsible for whatever bargain is struck, I frame the discussion as though the board itself is doing the bargaining.

2. On the general problem of public employees being in a position to elect the public officials who are their bosses, with special application to education, see Terry M. Moe, "Political Control and the Power of the Agent," *Journal of Law, Economics, and Organization* 22, no. 1 (Spring 2006): 1–29.

3. This document is available on the website of MEA Exposed at www.meaexposed.org/documents/SchoolBrdElectManual07.pdf.

4. Again, for an expansive discussion of this democratic dilemma, see Moe, "Political Control and the Power of the Agent."

5. For information on the powers and characteristics of school boards, see, for example, Frederick Hess, "School Boards at the Dawn of the 21st Century" (Alexandria, Va.: National School Boards Association, 2002);William G. Howell, ed., *Beseiged: School Boards and the Future of Education Politics* (Brookings, 2005); Frederick M. Wirt and Michael W. Kirst, *The Political Dynamics of American Education,* 2d ed. (Berkeley: McCutchin, 2006); and Thomas Sergiovanni, Paul Kelleher, Martha M. McCarthy, and Frances C. Fowler, *Educational Governance and Administration,* 6th ed. (Boston: Allyn and Bacon, 2008).

6. See William J. Bushaw and Alec M. Gallup, "Americans Speak Out: Are Educators and Policy Makers Listening? The 40th Annual Phi Delta Kappa/Gallup Poll of the Public's Attitudes toward the Public Schools," *Phi Delta Kappan* 90, no. 1 (September 2008): 9–20. I should add, however, that the advantage of localism has been slowly declining year by year, presumably because power and therefore expectations are shifting increasingly to the state and even national levels on public education.

7. See Wirt and Kirst, *The Political Dynamics of American Education*; Howell, *Beseiged*; and Michael B. Berkman and Eric Plutzer, *Ten Thousand Democracies: Politics and Public Opinion in America's School Districts* (Georgetown University Press, 2005). On the larger theme of democracy and the schools, see, for example, Amy Gutman, *Democratic Education* (Princeton University Press, 1999); Lorraine M. McDonnell, T. Michael Timpane, and Roger Benjamin, eds., *Rediscovering the Democratic Purposes of Public Education* (University of Kansas Press, 2000); and Michael W. Apple and James A. Beane, *Democratic Schools: Lessons in Powerful Education,* 2d ed. (Heinemann, 2007). On school boards and local democracy more generally, see, for example, Howell, ed., *Beseiged*; Sergiovanni and others, *Educational Governance and Administration*; Wirt and Kirst, *The Political Dynamics of American Education.*

8. See, for example, David Tyack, *The One Best System: The History of American Urban Education* (Harvard University Press, 1974); Paul E. Peterson, *The Politics of School Reform,* 1870–1940 (University of Chicago Press, 1985).

9. See especially Howell, *Beseiged*; Wirt and Kirst, *The Political Dynamics of American Education*; Hess, "School Boards at the Dawn of the 21st Century"; Berkman and Plutzer, *Ten Thousand Democracies.*

10. Sarah F. Anzia, "Election Timing and the Electoral Influence of Interest Groups," *Journal of Politics* (forthcoming 2011); Sarah F. Anzia, "The Election Timing Effect: Evidence From a Natural Experiment in Texas," Working Paper (Stanford University, Department of Political Science, 2010); Christopher R. Berry and Jacob E. Gerson, "Voters, Non-Voters, and the Implications for Election Timing for Public Policy," Working Paper (University of Chicago, 2010).

11. American Federation of Teachers, "Indiana Local's Political Action Pays Off in School Board Election," *American Teacher* (May-June, 2006): 6.

12. "Mayor to Back Bid to Control School Board," Associated Press State and Local Wire, September 12, 1998.

13. Rick Orlov, "Fed-Up Mayor Takes Fight to School Board," *Daily News of Los Angeles,* October 20, 1998.

14. One of the incumbents went over to the Riordan side and became part of its slate. See Kerry A. White, "LA Mayor Has Key Role in Board Race," *Education Week*, April 7, 1999.

15. "Mayor to Back Bid to Control School Board."

16. Kerry A. White, "Candidates Backed by Riordan Win in LA Board Races," *Education Week*, April 21, 1999. Also White, "LA Mayor Has Key Role in Board Race."

17. For an intensive study of Bersin's struggle with the unions over education reform, see Frederick Hess, ed., *Urban School Reform: Lessons from San Diego* (Harvard Education Press, 2005). Quote is from Hess's "Introduction," p. 1. See also Micah Sachs, "The Hardest Job in America," *San Diego Jewish Journal* (September 2003).

18. See Joe Williams, "The Labor-Management Showdown," in *Urban School Reform*, edited by Hess.

19. Cara Mia DiMassa, Duke Helfand, and Erika Hayasaki, "Trustee Tokofsky Reelected; With Korenstein Staying after Council Defeat, a Board Majority Is Allied with the Teachers Union," *Los Angeles Times*, May 21, 2003.

20. See, for example, Jeff Archer, "Early Bersin Exit Further Clouds San Diego Plans," *Education Week*, February 9, 2005.

21. See Lesli A. Maxwell, "Mayor's Candidates Win Board Seats in L.A.," *Education Week*, May 23, 2007; Howard Blume, "Two Union Candidates Win L.A. School Board Races," *Los Angeles Times*, March 4, 2009 (note that these victories still left Villaraigosa with a majority on the board); Patrick J. McDonnell and David Zahniser, "Villaraigosa Takes on Teachers Union," *Los Angeles Times*, December 10, 2010.

22. See McDonnell and Zahniser, "Villaraigosa Takes on Teachers Union"; also "Editorial: Ally of Teachers Sends Union a Strong Message," *Sacramento Bee*, December 9, 2010.

23. On minority groups, employment, and school politics, see, for example, Jeffrey R. Henig, Richard C. Hula, Marion Orr, and Desiree S. Pedescleaux, *The Color of School Reform: Race, Politics, and the Challenge of Urban Education* (Princeton University Press, 1999); Marion Orr, *Black Social Capital: The Politics of School Reform in Baltimore, 1986–1998* (University of Kansas Press, 1999).

24. For studies of mayoral control of the schools, see Jeffrey R. Henig and Wilbur C. Rich, eds., *Mayors in the Middle: Politics, Race, and Mayoral Control of Urban Schools* (Princeton University Press, 2004); Joseph P. Viteritti, ed., *When Mayors Take Charge: School Governance in the City* (Brookings, 2009); Kenneth K. Wong, Francis X. Shen, Dorothea Anagnostopoulos, and Stacey Rutledge, *The Education Mayor: Improving America's Schools* (Georgetown University Press, 2007).

25. This study is published. See Terry M. Moe, "Teachers Unions and School Board Elections," in *Beseiged*, edited by Howell.

26. There are often multiple candidates per district, and different candidates may have different views of how the local union is participating in politics. There are various ways these candidate responses might be aggregated to give a single measure for each district. To keep things simple, I have chosen to go with a majority-rule type of approach. Candidate responses for any given dimension of union activity are assigned a 1 for yes, a 0 for no, and averaged within each district. Districts are then coded as having that type of union activity

if their average is greater than 0.5, and they are categorized as not having it if their average is less than 0.5. For a relatively small number of districts, the average is exactly 0.5, and they can't be placed into one of these categories. They are labeled as "mixed."

27. The figures were calculated by first finding the median amount of money raised by the relevant set of candidates within each district and then taking the median of the district medians. As a method of aggregation, medians are more meaningful than averages in this case because a few candidates raised huge sums of money, and these outliers create averages that are sometimes misleading. Medians provide a better sense of what is typical.

28. To simplify things, I present these survey results without adding another table.

29. Charlene Haar, *The Politics of the PTA* (Transaction Publishers, 2002).

30. As mentioned earlier, these figures may tend to overstate the competitiveness of local elections, especially for smaller districts, because the sample is drawn entirely from the population of districts that actually held elections.

31. It is easy to think of particular cases in which business has played a huge role in school board politics. In both Los Angeles and San Diego, for example, the business community has been very active in promoting reform and taking on the unions, and similar examples can be found in other states. But these high-profile cases seem to be the exception rather than the rule.

32. For simplicity, I describe the findings here without presenting the data in a separate table.

33. The party registration data for each school district were gathered from county election offices. I score districts as Republican if at least 55 percent of the voters who register with one of the two major parties are Republican, Democrat if at least 55 percent are Democrat, and mixed-partisan if the party balance is somewhere in-between.

34. These dimensions are the same ones that appeared on the teacher survey in chapter 3. The lead-in wording is different, however. In the teacher survey, teachers were asked how collective bargaining affects public education. Here, candidates were asked, "When teachers unions do have influence, what do you consider the most likely effects on public education?"—followed by the same choice alternatives.

35. See, for example, Stephen Ansolabehere and James M. Snyder, "The Incumbency Advantage in U.S. Elections: An Analysis of State and Federal Offices, 1942–2000," *Election Law Journal: Rules, Politics, and Policy* 1, no. 3 (September 2002): 315–38; Gary C. Jacobson, *The Politics of Congressional Elections* (New York: Longman, 2009).

36. This study is published. See Terry M. Moe, "Political Control and the Power of the Agent," *Journal of Law, Economics, and Organization* 22, no. 1 (Spring 2006): 1–29.

37. I also have data for certain school elections held at the same time as the general elections, and the same general patterns emerge, but they are inevitably less dramatic, as the overall turnout among the general population is much higher.

38. For the details, district by district, see Moe, "Political Control and the Power of the Agent."

39. This is not the same as comparing the district medians that are set out in the figures. I am making a more finely grained comparison here. See Moe, "Political Control and the Power of the Agent" for a more detailed presentation of the data.

40. For the details of methodology, findings, and analysis, see Moe, "Political Control and the Power of the Agent."

41. There are plenty of news accounts of how politically active the unions often are in school districts that don't have collective bargaining. See, for example, Ericka Mellon, "Stipeche Wins HISD School Board Runoff," *Houston Chronicle*, December 1, 2010; "Locals Celebrate School Board Wins," on the website of the Texas State Teachers Association, available at www.tsta.org, with details at www.tsta.org/inside/locals/index.shtml); Lauren Roth, "Labor Groups Favor Virginia Beach Incumbents," *Virginia-Pilot*, September 11, 2008; "Chopra on the Chopping Block" (Goldwater Institute, February 12, 2007), available at www.freerepublic.com/focus/fnews/1783450/posts; Keung Hui, "Wake Teachers Announce School Board Endorsements," *News and Observer*, August 20, 2009, available at blogs.newsobserver.com/wakeed/wake-teachers-announce-school-board-endorsements.

Chapter Five

1. Again, I center my discussion here and throughout on school districts that have collective bargaining because it is the national norm. But I should point out that the issues I deal with in this chapter on teacher compensation are just as relevant for understanding schooling and labor relations in the southern and border-state districts that don't have collective bargaining. In these districts, decisions about teacher compensation are essentially policy decisions made by school boards (and sometimes and in some respects by state legislatures)—and the unions try to influence them through electoral politics and lobbying rather than through collective bargaining. The arguments that they make to bolster their case, however, are exactly the same: that teachers are underpaid, that more money needs to be spent on across-the-board raises for all teachers, and so on.

2. "Inflation Outpaces Teacher Pay, Study Finds" (Madison, Wis.: Wisconsin Education Association Council, November 16, 2006), available at www.weac.org/News_and_Publications/education_news/2006-2007/randing_inflation.aspx.

3. Linda Jacobson, "Teacher Salary Gains Tempered by Health-Benefit Costs, Says AFT," *Education Week*, 23, no. 42 (July 15, 2004).

4. Lowell C. Rose and Alec M. Gallup, "The 35th Annual Phi Delta Kappa/Gallup Poll of the Public's Attitudes toward the Public Schools," *Phi Delta Kappan* 85, no.1 (September 2003): 45–56.

5. William G. Howell, Paul E. Peterson, and Martin R. West, "Meeting of the Minds," *Education Next* 11, no. 1 (Winter 2011): 20–31.

6. Tony Foleno, Jean Johnson, and Steve Farkas, *A Sense of Calling: Who Teaches and Why* (New York: Public Agenda Association, 2000).

7. Findings from the General Social Survey can be calculated from data available on the survey's website. I have used "Data Anaysis Using SDA," which can be accessed at www.norc.uchicago.edu/GSS+Website/.

8. Rose and Gallup," "The 35th Annual Phi Delta Kappa/Gallup Poll of the Public's Attitudes toward the Public Schools."

9. William G. Howell and Martin R. West, "Is the Price Right?" *Education Next* (Summer 2008): 37–41.

10. Howell and West, "Is the Price Right?" p. 39.

11. For follow-up data and analysis, see William G. Howell, Paul E. Peterson, and Martin R. West, "The Persuadable Public," *Education Next* 9, no. 4 (Fall 2009): 20–29; Howell, Peterson, and West, "Meeting of the Minds."

12. That this strategy is rational for unions has long been recognized. See, for example, James N. Brown and Orley Ashenfelter, "Testing the Efficiency of Employment Contracts," *Journal of Political Economy* 94, no. 3 (1986): S40–S87.

13. Figures for 1955 and the 1970s and 1980s are taken from NCES, *Digest of Education Statistics* (Washington: NCES, various years). The teacher-student ratio for 2007–08 was calculated from the NCES's 2007–08 Schools and Staffing data set. At this writing, the latest teacher-student ratio figure from the *Digest of Education Statistics* (2009) was 15.5 for 2007.

14. Michael Podgursky, "Teacher Compensation and Collective Bargaining," in *Handbook of the Economics of Education*, edited by Eric Hanushek and Ludger Woessman (Amsterdam: Elsevier, forthcoming).

15. The 35 percent figure comes from "State Expenditure Report" (Washington: National Association of State Budget Officers, 2009), available at www.nasbo.org/Publications/StateExpenditureReport/tabid/79/Default.aspx.

16. Adam Schaeffer, "They Spend *What?* The Real Cost of Public Schools," Policy Analysis 662 (Washington: Cato Institute, March 10, 2010).

17. For a review of these studies, see Andrew J. Coulson, "The Effects of Teachers Unions on American Education," *Cato Journal* 30, no. 1 (Winter 2010): 155–70; also Joe A. Stone, "Collective Bargaining and Public Schools," in *Conflicting Missions: Teachers Unions and Education Reform*, edited by Tom Loveless (Brookings, 2000).

18. Caroline Hoxby, "How Teachers Unions Affect Education Production," *Quarterly Journal of Economics* 111, no. 3 (1996): 671–718. A more recent study, based on data from three midwestern states (Hoxby's study was based on a national sample), finds no union impact on salaries at all. See Michael F. Lovenheim, "The Effect of Teachers Unions on Education Production: Evidence from Union Election Certifications in Three Midwestern States" (Stanford University, December 2007). Another study, which looks at rural districts in Pennsylvania, finds a union impact of 7.6 percent. See Robert Lemke, "Estimating the Union Wage Effect for Public School Teachers When All Teachers Are Unionized," *Eastern Economic Journal* 30, no. 2 (2004): 273–91.

19. Jennifer D. Jordan, "Health Care: What Teachers Pay Is All over the Board," *Providence Journal*, August 27, 2007.

20. For a brief overview of the retiree health benefit situation for the public sector generally, see Government Accountability Office, "State and Local Government Retiree Benefits: Current Status of Benefit Structures, Protections, and Fiscal Outlook for Funding Future Costs," report to the Committee on Finance, U.S. Senate, November 15, 2007, available at www.gao.gov/new.items/d071156.pdf.

21. For an overview of sick leave policies in the public sector, which are similar to those specific to public education, see Employee Benefit Research Institute, "Leave

Programs in the Public Sector," in *Fundamentals of Employee Benefit Programs: Part 5, Public Sector,* ch. 45 (Washington: Employee Benefit Research Institute, 2005).

22. On the political logic of teacher pensions and the budget troubles it has led to, see Frederick M. Hess and Juliet P. Squire, "But the Pension Fund Was Just Sitting There . . .: The Politics of Teacher Retirement Plans," Working Paper 2009-04 (Washington: American Enterprise Institute, 2009).

23. See "Analysis of the 2005-06 Budget Bill: School District Financial Condition" (California Legislative Analyst's Office, February 2005), available at www.lao.ca.gov/analysis_2005/education/ed_06_school_district_financial_condition_anl05.htm. Also Greg Toppo, "School Systems Face Health Care Squeeze," *USA Today,* February 6, 2006. On GASB 45 and its effect on state and local governments more generally, see David Zion and Amit Varshney, "You Dropped a Bomb on Me, GASB: Uncovering $1.5 Trillion in Hidden OPEB Liabilities for State and Local Governments" (Credit Suisse, Americas/United States Equity Research Accounting and Tax, March 2007), available at online.wsj.com/public/resources/documents/DroppedB.pdf; Katherine Barrett and Richard Greene, "Promises with a Price: Public Sector Retirement Benefits" (Washington: Pew Center on the States, December 18, 2007), available at www.pewtrusts.org/our_work_report_detail.aspx?id=32390; Milt Freudenheim and Mary Williams Walsh, "The Next Retirement Time Bomb," *New York Times,* December 11, 2005.

24. Government Accounting Office, "State and Local Government Retiree Health Benefits: Liabilities Are Largely Unfunded, but Some Governments Are Taking Action," (Washington: GAO, November 2009), available at www.gao.gov/new.items/d1061.pdf.

25. Pew Center on the States, "The Trillion Dollar Gap: Underfunded State Retirement Systems and the Roads to Reform" (Washington: Pew Center on the States, February 2010), available at downloads.pewcenteronthestates.org/ The_Trillion_Dollar_Gap_final.pdf. See also Pew Center on the States, "Promises with a Price: Public Sector Retirement Benefits" (Washington: Pew Center on the States, December 2007), available at www.pewcenteronthestates.org/uploadedfiles/Promises with a Price.pdf.

26. Government Accounting Office, "State and Local Government Retiree Health Benefits."

27. The Census Bureau's 2009 survey of governments shows local full-time-equivalent employment to be 12.2 million and state full-time-equivalent employment to be 4.3 million. For employment data on state and local governments, see the Census Bureau's website at www.census.gov/govs/apes/.

28. Chris Edwards and Jagadeesh Gokhale, "Unfunded State and Local Health Costs: $1.4 Trillion," Tax and Budget Bulletin 40 (Washington: Cato Institute, October 2006).

29. Pew Center on the States, "The Trillion Dollar Gap."

30. Josh Barro and Stuart Buck, "Underfunded Teacher Pension Plans: It's Worse Than You Think," Civic Report 61 (New York: Manhattan Institute, April 2010).

31. See "Analysis of the 2005–06 Budget Bill"; Also Toppo, "School Systems Face Health Care Squeeze." On GASB 45 and its effect on state and local governments more generally, see Zion and Varshney, "You Dropped a Bomb on Me"; Barrett and Greene, "Promises with a Price"; Freudenheim and Walsh, "The Next Retirement Time Bomb."

32. From National Education Association, "Rankings and Estimates: Rankings of the States 2008 and Estimates of School Statistics 2009," NEA Research Report (Washington: NEA, December 2008), p. 78.

33. Michael Podgursky and Rattaya Tongrut, "(Mis-) Measuring the Relative Pay of Public School Teachers," *Education Finance and Policy* 1, no. 4 (2006): 425–40. Data from p. 437.

34. See, for example, the debate in National Council on Teacher Quality, "NCTQ Square-Off: Are Teachers Underpaid?" (Washington: NCTQ, July 2005), available at www.nctq.org/p/publications/docs/nctq_square_off_20071202080402.pdf.

35. Calculations from the 2007–08 Schools and Staffing Survey data set, obtained from the National Center for Education Statistics, put the precise figure to be 76 percent at that time, and it is surely about that now.

36. See, for example, National Education Association, "Rankings and Estimates: Rankings of the States 2008 and Estimates of School Statistics 2009." Also American Federation of Teachers, "Survey and Analysis of Teacher Salary Trends 2007."

37. This debate aside, there is also a fairly sizable scholarly literature on teacher wages, the teacher labor market, and the links between teacher compensation on such things as teacher quality and student outcomes. See, for example, Dan Goldhaber, Michael DeArmond, Albert Liu, and Dan Player, "Returns to Skill and Teacher Wage Premiums: What Can We Learn by Comparing the Teacher and Private Sector Labor Markets?" SFRP Working Paper 8 (Center on Reinventing Public Education, August 2008); Susanna Loeb and Tara Beteille, "Teacher Labor Markets and Teacher Labor Market Research," in *Teacher Quality: Broadening and Deepening the Debate*, edited by Greg Duncan and James Spillane (Northwestern University 2008); Susanna Loeb and Tara Beteille, "Teacher Quality and Teacher Labor Markets," in *Handbook of Education Policy Research*, edited by Gary Sykes, Barbara Schneider, and David Plank (New York: Routledge, 2009); Dan Goldhaber, "Teacher Quality and Teacher Pay Structure: What Do We Know, and What Are the Options?" *Georgetown Public Policy Review* 7, no. 2 (2002): 81–94.

38. Michael Podgursky, "Is Teacher Pay Adequate?" In *School Money Trials: The Legal Pursuit of Educational Adequacy*, edited by Paul E. Peterson and Martin R. West, pp. 131–158 (Brookings, 2007). See also Podgursky and Tongrut, "(Mis-) Measuring the Relative Pay of Public School Teachers"; and Jay P. Greene and Marcus A. Winters, "How Much are Public School Teachers Paid?" Civic Report 50 (New York: Manhattan Institute, January 2007), available at www.manhattan-institute.org/html/cr_50.htm.

39. See Podgursky, "Is Teacher Pay Adequate?" See also Podgursky and Tongrut, "(Mis-) Measuring the Relative Pay of Public School Teachers"; Benjamin Scafidi, David L. Sjoquist, and Todd R. Stinebrickner, "Do Teachers Really Leave for Higher Paying Jobs in Alternative Occupations?" Working Paper 20055 (University of Western Ontario, Department of Economics, CIBC Human Capital and Productivity Project, 2005); Michael Wolkoff and Michael Podgursky, "Wyoming School District Employee Compensation" (Sacramento: Management Analysis Planning, 2002).

40. Podgursky, "Is Teacher Pay Adequate?"; also Podgursky and Tongrut, "(Mis-) Measuring the Relative Pay of Public School Teachers."

41. See Sylvia A. Allegretto, Sean P. Corcoran, and Lawrence Mishel, *The Teaching Penalty: Teacher Pay Losing Ground* (Washington: Economic Policy Institute, 2008). See also Sylvia A. Allegretto, Sean P. Corcoran, and Lawrence Mishel, *How Does Teacher Pay Compare? Methodological Challenges and Answers* (Washington: Economic Policy Institute, 2004).

42. Again, for a head-to-head debate between the two sides, arranged by the National Council for Teacher Quality, see "NCTQ Square-Off: Are Teachers Underpaid?"

43. Social Security Administration, "FICA and SECA Tax Rates" (Washington: SSA, June 30, 2010), available at www.ssa.gov/OACT/ProgData/taxRates.html.

44. Social Security Administration, "Understanding the Benefit," SSA Publication 10024 (Washington: SSA, January 2010), available at www.socialsecurity.gov/pubs/10024.html.

45. Figures on defined-benefit plans are from Craig Copeland, "Individual Account Retirement Plans: An Analysis of the 2007 Survey of Consumer Finances, with Market Adjustments to June 2009," Issue Brief 333 (Washington: Employee Benefit Research Institute, August 2009). The 60 percent figure is for 2007. The $30,000 figure is an estimate for 2009.

46. Bureau of Labor Statistics, "National Compensation Survey: Employee Benefits in Private Industry in the United States" (Washington: Bureau of Labor Statistics, March 2007), table 1.

47. See Robert M. Costrell and Michael J. Podgursky, "Golden Peaks and Perilous Cliffs: Rethinking Ohio's Teacher Pension System" (Washington: Thomas B. Fordham Institute, June 2007).

48. Ibid.; also Michael J. Podgursky and Mark Ehlert, "Teacher Pensions and Retirement Behavior: How Teacher Pension Rules Affect Behavior, Mobility, and Retirement," Working Paper 5 (Washington: Urban Institute, National Center for Analysis of Longitudinal Data in Education Research, April 2007).

49. For convenience, I use the cost figures here for single coverage plans in which employees pay no monthly premium. See Bureau of Labor Statistics, "National Compensation Survey"; Bureau of Labor Statistics, "National Compensation Survey: Employee Benefits in State and Local Governments in the United States" (Washington: Bureau of Labor Statistics, September 2007).

50. Pennsylvania Legislative Budget and Finance Committee, "Final Report: A Study to Determine the Feasibility and Cost Effectiveness of Placing Public School Employees under the Commonwealth's Jurisdiction for the Purposes of Providing Health Benefits" (Alexandria, Va.: Hay Group, January 20, 2004).

51. The NCTQ database can be accessed at www.nctq.org/tr3/. The full data set includes another twenty-five contracts from the less populous states to ensure that each state is represented, but I do not include these cases. The top seventy-five districts are the largest districts in the country. Adding in the extra districts—for example, Burlington, Vermont, with an enrollment of 3,600, and Portland, Maine, with an enrollment of 7,100—skews the sample and makes it less representative.

52. These figures are based on districts in which the contracts specify the monetary amounts.

53. Jordan, "Health Care: What Teachers Pay."

54. Kaiser Family Foundation and Health Research and Educational Trust, "Employer Health Benefits, 2006 Summary of Findings" (Menlo Park, Calif.: Kaiser Family Foundation, 2006).

55. Stan Wisniewski and Lorel Wisniewski, "State Government Retiree Health Benefits: Current Status and Potential Impact of New Accounting Standards" (Washington: AARP Policy Institute, 2004).

56. New York State School Boards Association, "2008 Teacher Contract Survey" (Latham, N.Y.: New York State School Boards Association, 2008).

57. On the rise of civil service and the politics surrounding it, see, for example, Jack H. Knott and Gary J. Miller, *Reforming Bureaucracy: The Politics of Institutional Choice* (Englewood Cliffs, N.J.: Prentice-Hall, 1987). On the rise of tenure and other protections as they applied to teachers and the role and stance of the early teachers unions, see, for example, Marjorie Murphy, *Blackboard Unions: The AFT and the NEA, 1900–1980* (Cornell University Press, 1990).

58. Similar questions about the tenure-salary trade-off were asked in two other teacher surveys. In Public Agenda's *Stand by Me*, teachers were asked whether they would give up tenure for an additional $5,000 in salary, whether the pay increase would have to be a lot higher, or whether they would rather hold onto tenure: 31 percent of teachers said they would give up tenure for the $5,000 raise, 26 percent said the pay increase would have to be a lot higher, 29 percent said they would rather hold onto tenure (and thus, implicitly, that even a very large raise would not be enough to get them to give up tenure), and 14 percent were unsure. See Steve Farkas, Jean Johnson, and Ann Duffett, *Stand by Me: What Teachers Really Think about Unions, Merit Pay, and Other Professional Matters* (New York: Public Agenda, 2003). A study by Education Sector asked exactly the same question, revealing that, among tenured teachers, 25 percent would take the $5,000, 29 percent would require a much larger raise in salary, 29 percent would keep tenure regardless of the raise amount, and 25 percent were unsure. Untenured teachers were more receptive. See Ann Duffett, Steve Farkas, Andrew J. Rotherham, and Elena Silva, *Waiting to Be Won Over: Teachers Speak on the Professions, Unions, and Reform* (Washington: Education Sector, 2008).

59. See, for example, Caroline M. Hoxby, "What Has Changed and What Has Not," in *Our Schools and Our Future*, edited by Paul E. Peterson (Stanford, Calif.: Hoover Institution Press, 2003); Sean Corcoran, William Evans, and Robert Schwab, "Changing Labor Market Opportunities for Women and the Quality of Teachers, 1957–1992," NBER Working Paper 9180 (Cambridge, Mass.: National Bureau of Economic Research, 2002); Caroline M. Hoxby and Andrew Leigh, "Pulled Away or Pushed Out? Explaining the Decline of Teacher Aptitude in the United States," *American Economic Review* 94, no. 2 (May 2004): 236–40; Eric A. Hanushek and Steven Rivkin, "Teacher Quality," in *Handbook of the Economics of Education*, edited by Eric A. Hanushek and Finis Welch, pp. 1051–78 (Amsterdam: North-Holland, 2006).

60. Hanushek and Rivkin, "Teacher Quality"; Brian A. Jacob and Lars Lefgren, "The Impact of Teacher Training on Student Achievement: Quasi-Experimental Evidence from School Reform Efforts in Chicago," *Journal of Human Resources* 39, no. 1 (2004): 50–79;

Eric A. Hanushek, John F. Kain, Daniel M. O'Brien, and Steven Rivkin, "The Market for Teacher Quality," NBER Working Paper 11154 (Cambridge, Mass.: National Bureau of Economic Research, February 2005). For evidence of positive teacher-pay effects on student outcomes (although the data are aggregated to the state level), see Susanna Loeb and Marianne Page, "Examining the Link between Teacher Wages and Student Outcomes: The Importance of Alternative Labor Market Opportunities and Non-Pecuniary Variation," *Review of Economics and Statistics* 82, no. 3 (2000): 393–408. But see also Dale Ballou and Michael Podgursky, *Teacher Pay and Teacher Quality* (Kalamazoo, Mich.: W. E. Upjohn Institute for Employment Research, 1997).

Chapter Six

1. The Dade County contract is for 2006–09 and doesn't include the twenty-one pages of revisions that amend it for 2009–12. The Cleveland contract is for 2007–10. Both were accessed on the website of the National Council on Teacher Quality at www.nctq.org/tr3/search.jsp.

2. I invite readers to do this. The National Center on Teacher Quality has obtained the most recent labor contracts for the largest seventy-five districts in the country plus another twenty-five districts that are the largest in the states (like Wyoming or Idaho) that wouldn't otherwise be represented. These contracts can be read in their entirety. The NCTQ has also coded them along various dimensions and coded state laws as well. The NCTQ district database is located at www.nctq.org/tr3/search.jsp.

3. Terry M. Moe, "Collective Bargaining and the Performance of the Public Schools," *American Journal of Political Science* 53, no. 1 (January 2009): 156–74; Dale Ballou, *Teacher Contracts in Massachusetts* (Boston: Pioneer Institute, 2000); Pamela Riley, *Contract for Failure* (San Francisco: Pacific Research Institute, 2002).

4. See Emily Cohen, Kate Walsh, and RiShawn Biddle, "Invisible Ink in Collective Bargaining: Why Key Issues Are Not Addressed" (Washington: National Council on Teacher Quality, July 2008), available at www.nctq.org.

5. See, for example, Myron Lieberman, *The Teacher Unions* (New York: Free Press, 1997); Frederick M. Hess and Martin R. West, "A Better Bargain: Overhauling Teacher Collective Bargaining for the 21st Century" (Harvard University, Program on Education Policy and Governance, March 29, 2006); Lorraine McDonnell and Anthony Pascal, *Organized Teachers in Public Schools* (Santa Monica, Calif.: Rand Corporation, 1979).

6. Robert L. Walker, *The Teacher and Collective Bargaining* (Lincoln, Neb.: Professional Educators Publications, 1975), p. 29.

7. I'm referring here to their "reformist" demand for collaboration, which in some districts is used as a substitute for certain kinds of formal rules. In practice, collaboration means that committees with teacher (union) representation are set up to deal with particular issues—teacher transfers, say, or teacher assignments within schools—and the result is that the unions are given vetoes over school or district policies in those realms. This is just a different means by which the unions exercise power over school governance and organization. I deal with this in more detail in chapter 8, in my discussion of "reform unionism."

8. This conception of teachers as equal and interchangeable parts, a key component of the union ethos, has been dubbed the "widget effect" in a fascinating and informative recent study by the New Teacher Project. Daniel Weisberg, Susan Sexton, Jennifer Mulhern, and David Keeling, "The Widget Effect: Our National Failure to Acknowledge and Act on Differences in Teacher Effectiveness" (New York: New Teacher Project, 2009), available at www.tntp.org. Teachers are just widgets, one is as good as another, and distinctions are invidious and unwarranted.

9. The single salary schedule is not an invention of the unions. An outgrowth of Progressivism—see chapter 2—it was used by many districts well before the unions came to power, in the days when their monopolies were secure, they were under no accountability pressures to perform, and they had little to worry about if their compensation systems were inefficient and unproductive. In the years since, the unions have embraced the single salary schedule as their own and fought to keep it. The districts, meanwhile, have recently come under intense pressure to perform, and have shown growing interest in exploring ways that salaries can be used much more flexibly to promote the productivity of schools—most notably, through pay for performance, extra pay for teachers in shortage fields, and extra pay for teachers in disadvantaged schools. Now that the unions are under intense public criticism for blocking change, they are showing somewhat more flexibility on these scores—see chapters 8 through 10—but their moderation is a strategic accommodation to a hostile environment. They are trying to keep these reforms as weak and nonthreatening as possible.

10. This information was taken from the Prince George's County labor contract for teachers, as presented on the website of the National Council on Teacher Quality (www. nctq.org). Negotiated increases in teacher salaries are often reported as key parts of any bargaining settlement. When unions bargain for higher salaries, the end product is that the *entire salary schedule* is shifted upward—everyone gains across-the-board—although sometimes the unions will want (in response to member pressures or perceived inequities) gains that are asymmetric, with teachers at the higher or lower ends getting greater percentage raises. When the unions succeed in getting their members a "3 percent raise" for subsequent years, this refers to the shift in the *salary schedule*, not to what individual teachers actually get. The raise for the typical teacher is *bigger* than that, for each teacher is simultaneously moving up a step in the next year as well (and possibly over a column). To take one example: the Prince George's teacher with a master's degree and ten years of experience would get a 3 percent raise from the shift in the schedule, but another 2.9 percent from an automatic step increase in seniority.

11. For the Schools and Staffing Survey, see the National Center for Education Statistics website at /nces.ed.gov/surveys/sass/. For a more general discussion of salary schedules and their problems, see Michael Podgursky, "Teams versus Bureaucracies: Wage-Setting and Teacher Quality in Traditional Public, Charter, and Private Schools," in *Charter School Outcomes*, edited by Mark Barends, Matthew Springer, and Herbert Walberg, pp. 61–84 (Mahwah, N.J.: Lawrence Erlbaum Associates).

12. See, for example, Eric A. Hanushek and Steven G. Rivkin, "Teacher Quality," in *Handbook of the Economics of Education*, edited by Eric A. Hanushek and Finis Welch (Amsterdam: Elsevier, 2006).

13. NCTQ, "Human Capital in Seattle Public Schools: Rethinking How to Attract, Develop and Retain Effective Teachers" (Washington: NCTQ, 2009).

14. NCTQ, "Human Capital in Boston Public Schools: Rethinking How to Attract, Develop and Retain Effective Teachers" (Washington: NCTQ, 2010), p. 8.

15. Marguerite Roza and Raegen Miller, "Separation of Degrees: State-by-State Analysis of Teacher Compensation for Master's Degrees" (University of Washington, Center on Reinventing Public Education, July 2009).

16. Caroline M. Hoxby and Andrew Leigh, "Pulled Away or Pushed Out? Explaining the Decline of Teacher Aptitude in the United States," *American Economic Review* 94, no. 2 (May 2004): 236–40.

17. These figures are taken from the contracts on the website of the National Council on Teacher Quality at www.nctq.org/tr3/search.jsp.

18. On the Denver pay-for-performance program, see Denver Public Schools, "ProComp at a Glance: A Quick Reference Handbook" (Denver Public Schools, November 2006); Edward W. Wiley, Eleanor R. Spindler, and Amy N. Subert, *Denver ProComp: An Outcomes Evaluation of Denver's Alternative Teacher Compensation System, 2010 Report*, available on the Denver Public Schools website at static.dpsk12.org/gems/newprocomp/ProCompOutcomesEvaluationApril2010final.pdf.; Phil Gonring, Paul Teske, and Brad Jupp, *Pay-for-Performance Teacher Compensation: An Inside View of Denver's ProComp Plan* (Cambridge, Mass.: Harvard Education Press, 2007). On the Houston pay plan, see Center for Educator Compensation Reform, "Performance Pay in Houston" (Center for Educator Compensation Reform, December 2008), available at www.cecr.ed.gov/guides/summaries/HoustonCaseSummary.pdf. For an overview of the issue, see Michael J. Podgursky and Matthew G. Springer, "Teacher Performance Pay: A Review," *Journal of Policy Analysis and Management* 26, no. 4 (2007): 909–49.

19. These figures are taken from the contracts on the website of the National Council on Teacher Quality at www.nctq.org/tr3/search.jsp.

20. Ibid.

21. See Raegen T. Miller, Richard J. Murnane, and John B. Willett, "Do Teacher Absences Impact Student Achievement? Longitudinal Evidence from One Urban School District," *Educational Evaluation and Policy Analysis* 30, no. 2 (June 2008): 181–200, and the references therein.

22. NCTQ, "Human Capital in Seattle Public Schools," p. 6.

23. Ibid., p.47.

24. Ibid., p. 49.

25. Teachers get almost as much leave in the states without collective bargaining, but the explanation is that the unions have simply used their power at the state level to get leave requirements imposed through legislation. While almost no states that allow collective bargaining have any laws requiring personal leave, for instance, five of the seven states that prohibit collective bargaining have such laws. They are also much more likely to have laws requiring specific levels of sick leave.

26. Steve Farkas, Jean Johnson, and Ann Duffett, with Leslie Moye and Jackie Vine, *Stand by Me: What Teachers Really Think about Unions, Merit Pay, and Other Professional Matters* (New York: Public Agenda, 2003).

27. Steve Farkas, Jean Johnson, Ann Duffett, and Tony Foleno, with Patrick Foley, *Trying to Stay Ahead of the Game: Superintendents and Principals Talk about School Leadership* (New York: Public Agenda, 2001), pp. 27–28.

28. Bess Keller, "Phila. Middle School Teachers Fail 'Highly Qualified' Tests," *Education Week* 23, no. 30 (April 7, 2004): 9.

29. Quoted in Scott Reeder, "School Boards Lose Power to Fire Poor Teachers," in *The Hidden Costs of Tenure: Why Are Failing Teachers Getting a Passing Grade?* (Small Newspaper Group, 2005), available at thehiddencostsoftenure.com.

30. Farkas, Johnson, and Duffett, *Stand by Me*, p. 21.

31. Steve Farkas, Jean Johnson, and Ann Duffett, with Beth Syat and Jackie Vine, *Rolling Up Their Sleeves: Superintendents and Principals Talk about What's Needed to Fix Public Schools* (New York: Public Agenda, 2003), p. 33.

32. Weisberg and others, "The Widget Effect." The quote is from p. 17.

33. See his various articles, which are listed on thehiddencostsoftenure.com.

34. Weisberg and others, "The Widget Effect," p. 4.

35. Ibid., p. 6.

36. Reported in "Teacher Protection Racket," editorial, *USA Today*, July 17, 2008, p. 8A.

37. NCTQ, "Human Capital in Seattle Public Schools," p. 7; NCTQ, "Human Capital in Hartford Public Schools" (Washington: NCTQ, 2009), p. 6.

38. Jason Song, "Failure Gets a Pass: Firing Tenured Teachers Can Be a Costly and Tortuous Task," *Los Angeles Times*, May 3, 2009.

39. Both quotes are from Barbara Martinez, "Teacher Seniority Rules Challenged," *Wall Street Journal*, February 19, 2010.

40. Probably the most extensive study of the impacts of seniority rules is Jessica Levin, Jennifer Mulhern, and Joan Schunck, "Unintended Consequences: The Case for Reforming the Staffing Rules in Urban Teachers Union Contracts" (New York: New Teacher Project, 2005). See also the studies by the NCTQ: "Human Capital in Seattle Public Schools"; "Human Capital in Hartford Public Schools"; and "Human Capital in Boston Public Schools." Also Hess and West, "A Better Bargain." The factual material in this section is essentially a broad overview of material that is presented in greater detail in these sources.

41. Hess and West, "A Better Bargain," p. 27.

42. In recent years, the more progressive districts have begun to require that principals must agree before an excessed teacher will be placed in their school; this creates a situation in which some of these teachers cannot find any school that will accept them. Such teachers may then be let go after a period of time, if they never find a job within the system. This is rare.

43. See Levin, Mulhern, and Schunck, "Unintended Consequences," p. 24.

44. Ibid., p. 5. One of the New Teacher Project districts was New York City, which, thanks to the forceful efforts of Chancellor Joel Klein in insisting on work rule reform, has since removed some of the seniority rules from its contract (in return for which, however, the union received a big pay raise). I discuss this in chapter 7.

45. See, for example, Tamar Lewin and Sam Dillon, "Districts Warn of Deeper Teacher Cuts," *New York Times*, April 20, 2010; Nick Anderson, "100,000 Teachers

Nationwide Face Layoffs," *Washington Post*, May 27, 2010. How many teachers were actually laid off, however, remains entirely unclear, as the Obama administration worked with Congress to pass huge stimulus bills that infused funds into states and districts to avert the layoffs of teachers and other public sector workers.

46. For an overview of some of the problems that seniority creates as it applies to teacher layoffs, see NCTQ, "Teacher Layoffs: Rethinking 'Last-Hired, First-Fired' Policies" (Washington: NCTQ, February 2010).

47. Marguerite Roza, "Seniority-Based Layoffs Will Exacerbate Job Loss in Public Education" (University of Washington, Center on Reinventing Public Education, February 2, 2009).

48. See, for example, Eric A. Hanushek, John F. Kain, and Steven G. Rivkin, "Why Public Schools Lose Teachers," *Journal of Human Resources* 39, no. 2 (Spring): 326–54; Charles T. Clotfelter, Helen F. Ladd, and Jacob L. Vigdor, "Who Teaches Whom? Race and the Distribution of Novice Teachers," *Economics of Education Review* 24, no. 4 (2005): 377–92; Education Trust-West, "California's Hidden Teacher Spending Gap: How State and District Budgeting Practices Shortchange Poor and Minority Students and Their Schools," Special Report (Oakland, Calif.: Education Trust-West, March 2005); Marguerite Roza and Paul Thomas Hill, "How Within-District Spending Inequities Help Some Schools to Fail," in *Brookings Papers on Education Policy 2004*, edited by Diane Ravitch, pp. 201–18 (Brookings, 2004).

49. See Hanushek and Rivkin, "Teacher Quality."

50. See Terry M. Moe, "Bottom Up Structure: Collective Bargaining, Transfer Rights, and the Plight of Disadvantaged Schools" (Stanford University, Department of Political Science, May 2008). There is another quantitative analysis, by Koski and Horng, that finds no impact of seniority-based transfer rules on the distribution of teachers. Their analysis was explicitly based on an earlier (but nearly identical) version of my own paper—"borrowing" all of my ideas about theory and approach, but applying them to a new data set. For some reason, however, they measure transfer rules very differently, and they make some methodological missteps along the way. So it is no surprise, in my view, that they arrive at a "finding" of no impact. Null results are easy to get in any study with poor measures and methods, and in all likelihood say nothing credible about the true underlying effects that are being estimated. See William S. Koski and Eileen Horng, "Facilitating the Teacher Quality Gap? Collective Bargaining Agreements, Teacher Hiring and Transfer Rules, and Teacher Assignment among Schools in California," *Education Finance and Policy* 2, no. 3 (2007): 262–300.

51. The pandemonium and union hostility that resulted when Eva Moskowitz held city council hearings on teacher labor contracts in New York City is a nice illustration of the union preference for keeping the content of these contracts out of the spotlight and behind closed doors. The Moskowitz hearings are discussed in chapter 7.

52. The NCTQ data set is described on its website at www.nctq.org/tr3/search.jsp. It includes collective bargaining contracts from the largest seventy-five districts in the nation, plus another twenty-five from the largest districts in those states (Vermont, Wyoming, and the like) that aren't represented in the initial sample. Of the seventy-five largest districts, forty-nine have collective bargaining and twenty-six do not. The high

number without collective bargaining comes about partly because districts in the South tend to be organized by county, making them very large, and partly because Texas, in particular, is an extremely populous southern state that has lots of big cities and districts. With only forty-nine of the largest districts having collective bargaining, then, I expand the sample size as much as possible here by including all NCTQ districts with enrollments greater than 20,000. These districts are sufficiently large, in my view, to give them most of the characteristics (the bureaucracy, for example) of "large" school districts; and the data do not show that, in terms of their contracts, they are any different (for example, any less restrictive) than the other forty-nine. Because Arizona is difficult to categorize as having or not having collective bargaining, I have eliminated its two NCTQ districts from the analysis.

53. See, for example, Levin, Mulhern, and Schunck, "Unintended Consequences."

54. In this sample, all but one of these districts is located in Georgia, Mississippi, North Carolina, South Carolina, Texas, or Virginia, all of which prohibit collective bargaining. As noted, I have omitted Arizona (two districts) from the entire analysis because of its ambiguous status.

55. Eric A. Hanushek, "The Failure of Input-Based Schooling Policies," *Economic Journal* 113 (February 2003): F64–F98; Steven G. Rivkin, Eric A. Hanushek, and John J. Kain, "Teachers, Schools, and Academic Achievement," *Econometrica* 73, no. 2 (March, 2005): 417–58.

56. The data here refer to class size limits on grades nine to twelve. A focus on middle school or elementary school class size limits would show very similar results.

57. Districts were chosen from the Schools and Staffing Survey data set for 1999–2000. They were sampled randomly within size categories, giving roughly equal numbers for districts with enrollments greater than 20,000, from 10,000 to 20,000, from 5,000 to 10,000, and below 5,000. Districts so chosen were contacted and asked to submit the labor contract that was in effect during 2000. When districts did not respond, substitute districts were chosen randomly to replace them in the sample. For more information on the Schools and Staffing Survey data set, see the NCES website (nces. ed.gov/surveys/sass/).

58. In these contracts, I identify sixteen issues very much like those in table 6-1, code the rule(s) applying to each issue, and use factor analysis to construct a summary index of restrictiveness. For the methodology employed, see my discussion—for a sample of California districts—in Moe, "Collective Bargaining and the Performance of the Public Schools." Regarding the relationships illustrated in figures 6-1 and 6-2, a more finely grained statistical analysis—one that controls, for example, for state political culture, collective bargaining laws, and urbanicity of the district, and forces district size and minority composition to compete with one another for explanatory power—shows that *both* size and minority composition are statistically significant determinants of contract restrictiveness, and indeed are the most important factors. Size, however, is a far more powerful determinant than minority composition. Running the analysis without state fixed effects, for example, a shift in district size from low to high (two standard deviations) yields an increase in contract restrictiveness of 0.81 standard deviation—quite a large change—while a similar increase in minority composition leads to an increase in

restrictiveness of 0.31 standard deviation. When state fixed effects are introduced, the gap is even wider, but minority composition remains significant. One lesson here: minority composition is important in its own right and not just because minority kids tend to be found in large districts.

59. See especially Richard B. Freeman and James L. Medoff, *What Do Unions Do?* (New York: Basic Books, 1984). See also Richard B. Freeman, "Unionism Comes to the Public Sector," *Journal of Economic Literature* 24 (March 1986): 41–86; Charles Taylor Kerchner and Douglas E. Mitchell, *The Changing Idea of a Teachers Union* (London: Falmer Press, 1988); Charles Taylor Kerchner and Julia E. Koppich, *A Union of Professionals: Labor Relations and Educational Reform* (Teachers College Press, 1993); Charles Taylor Kerchner, Julia E. Koppich, and Joseph E. Weeres, *United Mind Workers: Unions and Teaching in the Knowledge Society* (San Francisco: Jossey-Bass, 1997).

60. Information is fundamental to the social science understanding of organizations. See, for example, the various chapters published in Robert Gibbons and John Roberts, *Handbook of Organizational Economics* (Princeton University Press, forthcoming). John Roberts, *The Modern Firm: Organizational Design for Performance and Growth* (Oxford University Press, 2007); Paul Milgrom and John Roberts, *Economics, Organization, and Management* (New York: Prentice Hall, 1992).

61. Professionalism is often understood and argued in combination with voice. See, for example, the argument of Leo Casey, a vice president of the AFT, in his "The Quest for Professional Voice," *American Educator* (Summer 2007), available on the AFT's website at www.aft.org/newspubs/periodicals/ae/summer2007/casey.cfm. See also Nina Bascia, *Unions in Teachers' Professional Lives: Some Social, Intellectual, and Practical Concerns* (Teachers College Press, 1994). The various works cited earlier on the topic of voice and input also point to the role of unions in enhancing professionalism and could just as well have been the main citations here. See Freeman and Medoff, *What Do Unions Do?*; Freeman, "Unionism Comes to the Public Sector"; Kerchner and Mitchell, *The Changing Idea of a Teachers Union*; Kerchner and Koppich, *A Union of Professionals*; and Kerchner, Koppich, and Weeres, *United Mind Workers*.

62. For just one example of how closely intertwined unionism and professionalism are in their own sense of themselves, see Casey, "The Quest for Professional Voice."

63. This chapter has already provided evidence on the kinds of rules they seek, but more can be found by simply taking a look at the details of the contracts made available on the NCTQ website (www.nctq.org/tr3/home.jsp).

64. For plenty of evidence, see, for example, the discussions in chapters 9 and 10 on union opposition to performance pay and performance-based teacher assessments. They have relented a bit over the last year, due to the pressures of Race to the Top and the shifting political sentiment against them, but they are still opposed and are doing what they can—sometimes in "collaboration" with reformers—to keep these reforms weak and nonthreatening.

65. The topic of professionals in organization was much studied from roughly the 1960s through the 1980s, but then tapered off. The more modern emphasis is on information and knowledge. For an example of the early literature, see Guy Benveniste, *Professionalizing the Organization: Reducing Bureaucracy to Enhance Effectiveness* (San Franciso:

Jossey-Bass, 1989). For examples of the more modern work, see David A. Klein, ed., *The Strategic Management of Intellectual Capital* (Maryland Heights, Mo.: Butterworth-Heinemann, 1998); Chun Wei Chu and Nick Bontis, eds., *The Strategic Management of Intellectual Capital and Organizational Knowledge* (Oxford University Press, 2002); Kimiz Dalkir, *Knowledge Management in Theory and Practice* (Maryland Heights, Mo.: Butterworth-Heinemann, 2005).

66. The most famous critical report on the nation's education schools is Arthur Levine, *Educating School Teachers* (Washington: Education Schools Project, September 2006), available at www.edschools.org/teacher_report_release.htm. Levine is the former president of Teachers College, one of the premier education schools in the country. See also "Transforming Teacher Education through Clinical Practice: A National Strategy to Prepare Effective Teachers," Report of the Blue Ribbon Panel on Clinical Preparation and Partnerships for Improved Student Learning, commissioned by the National Council for Accreditation of Teacher Education, November 2010, available at www.ncate.org/LinkClick.aspx?fileticket=zzeiB1OoqPk%3d&tabid=715; NCTQ, "Ed School Essentials: A Review of Illinois Teacher Preparation" (Washington: National Council on Teacher Quality, November 2010), available at www.nctq.org/edschoolreports/illinois/; Kate Walsh, "Teacher Education: Coming Up Empty" (Washington: Thomas B. Fordham Foundation, March 2006), available on the website of NCTQ at www.nctq.org/p/publications/docs/Teacher_Education_fwd_20080316034429.pdf.

67. See, for example, Frederick Hess, "How to Get the Teachers We Want," *Education Next* 9, no. 3 (Summer 2009): 34–39; Report of the Blue Ribbon Panel on Clinical Preparation and Partnerships for Improved Student Learning, "Transforming Teacher Education through Clinical Practice"; and Teach for America's discussion of their approach to teacher training on their website under "Training and Ongoing Support" (www.teachforamerica.org/the-corps-experience/training-and-ongoing-support/).

68. For an overview of the legal regulation of professions, the incentives of professional groups to seek it, and its economic and social consequences, see Morris M. Kleiner, "Occupational Licensing," *Journal of Economic Perspectives* 14, no. 4 (Fall 2000): 189–202. For more specific analyses, see, for example, Simon Rottenberg, ed., *Occupational Licensure and Regulation* (Washington: American Enterprise Institute, 1980); John R. Lott, "Licensing and Nontransferable Rents," *American Economic Review* 77, no. 3 (June 1987): 453–55; and Lee Benham and Alexandra Benham, "Regulating through the Professions: A Perspective on Information Control," *Journal of Law and Economics* 18, no. 2 (October 1975): 421–47.

69. For an overview, see Stephen Sawchuck, "Proof Lacking on Success of Professional Development," *Education Week*, November 10, 2010. See also Kwang Suk Yoon and others, "Reviewing the Evidence on Teacher Professional Development Affects Student Achievement" (Washington: National Center for Education Evaluation and Regional Assistance, Institute for Education Sciences, October 2007), available at /ies.ed.gov/ncee/edlabs/regions/southwest/pdf/REL_2007033.pdf. See also the overview in "Professional Development," *Education Week*, September 21, 2004. My point in the text is not that professional development can never be effective, because the evidence is that it can—if it consists of serious, rigorous course content. But all too many professional

development programs are not of that type. Here is a nice summary from the "Professional Development" piece: "Professional development has traditionally been provided to teachers through school in-service workshops. In the classic conception of that model, the district or school brings in an outside consultant or curriculum expert on a staff-development day to give teachers a one-time training seminar on a garden-variety pedagogic or subject-area topic. Such an approach has been routinely lamented in the professional literature . . . Even so, many teachers still appear to receive the bulk of their professional development through some form of the one-shot workshop."

70. Union leaders regularly say that firing is bad policy, and that the emphasis should be on ensuring quality through training. Here, for instance, is a recent quote from Randi Weingarten, president of the AFT. "It's cathartic to say 'fire the bad teachers,' but it doesn't do much to improve schools. The plain, unsexy fact is that the best way to improve teacher quality is to do a better job of developing and supporting the teachers to whom we entrust our children's educations." The quote is from Randi Weingarten, "Saving Our Schools: Superman or Real Solutions," *Huffington Post*, June 28, 2010, available at huffingtonpost.com.

71. Transcript of an ABC News *This Week* program, "Crisis in the Classroom," *ABC News,* August 15, 2010, available at abcnews.go.com/ThisWeek/week-transcript-crisis-classroom/story?id=11506701.

72. From the transcript of the National Public Radio story, "Leaders Tackle Challenges of Education Reform," *NPR,* September 29, 2010, available at www.npr.org/templates/story/story.php?storyId=130212968.

73. The Organization for Economic Cooperation and Development (OECD) provides comprehensive economic and social statistics on all its member countries, including Finland, on its website at www.oecd.org/home/0,3675,en_2649_201185_1_1_1_1_1,00.html.

74. For basic information about the history of labor relations and collective bargaining in Finnish education, see Erkki Aho, Kari Pitkanen, and Pasi Sahlberg, "Policy Development and Reform Principles of Basic and Secondary Education in Finland since 1968," Education Working Paper 2 (Washington: World Bank, May 2006). See also the website of the Trade Union of Education in Finland (www.oaj.fi/portal/page?_pageid=515,452376&_dad=portal&_schema=PORTAL). On the autonomy of Finnish schools from centrally imposed rules, see Pasi Sahlberg, "A Short History of Education Reform in Finland," available from his personal website at www.pasisahlberg.com/index.php?id=64.

75. See Randall W. Eberts and Joe A. Stone, *Unions and Public Schools: The Effect of Collective Bargaining on American Education* (Lexington, Mass.: Lexington Books, 1984); Randall W. Eberts and Joe A. Stone, "Teachers Unions and the Productivity of Public Schools," *Industrial and Labor Relations Review* 40, no. 3 (1987): 355–63; Martin Milkman, "Teachers Unions, Productivity, and Minority Student Achievement," *Journal of Labor Research* 18, no. 1 (1997): 137–50; Michael M. Kurth, "Teachers Unions and Excellence in Education: An Analysis of the Decline in SAT Scores," *Journal of Labor Research* 8 (Fall 1987): 351–67; Paul Grimes and Charles A. Register, "Teachers Unions and Student Achievement in High School Economics," *Journal of Economic Education*

21, no. 3 (1990): 297–308; Laura Argyris and Daniel I. Rees, "Unionization and School Productivity," *Research in Labor Economics* 14 (1995): 49–68; Sam Peltzman, "The Political Economy of the Decline of American Public Education," *Journal of Law and Economics* 36, no. 1 (1993): 331–70; Sam Peltzman, "Political Economy of Public Education: Non-College-Bound Students," *Journal of Law and Economics* 39, no. 1 (1996): 73–120; Hoxby, "How Do Teachers Unions Affect Education Production?"; Howard F. Nelson and Michael Rosen, "Are Teachers Unions Hurting American Education? A State-by-State Analysis of the Impact of Collective Bargaining among Teachers on Student Performance" (Milwaukee: Institute for Wisconsin's Future, 1996); Lala Carr Steelman, Brian Powell, and Robert M. Carini, "Do Teacher Unions Hinder Educational Performance? Lessons Learned from State SAT and ACT Scores," *Harvard Education Review* 70, no. 4 (Winter 2000): 437–65; Moe, "Collective Bargaining and the Performance of the Public Schools."

76. The SAT refers to what used to be called the Scholastic Aptitude Test, was renamed the Scholastic Assessment Test, and is now called the SAT Reasoning Test, with the initials not standing for anything. For a blow-by-blow on the name changes, as well as an overview of the history and content of the exam, see Wikipedia's account under "SAT," available at en.wikipedia.org/wiki/SAT#Name_changes_and_recentered_ scores. For similar information on the ACT exam (where the initials originally stood for American College Testing), see Wikipedia's account under "ACT (test)," available at en.wikipedia.org/wiki/ACT_(examination).

77. Eberts and Stone, *Unions and Public Schools*; Eberts and Stone, "Teachers Unions and the Productivity of Public Schools"; Argyris and Rees, "Unionization and School Productivity"; Milkman, "Teachers Unions, Productivity, and Minority Student Achievement."

78. Ibid. See also Grimes and Register, "Teachers Unions and Student Achievement in High School Economics."

79. For a more detailed discussion of these endogeneity problems, see Moe, "Collective Bargaining and the Performance of the Public Schools" and Hoxby, "How Do Teachers Unions Affect Education Production?" Hoxby does correct for endogeneity problems, using a "differences in differences" design in an analysis carried out at the district level on a national sample. In a recent working paper, Peter Dolton also corrects for endogeneity, using panel data with fixed effects, in an analysis carried out at the state level. See Peter Dolton, "Teacher Unions and Educational Outcomes: Some Further State Level Evidence" (University of London, Royal Holloway, December 2010). He finds that the impact of collective bargaining is negative.

80. Hoxby, "How Do Teachers Unions Affect Education Production?" Note that she uses drop-out rates as her measure of student performance because there are no test score measures of student achievement that are comparable across all the nation's school districts.

81. Moe, "Collective Bargaining and the Performance of the Public Schools."

82. See, for example, Levin, Mulhern, and Schunck, "Unintended Consequences." Also Hanushek, Kain, and Rivkin, "Why Public Schools Lose Teachers."

83. A rationale argued by some of the early research literature on collective bargaining is that union contracts, because filled with formal rules, have the effect of standardizing

public education—and that standardization tends to be good for average ("standard") children, but ill-suited to children from disadvantaged backgrounds, who need more specialized attention—for example, Eberts and Stone, *Unions and Public Schools*; Eberts and Stone, "Teachers Unions and the Productivity of Public Schools"; Milkman, "Teachers Unions, Productivity, and Minority Student Achievement"; Joe A. Stone, "Collective Bargaining and Public Schools," in *Conflicting Missions,* edited by Tom Loveless, pp. 47–68 (Brookings, 2000). The argument, then, is that the impact of collective bargaining is positive for average kids, but negative for disadvantaged kids. I am not persuaded by this argument, because union rules are pegged to the interests of teachers, and they are not intended to—and do not—standardize the education process around the needs of the average child. They easily come into conflict with the education of *all* children, not just those who are disadvantaged.

Chapter Seven

1. For data on charters in New Orleans, see National Alliance for Public Charter Schools, *A Growing Movement: America's Largest Charter Communities* (Washington: National Alliance for Public Charter Schools, November 2010), p. 5, available at www. publiccharters.org/files/publications/AllianceMarket Share Report_FINAL_Nov2010. pdf. On New Orleans, its school history, and its post-Katrina reforms, see Stacey M. Childress, "Reforming New Orleans Schools after Katrina" (Harvard University, Harvard Business School, July 2008); Erik W. Robelen, "New Orleans Schools Seize Post-Katrina Momentum," *Education Week*, August 25, 2010; Sarah Laskow, "Necessity Is the Mother of Invention," *Newsweek*, August 26, 2010; Paul Tough, "A Teachable Moment," *New York Times*, August 17, 2008; Walter Isaacson, "The Greatest Education Lab," *Time*, September 6, 2007; Adam Nossiter, "Against Odds, New Orleans Schools Fight Back," *New York Times*, April 30, 2008; Ron Schachter, "Fresh Chance for New Orleans Schools," *District Administration*, December 2006; Kathryn G. Newmark and Veronique De Rugy, "Hope after Katrina," *Education Next* 6, no. 4 (Fall 2006): 12–22. New Orleans' burst of innovation appears to have had a marked impact on student achievement. As *Education Week* observes, "State achievement data at various grade levels show considerable gains, and growth that has outpaced the state as a whole. For example, the percentage of 4th graders scoring at the 'basic' level or above in reading rose from 43 percent in 2005 to 62 percent in 2010, and in math from 47 percent to 59 percent." (Note that, while some students and their families did not return to the district after Katrina, most did, and the demographics of the student population are basically the same as before.) Quote is from Robelen, "New Orleans Schools Seize Post-Katrina Momentum." I don't emphasize the achievement gains in the text because I want to keep the focus on the labor contract and the organization of schooling, and because a serious analysis that attempts to determine the causal impacts of New Orleans' structural innovations on student achievement would require a more sophisticated statistical exercise (controlling for student characteristics and so on). Throughout the book, I will relegate most discussions about achievement impacts to the notes. It is easy to get bogged down in complicated assessments of whether a given change—charter schools, vouchers, pay for performance, and other

reforms—has an impact on student achievement. The data and existing studies rarely allow for definitive conclusions, and as a result these discussions threaten to distract from the main points I want to make in this book. Important as achievement is, I want to keep the focus on matters of organization and power so that the basic points about them can be clearly made.

2. For these and other data on charter school enrollments, see National Alliance for Public Charter Schools, *A Growing Movement: America's Largest Charter Communities* (Washington: National Alliance for Public Charter Schools, November 2010), p. 5, available at www.publiccharters.org/files/publications/AllianceMarket Share Report_FINAL_Nov2010.pdf.

3. An alternative way that reformers can try to weaken union power and free the districts from restrictive work rules is through changes in state law. But as we will see in chapters 9 and 10, this route is exceedingly difficult.

4. See, for example, Joseph Viteritti, ed., *When Mayors Take Charge: School Governance in the City* (Brookings, 2009); Jeffrey R. Henig and Wilbur C. Rich, eds., *Mayors in the Middle: Politics, Race, and Mayoral Control of Urban Schools* (Princeton University Press, 2004); Kenneth K. Wong, Francis X. Shen, Dorothea Anagnostopoulos, and Stacey Rutledge, *The Education Mayor: Improving America's Schools* (Georgetown University Press, 2007).

5. Information on enrollment is from the New York Department of Education website at schools.nyc.gov/AboutUs/default.htm. For the history of the city public school system and its many problems, see, for example, Diane Ravitch, *The Great School Wars: A History of the New York City Public Schools* (Johns Hopkins University Press, 2000). See also Marcia Chambers, "Politics and Patronage Dominate Community-Run School Districts," *New York Times*, June 26, 1980.

6. Catherine Gewertz, "NYC Mayor Gains Control over Schools," *Education Week*, June 19, 2002; "A Halfway Proposal on Schools," Editorial, *New York Times*, June 5, 2005.

7. Wayne Barrett, "Weingarten's War Byline," *Village Voice*, May 20, 2003.

8. "The Education Mayor's Big Win," editorial, *New York Times*, June 12, 2002.

9. Also see "Bloomberg Says Teacher Contract Depends on State," NY/Region, *New York Times*, May 13, 2002.

10. "Teach Us, Mr. Mayor; Education in New York," *The Economist*, January 20, 2007.

11. David Herszenhorn, "School Unions Want to Cancel Labor Hearings, Official Says," *New York Times*, November 11, 2003.

12. Lizzy Ratner, "Taking on Unions, and Paying a Price," *New York Observer*, December 8, 2003.

13. Ibid. On the pressures for Moskowitz to back off, see also David M. Herszenhorn, "School Unions Want to Cancel Labor Hearings, Official Says," *New York Times*, November 11, 2003.

14. David Saltonstall, with Joe Williams, "It's a Pointed Lesson in Political, School Ties," *New York Daily News*, November 14, 2003. Also Herszenhorn, "School Unions Want to Cancel Labor Hearings"; Alicia Colon, "A Principal Speaks Up on Teaching Standards," *New York Sun*, November 17, 2003.

15. Jeff Archer, "NYC Unions on Hot Seat at Hearings," *Education Week*, November 26, 2003.

16. Jessica Bruder, "Eva Moskowitz Runs in Manhattan Despite Randi Weingarten Ire," *New York Observer*, June 6, 2005.

17. Saltonstall, "It's a Pointed Lesson in Political, School Ties."

18. See, for example, Thomas Toch, "Liberal Reforms: A Conversation with Eva Moskowitz," *Education Sector*, June 12, 2006, available at www.educationsector.org/publications/liberal-reforms-conversation-eva-moskowitz.

19. AFT, "Grasping the Edu-Obvious: The Meaning of the Moskowitz Defeat—Updated," *EdWize,* September 14, 2005, available at edwize.org/wp-content/themes/edwize/print.php?p=76.

20. "School Wars in New York City," editorial, *New York Times*, December 3, 2003.

21. David M. Herszenhorn, "Mayor's Goal Is 'Thin' Pact with Teachers," *New York Times*, February 6, 2004.

22. Julia Levy, "Union Demands Teachers' Pay Rise by 19.1%," *New York Sun*, June 15, 2005.

23. David M. Herszenhorn, "City Reaches Tentative Deal with Teachers," *New York Times*, October 4, 2005.

24. Ibid. On the "groundbreaking" nature of this reform and its success in later operations, see Timothy Daly, David Keeling, Rachel Grainger, and Adele Grundless, "Mutual Benefits: New York City's Shift to Mutual Consent in Teacher Hiring," Policy Brief (New York: New Teacher Project, April 2008).

25. Sol Stern, "A Teachers' Contract for a New Era," *City Magazine*, July 21, 2009.

26. Ibid.

27. Elissa Gootman, "Teachers Agree to Bonus Pay Tied to Scores," *New York Times*, October 18, 2007.

28. Ibid.

29. Jennifer Medina, "Teacher Bonuses Total $27 Million, Nearly Double Last Year's," *New York Times*, September 5, 2009.

30. Diane Cardwell, "Bloomberg Seeks Further Changes for City Schools," *New York Times*, January 18, 2007.

31. Elissa Gootman, "A New Effort to Remove Bad Teachers," *New York Times*, November 15, 2007. By 2010 eight lawyers were working for the Teacher Performance Unit, and eight consultants (retired principals and administrators) were aiding their efforts. See Jennifer Medina, "Progress Slow in Bloomberg Goal to Rid Schools of Bad Teachers," *New York Times*, February 24, 2010.

32. Figure on tenure rate is from Gootman, "A New Effort to Remove Bad Teachers."

33. Jennifer Medina, "New York Measuring Teachers by Student Progress on Tests," *New York Times*, January 18, 2008.

34. David M. Herszenhorn, "Overhaul of Schools Would Let Teachers Rate Principals," *New York Times*, January 19, 2007.

35. Jennifer Medina, "Bill Would Bar Linking Class Test Scores to Tenure," *New York Times*, March 18, 2008.

36. Jennifer Medina, "Teachers to Be Measured Based on Students' Standardized Test Scores," *New York Times*, October 2, 2008.

37. Maura Walz, "Race to the Top: Bloomberg to Klein: Use Student Data in Tenure Decision This Year," *GothamSchools*, November 25, 2009, available at gothamschools. org. See also Jennifer Medina, "Mayor Says Student Scores Will Factor into Teacher Tenure," *New York Times*, November 26, 2009.

38. For the details of this controversy and its development over time, see Jennifer Medina, "$81 Million for Reserve of Teachers," *New York Times*, April 29, 2008; Jennifer Medina, "City and Teachers' Union Disagree on Reserve Pool," *New York Times*, June 7, 2008; Jennifer Medina, "City Teacher Pay Practice Comes in for Fresh Criticism," *New York Times*, September 22, 2008; Elizabeth Green, "Union, City Dig in Heels over Fate of Reserve Teachers," *New York Sun*, September 28, 2008; Anna Phillips, "Contract Sport: UFT and City Begin Contract Talks amid Questions over Pay, ATRs," *GothamSchools*, September 11, 2009, available at gothamschools.org; Jennifer Medina, "With Teachers' Contract Set to End, Talks Are Quiet," *New York Times*, October 30, 2009; Anna Phillips, "Contract Sport: Among City's Contract Demands: Flexibility to Lay Off Teachers," *GothamSchools*, February 23, 2010; Jennifer Medina, "City and Teachers' Union Near Contract Mediation," *New York Times*, February 25, 2010.

39. See, for example, Medina, "City and Teachers' Union Near Contract Mediation."

40. Daly and others, "Mutual Benefits: New York City's Shift to Mutual Consent in Teacher Hiring."

41. See, for example, Phillips, "Contract Sport: UFT and City Begin Contract Talks"; Phillips, "Contract Sport: Among City's Contract Demands."

42. To read Joel Klein's Temporary Reassignment Center agreement with Michael Mulgrew, president of the United Federation of Teachers, April 15, 2010, go to the United Federation of Teachers' website at www. uft.org/files/attachments/temporary-reassignment-centers-agreement-april-2010.pdf.

43. Again, I exclude New Orleans because it is a special case, because its local union was largely destroyed by Katrina and it hasn't had to fight a battle against union power.

44. Sharon Otterman and Jennifer Medina, "New York Schools Chancellor Ends 8-Year Run," *New York Times*, November 9, 2010.

45. See David Herszenhorn, "City Reaches Tentative Deal with Teachers," *New York Times*, October 4, 2005.

46. See, for example, Barbara Martinez, "More Teachers to Lose Positions—But Not Pay," *Wall Street Journal*, July 1, 2010; Medina, "Progress Slow in Bloomberg Goal to Rid Schools of Bad Teachers."

47. See, for example, Medina, "With Teachers' Contract Set to End, Talks Are Quiet."

48. Stern, "A Teachers' Contract for a New Era."

49. New York City's students appear to have made solid achievement gains during Bloomberg's tenure as mayor, both on the NAEP national exams and on state exams—but it is difficult, in the absence of carefully controlled statistical analyses, to draw any firm conclusions about the precise impact of their leadership on student learning. Plus, the state exams were recently recalibrated to make them tougher (in response to criticism that they

had gotten easier over the years), and the new results—with more kids doing poorly—have muddied the waters about the trends over time. My own view, in any event, is that it is a mistake to evaluate their leadership in these terms, because they have spent the past eight years in a pitched battle with the UFT trying to patch together a more effective organization—and *that* is the aspect of their leadership that really counts. The battle continues. In the meantime, they are saddled with a woefully ineffective organization and forced to do the best they can. For figures on New York City test scores, see the "district profiles" on the NAEP section of the National Center for Education Statistics website (nces.ed.gov/nation-sreportcard/districts/). See also Jennifer Medina, "Standards Raised, More Students Fail Tests," *New York Times*, July 28, 2010; "Beating the Odds: Analysis of Student Performance on State Assessments and NAEP, Results from the 2008–09 School Year" (Washington: Council of Great City Schools, March 2010), available at www.cgcs.org/Pubs/BT9.pdf.

50. The figure from fiscal 2009 is from Adam Schaeffer, "They Spend What? The Real Cost of Public Schools," Policy Analysis 662 (Washington: Cato Institute, March 10, 2010). The higher $28,000 figure is also from Shaeffer and comes from his in-depth study of spending in major districts around the country. See also Andrew J. Coulson, "D.C. Vouchers Solved? Generous Severance for Displaced Workers" (Washington: Cato Institute, December 17, 2009), available at www.cato-at-liberty.org/dc-vouchers-solved-generous-severance-for-displaced-workers/; June Kronholz, "D.C.'s Braveheart: Can Michelle Rhee Wrest Control of the D.C. School System from Decades of Failure?" *Education Next* 10, no. 1 (Winter 2010): 28–35.

51. The National Assessment of Educational Progress test score data are available on the web site of the National Center for Education Statistics. See especially the "state pro-files" section on NAEP (nces.ed.gov/nationsreportcard/states/).

52. Clay Risen, "The Lightning Rod," *Atlantic* (November 2008).

53. For the recent figure on charters, see Nick Anderson and Bill Turque, "Reading Scores Stalled under 'No Child' Law, Report Finds D.C. Fourth-Graders a Bright Spot in Disappointing 2009 Data," *Washington Post*, March 25, 2010.

54. David Nakamura, "Fenty's School Takeover Approved," *Washington Post*, April 20, 2007.

55. V. Dion Haynes, David S. Fallis, and April Witt, "Fenty's Agent of Change," *Washington Post*, July 2, 2007.

56. Theola Labb, "Teachers' Union Is Urged to Fight Plan; No. 2 Official Fears Prec-edent of Move at Central Office," *Washington Post*, October 18, 2007.

57. See, for example, Kronholz, "D.C.'s Braveheart."

58. V. Dion Haynes, "District Teachers Offered Buyout; As Many as 700 Could Accept Incentives to Leave," *Washington Post*, April 11, 2008; V. Dion Haynes, "Rhee Gets Say over Teacher Transfers; Some Denounce Agreement with Union President," *Washington Post*, April 29, 2008.

59. V. Dion Haynes, "Turmoil Racks Teachers Union; National Group Intervenes amid Officers' Battle, Recall Drive," *Washington Post*, May 5, 2008.

60. Sam Dillon, "School Chief Takes on Tenure, Stirring a Fight," *New York Times*, November 13, 2008.

61. Risen, "The Lightning Rod"; Jeff Chu, "Fixing Washington, D.C.'s School System," *Fast Company*, August 7, 2008, available at fastcompany.com.

62. See, for example, Bill Turque, "Pay-Hike Plan for Teachers in D.C. Entails Probation," *Washington Post*, July 24, 2008.

63. Bill Turque, "Rhee Says Consultant's Report Shows Pay Plan Is Sustainable," *Washington Post*, March 3, 2009.

64. Dillon, "School Chief Takes on Tenure, Stirring a Fight"; Bill Turque, "Pay Dispute Continues as Classes Near; D.C. Teachers Split along Age Lines," *Washington Post*, August 14, 2008.

65. Turque, "Pay-Hike Plan for Teachers in D.C. Entails Probation."

66. Bill Turque, "Rhee's Plan B Targets Teacher Quality; Strategy Might Include New Evaluation Process, Linking Licenses to Classroom Performance," *Washington Post*, September 8, 2008; Bill Turque, "Rhee Bypasses Talks, Imposes Dismissal Plan; Some Teachers Will Go on 90-Day Review," *Washington Post*, October 3, 2008.

67. Amanda Ripley, "Rhee Tackles Classroom Challenge," *Time*, December 8, 2008.

68. Bill Turque, "Long Battle Expected on Plan to Fire Teachers; D.C. Union Being Aided by National Organization," *Washington Post*, October 26, 2008.

69. Steven Pearlstein, "A Watershed Labor Negotiation," *Washington Post*, August 29, 2008.

70. Kronholz, "D.C.'s Braveheart"; Thomas B. Edsell, "Michelle Rhee Threatens End-Run around Teachers Union," *Huffington Post*, April 2, 2009, available at www.huffingtonpost.com; Bill Turque, "New D.C. Teacher Ratings Stress Better Test Scores," *Washington Post*, October 1, 2009.

71. Bill Turque, "D.C. Teacher Contracts Still Stuck; Fallout from Layoffs Is Cited, with No Bargaining Sessions Yet," *Washington Post*, October 21, 2009.

72. District of Columbia Public Schools, "D.C. Superior Court Denies Challenge to DCPS Reduction-In-Force," press release (Washington: D.C. Public Schools, November 24, 2009).

73. See, for example, Bill Turque, "D.C. Schools Insider," *Washington Post*, March 25, 2010; Bill Turque, "D.C. Teachers Contract May Be Close, Union Chief Says," *Washington Post*, March 26, 2010.

74. For details, see Washington Teachers Union, "Tentative Agreement Highlights," available at www.washingtonteachersunion.org. Also Sam Dillon, "A Tentative Contract Deal for Washington Teachers," *New York Times*, April 7, 2010; (although he gets the tenure provision wrong) Robert McCartney, "Teachers' Contract a Breakthrough for D.C.'s Schools' Rhee," *Washington Post*, April 11, 2010; Bill Turque, "D.C. Teachers' Union Ratifies Contract, Basing Pay on Results, Not Seniority," *Washington Post*, June 3, 2010.

75. Information on Weingarten's internal role in resisting Rhee's reforms was provided through confidential conversations with someone inside the D.C. administration who was privy to the negotiations. For examples of Weingarten's being given credit for the contract, see, for example, Andrew J. Rotherham and Richard Whitmire, "Making the Grade," *New Republic*, March 18, 2009; Tim Daly, "Weingarten Delivers the Goods: A Frequent Critic Praises the Union Head for Backing Bold Reforms," *New York Daily*

News, July 5, 2010; Andrew Rotherham, "Randi Weingarten Unplugged," *eduwonk*, June 18, 2010, available at eduwonk.com.

76. See Randi Weingarten, "D.C. Deal Has Few Lessons for N.Y.: Union Head Says Washington Contract Shouldn't Be a Model," *New York Daily News*, June 17, 2010.

77. See also the discussion in Steven Brill, "Teachers Unions Last Stand," *New York Times Sunday Magazine*, May 18, 2010.

78. Washington Teachers Union, "Tentative Agreement Highlights."

79. See Bill Turque, "D.C. Teacher Contract Undercut by Doubts on Private Funding," *Washington Post*, April 29, 2010.

80. Ibid.

81. Analysts argue that Fenty lost not just because his education reforms were resisted by many black residents (a resistance that was played upon by the unions during the campaign), but also because he was seen as arrogant, insensitive, and out of touch. Whatever the balance of causes, the unions spent heavily to have him defeated and clearly revealed where they stood. For overviews of the campaign from different angles, see Ben Smith, "Teachers Union Helped Unseat Fenty," *Politico*, September 15, 2010, available at politico.com; Andrew Rotherham, "Fenty's Loss in D.C.: A Blow to Education Reform?" *Time*, September 16, 2010; Nikita Stewart and Paul Schwartzman, "How Adrian Fenty Lost His Reelection Bid for D.C. Mayor," *Washington Post*, September 16, 2010; Ian Urbina, "Mayor's Loss May Imperil School Reform," *New York Times*, September 15, 2010. On Michelle Rhee's decision to leave, see Sean Cavanaugh and Mary Ann Zehr, "Rhee Resigns, Urging D.C.: 'Keep the Reforms Going,'" *Education Week*, October 13, 2010; Tim Craig and Bill Turque, "Michelle Rhee Resigns; Gray Huddles with Her Successor," *Washington Post*, October 13, 2010.

82. Bill Turque, "Washington Teachers' Union President George Parker Loses Run-Off Election," *Washington Post*, November 30, 2010. The election was supposed to have been held in May, but was postponed until November due to internal conflicts and intrigue.

83. Student achievement has increased significantly during Rhee's tenure, and the District of Columbia appears to have outpaced other big city districts, but I am not aware of any controlled statistical analyses of her impact and, done right, these assessments are rather complicated. In any event, Rhee never had the luxury of being able to govern her district under a favorable contract. She spent nearly three years battling the union and trying to clear away the district's dead wood, and her tenure was one of turmoil and conflict that couldn't fully benefit from the kind of organization she was trying to create. So it is really not of the essence to focus heavily on test score gains in the interim, as though this is the acid test of her leadership. For simple statistics on District of Columbia test scores, see "DCPS Secondary Students Demonstrate Significant Gains for Third Consecutive Year," July 13, 2010, available on the District of Columbia Public Schools website at dcps.dc.gov/DCPS/In+the+Classroom/How+Students+Are+Assessed/Assessments/DCPS+Secondary+School+Students+Demonstrate+Significant+Gains+for+Third+Consecutive+Year. See also Council of Great City Schools "Beating the Odds"; and "Test Scores Suggest the New D.C. School Model Is Working," editorial, *Washington Post*, May 21, 2010.

84. See, for example, Amanda Ripley, "Rhee Tackles Classroom Challenge," *Time*, November 26, 2008; Amanda Ripley, "'Waiting for Superman': A Call to Action for Our Schools," *Time*, September 23, 2010; Steven Brill, "Teachers Unions' Last Stand," *New York Times Magazine*, May 17, 2010; Evan Thomas, "Schoolyard Brawl," *Newsweek*, March 6, 2010; Jonathan Alter, "How Congress Keeps Screwing Up Education," *Newsweek*, July 2, 2010; Joe Klein, "Why We're Failing Our Schools," *Time*, January 28, 2010; "Potential Disruption? Ending D.C. School Vouchers Would Dash the Best Hopes of Hundreds of Children," editorial, *Washington Post*, March 2, 2009.

Chapter Eight

1. See, especially, Charles Taylor Kerchner and Douglas E. Mitchell, *The Changing Idea of a Teachers Union* (London: Falmer Press, 1988); Charles Taylor Kerchner and Julia E. Koppich, *A Union of Professionals: Labor Relations and Educational Reform* (Teachers College Press, 1993); Charles Taylor Kerchner, Julia E. Koppich, and Joseph E. Weeres, *United Mind Workers: Unions and Teaching in the Knowledge Society* (San Francisco: Jossey-Bass, 1997).

2. See, for example, Ann Bradley, "Unions Turn Critical Eye on Themselves," *Education Week*, February 16, 2000.

3. Again, the most prominent books are Kerchner and Mitchell, *The Changing Idea of a Teachers Union*; Kerchner and Koppich, *A Union of Professionals*; Kerchner, Koppich, and Weeres, *United Mind Workers*.

4. See, for example, Andrew J. Rotherham and Richard Whitmire, "Making the Grade: Can AFT President Randi Weingarten Satisfy Teachers and Reformers at the Same Time?" *New Republic*, March 18, 2009; Bob Herbert, "A Serious Proposal," *New York Times*, January 12, 2010; Jay Mathews, "Rare Alliance May Signal Ebb in Union's Charter Opposition," *Washington Post*, May 43, 2009.

5. A number of "reform" union leaders have been thrown out of office for getting out of step with the bread-and-butter interests of their members, even when their "reforms" have been quite modest. The incentives to stay away from real reform, in other words, are clear. See, for example, Vaishali Honawar, "A Union Chief's Defeat Stirs Debate on Leadership," *Education Week*, June 13, 2006; Bess Keller, "Elections Give No Easy Fix on Union Course," *Education Week*, March 15, 2005.

6. Kerchner, Koppich, and Weeres, *United Mind Workers*.

7. Quote is from Thomas Toch, "Tensions of the Shanker Era: A Speech That Shook the Field," *Education Week*, March 26, 1997. See that same article for basic information presented in this paragraph. See also Richard Kahlenberg, "The Agenda That Saved Public Education," *American Educator* (Fall 2007): 4–10.

8. Richard Kahlenberg's sympathetic biography of Shanker, which received a great deal of attention in the press and among reformers, is a good example of how the ideas of reform unionism shape assessments of what union leaders do and say. See Richard Kahlenberg, *Tough Liberal: Albert Shanker and the Battles over Schools, Unions, Race, and Democracy* (Columbia University Press, 2007). For a more hard-headed account, see

especially Myron Lieberman, *The Teacher Unions* (New York: Free Press, 1997), especially ch. 11, "Albert Shanker: Visionary or Union Apologist."

9. Robert Chase, "The New NEA: Reinventing Teacher Unions for a New Order," speech to the National Press Club, Washington, February 5, 1997. All quotes in the following paragraph are taken from the speech.

10. Quote is from Peter Brimelow, *The Worm in the Apple* (New York: Harper-Collins, 2003), p. 177. For a discussion of the Kamber report and "new unionism" more generally, see ch. 11, "The Same Old New Unionism."

11. Quote here (and prior) is from Kamber Group, "An Institution at Risk: An External Communications Review of the National Education Association," report to the National Education Association, January 14, 1997. For other discussions of the report, in addition to Brimelow's, see, for example, David Hill, "In the Line of Fire," *Education Week*, November 1, 1997; Mackinac Center for Public Policy, "NEA/MEA Remakes Image without Fundamental Change" (Midland, Mich.: Mackinac Center for Public Policy, January 7, 1999), available at www.mackinac.org/9412.

12. For general commentaries on Chase's speech, see Jeanne Ponessa, "Seeking 'Reinvention' of NEA, Chase Calls for Shift in Priorities," *Education Week*, February 12, 1997; Robert Lowe, "The New Unionism and the Very Old," *Education Week*, April 1, 1998; Hill, "In the Line of Fire."

13. Quoted in Lowe, "The New Unionism and the Very Old."

14. Quoted in Hill, "In the Line of Fire."

15. See, for example, Ann Bradley, "Network Seeks Union Role in Reform Efforts," *Education Week*, May 8, 1996; Vaishali Honawar, "Union Agitators," *Education Week*, February 1, 2006; Mark Simon and Naomi Baden, "The Power of Progressive Thinking," *Education Week*, January 30, 2008; Vaishali Honawar, "Mooney Institute Tries to Blend Unionism, School Reform," *Education Week*, April 9, 2008.

16. For overviews of peer review, see, for example, Project on the Next Generation of Teachers, *A User's Guide to Peer Assistance and Review* (Harvard University, Graduate School of Education, 2009), available at www.gse.harvard.edu/~ngt/par. Also American Federation of Teachers and National Education Association, *Peer Assistance and Peer Review: An AFT/NEA Handbook* (Washington: Shaping the Profession That Shapes the Future, an AFT/NEA Conference on Teacher Quality, 1998).

17. For these and other basic facts about peer review, see Ibid. On the Toledo Plan specifically, see, for example, Julia E. Koppich, "Toledo: Peer Assistance and Review (PAR)," Strategic Management of Human Capital, a project of the Consortium for Policy Research in Education (University of Wisconsin, October 2009). For a very sympathetic but detailed treatment of Toledo and discussion of peer review, see Ray Marshall, *The Case for Collaborative School Reform: The Toledo Experience* (Washington: Economic Policy Institute, 2008).

18. See, for example, Marshall, *The Case for Collaborative School Reform.*

19. For examples of the kinds of (essentially qualitative) studies that are done, see, for example, Linda Kaboolian and Paul Sutherland, "Evaluation of Toledo Public School District Peer Assistance and Review Plan" (Harvard University, John F. Kennedy School of Government, 2005); Jennifer Goldstein, "Easy to Dance to: Solving the Problems of

Teacher Evaluation with Peer Assistance and Review," *American Journal of Education* 113 (May 2007): 470–508; Koppich, "Toledo: Peer Assistance and Review"; Julia E. Koppich, "Toward Improving Teacher Quality: An Evaluation of Peer Assistance and Review in Montgomery County Public Schools," report prepared for the Montgomery County Public Schools, 2004; Marshall, *The Case for Collaborative School Reform*.

20. See Daniel Weisberg, Susan Sexton, Jennifer Mulhern, and David Keeling, "The Widget Effect: Our National Failure to Acknowledge and Act on Differences in Teacher Effectiveness" (New York: New Teacher Project, 2009), especially pp. 11, 15, 17, available at www.widgeteffect.org. Of course, it's possible that Toledo is managing to counsel-out its worst teachers and doing a better job of it than other districts are. But that hasn't been demonstrated, and the effects would have to justify the kinds of claims that are being made by proponents.

21. For critiques of peer review, see, for example, Thomas Toch and Robert Rothman, "Rush to Judgment" (Washington: Education Sector, January 2008), available at ww.educationsector.org/usr_doc/RushToJudgment_ES_Jan08.pdf ; Christina E. Murray and Gerald Grant, "Teacher Peer Review: Possibility or Pipe Dream?" *Contemporary Education* 69, no. 4 (Summer 1998): 202–05; Myron Lieberman, *Teachers Evaluating Teachers: Peer Review and the New Unionism* (New Brunswick, N.J.: Transaction Publishers, 1998).

22. See the cost figures for Toledo, presented in Koppich, "Toledo: Peer Assistance and Review." On Hillsborough County, see Tom Marshall, "Hillsborough School Board Gets First Look Monday at New Teacher Evaluation Spurred by Gates Grant," *St. Petersburg Times*, May 14, 2010. See also Lieberman, *Teachers Evaluating Teachers*.

23. Adam Urbanski and Roger Erskine, "School Reform, TURN, and Teacher Compensation," *Phi Delta Kappan* 81, no. 5 (January 2000): 367–70.

24. Even in districts that allow student test scores to enter into the equation, they usually have a very small role to play relative to other factors. See, for example, Vaishali Honawar, "Performance System Slow to Catch on in Minnesota," *Education Week*, January 17, 2007; Vaishali Honawar and Lynn Olson, "Advancing Pay for Performance," *Education Week*, January 26, 2008. For an overview of the teacher pay issue and of various reforms to the single salary schedule that have actually been adopted, see Michael J. Podgursky and Matthew G. Springer, "Teacher Performance Pay: A Review," *Journal of Policy Analysis and Management* 26, no. 4 (2007): 909–49.

25. See chapter 2; also Steve Farkas, Jean Johnson, and Ann Duffett, with Leslie Moye and Jackie Vine, *Stand by Me: What Teachers Really Think about Unions, Merit Pay, and Other Professional Matters* (New York: Public Agenda, 2003); Ann Duffett, Steve Farkas, Andrew J. Rotherham, and Elena Silva, *Waiting to Be Won Over: Teachers Speak on the Profession, Unions, and Reform* (Washington: Education Sector, May 2, 2008), available at www.educationsector.org; and Scholastic and the Bill and Melinda Gates Foundation, "Primary Sources: America's Teachers on America's Schools" (Scholastic and the Bill and Melinda Gates Foundation, 2010), available at www.scholastic.com/primarysources.

26. Douglas McGray, "Working with the Enemy," *New York Times*, January 16, 2005.

27. See Denver Classroom Teachers Association, "Straight Talk about ProComp" (Denver: Denver Classroom Teachers Association, September 2006).

28. See Denver Public Schools, "ProComp at a Glance: A Quick Reference Handbook," (Denver: Denver Classroom Teachers Association, November 2006).

29. A recent evaluation of the system's impact was carried out based on a few years' worth of data. It suggested that student achievement may have improved slightly, although there was no evidence that teachers who opted into ProComp boosted achievement more than teachers who didn't opt in. There was evidence, though, that teachers newly hired into ProComp were especially productive, suggesting that the program was attracting higher-quality people and thus having a positive selection effect. There was also evidence that retention levels were higher, especially among teachers at hard-to-staff schools (where turnover problems are usually greatest). All these findings are just suggestive, though, because the data do not allow for definitive conclusions about the program's impact; other factors might have been responsible for the observed outcomes. Edward W. Wiley, Eleanor R. Spindler, and Amy N. Subert, *Denver ProComp: An Outcomes Evaluation of Denver's Alternative Teacher Compensation System, 2010 Report* (Denver: Denver Public Schools, 2010), available at static.dpsk12.org/gems/newprocomp/ProCompOutcomes EvaluationApril2010final.pdf.

30. For more details on the politics and makeup of the Denver plan—and for an account more sympathetic than mine and more inclined to see it as a major reform—see Phil Gonring, Paul Teske, and Brad Jupp, *Pay-for-Performance Teacher Compensation: An Inside View of Denver's ProComp Plan* (Harvard Education Press, 2007).

31. See, for example, Steven Brill, "Teachers Unions' Last Stand," *New York Times Magazine*, May 17, 2010; Michele McNeil and Lesli A. Maxwell, "Schools up the Ante on Applications for Race to the Top," *Education Week*, June 9, 2010; Arne Duncan, "The Quiet Revolution: Secretary Arne Duncan's Remarks at the National Press Club" (Washington: U.S. Department of Education, July 27, 2010), available at www.ed.gov/ news/speeches/quiet-revolution-secretary-arne-duncans-remarks-national-press-club; Mary Bruce, "Controversy Surrounds White House Push for Increased Teacher Accountability," *ABC News*, July 29, 2010, available at abcnews.go.com/Politics/controversy-surrounds-white-house-push-increased-teacher-accountability /story?id=11279505.

32. See Bloomberg Businessweek, "Bill Gates' Latest Mission: Fixing America's Schools," *msnbc*, July 17, 2010; Nick Anderson, "Gates Foundation Playing Pivotal Role in Changes for Education System," *Washington Post*, July 12, 2010; Tom Marshall, "Hillsborough Hires 100 Peer Evaluators for Its $100 Million Gates Reforms," *St. Petersburg Times*, April 20, 2010; Marshall, "Hillsborough School Board Gets First Look Monday at New Teacher Evaluation Spurred by Gates Grant"; Karamagi Rujumba, "Bill Gates Lauds City's Steps to Improve Schools," *Pittsburgh Post-Gazette*, July 11, 2010; Jane Roberts, "Memphis Teachers Union OKs Contract with Raises," *Commercial Appeal*, February 17, 2010.

33. For an overview of Urbanski's ideas on collaboration, see, for example, Adam Urbanski and Clifford B. Janey, "A Better Idea," *Education Week*, May 23, 2001. The quote is from that article. See also Adam Urbanski, "Reform or Be Reformed," *Education Next* 1, no. 3 (Fall 2001): 51–54.

34. See, for example, Christine E. Murray and Gerald Grand, "Rochester's Reforms: The Right Prescription?" *Phi Delta Kappan* 79, no. 2 (October 1997): 148–55; Blake

Rodman, "Two Unions Gain Sharp Pay Hikes, Role in Decisions," *Education Week*, September 9, 1987.

35. Laura Mansnerus, "A Transformation on Hold," *New York Times*, July 6, 1993.

36. Ann Bradley, "Proposal to Retool Rochester Reforms Is Snubbed," *Education Week*, April 12, 1995.

37. Sewell Chan, "D.C.'s Schools Chief Gets Mixed Reviews; Some on Rochester Board Backed Janey," *Washington Post*, August 15, 2004.

38. Murray and Grand, "Rochester's Reforms," p. 148.

39. Adam Urbanski, "Take Peaceful Path to New Teachers Contract," *Rochester Democrat and Chronicle*, January 24, 2000.

40. Tim Louis Macaluso, "State of the Union: RTA's Adam Urbanski," *Rochester City Newspaper*, May 20, 2009.

41. David Andreatta, "Teacher Contract Talks Heat Up," *Rochester Democrat and Chronicle*, April 1, 2009.

42. Macaluso, "State of the Union."

43. Stephen Sawchuk, "Teacher Contract Called Potential Model for Nation," *Education Week*, October 28, 2009; also Neil King Jr., "Obama Wins a Battle as a Teachers Union Shows Flexibility," *Wall Street Journal*, October 17, 2009.

44. "Less Than 'Courage' in New Haven," editorial, *Washington Post*, November 10, 2009.

45. Ibid.

46. See, for example, Thomas W. Carroll, "New Haven's Teacher Contract a Model? Not So Fast," *Huffington Post*, October 21, 2009, available at www.huffingtonpost.com/thomas-w-carroll/new-havens-teacher-contra_b_328950.html; "Less Than 'Courage' in New Haven"; "The New Haven Model," editorial, *New York Times*, October 29, 2009.

47. "Less Than 'Courage' in New Haven."

48. "The New Haven Model."

49. For basic information about the history of Green Dot and the schools it operates, go to its website at www.greendot.org.

50. Barr recently stepped down as chief executive officer of Green Dot, but is still actively involved and has his sights on fomenting change throughout the country. See Lesli Maxwell, "Founder of Green Dot Charter School Network Steps Down," *Education Week*, November 23, 2009. On Barr, his social activism, and how he has channeled it into education reform, see, for example, Sam Dillon, "Union-Friendly Maverick Leads Charge for Charter Schools," *New York Times*, July 24, 2007; "The Rise of Green Dot Schools," *Administrator Magazine* (June 2008), available at www2.scholastic.com/browse/article.jsp?id=3749586.

51. See the Green Dot test scores from the California Department of Education, available at www.greendot.org/results/school_results.

52. See Dillon, "Union-Friendly Maverick Leads New Charge for Charter Schools." Also, for a graphic sense of what the UTLA is up to in Los Angeles, see Susan Estrich, "Los Angeles Shows Lack of Civic Engagement," *Fox News*, April 5, 2007, available at www.foxnews.com/story/0,2933,264083,00.html.

53. The entire contract can be downloaded from the Green Dot website at www.greendot.org/files/AMU Contract Final Version 2007-08.pdf.

54. See, for example, Maxwell, "Founder of Green Dot Charter School Network Steps Down." See also Thomas W. Carroll, "Behind the Unions' Shift on Charters," *New York Post*, October 9, 2009.

55. Trip Gabriel, "Despite Image, Union Leader Backs School Change," *New York Times*, October 15, 2010.

56. Quoted in Evan Thomas, "Schoolyard Brawl," *Newsweek*, March 6, 2010.

57. Quoted in Gabriel, "Despite Image, Union Leader Backs School Change."

58. We've already seen how this happens, but I discuss it in detail in chapters 9 and 10.

59. Vaishali Honawar, "AFT No Longer a Major Player in Reform Arena," *Education Week*, January 31, 2007.

60. Discussions are in the news media everywhere. See, for example, Amanda Ripley, "'Waiting for Superman': A Call to Action for Our Schools," *Time*, September 23, 2010; Brill, "Teachers Unions' Last Stand"; Thomas, "Schoolyard Brawl."

61. Quoted in Gabriel, "Despite Image, Union Leader Backs School Change."

62. Sam Dillon, "Head of Teachers Union Offers to Talk on Tenure and Merit Pay," *New York Times*, November 18, 2008.

63. See, for example, Randi Weingarten, "D.C. Deal Has Few Lessons for N.Y: Union Head Says Washington Contract Shouldn't Be a Model," *New York Daily News*, June 17, 2010.

64. Kathleen Byrne, "Eva Moskowitz and Randi Weingarten Duke It out over Charter Schools, Public Schools, and Unions," *Examiner*, May 1, 2009.

65. See their website at www.uftcharterschool.net/. They are not setting the world on fire. See, for example, James Merriman, "Mixed Review for UFT Charter School: Time for Some Humility?" *Centerpoint: The Charter Center Blog*, March 16, 2010, available at nyccharterschools.org/meet/blog/459-mixed-review-for-uft-charter-school.

66. See, for example, Anemona Hartocollis,"Crew Speaks Out against Charter School Plan," *New York Times,* December 16, 1998.

67. See the website of the Center for Education Reform at www.charterschoolresearch.com/laws/new-york.htm.

68. See, for example, Thomas W. Carroll, "Gutting Charters," *New York Post*, January 4, 2010; Thomas W. Carroll," The Unions' Plan to Kill Good Schools," *New York Post*, April 20, 2010; Carl Campanile, "Senate Charter OK Sparks Class War," *New York Post*, May 4, 2010; Glenn Blain and Rachel Monohan, "State Senate OKs Move to Double Number of Charter Schools; Makes Deadline for Race to the Top Cash," *New York Daily News*, May 29, 2010; Joshua Greenman, "State Teachers Union Is the Big Loser in New York's Win of $700 Million for Education," *New York Daily News*, August 25, 2010; Wayne Barrett, "Bloomberg and the Teachers Union," *Village Voice*, May 13, 2009.

69. "Friends to Failure: Teachers Union Battles to Keep Dismal Harlem Schools Alive," editorial, *New York Daily News*, April 5, 2009; Elizabeth Green, "Parents, Weingarten Sue DOE, Klein over Charter School Siting," *GothamSchools,* March 24, 2009, available at gothamschools.org; Jason L. Riley, "Charter Schools Flourish in Harlem but Teachers Unions Are Still Trying to Stop Their Growth," *Wall Street Journal*, March 8, 2010; Barrett, "Bloomberg and the Teachers Union."

70. This quote is taken from her January 14, 2004, address to the Association for a Better New York. The address was posted, word for word, on the UFT website as "UFT President Randi Weingarten Address before ABNY Jan 14, 2004," and I accessed and downloaded it on February 24, 2010, but it is apparently no longer posted on that website—or anywhere, so far as I can tell. For an account of the speech, see David Herszenhorn, "Failing City Teachers Face a Faster Ax," *New York Times*, January 15, 2004.

71. Quoted in Dana Goldstein, "The Education Wars," *American Prospect*, March 23, 2009. See also Dillon, "Head of Teachers Union Offers to Talk on Tenure and Merit Pay."

72. Andrew Rotherham and Richard Whitmire, "Making the Grade," *New Republic*, March 18, 2009.

73. Randi Weingarten, "Reflections and Thank Yous," *Huffington Post*, June 25, 2009, available at huffingtonpost.com.

74. Again, for the details see chapter 7.

75. Barbara Martinez, "More Teachers to Lose Positions—But Not Pay," *Wall Street Journal*, July 1, 2010.

76. See Jennifer Medina, "Bill Would Bar Linking Class Test Scores to Tenure," *New York Times*, March 18, 2008.

77. Vaishali Honawar, "New AFT Leader Vows to Bring Down NCLB Law," *Education Week*, July 30, 2008. See also Sam Dillon, "New Vision for Schools Proposes Broad Role," *New York Times*, July 15, 2008.

78. Honawar, "New AFT Leader Vows to Bring Down NCLB Law."

79. See, for example, Dan Brown, "Public School Teachers Endorse Hillary Clinton," *Huffington Post*, October 9, 2007, available at huffingtonpost.com; Michele McNeil, "Clinton Calls Merit Pay for Teachers 'Demeaning,'" *Education Week*, November 20, 2007.

80. Rebecca Harshbarger, "DC Ed Chief Slams Randi," *New York Post*, September 27, 2010.

81. Steven Greenhouse, "Union Chief Seeks to Overhaul Teacher Evaluation Process," *New York Times*, January 13, 2010. Also Bob Herbert, "A Serious Proposal," *New York Times*, January 12, 2010. Also Stephen Sawchuk, "AFT Chief Promises Due Process Reform," *Education Week*, January 20, 2010.

82. On the position of the *New York Times*, see, for example, "The New Haven Model," editorial, *New York Times*, October 29, 2009; "Walking the Walk on School Reform," editorial, *New York Times*, January 16, 2010.

83. Quoted in Goldstein, "The Education Wars."

84. Randi Weingarten, "Stop Vilifying Teachers Unions: Politicians, Parents, and Labor Leaders Share Responsibility," *New York Daily News*, August 3, 2009.

85. Randi Weingarten, testimony before the House Committee on Education and Labor, May 4, 2010.

86. See chapter 10. On the New York agreement in particular, see, for example, Jennifer Medina, "New York State Votes to Expand Charter Schools," *New York Times*, May 28, 2010; Jennifer Medina, "Agreement Will Alter Teacher Evaluations," *New York Times*, May 10, 2010; Maura Walz, "What to Expect from Today's Teacher Evaluation Agreement," *GothamSchools*, available at gothamschools.org. That same site has a copy of the agreement (which became legislation).

87. See, for example, Jeremy P. Meyer and Colleen O'Connor, "Smaller Teachers Union Backs Colo. Reform Bill," *Denver Post*, May 10, 2010; Stephanie Banchero, "Teacher Evaluation Bill Approved in Colorado," *Wall Street Journal*, May 14, 2010.

88. On the New York reform, see Medina, "New York State Votes to Expand Charter Schools"; Medina, "Agreement Will Alter Teacher Evaluations"; Walz, "What to Expect from Today's Teacher Evaluation Agreement." On Colorado, see Jeremy P. Meyer, "After the Signing of Teacher-Evaluation Measure, Factions Dig into Law's Details," *Denver Post*, May 21, 2010.

89. For positive takes on Weingarten's contributions to reform in recent years, see, for example, Rotherham and Whitmire, "Making the Grade"; Tim Daly, "Weingarten Delivers the Goods: A Frequent Critic Praises the Union Head for Backing Bold Reforms," *New York Daily News*, July 5, 2010; Andrew Rotherham, "Randi Weingarten Unplugged," *eduwonk*, June 18, 2010, available at eduwonk.com; Goldstein, "The Education Wars"; Dana Goldstein, "Grading 'Waiting for Superman,'" *Nation*, September 23, 2010.

90. Honawar, "A Union Chief's Defeat Stirs Debate on Leadership"; Keller, "Elections Give No Easy Fix on Union Course."

91. Weingarten, "Stop Vilifying Teachers Unions."

Chapter Nine

1. For basic information on the structure of American education and on the division of authority among local, state, and national governments and officials, see, for example, Michael W. Kirst and Frederick M. Wirt, *The Political Dynamics of American Education*, 4th ed. (Richmond, Calif.: McCutchan, 2009); Carl F. Kaestle, Alyssa E. Lodewick , and Jeffrey R. Henig, eds., *To Educate a Nation: Federal and National Strategies of School Reform* (University of Kansas Press, 2007).

2. On NCLB, the political lead-up to it, and the growing federal role in American education, see, for example, Patrick McGuinn, *No Child Left Behind and the Transformation of Federal Education Policy* (University of Kansas Press, 2006); Paul Manna, *School's In: Federalism and the National Education Agenda* (Georgetown University Press, 2006).

3. While policymakers and opinion leaders are increasingly recognizing that this is so, and indeed are increasingly open and vocal about it—something that is discussed in chapter 1 and discussed again in much greater detail in chapter 10—academic scholarship (aside from my own) does not emphasize this theme at all. There are two reasons for this. The first is that, even though public education is thoroughly political, education researchers and political scientists have barely studied the politics of education over the decades, and they have done even less to study and lay bare the political role of the teachers unions. The second is that, in recent years, scholars who *have* studied the politics of education have focused on the *national* politics of education, especially No Child Left Behind, and they have not focused on (or studied) the *state-level* politics of education, where the vast majority of important policy decisions about education are made. I should add that NCLB was the unions' single greatest defeat in the modern reform era and not at all representative of their overall influence. More generally, the teachers

unions tend to be weaker at the national level than in most of the states, because more groups are involved in national issues, the issues are more salient to the public and get more media attention, and the unions are less politically advantaged. As a result, the academic literature on the politics of education has little to say about the state-level politics of education and is not a good basis for trying to understand the power of the teachers unions in education generally. It is, however, helpful for understanding the politics of NCLB and national developments. See, for example, McGuinn, *No Child Left Behind and the Transformation of Federal Education Policy*; Manna, *School's In*; Lee W. Anderson, *Congress and the Classroom: From the Cold War to "No Child Left Behind"* (Pennsylvania State University Press, 2007); Kaestle, Lodewick, and Henig, eds., *To Educate a Nation*; Elizabeth Debray and Carl Kaestle, *Politics, Ideology, and Education: Federal Policy during the Clinton and Bush Administrations* (Teachers College Press, 2006); Kevin Kosar, *Failing Grades: The Federal Politics of Education Standards* (Boulder, Colo.: Lynne Rienner Publishers, 2005); Lawrence McAndrews, *The Era of Education: The Presidents and the Schools, 1965–2001* (University of Illinois Press, 2008).

4. See, of course, chapter 2. Also see Marjorie Murphy, *Blackboard Unions: The AFT and the NEA, 1900–1980* (Cornell University Press, 1990); Terry M. Moe, "Teachers Unions and the Public Schools," in *A Primer on America's Schools*, edited by Terry M. Moe (Stanford, Calif.: Hoover Institution Press, 2001); Myron Lieberman, *The Teachers Unions* (New York: Free Press, 1997).

5. For a comparable argument, made early on, that the rise of union power led to a qualitatively different kind of system, see William Grimshaw, *Union Rule in the Schools* (Lexington, Mass.: Lexington Books, 1979).

6. For earlier statements of these views and the surrounding facts, see Moe, "Teachers Unions and the Public Schools"; also Terry M. Moe, "Union Power and the Education of Children," in *Collective Bargaining in Education: Negotiating Change in Today's Schools*, edited by Jane Hannaway and Andrew J. Rotherham (Harvard Education Press, 2006); Terry M. Moe and John E. Chubb, *Liberating Learning: Technology, Politics, and the Future of American Education* (San Francisco: Jossey-Bass, 2998); Terry M. Moe, "The Politics of the Status Quo," in *Our Schools and Our Future: Are We Still at Risk?* edited by Paul E. Peterson (Stanford, Calif.: Hoover Press, 2003); Terry M. Moe, "Politics, Control, and the Future of School Accountability," in *Leave No Child Behind? The Politics and Practices of School Accountability*, edited by Paul E. Peterson and Martin West (Brookings, 2003). See also Lieberman, *The Teachers Unions*; Peter Brimelow, *The Worm in the Apple: How the Teachers Unions Are Destroying American Education* (New York: HarperCollins, 2003); G. Gregory Moo, *Power Grab: How the National Education Association Is Betraying Our Children* (Washington: Regnery Publishing, 1999).

7. These features of American government are well known. For a theoretical treatment of how veto points and veto politics shape the making (and not making) of public policy, see George Tsebelis, *Veto Players: How Political Institutions Work* (Princeton University Press, 2002). Political scientists have written quite a bit about the obstacles to change and the stickiness of the status quo. My emphasis in this book is on veto points, but there are other explanations for status quo biases as well—often having to do with the power of interest groups, vested interests, and their capacity for preventing change.

See, for example, Paul Pierson, "When Effect Becomes Cause," *World Politics* 45, no. 4 (July 1993): 595–628; Paul Pierson, *Placing Politics in Time* (Princeton University Press, 2004); Carter Wilson, "Policy Regimes and Policy Change," *Journal of Public Policy* 20, no. 3 (1995): 247–74; E. E. Schattschneider, *The Semi-Sovereign People: A Realist's View of Democracy in America* (New York: Holt, Rinehart, and Winston, 1960); Theodore Lowi, *The End of Liberalism: Ideology, Policy, and the Crisis of Public Authority* (New York: Norton, 1969); Karen Orren and Stephen Skowronek, *The Search for American Political Development* (Cambridge University Press, 2004).

8. Ronald G. Shaiko, "Making the Connection: Organized Interests, Political Representation, and the Changing Rules of the Game in Washington Politics," in *The Interest Group Connection: Electioneering, Lobbying, and Policymaking in Washington*, 2d ed., edited by Paul S. Herrnson, Ronald G. Shaiko, and Clyde Wilcox (Washington: CQ Press, 2005).

9. For detailed discussions of the political resources of both the NEA and the AFT, see Lieberman, *The Teacher Unions*; Brimelow, *The Worm in the Apple*.

10. Political scientists have studied campaign contributions extensively, but have had a very difficult time arriving at confident conclusions about whether money buys influence because the causality is very difficult to show. For one prominent (and especially creative) study that seems to have done so, see Richard L. Hall and Frank W. Wayman, "Buying Time: Moneyed Interests and the Mobilization of Bias in Congressional Committees," *American Political Science Review* 84, no. 3 (September 1990): 797–820. For recent overviews of the political science literature on money and elections, see, for example, Marian L. Currinder and John C. Green, "Money and Elections," in *The Electoral Challenge: Theory Meets Practice*, edited by Steven C. Craig and David B. Hill (Washington: CQ Press, 2010); Stephen Wayne, *Is This Any Way to Run a Democratic Election?* 4th ed. (Washington: CQ Press, 2010). For an interesting quantitative analysis and overview, see Stephen Ansolabehere, John M. De Figueiredo, and James M. Snyder, "Why Is There So Little Money in U.S. Politics?" *Journal of Economic Perspectives* 17, no. 1 (Winter 2003): 105–30.

11. On the latter, see the Initiative and Referendum Institute at the University of Southern California website at www.iandrinstitute.org/statewide_i%26r.htm.

12. The national figures are from the Center for Responsive Politics, at www.opensecrets.org. The state figures are from the National Institute on Money in State Politics, at www.followthemoney.org.

13. The rules surrounding independent expenditures were significantly loosened in 2010 by the Supreme Court's Citizens United decision, which essentially allowed corporations and unions (and other entities) to spend unlimited amounts of money on elections, even in support of or opposition to candidates, as long as their contributions and strategies are not coordinated with those of candidates or parties. In the 2010 federal election, these independent contributions soared as a result, but it is difficult to know the actual sources of much of the spending. The court case is *Citizens United* v. *Federal Election Commission*, S.Ct. 876 (2010). For a discussion of independent expenditures and their magnitudes over the years, see the website of the Center for Responsive Politics at www.opensecrets.org/outsidespending/index.php. For a nice explanation of the Citizens

United decision and its consequences, see McKenna Long & Aldrich Attorneys at Law, "Citizens United Supreme Court Decision Changes Rules of Road for Political Participation with Corporate and Labor Funds" (McKenna Long & Aldrich, January 25, 2010), available at www.mckennalong.com/news-advisories-2235.html. See also Adam Liptak, "Justices, 5-4, Reject Corporate Spending Limit," *New York Times,* January 21, 2010.

14. These national figures and those that follow in the text below are all from the Center for Responsive Politics, at www.opensecrets.org/orgs/list.php?order=A.

15. Again, the national figures are from the Center for Responsive Politics, at www.opensecrets.org. The state figures are from the National Institute on Money in State Politics, at www.followthemoney.org.

16. Note that the percentage going to Democrats is not the same as in table 9-3. This is because the figure here is solely for the Pennsylvania Teachers Association, and the figure in table 9-3 is for all teachers unions in Pennsylvania, including local affiliates that contribute to state campaigns as well as any NEA or AFT contributions.

17. Here and throughout this section, the data on money amounts, as well as details about the contributions going to Republicans, Democrats, and specific individuals, all come from the website of the National Institute on Money in State Politics, at www.followthemoney.org.

18. Here again, the percentage going to Democrats does not exactly match the corresponding figure in table 9-3 because the latter includes all contributions from teachers union sources and is not just for the state association itself.

19. Again, this figure for percent Democrat does not match the figure in table 9-3 because the latter is a summary figure for all teachers unions making contributions to Utah state campaigns.

20. Data from the website of the National Institute on Money in State Politics, at www.followthemoney.org.

21. Ibid.

22. Ibid.

23. Because I need to combine the contributions of the affiliates of both the NEA and the AFT and because these contributions often come not just from the state associations but also from the local associations and sometimes from the nationals themselves, I have used the contribution figures that followthemoney provides for "teachers unions" generally. Although this measure sometimes includes contributions from faculty unions and other sources that are not K–12 teachers unions, these extraneous contributions are always very small, so the figures in table 9-3 are (with some measurement error) what we want. One issue to keep in mind, though, is that, in coming up with the rankings in table 9-3, I have simply compared the "teachers unions" contributions to those of other interest groups listed in followthemoney's top twenty contributors to candidates and parties, a list that was provided to me personally by staff at the National Institute on Money in State Politics and isn't calculated from the data tools available on the website. If these contributors have local or national affiliates that are also making contributions, these contributions aren't taken into account in my rankings—although they are for the teachers unions—and that obviously threatens to bias the rankings somewhat in favor of the teachers unions. Except in rare cases, however, this is not a problem. The only

groups that have local or national affiliates that might make sizable contributions are other unions—particularly AFSCME and SEIU—and possibly business associations like the Chamber of Commerce. In table 9-4, I provide supplementary information on how the teachers unions stack up to all three of these contributors. AFSCME and SEIU are not competitors to the teachers unions anyway. They are basically on the same team. Business associations are another matter—although most of the time, of course, they are concerned about issues other than education and use their power accordingly. Be that as it may, the teachers unions out-contribute them anyway, even when the contributions of all business associations of all types are aggregated.

24. Note that one of the two states where the unions are out-contributed by business associations is Vermont, which only recently entered the strong-law category.

25. The SEIU organizes both public and private sector workers. On AFSCME, the SEIU, and other public sector unions, see, for example, Chris Edwards, "Public Sector Unions," Cato Institute Tax and Budget Bulletin 61 (Washington: Cato Institute, March 2010); Leo Troy, *The New Unionism in the New Society: Public Sector Unions in the Redistributive State* (George Mason University Press, 1994); Richard B. Freeman, "Unionism Comes to the Public Sector," *Journal of Economic Literature* 24 (March 1986): 41–86.

26. Andy Stern has since announced his retirement as president, but the SEIU's influence continues. See, for example, Stephen Spruiell, "Unholy Union," *National Review*, November 29, 2009; Steven Greenhouse, "Andy Stern to Step Down as Chief of Politically Active Union," *New York Times*, April 13, 2010; Steven Greenhouse, "New Union Leader Wants Group to Be More of a Political Powerhouse," *New York Times*, May 8, 2010.

27. On the Citizens United case and independent spending, see McKenna Long and Aldrich, "Citizens United Supreme Court Decision"; Liptak, "Justices, 5-4, Reject Spending Limit."

28. Brody Mullins and John D. McKinnon, "Campaign's Big Spender," *Wall Street Journal*, October 22, 2010.

29. For each state, the spending figures are based on spending by all the national, state, and local affiliates of the teachers unions, AFSCME, and the SEIU. The spending is for candidates and parties and does not include money for ballot measures.

30. For a recent retrospective that discusses Bush's emergence as a national reform leader, see Sean Cavanagh, "Jeb Bush's Influence on Education Policy Spreads," *Education Week*, December 29, 2010. For an overview and discussion of the Bush-era Florida reforms, as well as an assessment of the state's performance—test scores have risen and the achievement gap separating minorities and whites has been dramatically narrowed (but the graduation rate has not gone up)—see Matthew Ladner and Lindsey M. Burke, "Closing the Achievement Gap: Learning from Florida's Reforms," Backgrounder 2468 (Washington: Heritage Foundation, September 17, 2010), available at thf_media. s3.amazonaws.com/2010/pdf/bg2468.pdf. See also Paul E. Peterson, ed., *Reforming Education in Florida: A Study Prepared by the Koret Task Force on K–12 Education* (Stanford, Calif.: Hoover Press, 2006). The Florida reforms also have their critics. See, for example, Kathryn M. Borman and Sherman Dorn, eds., *Education Reform in Florida* (State University of New York Press, 2007); also Valerie Strauss, "A Sobering Look at Florida School Reform," *Washington Post*, December 21, 2010.

31. See, for example, Wes Allison and Steve Bousquet, "Another Florida Election in Doubt," *St. Petersburg Times*, September 11, 2002; "Polls Show Reno in Dead Heat in Florida Governor Primary," *New York Times*, September 1, 2002; Jeff Archer, "Governor's Race Tests Power of Merged Teachers' Union," *Education Week*, October 30, 2002; Sol Stern, "What the Voucher Victory Means," *City Journal* (Autumn 2002).

32. Wes Allison and Adam C. Smith, "McBride Campaign Entwines with Teachers Union (FEA)," *St. Petersburg Times*, September 17, 2002.

33. See Bernadette Malone, "The Zeal against Jeb: For Florida Democrats, It's Payback Time," *National Review*, November 2002. The FEA denies taking out the mortgage to finance its political campaign, but see the discussion in Rod Paige, *The War against Hope* (Nashville: Thomas Nelson, 2006), p. 215, n. 65.

34. Allison and Smith, "McBride Campaign Entwines with Teachers Union (FEA)."

35. Eric Boehlert, "Florida: The Sequel," *Salon*, November 1, 2002, available at www.salon.com/news/feature/2002/11/01/florida.

36. A Zogby poll showed McBride pulling to within three points of Bush in early October of 2002. See John-Thor Dahlburg, "Jeb Bush's Lead Shrinks as Race Is a Dead Heat," *Los Angeles Times*, October 17, 2002.

37. Dana Canedy, "The 2002 Elections: Florida; Bush Looks to 2nd Term as Analysts Point to 2004," *New York Times*, November 7, 2002. See also Allison and Smith, "McBride Campaign Entwines with Teachers Union (FEA)"; Bob Mahlburg, "Top Labor Officials Visit State to Back McBride," *Orlando Sentinel*, October 15, 2002; Tim Padgett, "Why Jeb Bush Won Big," *Time*, November 6, 2002.

38. There is a growing political science literature on the role of money in ballot measure campaigns and whether high-spending interest groups are able to get their way. Causality in these matters is difficult to determine. Clearly, groups would not be contributing if they didn't think their money was having an impact, but researchers have not been able to document the connection between money and outcomes with confidence. See, for example, Thomas Stratmann, "The Effectiveness of Money in Ballot Measure Campaigns," *Southern California Law Review* (May 2005): 101–24; Shaun Bowler and Todd Donovan, *Demanding Choices: Opinion, Voting, and Direct Democracy* (University of Michigan Press, 2000); Elisabeth Gerber, *The Populist Paradox: Interest Group Influence and the Promise of Direct Legislation* (Princeton University Press, 1999).

39. See the discussion in Terry M. Moe, *Schools, Vouchers, and the American Public* (Brookings, 2001).

40. See Jordan Rau, "Powerful Teachers Union Is in the Thick of Ballot Battles," *Los Angeles Times*, September 28, 2005.

41. See Clea Benson, "Teachers Put Governor in the Corner; Unions Are Spending Millions to Rip Schwarzenegger Proposals," *Sacramento Bee*, April 13, 2005.

42. Calculated from the data on www.followthemoney.org.

43. For background on this campaign, see Rau, "Powerful Teachers Union Is in the Thick of Ballot Battles."

44. All of these figures are calculated from the data on www.followthemoney.org.

45. See Census Bureau, *The 2010 Statistical Abstract* (Washington: U.S. Census

Bureau, 2010), table 424, "State and Local Governments—Revenue and Expenditure by Function: 2005 and 2006."

46. Again, all of these figures are calculated from the data on www.followthe money.org.

47. Ibid.

48. See the earlier citations to the research literature on money and elections.

49. Given its importance, one might expect to see a big scholarly literature on the politics of education reform. But, aside from journalistic accounts (which are often quite informative), there is surprisingly little research on the topic. The most significant development is that, in recent years, a number of books and articles have appeared on the politics of No Child Left Behind, often tracing the political and historical linkages back to the original Elementary and Secondary Education Act of 1965. As discussed in an earlier note, this scholarly work is surely valuable, but its focus is on national politics—which not only is very different from politics at the state level (in part because political constituencies are much bigger, many more groups are involved, and the teachers unions have many more competitors), but is also not nearly as important in the grander scheme of things. NCLB aside, almost all the major issues and battles in American education reform have been fought out at the state level, where the unions' role is typically huge, and any account of the politics of reform needs to recognize as much. A national-level focus is easily very misleading. See, for example, McGuinn, *No Child Left Behind and the Transformation of Federal Education Policy*; Manna, *School's In*; Anderson, *Congress and the Classroom*; Kaestle, Lodewick, and Henig, eds., *To Educate a Nation*; Debray and Kaestle, *Politics, Ideology, and Education*; Kosar, *Failing Grades*; McAndrews, *The Era of Education*.

50. For an excellent overview and assessment of the early reform era, see Thomas Toch, *In the Name of Excellence* (Oxford University Press, 1991).

51. For high-profile reports, see, for example, Carnegie Forum on Education and the Economy, Task Force on Teaching as a Profession, *A Nation Prepared: Teachers for the 21st Century* (New York: Carnegie Corporation of New York, 1986); Holmes Group, *Tomorrow's Teachers* (Michigan State University, 1986); Twentieth Century Fund, Task Force on Federal Elementary and Secondary Education Policy, *Making the Grade* (New York: Twentieth Century Fund, 1983).

52. For an informative account of various ways in which the unions engaged in politics and blocked reform efforts, see Toch, *In the Name of Excellence*. For a discussion of how the unions used the reform climate to pursue their traditional objectives, see, for example, Cindy Currence, "Teachers' Unions Bringing Reform Issues to Bargaining Table," *Education Week*, May 15, 1985.

53. National Center on Education Statistics, *Digest of Education Statistics, 2008* (Washington: NCES, 2008).

54. See Eric A. Hanushek, "The Failure of Input-Based Schooling," *Economic Journal* 113 (2003): 64–98.

55. See, for example, the evidence and discussion in Caroline M. Hoxby, "What Has Changed and What Has Not," in *Our Schools and Our Future*, edited by Paul E. Peterson (Stanford, Calif.: Hoover Institution Press, 2003).

56. Toch, *In the Name of Excellence*, p. 102.

57. On the teachers unions' political activities on these issues, see Toch, *In the Name of Excellence*, for accounts during the early reform period. For more modern developments, see, for example, Dale Ballou and Michael Podgursky, "Gaining Control of Professional Licensing and Advancement," in *Conflicting Missions?* edited by Tom Loveless (Brookings, 2000); Hess and West, *A Better Bargain*.

58. See, for example, Hanushek, "The Failure of Input-Based Schooling"; Eric A. Hanushek and Steven Rivkin, "Teacher Quality," in *Handbook of the Economics of Education*, edited by Eric A. Hanushek and Finis Welch, pp. 1051–78 (Amsterdam: Elsevier, 2006); Thomas J. Kane, Jonah E. Rockoff, and Douglas O. Staiger, "What Does Certification Tell Us about Teacher Effectiveness? Evidence from New York City," NBER Working Paper 12155 (Cambridge, Mass.: National Bureau of Economic Research, 2006).

59. Eric Hanushek, "Teacher Deselection," in *Creating a New Teaching Profession*, edited by Dan Goldhaber and Jane Hannaway, pp. 165–80 (Washington: Urban Institute Press, 2009).

60. Examples of union opposition are legion. See, for example, Joanna Richardson, "Critics Target State Teacher Tenure Laws," *Education Week*, March 1, 1995; Jennifer Medina, "Bill Would Bar Linking Class Test Scores to Tenure," *Education Week*, March 18, 2008; Toch, *In the Name of Excellence*.

61. See, for example, "Colorado Reforms Teacher Tenure," *Teacher Magazine,* June 14, 2010. Also Steve Sawchuck, "States Strive to Overhaul Teacher Tenure," *Education Week*, April 7, 2010.

62. "Colorado Reforms Teacher Tenure."

63. Michael Finnegan and Robert Salladay, "Voters Reject Schwarzenegger's Bid to Remake State Government," *Los Angeles Times*, November 9, 2005.

64. See, for example, Patrick McGuinn, "Ringing the Bell for K–12 Tenure Reform" (Washington: Center for American Progress, February 2010); Linda Jacobson, "Georgia Reform Law Stirs Political Pot," *Education Week*, September 20, 2000.

65. James Salzer, "Teacher Vote at Center of Race," *Atlanta Journal-Constitution*, June 20, 2010.

66. For a review of evidence, see Kate Walsh, *Teacher Certification Reconsidered: Stumbling for Quality* (Baltimore, Md.: Abell Foundation, 2001).

67. See Toch, *In the Name of Excellence*; also Kathleen Kennedy Manzo, "NC Lawmakers Revoke Teacher-Testing Plan," *Education Week*, June 17, 1998; Bess Keller, "Pennsylvania Teachers Put to Test," *Education Week*, January 9, 2002. Also, with regard to the "high-quality teacher" provision of NCLB (which was a union victory on the issue of veteran teacher testing), see Julie Blair, "Unions' Positions Unheeded on ESEA," *Education Week*, November 6, 2002.

68. Keller, "Pennsylvania Teachers Put to Test."

69. See, for example, G. G. Milkovich and J. M. Newman, *Compensation*, 8th ed. (New Delhi: Tata McGraw-Hill, 2005).

70. See, for example, Michael J. Podgursky, "Teams versus Bureaucracies: Personnel Policy, Wage Setting, and Teacher Quality in Traditional Public, Charter, and Private Schools," in *Charter School Outcomes*, edited by Mark Berends, Matthew G. Springer, and Herbert J. Walberg (New York: Lawrence Erlbaum Associates, 2007).

71. See, for example, Hanushek and Rivkin, "Teacher Quality"; Steven Rivkin, Eric A. Hanushek, and John F. Kain, "Teachers, Schools, and Academic Achievement," *Econometrica* 73, no. 2 (March 2005): 417–58; William L. Sanders and Sandra P. Horn, "Research Findings from the Tennessee Value-Added Assessment System (TVAAS) Data Base: Implications for Educational Evaluation and Research," *Journal of Personnel Evaluation in Education* 12, no. 3 (1998): 247–56.

72. For overviews, see Michael J. Podgursky and Matthew G. Springer, "Teacher Performance Pay: A Review," *Journal of Policy Analysis and Management* 26, no. 4 (2007): 909–49. Also Robin Chait and Reagen Miller, "Paying Teachers for Results: A Summary of Research to Inform the Design of Pay for Performance Programs for High-Poverty Schools" (Washington: Center for American Progress, 2009). For overviews of experiments under way to assess the effectiveness of different pay-for-performance designs, see Michael J. Podgursky and Matthew G. Springer, "Market and Performance Based Reforms of Teacher Compensation: A Review of Recent Practices, Policies, and Research," paper prepared for the PEPG conference, Merit Pay: Will It Work? Is It Politically Viable? Harvard University, Kennedy School of Government, Cambridge, Mass., June 3–4, 2010. At this writing, a recent pay-for-performance experiment in Nashville came up with much-publicized negative results, showing that teachers who received bonuses for exemplary student learning gains did not perform better than teachers who didn't receive such bonuses. This is just one experiment of a particular bonus program, though, and it says nothing about the selective-attraction dimension of pay for performance, which is crucial to its overall impact. The study does underline the point I've made in the text: there are many ways to design these programs, some work better than others, and the challenge over time is to build on research and experience to arrive at systems that work effectively. Not just any pay-for-performance regime will do the job. See Matthew G. Springer and others, *Teacher Pay for Performance: Experimental Evidence from the Project on Incentives in Teaching* (Vanderbilt University, National Center on Performance Incentives, September 2010).

73. In its 2010–11 resolutions, for example, the NEA states, "Any additional compensation beyond a single salary schedule must not be based on education employee evaluation, student performance, or attendance" (F-10). It also states, "Performance pay schedules, such as merit pay or any other system based on an evaluation of an education employee's performance, are inappropriate" (F-9). See National Education Association, "2010–11 NEA Resolutions," on the NEA's website at www.nea.org/assets/docs/resolutions-documnent-2010-2011.pdf.

74. Douglas McGray, "Working with the Enemy," *New York Times*, January 16, 2005.

75. On the politics of union blocking efforts—which have been quite successful—see Stuart Buck and Jay P. Greene, "Blocking, Diluting, and Co-Opting Merit Pay," paper presented at the PEPG conference Merit Pay: Will It Work? Is It Politically Viable? Harvard University, Kennedy School of Government, June 3–4, 2010. On the rising support for pay for performance (prior to Race to the Top), see, for example, Vaishali Honawar, "Teacher Performance Pay Plans Expand across U.S.," *Washington Times*, April 10, 2009; Vaishali Honawar, "Merit Pay Gaining Bipartisan Favor in Federal Arena," *Education Week*, August 1, 2007; Lynn Olson, "Teacher Pay Experiments Mounting amid Debate," *Education Week*, October 3, 2007.

76. On these programs, see, for example, Paula Vu, "States Venture into Teacher Performance," *Stateline,* October 9, 2007, available at www.stateline.org/live/details/story?contentId=246599; Center for Educator Compensation Reform, "Texas State-Level Pay for Performance Programs: Overview and Discussion" (Washington: Center for Educator Compensation Reform, August 2007), available at www.cecr.ed.gov/guides/summaries/TexasCaseSummary.pdf; Minnesota, Office of the Legislative Auditor, "Q Comp: Quality Compensation for Teachers" (St. Paul: State of Minnesota, Office of the Legislative Auditor, February 2009), available at www.auditor.leg.state.mn.us/ped/pedrep/qcompsum.pdf; Dorie Turner, "States Push to Pay Teachers Based on Performance," *USA Today,* April 8, 2010.

77. On Houston, see Center for Educator Compensation Reform, "Performance Pay in Houston" (Washington: Center for Educator Compensation Reform, December 2008), at ww.cecr.ed.gov/guides/summaries/HoustonCaseSummary.pdf. Regarding recipients of the Gates Foundation grant, I have not put Pittsburgh in the same category as Memphis and Hillsborough County because its pay-for-performance plan is designed to give bonuses to teachers in low-performing schools and to teachers working in teams; it is not a general plan for all teachers. For information on all three plans, see Bloomberg Businessweek, "Bill Gates' Latest Mission: Fixing America's Schools," *msnbc,* July 17, 2010; Nick Anderson, "Gates Foundation Playing Pivotal Role in Changes for Education System," *Washington Post,* July 12, 2010; Tom Marshall, "Hillsborough Hires 100 Peer Evaluators for Its $100 Million Gates Reforms," *St. Petersburg Times,* April 20, 2010; Tom Marshall, "Hillsborough School Board Get First Look Monday at New Teacher Evaluation by Gates Grant," *St. Petersburg Times,* May 14, 2010; Karamagi Rujumba, "Bill Gates Lauds City's Steps to Improve Schools," *Pittsburgh Post-Gazette,* July 11, 2010; Jane Roberts, "Memphis Teachers Union OKs Contract with Raises," *Commercial Appeal,* February 17, 2010.

78. See, for example, Ann Bradley, "DC Unions Assail Plan to Tie Pay to Student Achievement," *Education Week,* April 19, 1995; Alyson Klein and David J. Hoff, "Unions Assail Teacher Ideas in NCLB Draft," *Education Week,* September 19, 2007; also Toch, *In the Name of Excellence*; Olson, "Teacher-Pay Experiments Mounting amid Debate."

79. Kate Walsh and Sandi Jacobs, "Alternative Certification Isn't Alternative" (Washington: Thomas B. Fordham Foundation, NCTQ, September 2007).

80. Kate Walsh, "Teacher Certification Reconsidered: Stumbling for Quality" (Abel Foundation, 2001), available at www.abell.org/pubsitems/ed_cert_1101.pdf. See also Kane, Rockoff, and Staiger, "What Does Certification Tell Us about Teacher Effectiveness?"; Hanushek, "The Failure of Input-Based Schooling"; Debra Viadero, "Draw Called over Routes to Teaching," *Education Week,* May 12, 2010; Arthur Levine, *Educating School Teachers* (Washington: Education Schools Project, 2006).

81. See Frederick M. Hess, "Tear Down This Wall: The Case for a Radical Overhaul of Teacher Certification," Progressive Policy Institute 21st Century Schools Project (November 2001), available at www.ppionline.org/documents/teacher_certification.pdf.

82. For an overview of the issue, see Walsh and Jacobs, "Alternative Certification Isn't Alternative."

83. Note that the education schools themselves are politically powerful.

84. Quoted in Daniel Nadler and Paul E. Peterson, "What Happens When States Have Genuine Alternative Certification?" *Education Next* 9, no. 1 (Winter 2009): 70–76.

85. For basic information on the program, see its website at www.teachforamerica.org.

86. "Teach for (Some) America," editorial, *Wall Street Journal*, April 25, 2009.

87. For details on Teach for America, see www.teachforamerica.org/. See also Lucia Graves, "The Evolution of Teach for America," *U.S. News and World Report*, October 17, 2008; "Eight Questions for Wendy Kopp," *The Economist*, April 3, 2010. For studies of TFA's effectiveness, see Zeyu Xu, Jane Hannaway, and Colin Taylor, *Making a Difference: The Effects of Teach for America in High School* (Washington: Urban Institute, 2008); George H. Noell and Kristin A. Gansle, *Teach for America Teachers' Contribution to Student Achievement in Louisiana in Grades 4–9: 2004–2005 to 2006–2007* (Louisiana State University, 2009); Paul T. Decker, Daniel P. Mayer, and Steven Glazerman, *The Effects of Teach for American on Students* (New York: Mathematica, 2004); Gary Henry and Charles Thompson, "Impacts of Teacher Preparation on Student Test Scores in North Carolina: Teacher Portals" (University of North Carolina, Carolina Institute for Public Policy, 2010); Kane, Rockoff, and Staiger, "What Does Certification Tell Us about Teacher Effectiveness?"; Julien Vasquez Heilig and Su Jin Jez, "Teach for America: A Review of the Evidence" (East Lansing, Mich.: Great Lakes Center for Education Research and Practice, 2010).

88. Greg Toppo, "Teach for America: Elite Corps or Costing Older Teachers Jobs?" *USA Today*, July 29, 2009.

89. "Teach for (Some) America."

90. See, for example, Jennifer A. O'Day and Marshall S. Smith, "Systemic School Reform and Educational Opportunity" in *Designing Coherent Education Policy: Improving the System,* edited by Susan Fuhrman, pp. 250–312 (San Francisco: Jossey-Bass, 1993).

91. See "Clinton Plan: 100,000 More Teachers, Smaller Class Sizes," *Education Week*, February 4, 1998; Ann Bradley, "Plan for Smaller Classes Sets Off Hiring Spree in Calif.," *Education Week*, September 4, 1996; Alan Richards, "Florida Debates How to Shrink Class Sizes," *Education Week*, February 5, 2003.

92. See, for example, Hanushek, "The Failure of Input-Based Schooling"; Eric Hanushek, "Evidence, Politics, and the Class Size Debate," in *The Class Size Debate*, edited by Lawrence Mishel and Richard Rothstein (Washington: Economic Policy Institute, 2002).

93. In other writings, I have argued for moving from a top-down system to one that takes greater advantage of choice and competition, with schools being held accountable mainly from below. See John E. Chubb and Terry M. Moe, *Politics, Markets, and America's Schools* (Brookings, 1990). There is good reason, however, that even a system based largely on choice and competition can benefit considerably from an overarching structure of rules designed to discourage unwanted behaviors, to encourage productive behaviors, and to impart the right incentives. Indeed, I believe a mixed system of markets and government is necessary if markets are to work to greatest social advantage. That is essentially the strategy the nation has followed in the economic realm, where a supposedly "free market" economy is combined with a governmentally imposed structure of rules and regulations. In the current education system, which is almost entirely top-down,

accountability clearly has a crucial role to play in ensuring productive performance and proper incentives. But it would continue to be desirable in a system based largely on choice and competition. For my views on a mixed system, see Terry M. Moe, "Beyond the Free Market: The Structure of School Choice," *Brigham Young University Law Review* 2008, no. 1 (2008): 557–92.

94. For a perspective on the how the politics of accountability has unfolded across states, see Lance T. Izumi and Williamson M. Evers, "State Accountability Systems," in *School Accountability*, edited by Williamson M. Evers and Herbert J. Walberg (Stanford, Calif.: Hoover Institution Press, 2002).

95. See, for example, American Federation of Teachers, "Sizing up State Standards, 2008" (Washington: AFT, 2008), available at www.aft.org. It has been regularly issuing such reports on state academic standards since 1995.

96. See, for example, Richard Phelps, *Defending Standardized Testing* (Mahwah, N.J.: Lawrence Erlbaum Associates, 2005).

97. John Gehring, "Mass. Teachers Blast State Tests in New TV Ads," *Education Week*, November 22, 2000.

98. See, for example, National Education Association, "Testing Plus: Real Accountability with Real Results" (Washington: NEA, 2001), available at www.fairtest.org/testing-plus-real-accountability-real-results; also Vaishali Honawar, "NEA Opens Campaign to Rewrite Federal Education Law," *Education Week*, July 12, 2006.

99. See, for example, Alfie Kohn and Lois Bridges, *The Case against Standardized Testing; Raising Scores, Ruining the Schools* (Portsmouth, N.H.: Heinemann, 2000); Sharon L. Nichols and David C. Berliner, *Collateral Damage: How High-Stakes Testing Corrupts America's Schools* (Harvard Education Press, 2007); Richard Rothstein, Rebecca Jacobsen, and Tamara Wilder, *Grading Education: Getting Accountability Right* (Teachers College Press, 2008); Daniel Koretz, *Measuring Up: What Educational Testing Really Tells Us* (Harvard University Press, 2008); Mark J. Garrison, *A Measure of Failure: The Political Origins of Standardized Testing* (State University of New York Press, 2009). See also the website of the National Center for Fair and Open Testing at www.fairtest.org.

100. Hanushek and Rivkin, "Teacher Quality"; Rivkin, Hanushek, and Kain, "Teachers, Schools, and Academic Achievement"; Sanders and Horn, "Research Findings from the Tennessee Value-Added Assessment System (TVAAS) Data Base."

101. The unions argue that, when schools and teachers perform poorly, they should be provided with additional resources, support, and training. In what it calls its "positive agenda" for NCLB reform—a good label for it, as it is an agenda entirely lacking in sanctions—the NEA says, "Schools that fail to close achievement gaps after receiving additional financial resources, technical assistance, and other supports should be subject to supportive interventions." No sanctions, no jobs put at risk, just support. It also says that, when measures of student achievement are employed, they "should be used as a guide to revise instructional practices and curriculum, to provide individual assistance to students, and to provide appropriate professional development to teachers and other educators. They should not be used to penalize schools or teachers." See National Education Association, *ESEA: It's Time for a Change; NEA's Positive Agenda for the ESEA Reauthorization* (Washington: NEA, July 2006), available at www.nea.org/esea/posagendaexecsum.html.

102. Jennifer Medina, "Bill Would Bar Linking Class Test Scores to Tenure," *New York Times*, March 18, 2008.

103. For a more extensive discussion of these issues, see Moe and Chubb, *Liberating Learning*.

104. Data Quality Campaign, "2007 NCEA State P–12 Data Collection Survey Results: State of the Nation" (Washington: Data Quality Campaign, 2007), available at www.dataqualitycampaign.org/survey_results/state_of_nation.cfm.

105. California Assembly Committee on Education, Hearing on AB 1213, April 20, 2005, available at www.leginfo.ca.gov/pub/05-06/bill/asm/ab_1201-1250/ab_1213_cfa_20050419_101222_asm_comm.html.

106. California Senate Bill 1614 (2006), available at www.leginfo.ca.gov/pub/05-06/bill/sen/sb_1601-1650/sb_1614_bill_20060930_chaptered.pdf.

107. See the account in Moe and Chubb, *Liberating Learning*.

108. See, for example, Lesli A. Maxwell, "California 'Firewall' Becomes 'Race to Top' Issue," *Education Week*, August 11, 2990; Associated Press, "California Passes Major School-Reform Package," *USA Today*, January 7, 2010. I should add that California lost the Race to the Top and then lightning struck yet again: citing the state's catastrophic budget deficit as well as various technical failings of the system, Governor Schwarzenegger *vetoed* newly appropriated funding for it, leaving its future highly uncertain. Sean Cavanagh, "Veto Stirs Concerns over California Data System," *Education Week*, October 22, 2010.

109. See "Los Angeles Teacher Ratings," *Los Angeles Times*, available at projects.latimes.com/value-added/. See also Nick Anderson, "Education Secretary Arne Duncan Wants Schools to Give Parents, Teachers More Data," *Washington Post*, August 25, 2010; Andrew Rotherham, "Rating Teachers: The Trouble with Value-Added Data," *Time*, September 23, 2010.

110. See, for example, Rotherham, "Rating Teachers."

111. "Los Angeles Teacher Ratings."

112. "Teachers, by the Numbers," editorial, *Los Angeles Times*, August 17, 2010.

113. Ibid.

114. "Los Angeles Unified Votes to Overhaul Teacher Evaluation Process," *Southwest Riverside News Network*, September 2, 2010, available at www.swrnn.com/southwest-riverside/2010-09-02/news/los-angeles-unified-votes-to-overhaul-teacher-evaluation-process; Howard Blume, "L.A. Teachers Union Won't Accept Pay Cuts, 'Value-Added' Evaluations," *Los Angeles Times*, December 16, 2010.

115. Anderson, "Education Secretary Arne Duncan Wants Schools to Give Parents, Teachers More Data."

116. National Education Association, "NEA's 8 Principles for ESEA Reauthorization," available on the NEA's website at www.nea.org/home/1335.htm.

117. Most accounts of the politics of education put too much emphasis on Republican resistance to accountability. The reason is that virtually all these accounts focus (as pointed out in earlier notes) on politics at the national level rather than at the state level where most education policy of consequence is actually made. What Republicans *have* resisted is federal intrusion in state affairs. They have long been much more supportive of

accountability at the state level, and that is where most of the action has taken place. For accounts of national politics and Republican resistance to violations of local control, see, for example, McGuinn, *No Child Left Behind and the Transformation of Federal Education Policy*; Manna, *School's In*; and Debray and Kaestle, *Politics, Ideology, and Education.*

118. On the unions' centrality, see, for example, Joe Williams, "Echo Chamber: The National Education Association's Campaign against NCLB" (Washington: Education Sector, Connecting the Dots, July 2006), available at www.educationsector.org/sites/default/files/publications/CTDNEADollarsWITH_CORRECTION_NOTE.pdf; David Hoff, "NEA Lobbies against NCLB," *Education Week*, November 9, 2007; Vaishali Honawar, "New AFT Leader Vows to Bring Down NCLB Law," *Education Week*, July 30, 2008. On the ambivalent role of civil rights groups, see, for example, Karla Scoon Reid, "Civil Rights Groups Split on NCLB," *Education Week*, August 31, 2005.

119. See McGuin, *No Child Left Behind and the Transformation of Federal Education Policy*; Kosar, *Failing Grades*; Debray and Kaestle, *Politics, Ideology, and Education.*

120. See, for example, John E. Chubb, ed., *Within Our Reach: How America Can Educate Every Child* (New York: Rowman and Littlefield, 2005).

121. See, for example, Julie Blair, "Unions' Positions Unheeded on ESEA," *Education Week*, November 6, 2002; Terry M. Moe, "A Highly Qualified Teacher in Every Classroom," in *Within Our Reach*, edited by Chubb.

122. Joe Williams, "District Accountability: More Bark Than Bite?" In *No Remedy Left Behind: Lessons from a Half-Decade of NCLB*, edited by Frederick M. Hess and Chester E. Finn Jr. (Washington: AEI Press, 2007).

123. The details of state accountability systems can be found on the website of the Council of Chief State School Officers at www.ccsso.org and the website of the Education Commission of the States at www.ecs.org. For overviews, see Evers and Walberg, *School Accountability*; Chubb, ed., *Within Our Reach.*

124. The impact of NCLB on student achievement is difficult for researchers to determine, at least at this point. Many factors influence student achievement and need to be controlled, of course. The situation is further complicated by the fact that many states already had accountability systems—of various sorts, from weak to strong—prior to NCLB; once NCLB was enacted, states began fully participating at somewhat different rates. In addition, there are various considerations—such as teaching to the test, cheating, and possible impacts on nontested subjects (science, history)—that make the impact of accountability still more difficult to explore. For now, the best available studies tend to suggest that NCLB has had some positive effects on student achievement, but that its effects are spotty and by no means the sort of sea change that reformers were trying to bring about. This is what we ought to expect, given NCLB's flaws and given the political obstacles that prevented it from being designed as effectively as possible. For studies of NCLB's impact, see Thomas S. Dee and Brian Jacob, "The Impact of No Child Left Behind on Student Achievement," NBER Working Paper 15531 (Cambridge, Mass.: National Bureau of Economic Research, November 2009); Eric A. Hanushek and Margaret E. Raymond, "Does School Accountability Lead to Improved Student Performance?" *Journal of Policy Analysis and Management* 24, no. 2 (2005): 297–327; Martin Carnoy and Susanna Loeb, "Does External Accountability Affect Student Outcomes?"

Educational Evaluation and Policy Analysis 24, no. 4 (Winter 2002): 305–31; Brian Jacob, "Accountability, Incentives, and Behavior: Evidence from School Reform in Chicago," *Journal of Public Economics* 89, no. 5-6 (2005): 761–96; for a review, see David N. Figlio and Helen Ladd, "School Accountability and Student Achievement," in *Handbook of Research in Education Finance and Policy*, edited by Helen Ladd and Edward B. Fiske, pp. 166–82 (New York: Routledge, 2008).

125. This problem—that policy frameworks tend to be partly designed by actors who want them to fail—is in fact quite general and occurs across virtually all policy areas. It is not unique to education. See Terry M. Moe, "The Politics of Bureaucratic Structure," in *Can the Government Govern?* edited by John E. Chubb and Paul E. Peterson (Brookings, 1989).

126. Bess Keller, "NEA Files 'No Child Left Behind' Lawsuit," *Education Week*, April 20, 2005.

127. Dean Vogel, vice president of the California Teachers Association, quoted in Alyson Klein and David J. Hoff, "Unions Assail Teacher Ideas in NCLB Draft," *Education Week*, September 19, 2007.

128. On the union's attack on NCLB reauthorization generally, see, for example, Vaishali Honawar, "NEA Opens Campaign to Rewrite Federal Education Law," *Education Week*, July 12, 2006; Vaishali Honawar, "New AFT Leader Vows to Bring Down NCLB Law," *Education Week*, July 28, 2008; Klein and Hoff, "Unions Assail Teacher Ideas in NCLB Draft."

129. On the benefits that school choice stands to offer, see, for example, Moe, "Beyond the Free Market: The Structure of School Choice"; Chubb and Moe, *Politics, Markets, and America's Schools*; Andrew J. Coulson, *Market Education* (New Brunswick, N.J.: Transaction Publishers, 1999); Milton Friedman, *Capitalism and Freedom* (University of Chicago Press, 1962); John E. Coons and Stephen D. Sugarman, *Education by Choice: The Case for Family Control* (University of California Press, 1979).

130. See, for example, Bengt Holmstrom, "Agency Costs and Innovation," *Economic Behavior and Organization* 12, no. 3 (1989): 305–27.

131. Choice tends to be characterized as a free market approach to education, and many of the criticisms leveled against it are premised on that notion—arguing, for example, that a free market approach would lead to discrimination against the poor (because choice schools would not admit them), that parents would be too uninformed to make good choices, and so on. These and other problems could indeed arise in a free market educational setting. But as I have argued extensively in my own work, the point of *designing* a choice system is precisely to mitigate such problems and, more generally, to ensure that choice and competition work in ways that are socially beneficial. This is accomplished through the adoption of an appropriate set of governmental rules that structure how the system is to operate. Just as the American economy is a mixed system of government and markets, with choice and competition operating within a framework of governmental rules (about price fixing, deceptive practices, taxes, and so on), so school choice is best viewed as a mixed system as well, and the challenge, in putting choice to best use for kids and society, is *not* simply to introduce more choice and competition, but also to *get the structure right* and thus to ensure that these market forces work to

greatest social advantage. For an extensive discussion of design issues and of choice as a mixed system, see Moe, "Beyond the Free Market." See also R. Kenneth Godwin and Frank R. Kemerer, *School Choice Tradeoffs* (University of Texas Press, 2002). For some of the standard criticisms of school choice, see, for example, Peter W. Cookson Jr., *School Choice: The Struggle for the Soul of American Education* (Yale University Press, 1994); Bruce Fuller and Richard Elmore, eds., *Who Chooses, Who Loses? Culture, Institutions, and the Unequal Effects of School Choice* (Teachers College Press, 1996); Jeffrey R. Henig, *Rethinking School Choice* (Princeton University Press, 1995); Kevin B. Smith and Kenneth J. Meier, *The Case against School Choice: Politics, Markets, and Fools* (Armonk, N.Y.: M. E. Sharpe, 1995); Amy Stuart Wells, *Time to Choose: America at the Crossroads* (New York: Hill and Wang, 1993).

132. For a discussion of the political coalitions involved in the school choice issue, see Moe, *Schools, Vouchers, and the American Public*; Hubert Morken and Jo Renee Formicola, *The Politics of School Choice* (London: Rowman and Littlefield, 1999); Godwin and Kemerer, *School Choice Tradeoffs*; Paul T. Hill and Aschley E. Jochim, "Political Perspectives on School Choice," in *Handbook of Research on School Choice*, edited by Mark Berends, Matthew G. Springer, Dale Ballou, and Herbert J. Walberg, pp. 3–18 (New York: Routledge, 2009).

133. Milton Friedman, "The Role of Government in Education," in *Economics and the Public Interest*, edited by Robert A. Solow (Rutgers University Press, 1955); Friedman, *Capitalism and Freedom*. For information on the history of school choice, see Coulson, *Market Education*.

134. For historical perspective, see Coulson, *Market Education*; Chester E. Finn Jr., *Troublemaker: A Personal History of School Reform since Sputnik* (Princeton University Press, 2008). See also, for a different historical slant, Cookson, *School Choice*; Henig, *Rethinking School Choice*.

135. On the Milwaukee voucher plan, see John F. Witte, *The Market Approach to Education* (Princeton University Press, 2000); Moe, *Schools, Vouchers, and the American Public*; Patrick Wolf, "The Comprehensive Longitudinal Evaluation of the Milwaukee Parental Choice Program: Summary of Third Year Reports," SCDP Milwaukee Evaluation Report 4 (University of Arkansas, Department of Education Reform, April 2010).

136. See, for example, William G. Howell, Paul E. Peterson, and Martin R. West, "The 2009 Education Next-PEPG Survey of Public Opinion," *Education Next*, November 23, 2009, available at educationnext.org/files/pepg2009.pdf. See also Moe, *Schools, Vouchers, and the American Public*.

137. See, for example, Mark Walsh, "Voucher Initiatives Defeated in Calif., Mich.," *Education Week*, November 15, 2000.

138. See, for example, Karen Diegmueller, "Despite Defeat, Choice Bill Likely to Resurface in Pa.," *Education Week*, January 8, 1992; Drew Lindsay, "Grassroots Lobbying Kills Ariz. Voucher Proposals," *Education Week*, April 26, 1995; John Gehring, "Voucher Battles Head to State Capitals," *Education Week*, July 10, 2002; Alan Richard, "School Choice Loses Legislative Momentum," *Education Week*, June 8, 2005.

139. See, for example, Witte, *The Market Approach to Education*; Drew Lindsay, "Wisconsin, Ohio Back Vouchers for Religious Schools," *Education Week*, July 12, 1995;

Jessica L. Sandham, "Florida Oks 1st Statewide Voucher Plan," *Education Week*, May 5, 1999; for an overview of voucher plans across the nation, see Friedman Foundation, *The ABC's of School Choice 2007–08*, available at www.friedmanfoundation.org. See also the website of the American Federation for Children at www.federationforchildren.com/existing-programs.

140. Michele McNeil, "Utah Vouchers Rejected in Overwhelming Vote," *Education Week*, November 7, 2007.

141. See, for example, Marianne D. Hurst, "Colo. Supreme Court Strikes Down Voucher Law," *Education Week*, June 29, 2004; Alan Richard, "Fla. Court: Vouchers Unconstitutional," *Education Week*, January 11, 2006; Pat Kossan, "Ariz. School Voucher Programs Ruled Unconstitutional," *Arizona Republic*, May 16, 2008.

142. Sam Dillon, "Democrats Limit Future Financing for Washington Voucher Program," *New York Times*, February 27, 2009; "Presumed Dead: Politics Is Driving the Destruction of the District's School Voucher Program," editorial, *Washington Post*, April 11, 2009.

143. *Zelman v. Simmons-Harris*, 536 U.S. 639, 652 (2002); David Stout, "Public Money Can Pay Religious-School Tuition, Court Rules," *New York Times*, June 27, 2002.

144. Computed from figures provided by the American Federation for Children at www.federationforchildren.com/existing-programs. The Maine and Vermont "tuitioning" programs were not included; neither were programs that simply allow parents to take a tax deduction or tax credit for educational expenses when calculating income tax. The only tax credit programs included here are those that create scholarship organizations for distributing vouchers to qualifying children.

145. See www.floridaschoolchoice.org/information/mckay/www.stepupforstudents.org/.

146. There is a research literature that studies the impact of vouchers on student achievement, but I don't discuss it in the text and don't explore it in any detail here because my focus is on the *politics* of vouchers. The teachers unions are opposed to vouchers for reasons that have nothing to do with what these impacts might be or what the research might show, and to dwell on the research (and do it justice) would be a distraction from the political themes that need to be highlighted here. Suffice it to say that good studies of voucher impacts are methodologically very difficult to carry out, and partly for that reason the findings from this research—as from much educational research on other topics (like accountability)—are mixed. The best research, in my view, has been carried out by Paul Peterson and a number of colleagues. They conducted a series of eight random-assignment studies—the gold standard in this kind of work—taking advantage of the fact that voucher programs used lotteries to determine, by luck of the draw, which applying kids would get vouchers and which applying kids would not (and would thus have to return to the public schools). They found that vouchers led to significant achievement gains for African American students, who are the most numerous in these programs, but that there were no comparable effects for Hispanic students (although it is unclear why). See William G. Howell and Paul E. Peterson, *The Education Gap: Vouchers and Urban Schools* (Brookings, 2002). There are also well-done studies indicating that, by threatening public schools with a loss of students and money, vouchers give rise to competitive pressures that increase achievement in the public schools.

See, for example, Caroline Hoxby, "School Choice and School Competition: Evidence from the United States," *Swedish Economic Policy Review* 10 (2003): 9–65; also Rajashri Chakrabarti, "Impact of Voucher Design on Public School Performance: Evidence from Florida and Milwaukee Voucher Programs," Working Paper (Federal Reserve Bank of New York, 2005). There are also studies that tend to put these findings in question. In a detailed assessment of the research literature as a whole, David Figlio concludes, "The weight of the evidence indicates that vouchers lead to improvements in satisfaction for users; they may have positive test score benefits for some segments of the United States population; and there may be some positive spillovers to the overall public school population." See David Figlio, "Voucher Outcomes," in *Handbook of Research on School Choice*, edited by Berends and others, pp. 321–37. The quote is from p. 336. In another recent review, Patrick Wolf sums up his assessment by saying, "We know that parents are much more satisfied with their child's school if they have used a voucher to choose it. We know . . . that the effect of vouchers on student achievement tends to be positive; however, achievement impacts are not statistically significant for all students in all studies and they tend to require several years to materialize." (He does not look at competitive effects.) See Patrick J. Wolf, "School Voucher Programs: What the Research Says about Parental School Choice," *Brigham Young University Law Review* 2 (April 2008): 415–46. The quote is from p. 446.

147. For Budde's ideas, see Ray Budde, "Education by Charter: Restructuring School Districts" (Andover, Mass.: Regional Laboratory for Educational Improvement of the Northeast and Islands, 1988); Ray Budde, "The Evolution of the Charter Concept," *Phi Delta Kappan* 78, no. 1 (September 1996): 72–73. For Shanker's ideas, see Albert Shanker, speech to the National Press Club, Washington, March 31, 1988; Albert Shanker, "Restructuring Our Schools," *Peabody Journal of Education* 65, no. 3 (Spring 1988): 88–100.

148. For the early history of the charter movement, including discussions of the key actors and ideas, see, for example, Joe Nathan, *Charter Schools: Creating Hope and Opportunity for American Education* (San Francisco: Jossey-Bass, 1996); Chester E. Finn Jr., Bruno V. Manno, and Gregg Vanourek, *Charter Schools in Action* (Princeton University Press, 2000).

149. For an account of the politics of the Minnesota charter law in 1991, see Nathan, *Charter Schools*.

150. Ibid., p. 69.

151. Ibid., p. 70. The reformers kept pushing for a loosening of restrictions in future years and later succeeded in raising the ceiling—to forty schools.

152. On the politics of charters during the 1990s, see Nathan, *Charter Schools*; Finn, Manno, and Vanourek, *Charter Schools in Action*. See also Michael Mintrom, *Policy Entrepreneurs and School Choice* (Georgetown University Press, 2000); Hubert Morken and Jo Renee Formicola, *The Politics of School Choice* (New York: Rowman and Littlefield, 1999); Lance D. Fusarelli, *The Political Dynamics of School Choice: Negotiating Contested Terrain* (New York: Palgrave Macmillan, 2003); Bryan Hassel, *The Charter School Challenge* (Brookings, 1999). For a rather typical news account of charter battles, see, for

example, Raymond Hernandez, "Charter Schools Gaining Support," *New York Times*, February 28, 1996.

153. See Gary K. Hart and Sue Burr, "The Story of California's Charter School Legislation," *Phi Delta Kappan* 78, no. 1 (September 1996): 37–40.

154. Thomas Toch, "Union Man" (Washington: Education Sector, August 17, 2007), available at www.educationsector.org/publications/union-man. For a labor-sympathetic account of Shanker and charters, see Richard D. Kahlenberg, "The Charter School Idea Turns 20," *Education Week*, March 26, 2008.

155. In addition to the works on charter politics cited earlier, see, for example, Hill and Jochim, "Political Perspectives on School Choice." See also the website of the Democrats for Education Reform at www.dfer.org/. For survey results on the popularity of charters among citizens, especially minorities, see William Howell, Paul E. Peterson, and Martin West, "Meeting of the Minds," *Education Next* 11, no. 1 (Winter 2011): 20–31. For news accounts, see Elizabeth Green, "How New Generation of Reformers Target Democrats on Education Reform," *New York Sun*, May 31, 2007; David J. Hoff, "Key Democrat's Plan Would Boost Charter Schools," *Education Week*, March 19, 2008.

156. There were other elements to the agreement besides increasing the cap. Hastings won provisions allowing charter operators to appeal to county and state school boards if they are turned down for authorization at the local level, requiring districts to turn over unused facilities to charters needing space, and allowing nonprofit groups to run charters. The CTA also got some concessions, requiring that charter schools would henceforth have to hire only certified teachers and that there would be additional financial oversight of their operations. See Robert C. Johnston, "Calif. Reaches 'Historic' Charter School Agreement," *Education Week*, May 6, 1998; George A. Clowes, "New Charter Law Boosts School Choice," *School Reform News,* June 1998; Morken and Formicola, *The Politics of School Choice.*

157. Again, see the works cited earlier on the politics of charters.

158. Karla Scoon Reid, "Proposal for Charter Schools Roils Detroit," *Education Week*, October 8, 2003.

159. See the works cited earlier on the politics of charters. See also Paul T. Hill, *Charter Schools against the Odds* (Stanford, Calif.: Hoover Institution Press, 2006). For a quantitative study showing that strong unions are associated with weak charter laws (or no charter laws at all), see Christiana Stoddard and Sean P. Corcoran, "The Political Economy of School Choice: Support for Charter Schools across States and Districts," *Journal of Urban Economics* 62, no. 1 (2007): 27–54; see their overview discussion in Christiana Stoddard and Sean P. Corcoran, "Charter Politics," *Education Next* 8, no. 2 (Spring 2008): 72–78. See also Francis X. Shen and Kenneth K. Wong, "Beyond Weak Law, Strong Law: Political Compromises and Legal Constraints on Charter School Laws," paper presented for the 2006 annual meeting of the American Political Science Association, Philadelphia, August 31–September 3, 2006. For a comprehensive overview of state charter laws and assessments of their strengths and weaknesses, see Center for Education Reform, *Charter School Laws across the States 2010* (Washington: Center for Education Reform, 2010), available at www.edreform.com. See also National Alliance of

Public Charter Schools, "State Charter Law Rankings Data Base" (Washington: National Alliance of Public Charter Schools, 2006–09), available at www.publiccharters.org/charterlaws.

160. See Diana Jean Schemo, "Charter Schools Trail in Results, U.S. Data Reveal," *New York Times*, August 17, 2004; F. Howard Nelson, Bella Rosenberg, and Nancy Van Meter, *Charter School Achievement on the 2003 National Assessment of Educational Progress* (Washington: American Federation of Teachers, 2004).

161. Assessing whether charter schools make a difference for student performance and exactly how and to what extent is very difficult to do methodologically. So not surprisingly, the research literature is rather mixed—although in general it is positive. A 2009 national study by CREDO, a Stanford-based research organization, finds that, while 17 percent of charters outperformed their traditional public school counterparts, another 37 percent did not; the unions and other charter critics have been highlighting this study ever since. Although its methodology (which employs "matching") is much more sophisticated than that of many earlier studies, it has been severely criticized by Caroline Hoxby on technical grounds. Hoxby soon released a study of her own, relying on randomization, showing (for the state of New York) that charters do significantly better than regular public schools. She has done several other studies in the past, on different samples, arriving at the same basic conclusion. For the relevant studies, see Caroline Hoxby, "Multiple Choice: Charter Performance in 16 States" (Stanford, Calif.: CREDO, June 2009); Caroline Hoxby, Sonali Murarka, and Jenny Kang, "How New York City's Charter Schools Affect Achievement" (Cambridge, Mass.: New York City Charter Schools Evaluation Project, September 2009). The critiques and responses can be found at credo.stanford.edu/. See also the critique written by Nelson Smith of the National Alliance for Public Charter Schools, who notes that the CREDO results for charters turn positive when the students have been in charters for more than one year. See Nelson Smith, "CREDO Report Reconsidered," on his organization's website at www.publiccharters.org/files/publications/CREDOReconsidered-final.pdf. For a review (written prior to the recent CREDO-Hoxby exchange) of a large number of studies on the impact of charters on achievement, see Bettie Teasley, "Charter School Outcomes," in *Handbook of Research on School Choice*, edited by Berends and others, pp. 209–26. Echoing Nelson's point about the time-and-experience element, she notes, "Older more established charter schools tend to produce stronger academic outcomes than their traditional public counterparts."(p. 224). See also Berends, Springer, and Walberg, eds., *Charter School Outcomes*.

162. For background on Mooney, who died in 2006, see "About Tom Mooney" on the website of the Tom Mooney Institute for Teacher and Union Leadership at www.mooneyinstitute.org/about-tom-mooney.

163. Eric W. Robelen, "Ohio Supreme Court Narrowly Upholds State Charter Law," *Education Week*, November 1, 2006.

164. From the OEA website at www.ohea.org. See their press release announcing their filing of the suit. Stephen Ohlemacher, "Ohio Educators File Federal Lawsuit; Teachers Union Deems Charters Illegal," *Cleveland Plain Dealer*, June 10, 2004; Catherine Candinsky, "Charter Schools Face Another Lawsuit," *Columbus Dispatch*, March 24, 2007.

165. Catherine Candinsky, "Teachers behind Dann's Strategy?" *Columbus Dispatch*, October 2, 2007.

166. See, for example, William Hershey and Laura Bischoff, "Strickland Targets Charter Schools, Vouchers," *Dayton Daily News*, March 14, 2007; "Assault on Education: Strickland's Budget Takes Aim at Charter Schools But Students Would Be the Biggest Victims," *Columbus Dispatch*, March 1, 2009; Jim Siegel, "Charter Schools: Strickland's Plan for Cuts Is Unfair," *Columbus Dispatch*, February 6, 2009, available at dispatchpolitics.com,; Dave Larson, "Charter Schools Focus of Hearing," *Dayton Daily News*, March 17, 2009.

167. These figures are from the "Reports" section of the National Alliance for Public Charter Schools' website at www.publiccharters.org/dashboard/home. Data are for 2009–10, the most recent they make available. Data are also available on the Center for Education Reform's website at www.edreform.com, especially their statistics page at www.edreform.com/_upload/CER_charter_numbers.pdf.

168. Stephen Brill, "Teachers Unions' Last Stand," *New York Times Sunday Magazine*, May 17, 2010.

169. Data are from the "Reports" section of the National Alliance for Public Charter Schools' website at www.publiccharters.org/dashboard/home.

170. The figures in this paragraph are taken from National Alliance for Public Charter Schools, *A Growing Movement: American's Largest Charter School Communities*, 5th ed. (Washington: National Alliance for the Public Schools, November, 2010), available at www.publiccharters.org/files/publications/AllianceMarket Share Report_FINAL_Nov2010.pdf.

171. For figures on charter school enrollments, see the "public charter school dashboard" data on the website of the National Alliance of Public Charter Schools at www.publiccharters.org/dashboard/students/page/overview/year/2010. For perceptive, informative accounts of the many difficulties faced by charters, see Hill, *Charter Schools against the Odds*.

172. For an official NEA statement on the issue, see "Privatization" on its website at www.nea.org/privatization/index.html. For the AFT's position, see "Privatization" on its website at www.aft.org/topics/privatization/index.htm.

173. For a discussion of these cases and their politics, see Terry M. Moe, "Democracy and the Challenge of Education Reform," in *Advances in the Study of Entrepreneurship, Innovation, and Economic Growth*, vol. 9, edited by Gary D. Libecap (Greenwich, Conn.: JAI Press, 1997).

174. See, for example, Paul E. Peterson and Matthew M. Chingos, "For-Profit and Nonprofit Management in Philadelphia Schools," *Education Next* (Spring 2009): 65–70.

175. See, for example, Mark Walsh, "Baltimore to Terminate EAI Schools Contract," *Education Week*, November 29, 1995; Mark Walsh, "Hartford Ousts EAI in Dispute over Finances," *Education Week*, January 31, 1996; Mark Walsh, "Reports Paint Opposite Pictures of Edison Achievement," *Education Week*, March 5, 2003.

176. See Paul Socolar, "Phaseout of EMOs Accelerates," Philadelphia Public School Notebook blog, May 12, 2010, available at thenotebook.org/blog/102514/phaseout-emos-accelerates. See also Keith B. Richberg, "Setback for Philadelphia Schools Plan," *Washington Post*, June 2, 2008, p. A03.

Chapter Ten

1. See, for example, Paul Pierson and Theda Skocpol, "Historical Institutionalism in Contemporary Political Science," in *Political Science: The State of the Discipline*, edited by Ira Katznelson and Helen V. Milner (New York: W.W. Norton, 2002); Paul Pierson, *Politics in Time: History, Institutions, and Social Analysis* (Princeton University Press, 2004); Ruth Berins Collier and David Collier, *Shaping the Political Arena: Critical Junctures, the Labor Movement, and Regime Dynamics in Latin America* (Princeton University Press, 1991).

2. See, for example, Citizens' Commission on Civil Rights, "Title I at Midstream: The Fight to Improve Schools for Poor Kids" (Washington: Citizens' Commission on Civil Rights, Summer, 1999).

3. On the politics of No Child Left Behind, see, for example, Patrick J. McGuinn, *No Child Left Behind and the Transformation of Federal Education Policy, 1965–2005* (University of Kansas Press, 2006); Paul Manna, *School's In: Federalism and the National Education Agenda* (Georgetown University Press, 2006); Lee W. Anderson, *Congress and the Classroom: From the Cold War to "No Child Left Behind"* (Pennsylvania State University Press, 2007); Carl F. Kaestle and Alyssa E. Lodewick, eds., *To Educate a Nation: Federal and National Strategies of School Reform* (University of Kansas Press, 2007); Elizabeth Debray and Carl F. Kaestle, *Politics, Ideology, and Education: Federal Policy during the Clinton and Bush Administrations* (Teachers College Press, 2006); Kevin Kosar, *Failing Grades: The Federal Politics of Education Standards* (Boulder, Colo.: Lynne Rienner Publishers, 2005).

4. See, for example, William G. Howell, Paul E. Peterson, and Martin R. West, "2009 Education Next-PEPG Survey of Public Opinion," *Education Next* (Fall 2009): 1–9, available at educationnext.org/files/pepg2009.pdf. See also Terry M. Moe, *Schools, Vouchers, and the American Public* (Brookings, 2001).

5. This quote is taken from McGuinn, *No Child Left Behind and the Transformation of Federal Education Policy*, p. 171.

6. See, among many possible examples, Jonathan Alter, "Obama's No-Brainer on Education," *Newsweek*, July 12, 2008; "'Potential Disruption?' Ending D.C. School Vouchers Would Dash the Best Hopes of Hundreds of Children," editorial, *Washington Post*, March 2, 2009; Evan Thomas and Pat Wingert, "Why We Must Fire Bad Teachers," *Newsweek*, March 6, 2010.

7. Nicholas Kristof, "Obama Takes on the Teacher Unions," *New York Times*, March 10, 2009.

8. Joe Klein, "Why We're Failing Our Schools," *Time*, January 28, 2010.

9. See, for example, Michele McNeil, "Civil Rights Groups Call for New Federal Education Agenda," *Education Week*, July 26, 2010; Ruth Marcus, "Civil Rights Groups Are Picking the Wrong Fight with President Obama," *Washington Post*, August 5, 2010.

10. See the Democrats for Education Reform website at www.dfer.org/about/principles/. The mission statement for the Education Equality Project can be read at www.educationequalityproject.org/what_we_stand_for/our_mission.

11. Dana Goldstein, "The Democratic Education Divide," *American Prospect*, August 25, 2008, available at www. prospect.org/cs/articles?article=the_democratic_education_divide.

12. For details on Teach for America, visit www.teachforamerica.org/. See also Lucia Graves, "The Evolution of Teach for America," *U.S. News and World Report*, October 17, 2008; "Eight Questions for Wendy Kopp," *The Economist*, April 3, 2010.

13. On this reformist network and its roots in Teach for America, see, for example, Stephen Brill, "Teachers' Unions' Last Stand," *New York Times Sunday Magazine*, May 18, 2010; Evan Thomas and Pat Wingert, "Why We Can't Get Rid of Failing Teachers," *Newsweek*, March 15, 2010.

14. See, for example, Richard Lee Colvin, "The New Philanthropists," *Education Next* (Fall 2005): 34–41. See also Frederick M. Hess, "The Challenge of Giving," *Education Week*, January 18, 2006; "Gates Foundation Announces Expanded Education Grantmaking," *Philanthropy News Digest*, November 13, 2008.

15. Ibid. See, in addition, Bill Gates, Speech to National Charter Schools conference, June 29, 2010, available at www.gatesfoundation.org/speeches-commentary/Pages/bill-gates-2010-national-charter-schools-conference.aspx. See also "Gates Foundation Program Aimed at Schools," *United Press International*, November 18, 2009, available at www.upi.com/Top_News/US/2009/11/18/Gates-Foundation-program-aimed-at-schools/UPI-46821258569176/; Bloomberg Businessweek, "Bill Gates' Latest Mission: Fixing America's Schools," *msnbc*, July 17, 2010; Nick Anderson, "Gates Foundation Playing Pivotal Role in Changes for Education System," *Washington Post*, July 12, 2010; Tom Marshall, "Hillsborough Hires 100 Peer Evaluators for Its $100 Million Gates Reforms," *St. Petersburg Times*, April 20, 2010; Tom Marshall, "Hillsborough School Board Get First Look Monday at New Teacher Evaluation Spurred by Gates Grant," *St. Petersburg Times*, May 14, 2010; Karamagi Rujumba, "Bill Gates Lauds City's Steps to Improve Schools," *Pittsburgh Post-Gazette*, July 11, 2010; Jane Roberts, "Memphis Teachers Union OKs Contract with Raises," *Commercial Appeal*, February 17, 2010.

16. For a reasonable account of the various candidates' issue positions during the 2008 Democratic presidential primaries, see the OnTheIssues website at www.ontheissues.org/2008.htm.

17. See, for example, Associated Press, "Obama Unveils Plans for Education Reform," *USA Today*, September 10, 2008.

18. See, for example, the summary in Wikipedia, "American Recovery and Reinvestment Act of 2009," available at en.wikipedia.org/wiki/American_Recovery_and_Reinvestment_Act_of_2009.

19. See, for example, Sam Dillon, "For Education Chief, Stimulus Means Power, Money, and Risk," *New York Times*, February 17, 2009; Maria Glod, "Stimulus Includes $5 Billion Flexible Fund for Education Innovation," *Washington Post*, February 14, 2009.

20. "'Potential Disruption?' Ending DC School Vouchers Would Dash the Best Hopes of Hundreds of Children," editorial, *Washington Post*, March 2, 2009.

21. "President Obama's Remarks to the Hispanic Chamber of Commerce," *New York Times*, March 10, 2009.

22. For informative overviews of Race to the Top, up to about June 2010, see Brill, "Teachers Unions' Last Stand"; Andy Smarick, "The Full Story on Race to the Top," Education Stimulus Watch Special Report 3 (Washington: American Enterprise Institute, March 2010); Michele McNeil and Lesli A. Maxwell, "Schools Up the Ante on Applications for Race to the Top," Education Week, June 9, 2010.

23. See, for example, Neil King Jr., "Only Two States Win Race to Top," Wall Street Journal, March 29, 2010. For assessments of the Delaware and Tennessee applications and some details on what they proposed, see "Navigating the Race to the Top Traffic Jam" (Washington: National Council on Teacher Quality, 2010), available at www. nctq.org.

24. Amanda Paulson, "Race to the Top Winners: How Did Delaware and Tennessee Succeed?" Christian Science Monitor, March 29, 2010.

25. Nick Anderson, "Input of Teachers Unions Key to Successful Entries in Race to the Top," Washington Post, April 3, 2010. See also Paulson, "Race to the Top Winners"; King, "Only Two States Win Race to Top."

26. On the California education budget numbers, see "2010 Budget Act and Related Legislation" (Sacramento: California Department of Education, 2010), available at www. cde.ca.gov/fg/fr/eb/.

27. Brill, "Teachers Unions' Last Stand."

28. Stephen Sawchuk, "Unions' Tactics Diverge in Engaging Obama Agenda," Education Week, September 16, 2010 (updated version of article originally published on August 25, 2010).

29. See, for example, Andy Smarick, "Advancing Performance Pay in the Obama Administration: The Influence of Political Strategy and Alternative Priorities," paper prepared for the PEPG conference, Merit Pay: Will It Work? Is It Politically Viable? Harvard Kennedy School, Cambridge, Mass., June 3–4, 2010.

30. See, for example, the discussion in Smarick, "The Full Story on Race to the Top."

31. "Partners in Reform: Remarks by Arne Duncan to the National Education Association," July 2, 2009, available on the U.S. Department of Education's website at www2. ed.gov/news/speeches/2009/07/07022009.html.

32. Sam Dillon, "Easter States Dominate in Winning School Grants," New York Times, August 24, 2010.

33. See, for example, Amanda Paulson, "Race to the Top Losers: Why Did Louisiana and Colorado Fail?" Christian Science Monitor, August 24, 2010.

34. Daniel H. Bowen, "Politics and the Scoring of Race to the Top Applications," Education Stimulus Watch Special Report 4 (Washington: American Enterprise Institute, September 2010).

35. See, for example, Frederick M. Hess, "Race to the Top Limps to a Finish," National Review Online, August 31, 2010; Nancy Mitchell, "How Colorado Lost Race to the Top," Education Week, August 27, 2010; Stephen Sawchuk, "Updated: No Clear Teacher Narrative in Race to Top Phase Two Winners," Education Week, August 24, 2010; Paulson, "Race to the Top Losers." Maryland, whose case should have been weak to begin with, managed to win despite having only 8 percent union buy-in.

36. Michael J. Petrilli, "A Big Flop on Race to the Top," *Flypaper*, August 24, 2010, available on the website of the Thomas Fordham Institute at www.educationgadfly.net/flypaper/index.php/2010/08/a-big-flop-on-race-to-the-top/.

37. Michele McNeil, "Race to Top Buy-In Level Examined," *Education Week*, June 16, 2010.

38. See, for example, Stephen Sawchuk, "More than Two-Thirds of States Adopt Core Standards," *Education Week*, updated August 23, 2010; Catherine Gewertz, "Federal-Intrusion Talk on Common Standards: A Win-Win?" *Education Week*, August 24, 2010.

39. Mississippi enacted a very restricted law that allows for low-performing public schools to convert to charters with a parent vote, but does not allow private groups to start up charters in the usual manner. This doesn't really count as a charter law. See, for example, Stephanie Banchero, "Race to Top Leaves Some School Reformers Weary," *Wall Street Journal*, June 1, 2010.

40. Jennifer Medina, "New York State Votes to Expand Charter Schools," *New York Times*, May 28, 2010; Eric W. Robelen, "State Picture on Charter Caps Still Mixed," *Education Week*, August 12, 2009 (updated May 8, 2010); Smarick, "The Full Story on Race to the Top."

41. See, for example, Alexander Russo, "USDE: List of States Making RTT-Related Changes," *Alexander Russo's This Week in Education*, June 4, 2010. His blog can be found on the website of Scholastic at www.scholastic.com/administrator/; Sam Dillon, "Education Grant Effort Faces Late Opposition," *New York Times*, January 18, 2010; Paulene Meyers, "The Effect of Race to the Top on States' Policies Regarding Linking Student Achievement Data to Teacher Evaluations," Undergraduate honors thesis, Stanford University, Department of Political Science, 2010.

42. See, for example, Jeremy P. Meyer, Lynn Bartels, and Jessica Fender, "Tenure Bill Nears Passage," *Denver Post*, May 12, 2010; Lynn Bartels, "Tenure Bill Signed into Law after Roller-Coaster Legislative Journey," *Denver Post*, May 21, 2010; Bill Barrow, "Jindal Signs New Teacher Evaluation System into Law," *Times-Picayune*, May 27, 2010; Associated Press, "Florida Governor Vetoes Measure on Merit Pay, Tenure," *Education Week*, April 21, 2010.

43. It also endorsed the Democratic candidate, who was hardly happy about having to share its largesse with Crist. Adam C. Smith, "Educators Union Splits Senate Endorsement," *St. Petersburg Times*, May 23, 2010. On the veto, see "Florida Governor Vetoes Measure on Merit Pay, Tenure," *Associated Press*, April 21, 2010.

44. See the discussions in, for example, Smarick, "The Full Story of Race to the Top"; Brill, "Teachers Unions' Last Stand."

45. For both Tennessee and Delaware, the applications are available in full on the U.S. Department of Education's website at www2.ed.gov/programs/racetothetop/phase1-applications/index.html.

46. Lesli A. Maxwell, "Race to Top Win Poses $100 Million Test for Delaware," *Education Week*, April 7, 2010.

47. Jeremy P. Meyer, "After the Signing of Teacher-Evaluation Measure, Factions Dig into Law's Details," *Denver Post*, May 21, 2010.

48. Meyer, Bartels, and Fender, "Tenure Bill Nears Passage"; Bartels, "Tenure Bill Signed into Law after Roller-Coaster Legislative Journey."

49. See, for example, "The New Haven Model," editorial, *New York Times*, October 29, 2009; "Walking the Walk on School Reform," editorial, *New York Times*, January 16, 2010.

50. Leo Casey, "Teacher Evaluation and Improvement Plan: Frequently Asked Questions," *EdWize*, May 12, 2010, available at www.edwize.org/teacher-evaluation-and-improvement-plan-frequently-asked-questions. For additional information on the legislation, see, for example, Medina, "New York State Votes to Expand Charter Schools"; Jennifer Medina, "Agreement Will Alter Teacher Evaluations," *New York Times*, May 10, 2010; Maura Walz, "What to Expect from Today's Teacher Evaluation Agreement," *GothamSchools*, available at gothamschools.org. That same site has a copy of the agreement (which became legislation).

51. See Brill, "The Teachers Unions' Last Stand"; McNeil, "Race to Top Buy-In Level Examined."

52. Ron Matus, "As Florida Vies Again for Federal Schools Grant, Some Still Worry about Union Support," *St. Petersburg Times*, June 1, 2010; See also "Three More Side Agreements for Florida's Race to the Top," *Gradebook*, June 3, 2010, available at blogs.tampabay.com/schools/2010/06/three-more-side-agreements-for-floridas-race-to-the-top.html; McNeill, "Race to Top Buy-In Level Examined."

53. Smarick, "The Full Story on Race to the Top," taken from pp. 4, 8.

54. See, for example, Sam Dillon, "Obama Calls for Major Change in Education Law," *New York Times*, March 13, 2010; Nick Anderson, "Obama: Revise No Child Left Behind Law," *Washington Post*, March 14, 2010.

55. I am in the early stages of writing a book (with Michael Henderson) on the post-Katrina experience in New Orleans and its lessons for American education reform more generally. To go into the New Orleans case in great depth here—by explaining, for example, what its pre-Katrina power structure looked like, what role the local union played, how Katrina and the destruction of the local union affected the politics of education at both the local and state levels, how reformers saw and took their opportunities, what resistance they faced, and so on—would obviously require a lengthy analysis and a full-blown research project to support it. For now, I think it is best simply to outline why New Orleans is an interesting and instructive case, and to leave the details for later research. I should emphasize, though, that I am not claiming that the destruction of the local teachers union was the only factor that explains the post-Katrina renaissance, just that it was enormously important; the full story (on both the local and state levels) is of course more complicated. On New Orleans, its school history, and its post-Katrina reforms, see Stacey M. Childress, "Reforming New Orleans Schools after Katrina" (Harvard University, Harvard Business School, July 2008); Erik W. Robelen, "New Orleans Schools Seize Post-Katrina Momentum," *Education Week*, August 25, 2010; Sarah Laskow, "Necessity Is the Mother of Invention," *Newsweek*, August 26, 2010; Paul Tough, "A Teachable Moment," *New York Times*, August 17, 2008; Walter Isaacson, "The Greatest Education Lab," *Time*, September 6, 2007; Adam Nossiter, "Against Odds, New Orleans Schools Fight Back," *New York Times*, April 30, 2008; Ron Schachter, "Fresh Chance for New

Orleans Schools," *District Administration*, December 2006; Kathryn G. Newmark and Veronique De Rugy, "Hope after Katrina," *Education Next* 6, no.4 (Fall 2006): 12–22. For data on charters in New Orleans, see National Alliance for Public Charter Schools, *A Growing Movement: America's Largest Charter Communities* (Washington: National Alliance for Public Charter Schools, November 2010), p. 5, available at www.publiccharters. org/files/publications/AllianceMarket Share Report_FINAL_Nov2010.pdf.

56. Needless to say, the institution builders in these cases were heavily influenced by the United States. So another way of telling this particular story is that the United States was much better able to create democratic political systems and market-based economies in postwar Germany and Japan because their prior institutions and power structures had been destroyed and were not able to resist and heavily constrain the new institutional forms. See Mancur Olson Jr., *The Rise and Decline of Nations: Economic Growth, Stagflation, and Social Rigidities* (Yale University Press, 1984).

57. See, for example, Kevin Boyle, *The UAW and the Heyday of American Liberalism, 1946–1968* (Cornell University Press, 1995). For membership numbers over time, see "United Auto Workers," on Wikipedia at en.wikipedia.org/wiki/United_Auto_Workers.

58. Much has been written on the decline of the American auto industry. Here and below, see, for example, Paul Ingrassia, *Crash Course: The American Automobile Industry's Road from Glory to Disaster* (New York: Random House, 2010); Micheline Maynard, *The End of Detroit: How the Big Three Lost Their Grip on the American Car Market* (New York: Broadway Business, 2004); Tanvir Orakzai, "U.S. Auto Industry Decline: Lessons from Ford and GM," *American Chronicle*, July 8, 2010; Xiaohua Yang, *Globalization of the Automobile Industry* (Westport, Conn.: Praeger, 1995).

59. For a broader perspective on competition and the decline of unions generally, see Barry T. Hirsch, "Sluggish Institutions in a Dynamic World: Can Unions and Industrial Competition Coexist?" *Journal of Economic Perspectives* 22, no. 1 (Winter 2008): 153–76; Henry S. Farber and Bruce Western, "Accounting for the Decline of Unions in the Private Sector, 1973–1998," *Journal of Labor Research* 22, no. 3 (2001): 459–85.

60. Associated Press Business Staff, "UAW Membership Down during Tough 2009 for Autos," *Cleveland Live*, March 29, 2010, available at cleveland.com.

61. See, for example, Thomas L. Friedman, *The World Is Flat: A Brief History of the Twenty-First Century* (New York: Farrar, Straus, and Giroux: 2006).

62. Terry M. Moe and John E. Chubb, *Liberating Learning: Technology, Politics, and the Future of American Education* (San Francisco: Jossey-Bass, 2009).

63. On the enormous benefits of technology for education, see, in addition to *Liberating Learning*, Clayton Christensen, Curtis W. Johnson, and Michael B. Horn, *Disrupting Class: How Disruptive Innovation Will Change the Way the World Learns* (New York: McGraw-Hill, 2008); Paul E. Peterson, *Saving Schools* (Harvard Education Press, 2010); Office of Educational Technology, "Transforming American Education: Learning Powered by Technology" (Washington: U.S. Department of Education, March 2010).

64. See, for example, Project Tomorrow, "Creating Our Future: Students Speak Up about Their Vision for 21st Century Learning: Speak Up 2009; National Findings K–12 Students and Parents" (Irvine, Calif.: Project Tomorrow, 2009); Project Tomorrow, "Unleashing the Future: Educators 'Speak Up' about the Use of Emerging Technologies

for Learning" (Irvine, Calif.: Project Tomorrow, 2010); other Project Tomorrow reports on that organization's website at www.tomorrow.org/index.html.

65. In addition to sources cited earlier, see Bill Tucker, "Laboratories for Reform: Virtual High Schools and Innovation in Public Education," Education Sector Report (Washington: Education Sector, 2007); John Watson, Amy Murin, Lauren Vashaw, Butch Gemin, and Chris Rap, *Keeping Pace with K–12 Online Learning 2010: An Annual Review of Policy and Practice* (Evergreen, Colo.: Evergreen Research Group, 2010), available at www.kpk12.com/wp-content/uploads/KeepingPaceK12_2010.pdf.

66. Matthew Wicks, *A National Primer on K–12 Online Learning, Version 2* (International Association for K–12 Online Learning. 2010), available at www.inacol.org/research/docs/iNCL_NationalPrimerv22010-web.pdf.

67. See Watson and others, *Keeping Pace with K–12 Online Learning 2010* for up-to-date information and statistics on the developments in virtual learning.

68. Ibid.

69. Ibid.

70. Ibid. Additional data on virtual charters and their enrollments are available from the Center for Education Reform at www.edreform.org.

71. For a discussion of hybrids, see Watson and others, *Keeping Pace with K–12 Online Learning 2010.*

72. See the Rocketship website (rsed.org/schools/) for information on the history, organization, and academic accomplishments of its hybrid model. There are currently three Rocketship schools in operation, but two are in their first year. For another example of a hybrid school, see the new San Francisco Flex Academy, pioneered by Mark Kushner of K12 (www.k12.com/sfflex/).

73. See Moe and Chubb, *Liberating Learning*, for the political details of these cases.

74. See William J. Baumol and William G. Bowen, *The Performing Arts: An Economic Dilemma* (New York: Twentieth Century Fund, 1966).

75. For an application of Baumol's disease to virtual education, see Peterson, *Saving Schools*; Moe and Chubb, *Liberating Learning.*

76. On the connection between union membership and political power, see, for example, Joseph B. Rose and Gary N. Chaison, "Linking Union Density and Union Effectiveness: The North American Experience," *Industrial Relations* 35, no. 1 (January 1996): 78–105; Elimane Kane and David Marsden, "The Future of Trade Unionism in Industrialized Market Economies," *Labor and Society* 13 (April 1988): 109–24; Margaret Levi, "Organizing Power: The Prospects for an American Labor Movement," *Perspectives on Politics* 1, no. 1 (March 2003): 45–68.

77. These figures are taken from the National Center for Education Statistics, Schools and Staffing Survey, 2007–08.

78. Gary Chaison, "Information Technology: The Threat to Unions," *Journal of Labor Research* 23, no. 2 (Spring 2002): 249–59. The first portion of the quote is taken from p. 250, the second from p. 256. On the other side of the ledger, certain unionists and scholars have expressed optimism that unions might be able to use information technology to enhance their organizing efforts—creating their own websites, reaching

out to members and potential members, using communication to coordinate member behavior, and so on—but there is little evidence that these efforts, although vigorously pursued, have yielded any real gains to speak of. Membership has continued to slide. See the entire symposium in the *Journal of Labor Research*, of which the Chaison article is a part. See especially the article written by staff members of the NEA: Sam Pizzigati, Barbara Yentzer, and Ronald D. Henderson, "The School of Hard Knocks: NEA's Experience," *Journal of Labor Research* 23, no. 2 (Spring 2002): 175–99.

Appendix A

1. In this analysis, the variable on union membership is taken from the national teacher survey, which was carried out in 2003, but some of the state-level variables are measured in 2004. I retained the 2004 variables, rather than using measures from an earlier year, in order to enhance comparability with the aggregate data analysis from table A-1. There appears to be little downside to doing so. The purpose of these variables, in effect, is to allow for cross-sectional comparisons across the states—indicating that some states are more liberal than others, for example, or that some are more industrialized than others—and as these variables change only slowly over time, the cross-sectional comparisons would be virtually the same if earlier data points were used. In any event, there is nothing magical about 2003 as a "date" placed on union membership, as most teachers first joined their unions (or chose not to) at some earlier time—often ten or twenty or even thirty years earlier; moreover, with each passing year, they are free to change their decisions. The role of the state-level variables is to make cross-sectional comparisons that essentially indicate what *type* of state each teacher works in, by reference to factors that have changed only slowly over time. A more finely grained analysis would obviously want to go well beyond the simple analysis I am providing here, which I offer as an interesting and informative first cut.

2. Because an interaction term is present, the impact of being a Republican is estimated in two parts. The coefficient on the Republican variable tells us the impact of being Republican *when agency fees are not present*. The coefficient on the interaction term (agency fees*repub) tells us how the impact of being Republican changes—relative to the no-agency-fee base—when agency fees *are* present. In this model, the impact of being Republican is –0.23 in states without agency fees, but the impact goes up by 0.16 in states with agency fees—yielding a net impact of –0.07. In states with agency fees, then, Republicans are still less likely to be union members, but the impact of their partisanship is quite a bit smaller than in states without agency fees. This same sort of calculation is carried out for all the other variables whose impacts involve interaction terms.

Appendix B

1. Even so, for states in which collective bargaining is prohibited—and where any bargaining-like relationships must be meet-and-confer arrangements—I code all districts as not having collective bargaining even if teachers reported that they do.

Appendix C

1. These figures are for teachers generally, not just union members. If we look just at union members, the relationship between youth and voluntarism is again the same.

2. All figures are for union members in districts with collective bargaining.

3. Ibid.

4. Figures are for all teachers in districts without collective bargaining, not just union members.

Index

Page numbers followed by *f* or *t* refer to figures or tables, respectively.